LIFE'S IMPONDERABLES™

The Answers to Civilization's Most Perplexing Questions

Why Do Clocks Run Clockwise?

When Do Fish Sleep?

Why Do Dogs Have Wet Noses?

DAVID FELDMAN

GALAHAD BOOKS
NEW YORK

Contents

Introduction

In 1986, my first book, *Imponderables™: The Solution to the Mysteries of Everyday Life*, was foisted upon an innocent world. The book was full of enigmas of mundane life that drove me nuts—questions that couldn't be answered by numbers, facts, or standard reference books.

I knew that *I* wanted to know why we don't ever see baby pigeons, why Kellogg's Sugar Flakes have the same number of calories per ounce as Kellogg's Corn Flakes, and why women open their mouths when applying mascara. But how would I find answers to my Imponderables™?

I quickly realized that the best way to find the answers was to speak directly to experts: in these cases, to ornithologists; nutritionists; all the major cereal companies; cosmetic companies; beauty demonstrators at department stores; and plastic surgeons. Experts in every field imaginable have generously shared their knowledge with me.

But would there be actual human beings that would buy a book filled with these questions? Much to my astonishment, soul mates abounded. At the end of my first book, I asked for readers to unburden their Imponderables™, and ever since I've been flooded. Most of the content of *Why Do Clocks Run Clockwise?*, and all my subsequent books, come from reader questions.

I'm delighted that the first three books of Imponderables™ to include reader participation have been assembled together in their original form. You might find an occasional passage that seems out of date, inevitable in books written more than ten years ago. Ignore all the entreaties to help solve Frustables (short for "Frustrating Imponderables™"), which readers have tried to vanquish for more than a decade. But I still welcome your feedback and even a new Imponderable™ or two. You can reach me at feldman@imponderables.com, at my web site at http://www.imponderables.com, or via pony express at:

Imponderables
P.O. Box 905
Planetarium Station
New York, NY 10024-0546

WHY DO CLOCKS RUN CLOCKWISE?
and other
IMPONDERABLES™

For Michael Leo Feldman

Contents

doughnuts. Why do they then put the same tissue in with the doughnuts for the customer to carry home—germs and all?

Preface

If you read the first volume of *Imponderables*, you now know why you don't ever see baby pigeons, why women open their mouths while applying mascara, and why people look up when thinking. But the last frontiers in human knowledge haven't quite yet been plumbed. Thus the burning need for *Why Do Clocks Run Clockwise? and Other Imponderables*.

Imponderables are the everyday mysteries of life that aren't very important—until they occur to you. Then they begin to gnaw at your brain like termites boring through wood. An Imponderable is a mystery that cannot be solved by numbers or measurements or standard reference books. You will sleep better when you find out where flies go in winter, what happens to the tread that wears off tires, and why hamburger-bun bottoms are so thin that they disintegrate under the weight of the patty. You will be a better person for knowing this stuff.

Most of the new Imponderables come from readers of the first book. It is humbling to discover that the readers of *Imponderables* are at least as imaginative (crazed?) as its author.

Many readers asked for a subject index in the next volume of *Imponderables*. Your wish is our command. We've also added a new feature, "Frustables," short for Frustrating Imponderables, a top-ten list of Imponderables whose answers eluded us. We are offering a free copy of the next edition of *Imponderables* to the first person who provides evidence or referrals that lead us to solutions of these ultimate mysteries.

And, of course, we still offer a free copy of the next edition of *Imponderables* to the first person who poses an Imponderable we answer in our next volume.

What Is the Purpose of the Warning Label on a Mattress? And What Happens If I Rip It Off?

Here is an Imponderable that happens to be one of the foremost moral issues plaguing our society today. Many transgressors are consumed with guilt over having ripped off mattress tags. Some are almost as upset about impetuously doing in pillow tags, as well.

We are here to say: do not be hard on yourself. You have done nothing legally wrong. You have not even done anything morally wrong.

Those warning labels are there to protect you, not to shackle you. If you look carefully at the language of the dire warning, there is always a proviso that the label is not to be removed "except by the consumer." Labeling laws are up to the individual states. Thirty-two of the fifty states have laws requiring mattress tags, and none of the states cares whether the purchaser of a mattress rips up the tag.

So how do these warning labels protect you? Most important, they inform the consumer exactly what the filling material is made of, because the fill is not visible. The label also notifies the consumer that the manufacturer is registered with all of the appropriate government agencies and has fulfilled its obligations in complying with their regulations. There is also manufacturing information on the tag that may help the consumer when and if a warranty adjustment is desired (though this is a good argument for keeping the tag on the mattress, or at least filing it for future reference).

One of the reasons why mattress warning label laws were imposed in the first place is that some less-than-ethical merchants used to palm off secondhand mattresses as new ones. It is legal, in most states, to sell secondhand mattresses as long as they are properly sterilized. A white tag guarantees a new mattress; a sterilized secondhand mattress carries a yellow tag.

Submitted by the Reverend Ken Vogler, of Jeffersonville, Indiana. Thanks also to: Mike Dant, of Bardstown, Kentucky, and Owen Spann, of New York, New York.

Why Do Dogs Walk Around in Circles Before Lying Down?

The most common and logical explanation for the phenomenon is that in the wild, circling was a method of preparing a sleeping area or bed, particularly when it was necessary to flatten down an area among tall grass, leaves, and rocks.

Some experts also believe that circling is a way for dogs to map territory, to define an area of power. Dog writer Elizabeth Crosby Metz explains the habit this way:

I believe it also has to do with spreading their proprietary scent around their nesting site, to say: "Keep away, this is MY nest!"

In fact, as a breeder I know that mother dogs will circle many times before lying down to feed their sightless, deaf newborns as a way of spreading her scent and indicating to them exactly where she is and how far they have to go to reach her. Think about it: How else can blind, deaf newborns so surely find the milk bar?

Submitted by Daniel M. Keller, of Solana Beach, California. Thanks also to: Joanna Parker, of Miami, Florida.

If Nothing Sticks to Teflon, How Do They Get Teflon to Stick to the Pan?

"They," of course, is Du Pont, which owns the registered trademark for Teflon and its younger and now more popular cousin, Silverstone. G. A. Quinn, of Du Pont, told *Imponderables* that the application of both is similar:

> When applying Silverstone to a metal frypan, the interior of the pan is first grit-blasted, then a primer coat is sprayed on and baked. A second layer of Polytetrafluoroethylene (PTFE) is applied, baked and dried again. A third coat of PFTE is applied, baked and dried.
>
> About the only thing that sticks to PTFE is PTFE. So, the 3-coat process used in Silverstone forms an inseparable bond between the PTFE layers and the primer coat bonds to the rough, grit-blasted metal surface.

Du Pont has recently introduced Silverstone Supra, also a three-layer coating that is twice as durable as conventional Silverstone.

Submitted by Anthony Virga, of Yonkers, New York.

Why Is the Scoring System in Tennis So Weird?

Tennis as we know it today is barely over a hundred years old. A Welshman, Major Walter Clopton Wingfield, devised the game as a diversion for his guests to play on his lawn before the real purpose for the get-together—a pheasant shoot. Very quickly, however, the members of the Wimbledon Cricket Club adopted Wingfield's game for use on their own underutilized lawns, empty since croquet had waned in popularity in the late eighteenth century.

Long before Wingfield, however, there were other forms of tennis. The word "tennis" first appeared in a poem by John Gower in 1399, and Chaucer's characters spoke of playing "rackets" in 1380. Court tennis (also known as "real" tennis) dates back to the Middle Ages. That great athlete, Henry VIII, was a devotee of the game. Court tennis was an indoor game featuring an asymmetrical rectangular cement court with a sloping roof, a hard ball, a lopsided racket, and windows on the walls that came into play. Very much a gentleman's sport, the game is still played by a few diehards, though only a handful of courts currently exist in the United States.

Lawn tennis's strange scoring system was clearly borrowed from court tennis. Although court tennis used a fifteen-point system, the scoring system was a little different from modern scoring. Each point in a game was worth fifteen points (while modern tennis progresses 15–30–40–game, court tennis progressed 15–30–45–game). Instead of the current three or five sets of six games each, court tennis matches were six sets of four games each.

The most accepted theory for explaining the strange scoring system is that it reflected Europeans' preoccupation with astronomy, and particularly with the sextant (one-sixth of a circle). One-sixth of a circle is, of course, 60 degrees (the number of points in a game). Because the victor would have to win six sets of four games each, or 24 points, and each point was worth 15 points, the game concluded when the winner had "completed" a circle of 360 degrees (24 × 15).

Writings by Italian Antonio Scaino indicate that the sextant scoring system was firmly in place as early as 1555. When the score of a game is tied after six points in modern tennis, we call it "deuce"—the Italians already had an equivalent in the sixteenth century, *a due* (in other words, two points were needed to win).

Somewhere along the line, however, the geometric progression of individual game points was dropped. Instead of the third point scoring 45, it became worth 40. According to the *Official Encyclopedia of Tennis,* it was most likely dropped to the lower number for the ease of announcing scores out loud, because "forty" could not be confused with any other number. In the early 1700s, the court tennis set was extended to six games, obscuring the astronomical origins of the scoring system.

When lawn tennis began to surpass court tennis in popularity, there was a mad scramble to codify rules and scoring procedures. The first tennis body in this country, the U.S. National Lawn Tennis Association, first met in 1881 to establish national standards. Prior to the formation of the USNLTA, each tennis club selected its own scoring system. Many local tennis clubs simply credited a player with one point for each rally won. Silly concept. Luckily, the USNLTA stepped into the breach and immediately adopted the English scoring system, thus ensuring generations of confused and intimidated tennis spectators.

There have been many attempts to simplify the scoring system in order to entice new fans. The World Pro Championship League tried the table-tennis scoring system of twenty-one–point matches, but neither the scoring system nor the League survived.

Perhaps the most profound scoring change in this century has been the tie breaker. The U.S. Tennis Association's Middle States section, in 1968, experimented with sudden-death playoffs, which for the first time in modern tennis history allowed a player who won all of his regulation service games to lose a set. The professionals adopted the tie breaker in 1970, and it is used in almost every tournament today.

Submitted by Charles F. Myers, of Los Altos, California.

Why Have Humans Lost Most of Their Body Hair?

Anthropologists have debated this issue for a long time. Hair on most creatures is an important means of maintaining heat in the body, so the reasons for humans losing this valuable form of insulation are unlikely to be trivial. Here are some of the more logical theories advanced about why hair loss made sense for humans, along with the opinions of Desmond Morris, whose book *The Naked Ape* derives its title from this very Imponderable.

1. Hair loss allowed primitive people to cope better with the myriad of skin parasites, such as ticks, mites, and vermin, that bothered them. Parasites were more than a nuisance; they spread many potentially fatal infectious diseases. Although this theory makes sense, it doesn't explain why other relatives of man, equally bothered by parasites, have not evolved similarly.

2. Naked skin could have been a social rather than a func-

tional change. Most species have a few arbitrarily selected characteristics that differentiate them from other species—what Desmond Morris calls "recognition marks." Morris doubts the validity of the "recognition mark theory," for hair loss is a far more drastic step than is necessary to differentiate humans from other primates.

3. Hair loss might have had a sexual and reproductive basis. Male mammals generally are hairier than their female counterparts. This type of sex-based physiological difference helps make one sex more attractive to the other. Morris also mentions that hair loss served to heighten the excitement of sex—there is simply more tactile sensation without fur. Now that we are in the midst of a worldwide population explosion and trying to slow the birth rate, it is easy to forget that nature has built into our species characteristics to help increase our numbers.

4. Some anthropologists believe that before humans became hunting animals, stalking the savannas of East Africa, we went through a phase as an aquatic animal, seeking food at tropical seashores rather than on the more arid open plains. Without hairy bodies, humans became more streamlined in the water, able to swim and wade effectively. This is also a possible explanation for our hair being so plentiful on the head: if we spent much of our time wading in the water, only the top of the head need be covered, as protection against the sun. According to this theory, man left the water only after he developed the tools necessary to hunt.

5. Even if the aquatic phase never existed, hair loss helped humans regulate their body temperature after they moved from the forests to a plains-based hunting culture. Morris questions this theory: after all, other mammals, such as lions and jackals, made a similar switch of terrains without accompanying hair loss. Furthermore, the loss of body hair had a negative effect in that it subjected humans to dangerous ultraviolet radiation from the sun.

6. Hair loss kept primitive humans from overheating during the chase when hunting. This is Morris's pet theory. When our

ancestors became hunters, their level of physical activity increased enormously. By losing their heavy coat of hair, and by increasing the number of fat and sweat glands all over the body, humans could cool off faster and more efficiently. Sweat glands could not deliver their cooling effect nearly as effectively if fur trapped perspiration.

As divorced as we are from the problems of our primate forebears, Morris believes that human genetics will always countermand our attempts to elevate our culture. "[Man's] genes will lag behind, and he will be constantly reminded that, for all his environment-moulding achievements, he is still at heart a very naked ape."

Submitted by Sean S. Gayle, of Slidell, Louisiana.

Why Don't People Get Goosebumps on Their Faces?

Be proud of the fact that you don't get goosebumps on your face. It's one of the few things that separate you from chimpanzees.

We get goosebumps only on parts of our bodies that have hair. As you have learned from the exciting previous entry, the purpose of body hair is to protect us from the cold. But when our hair doesn't provide enough insulation, the small muscles at the bottom of each hair tighten, so that the hair stands up.

In animals covered with fur, the risen strands form a protective nest of hairs. Cold air is trapped in the hair instead of bouncing against delicate skin. The hair thus insulates the animals against the cold.

Although humans have lost most of their body hair, the same muscular contractions occur to defend against the cold. Instead of a mat of hair, all we have to face the elements are a few wispy tufts and a multitude of mounds of skin, which used to support an erect hair and now must go it alone. When a male lion gets "goosebumps," his erect hair makes him ferocious; our goosebumps only make us look vulnerable.

Submitted by Pam Cicero, of Madison, Ohio.

Why Doesn't Countdown Leader on Films Count All the Way to One?

Remember watching the leader on sixteen-millimeter films in school, waiting for the countdown to go 10–9–8–7–6–5–4–3–2–whoops? It *never* got down to one.

Countdown leader, of course, is there to help the projectionist time when a film is going to start. Each number is timed to appear precisely one second after the other. The projectionist usually uses the number two as the cue to allow the projector light to hit the screen and begin the show. What would be number one is simply the start of the picture.

Wouldn't it work just as well to have zero represent the beginning of the movie, so that frustrated audiences could have the satisfaction of counting down from ten to one? Of course it would. But as in most areas, tradition and inertia rule. As Bob Dylan wrote, "Don't follow leaders."

Submitted by Ronald C. Semone, of Washington, D.C.

When a Company Sells Lobster Tails to Restaurants and Stores, What Do They Do with the Rest of the Lobster?

The American or Maine lobster is usually delivered to stores and restaurants whole and served in the shell. The claws, legs, and body all contain good lobster meat, and aficionados covet the green "tomalley" or liver and the red roe often found in female lobsters. As Richard B. Allen, vice-president of the Atlantic Offshore Fishermen's Association, put it, "If they are not eating almost everything except the shell, they are missing a fine eating experience."

If you find "lobster tails" listed on a restaurant menu, chances are you are ordering rock or spiny lobsters. Unlike Maine lobsters, spiny lobsters do not have big claws, but rather two large antennas. We spoke to Red Lobster's purchaser, Bob Joseph, who told us that most of Red Lobster's tails come from Brazil, Honduras, and the Bahamas. Red Lobster buys about two million pounds of spiny lobster a year (as well as a similar poundage of Maine lobster). The nontail meat of the spiny lobster is stringy and watery compared to the tails, and not as good-looking. Consumers seem to prefer the big, steaklike chunks of the tail rather than the shreds of meat found on other parts of the crustacean.

Although some restaurants and fish stores will buy the relatively small claws of spiny (and rock) lobsters, what happens to the nontail meat that isn't in demand? The claw, thorax, and head meat is sold as "meat packs," which are used for soups (lobster bisque, gumbos) and reconstituted for seafood salads. Seafood and Italian restaurants often use "meat-pack" lobster for pastas. And, surprisingly, one of the biggest users of lobster "meat pack" is egg-roll makers.

Submitted by Claudia Wiehl, of North Charleroi, Pennsylvania.

Why Do They Need Twenty Mikes at Press Conferences?

If you look carefully at a presidential press conference, you'll see two microphones. But at other press conferences, you may find many more. Why the difference?

Obviously, all the networks have access to the president's statements. How can they each obtain a tape when there are only a couple of microphones? They use a device called a "mult box" (short for "multiple outlet device"). The mult box contains one input jack but numerous output jacks (usually at least eight outputs, but sixteen- and thirty-two–output mult boxes are common). Each station or network simply plugs its recording equipment into an available output jack and makes its own copy. The second microphone is used only as a backup, in case the other malfunctions. The Signal Corps, which runs presidential news conferences, provides the mult boxes at the White House.

It's more likely, though, that a press conference will be arranged hastily or conducted at a site without sophisticated electronics equipment. It is at such occasions that you'll see multiple microphones, with each news team forced to install its own equipment if it wants its own tape.

All networks and most local television stations own mult boxes. Of course, the whole purpose of the mult box is to promote pooling of resources, so the networks, on the national level, and the local stations, in a particular market, alternate providing mult boxes. There usually isn't a formal arrangement for who will bring the mult box; in practice, there are few hassles.

Some media consultants like the look of scores of microphones, believing it makes the press conference seem important. A more savvy expert will usually ask for a mult box, so that the viewing audience won't be distracted by the blaring call letters on the microphones from a single pearl of wisdom uttered by the politician he works for.

Why Do Some Localities Use Salt and Others Use Sand to Treat Icy Roads?

Gabriel Daniel Fahrenheit, creator of the Fahrenheit temperature scale, discovered that salt mixed with ice (at a temperature slightly below the freezing point) creates a solution with a lower freezing point than water alone. Thus, salt causes snow and ice to melt.

Most localities haven't found a better way to de-ice roadways and sidewalks than salt. Salt is also effective in keeping hard packs of ice from forming in the first place. While a number of chemicals have been developed to melt ice, salt remains a much cheaper alternative.

So why don't all localities use salt to treat icy roads? Ecological problems have led some municipalities to ban the use of salt outright. Salt causes corrosion of vehicles, pavement, bridges, and any unprotected steel in surrounding structures. Salt also harms many kinds of vegetation.

The effectiveness of salt as an ice remover also has distinct limitations. Salt is best used in high-traffic areas; without enough traffic to stimulate a thorough mixing of ice and salt, hard packs can still develop. Below approximately 25° F, salt isn't too effective, because ice forms so fast that the salt doesn't have a chance to lower the freezing point. And salt applied on top of ice doesn't provide traction for drivers or pedestrians.

Sand, by contrast, provides excellent traction for vehicles when grit comes in contact with tires, whether the sand is exposed on top of the surface of the ice or mixed in with slush or snow. Sand doesn't require high-volume traffic areas to work effectively, it does little or no harm to vegetation, vehicles, or road, and is (pardon the expression) dirt cheap.

There is only one problem with sand: it doesn't melt snow or ice. Salt tries to cure the problem. Sand attempts to treat the symptoms.

Some localities have experimented with sand-salt combinations. Actually, most sand spread on pavements already contains some salt, used to keep the sand from freezing into clumps when mixed with the snow.

While salt is considerably more expensive than sand, cost is rarely the main criterion for choosing sand over salt. Joseph DiFabio, of the New York State Department of Transportation, told *Imponderables* that salt costs approximately twenty dollars per ton, compared to five dollars per ton for sand. In fact, sand must be applied in a greater concentration than salt, about three times as much. Because maintenance crews must use three times as much sand to treat the same mileage of roadway, they must return to reload their trucks with sand three times as often as with salt. The eventual cost differential, therefore, is negligible.

Submitted by Daniel A. Placko, Jr., of Chicago, Illinois.

Why Is the Telephone Touch-Tone Key Pad Arranged Differently from the Calculator Key Pad?

Conspiracy theories abound, but the explanation for this Imponderable reinforces one of the great tenets of Imponderability: when in doubt, almost any manmade phenomenon can be explained by tradition, inertia, or both. A theory we have often heard is that the phone company intentionally reversed the calculator configuration so that people who were already fast at operating calculators would slow down enough to allow the signals of the phone to register. It's a neat theory, but it isn't true. Even today, fast punchers can render a touch-tone phone worthless.

Both the touch-tone key pad and the all-transistor calculator were made available to the general public in the early 1960s. Calculators were arranged from the beginning so that the lowest digits were on the bottom. Telephone keypads put the 1–2–3 on the top row. Both configurations descended directly from earlier prototypes.

Before 1964, calculators were either mechanical or electronic devices with heavy tubes. The key pads on the first calculators actually resembled old cash registers, with the left row of keys numbering 9 on top down to 0 at the bottom. The next row to the right had 90 on top and 10 on the bottom, the next row to the right 900 on top, 100 on the bottom, and so on. All of the early calculators were ten rows high, and most were nine rows wide. From the beginning, hand-held calculators placed 7–8–9 on the top row, from left to right.

Before the touch-tone phone, of course, rotary dials were the rule. There is no doubt that the touch-tone key pad was designed to mimic the rotary dial, with the "1" on top and the 7–8–9 on the bottom. According to Bob Ford, of AT&T's Bell Laboratories, a second reason was that some phone-company research concluded that this configuration helped eliminate dialing errors. Ford related the story, which may or may not be apocryphal, that when AT&T contemplated the design of their key pad, they called several calculator companies, hoping they would share the research that led them to the opposite configuration. Much to their chagrin, AT&T discovered that the calculator companies had conducted no research at all. From our contacts with Sharp and Texas Instruments, two pioneers in the calculator field, it seems that this story could easily be true.

Terry L. Stibal, one of several readers who posed this Imponderable, suggested that if the lower numbers were on the bottom, the alphabet would then start on the bottom and be in reverse alphabetical order, a confusing setup. This might have entered AT&T's thinking, particularly in the "old days" when phone numbers contained only five digits, along with two exchange letters.

Submitted by Jill Gernand, of Oakland, California. Thanks also to: Lori Bending, of Des Plaines, Illinois, and Terry L. Stibal, of Belleville, Illinois.

What Is the Difference Between a "Kit" and a "Caboodle"?

Anyone who thinks that changes in the English language are orderly and logical should take a look at the expression "kit and caboodle." Both words, separately, have distinct meanings, but the two have been lumped together for so long that each has taken on much of the other's meaning.

Both words have Dutch origins: "Kit" originally meant tankard, or drinking cup, while "Boedel" meant property or house-

hold stuff. By the eighteenth century, "kit" had become a synonym for tool kit. For example, the knapsacks carried by soldiers that held their eating utensils and nonmilitary necessities were often called "kits." "Boodle" became slang for money, especially tainted money. By the nineteenth century, "caboodle" had taken on connotations of crowds, or large numbers.

Yet the slurring of meanings occurred even before the two terms became inseparable. The *Oxford English Dictionary* quotes from Shelley's 1785 *Oedipus Tyrannus*, "I'll sell you in a lump the whole kit of them." In this context, "caboodle" would seem more appropriate than "kit."

By the mid-nineteenth century, "kit" had found many companion words in expressions that meant essentially the same thing: "kit and biling"; "whole kit and tuck"; "whole kit and boodle" and "whole kit and caboodle" were all used to mean "a whole lot" or "everything and everyone." The *Dictionary of Americanisms* cites a 1948 *Ohio State Journal* that stated: "The whole caboodle will act upon the recommendation of the *Ohio Sun*."

The expression "kit and caboodle" was popularized in the United States during the Civil War. The slang term was equally popular among the Blue and the Gray. Although the expression isn't as popular as it used to be, it's comforting to know that old-fashioned slang made no more sense than the modern variety.

What Is the Purpose of the Ball on Top of a Flagpole?

We were asked this Imponderable on a television talk show in Los Angeles. Frankly, we were stumped. "Perhaps they were installed to make the jobs of flagpole sitters more difficult," we ventured. "Or to make flagpole sitting more enjoyable," countered host Tom Snyder. By turns frustrated by our ignorance and outwitted by Mr. Snyder, we resolved to find the solution.

According to Dr. Whitney Smith, executive director of the Flag Research Center in Winchester, Massachusetts, the ball may occasionally be combined with a mechanism involved with the halyards that raise and lower a flag, but this juxtaposition is only coincidental. Much to our surprise, we learned that the ball on top of a flagpole is purely decorative.

Actually, the earliest flaglike objects were emblems—an animal or other carved figure—placed atop a pole. Ribbons beneath these insignia served as decoration. According to Dr. Smith, the importance of the two was later reversed so that the design of the flag on a piece of cloth (replacing the ribbons) conveyed the message while the finial of the pole became ornamental, either in the form of a sphere or, as the most common alternatives, a spear or (especially in the United States) an eagle.

George F. Cahill, of the National Flag Foundation, believes that a pole just isn't as pleasing to the eye without something on top. Spears don't look good on stationary poles, and eagles, while visually appealing, are more expensive than balls or spears. Cahill adds another advantage of the ball: "On poles that are carried, a spear can be a hazard, not only to individuals, but to woodwork and plaster, and eagles are cumbersome and easily breakable. So, the ball gives the pole a safe and rather attractive topping and finish."

We speculated that perhaps birds were less likely to perch on a sphere than a flat surface, thus saving the flag from a less welcome form of decoration. But Cahill assures us that birds love to perch on flagpole balls.

We may never have thought of these balls as aesthetic objects, but *objets d'art* they are.

Why Does Wayne Gretzky Wear a Ripped Uniform?

Hockey players don't tend to make as much money as, say, top basketball players, but surely the biggest star in hockey can afford an unmangled uniform. Can't he?

Actually, Gretzky's uniform isn't ripped, and he is not trying to affect a "punk" look. Gretzky always tucks one corner of his shirt into the back of his pants, which only makes his shirt *appear* to be torn. The story of how Gretzky started this practice is a fascinating one, told to us by the National Hockey League's Belinda Lerner:

> It began when Wayne was a young hockey player competing with older boys. His uniform shirt, if left out of his pants, would hang down to his knees. Wayne tucked the shirt inside his pants to give a taller appearance. Now Wayne, who is six feet tall, tucks in the corner of his shirt out of habit and superstition. Bill Tuele, Public Relations Director for the Edmonton Oilers, tells me Wayne has a piece of Velcro sewn into his pants so the shirt is securely fastened throughout the game.

Submitted by Lorin Henner, of New York, New York.

Why Is There Always Pork in Cans of Pork and Beans? Does That Tiny Little Hunk of Fat, Which Is Presumably Pork, Really Add Flavor? It's Disgusting to Look at, So Why Do They Put It In? Why Not "Lamb and Beans" or "Crickets and Beans"? Why Always Pork?

Perhaps it will comfort you to know that yes, indeed, the pork is placed into the can for flavor. Pork and beans are actually cooked in the can. One fairly large piece of pork is placed in the can before cooking. After being heated during processing, it melts down to the size you see in the can, its flavor having permeated the beans.

We spoke to Kathy Novak, a Consumer Response Representative at Quaker Oats, the parent company of Stokely-Van Camp, who told us that they receive quite a few inquiries about the pork from fans of Van Camp's Pork and Beans, including more than a few angry missives from those who opened a can that inexplicably did not contain the piece of pork. So there is no doubt that the pork does have its fans. James H. Moran, of Campbell's Soup Company, says that many of his company's customers eat the pork, while others do not.

Do manufacturers have to include a piece of pork to call the product "Pork and Beans"? Not really. Some producers use rendered pork liquid instead of a solid piece of meat, and are legally entitled to call their product "Pork and Beans."

Submitted by Joel Kuni, of Kirkland, Washington.

How Do Military Cadets Find Their Caps After Tossing Them in the Air upon Graduation?

Be it West Point, Annapolis, or Colorado Springs, the tradition is the same: at the end of graduation ceremonies, after the class is called to attention for the last time and the immortal words "You are dismissed" are uttered, the former cadets fling their caps in the air. Occasionally, hats will fly at sporting events as well. How are they retrieved?

The press and relatives grab a few. But the vast majority of the caps are claimed by children. Lieutenant Colonel James A. Burkholder, Commandant of Cadets at the U.S. Air Force Academy, wrote that after most, but not all, of the graduates throw their hats in the air, "children under 12 are allowed to scramble to get [the hats]. It becomes 'finders keepers.' Keeping the children off the field prior to that moment is also a sight to see. Thus, after graduation, you will see chil.ren with their 'treasures' and others, without hats, in all sorts of despair."

Could the cadets find their caps if they did want them? Possibly. Caps have a pocket with a piece of cardboard in the inside lining, on which cadets write their names with a felt pen. More often than not, however, the ink will have worn off or become smeared. As the graduating classes at West Point usually number about a thousand, the chances of someone actually finding his own hat are remote.

Is the hat tossing rehearsed? Choreographed? No. It is a spontaneous gesture, albeit a spontaneous gesture repeated yearly. Is it frowned upon? Not really. As Al Konecny, Assistant Public Affairs Officer at West Point, told us, there is nothing wrong with the graduates tossing away a part of their uniform— it's no longer their proper uniform, anyway. They've just been promoted!

Submitted by Merry Phillips, of Menlo Park, California. Thanks also to: Paul Funn Dunn, of WSOY, Decatur, Illinois.

Why Does American Electricity Run on A.C. Rather Than D.C.?

Direct current flows only in one direction. Alternating current flows back and forth continuously. Thomas Edison was a proponent of direct current (he had a financial stake in it), which worked fine in the early days of electric light, because the generators were very close to the lights that used electricity.

But as demand for electric light increased, D.C. proved inadequate. Electric current loses the least energy when traveling at high voltages. It was then uneconomical to transform D.C. to the high voltages necessary for long-distance transmissions. Direct current circuits would have required generating stations every three or four miles, unfeasible in the sprawling United States.

In 1885, a young man named George Westinghouse bought the U.S. patent for alternating current from inventor Nikola Tesla. Not only could A.C. transmit higher voltages more cheaply than D.C., the voltages could be raised or lowered by switching only one transformer. With its relative flexibility and lower cost, A.C. quickly became the U.S. standard.

Submitted by Larry Hudson, of Nashville, Tennessee. Thanks also to: John Brandon, of Davis, California.

What Is That Sniffing Noise Boxers Make When Throwing Punches?

Listen carefully to any boxing match, or to any boxer shadow-boxing, and you will hear a sniffing sound every time a punch is thrown. This sound is known to many in the boxing trade as the "snort."

A "snort" is nothing more than an exhalation of breath. Proper breathing technique is an integral part of most sports, and many boxers are taught to exhale (usually, through their nose) every time they throw a punch. Scoop Gallello, president of the International Veteran Boxers Association, told *Imponderables* that when a boxer snorts while delivering a punch, "he feels he is delivering it with more power." Gallello adds: "Whether this actually gives the deliverer of the punch added strength may be questionable." Robert W. Lee, president and commissioner of the International Boxing Federation, remarked that the snort gives a boxer "the ability to utilize all of his force and yet not expend every bit of energy when throwing the punch. I am not sure whether or not it works, but those who know much more about it than I do continue to use the method and I would tend to think it has some merit."

The more we researched this question, the more we were struck by the uncertainty of the experts about the efficacy of the snorting technique. Donald F. Hull, Jr., executive director of the International Amateur Boxing Association, the governing federation for worldwide amateur and Olympic boxing, noted that "While exhaling is important in the execution of powerful and aerobic movements, it is not as crucial in the execution of a boxing punch, but the principle is the same." Anyone who has ever watched a Jane Fonda aerobics videotape is aware of the stress on breathing properly during aerobic training. Disciplines as disparate as weightlifting and yoga stress consciousness of inhalation and exhalation. But why couldn't any of the boxing experts explain why, or if, snorting really helps a boxer?

Several of the authorities we spoke to recommended we contact Ira Becker, the doyen of New York's fabled Gleason's Gymnasium, who proved to have very strong opinions on the subject of snorting: "When the fighter snorts, he is merely exhaling. It is a foolish action since he throws off a minimum of carbon dioxide and some vital oxygen. It is far wiser to inhale and let the lungs do [their] own bidding by getting rid of the CO_2 and retaining oxygen."

The training of boxing, more than most sports, tends to be ruled by tradition rather than by scientific research. While most aspiring boxers continue to be taught to snort, there is obviously little agreement about whether snorting actually conserves or expends energy.

Why, in Any Box of Assorted Chocolates, Are the Caramels Square, the Nougats Rectangular, the Nuts Oval, and the Creams Circular?

Before we are inundated with letters, let's square away one fact. Not all chocolatiers conform to the geometric code stated in the Imponderable above. But most do. Who invented the scheme?

Despite contacting all of the biggest chocolate makers in the United States, and some of the older smaller ones, we couldn't come up with a definitive answer. Whether it was the venerable Thompson Candy Company in Meriden, Connecticut, See's Candies in South San Francisco, California, or Whitman's, all simply said that these shapes were "traditional."

When most chocolates were dipped by hand, many companies put an easily identifiable code on each chocolate, usually in the form of a swirly script on top of each piece. At Whitman's, for example, the code ran like this:

> A "V" usually signified a vanilla cream center; flat-topped chocolates with an open "C" often indicated a chocolate butter cream center; dome-shaped chocolates inscribed with a closed "C" would reveal a cherry cordial. Square-shaped chocolates with a "V" indicated a vanilla caramel center. An "O" stood for an orange cream; "P" for pineapple cream; and "R" for raspberry cream.

In the past, these fillings were coated with chocolate by a person who quickly dipped the centers in hot melted chocolate and then set aside the pieces to cool and solidify. Most boxed centers today are coated with an automatic enrober. Charlotte H. Connelly, of Whitman's, describes the process:

> In the enrobing process, candy centers are arranged on a moving belt which passes over a pool of chocolate which coats the underside. Then the centers move under a curtain of chocolate which coats each piece with precisely the right amount of melted chocolate. . . . In many instances, with the demise of the hand-dipper, the individual codes have ceased to exist. Although the shapes are

used by many confectionary manufacturers, this is certainly not industrywide as many boxed chocolates suppliers do not conform to these patterns.

How right she is. Most of Fanny Farmer's creams, for example, are circular, but their cream caramels and walnut creams are square. See's Candies produces approximately 130 different pieces of confection. And although each piece does have an individual marking, only the most diehard customer could possibly commit them all to memory.

What the world is clamoring for is a visual guidebook to chocolate centers, to stop the needless despair caused when an innocent person selects a nougat when he thinks he has chosen a caramel. Excuse us, while we call our editor. . . .

Submitted by Mrs. Marjorie S. Fener, of Hempstead, New York.

Whatever Happened to Pay Toilets?

Going to the bathroom is one of the few activities that has gotten cheaper of late. Pay toilets used to be the rule in airports and bus and train stations, and one would often encounter them in gas stations and restaurants.

Pay toilets were never meant to be profit-making enterprises, but merely a method to help defray the costs of cleaning the bathrooms. It was presumed that the dime or quarter "entrance fee" would motivate users to keep the pay stalls cleaner.

It didn't work, though, for instead of encouraging users to exercise best behavior, bathrooms with pay toilets were often trashed by angry patrons.

The vast majority of pay toilets in the 1950s and 1960s were operated by municipalities. According to Ben Castellano of the Federal Aviation Administration, the small amount of revenue generated by pay toilets in airports simply was not worth the attendant hassles: the numerous complaints about their presence and the constantly broken locks that rendered toilets unusable.

But the real death knell of the pay toilet came with several lawsuits filed against municipalities by women's groups. Pay toilets were sexually discriminatory, they argued, because women, unlike men, were forced to pay to urinate. Instead of putting women on the honor code or installing human or video monitors, most cities relented and abandoned the pay toilet. Even male chauvinists were forced to admit that the women's movement had struck a blow for humankind.

When a Pothole Is Formed on the Road, Why Don't We See the Displaced Concrete?

Of course, the endless procession of automobiles and trucks weakens concrete, but the real culprit in the creation of potholes is moisture. Potholes are usually formed when moisture penetrates the pavement. Combined with the destructive effects of alternating cycles of freeze and thaw, especially in the spring, and various chemicals, moisture weakens the concrete from within.

Eugene W. Robbins, president of the Texas Good Roads/ Transportation Association, gave us the most succinct explanation of what happens to the "missing" concrete: "When the pothole forms, the material is broken loose, is pulverized or thrown to the side of the road by vehicle tires, and is blown away by wind or washed away by rain."

Submitted by Chuck Appeldoorn, of Woodbury, Minnesota.

Why Do Most Cities in the United States Put a Maximum-Height Restriction on a Fence a Homeowner May Put Around His Residence, and How Do They Decide on the Maximum?

Our *Imponderables* research team looked into this pesky problem and found that virtually all cities have local ordinances defining maximum heights for fences in residential neighborhoods. Are these restrictions fussy and capricious?

Before we can answer this Imponderable, we must not shrink from asking, without trepidation, the Big Question: what is the purpose of a fence? There are at least six common reasons why homeowners erect fences:

1. To block visual access to their property
2. To demarcate property lines
3. To inhibit access by unwanted people or animals
4. To protect property from the elements
5. To improve climatic conditions (particularly, to break up strong winds)
6. To enhance the appearance of the property

We can all agree, then, that the fence is a noble and worthwhile institution. So why can't homeowners build them to their preferred height specifications?

Because fences also cause problems. Enormous problems. And problems relating to their height are high on the list, all considerations in the decision to codify height restrictions:

1. *High fences are a safety hazard.* This is the number one reason why most localities enact restrictive ordinances. High fences at intersections or near driveways obstruct the vision of motorists and pedestrians. Fences of more than three feet near driveways are particularly dangerous, for they block the view of small children. Most cities also severely restrict the height of fences in the front of corner houses.

2. *As any regular viewer of* The People's Court *or regular reader of Ann Landers can testify, neighbors constantly fight about fences.* They fight about how high they are, what color they are, whose property they are on, and whose responsibility it is to maintain them. Many fences are built solely to irritate neighbors; these are called "spite fences." Without zoning ordinances, municipal governments were without the means to settle such disputes.

3. *Fences can block or obstruct the view, the available light, and the air flow of adjoining properties.* Just as the construction of a skyscraper can totally disrupt the surrounding en-

vironment, so can a relatively low fence in a residential neighborhood.

4. *Many people feel that fences are ugly.* But try to argue this point with a neighbor who has built a fence solely to secure more privacy.

5. *Fences can change the feel of a neighborhood.* Nothing warms up Elm Street like a nice six-foot high barbed wire topped electric chain-link fence.

6. *The same fence that diminishes wind in the winter blocks out cool breezes for the homeowner AND HIS NEIGHBOR during the summer.* The next-door neighbor becomes a passive victim of the fence.

You can imagine, then, the quandary that the city planner faces when trying to determine the proper height levels for residential fences. Zoning ordinances must regulate not only the height of fences, but their degree of openness, which materials can be used to construct fences, how a fence is defined, and how these regulations are to be enforced.

Laws must be enacted to allow homeowners to build fences without receiving permission from abutting neighbors, or the city risks needless delays and squabbles. And laws must be written to provide for exceptions. Fences around tennis courts, for example, must be built higher than other residential fences or there will be safety risks to neighbors and some rather angry tennis players. In mixed-use zones, the law must discriminate between commercial and residential property. The risk of children or criminals climbing into dangerous factories or near hazardous substances far outweighs the aesthetic damage done by a high fence.

So have a little compassion for these zoning ordinances, as arbitrary as they may seem. Sheaves of material sent by the American Planning Association indicate that planners are trying to give you a break. For example, in most localities, fences in side- and backyards are allowed to be higher than in front yards, because high fences in less public territory pose less of a safety risk.

Corner houses are likely to face the most restrictions. In Salt Lake City, for example, fences within thirty feet of an intersection or on any corner lot can be built no higher than three feet. A Coral Gables, Florida, ordinance restricts walls or fences to three feet high if they are within twenty feet of a street or alley intersection. Other cities also restrict any other structure, man-made or natural, from blocking visual access near an intersection.

As crime rates have escalated in surburban as well as urban neighborhoods, many cities have raised their height limits, often from four to six feet. Many residents feel more secure with a high fence around the perimeter of their property. Los Angeles has even considered upping its maximum height from six to eight feet for this very reason.

While the current trend is toward higher fences, don't wait for deregulation to hit local ordinances. High fences are still considered by most property associations to be eyesores and can adversely affect the property value of a single home or a whole neighborhood. When the subject of property values rears its ugly head, other considerations often have a way of fading from view.

Submitted by Bert Sailer, of Los Angeles, California.

Why Do Your Feet Swell Up So Much in Airplanes?

We talked to two specialists in aviation medicine who assured us that there is no reason why atmospheric changes in airplanes would cause feet to swell. Both assured us that the reason your feet swell up on a plane is the same reason they swell up on the ground—inactivity.

Your heart is not the only organ in the body that acts as a pump; so do the muscles of the legs. Walking or flexing a leg muscle assists the pumping effect. On a plane, you are not only confined in movement but sitting with the legs perpendicular to the floor. If you sit for prolonged periods without muscular activity, blood and other fluids collect in the foot with the assistance of gravity.

It doesn't really matter whether you leave your shoes on or off during periods of inactivity. If left on, they will provide external support, but they will inhibit circulation, feel tight—and will not prevent feet from swelling, in any case. If you take your shoes off, you will feel more comfortable, but you'll have a tough time putting your shoes back on, and most of us don't take our shoehorns along on planes.

The pooling of fluids in the feet can happen just as easily in a bus, a train, or an office. Most people's feet swell during the day, which is why the American Podiatric Association recommends buying shoes during the middle of the afternoon. Many people require a shoe a half size to a full size larger in the afternoon than when they wake up.

If your feet swelling becomes a problem, consider airplane aerobics. A few laps around a wide-body plane will do wonders for your feet and will build up your appetite for that wholesome and delicious airplane meal that awaits you.

Submitted by Christal Henner, of New York, New York.

Why Are Hamburger-Bun Bottoms So Thin?

An irate caller from Champaign, Illinois, hit us with this Imponderable, and we immediately empathized. Who hasn't taken a juicy burger off the barbecue, placed a Bermuda onion, some ketchup, maybe a dollop of mustard on the patty, only to find the bun bottom wilting in his fingertips? The bun top only gets mangled by the fingertips of the eater. The bottom carries the weight of the burger, the bun, the eater's fingers, plus the grease from the meat itself. Halfway through eating the sandwich, the bun top looks like Grace Kelly; the bun bottom looks like Sam Kinison.

All of the commercial retail bakeries we spoke to were eager to fault the slicers. Of course, all commercial slicers come with adjustable blades, so the bun *could* be sliced at any height. Surely, not all hamburger buns are missliced, so why don't they slice them higher?

We did find some explanations for the mystery of the puny bun bottom. Most hamburger buns purchased in the grocery store are approximately one and a quarter inches high. They are baked in molds that are half an inch high. Many bakeries slice the bun at this half-inch mark rather than the true midpoint. This is necessary because the tops of the hamburger buns puff up (three-quarters of an inch above the mold), and the top is relatively fragile. The lowest point of this fragile area is called the "shred line." Slices made above the shred line tend to be less clean. One of the reasons that the bottoms of McDonald's Big Mac buns stand up so well is that they are baked in one-inch molds, producing a higher shred line, so that they can be sliced at a proportionately higher point.

The hamburger-bun tops are, in fact, much more important from a marketing point of view. Nothing pleases browsers at the bakery shelf more than buns with a pronounced mushroom top. Because the mushroom top is above the shred line, bakers must decide between good looks and practicality when it comes time to slice the buns—guess which one they choose.

B. W. Crosby, of Pepperidge Farm, adds that "The flavor and texture of the bun comes from the top; therefore, the top needs to be substantial in size." Although the ingredients on the top of the bun are identical to those on the bottom, there is some substance to this argument. The sugar in the dough caramelizes on the top of the bun during baking (that's why the top of the bun is browner than the rest), adding some flavor to what is essentially an exceptionally bland product. Any other flavor enhancements, such as sesame seeds or onions, are also generally loaded on the top of the bun.

One bun expert we spoke to, Bill Keogh of American Bakeries, offered a unique and practical solution to the bun bottom crisis. When he eats a large, juicy hamburger and anticipates a potential problem, he simply turns over the hamburger and eats it bun-bottom up. The so-called bun top, now on the bottom, easily soaks up any footloose grease, for not only is it heavier, it is also wider; thus he simultaneously solves the common problem of trying to eat a sandwich when the patty is wider than the bun bottom. This type of ingenuity is what separates us from the anthropoids.

Why Do Golfers Yell "Fore" When Warning of an Errant Golf Shot?

This expression, popularized by former President Gerald Ford, actually started as an English military term. When the troops were firing in lines, the command " 'ware before" indicated that it might be prudent for the front line to kneel so that the second line wouldn't blow their heads off.

"Fore" is simply a shortened version of the "before" in " 'ware before."

Submitted by Cassandra A. Sherrill, of Granite Hills, North Carolina.

Why Are All Executions in the United States Held Between Midnight and Seven A.M.?

Executions in the United States were not always held in the wee hours. Until the 1830s, most executions were hangings, public affairs that were usually performed at noontime in town squares. Government and penal officials generally believed that public executions acted as a deterrent to would-be felons, so they timed them to attract the largest crowd possible.

Public executions were not without problems even for proponents of capital punishment. Condemned criminals were allowed to give a last statement, which often turned into a tirade against the government and the church. The public execution gave often deranged individuals an opportunity to mock the values and institutions that the justice system was designed to protect. Some criminals successfully played upon the sympathy of the crowd, portraying themselves as martyrs.

About this time, opposition to public executions began to be heard, with both philosophical and practical objections being raised. Many found public executions barbaric, especially because the crowd more resembled crazed football fans than witnesses to a human death. Local merchants in big cities usually disliked public executions because they disrupted business (for the same reason, small-town merchants liked public executions —they attracted potential customers).

Sociologist Richard Moran of Mount Holyoke College, a leading expert on the history of capital punishment, stresses that throughout American history, those against it have sought public executions, believing that if the American public were exposed to the barbarity of executions, it would reject them.

Those in favor have always sought to make executions private. This trend was first manifested in the 1830s, when several states decided to perform executions within prison walls. Rhode Island was the first state to abolish public executions, in 1833, and Pennsylvania followed the year after. Actually, the public could still attend hangings inside prison, but only by purchasing tickets. During this period, most executions were still held during the afternoon.

Slowly, many states began to move their execution times to late evening, midnight, and even predawn hours. The practice of execution at dawn dates back centuries, when the military of many countries had firing squads execute the condemned as soon as there was enough light for the gunmen to see their target. Professor Moran, however, provides another reason for the early-morning hours: concealment. Even in the nineteenth century, most prison and government officials tried to diminish press coverage of executions, in order to minimize protest. Executions were held in the early morning so that the press couldn't print stories about the execution in that morning's newspaper. If they chose to cover the execution at all, the story had to appear on the following day, when it was likely to receive less prominence.

Some of the penal authorities we spoke to stressed the practical advantages of early-morning executions. Anthony P. Travisono, executive director of the American Correctional Association, told *Imponderables* that between midnight and six A.M., "there is very little activity at the institution and all is fairly quiet." He added, rather eerily, "also, the surge of power is stronger."

Professor Moran also suggests that prisoners are more disorderly on days of executions, so that performing executions while the inmates sleep is prudent.

We asked Moran if early-morning executions could be an expression of collective, if unconscious, shame about the whole enterprise. Although he didn't take a definitive stand on the issue, Moran acknowledged the possibility and bolstered the contention with an interesting fact about electrocutions. Not only are today's executions indoors and closed to the public, but electrocutions, without exception, are performed in rooms without windows. The grim task of taking a human life is accomplished without any natural light entering the chamber. We used to make executions a public ritual, symbolic of our repudiation of the criminal act and our affirmation of the need for justice. We now perform executions privately, almost furtively—as if we were the criminals.

Why Do Ants Tend to Congregate on Sidewalks?

With the help of several entomologists and pest control experts, we pieced together several reasons for this phenomenon.

1. Some species, particularly one actually called "pavement ants," prefer to nest on sidewalks and under rocks and other hard surfaces.

2. As John J. Suarez, technical manager of the National Pest Control Association, so elegantly put it: "Sidewalks are a favorite place for people to drop candy, fast food, food wrappers and soft drink containers." Ants are known for their industriousness, but they aren't dumb. If they are given offerings that require no effort on their part, they won't decline the largess.

3. Ants release pheromones, a perfume trail left from the nest to food sources. Pheromones are easily detected on sidewalks, which, as we have already learned, are often repositories

for food. Ants on sidewalks, then, are often merely picking up the scent left by scouts before them.

4. Sidewalks absorb and store heat. Ants run around naked. They prefer warmth.

5. The most popular explanation: darkish ants are more easily visible in contrast to the white sidewalk than on grass or dirt. Suarez speculates that the greater warmth of sidewalks may make the ants more active as well as more visible. But don't assume that because you can't see ants on your front lawn they aren't there. THEY ARE EVERYWHERE.

Submitted by Daniel A. Placko, Jr., of Chicago, Illinois.

Why Do American Cars Now Have Side-View Mirrors on the Passenger Side with the Message, "Objects in the Mirror Are Closer Than They Appear"?

A reasonable person might ask why the American automobile industry had to "improve" on those hopelessly old-fashioned side-view mirrors that didn't distort one's perception of distance. And why, if the inside rear-view mirror shows objects without distortion, can't the side mirror do the same?

Car manufacturers are required to provide flat, unit magnification mirrors on the driver's side of the car. The driver-side mirrors offer the same undistorted image as the mirror in your medicine cabinet.

The new mirrors are convex (for those who forgot their high-school science, convex surfaces curve outward, as opposed to a spoon, which has a concave surface). Convex mirrors have one huge advantage over flat mirrors—they allow a much wider angle of vision. Engineers have found that convex side-view mirrors afford drivers a much clearer view of the passenger side of the car than the old combination of rear-view mirror and conventional side-view mirror. The rear-view mirror, if used alone, leaves blind spots that can lull drivers into complacency when they are considering making lane changes. Drivers are less likely to be sideswiped when consulting a wide-angle side-view mirror, even if an oncoming car is closer than it appears, because they are more likely to spot the car in the first place.

The immortal words, "Objects in the mirror are closer than they appear," are mandated by federal law on all convex mirrors. The government has also set specific standards for the curvature of convex mirrors. The average radius of the curvature for convex mirrors should be no less than thirty-five inches and no greater than sixty-five inches.

Ed Stuart, a representative of Chrysler Motors, told *Imponderables* that the convex mirrors are particularly popular with freeway and turnpike drivers, who can see oncoming cars streaming in from entry ramps much more easily. The biggest danger of the convex mirror is that because objects in the mirror are closer than they appear, drivers will think they have more room to pass another car than they really do. But most drivers look through the undistorted rear-view mirror rather than the side-view mirror before making a lane change anyway, and the prudent driver should check over his shoulder before making his move.

Submitted by Loretta McDonough, of Richmond Heights, Missouri.

Why Do Dogs Smell Funny When They Get Wet?

Having once owned an old beaver coat that smelled like a men's locker room when it got wet, we assumed that the answer to this Imponderable would have to do with fur. But all of the experts we spoke to agreed: the funny smell is more likely the result of dogs' skin problems.

First of all, not all dogs do smell funny when they get wet. Shirlee Kalstone, who has written many books on the care and grooming of dogs, says that certain breeds are, let us say, outstanding for their contribution to body odor among canines. Cocker spaniels and terriers (especially Scotties) lead the field, largely because of their propensity for skin conditions. (Cockers, for example, are prone to seborrhea.) Jeffrey Reynolds, of the National Dog Groomers Association, adds that simple rashes and skin irritations are a common cause of canine body odor, and that water exacerbates the smell. In his experience, schnauzers are particularly susceptible to dermatological irritations.

Of course, dogs occasionally smell when they get wet because they have been rolling in something that smells foul. Gamy smells are usually caused by lawn fertilizer, for example.

Regular grooming and baths can usually solve the odor problem, according to Kalstone. Don't blame the water, in other words—blame the owner.

Submitted by Robert J. Abrams, of Boston, Massachusetts.

Why Do All Dentist Offices Smell the Same?

You are smelling what Dr. Kenneth H. Burrell, assistant secretary of the Council on Dental Therapeutics, calls the "mixture of essential oils dentists frequently use in the course of treatment." Many of these oils are natural or synthetic derivatives of products found in your household. A number of dental medicaments contain camphor, the same pungent substance that repels moths, while others are derivatives of items found on the spice rack: thyme and clove.

The most prominent scent in the dentist's office, the one that makes you claim that all dentist offices smell alike, is probably eugenol, a colorless or pale liquid that is the essential chemical constituent of clove oil. Dentists combine solutions of clove oil or eugenol with a mixture of rosin and zinc oxide to prepare a protective pack after gum surgery or as a temporary cement. Eugenol is also used as an antiseptic, especially in root-canal therapy, and as an anodyne (painkiller). This versatile liquid is also part of the mixture for temporary fillings, impression materials, and surgical dressings after periodontal work.

We at *Imponderables* have pondered of late why clove candies and gum have come and gone. Our pet theory is that rejection of this once-popular flavor comes from a generation of sense memories unconsciously associating cloves with the dentist's office.

Submitted by Julie Lasher and Brian Scott Rossman, of Sherman Oaks, California.

What Are Those Large Knobs Between Sets of Escalators in Department Stores?

The knobs' sole purpose in life is to keep miscreants from sliding down the flat space between the escalators—or at least to guarantee that if misceants *do* slide down in between the escalators, they'll have a bumpy ride.

At Westinghouse Electric Corporation, the knobs are known as an "Anti-Slide Device" and are used on the wide decking between escalators or between an escalator and a wall. As Westinghouse engineer Robert L. Meckley points out, the knobs not only prevent rowdy kids from sliding down, but also keep purses and other baggage (such as Baccarat crystal) from flying down and crashing on the floor. Although the Anti-Slide Devices are hardly high-tech, they do the job.

Submitted by Liz Sblendorio, of Hoboken, New Jersey.

Why Is Jack the Nickname for John?

Believe it or not, a whole book has been written on this subject: *The Pedigree of Jack and of Various Allied Names* by E. W. B. Nicholson. (Don't look for it in your bookstore; it was published in 1892.)

The history of Jack as a pet name for John is a long and tangled one, as these things usually are. Most people assume that Jack is derived from the French Jacques, and that Jack should therefore be short for James rather than John. Nicholson debunked this notion, claiming that there is no recorded example of Jack ever being used to represent Jacques or James.

Jack is actually derived from the name Johannes, which was shortened to Jehan and eventually to Jan. The French were fond of tacking the suffix *-kin* onto many short names. French nasalization resulted in the new combination being pronounced Jackin instead of Jankin. The name Jackin was shortened to Jack. The Scottish version, Jock, was a similar contraction of Jon and *-kin.*

By the fourteenth century, Jack had become a synonym for *man* or *boy,* and later was also used as a slang name for sailors (thus the Jack in Cracker Jack).

In the mid-nineteenth century, Jack became popular as a Christian name, and it remained so until its use peaked in the 1920s. At that point, the diminutive Jackie became popular, propelled by child stars Jackie Cooper and Jackie Coogan. The feminine equivalent, Jacqueline, became the rage in the 1930s, and Jackie, for a short period, became a unisex name. Jack never regained its prominence, though there was a small surge after the United States elected a popular president named John, whose pet name was Jack.

Submitted by Michael Jeffreys and Krissie Kraft, of Marina del Rey, California.

Which Side Gets the Game Ball When a Football Game Ends in a Tie?

Jim Heffernan, director of public relations for the National Football League, told *Imponderables* that NFL rules require that each home team provide twenty-four footballs for the playing of each game. The home team and the visiting team each provide additional balls for their pregame practice.

A "game ball," contrary to popular belief, is not one football given to the winning side. Game balls are rewards for players and coaches who, as Heffernan puts it, "have done something special in a particular game." The game-ball awards are usually doled out by the coach; on some teams, the captains determine the recipients.

The same holds true in college football. James A. Marchiony, director of media services for the National Collegiate Athletic Association, says, "Game balls are distributed at the sole discretion of each team's head coach; a winning, losing or tying coach may give out as many as he or she wishes."

Submitted by Larry Prussin, of Yosemite, California.

Why Do Ketchup Bottles Have Necks So Narrow That a Spoon Won't Fit Inside?

Heinz has had a stranglehold on the ketchup business in the Western world for more than a century, so the story of ketchup bottle necks is pretty much the story of Heinz Ketchup bottle necks. Ironically, although Heinz ads now boast about the *difficulty* of pouring their rather thick ketchup, it wasn't always so.

When Heinz Ketchup was first introduced in 1876, it was considerably thinner in consistency. It came in an octagonal bottle with a narrow neck intended to help impede the flow of the product. Prior to the Heinz bottle, most condiments were sold in crocks and sharply ridged bottles that were uncomfortable to hold.

Over the last 111 years, the basic design of the Heinz Ketchup bottle has changed little. The 1914 bottle looks much like today's, and the fourteen-ounce bottle introduced in 1944 is identical to the one we now use. Heinz *was* aware that as their ketchup recipe yielded a thicker product, it poured less easily through their thin-necked bottle. But they also knew that consumers preferred the thick consistency and rejected attempts to dramatically alter the by-now-familiar container.

Heinz's solution to the problem was the marketing of a twelve-ounce wide-mouth bottle, introduced in the 1960s. Gary D. Smith, in the communications department of Heinz USA, told *Imponderables* that the wide-mouth bottle, more than capable of welcoming a spoon, is the "least popular member of the Heinz Ketchup family." He added, though, that "its discontinuance would raise much fervor from its small band of loyal consumers who enjoy being able to spoon on" their ketchup.

In 1983, Heinz unveiled plastic squeeze bottles, which not only solved the pourability problem but also solved the breakability problem. The sixty-four–ounce plastic size, while mammoth, still has a relatively thin neck.

Until 1888, Heinz bottles were sealed with a cork. The neckband at the top of the bottle was initially designed to keep a foil cap snug against its cork and sealing wax. Although it was rendered obsolete by the introduction of screw-on caps, the neckband was retained as a signature of Heinz Ketchup.

Submitted by Robert Myers, of Petaluma, California.

Ivory Soap Advertises Its Product as 99 and ⁴⁴/₁₀₀ Percent Pure—99 and ⁴⁴/₁₀₀ Percent *What?* And What Is the Impure ⁵⁶/₁₀₀ Percent of Ivory Soap?

Procter & Gamble, in the late nineteenth century, sold many products made of fats, such as candles and lard oil, as well as soap. Ivory Soap was originally marketed as a laundry soap, but the company was smart enough to realize its product's potential as a cosmetic soap. The only problem was that most consumers were buying castile soaps (hard soaps made out of olive oil and sodium hydroxide) and considered laundry soap inappropriate for their personal grooming.

In order to convince consumers that its soap was wholesome, Procter & Gamble employed an independent scientific consultant in New York City to determine exactly what a pure soap was. The answer: a pure soap should consist of nothing but fatty acids and alkali; anything else was foreign and superfluous.

Samples of Ivory Soap were sent to the same chemist for analysis. Much to the manufacturer's surprise, Ivory, by the consultant's definition, was "purer" than the competing castile soaps—containing only 0.56 percent "impurities." The impurities, then and now, were rather innocent:

> Uncombined alkali 0.11 percent
> Carbonates 0.28 percent
> Mineral matter 0.17 percent

The first Ivory advertisement was placed in a religious weekly, *The Independent,* on December 21, 1881. Procter & Gamble decided to emphasize the positive, and right away hammered at their product's advantages. Ivory Soap was trumpeted as "99 and 44/100 percent pure," a rare advertising slogan in that it has lasted longer than a century.

Submitted by Linda A. Wheeler, of Burlington, Vermont.

Why Do We Grow Lawns Around Our Houses?

At first blush, this Imponderable seems easily solved. Lawns are omnipresent in residential neighborhoods and even around multiunit dwellings in all but the most crowded urban areas. Lawns are pretty. Enough said.

But think about it again. One could look at lawns as a monumental waste of ecological resources. Today, there are approximately 55 million home lawns in the United States, covering 25 to 30 million acres. In New Jersey, the most densely populated state, *nearly one-fifth of the entire land area is covered with turfgrass,* twice as much land as is used for crop production. Although turfgrass is also used for golf courses and public parks, most is planted for lawns. The average home lawn, if used for growing fruits and vegetables, would yield two thousand dollars worth of crops. But instead of this land becoming a revenue generator, it is a "drainer": Americans spend an average of several hundred dollars a year to keep their lawns short and healthy.

If the purpose of lawns is solely ornamental, why has the tradition persisted for eons, when most conceptions of beauty change as often as the hem length of women's dresses? The Chinese grew lawns five thousand years ago, and circumstantial evidence indicates that the Mayans and Aztecs were lawn fanciers as well. In the Middle Ages, monarchs let their cattle run loose around their castles, not only to feed the animals, but to cut the grass so that advancing enemy forces could be spotted at a distance. Soon, aristocrats throughout Europe adopted the lawn as a symbol of prestige ("if it's good enough for the king, it's good enough for me!"). The games associated with lawns—bowls, croquet, tennis—all started as upper-class diversions.

The lawn quickly became a status symbol in colonial America, just as it was in Europe. Some homeowners used scythes to tend their lawns, but most let animals, particularly sheep, cows, and horses, do the work. In 1841, the lawn mower was introduced, much to the delight of homeowners, and much to the dismay of grazing animals and teenagers everywhere.

Dr. John Falk, who is associated with the educational research division of the Smithsonian Institution, has spent more time pondering this Imponderable than any person alive, and his speculations are provocative and convincing. Falk believes that our desire for a savannalike terrain, rather than being an aesthetic predilection, is actually a genetically encoded preference. Anthropologists agree that humankind has spent most of its history roaming the grasslands of East Africa. In order to survive against predators, humans needed trees for protection and water for drinking, but also grassland for foraging. If primitive man wandered away into rain forests, for example, he must have longed to return to the safety of his savanna home. As Falk commented in an interview in *Omni* magazine: "For more than ninety percent of human history the savanna was home. Home equals safety, and that information has to be fairly hard-wired if the animal is going to respond to danger instantaneously."

When we talked to Dr. Falk, he added more ammunition to support his theories. He has conducted a number of cross-cultural studies to ascertain the terrain preferences of people all over the world. He and psychologist John Balling showed subjects photographs of five different terrains—deciduous forest, coniferous forest, tropical rain forest, desert, and savanna—and asked them where they would prefer to live. The savanna terrain was chosen overwhelmingly. Falk's most recent studies were conducted in India and Nigeria, in areas where most subjects had never even seen a savanna. Yet they consistently picked the savanna as their first choice, with their native terrain usually the second preference.

Falk and Balling also found that children under twelve were even more emphatic in their selection of savannas, another strong, if inconclusive, indication that preference for savanna terrain is genetic.

In the *Omni* article, Falk also suggested that even the way we ornament our lawns mimics our East African roots. The ponds and fountains that decorate our grasses replicate the natural water formations of our homeland, and the popularity of umbrella-shaped shade trees might represent an attempt to recreate the acacia trees found in the African savanna.

Of course, psychologists have speculated about other reasons why we "need" lawns. The most common theory is that lawns and gardens are a way of taming and domesticating nature in an era in which affluent Westerners are virtually divorced from it. Another explanation is that lawns are a way of mapping territory, just as every other animal marks territory to let others know what property it is ready to defend. This helps explain why so many homeowners are touchy about the neighborhood kid barely scraping their lawn while trying to catch a football. As Dr. Falk told *Imponderables,* "People create extensions of themselves. When people create a lawn as an extension of themselves, they see a violation of their lawn as a violation of their space."

Lawns are also a status symbol, for they are a form of property that has a purely aesthetic rather than economic purpose. Historically, only the affluent have been able to maintain lawns —the poor simply didn't have the land to spare. Fads and fashions in lawns change, but there are usually ways for the rich to differentiate their lawns from the hoi polloi's. Highly manicured lawns have usually been the preference of the rich, but not always. In the Middle Ages, weeds were considered beautiful. In many parts of the world, mixed breeds of turf are preferred.

American taste has become increasingly conservative. Ever since World War II, the "ideal" American lawn has been a short, monoculture, weed-free lawn, preferably of Kentucky bluegrass. Falk sees these preferences as carry-overs from the technology used by American agronomists to develop grass for golf courses. Americans always want to build a better mousetrap; our "ideal lawn" has become just about the only type.

Americans have largely resisted the inroads of artificial grass. Although many team owners endorse it, sports fans by and large recoil at artificial turf in sports stadiums—perhaps another genetically determined predisposition.

Submitted by Rick Barber, of Denver, Colorado.

Why Do Many Exterminators Wear Hard Hats?

Our correspondent wondered why one of the largest exterminator companies, in its television commercials, dresses its exterminators with nice pants, a dressy shirt, and a hard hat. Is there any practical reason for the hard hat in real life? Is there a marketing reason?

The practical reason: pest-control operators often have to inspect crawl spaces, basements, and cellars full of obstacles—nails, heat ducts, spider webs, and other protruding objects from above. The hard hat helps reduce accidents.

The marketing reason: the hard hat conveys a professional image. Subliminally, the hard hat is supposed to make the customer think: "If the exterminator has to wear a hard hat, this work must be too dangerous for a civilian like me! Better leave it to the experts."

Submitted by Phil Feldman, of Los Angeles, California.

Who Was the Emmy That the Emmy Award Is Named After?

Not who, but what? Unlike the premier theater (Tony) and movie (Oscar) awards, the Emmy isn't named after a person.

In 1948, the president of the budding National Academy of Television Arts and Sciences, Charles Brown, formed a committee to select the outstanding achievements in television that year. He also asked for suggestions for a name and symbol for the award.

From the start, technological terms were the top contenders. "Iconoscope" (a large orthicon tube) was an early favorite, but the committee was afraid the name would be shortened to "Ike." "Tilly" (for television) was suggested, but cooler heads prevailed. Harry Lubcke, a pioneer television engineer and future president of the academy (1949–1950) offered "Emmy," a nickname for the image orthicon tube (state-of-the-art circuitry at that time), and it prevailed.

The statue itself was designed by Louis McManus, who received a gold lifetime membership in the academy and one of the six statuettes presented at the first Emmy Awards banquet on January 25, 1949. As McManus went up to receive his award, he is reputed to have been told, "Louis, here she is . . . our baby. She'll be here long after we're gone." Indeed, long after the image orthicon tube was gone.

Why Don't Dogs Develop Laryngitis, Sore Throats, Voice Changes, or Great Discomfort After Barking Continuously?

A caller on a talk show hit us with this Imponderable. The dog next door, left alone by his master, had been barking, continuously, for hours. Why didn't it hurt the dog's throat at least as much as the caller's ears?

We approached several vets and stumped some, but the consensus answer was best expressed by William E. Monroe, D.V.M., Diplomate, of the American College of Veterinary Internal Medicine:

> Dogs do occasionally get laryngitis and voice changes from excessive barking. It is not as common in dogs as in people because the motor control of the canine larynx (voice box) is not as refined as

that of humans for sound production. Therefore, the voice range is narrower and subsequent stress from phonation is probably not as severe. Since barking is not much a part of daily living for most pet dogs as speaking is for people, laryngitis manifested as a voice change is also not as frequently observed in dogs, even though it may be present.

Why Are There Eighteen Holes on a Golf Course?

In Scotland, the home of golf, courses were originally designed with varying numbers of holes, depending on the parcel of land available. Some golf courses, according to U.S. Golf Association Librarian Janet Seagle, had as few as five holes.

The most prestigious golf club, the Royal and Ancient Golf Club of St. Andrews, originally had twenty-two holes. On October 4, 1764, its original course, which had contained eleven holes out and eleven holes in, was reduced to eighteen holes total in order to lengthen them and make it more challenging. As a desire to codify the game grew, eighteen holes was adopted as the standard after the St. Andrews model.

What Does 0° in the Fahrenheit Scale Signify?

During our school days, we were forced to memorize various points in the Fahrenheit scale. We all know that the freezing point is 32° and that the boiling point is 212°. The normal human body temperature is the inelegantly unround number of 98.6°.

Countries that have adopted the metric system have invariably chosen the Celsius system to measure heat. In the Celsius scale, 0° equals the freezing point.

The Fahrenheit temperature scale was created by a German physicist named Gabriel Daniel Fahrenheit, who invented both the alcohol thermometer and the mercury thermometer. The divisions of his scale aren't quite as arbitrary as they might seem. Zero degrees was chosen to represent the temperature of an equal ice-salt mixture, and 100° was originally supposed to signify the normal body temperature. But Fahrenheit screwed up. Eventually, scientists found that the scale didn't quite work, and the normal body temperature was "down-scaled" to 98.6°.

Submitted by James S. Boczarski, of Amherst, New York.

What Does Each One-Degree Increment in the Fahrenheit Scale Signify?

Although his scale was not based on the freezing and boiling points, Fahrenheit recognized their significance. The interval between the boiling point (212°) and freezing point (32°) numbers exactly 180 degrees on the Fahrenheit scale, a figure with which scientists and mathematicians were used to working.

The increments in a temperature scale have no cosmic significance in themselves. The Celsius system, for example, is less precise than the Fahrenheit in distinguishing slight variations in moderate temperatures. Thus while 180 increments on the Fahrenheit scale are necessary to get from the freezing to the boiling point, the freezing point (0°) on the Celsius scale and the boiling point (100° C) are closer, only 100 increments apart.

In most cases, the meaning of the one-degree increments in temperature scales has more to do with what is intended to be measured by the scale than with any particular mathematical requirements. The Fahrenheit scale, intended for use in human thermometers, was designed originally to have 100°F represent the normal body temperature. Temperature scales now used by scientists, such as the Kelvin and Rankine scales, use absolute zero (the equivalent of −273.15° C or −459.67° F) as the base point. Rankine uses the same degree increments as Fahrenheit; Kelvin uses the Celsius degree.

Submitted by James L. Foley, of Calabasas, California.

Why Doesn't Rain Come Down the Chimney into the Fireplace When Smoke Can Get out of the Chimney?

Some residential buildings contain chimney caps, sloping structures that stand atop the chimney, as pictured below:

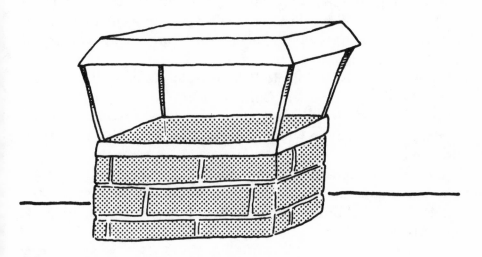

While the rain slides down the slopes, the smoke can easily escape under the cap.

But most buildings don't contain chimney caps and don't need them, for even large amounts of water can be absorbed by the bricks and masonry in a chimney. Indeed, the high absorbency of bricks is one of the reasons they are used in chimneys. In buildings of four or more stories, almost any quantity of water will be absorbed without the need of a chimney cap.

Submitted by Michael Jeffreys and Krissie Kraft, of Marina del Rey, California. Thanks also to: Leonard Scarpace, of Newhall, California.

Why Do Curad Bandage Wrappers Sparkle in the Dark When You Open Them?

Whenever we did promotion for the first volume of *Imponderables* and talked about why wintergreen Life Savers glow in the dark when you bite into them, we invariably received a phone call from someone asking why opening Curad wrappers caused the same phenomenon.

So we wrote to Colgate-Palmolive to unravel this mystery. The adhesive used to seal Curad bandage wrappers contains an ultraviolet dye. Most likely, the excitation and friction caused in the act of opening the wrapper causes the glow, which is visible only in the dark.

The research-and-development department of Colgate-Palmolive adds that static electricity might add to the sparkling effect. The sparkling is perfectly harmless and, if you are cut, a nice diversion from your pain.

Why Do Garment Labels Often Say *"Professionally* Dry-Clean Only"?

When was the last time you were propositioned by an *amateur* dry cleaner? Most folks don't take up dry-cleaning as an avocation, so when we were posed this Imponderable by a caller on the *Owen Spann Show,* we resolved to ferret out exactly who these dangerous amateur dry cleaners were.

It turns out that the veiled reference in "Professionally Dry-Clean Only" labels is not to incompetent practitioners, but to incompetent machines. What these labels are actually warning you against is cleaning the garments in the coin-op bulk dry-cleaning machines that used to be found frequently in laundromats. As much as anything, the labels are a convenient way for clothing manufacturers to avoid liability for the havoc the machines have wreaked. Molly Chillinsky, of the Coin Laundry Association, says that these bulk dry-cleaning devices are almost extinct; in time, the labels might become so as well.

Karen Graber, communications director of the International Fabricare Institute, the Association of [ahem] Professional Dry Cleaners and Launderers, adds that the Federal Trade Commission stipulates that along with the "Professionally Dry-Clean Only" warning, garment manufacturers should inform the consumer of any necessary modification in the basic dry-cleaning process. "Even the most professional dry cleaner might not know without being told that something should be dried at a low temperature, for example, or should not be pressed with steam." The clothing industry, unfortunately, often forgets to add these warnings.

Overcome by the spirit of Imponderables, Karen Graber added one of her own. Another clothing label warning that is sprouting up is the incantation: "Dry-clean only. Do not use petroleum or synthetic solvent." As there are only two kinds of solvent (you guessed it—petroleum and synthetic), her Imponderable is: what do you do with such a garment?

Graber's answer: "Leave it in the store, along with anything else you know from the label is bound to cause you and your dry cleaner some sleepless nights."

What Is the Difference Between "Flotsam" and "Jetsam"?

Although they sound suspiciously like two of Santa's missing reindeer, flotsam and jetsam are actually two different types of debris associated with ships. We rarely hear either term mentioned without the other close behind (and saying "jetsam" before "flotsam" is like saying "Cher" before "Sonny"). When we talk about "flotsam and jetsam" today, we are usually referring metaphorically to the unfortunate (for example, "While visiting the homeless shelter, the governor glimpsed what it is like to be the flotsam and jetsam of our society").

At one time, however, "flotsam" and "jetsam" not only had different meanings, but carried important legal disinctions. In English common law, "flotsam" (derived from the Latin *flottare*, "to float") referred specifically to the cargo or parts of a wrecked ship that float on the sea.

"Jetsam" (also derived from Latin—*jactare*, "to throw") referred to goods purposely thrown overboard in order either to lighten the ship or to keep the goods from perishing if the ship did go under.

Although the main distinction between the two terms was the way the goods got into the water, technically, to become jetsam, the cargo had to be dragged ashore and above the high-water line. If not, the material was considered flotsam, which included all cargo found on the shore between the high- and low-water lines.

Actually, two more terms, "lagan" and "derelict," were also used to differentiate cargo. "Lagan" referred to any abandoned wreckage lying at the bottom of the sea; "derelict" was the abandoned ship itself.

While insurance companies today have to pay out for flotsam, jetsam, lagan, *and* derelict, the old distinctions once dictated who got the remains. Jetsam went to the owner of the boat, but flotsam went to the Crown. The personal effects of nonsurviving crewmen could become flotsam or jetsam—depending on how far the debris traveled and whether it floated.

Why Do Doughnuts Have Holes?

The exact origins of doughnuts and their holes are shrouded in mystery and are a topic of such controversy that we have twice been caught in the middle of heated arguments among professional bakers on radio talk shows. So let us make one thing perfectly clear: we offer no conclusive proofs here, only consensus opinion.

Some form of fried cake has existed in almost every culture. "Prehistoric doughnuts"—petrified fried cakes with holes— have been found among the artifacts of a primitive Indian tribe. The Dutch settlers in America, though, are usually credited with popularizing fried cakes (without holes) in the United States, which they called "oily cakes" or *olykoeks*. Washington Irving, writing about colonial New York, described "a dish of balls of sweetened dough fried in hog's fat, and called dough nuts or oly koeks." Fried cakes became so popular in New York and New England that shops sprouted up that specialized in serving them with fresh-brewed coffee. In 1673, the first store-bought fried cakes were made available by Anna Joralemon in New York. Mrs. Joralemon weighed 225 pounds and was known affectionately as "the Big Doughnut."

The gentleman usually credited with the "invention" of the doughnut hole was an unlikely candidate for the job—a sea captain named Hanson Gregory. Supposedly, Captain Gregory was at the helm of his ship, eating a fried cake one night, when stormy weather arose. Gregory, needing both hands to steer the ship, spontaneously rammed the cake over one of the spokes. Impressed with his creation, Gregory ordered the ship's cook to make fried cakes with holes from then on.

Many other legends surround the creation of the doughnut hole. Plymouth, Massachusetts, advances the notion that the first doughnut hole was created when, in the seventeenth century, a drunken Indian brave shot an arrow through a kitchen window, punching out a piece of dough from the center of a cake just about to be fried. Pretty lame, Plymouth.

Regardless of the origin of the holes in doughnuts, we have learned that bakers disagree about its role in the making of a quality doughnut. Certainly, good doughnuts can be made without holes.

Thomas A. Lehmann, director of bakery assistance at the American Institute of Baking, told us that yeast-raised doughnuts can be made quite easily without the hole and points to the bismarck, or jelly-filled doughnut, as a perfect example. Lehmann adds, though, that if bismarcks were fried on the surface, the same way as conventional yeast-raised doughnuts, the holeless dough would tend to overexpand, turning into a ball shape. That is why most bakers prefer submersion frying, which results in a more uniform and symmetrical finished product.

"Cake" doughnuts, which are chemically leavened, can also be made without holes, but many experts believe that they lose their desired consistency without them. Glenn Bacheller, director of product marketing for Dunkin' Donuts, explains why the hole is important: "Heat does not penetrate the donut as readily [without the hole] and the interior of the donut tends to have a doughy texture. The only way to prevent this is to fry the donut longer, which results in the exterior of the donut being over fried."

Why Does a Newspaper Tear Smoothly Vertically and Raggedly Horizontally?

Newsprint is made up of many wood fibers. The fibers are placed on printers in pulp form, consisting of 80 to 90 percent water— the newsprint dries while in the machine. The printing machines are designed to line up the fibers in a horizontal position to add tear strength to the sheet vertically.

The basic purpose of lining up the fibers in one direction is simply to add stability to the sheet when the press is running. According to Ralph E. Eary, national director of production and engineering for the newspaper division of Scripps Howard, "All standard size newspapers are printed vertically on an unwound sheet of newsprint." A rip in one sheet endangers the whole printing process, and at best costs money and time.

In other words, the finished newspaper has a grain, just as a piece of meat or linen has a grain. (Even notice how hard it is to tear a bedsheet in one direction and how easy in another?) When you rip the newspaper vertically, you are tearing with the grain, or more accurately, between grains. The same principle is in effect when one consumes Twizzlers brand licorice. Individual pieces rip off easily if you tear between the slices; only Conan could rip off pieces horizontally.

Submitted by L. Stone, of Mamaroneck, New York. Thanks also to: Julia Berger, of Richmond, Virginia, and Virginia E. Griffin, of Salinas, California.

Why Are The Netherlands also Called Holland and the Low Countries? And Why Are Its People Called Dutch?

Our pet theory was that the official name of the country was "the Netherlands," but that "Holland" was used to make it easier for mapmakers to fit the name within the confined borders. Actually, the official name of the country is Nederland, the name native inhabitants call it—"Netherlands" is simply the closest English equivalent.

The word "nether" means below the earth's surface. The low and marshy lands near the mouth of the estuary of the Rhine River are responsible for the name, "the Low Countries." The German name "Niederlande" and the French name "les Pays-Bas" are exact translations.

By why "Holland"? Holland was the name of a province, not the whole country. In the sixteenth, seventeenth, and eighteenth centuries, it was by far the most important province commercially, and Hollanders displayed more devotion to their province than to the nation as a whole. Holland eventually became so dominant that, much in the same way that the Soviet Union is mislabeled "Russia," Holland came to represent all of the Netherlands.

Further confusing the issue is the term "Dutch," used to describe the citizens of the Netherlands. "Dutch" is actually older than "the Netherlands." Until the sixteenth century, inhabitants of the Netherlands called themselves Diets (which means "the people"). This word, pronounced "deets," was corrupted in English as "Dutch." The British continued to use the medieval name long after Netherlanders stopped using it themselves.

Americans tend to use the word "Dutch" not only to describe Netherlanders, but also Germans. Thus, while the Holland Dutch from Michigan are true descendants of Netherlanders, the Pennsylvania Dutch are actually German.

(The "Dutch" in Pennsylvania Dutch almost certainly stems from a corruption of the German name for their country, Deutschland.) According to the Netherlands Chamber of Commerce: "To stop this confusing multiplicity of names the Netherlands Government has tried to use the words 'The Netherlands' as the name for the country and 'Netherlander' as the name for an inhabitant of the Netherlands. It is easy to decree such a thing, but it takes much time to suppress a time-honoured word used in foreign countries."

Netherlanders have to deal with confusion not only about the name of their country, but about the name of their capital. Amsterdam is the official capital, but the seat of government is at The Hague. The official name of The Hague is 's-Gravenhage, "the count's hedge," except nobody calls the city 's-Gravenhage, preferring the colloquial Den Haag (the hedge).

For such a small country, the Netherlands has its share of identity problems.

Submitted by Daniel Marcus, of Watertown, Massachusetts.

What Are Those Twitches and Jerks That Occasionally Wake Us Just as We Are Falling Asleep?

It has probably happened to you. You are nestled snugly under the covers. You aren't quite asleep but you're not quite awake. Just as your brain waves start to slow, and as you fantasize about owning that Mercedes Benz convertible, you are jolted awake by an unaccountable spasm, usually in a leg.

You have been a victim of what is called a "hypnic jerk," a phenomenon explained in David Bodanis's marvelous *The Body Book*:

> They occur when nerve fibers leading to the leg, in a bundle nearly as thick as a pencil, suddenly fire in unison. Each tiny nerve in the bundle produces a harsh tightening of a tiny portion of muscle fiber that is linked to it down in the leg, and when they all fire together the leg twitches as a whole.

Sleep specialists haven't pinned down what causes hypnic jerks or why they occur only at the onset of sleep. Although some people experience them more often than others, their appearance is unpredictable, unlike myoclonic jerks, spasms that occur at regular intervals during deep sleep.

Submitted by Cathy C. Bodell, of Fullerton, California. Thanks also to: Daniel A. Placko, Jr., of Chicago, Illinois.

Why Are There Twenty-one Guns in a Twenty-one–Gun Salute?

The original intention of gun salutes was probably to assure the royalty or nation being honored that they were physically secure —that the weapons that were meant to pay tribute could also be used to kill. Before any recorded history of formal gun salutes, many cultures were known to discharge ordnance indiscriminately at festivals and holidays. Some good old-fashioned noise, be it fireworks in China or cheering at football games, has always been an accompaniment to joyous rituals.

Twenty-one–gun salutes have existed since at least the sixteenth century (the final scene from *Hamlet* mentions one), but the number of guns fired evolved gradually and inconsistently from country to country. The English were the first to codify the practice. According to a study conducted in 1890 by C. H. Davis, a commander and chief intelligence officer in the U.S. Navy, the earliest English regulation, formulated in 1688, prescribed that the birthdays and coronations of royalty should be solemnized "by the Fleet, Squadrons, and every single ship of war, by the discharge of such number of their great guns," but allowed that the number of guns used should be decided upon by the chief officer. By 1730, the British Naval Regulations were amended so that the number of guns discharged was still at the discretion of the chief officer, but was not to exceed twenty-one for each ship.

The notion of twenty-one as the highest gun salute undoubtedly stems from this royal origin. Salutes were always in odd numbers in the British military, with lower-ranking officers receiving, say, a five-gun salute and each increasing rank offered two more guns. The 1730 regulation was probably a response to rampant inflation in gun salutes; the Navy wanted to assure that no one received more guns than the royalty. In 1808, twenty-one guns was mandated as the *only* proper salute for royalty.

Although the United States, in its infancy, adopted gun salutes, there were no specific regulations governing the practice. Until 1841, the U.S. Navy fired one gun for each state in the Union. As our nation grew, and what with the price of ammunition, we prudently decided to limit our salutes to twenty-one guns. This change was codified in 1865 and has remained the practice ever since. The establishment of a maximum standard was not arbitrary or capricious. Gun salutes were a form of international diplomacy, and any deviation from the norm had possible ramifications. Commander Davis stressed the importance of conforming to international practice: "According to the present regulations and long established custom, a vessel of war, on her arrival in a foreign port, salutes the flag of the nation to which that port belongs, after having ascertained that the salute will be returned, with 21 guns. The salute is immediately returned gun for gun. This rule is universal and invariable in all countries in the world."

Davis believed that if the United States had continued its

practice of discharging one gun for each state, it could have had serious consequences. He feared that other countries would assume that by exceeding twenty-one guns, we were trumpeting our own power and superiority.

A last objection to the one gun/one state idea was that gun salutes have always involved an odd number. Even numbers have traditionally been fired in mourning and at funerals. While modern communications equipment has largely obviated the need to use gun salutes as a symbol of peace and goodwill, the twenty-one–gun salute is alive and well as a ritual to express celebration and honor. Although we can't pinpoint exactly why the British first arrived at twenty-one (some speculate that the combination of three multiplied by seven might have been adopted for mystical or religious reasons), we clearly owe our custom to the British military's desire to salute royalty with the utmost hoopla.

Submitted by Debra Kalkwarf, of Columbus, Indiana. Thanks also to: Douglas Watkins, Jr., of Hayward, California.

Why Do Women Tend to Have Higher Voices Than Men? Why Do Short People Tend to Have Higher Voices Than Tall People?

Daniel Boone, a University of Arizona professor and expert on vocal mechanisms, provides the answer: "Fundamental frequency or voice pitch level is directly related to the length and thickness of the individual's vocal folds [or vocal cords]." The average man's vocal-fold length is approximately eighteen millimeters; the average woman's is ten millimeters.

The tall person of either gender is likely to have longer vocal cords than a shorter person of the same sex.

Washington, D.C. Streets Are Named
Alphabetically. Why Is There No "J" Street?

We posed this Imponderable to Nelson Rimensnyder, historian of the House of Representatives Committee on the District of Columbia. Although Rimensnyder stated that there was no definitive answer, he did offer two main theories:

1. *J*, as written during the eighteenth century, was often confused with other letters of the alphabet, particularly *I*.

2. Pierre L'Enfant and other founders of Washington, D.C., were political, professional, and personal enemies of John Jay and therefore snubbed him when naming the streets in 1791.

Rimensnyder adds that there *is* a two-mile-long "Jay" Street in the Deanwood section of northeast Washington. Although this street presumably honors our first Supreme Court Chief Justice, its naming didn't upset Pierre L'Enfant in the slightest: "Jay" Street wasn't adopted until after 1900.

Submitted by M. Babe Penalver, of Bronx, New York.

What Happens to the Tread That Wears Off Tires?

The tread wears gradually off our tires. After a few years of heavy mileage, it eventually becomes bare. But we don't see bits of tread on the road (except from premature blowouts, of course). Highways are not discolored with blackened tread bits. Does tire tread disappear along with our socks?

The automobile industry, the tire industry, and some independent pollution experts have long been concerned about what may seem to be a trivial problem. Two specialists in the chemistry department of the Ford Motor Company have estimated that 600,000 metric tons of tire tread are worn off American vehicles every year. The possibility was more than remote that all of this material might remain in the air, in suspendable particles, which could be dangerous to humans. So they sought a way to measure what happens to the disappearing tread.

Tests to determine the presence of tire tread were held in three different sites, all of which presented some problems. First, indoor tests were designed to simulate driving wear on a tire. Unfortunately, without ambient weather conditions, worn rubber simply tended to stick to the simulated road surface. Scientists knew this wasn't what happened under real conditions, for the second type of tests, on real highways, indicated that virtually no rubber stayed on the road, due to wind, rain, and movement of surrounding traffic. Additionally, surface areas around highways were sometimes cleaned by maintenance crews, hindering efforts to measure long-term accumulation of tire tread. The third type of test, in tunnels, might be thought to show the maximum possible buildup of tire tread, except that road surfaces in tunnels tend to wear tires less than surface streets, and the lack of natural wind and rain in the tunnel made any extrapolation difficult.

Still, the combined results of these experiments did provide quite a lot of information about exactly what happens to tire tread. Whereas the most common substance in exhaust fumes is dangerous lead, the most plentiful tire debris is in the form of styrene-butadiene rubber (SBR), the most common rubber hydrocarbon in treads. Most of the tread debris is not in the form of gas, but rather in microscopic particles that are heavy enough to fall to the ground.

All road and tunnel tests seem to confirm that particle debris found along roadsides accounted for at least 50 percent of the total missing tire tread, and possibly much more. One study indicated that 2 percent of all roadside dustfall consisted of worn tread material. Another study, in Detroit, found that of the total particulate loading in the air, only 1 percent was tread dust. Even in tunnel tests, tire tread comprised only 1 to 4 percent of the total airborne particulate matter generated—a percentage far less than that of the exhaust emissions of gasoline- and diesel-powered vehicles.

All the tests concur, then, that the vast majority of worn tread in particle form falls on the ground instead of staying in the air.

What happens to the rest of the worn tread? Much of it is dissolved through oxidation and devulcanization (a chemical reaction that reverses the process used to harden rubber). One estimate speculated that devulcanization accounted for 30 percent of the disappearing SBR. Wind, water runoff, oxygen, and microbial attack all act to help degrade tread particulates, which degenerate faster than the tread rubber on tires in any case.

In fact, nobody could get very excited about the possible environmental dangers of worn tire tread. If the tread particulate were light enough to remain airborne, it could cause some harm, but the 95 percent plus that settles into the ground near the roadway poses no health hazard. K. L. Campbell, of Firestone Tire & Rubber Company, points out that "Tire tread rubber is essentially an inert material so it doesn't contribute to acid rain or soil pollution." And because worn tire-tread particles on the ground are in too small a form even to see with the naked eye, we aren't even aware that they are there. Which proves again that what you can't see can't hurt you.

Submitted by Larry Orbin, of Florissant, Missouri. Thanks also to: Brad Miles, of Victoria, British Columbia; G. William Foster, Jr., of Tulsa, Oklahoma; and Art Lombard, of Oakland, California.

Why Do Whips Make a Cracking Sound When Snapped?

Whips can attain a speed of more than seven hundred miles per hour when snapped, breaking the sound barrier. What you are hearing is a mini sonic boom.

How Did Xmas Come to Stand for Christmas?

The use of the colloquial "Xmas" has often been singled out as an example of how the holiday has been commercialized and robbed of its religious content. The X in Xmas is actually the descendant of the Greek equivalent of *Ch*, as in "Christos," which means "Christ." The letter X has stood for Christ (look up X in any dictionary) since at least A.D. 1100, and the term "Xmas" was first cited in 1551. Word expert Eric Partridge points out that the scholarly abbreviation for "Christianity" is "Xianity."

So many people dislike "Xmas" for its supposed crassness that its use is now virtually confined to commercial literature and banners. The *New York Times Manual of Style and Usage*, for example, offers this simple recommendation for when "Xmas" is acceptable: "Never use."

Submitted by Bobby Dalton, of Maryland Heights, Missouri. Thanks also to: Andrew Neiman, of Dallas, Texas.

Do Batteries Wear Out Faster If You Turn Up the Volume of a Radio?

Absolutely.

The battery applications manager of Eveready Battery Company, Inc., B. G. Merritt, told us about some research that proved the point conclusively:

> We recently tested a major manufacturer dual cassette "boom box" powered by 6 "D" size cells. From lowest setting to highest setting on the volume control, the power necessary to drive the "box" increased three times. This power increase directly translates into one third battery life at full volume when compared with zero volume. This power increase is necessary to drive the speakers.
>
> By comparison, a personal stereo (portable type) cassette player current increased only 30% when adjusted from zero volume to full volume. Battery life would be decreased only 30% for this device.

WHY DO CLOCKS RUN CLOCKWISE?

Don French, a battery expert at Radio Shack, confirmed Eveready's findings. He estimated that a shirt-pocket portable radio would use at least 200 percent more battery charge at the loudest volume setting than at the softest. French pointed out that even tiny radios have audio amplifiers that must be powered. A home stereo might require fifty watts and a shirt-pocket radio two hundred milliwatts, but the principle is the same—the more power required, the more juice required.

Submitted by Allen Kahn, of New York, New York.

Why Do Some Ranchers Hang Old Boots on Fenceposts?

It all started with an innocent call from a listener to Tannah Hirsch's KMBZ talk show in Kansas City. The listener asked the Imponderable above, and we admitted that we didn't have the slightest idea why some ranchers hang old boots on fenceposts. In fact, being urban folks, we had never seen this phenomenon at all. But it was an intriguing question, and we decided to investigate. The results will show you some of the trials and tribulations of tracking down answers to Imponderables.

A few weeks later, we received a letter from Rick Miller, who works at Kansas State University as an agricultural agent in Johnson County, Kansas. Rick had previously worked in southwestern Kansas, had seen boots hanging on fences, and had investigated. His conclusion was intriguing: "The boots are hung on the fence to discourage predators such as coyotes from entering fields where livestock are. The coyotes, with their keen sense of smell, pick up the human odor from the boots. Thinking humans are around, the coyotes won't cross the fence." Having read *All the President's Men* and faithfully watched *Lou Grant*, we were determined to dig up a second source to corroborate Mr. Miller's story.

First we wrote to several ranchers' organizations. All were familiar with the practice, but none mentioned the coyote angle, and only one had any theory at all—Rhoda G. Cook, executive secretary of the Montana Outfitters and Guides Association: "My late husband, who was a long-time packer and breaker of mules for the Forest Service said several times his boots were on the fence so everybody would know that a real cowboy lived there. I can vouch for the fact that they certainly smelled better out there than under the bed."

Still missing the "smoking gun" that could definitively answer the Imponderable, we contacted all of the largest manufacturers of cowboy boots. Nobody could help us, but Frye sent us to *Western Horseman* magazine, where we spoke to writer Darrell Arnold and publisher Dick Spencer. Mr. Spencer didn't put much stock in the coyote theory, but he remembered seeing long stretches of boots on fenceposts along Windless Hills, near Ogallala, Nebraska. He recommended that we contact someone in that area.

We found out that the newspaper of record in Ogallala was the Keith County *News*, published by Jack Pollack. Mr. Pollack was quite familiar with the stretches of boots on fenceposts, but didn't know why they were there. He suggested we speak to some ranchers in the area and was kind enough to supply some phone numbers.

We contacted several ranchers, none of whom could say how the practice began. But one rancher, Waldo Haythorne, asked if we wanted to get in touch with the son of the man who started the tradition. We sure did!

And we found out that the pioneer in the practice of hanging boots from fenceposts was none other than Henry Swanson. According to his son, Virgil Swanson, after Henry put some worn boots on his fenceposts his neighbors followed his example, until the path from the town of Arthur to the cemetery about a quarter-mile away was marked by boots at every ranch. Others copied the practice, and up in the hills above Arthur, there are longer stretches of boot-strewn fences (probably the ones Dick Spencer had spotted).

So, with great anticipation, we asked Virgil Swanson the question that had come to obsess us: WHY did your father hang the boots from the fencepost? He paused for a moment, and then replied, "Gee. I really don't know. I guess he just did it to do it."

Dejected, we were back to first base. But quitters we are not. We called up our original correspondent, Rick Miller, to find out more about the coyote angle. Rick told us that coyotes have a keen sense of smell, and are uncommonly smart animals. Coyotes don't like to mess around with people, and boots trapped the human scent better than anything else. Rick said that some ranchers in southwestern Kansas put boots on every single fencepost surrounding their fields, and it seemed to work for them. We were still a tad skeptical, because we couldn't get anyone else, including a few vets we consulted, to confirm Rick Miller's explanation. Rick suggested we speak to Bob Henderson, who works for the Kansas State Wildlife Department.

Bob Henderson, of course, did *not* confirm Rick's theory. He felt that coyotes are too smart to be fooled more than once or twice by boots on fenceposts, and that coyotes are not as frightened by human odors as most people think. The problem with the boot-as-repellent theory is that coyotes, despite their excellent sense of smell, do not rely only on that sense. The coyote also uses its sight to determine whether it is safe to prey; once it becomes accustomed to seeing the same boots on the same fenceposts day after day, it won't be timid about scaling the fence. In fact, Henderson said, coyotes are not afraid of human scent (human urine has even been used as an attractant to trap coyotes)—they are afraid of people.

Just as we were about ready to give up on this Imponderable

(or put it in the Frustrables section), we received a letter from Lynda Frank, of Omaha, Nebraska, posing the same Imponderable. We called her immediately. Although Lynda had no concrete theories, she assumed that the practice was simply a traditional one, without any practical purpose.

We then spoke to five or six experts in Animal Damage Control. These are local or regional governmental agencies that attempt to rid areas of coyotes and other pests. None of them was familiar with the boot-repellent theory. One person referred us to Dr. Mike Fall, at the Denver Wildlife Research Center, a specialist in predator control. Like most good scientists, Dr. Fall was circumspect about speculating on a topic he had not researched himself, but he had grave doubts about whether boots on fenceposts would have any long-lasting effect on deterring coyotes from trespassing.

Dr. Fall emphasized that to discourage coyotes, you must chip away at one of their strengths—their adaptability. You must disrupt the patterns they encounter, for they can become accustomed to just about anything, including human odors. Scientists still don't fully understand the impact of odors on coyotes. Scents have been developed that can consistently attract coyotes, but nothing yet can consistently repel them.

Fall predicted that boots on fenceposts would work over time only if the footwear were constantly rearranged, making the coyote insecure about whether humans were afoot. Experiments have been conducted using electric fences, guard dogs, and other animals, lights, and loud radios and tape recordings to deter coyotes, all with some, but limited success. The most promising approach, according to Dr. Fall, is a multistimulus deterrent, flashing lights with high-frequency sounds produced in *random patterns*, so that the coyotes are thrown off guard.

So—after consulting nearly thirty people, we still don't have a definitive answer to this Imponderable. It has thoroughly humbled us. We would love to hear from readers who might have the answer. Until then, we can only offer the three theories offered to us that make sense:

1. The boots scare away coyotes.
2. It is far wiser to stink up a fencepost than to stink up a house.
3. To paraphrase Virgil Swanson, "Some people just do things to do things."

Submitted by Rick Miller, of Gardner, Kansas. Thanks also to: Lynda Frank, of Omaha, Nebraska.

Why Do Bananas, Unlike Other Fruits, Grow Upward?

If you knew about the tumultuous birth process of the banana, perhaps you would be more charitable the next time you encounter some bruised specimens at the supermarket.

The banana is actually a giant herb in the same biological family as lilies, orchids, and palms. It is the largest plant on earth without a woody stem—a banana stalk is 93 percent water—and is consequently extremely fragile. Although it can reach a full height of fifteen to thirty feet in one year, even moderate winds can blow down a plant.

The fruit stem or bunch originates at ground level. At this stage, the bunch consists of all of the fruit enclosed in leaf bracts. The individual fruit "fingers" (the technical name for a single banana) are pointed upward. As the bunch or bud is pushing its way through the mass of tightly packed leaf sheaths known as the pseudostem, the fruit fingers remain pointed upward until they emerge at the top of the plant.

The bananas exert tremendous pressure on the pseudostem. Before the fruits expand, the leaves enclosing them roll around on themselves inside the trunk. After the fruit emerges from the leaves, the fingers point downward, but only because the bud surrounding them has changed direction.

Once the entire bunch of bananas is mature, fully emerged from its sheath, and pointing downward, the individual leaf bracts enclosing the hands (the female flower cluster) fall away, exposing the fruit. At this point, the individual flowers grow rapidly, filling out. Their increased weight bends the main stalk so that the individual fruits on the hand start to turn upward in about seven to ten days.

Dr. Pedro Sole, of Chiquita Brands, points out that in the past, "primitive bananas grew upwards, like the seeds of most grasses forming a spike."

So is there a logical reason for the banana's tortuous up-and-down birthing process now? Jack D. DeMent, of the Dole Fresh Fruit Company, sees the answer in the behavior of the traditional noncommercial banana plant:

> A flower is found on the tip of each individual fruit. This flower is removed during [commercial] packing but is present during fruit development. As the hands turn up, the flower is better exposed to insects and nectar eating birds and bats. Their feeding would normally aid in fertilization of the fruit. Today's commercial banana is sterile and rarely—almost never—produces a viable seed.

DeMent theorizes that the commercial banana's tendency to grow upward is a holdover from its ancestors that needed to point upward for their very survival.

Presumably, natural selection will simplify the growth process of the banana over the next few hundred thousand years or so.

Submitted by Lynda J. Turner, of Hackettstown, New Jersey.

Why Is There a Black Dot in the Middle of Otherwise White Bird Droppings?

An important question, one that philosophers throughout the ages have pondered. Luckily, ornithologists know the answer.

That black dot is fecal matter. The white stuff is urine. The urine and fecal matter of birds collect together and are voided simultaneously out of the same orifice. Feces tend to sit directly in the middle of droppings because the urine, slightly sticky in consistency, clings to them.

Submitted by Ann Marie Byrne, of Queens, New York.

Do Toilet-Seat Covers Really Protect Us Against Anything?

We became suspicious about the efficacy of toilet-seat covers when we pondered, one day: why don't they sell toilet-seat covers for home use? You see them only in public rest rooms. Perhaps the idea is not to protect you from disease, but from the thought of exposing your bare backside to the same surface area occupied by heaven knows who before you.

We were on the right track. Not only are venereal diseases *not* spread by toilet seats, but nothing else is, either. Although there was one report suggesting that the herpes virus *may* survive *briefly* in such an environment, the secretary of the American Society of Colon and Rectal Surgeons, Dr. J. Byron Gathright, Jr., echoed the sentiments of other doctors we spoke to: "There is no scientific evidence of disease transmission from toilet seats."

Submitted by Jean Hanamoto, of Morgan Hill, California.

Why Do Sailors Wear Bell-Bottom Trousers?

Nobody knows for sure if there was one particular reason why this custom started, but three theories predominate:

1. The flared leg allows bell-bottoms to fit over boots easily. Sailors traditionally sleep with their boots at the side of the bed, so that, in case of emergency, they don't have to waste time trying to position their pants over their footwear. Once a sailor arrives on deck, having the trouser legs fully cover the top of the boot has practical advantages as well—it protects him from spray and rain entering his boots.

2. Bell-bottoms are easily rolled up. Because sailors often work with potentially harmful chemicals (scrubbing the deck with lye, for example), rolling up the cuffs prevents permanent damage to the pants. Also, if a sailor needs to wade ashore, bell-bottoms can easily be rolled up above the knee.

3. If a sailor is thrown overboard, bell-bottoms are also easier to remove than conventional trousers. And the loose fit of the bell-bottom also makes it easier to remove boots in the water.

Sailors in boot camp are taught another practical use for bell-bottom trousers. If the legs are tied at the ends, bell-bottoms can hold quite a lot of air; in a pinch, they can be used as flotation devices.

Why Doesn't Sugar Spoil or Get Moldy?

Virtually all living organisms can digest sugar easily. So why isn't sugar prone to the same infestation as flour or other kitchen staples?

Because sugar has an extremely low moisture content—usually about 0.02 percent—it dehydrates microorganisms that might cause mold. As John A. Kolberg, vice-president of operations at the Spreckels Division of Amstar Corporation, explains it, "Water molecules diffuse or migrate out of the microorganism at a faster rate than they diffuse into it. Thus, eventually the microorganism dies due to a lack of moisture within it." Sugar's low moisture level also impedes chemical changes that could cause spoilage.

All bets are off, however, if sugar is dissolved in water. The more dilute the sugar solution, the more likely yeasts and molds will thrive in it. Even exposure to high humidity for a few days will allow sugar to absorb enough moisture to promote spoilage and mold.

Storing sugar in an airtight container will retard the absorption of moisture even in humid conditions. If stored in an atmosphere unaffected by swings in temperature and humidity, sugar retains its 0.02 percent moisture level and has an unlimited shelf life.

Submitted by Joel Kuni, of Kirkland, Washington.

AND OTHER IMPONDERABLES

Why Do Nurses Wear White? Why Do Surgeons Wear Blue or Green When Operating?

Florence Nightingale always wore a white uniform. White, of course, is a symbol of purity, and in the case of a nurse, an appropriate and practical one—white quickly shows any dirtiness.

Surgeons also wore white until 1914, when a surgeon decided that red blood against a white uniform was rather repulsive and needlessly graphic. The spinach green color he chose to replace it helped neutralize the bright red.

At the end of World War II, the lighting was changed in operating rooms, and most surgeons switched to a color called "misty green." Since about 1960, most surgeons have used a color called "seal blue," which contains a lot of gray. Why this latest switch? According to Bernard Lepper, of the Career Apparel Institute of New York City, seal blue shows up better on the TV monitors used to demonstrate surgical techniques to medical students.

> *Submitted by Norman J. Sanchez, of Baton Rouge, Louisiana. Thanks also to: Lori Bending, of Des Plaines, Illinois; Andrew Neiman, of Dallas, Texas; and Reverend Ken Vogler, of Jeffersonville, Indiana.*

Why Doesn't a "Two-by-Four" Measure Two Inches by Four Inches?

Before the invention of mass-scale surfacing equipment, most lumber was sold to the construction trade in rough form. In the "good old days," a "two-by-four" was approximately two inches by four inches. Even then, two inches by four inches was a rough estimate—cutting equipment trimmed too thick or too thin on occasion.

As the construction trade demanded smooth edges, surfacing machinery was created to handle the task automatically. These devices reduced the dimensions of the rough lumber by at least one-eighth of an inch in thickness and width.

The radio talk-show caller who posed this Imponderable wondered why he got gypped by buying finished "two-by-fours" that measured 1⅝ inches thick by 3⅝ inches wide. The answer comes from H. M. Niebling, executive vice-president of the North American Wholesale Lumber Association, Inc.:

> [After the early planers were used,] profile or "splitter" heads were developed for planers, wherein one could take a 2″ × 12″ rough piece and make 3 pieces of 2 × 4s in one surfacing operation [i.e., as the lumber went through the planer it was surfaced on four sides and then, at the end of the machine, split and surfaced on the interior sides]. Unfortunately, the "kerf," or amount of wood taken out in this splitting operation, further reduced the widths.

The size of these "kerfs," three-eighths of an inch, didn't allow processors to make three pieces 3⅞ inches wide (three times 3⅞ plus three times ⅜, to represent the "wastage" of the kerfs, equals 12¾ inches, wider than the original 12-inch rough piece). This is why the dimensions of the finished piece were reduced to 1⅝ inches thick by 3⅝ inches wide.

If you think this is complicated, Niebling recounts other problems in settling the dimensions of lumber. Fresh-cut lumber is called "green" lumber, whether or not it is actually green in color at the time. Green lumber must be dried by natural or artificial means. When lumber dries, it shrinks and becomes stronger. Some lumbermen believed that either dry lumber should be sold smaller in size or that green lumber should be sold larger. Recounts Niebling: "The result was that 2 × 4s surfaced dry comes out at 1½″ by 3½″ instead of 1⅝″ by 3⅞″. To settle the fight between green and dry producers, a green 2 × 4 is surfaced to 1⁹⁄₁₆″ by 3⁹⁄₁₆″. In effect, they reduced the green size too to settle the fight."

The lumbermen we spoke to agreed that the pint-sized two-by-fours provided the same strong foundation for houses that the rough original-sized ones would. One expert compared the purchase of a two-by-four to buying a steak. You buy a nice steak and it is trimmed with fat. Sure, the butcher will trim off the fat, but then he'll raise the price per pound. One way or the other, you pay.

Why Is an Acre 43,560 Square Feet?

"Acre" is an Anglo-Saxon word that means, literally, the amount of land plowable in one day. The term was used before the tenth century, the acre originally referring to the area that could be plowed by a yoke of oxen in one day. The actual footage of the acre varied from region to region.

In the late thirteenth and early fourteenth centuries, Edward I and Edward III tried to codify English measurements. Although the quantity of land that could be plowed in one day was obviously variable, depending upon such factors as the durability of the animals pulling the plow, the plowing equipment, and the topography of the land, there were obvious advantages to standardization. By the reign of Henry VIII, there was universal agreement that an acre should be 40 poles long by 4 poles wide (or 160 square rods). These nice round units of measurement (one rod = 16.5 feet; one pole = one square rod), popular in agricultural societies, translate exactly to our current standard of the acre as 43,560 square feet. With modern machinery, any farmer can plow considerably more than one acre in a day, but the acre has proved to be an enduring unit of measurement.

Why Do Men's Bicycles Have a Crossbar?

We're sure you'll be overjoyed to learn that everyone we talked to agreed on the paramount issue: that crossbar at the top of the frame makes men's bikes far sturdier than women's. After centuries of experimentation, manufacturers have found that the best strength-to-weight ratio is maintained by building frames in the shape of diamonds or triangles. Without the crossbar, or as it is now called, the "top tube," part of the ideal diamond structure is missing.

A man's bicycle has its top tube parallel to the ground; on a ladies' bicycle, the top tube intersects the seat tube several inches above the crank axle. Why is the women's top tube lower than the male's?

The tradition is there for no other reason than to protect the dignity and reputations of women riding a bicycle while wearing a skirt or dress. Now that most women bicyclists wear pants or fancy bicycle tights, the original purpose for the crossbar is moot, although Joe Skrivan, a product-development engineer for Huffy, points out an additional bonus of the lower top tube: it allows for easy mounting and dismounting.

Skrivan notes that the design difference creates few complaints from women. Casual women bicyclists don't necessarily need the rigidity of the higher crossbar. Serious female bicyclists buy frames with exactly the same design as men's.

Submitted by Linda Jackson, of Buffalo, New York.

Why Is Royalty Referred to as "Blue-Blooded"?

In the eighth century, a group of Islamic warriors, the Moors, invaded and occupied Spain. And they ruled over the country for five centuries.

This didn't sit too well with the aristocrats of Castile, who began referring to themselves as *sangre azul* ("blue blood") to differentiate themselves from the Moors. No, the Castilians' blood was no different in color than the Moors, but their skin complexion was lighter than their conquerors.

The Castilian pride in their "blue blood" was a thinly veiled proclamation of pride in their light complexions, and a subtle way of indicating that they were not, as the *Oxford English Dictionary* puts it, "contaminated by Moorish, Jewish, or other foreign admixture." For the paler the complexion of the skin, the more blue the veins appear.

Submitted by Daniel A. Placko, of Chicago, Illinois.

Why Are People Immune to Their Own Body Odor?

How can so many otherwise sensitive people expose others to their body odors? Surely, they must not know that they (or their clothes) are foul-smelling, or they would do something about it. Right?

Right. Compared to most animals, humans don't have an acutely developed sense of smell. According to Dr. Pat Barelli, secretary of the American Rhinologic Society, "The olfactory nerve easily becomes 'fatigued' in areas where there are odors." In order not to be overloaded with information, your nervous system decides not to even try being "bothered" by your body odor unless it changes dramatically. Whether you regularly smell like a spring bouquet or like last night's table scraps, you are unlikely to notice—even if you are sensitive to the body odor of other people.

Dr. Morley Kare, director of the Monell Institute at the University of Pennsylvania, adds that this fatigue principle applies to many of the senses. Workers at automobile factories must learn to block out the sounds of machinery or risk being driven insane. Residents of Hershey, Pennsylvania, stop noticing the smell of chocolate that permeates the town.

Students often can't discriminate the taste of different dishes served in their school cafeteria. Of course, this phenomenon might be explained by the fact that all the cafeteria dishes *do* taste alike, but we would need a government grant to confirm the thesis.

Submitted by Karole Rathouz, of Mehlville, Missouri.

Why Are the Outside Edges of the Pages of Many Paperback Books Colored?

In the early days of paperback books, the paper used was of very low quality, usually newsprint. Consumers rejected the soiled and discolored appearance of the pages. Publishers hit upon the notion of "staining," which made the paper look fresh, even pretty, and most important, prolonged the shelf life of their books.

Some publishers used the same color stain for long periods of time, in an attempt to make their company's product easily identifiable in the bookstore. For a long time, Dell's paperbacks were stained blue; Bantam's were yellow; Pocket Books favored red.

As the paper quality improved, the necessity for staining decreased. Some publishers still stain some of their mass-market (small-sized) paperback books. Occasionally, even today, the paper quality is low, or the paper within one book varies slightly in color—staining eliminates these problems. Trade (larger-sized) paperbacks use higher-quality paper, so staining is rare. Ironically, the tradition of staining dates back to the days of Gutenberg, when Bibles were stained for aesthetic purposes. Some expensive hardcover books are stained today to add a touch of panache.

Paperback books are stained by machine after they are completely bound. The books are moved on a conveyor belt that has sides and walls to protect the books from errant ink. Two jets spray ink all over the top, bottom, and nonbound side of the paper.

The staining of hardbound books used to be done by machine, but since the practice has almost completely died out the machinery has been sold off. Today, staining of hardbounds is done by hand, with a spray gun. The books are taken off the assembly line before they are cased. Protected by backboards and wings, the books are sprayed three at a time. The ink dries exceptionally fast.

Although staining adds some expense to the production cost, publishers must wonder: Does anyone notice? Does anybody care? The production experts we spoke to felt that the custom of staining persisted more because of inertia than for any practical purpose.

Submitted by Pat O'Conner, of Brooklyn, New York.

How Do They Shell Pine Nuts?

With great difficulty.

Paul Wallach, who hosts a popular interview show in Los Angeles concerned largely with food and restaurants, told us that this Imponderable had stumped him for a long time. What machine, he wondered, could possibly be fitted to work on pine nuts?

It turns out that no machine works consistently well in shelling pine nuts. Most pine-nut processors use almond shellers, which do only a decent job of shelling without ruining the nutmeat.

Many of the pine nuts from China are shelled by hand. Or rather, by a hammer held by a human hand. Not high-tech. Not fast. Labor intensive. But effective.

Submitted by Paul Wallach, of Los Angeles, California.

How Can Owners of Small Cemeteries Make Money? How Can They Plan Their Finances When They Have to Wait for People to Die Before They Derive Income?

We were asked this Imponderable several times on radio talk shows. And we were stumped. The income of a small cemetery owner must be severely limited by the population the cemetery serves. In many cases, privately owned cemeteries and funeral homes even in the smallest towns must "compete" against their church-owned or municipal counterparts. Church-owned cemeteries often charge only for the cost of digging a grave; the privately owned cemetery charges Tiffany prices in comparison.

We found out that more than a few cemetery owners in small towns are not millionaires. Many funeral directors and a few cemeterians need second jobs to provide more income. How do the small cemeterians survive? Are there any (legal) ways of "drumming up" business?

We were lucky enough to find Howard Fletcher, the chairman of the Small Cemetery Advisory Committee of the American Cemetery Association. Mr. Fletcher, who owns a memorial park in Muscatine, Iowa, helps fellow small cemeterians contend with the very financial problems we have discussed. Despite all the jokes about the business (such as "*everybody* is a potential customer"), a small cemeterian must do more than sit around and wait for people to die in order to survive. Howard Fletcher is unusually frank and unsanctimonious about his profession, and unashamed about the methods he uses to maximize his income. He developed a pamphlet called "50 Sources of Income for Small Cemeteries," from which most of the material below was adapted.

Within Fletcher's fifty sources of income are at least five broad categories: preselling; upgrading; maximizing underutilized assets; creative financing; and expanding services and products.

Preselling

To Fletcher, this is the key ingedient in a successful small cemetery operation. Most funeral directors have to wait until a death before seeing any income. Fletcher tries to sell his community on the advantages of buying space, vaults, caskets, and even memorial markers "preneed" rather than "at need." He has many arguments in his arsenal: a preneed purchase saves the bereaved family from the emotional strain of making funeral arrangements at the time a loss occurs; the decision can be made at the home of the buyer; prices will be lower now than when bought in the future; no cash is necessary right away, while most funeral directors would require some cash "at need"; making arrangements now will provide the buyer with peace of mind, not only for him or herself, but in knowing that the family will not be saddled with the unpleasant task; spouses can make decisions about funeral arrangements together; terms are negotiable—the buyer is likely to have more leverage when he or she is hale and hearty. To quote Mr. Fletcher: "It is not a question of if these arrangements will be made, it is only a question of who is going to make them and when!"

Here are some of the successful variations of preneed selling:

1. Sell child burial protection. Child protection doesn't cost much, but it does provide great cash flow. By the time the child is likely to die, compound interest has made this presell very profitable.

2. Presell grave opening and closing charges.

3. Offer one free burial space or two-for-one sales to married couples. Presumably, married couples want to be buried together, so the free space for one turns out to be the same deal as the two-for-one—these offers are always nonassignable and nontransferable (thus solving the possible divorce problem).

Upgrading

1. Sell marker refinishing kits. Bronze markers often tarnish because of oxidation.

2. Sell granite bases as upgrades from concrete bases.

3. Sell larger memorials.

4. "Reload." Use existing customers as a base to sell new or improved products. This is one reason cemeterians like to deliver by hand all deeds and official papers. They can discreetly get referrals or find family members who have not yet made funeral plans. Fletcher issues two newsletters per year with return cards and pitches for upgrading products.

5. Sell wreath and grave coverings for Christmas, Memorial Day, and other holidays.

6. Sell vesper lights.

7. Sell carillon chimes with the donor's name on plaque.

Maximizing Underutilized Assets

1. Launch a lawn-care business to more fully utilize landscaping equipment.
2. Sell double-depth privileges.
3. Grow and sell sod.
4. Raise and sell nursery stock from open land.
5. Cut and sell firewood from open land.
6. Sell excess trees on property.
7. Lease extra acreage to farmers.
8. Sell excess materials from graves as fill dirt.

Creative Financing

Many of these tips consist of charging separate fees for services that might or might not be included in the usual package deal:

1. Charge a filing and recording fee.
2. Charge for deed transfer and replacement.
3. Offer discount for cash payment of open accounts in order to generate cash flow.
4. Sell accounts receivable for cash flow.
5. Charge interest on house accounts.
6. Increase price of lots by having care charge paid separately.
7. Increase price of memorial by having installation and care charges paid separately.
8. Sell for allied businesses, such as monument dealers.
9. Sell extra-care charge for special care.
10. Where cemetery has historic value, apply for federal, state, or local registry in historical society for funding purposes.
11. Hire professional collectors for delinquent accounts.
12. Offer a discount on a new marker if purchased within one month of burial.

Expanding Services and Products

Here are some of the more creative ideas, all potentially practical:

1. Start a pet cemetery, with preneed and at need sales.
2. Manufacture vaults.
3. Build a funeral home that offers preneed as well as at need follow-up.
4. Start a trailer park on extra acreage where feasible.
5. Rent the chapel tent for weddings and lawn parties.
6. Raise and sell livestock.
7. Develop a flower shop.
8. Sell garden features and entrance features.
9. Sell trees—lining drives and/or walks.
10. Sell benches in cemetery.
11. Sell stained-glass windows.
12. Sell pews in chapel.
13. Sell furniture in mausoleum or committal area.

Some of these "money-making tips" might be offensive to your sensibilities. The image of a trailer park next to the memorial park is less than pleasing, and the thought of discussing preneed services at your kitchen table might dull the appetite a bit. The alternative, though, is usually a full-court press at the time of death.

Howard Fletcher is providing a service, but is also willing to admit that he is in business to make money. He wants the public to know what the business is like, so that the public can understand the industry's problems. Most small cemeteries make less than $100,000 in sales per year and conduct fewer than 150 burials. In order to survive, the small cemetery owner must often hustle as aggressively as any other salesperson.

Why Are Most Homes Painted White?

Most homes in the United States have always been painted white. Paint was first used as a preservative as much as an aesthetic expression. White was evidently believed to be more durable than other mixtures, but there were also historical reasons for its popularity. White was associated with the classic Greek and Roman architectural forms. Furthermore, Puritans viewed color as frivolous; the "seriousness" of white continued to appeal to Americans as late as the mid-nineteenth century.

In 1842, American architect Andrew Jackson Downing launched an attack against the color white for homes (a large proportion of American homes were then painted white with green shutters):

> There is one colour ... frequently employed by house painters, which we feel bound to protest against most heartily, as entirely unsuitable, and in bad taste. This is white, which is so universally

applied to our wooden houses of every size and description. The glaring nature of this colour, when seen in contrast with the soft green foliage, renders it extremely unpleasant to an eye attuned to harmony of coloring, and nothing but its very great prevalence in the United States could render even men of some taste so heedless of its bad effect.

Downing argued for muted earth tones as the best alternative to white, and for a while his aesthetic was influential, especially after the paint industry developed the technology to premix paints of various shades and ship them safely throughout the country by rail. (Until after the Civil War, local painters had had to mix dry colors with lead and oil to create nonwhite shades of paint.)

In the late nineteenth century, white houses became the vogue once again, and although tastes in home colors have gone through many cycles in the past hundred years, white has never become unfashionable. A survey of paint authorities yielded some reasons for its endurance as our most popular color:

1. The choice of white can never be a disaster. Although you risk seeming unchic by avoiding a more "daring" color, you can never be accused of tackiness. Shari Hiller, the color stylist for Dutch Boy Paints, thinks this is the most important reason for the popularity of white:

I have found in putting together color cards for our brands, that the homeowner is pleading for suggestions in the exterior color scheme areas. When we finally answer our customers' needs and provide them with enough advertising, photos, and helpful suggestions that they feel more comfortable making a color decision, I think we may see many other colors gaining in popularity.

2. White has so many pleasant associations. White connotes cleanliness, peace, strength, and purity.

3. White is classic. Much like the basic black dress, white is unlikely ever to go out of style. Our president, after all, doesn't live in the Puce House. Of our nation's major monuments, only the Statue of Liberty isn't white (and the statue, of course, was a French import).

4. White goes well with other colors. White mixes well with any shutter trim the homeowner desires, and with all roof colors.

Submitted by Mark Carroll, of Nashville, Tennessee.

Why Is One Side of Reynolds Wrap Aluminum Foil Shiny and the Other Side Dull?

Grown people, though no personal friends of ours, have been known to argue about whether the shiny side of Reynolds Wrap is supposed to cover the food or to be the side exposed to the outside elements. According to the folks at Reynolds Metals, it makes little difference which side of Reynolds Wrap you use. There is a slight difference in the reflectivity of the two sides, but the difference is so small that it can only be measured by laboratory instruments. Nikki P. Martin, Reynolds's consumer services representative, puts it succinctly if self-servingly: "Both sides do the same fine job of keeping hot foods hot, cold foods cold, wet foods wet, dry foods dry and all foods fresh longer."

Foil starts as a large block of solid aluminum. The block is rolled like a pie crust until it becomes one long, thin, continuous sheet. The dissimilar finishes of Reynolds Wrap are the result rather than the intention of its manufacturing process. Martin explains that "In the final rolling step, two layers of aluminum foil are passed through the rolling mill at the same time. The side coming in contact with the mill's highly polished steel rollers becomes shiny. The other side, not coming in contact with the heavy roller, comes out with a matte finish."

Submitted by Frank Russell, of Columbia, Missouri.

Why Do Superficial Paper Cuts Tend to Hurt More Than Grosser Cuts?

Perhaps paper cuts hurt more because they are so emotionally maddening. How can such a trivial little cut, sometimes without a hint of blood, cause such pain?

The sensory nerve endings are located close to the skin surface, and the hands, where most paper cuts occur, contain more nerve endings than almost any other area of the body. Dr. John Cook, of the Georgia Dermatology and Skin Cancer Clinic, adds that a trivial laceration such as a paper cut creates the worst of both worlds: "It irritates these nerve endings but doesn't damage them very much." Damaged nerve endings can lead to more serious complications, but sometimes to less pain than paper cuts.

Dr. Cook and Dr. Elliot, of the American Dermatological

Association, also mentioned that most patients tend not to treat paper cuts as they would grosser ones. After any kind of cut, the skin starts drying and pulling apart, exposing nerve endings. Cuts are also exposed to foreign substances, such as soap, liquids, perspiration, and dirt. Putting a bandage over a paper cut will not make it heal faster, necessarily, but if the cut stays moist, it won't hurt as much.

Why Does the Brightest Setting of a Three-Way Light Bulb Always Burn Out First?

As we sit typing this in the light of a General Electric 50/200/250-watt three-way light bulb, having experienced this plight many a time in the past, we took a personal interest in solving this Imponderable. If you have read the following Imponderable (and shame on you if you are reading out of order), you have already figured out the answer. When you can no longer get the 250-watt light, the reason is that the 200-watt filament has burnt out. All that is left is the 50-watt filament, lovely for helping plants grow, but hardly sufficient illumination in which to create literary masterpieces.

However, the higher-wattage filament doesn't *necessarily* burn out first. It does have a shorter rated life than the low-wattage filament. General Electric's research has shown that because the lower filament is often used as a night light or background light, it tends to get more use than the higher-wattage filament, so it is intentionally designed to have a longer life.

Submitted by Tom O'Brien, of Los Angeles, California.

How Do Three-Way Light Bulbs Work? How Do the Bulbs "Know" at Which Intensity to Shine?

Each three-way light bulb contains two filaments. Let's take as an example the popular 50/100/150-watt three-way bulb. When you turn the switch to the first setting, the lower wattage (50-watt) filament lights. When you turn to the next setting, the 100-watt filament lights and the 50-watt filament turns off. When you turn the switch for the third time, both the 50- and the 100-watt filaments light. This explains why the highest wattage rating for a three-way bulb is always the sum of the two lower wattage figures.

James Jensen, of the General Electric Lighting Business Group, is quick to explain that three-ways will work only in sockets designed to accept this type of bulb. While the three-way bulb, like conventional bulbs, makes contact in the socket through its screw shell and through an eyelet contact at the bottom of the base, it also contains a third feature. Says Jensen: "In addition, there is a contact ring surrounding the eyelet. This ring contacts a small post contact in the socket. Sometimes, a three-way bulb will flicker or fail to light on all settings. This is often due to poor (or no) contact in the socket. Sometimes merely tightening the bulb in the socket will remedy this."

Submitted by Elaine Murray, of Los Gatos, California.

Why Do Snakes Dart Out Their Tongues?

Although snake watchers at zoos love to see the reptiles flick their tongues, imagining they are ready to pounce on some unsuspecting prey, the tongues are perfectly harmless. Snakes don't sting or use their forked tongues as weapons.

The tongue is actually an invaluable sensory organ for the snake. It enables the reptile to troll for food (just as a fisherman sticks his line out in the water and hopes for the best), while feeling its way over the ground. It does this by bringing in bits of organic matter that it can smell or taste, alerting it to a potential food source. Some evidence suggests that a snake's tongue is equally sensitive to sound vibrations, warning it of potential prey or predators.

Where Do They Get That Organ Music in Skating Rinks?

As we discussed in our first volume of Imponderables, skaters are not allowed to use music with vocals in competitions, and we explained some of the reasons why that music sounds so awful. The inevitable follow-up question: what about the music in ice and roller skating rinks?

Chances are very, very good that any organ music you hear in skating rinks comes from a company called Rinx Records, the only known source for tempo organ music. Competitive skaters need all-instrumental music of specific lengths (usually three or four minutes, exactly) for competitions and achievement tests. Not only do these songs need to be an exact length, but many need to be an exact number of beats per minute. Rinx Records, for example, provide waltzes with 108, 120, and 138 beats per minute. The records must have a strong beat so that skaters can synchronize their movements with music often piped through horrendous sound systems.

Rinx Records was founded in 1950, in Denver, Colorado, by Fred Bergen, a man who not only was involved in skating, but was an organist who played on many records. In 1968, Bergen sold Rinx Records to Dominic Cangelosi, who still operates the business from the roller rink he owns. Cangelosi has played keyboards on all of the records he has released since 1968. His music is heard throughout the world, but like the baseball stadium organist, he labors in semiobscurity, unmolested by rabid fans on the street.

Rinx is a nice business. Although a few other individuals besides Cangelosi market tapes, Cangelosi has the record end of the field sewn up. He has a big market, with a mailing list of more than five thousand customers, including not only rinks but skating instructors and individual skaters as well. Ice skating and roller skating share many of the same tempos (though some ice skating music is much faster), so Rinx sells to both markets. In all, Rinx has more than thirteen hundred *different* records in stock, on seven-inch 45 rpm. If your heart prompts, you can find out more about Rinx Records by contacting Dominic Cangelosi at: P. O. Box 6607, Burbank, CA 91510.

Although Rinx's variety of organ music is associated with bygone days, Cangelosi has tried to spice up his arrangements with synthesizers, pianos, and electronic and Hammond organs in addition to the traditional acoustic and pipe organs. On some records, he adds guitar, drums, or other accompaniment. Cangelosi also "covers" popular songs, for which he pays a fee to ASCAP or BMI. Rink operators likewise have to pay a nominal fee to these licensing organizations for playing contemporary songs in their rinks.

George Pickard, executive director of the Roller Skating Rink Operators Association, says that most rinks have abandoned old-fashioned music for rock and disco. But many have special adult sessions that use Rinx and other more traditional records. There are even a few rinks that still have live organ music, the last echo of bygone days.

Submitted by Gail Lee, of Los Angeles, California. Thanks also to: Joy Renee Grieco, of Park Ridge, New Jersey.

What Do Federal Express Delivery People Do After 10:30 A.M.?

Federal Express is justly famous for its pledge to deliver Priority One packages before 10:30 A.M. the next business day. What, then, do delivery people do after the last priority package is delivered? Take a siesta? Smoke cigars? Play poker with U.S. Post Office employees who haven't delivered their first-class mail yet?

   Actually, Federal Express keeps its employees hopping all day long. In some cities, packages are delivered as early as 7:30 A.M. (The pickup and delivery cycles of packages tend to be earlier in the West, because *all* packages are routed through Federal Express headquarters in Memphis, Tennessee prior to shipment to their eventual destinations.) Before any packages can be delivered, they must be sorted by routes; in smaller stations, the courier often does the sorting himself.

After all Priority One packages are delivered, the courier tries to drop off all second-day deliveries before noon. If he succeeds, he is likely to take a lunch break around midday.

After lunch, the pickup cycle begins. By the time the courier has gathered all the incoming packages, he has worked a full day. If there is any spare time at all, paper work has a way of filling it.

In large stations, the process of sorting routes, delivering Priority One packages, delivering second-day packages, picking up all packages, and filling out paper work can consume more than eight hours. For this reason, about 25 percent of all Federal Express employees are part-timers, often used for sorting packages for delivery by couriers. When a Federal Express courier drops off his last Priority One package before the 10:30 A.M. deadline, his workday has just begun.

Submitted by Merle Pollis, of Cleveland, Ohio.

Why Do So Many Mass Mailers Use Return Envelopes With Windows?

It's easy to figure out why many mass mailers (such as utilities or credit card companies) use window envelopes for the bills they send to you. Bills are prepared by computers and are stuffed into envelopes by inserting machines. The window eliminates the costly process of addressing each envelope separately.

But why the window on the return envelope? Couldn't the companies simply preprint their address, avoiding the problem of customers inserting the reply portion of the statement upside down or wrong side out?

There is a good reason for window reply envelopes. Many large companies use various geographical locations for receiving remittances. The window envelope saves the company the cost of printing several different addresses on reply envelopes.

Although the dire warnings on the back or flap of envelopes have almost eliminated the problem of incorrectly stuffed reply stubs, Pavey Envelope and Tag Corporation, of Jersey City, New Jersey, has recently developed the idea of clipping a corner on the return stub and gluing a corner of the envelope so that the stub can be inserted only one way—the correct way.

Submitted by Pat O'Conner, of Brooklyn, New York.

Why Does the Skin on the Extremities Wrinkle After a Bath? And Why Only the Extremities?

Despite its appearance, your skin isn't shriveling after your bath. Actually, it is expanding.

The skin on the fingers, palms, toes, and soles wrinkles only after it is saturated with water (a prolonged stay underwater in the swimming pool will create the same effect). The stratum corneum—the thick, dead, horny layer of the skin that protects us from the environment and that makes the skin on our hands and feet tougher and thicker than that on our stomachs or faces —expands when it soaks up water. This expansion causes the wrinkling effect.

So why doesn't the skin on other parts of the body also wrinkle when saturated? Actually, it does, but there is more room for the moisture to be absorbed in these less densely packed areas before it will show. One doctor we contacted said that soldiers whose feet are submerged in soggy boots for a long period will exhibit wrinkling all over the covered area.

Submitted by Michelle L. Zielinski, of Arnold, Missouri.

Submitted by Marley Sims, of Van Nuys, California. ▶

What Happens to the Razor Blades That Are Thrown Down Used-Blade Slots in Hotels?

Absolutely nothing. They are left to collect indefinitely between the studs of the walls. If you ever try to put a used blade down the razor slot and find the slot stuffed to the gills, you may assume that you are either in a very old hotel or in one that caters to a particularly hirsute clientele. Of course, there are fewer of those blades being deposited than there were years ago, because disposable razors are particularly popular among travelers; disposables won't fit in the skinny opening.

If our civilization goes the way of the dodo and the remnants of our culture are buried in layers, we will certainly have some nasty surprises for future archaeologists. Between used razor blades and pop top can tabs, we will literally keep future diggers on their toes, or at least in very durable shoes.

Why Doesn't Evaporated Milk Have to Be Refrigerated?

Evaporated milk, of course, is thickened solely by evaporation; it is often confused with condensed milk, which is made by evaporating some of the cow's milk and adding sugar. Evaporated milk has a long shelf life because it is sterilized in the can, a steam-heat process that destroys potentially harmful micro-organisms. Evaporated milk often develops a darkish off-color after about a year, but it is still safe to consume.

Submitted by Cassandra A. Sherrill, of Granite Hills, North Carolina.

Why Is Evaporated Milk Sold in Soldered Cans?

Can openers, and the people who use them, have difficulty with soldered cans. Is there a real advantage to using them?

Soldered cans are stronger than regular aluminum or tin cans. As we have just learned, evaporated milk is actually sterilized in the can, and manufacturers have found soldered cans to be more dependable and durable during the intense heating process. Marsha McLain, of Pet, Inc., told us that all of their cans are welded with double seams in two pieces. The bottom and sides are actually one piece, and are filled with liquid. Only after the milk is put into the container is the top soldered on.

What Causes the Ringing Sound You Get in Your Ears?

Unless you are listening to a bell, a ringing sensation means you are suffering from tinnitus. Someone with tinnitus receives auditory sensations without any external auditory source. While most of us rarely experience tinnitus, it is a chronic problem for over 30 million Americans.

Tinnitus is a symptom, not a disease in itself. Virtually anything that might disturb the auditory nerve is capable of causing tinnitus. Because the function of the auditory nerve is to carry sound, when the nerve is irritated for any reason the brain interprets the impulse as noise.

Some of the most common causes for temporary tinnitus are:

1. Reaction to a loud noise.
2. Vascular distress after a physical or mental trauma.
3. Allergic reaction to medication. (Aspirin is the most common pharmaceutical cause of tinnitus. Many people who take more than twenty aspirin per day are subject to tinnitus attacks). Luckily, the symptoms usually disappear upon discontinuance of the drug.

Causes of more chronic tinnitus conditions are myriad. Here are some of the most common: clogging of the external ear with earwax; inflammation of any part of the ear; drug overdoses; excessive use of the telephone; vertigo attacks; nutritional deficiencies (particularly a lack of trace minerals); muscle spasms in the ear; infections; allergies.

Chronic tinnitus sufferers have to live not only with annoying buzzing, but usually with accompanying hearing loss. Unfortunately, there is no simple cure for the condition. Much research is being conducted on the role of nutrition in helping treat tinnitus, but for now, the emphasis is on teaching sufferers how to live with the problem. Devices are sold to mask the ringing sound. Techniques such as hypnosis and biofeedback are used to distract the patient from the annoying ringing.

Ear problems may not be the most glamorous medical problems, but they are the most prevalent, as a booklet from the House Ear Institute, prepared by the Otological Medical Group, Inc., of Los Angeles, explains: "Loss of hearing is America's largest, yet least recognized, physical ailment. More people suffer from it than heart disease, cancer, blindness, tuberculosis, multiple sclerosis, venereal disease, and kidney disease combined."

Submitted by Bobby Dalton, of Maryland Heights, Missouri.

HOW Did Chocolate Bunnies for Easter Come About?

No doubt, the chocolate bunny was introduced for the same reason that candy corn was introduced for Halloween—in order to make more money for the candy industry. Purveyors of nonessential gift items (flowers, greeting cards, candy) are always looking for new reasons to compel customers to buy their products. If one were inclined toward conspiracy theories, one could look on everything from Mother's Day to National Secretary's Week as nothing but blatant attempts to pry discretionary dollars from hapless citizens.

Chocolate bunnies date back to the 1850s in Germany. Along with bunnies, chocolatiers sold chocolate eggs and chickens. Switzerland, France, and other European chocolate producers followed soon after. Most of the chocolate companies we contacted felt that the bunnies symbolized renewal and rejuvenation, and were intended to symbolize the "Rites of Spring," not strictly Easter. As Charlotte H. Connelly of Whitman's Chocolates told us, the chocolate bunnies spread rapidly to the United States from Europe.

At present, chocolate eggs and bunnies help bridge the "chocolate gap" that befalls the confectionary industry between St. Valentine's Day and Mother's Day.

Monsieur Blue hair rinses our specialty

We Proudly
Use and
Recommend
"True Blue"
Hair
Products

HAIRDO

Why Do Old Women Dye Their Hair Blue?

In the 1960s, it was fashionable to tint or bleach hair in pastel shades. Some older women, perhaps, are choosing to stick with a trend that has come and gone.

The majority, however, use a blue rinse (not a dye or tint) to combat the yellow shadings that discolor their gray or white hair. Blue helps mask yellow.

Advancing age is not the sole reason for yellow hair. Some chemicals used in other hair preparations can cause yellowing. But the biggest culprit of all is smoke. Cosmetician Richard Levac told *Imponderables* that as we get older, the hair becomes more porous. Smoke coats the hair and embeds itself in the hair shaft, causing yellowing.

Levac adds that very few women are intentionally trying to emerge from a salon with blue hair. Blue rinses are much lighter than they were twenty years ago. If you can notice the blue, the hairdresser has done a poor job.

Ironically, blue hair has now made a comeback of sorts with young girls, thanks to new wave music. And with Cyndi Lauper around, any primary color is fair game.

Submitted by Daniel A. Placko, Jr., of Chicago, Illinois.

What Are the Criteria for the Placement of a "Dangerous Curve" or "Dangerous Turn" Sign?

The answer comes from the encylopedic *Manual on Uniform Traffic Devices.* Individual states are free to deviate from the standards cited in this federal publication, but few do.

How do they determine if a turn is dangerous enough to warrant a warning sign? The *Manual*'s criterion for a turn sign (the black arrow at a right angle against a yellow background) is explicit:

> The Turn sign is intended for use where engineering investigations of roadway, geometric, and operating conditions show the recommended speed on a turn to be 30 MPH or less, and this recommended speed is equal to or less than the speed limit established by law or by that regulation for that section of a highway. Where a Turn sign is warranted, a Large Arrow sign may be used

on the outside of the turn. Additional protection may be provided by use of the Advisory Speed plate.

Note that these guidelines reflect the reality that actual traffic speeds usually exceed the law. Warning signs can be posted even if the "safe" speed is identical to the posted speed limit.

The criterion for the curve sign is similar: a curve sign can be placed any time tests demonstrate that the recommended speed should be between thirty and sixty miles per hour and that speed is equal to or less than the posted speed limit.

Submitted by Robert J. Abrams, of Boston, Massachusetts.

Why Don't We Ever See Dead Birds?

We see hundreds of birds on an average day, and occasionally spot one run over by a car, but why don't we ever see one dead from natural causes? Don't they ever keel over in flight? Do birds go someplace special to die?

Surprisingly, birds don't fly anywhere particular to die. The reason we don't see dead birds is that they are quickly scavenged by other animals. Although this sounds like a cruel fate, bird expert Starr Saphir views it differently, marveling at the efficiency of the natural world. The moment a bird can no longer function, it is used as valuable fuel. Birds are eaten by cats, dogs, rats, opossums, small insects, and even bacteria. Saphir told us that she has led birdwatching walks and seen the intact but dead body of a bird on the ground on the first leg of the walk; on the way back, an hour later, the majority of the body was already scavenged. Within twenty-four hours, the remains of most birds, in the wild or in an urban area, would presumably become only a pile of feathers.

Richard C. Banks, vice-president of the U.S. Ornithologist's Union, told *Imponderables* that a few birds might actually die in flight (although he had not personally ever seen this happen). The most likely candidates would be migrating birds flying over the ocean, far away from food sources and without convenient landing spots to fight off exhaustion. Sick birds generally don't take wing in the first place.

Submitted by Cecilia F. Boucher, of Roslindale, Massachusetts. Thanks also to: Walter Bartner, of New York, New York; Thomas Cunningham, of Pittsburgh, Pennsylvania; L. T. Quirk, of Red Bank, New Jersey; and Richard Rosberger, of Washington, D.C.

Why Do All Packaged Bakery Goods Seem to Be Registered by the Pennsylvania Department of Agriculture?

In 1933, the state of Pennsylvania passed a Bakery Inspection Act mandating that all bakery goods must be inspected and registered in order to be sold in the state. Further, no packaged bakery goods could be sold in Pennsylvania unless the registration notice was printed on its wrapping. The law was enacted to ensure not only the wholesomeness of the food but the accuracy of the weight stated on the package and the health of the employees handling the food (all bakery employees must have an annual physical examination).

It is easy to understand why Pennsylvania would want to protect the welfare of its citizens, but why are Pepperidge Farm cookies, Hostess cupcakes, Wonder bread, and other nationally distributed baked goods also registered by the Pennsylvania Department of Agriculture? Because the law does not exempt out-of-state bakeries from having to print "Registered by the Pennsylvania Department of Agriculture" on its packaging —without it, the goods cannot be sold anywhere in Pennsylvania. Instead of going to the extra expense of printing separate wrappers for the state of Pennsylvania, manufacturers include its registration on their labels all across the country.

How does Pennsylvania monitor the wholesomeness in bakeries out of state or out of country? According to Dick Elgin, of the Pennsylvania Department of Agriculture, the state has reciprocal agreements with food inspection units in other states. Most states have laws regulating the wholesomeness of bakeries; it is only the requirement to print the state's "seal of approval" that differentiates Pennsylvania.

Meat, poultry, and eggs are the only foodstuffs that require inspections by the federal government. While the Pennsylvania Department of Agriculture registration won't promise you great taste or even good nutrition, it will reassure you that the plant where your cookie was baked was inspected at least once a year and that some inspector lived after popping a similar cookie into his or her mouth.

Submitted by Carol Jewett, of New York, New York.

How Do They Keep All the Raisins in Cereal Boxes from Falling to the Bottom?

The Rule of Popcorn Physics, which states that unpopped popcorn kernels fall to the bottom of the bowl, has saved many a tooth for generations. The explanation for this immutable law is easy enough to comprehend: unpopped kernels fall to the bottom both because their density is greater than expanded popcorn and because our handling of the corn creates crevices for the unpopped kernel to slide down.

Many inquisitive types have searched for corollaries to the Popcorn Physics rule. For example, the tenet of Slithery Sundaes posits that regardless of how much syrup or toppings one puts atop ice cream in a sundae, it will all fall to the bottom of the bowl anyway, collecting in a pool of glop.

So it was not without a feeling of reverence and awe that we approached the subject of raisins in cereal boxes, tiny dried grapes that seem to defy the usual laws of food gravity. Linda E. Belisle, at General Mills, supplied the simple but elegant solution.

Raisins are added to boxes only after more than half of the cereal has already been packed. The cereal thus has a chance to settle and condense. During average shipping conditions, boxes get jostled a bit (the equivalent of our stirring the contents of a popcorn bowl while grabbing a fistful), so the raisins actually sift and become evenly distributed throughout the box.

The tendency of cereal to condense within the package is responsible for the warning on most cereal packages that the contents are measured by weight rather than volume. Little did you know that this condensation was also responsible for the Law of Rising Raisins.

Submitted by James A. Hoagland, of Stockton, California.

Why Do Runs in Stockings Usually Run Up?

A complicated issue, it turns out, but one that the folks at Hanes and L'eggs were happy to tackle. The direction in which runs will go is determined by the type of stitching used in the construction of the hosiery. The leg portions of most panty hose and sheer nylons are woven in what is called the "jersey stitch" or "stocking stitch." The jersey stitch is produced by one set of needles when all of the needles produce plain stitches at every course. Hosiery made from jersey stitches runs or "ladders" both up and down.

Most manufacturers use the jersey stitch for their basic panty hose and stocking styles. Jersey stitches provide a smoother feel and a sheerer look than other constructions, yet they are still durable and stretch well.

Other often-used stitches include the "run resist," the "float," and most popular, the "tuck," all of which *will only run up*. L'eggs, for example, uses the tuck stitch on their control-top panties. When the yarn in the stitch is severed, it will only run upward. The purpose, according to L'eggs, is "to prevent the run from encroaching onto the part of the hose that you can see."

Why don't the manufacturers always use a stitch that will ladder up, then, as this construction will most often prevent the run from being visible? Hanes Hosiery's answer is that tucks, run-resist, and float stitches all feel rough on the leg and look heavier on the leg than the jersey stitch. Most manufacturers use the float and tuck stitches for stockings that are designed to look heavier, particularly patterned and mesh hosiery.

Submitted by Sara Vander Fliet, of Cedar Grove, New Jersey.

Does Putting Women's Hosiery in the Freezer Forestall Runs?

On one thing L'eggs and Hanes can agree. Despite all folk wisdom and advice columns to the contrary, putting hosiery in the freezer does not forestall runs. Mary S. Gilbert of L'eggs states that "hosiery is made of synthetic fibers which are not affected by cold."

Eleanor Pardue, product evaluation manager at Hanes, was familiar with the nylon in the freezer claim, but remains firm:

> Based on the physical testing I am familiar with, there is no difference in the breaking strength of nylon which has never been frozen and nylon that has been frozen. I do know that one can wear two identical pairs of stockings manufactured at the same time under identical circumstances and one pair may run the first time worn while the other pair may last through ten wears.

Submitted by Bonnie Gellas, of New York, New York.

Why Do Traffic Signals Use Red, Yellow, and Green Lights? Why Is the Red Light on Top, Green Light on the Bottom, and Yellow Light in Between?

Traffic signals actually predate the existence of the automobile. One was installed outside of British Parliament in 1868. This signal (and some early American variations) had two semaphore arms, like a railroad signal, that acted as a physical impediment to oncoming traffic.

The English device was designed to control the flow of pedestrians, and some feature was needed to make it functional at night. The easiest solution was to adapt the system used for railroad signals—red and green gas lamps would signify when one could proceed (green) or had to stop (red). This British prototype wasn't a rousing success—it blew up shortly after its introduction, killing a London policeman.

A lively controversy has developed over where the first modern traffic signal designed to control automobile traffic was in use. Although Salt Lake City and St. Paul lay claim to the crown, the green-red signal installed on Euclid Avenue in Cleveland, Ohio, in 1914 is generally credited with being the first.

Although the traffic signal's colors might have been arbitrarily lifted from the railroad's, there is an important safety reason for the consistency of the configuration today. As recently as the 1950s, many traffic signals, especially in busy urban intersections, were displayed horizontally rather than vertically. The current vertical design with red on top was adopted in order to aid color-blind individuals who might be confused by different layouts. According to Eugene W. Robbins, president of the Texas Good Roads/Transportation Association, the red in traffic signals has some orange in it and the green has some blue in order to make it even easier for the color blind to distinguish them.

Submitted by John Branden, of Davis, California. Thanks also to: Maya Vinarsky, of Los Angeles, California; Sean Gayle, of Slidell, Louisiana; Eddie Haggerty, of Waseca, Minnesota; William Debovitz, of Bernardsville, New Jersey.

This side for milking   See udder side

Why Are Cows Usually Milked from the Right Side?

Although this subject is usually not part of the veterinary school curriculum, we went right to the organization best suited to answer the Imponderable: the American Association of Bovine Practitioners and its officer Dr. Harold E. Amstutz. Although Dr. Amstutz said he had never considered this question before we posed it, he was ready with a sensible explanation:

> Since most people are right handed, it is more logical to sit down on the right side of the cow and have more room to maneuver the milk bucket with the right hand between the cow's front and rear legs. There would not be nearly as much room to maneuver the bucket with the right hand if a right handed person were to sit on the left side.
>
> In general, we think of "right" as correct and "left" as being wrong. Cows have no preference since we milk them from either

side in today's milking parlors. The only ones that would have a preference are those that were trained to be milked on one side and then someone tried to milk them from the other side. The milker would probably be kicked in that case.

Submitted by Marci Perlmutter, of Warren, New Jersey.

Why Do Many Merchants Ask Customers to Put Their Addresses and Phone Numbers on Credit Card Slips?

If Visa or MasterCard or American Express needed your address or phone number, wouldn't they reserve a spot on their credit-card slips for them? Clearly, it is the stores that want such data.

But why do the stores need this information? If you charge goods on a stolen credit card, it is the creditor, not the merchant, who gets stuck with the bill, as long as the merchant complies with all of the security arrangements (such as verifying all purchases above a certain amount).

The credit-card companies themselves couldn't think of a good reason for stores to ask for address and phone number. After all, if somebody is going to steal a credit card, he is unlikely to provide accurate instructions on how to locate him. Perhaps, one credit-card executive speculated, the stores make this request in order to compile a mailing list.

So we talked to merchants. Their reasons turned out to be prosaic. Some of them mentioned that they carry insurance on bad checks, and that part of the agreement with insurance companies is that all customers must supply addresses, phone numbers, and driver's license or social security number. If they don't include these data, merchants aren't reimbursed for bad checks. Although they realize that such precautions are irrelevant when it comes to collecting money from credit cards, some merchants believe that by forcing employees to collect addresses and phone numbers from all noncash customers, clerks would be less likely to forget to ask for the information from people using checks.

All of the merchants in New York City gave one reason, and several mentioned it as the only reason, for asking customers to include address and phone numbers, and this explains why the practice is uncommon in small towns. With the information provided they can contact customers when they leave their credit card at the store by mistake!

Submitted by Mark Schulman of Altamonte Springs, Florida.

On Airplanes, Why Do Our Ears Pop and Bother Us More on Descent Than on Ascent?

The ear is composed of three parts:

1. The outer ear, which includes the part of the ear that is visible, plus the ear canal connected to the eardrum.
2. The middle ear, which includes the eardrum, the ear bones (ossicles), and the air spaces behind the eardrum and in the mastoid cavities.

3. The inner ear, which contains the nerve endings that facilitate hearing and equilibrium.

The middle ear is what bothers travelers on airplanes because it is, in part, an air pocket vulnerable to changes in air pressure. On the ground, when you swallow, your ears make a little click or popping sound. This noise marks the passage of a small air bubble up from the back of your nose, through the eustachian tube, and into your middle ear. According to the American Council of Otolaryngology, "the air in the middle ear is constantly being absorbed by its membranous lining, but it is frequently re-supplied through the eustachian tube during the process of swallowing. In this manner air pressure on both sides of the eardrum stays about equal. If, and when, the air pressure is *not* equal, the ear feels blocked."

If the eustachian tube is blocked, no air can be replenished in the middle ear; any air present absorbs and a vacuum occurs, sucking the eardrum inward. Blocked eustachian tubes can cause a loss of hearing and pain.

A clear and properly functioning eustachian tube is the key to problem-free ears on plane flights; if it can open wide enough and often enough, the eustachian tube can moderate changing air-pressure conditions. When you ascend on an airplane, it is to less pressure, so the air expands in the middle ear. The eustachian tube works much like a flutter valve on an automobile. When you ascend, the air in your ear is forced through the tube in a steady stream without any problem.

When you descend, it is to greater air pressure. A vacuum forms even faster in the middle ear, making it harder for the air to go back through the membranous part of the eustachian tube. According to Dr. Andrew F. Horne, in the Office of Aviation Medicine of the Federal Aviation Administration, the ear popping is caused when the valve of the eustachian tube opens and closes. On ascent, the air runs through the eustachian tube in a steady stream; on descent, the air must contend with the membranous part of the eustachian tube. Without the steady air flow, it takes longer to equalize air pressure inside and outside your ear.

Airplane pilots are taught how to counteract differences in air pressure. The simple act of swallowing pulls open the eustachian tube, which is why gum chewing or candy sucking has become a takeoff and landing ritual for many passengers. Yawning is even more effective, for it pulls the muscle that opens the eustachian tube even harder than swallowing.

If neither swallowing nor yawning works, the American Council of Otolaryngology recommends this procedure:

1. Pinch your nostrils shut.
2. Take in a mouthful of air.
3. Using your cheek and throat muscles, force the air into the back of your nose as if you were trying to blow your thumb and fingers away from your nostrils.
4. When you hear a loud pop in your ears, you have succeeded, but you may have to repeat the process again during descent.

Where Do Houseflies Go During the Winter?

To heaven, usually. Some flies survive winter, but only under extremely favorable conditions, when they can take shelter in barns or inside human residences where they can find enough organic matter and warmth to eat and breed.

Even under the best of circumstances, the normal life-span of a housefly north of the equator is approximately seven to twenty-one days. The most important variable in the longevity of these insects is the ambient temperature—they die off in droves when it falls below freezing or becomes excessively hot.

Although they actually live longest in cool temperatures, because they are less active, flies breed most prolifically when temperatures are warm, food is abundant, and humidity is moderate. Winter tends to deprive them of all of these favorable conditions, so that they not only die off themselves, but do so without having been able to breed successfully. The U.S. Department of Agriculture claims that no housefly has been proved to live from autumn to spring (which answers another Imponderable: why do we see so few houseflies in the spring?).

So how can they regenerate the species? Most people believe that flies hibernate or become dormant, like some other insects, but this theory has proved to be untrue. The few flies that we find in the spring are mainly the descendants of the adult flies that managed to find good hiding places during the previous winter. These spring flies breed their little wings off, just in time to harrass you on your picnics when the weather gets good.

Some of the flies that survive winter are not adults, but rather flies in their earlier developmental stages. Fly eggs are usually deposited in the ground, in crevices, in wood, or in a particular favorite, cow manure. These eggs hatch, literally, in a few hours, and turn into larvae, a phase that can last anywhere from one to four days. Larvae feed on decaying plant or animal matter (such as other insect larvae). As the fly larva grows, it undergoes pupation, a phase that lasts about five days, in which the fly rests as its larval features are transformed into adult ones. Many entomologists used to answer this Imponderable by speculating that most flies that survive the winter do so in the form of larvae or pupae, but scientists now believe that adult flies have a much better chance of surviving the winter than their younger brethren, who have a hard time coping with cold weather. Still, some larvae and pupae do stay alive during the very end of winter and develop into adults in the spring.

The fecundity of the *Musca domestica* is truly awesome. One scientist estimated that a single mating pair of houseflies could generate as many as 325,923,200,000,000 offspring in one summer. One-sixth of a cubic foot of soil taken in India revealed 4,024 *surviving* flies. Maybe the Imponderable should read: why isn't the entire world overcome with flies?

Any notion that flies migrate south during the winter is easily dispelled. The average flight range of a housefly is a measly one-quarter of a mile. Scientists have tracked the flight of flies: they rarely go beyond a ten-mile radius of their birthplace during their entire lifetime.

Where Does White Pepper Come From?

From black pepper. The most popular of all spices (salt is not a spice) is not related to sweet red, green, or hot peppers, but is the dried berry of a woody, climbing vine known as *Piper nigrum L.*

On the vine the peppercorn is neither white nor black. As the fruit ripens, it turns from green to yellow and then to red. To make black pepper, the berries are picked while somewhat immature and then dried. As they dry, their skin turns a dark color. When ground, the pepper contains both light and dark particles —because the whole peppercorn is used—but the general appearance is dark.

White pepper is left on the vine to mature, at which point it is easier to separate the dark skin. The berries are soaked to loosen the skin as much as possible and then rubbed to remove it entirely. After the dark skin is discarded, the naked white peppercorns are put out in the sun to dry.

Technology has caught up with the spice world. Some white pepper, usually known as "decorticated white pepper," is now produced by removing the skin of dried *black* peppercorns by machine. Decorticated pepper looks like white pepper but tastes more like black pepper.

Why bother with white pepper? Often it is used solely for aesthetic purposes, such as in light-colored sauces and soups where little black specks may upset the chef's carefully orchestrated balance (or be misconstrued as little black insect fragments). Some spice wimps also prefer white pepper for its milder taste and smell.

Ted Turner does not have a monopoly on colorization. Go into any gourmet store and you will encounter green peppercorns. These immature berries are not left out in the sun but either packed in liquid (usually wine vinegar or brine) or freeze-dried in order to retain the distinctive green color. Because green peppercorns are harvested at an early stage of the berry's development, they are quite mild, but they do have a distinctive taste, which is prized by nouvelle cuisine restaurateurs.

Submitted by Kathy Cripe, of South Bend, Indiana.

What Purpose Do Wisdom Teeth Serve?

They serve a powerful purpose for dentists, who are paid to extract them. Otherwise, wisdom teeth are commonly regarded as being useless to modern man. But because nature rarely provides us with useless body parts, a little investigation yields a more satisfying answer.

Primitive man ate meats so tough that they make beef jerky feel like mashed potatoes in comparison. The extra molars in the back of the mouth, now known as wisdom teeth, undoubtedly aided in our ancestors' mastication.

As humans have evolved, their brains have gotten progressively larger and the face position has moved farther downward and inward. About the time that primitive man started walking in an upright position, other changes in the facial structure occurred. The protruding jawbones of early man gradually moved backward, making the jaw itself shorter and leaving no room for the wisdom teeth (also known as third molars). Most people's jaws no longer have the capacity to accommodate these four, now superfluous, teeth.

Why Are Ancient Cities Buried in Layers? And Where Did the Dirt Come From?

This Imponderable assumes two facts that aren't always true. First, not all ruins are the remains of cities. Many other ancient sites—such as forts, camping sites, cave dwellings, cemeteries, and quarries—are also frequently buried. Second, not all ancient cities are buried; once in a while, archaeologists are given a break and find relics close to or at the surface of the ground.

Still, the questions are fascinating, and we went to two experts for the answers: George Rapp, Jr., dean and professor of geology and archaeology of the University of Minnesota, Duluth, and coeditor of *Archaeological Geology*; and Boston University's Al B. Wesolowsky, managing editor of the *Journal of Field Archaeology*. Both stressed that most buried ruins were caused by a combination of factors. Here are some of the most common:

1. Wind-borne dust (known to archaeologists as "Aeolian dust") accumulates and eventually buries artifacts. Aeolian dust can vary from wind-blown volcanic dust to ordinary dirt and house dust.

2. Water-borne sediment accumulates and eventually buries artifacts. Rain carrying sediment from a high point to a lower spot is often the culprit, but sand or clay formed by flowing waters, such as riverine deposits gathered during floods, can literally bury a riverside community. Often, water collects and carries what are technically Aeolian deposits to a lower part of a site.

3. Catastrophic natural events can cause burials in one fell swoop, though this is exceedingly rare, and as Dr. Rapp adds, "In these circumstances the site must be in a topographic situation where erosion is absent or at least considerably slower than deposition." Even when a city is buried after one catastrophe, the burial can be caused by more than one factor. Dr. Wesolowsky notes that although both Pompeii and Herculaneum were buried by the eruption of Mt. Vesuvius in A.D. 79, one was buried by mudflow and the other by ashflow.

4. Manmade structures can collapse, contributing to the burial. Sometimes this destruction is accidental (such as floods, earthquakes, fires), and sometimes intentional (bombings, demolitions). Humans seem incapable of leaving behind no trace of their activities. Says Rapp: "Even cities as young as New York City have accumulated a considerable depth of such debris. Early New York is now buried many feet below the current surface."

5. Occasionally, ancient civilizations did their own burying. Wesolowsky's example:

When Constantine wanted to build Old St. Peter's on the side of the Vatican Hill in the early fourth century, his engineers had to cut off part of the slope and dump it into a Roman cemetery (thereby preserving the lower part of the cemetery, including what has been identified as the tomb of Peter himself) to provide a platform for the basilica. When Old St. Peter's was demolished in the sixteenth century to make way for the current church, parts of the old church were used as fill in low areas in the locale.

Rapp's example:

> This phenomenon is best seen in the tels of the Near East. Often they are tens of feet high. Each "civilization" is built over the debris of the preceding one. The houses were mostly of mud brick, which had a lifetime of perhaps sixty years. When they collapsed the earth was just spread around. In two thousand or three thousand years these great habitation mounds (tels) grew to great heights and now rise above the surrounding plains. Each layer encloses archaeological remains of the period of occupation.

While we self-consciously bury time capsules to give future generations an inkling of what our generation is like, the gesture is unnecessary. With an assist from Mother Nature, we are unwittingly burying revealing artifacts—everything from candy wrappers to beer cans—every day.

Submitted by Greg Cox, of San Rafael, California.

What's the Difference Between an X-Rated Movie and an XXX-Rated Movie? Why Isn't There an "XX" Rating?

The Motion Picture Association of America issues the movie ratings you see in the newspaper. Motion picture companies are under no legal obligation to have their movies rated, but they are not allowed to affix their own rating. In order to obtain a G, PG, PG-13 or R rating, a fee must be paid to the MPAA. An MPAA committee views each film and issues an edict that sets the rating, subject to appeal. None of the major film companies is willing to bypass the MPAA ratings. Since the rating codes were instituted in the 1960s, there has actually been much less pressure on the studios to reduce violence and sexual content. Also, some newspapers refuse to accept advertising for non-MPAA-rated movies, and most film executives feel that the rating system has worked reasonably well as a warning device for concerned parents.

The X-rating was originally conceived as the designation for any movie suitable only for adults, regardless of genre. Such critics' favorites as the Best Picture Oscar-winning *Midnight Cowboy* were rated X because of their mature subject matter, and *A Clockwork Orange* was rated X for its violence and intensity.

With only a few other exceptions, nonpornographic X-rated movies have bombed at the box office. Any film that catered to adults automatically excluded many of the most rabid moviegoers—teenagers. The advertisements for so-called "adult films" gladly trumpeted their X ratings: how better to prove the salaciousness of a movie than by prohibiting children from viewing it? Even better, MPAA rules allowed companies to rate their films X without the association's certification, a policy that enabled low-budget film companies to nab an X rating without paying the fee of nearly a thousand dollars. As the few mainstream X-rated films were overwhelmed by the multitude of X-rated porn movies, major film companies like Paramount and Columbia refused to release any X-rated movies, for X had become synonymous with smut.

The producers of adult films had the opposite problem. Here they were, trying to purvey their X-rated product, when prestigious films like *Midnight Cowboy* were sullying the reputation of the adults-only rating by containing redeeming social value.

David F. Friedman, board chairman of the Adult Film Association of America, told us that the XXX rating was actually started as a joke, to distinguish "straight films," with mature content, from pornography. There is not now and has never been a formal XXX rating for movies; it has always been a marketing ploy adopted by film distributors and/or movie exhibitors.

Is there any difference between an X- and an XXX-rated movie? According to Friedman, no. Although some customers might believe that an XXX-rated movie is "harder" than the simple X, this has never been the case. Many pornographic films are made in several versions: hard-core X-rated; a "soft" X, used for localities where hard-core is banned; a "cable" version, a doctored once-explicit version; and an expurgated R-rated version, designed for playoffs in nonporno theaters, such as drive-ins. Whether or not any of these versions of a pornographic movie is billed as X or XXX is more dependent on the whims of the producer or the theater management than on the content of the movie.

Why no XX rating? Who knows? Once someone started the XXX, who was going to say that their movie wasn't quite as sexy? X-inflation is likely to remain rampant as long as there are pornographic theaters.

Submitted by Richard Rosberger, of Washington, D.C. Thanks also to: Curtis Kelly, of Chicago, Illinois, and Thomas Cunningham, of Pittsburgh, Pennsylvania.

Where Does a New Speed Limit Begin? Does It Start at the Speed Limit Sign, at Some Point Beyond the Sign, or Where the Sign Becomes Clearly Visible?

If a speed limit drops from fifty-five miles per hour to thirty-five miles per hour, isn't it clearly legal to drive at fifty-five miles per hour until you pass the thirty-five miles per hour sign? But how are we expected to drop twenty miles per hour instantaneously? Is there a grace period, a distinct length of road on which we are exempt from the new speed limit?

No such luck. The speed-limit sign is posted precisely where the new limit takes effect. How you slow down to the new speed is your business, and your problem.

Of course, traffic laws are up to the individual states, but most legislatures rely on the provisions of the federal government's *Manual on Uniform Traffic Control Devices*. And the manual is unambiguous: "Speed limit signs, indicating speed limits for which posting is required by law, shall be located at the points of change from one speed limit to another. . . . At the end of the section to which a speed limit applies, a Speed Limit sign showing the next speed limit shall be erected." The one provision intended to help drivers slow down before a new speed limit is the "Reduced Speed Ahead" sign. These are placed primarily in rural areas where drops in speed limits can easily reach twenty to thirty-five miles per hour. But these warning signs must be followed by a speed-limit sign that marks precisely where the altered speed limit applies.

Submitted by Glenn Worthman, of Palo Alto, California.

If the National Speed Limit is 55 Miles per Hour, Why Do Speedometers Go up to 85 Miles per Hour and Higher?

The Department of Transportation mandated the maximum speedometer reading effective September 1, 1982. The rule read:

> No speedometer shall have graduations or numerical values for speeds greater than 140/km/h and 85 mph and shall not otherwise indicate such speeds. Each speedometer shall include "55" in the mph scale. Each speedometer, other than an electronic digital speedometer, shall highlight the number 55 or otherwise highlight the point at which the indicated vehicle speed equals 55 mph.

Benn Dunn, manager of product technical communications for American Motors, says that the National Highway Traffic Safety Administration offered two reasons for the 85 mile per hour limit. First, the limit would allow speedometer dials to be more precisely graduated and more readable in the range of reasonable driving ranges. Second, the upper limit presumably "reduced the temptation for immature drivers to test the upper speeds of their vehicles on public roads."

The regulation simply didn't work. Although there are no current federal regulations concerning what speeds should be shown on speedometers, all of the big four automakers continue, voluntarily, to maintain 85 miles per hour as the maximum speed indication on the analogue speedometers of most of their cars. Mr. Dunn predicted, however, that we will soon begin to see higher markings on analogue speedometers.

On their high-performance cars, U.S. automakers all exceed the 85 mile per hour standard. Obviously, the auto companies are not trying to encourage reckless driving, but the speedometer with a 125 mile per hour capacity is an effective marketing ploy. A car with a high maximum reading sends a message to the consumer that the car must be capable of attaining these speeds.

The automakers give three main reasons why it is important to maintain indications beyond the federal speed limit:

1. As P. M. Preuss, of Ford Motor Company, explained it, "Car speedometers are labeled beyond 55 mile per hour speeds because people drive in excess of 55 miles per hour. Obviously, some of these drivers are reckless, but by no means all. Automakers are under no obligation to produce cars that can go only 55 miles per hour; drivers who exceed the legal limit should be aware of how fast they are going." Law-abiding citizens exceed the speed limit under many circumstances. Passing maneuvers often require bursts of speed for brief periods of time. Drivers approaching a steep upgrade, reasonably enough, want to gather a head of steam before the climb. And drivers entering expressways must often speed up for their own and others' protection.

2. Speed limits can change. Particularly in rural areas, the 55 mile per hour limit has never been accepted and has been viewed as an affront to basic liberties.

3. Automobile engineers need speedometers with more generous indications. Many of the procedures they use to assess the safety and performance of cars, including tire, brake, and component tests, are carried out at speeds greater than 55 miles per hour.

Soon, analogue speedometers will probably give way to electronic speedometers. At present, electronic models are in short supply, so they are primarily a luxury option. Electronic speedometers feature continuous digital readouts, usually in two mile per hour increments, that register accurately whatever speed the car is traveling, regardless of the speed limit.

Submitted by Daniel C. Papcke, of Lakewood, Ohio.

What Is the Purpose of Pubic and Underarm Hair, the Only Body Hair That Men and Women Share in Abundance?

Even though humans have lost most of their fur, pubic hair and underarm hair remain in both sexes (at least, in most of the world —the majority of American women shave their armpits, for some reason we at *Imponderables* are still trying to ascertain). Any logical reason for this?

The most popular explanation is that pubic hair and armpit hair both trap the milky fluid secreted by the sebaceous glands. When the secretion is broken down by bacteria, a strong odor that acts as an aphrodisiac is generated. Isn't it ironic, then, that deodorants and antiperspirants are trumpeted for their ability to mask offensive odors? We are so worried about carrying bad smells that we neglect to realize that body odor can attract others. Perhaps deodorants should be marketed for people who *want* to get rid of the opposite sex.

Zoologists offer another explanation for pubic hair. Many animals, especially primates, have striking visual features around their genitals to help attract potential mates (have you seen a baboon lately?). The wide patch of pubic hair on an otherwise naked skin might have remained on humans for the very same reason.

Submitted by Barbara and Celeste Hoggan, of El Paso, Texas.

Why Do Construction Crews Put Pine Trees on Top of Buildings They Are Working On?

The tree atop buildings (and bridges) under construction is known as the "topping out" tree and celebrates the completion of the basic skeleton of the structure. In skyscrapers, an evergreen is attached to the top beam as it is hoisted, a signal that the building has reached its final height. For some builders, the evergreen symbolizes that none of the construction crew died in the effort. For others, the tree is a talisman for good luck and prosperity for the future occupants of the building.

While the topping-out ceremony of today is often accompanied by a celebration, complete with boring speeches by local politicians and the popping of flashbulbs, the precursors of topping out are ancient. Like many of our benign rituals, topping-out celebrations stem from ancient superstitions. The Romans marked the completion of the Pons Sublicius over the Tiber River in 621 B.C. by throwing some humans into the river as a sacrifice to the gods. While we now launch ships by banging them with champagne bottles, a different liquid—human blood —was used in earlier times. In ancient China, the ridgepoles of new buildings were smeared with chicken blood in an attempt to fool the gods into believing they were receiving the human counterpart. Many cultures feared that evil spirits occupied new structures, so well into the Middle Ages, priests and rabbis performed special blessings on new homes and public buildings.

The first evidence of trees being hoisted atop buildings was in A.D. 700 in Scandinavia, when they signaled that a completion party was about to begin. Black Forest Germans celebrated the nativity of Jesus Christ with the hoisting of Christmas trees. Today, topping-out trees are still most prevalent in northern Europe, particularly Germany and the Scandinavian countries. Indeed, Scandinavia's greatest playright, Henrik Ibsen, had his protagonist in *The Master Builder* meet his doom by falling while placing a topping-off wreath on one of his new buildings.

The evergreen has been joined by the stars and stripes as a topping-off symbol in the United States. According to *The Ironworker* magazine, "When the last strands of cable were laid for the Brooklyn Bridge a hundred years ago, the wheel operated by Ironworkers was decorated with American flags. By 1920 ironworkers were again draping their work with American flags, this time while driving the first rivet on the Bank of Italy in San Francisco." Flags atop buildings today signify not only the patriotism of the construction crew but also, in some cases, that the building was financed by public funds.

Submitted by Robert J. Abrams, of Boston, Massachusetts.

Why Aren't Whitewall Auto Tires as Wide as They Used to Be?

The sole purpose of white sidewall tires is to look pretty. At one time, whitewalls were all the rage and an option that most Americans bought. A caller on a radio talk show, who posed this Imponderable, questioned why, although he paid a hefty premium for the whitewalls, he got much less white for his money than he did years ago.

Talks with tire experts yielded two explanations. First, as whitewalls are a totally cosmetic option, their appearance is subject to the whims of fashion. Tire design, like high-fashion design, tends to follow the lead of Europeans. Porsche has evidently made a huge impact with its all black tires. Whitewalls are not particularly hip at the moment, so a flashy display of white on the sidewalls at this time is as likely to impress the opposite sex as a panoply of gold chains.

Second, the thickness of white sidewalls has been reduced to conform to a general decrease in the thickness of tires and tire components, part of an industrywide attempt to make tires run cooler in order to meet the requirements of high speeds on interstate highways and of federal high-speed safety standards.

The extra charge for whitewalls actually does reflect higher expenses in manufacturing them. According to Firestone Tire & Rubber Company, white rubber is slightly more expensive than black rubber per pound, but there are two other factors that increase the cost of whitewalls: extra time and steps are necessary to manufacture and finish whitewalls, and the black rubber adjacent to the white rubber must be treated to keep the white from being stained by what would be a normal migration of materials within the tire.

Why Do Clocks Run "Clockwise"?

In baseball, horse racing, and most forms of skating, we are accustomed to seeing a counterclockwise movement. Is there any particular reason why clocks run "clockwise"?

Henry Fried, one of the foremost horologists in the United States, gives a simple explanation for this Imponderable. Before the advent of clocks, we used sundials. In the northern hemisphere, the shadows rotated in the direction we now call "clockwise." The clock hands were built to mimic the natural movements of the sun. If clocks had been invented in the southern hemisphere, Fried speculates, "clockwise" would be the opposite direction.

Submitted by William Rogers, of St. Louis, Missouri.

On Clocks and Watches with Roman Numerals, Why Is Four Usually Noted as IIII Rather than IV?

Watch and clock designers are given great latitude in designating numbers on timepiece faces. Some use arabic numbers, most use roman numerals, and a few use no numbers at all.

But have you noticed that while the number nine is usually designated as "IX" on timepieces, four is almost universally designated as "IIII"? We contacted some of the biggest manufacturers of watches, and even they couldn't pinpoint the derivation of this custom. But they sent us to our friend, Henry Fried, who swatted away this Imponderable as if it were a gnat.

When mechanical clocks were first invented, in the fourteenth century, they were displayed in public places, usually on cathedrals. The faces themselves were only ornamental at first, for the early models had no hour or minute hand but merely gonged once for every hour of the day.

Clocks were thus of special value to the common people, who were almost universally illiterate. Most peasants, even in Italy, could not read roman numerals, and they could not subtract. They performed calculations and told time by counting on their fingers. Four slash marks were much easier for them to contend with than "IV," taking one away from five.

Many early clocks displayed twenty-four hours rather than twelve. While some German clocks in the fifteenth and sixteenth centuries used roman numerals to denote A.M. and arabic numbers for P.M., all-day clocks remained especially troublesome for the illiterate. So some clock designers always displayed all numbers ending with four or nine with slash marks rather than "IV" or "IX."

Why do clockmakers persist in using roman numerals today? Primarily because the touch of antiquity pleases consumers. At a time when dependable clocks and watches can be produced for less than they could decades ago, manufacturers need design elements to convince consumers to spend more. Although some argue that roman numerals are easier to read upside down and at a distance, the touch of class they connote is still their biggest selling point.

The delicious irony, of course, is that this touch of class stems from a system designed for peasants.

Why Are Rain Clouds Dark?

Rain is water. Water is light in color. Rain clouds are full of water. Therefore, rain clouds should be light. Impeccable logic, but wrong.

Obviously, there are always water particles in clouds. But when the particles of water are small, they reflect light and are perceived as white. When water particles become large enough to form raindrops, however, they absorb light and appear dark to us below.

Why Are So Many Corporations Incorporated in Delaware?

We blanched when we noticed that two of the largest New York banks, Citibank and Chase Manhattan, were incorporated in Delaware. Both banks' names betray their New York roots, so surely there must be some practical reasons why they chose to incorporate in another state.

Then we encountered a November 1986 *Forbes* article, which reported that Delaware houses more than thirty out-of-state banks. A call to the Delaware Chamber of Commerce yielded even more startling statistics. More than 170,000 companies are incorporated in Delaware, including more than one-half of all Fortune 500 companies, 42 percent of all New York Stock Exchange listees, and a similar proportion of AMEX companies.

How could Delaware, the home of fewer than 700,000 people, house so many corporations? The answer is a textbook illustration of the ways a small state can attract big business by changing its laws and tax structure to attract outsiders. One of the reasons that Delaware attracted so many banks, for example, is that it abolished usury ceilings, which are set by the state rather than by the federal government. Let's look at the other inducements that Delaware offers corporations seeking a home.

Favorable Tax Laws

1. No state sales tax.
2. No personal property tax.
3. No corporate income tax for corporations maintaining a corporate office in Delaware but not doing business in the state. If Chase Manhattan were incorporated in New York, New York State would demand a share of the income generated beyond its borders.
4. No corporate income tax for holding companies handling intangible investments or handling tangible properties located outside Delaware.
5. An extremely low franchise tax, based on authorized capital stock (the minimum is a staggeringly low $30; but there is also a maximum, $130,000 per year, that is very attractive to big corporations). Even with the low rate, the franchise tax generates 14 percent of the state's general fund revenues—Delaware collected over $126 million in 1986.
6. The corporate tax rate itself is a low 8.7 percent and is collected only on money generated inside Delaware. Compare this to the 10 percent New York State tax and the total burden of 19 percent for companies operating within New York City.

Favorable Corporation Law

1. Delaware's court of Chancery sets the nation's standards for sophistication and timeliness in shaping corporate law. Don-

ald E. Schwartz, professor of law at Georgetown Law Center, says: "There is, by an order of several magnitudes, a larger body of case law from Delaware than there is from any other jurisdiction, enabling not only lawyers who practice in Delaware, but lawyers everywhere who counsel Delaware corporations to be able to render opinions with some confidence." By quickly establishing precedents on the issues that confront corporate heads today, Delaware has defined the legal parameters for doing business faster and more comprehensively than any other state. Business leaders feel more secure in making decisions and planning for the future, because the law is set early; as Schwartz puts it, "Corporate managers and their lawyers seek predictability."

2. In Delaware, only a majority of shareholders of a company need agree to incorporate a company. Many states require a two-thirds majority.

3. Delaware allows mergers to proceed with less intrusion than just about any other state.

4. Once incorporated, a corporation can change its purpose of business without red tape from the state.

5. The corporation's terms of existence is perpetual in Delaware. Some states require renewals, which involve paper work and extra expense.

Favorable Treatment of Corporate Leaders

Delaware has recently enacted several laws designed to make life easier for corporate heads, particularly boards of directors.

1. Delaware law allows corporations to indemnify directors, officers, and agents against expenses and often against judgments, fines, and costs of settlements incurred in suits against them filed by third parties.

2. Delaware law makes it difficult to unseat directors of a corporation.

3. Directors of a Delaware corporation do not necessarily have to meet in Delaware. Decisions can be made by conference

call; they can even take an action without any meeting if there is unanimous written consent.

4. Perhaps most important in this category, Delaware passed an enabling act that allowed corporations to limit or eliminate outside directors' personal financial liability for violations of their fiduciary duty (including potential liability for gross negligence). This rule makes it much easier to attract directors to Delaware corporations; would-be directors in many states are forced to pay high liability insurance premiums to protect themselves against just such lawsuits. Although Delaware law does not allow directors to escape unscathed for perpetrating fraud, the knowledge that they won't be held up for making a mistake (even a "gross" one) makes directors happy to work in the state.

Other factors also make Delaware attractive to corporations. Unions are not as entrenched in Delaware as in most areas of the Mid-Atlantic and Northeast. Pay and cost-of-living scales are lower than in surrounding regions.

Perhaps the most enticing nontangible asset of Delaware in attracting business is the accessibility of government officials to business people. State Insurance Commissioner David Levinson was quoted in the *Forbes* article on this subject: "If you have a problem and you're operating a company in Delaware, within 48 hours you can have in one room the governor, the insurance commissioner, the president pro tem of the senate and the speaker of the house."

Delaware's probusiness slant has revived what was once a stagnant economy. But has this infusion of incorporations helped the average citizen of Delaware, when most companies do not relocate there? Evidence suggests that money has trickled down. Although there are pockets of poverty in Delaware, unemployment is now well below the national average.

The secret weapon of Delaware is its small size. A bigger state would need promises of a large number of jobs before offering financial concessions to corporations. But a small state like Delaware can siphon off the gravy and thrive. For example, Delaware offers some tax breaks to out-of-state banks if they incorporate in Delaware and maintain an office with at least one hundred employees. To a multinational bank, one hundred jobs is a drop in the bucket. To a state with fewer than twenty thousand unemployed people, one hundred jobs represents a substantial opportunity.

Why Does Coca-Cola From a Small Bottle Taste Better Than Coca-Cola From a Large Bottle or Can?

Scratch any Coca-Cola diehard, and you are likely to find someone who insists that Coke tastes best out of 6½-ounce glass bottles. While purists can handle the 12-ounce glass bottles, their eyes inevitably become glazed or downcast as soon as the words "plastic" or "can" or "three-liter" are bandied about.

We must confess. We have the same conviction. Yet the small Coke bottles are almost impossible to find in many parts of the country. A friend of ours, Chris Geist, who lives in Bowling Green, Ohio, once wrote a letter to Coca-Cola complaining that his family couldn't find the small bottles anywhere. A representative from Coca-Cola came to his door, one day, like Michael Anthony on *The Millionaire,* with a case of 6½-ounce glass bottles. The Coca-Cola man bewailed the demise of the small glass bottles himself, but explained that supermarkets refuse to stock them. Grocery stores don't like the breakability of glass, and they prefer the higher profit margins provided by the larger sizes.

Despite many attempts, we could not get Coca-Cola to respond to this Imponderable, on or off the record, but we consulted several other soft-drink companies and soft-drink technologists and got pretty much the same answer from all. The response of the National Soft Drink Association is typical: "What many people do not realize is that the exact same product that goes into small bottles also goes into large bottles and cans. We have found in the past that most perceived taste preferences disappear when a blind taste test is administered using a similar sample container such as a paper cup." Our guess, however, is that these comparisons were made under ideal conditions; the consumer is not always granted such favorable benefits. For one, the polyester resin material used in two- and three-liter soft drink bottles does not retain CO_2 as well as glass or aluminum. And although polyester resin provides a decent shelf life in the supermarket, the carbonation retention is not nearly as good as in other containers.

Most important, any amount of air in the head space (the top of the bottle) adversely affects the taste of the liquid. Once a bottle is opened, even if the closure is reapplied tightly, the carbonation and the taste are never quite the same again. Indeed, one of our pet theories is that simply in the time that it takes to fill a three-liter bottle, more air is trapped inside than in a small bottle. The amount of CO_2 in a bottle affects not only our sense of its carbonation but also our taste perception.

We didn't get far on the can versus bottle argument. We assumed that canned soft drinks didn't taste as good as bottled ones because traces of the metal affected the flavor. Soft-drink experts insist that in blind taste tests, consumers can't tell the difference, and buyers like the convenience and durability of the can. Bah humbug!

Submitted by Ronald C. Semone, of Washington, D.C.

Why and When Was 1982–1984 Chosen to Replace 1967 as the Base Year for the Consumer Price Index? Why Wasn't It Changed After Ten Years?

The Consumer Price Index measures the average change in prices over time in a fixed market basket of goods and services. The CPI tracks the prices of food, clothing, housing, utility costs, medical care, drugs, transportation, and many other goods and services, as well as the taxes on all of these items. Prices are collected from 85 urban areas, including about 4,000 food stores, 24,000 rental units, and 28,000 business establishments, both commercial enterprises and nonprofit institutions such as hospitals.

The Consumer Price Index is based on data compiled from

the Consumer Expenditure Surveys. The accuracy of these data is important not only in the abstract, to economists and researchers, but in the pocketbook, to workers, whose cost-of-living provisions are keyed to the CPI. The reference base year is changed to make comparisons of rates of change easier for the public to understand. By changing the base year every ten years or so, the numbers don't get unwieldy. Until 1987, the base year for the CPI was 1967; the index was expressed as 1967 = 100. If the 1972 index had increased by 50 percent since 1967, it would have been expressed as 150. An index rating of 250 would mean a 150 percent jump since the reference base year.

The Bureau of Labor Statistics is not under any statutory requirement to change its base year at any particular time, though it strives to do so approximately every decade. Originally, BLS intended to change the base year to 1977, which would have been a fortuitous choice for two reasons. First, the then most recent quinquennial (five-year) economic censuses were taken for 1977, and many economic time series are tied to economic censuses. Second, the expansion of the economy in 1977 after the recession of 1974–1975 was relatively balanced, which meant that there were few extreme conditions in particular segments of the economy that would have made 1977 unrepresentative of the recent period.

The most difficult part of compiling the CPI isn't the collection of raw data (it is time consuming, but not hard, to find out the cost of, say, dairy products in different localities throughout the country), but rather the weighting of the various sectors that the CPI measures. In order for the index to be accurate, it must measure not only how much goods and services cost the consumer, but also what percentage of consumer expenses each category represents. It matters little if the cost of maraschino cherries skyrockets if very few consumers buy them in the first place. But if the price of a staple such as oil zooms during an energy crisis, it will have a more substantial effect on the CPI.

In the late 1970s, the Bureau of Labor Statistics was in the process of developing new systems to "weight" the different components of the index, so the plan was to wait to implement 1977 as the base year until 1981, after the new weighting system was introduced. No base-year changes can be made without review by the Office of Federal Statistical Policy and Standards, Office of Management and Budget. According to Patrick Jackman, at the Office of Prices and Living Conditions of the Bureau of Labor Statistics, severe budget constraints led the BLS to ask for a postponement of the change, and they were granted it. Without these budget problems, 1977 would have been the reference base year, at least through the late 1980s. In other words, Reaganomics killed the planned base-year change.

So why have they finally made the decision to adopt the three-year 1982–1984 period as the reference base? Historically, the reference base period has tended to be three years (before 1967, 1957–1959 and 1947–1949 were the reference bases), mainly because it was believed there would be less volatility in the index if it reflected a fairly lengthy time period. Then a government interagency task force decided that the Bureau of Labor Statistics should designate a *single* year as the reference base period, and 1967 was chosen. The intent was to key several economic indexes to the same base year. The Office of Management and Budget abandoned this attempt and reverted to a three-year period—1982–1984—largely because this particular period was already being used in determining the expenditure base weights.

Submitted by Daniel Marcus, of Watertown, Massachusetts.

Why Do Firehouses Have Dalmatians?

Although today dalmatians serve primarily as firehouse mascots, back in the days of horse-drawn hose carts, they provided a valuable service. Dalmatians and horses get along swimmingly, so the dogs were easily trained to run in front of the carts and help clear a path for the firefighters to get to a fire quickly.

The breed eventually became so popular in New York City firehouses that the Westminster Kennel Club offered a special show class for dalmatians owned by New York Fire Department members. In their book, *Dalmatians: Coach Dog, Firehouse Dog*, Alfred and Esmeralda Treen tell the story of a Lieutenant Wise of the NYFD who had such a close attachment to his firehouse mascot, Bessie, that she followed him home on his days off, literally hopping on the streetcar to accompany him. If Bessie missed the car, she knew where to stand to catch the next one. Bessie also followed Lieutenant Wise into burning buildings but stayed one floor below the fighting line, "for fear a dog might cause a man to stumble if retreat was ordered."

Dalmatians have been used throughout history for serious work: as sentinels on the borders of homeland Dalmatia and Croatia, during wars; as shepherds; as draft dogs; as hound dogs; as retrievers; and as performing dogs (dalmatians not only are intelligent, but have excellent memories). Dalmatians' speed and endurance and lack of fear of horses enabled them to become superb coach dogs for fire carts. As the Dalmatian Club of America puts it, the breed was able "to coach under the rear axle, the front axle, or most difficult of all, under the pole between the leaders and the wheelers."

The death knell of the dalmatian as a coaching dog for fire departments sounded with the introduction of motorized cars. Dalmatians like Bessie lost their function, as we can see from this sentimental lament from Lieutenant Wise:

> For five and a half long years Bessie cleared the crossing at Third
> Avenue and Sixty-seventh Street for her company, barking a warn-

ing to surface-car motormen, truck drivers, and pedestrians, and during all that time she led the way in every one of the average of forty runs a month made by No. 39. Then like a bolt from the sky the white horses she loved were taken away, even the stalls were removed, and the next alarm found her bounding in front of a man-made thing that had no intelligence—a gasoline-driven engine. Bessie ran as far as Third Avenue, tucked her tail between her legs and returned to the engine house. Her heart was broken. She never ran to another fire.

Today's dalmatian is as likely to help in quashing fires as is Smokey the Bear. But firehouse mascots still abound, and the dalmatian is still often chosen by many firefighters in honor of its heroism in the past.

Doughnut-Shop Employees Always Pick Up the Doughnuts With a Tissue So That Their Hands Never Touch the Doughnuts. Why Do They Then Put the Same Tissue in with the Doughnuts for the Customer to Carry Home—Germs and All?

Imponderables must have the most discerning readership in the cosmos. Who else but an *Imponderables* reader would raise such an important health issue, hitherto hidden in obscurity?

We contacted all of the biggest doughnut-store companies. Those that responded sheepishly admitted that the tissue, usually Sav-R-Wrap tissue, is used by employees for sanitary reasons, but couldn't explain why the tissue, "germs and all," is stuffed in the bag, except that it is, as Carl E. Hass, president of Winchell's says, "placed on top of the donuts so that the customer may use it to remove the product from the bag." The director of product marketing at Dunkin' Donuts, Glenn Bacheller, agreed that perhaps the custom isn't the greatest idea, and said that the Dunkin' Donuts training department is looking into the possibility of not stuffing in the "used" tissue. Our reader may have earned a niche in doughnut history.

Submitted by Karen Simmons, of West Palm Beach, Florida.

Why Is Scoring Three Goals in Hockey Called a Hat-Trick?

"Hat-trick" was originally an English cricket term used to describe the tremendous feat of a bowler's taking three wickets on successive balls. The reward for this accomplishment at many cricket clubs was a new hat. Other clubs honored their heroes by "passing the hat" among fans and giving the scorer the proceeds. The term spread to other sports in which scoring is relatively infrequent—"hat-trick" is also used to describe the feat of scoring three goals in soccer.

According to Belinda Lerner, of the National Hockey League, the expression surfaced in hockey during the early 1900s: "There is some confusion about its actual meaning in hockey. Today, a 'true' hat-trick occurs when one player scores three successive goals without another goal being scored by other players in the contest."

Submitted by Ron Fishman, of Denver, Colorado.

What Are the Names on the Bottom of Grocery Sacks?

The kraft paper grocery sack celebrated its hundredth anniversary in 1986. Innovation is necessary to keep most venerable products fresh and appealing. But aren't designer grocery sacks a little much? What will we have next—generic paper sacks?

The largest manufacturer of grocery bags, Stone Container Corporation, of Huntington, Long Island, makes over 25 billion bags and sacks every year (a "sack" is technically a large grocery bag). These numbers are impressive, but let's face it: making the same paper bags day in and day out is not the most exciting job in the world. So many manufacturers have decided that, in order to promote pride and a sense of responsibility in the workers, employees would "sign" their work.

In most cases, the name you see on the bottom of the bag (usually just a first name) is that of the person who actually made the bag. Sometimes it is the name of the inspector responsible for supervising the production of the bags by other workers. While inspection certificates in clothing (such as "Inspected by No. 7") are there to monitor quality control, the names on grocery bags are intended solely to add to the esprit de corps.

At the Stone Container Corporation, many of the workers who run the bag machines have their full names on the bag, preceded by the words, "Produced with Pride by:" If most manufacturers included that inscription, this Imponderable wouldn't exist, and the mystique of "Toms," "Dicks," and "Harriets" on the bottom of shopping bags wouldn't linger.

Submitted by Kathi Sawyer Young, of Encino, California.

Why Do Chinese Restaurants Use Monosodium Glutamate? Other Ethnic Restaurants Don't Use It And It Certainly Is Not a Traditional Part of the Native Cuisine.

Actually, you are just as likely to encounter MSG in a Japanese or Indian restaurant as in a Chinese restaurant. And MSG *has* been a traditional part of Chinese cuisine. Sort of.

Glutamate has been used by Oriental cooks for more than two millennia, but not glutamate out of a shaker. Chefs noticed that soup stock made from *Laminaria japonica*, a certain seaweed, tasted better. They didn't know at the time that what was special about this strain of seaweed was that it contained large amounts of natural glutamate.

The discovery of the links between seaweed, monosodium glutamate, and flavor is credited to Professor Kikunae Ikeda of the University of Tokyo, who, in 1908, isolated the specific component of *Laminaria japonica* that enhanced flavor. While Western scientists believed there were only four basic tastes—sweet, sour, salty, and bitter—Ikeda believed in what the Japanese call *umami*, or tastiness, as a separate component. The mystery of *umami* is what the professor was trying to discover by unraveling the composition of the seaweed.

Dr. Ikeda was so enthusiastic about the power of MSG that commercial production of the substance was soon undertaken in Japan. MSG is essentially a concentrated form of sodium. It is extracted from seaweed in the Orient and from seaweed, beets, and grains in the West. Bean curd and soy sauces also tend to contain MSG. Japan and China are still the largest consumers of MSG, but it is used throughout the world (about 200,000 tons of it annually), and the United States, which didn't start producing it until the 1940s, eats its share—not only in Chinese and Japanese restaurants, but in many prepared foods.

One of the reasons many people associate MSG with Chinese food is the dreaded "Chinese restaurant syndrome," whose sufferers insist that they have strong allergic reactions to the chemical. One Chinese restaurant in New York City was so beset by requests from Occidentals to omit the ingredient from its food that all the waitresses donned white aprons with large block letters emblazoned with the immortal words, "No MSG."

The Glutamate Association (yes, there is a trade organization just for glutamate producers) insists that MSG is perfectly safe. They argue that MSG is no different from the glutamate that is liberated by our bodies when we eat food protein, and that MSG added to food represents only a small fraction of the glutamate contained naturally in most foods. For example, most recipes call for half a teaspoon of MSG per pound of meat. With these proportions, the MSG in a serving of chicken would constitute less than 10 percent of the glutamate already found in the chicken.

While the U.S. Food and Drug Administration lists MSG as "Generally Recognized as Safe," a category that includes other common food additives such as salt, pepper, and sugar, many Americans feel that any food that can cause intense allergic reactions must be harmful, and despite its advocacy even the Glutamate Association cites the World Health Organization's recommendation to limit MSG consumption to a maximum of one-third of an ounce a day (far more than the average American eats). So the question persists: why do restaurateurs and food packagers insist on including an additive that many people don't want and can't really distinguish by taste even if included?

MSG's greatest attribute is its ability to blend flavors well, especially the flavor of mixed spices, which is a reason why Indian cooks, so spice-conscious, tend to use MSG in great quantities. MSG tends to soften the astringent qualities of some foods. Tomatoes taste less acidic with MSG; potatoes less earthy; onions less strong.

For many of the same reasons, a number of chefs disdain MSG, believing that it deadens the taste of foods and is too often used to compensate for inferior products. Others feel there is a thin line between "blending" and "harmonizing" tastes and making all foods taste the same. Some object, in principle, to the idea of using any additive (even a naturally derived one) to enhance the natural taste of a meat, though this same argument could be made against using salt or pepper.

Many consumers confuse MSG with meat tenderizers (which often contain MSG as an ingredient). MSG does not act as either a spice or a tenderizer. Tenderizers act through the use of purified papain, a protein-splitting enzyme extracted from the juice of unripe papayas. It is confusion between MSG and tenderizers that is often the cause of nervous confrontations in Chinese restaurants. The waiters think that the Americans are being oversensitive to MSG, particularly because, more often than not, MSG will be contained in the base of sauces even if your "no MSG" orders are followed—your request will merely prevent additional MSG from being sprinkled on. The customer is sure that MSG is an ingredient the sole purpose of which is to reduce tough, rubbery meat into something edible, while the cook is likely to dash a few more sprinkles of MSG on his own food if he has the chance.

Submitted by Ronald C. Semone, of Washington, D.C.

Why Do Old Men Wear Their Pants Higher Than Young Men?

We couldn't find too many clothing or gerontological authorities who specialized in this subject, but just about everyone we contacted was more than happy to offer speculations. So, until the *Encyclopaedia Britannica* prints an entry on "Pants Height," we'll just have to write the definitive treatment ourselves.

The most common explanation we received from clothiers is that as men get older, they lose a little height and the spine curves a bit. Thus, a pair of pants that might have hung at waist level a few years ago will now creep upward. The one problem with this theory: when old men go to buy new pants, they still buy pants that hang high.

The second most popular explanation of this nagging social problem is the "Paunch Theory," which postulates that high-riding pants are a pathetic attempt to hide abdominal excesses. While this idea makes eminent sense, it doesn't explain why younger men with truly awesome beer bellies wear their pants low and let their stomachs hang unfettered.

But one wise man, Fred Shippee, of the American Apparel Manufacturers Association, offered the most logical explanation. Pants were cut relatively high until the jeans craze of the 1960s. Most men above the age of fifty, let alone much older men, never had the experience of wearing pants designed to hang on the hips rather than on the waist, and they feel uncomfortable starting now. To someone used to wearing high-cut pants, hip huggers feel as if they are always on the verge of falling off.

The low cut of jeans (called "low-rise") truly revolutionized menswear and literally lowered our sights. When we see "high-rise" pants, we think "old" or "nerd." While much has been written about the ups and downs of women's hemlines, we hope that this chapter will stir compassion for men who wear their pants high or low, and eventually bring about world peace.

Why Are Oreos Called "Oreos"?

Although the world's most popular cookie recently celebrated its seventy-fifth anniversary, the origin of its name is shrouded in mystery. It was first marketed in Hoboken, New Jersey, on March 6, 1912 as the Oreo Biscuit. In 1921, the name was changed to the Oreo Sandwich. In 1948, the same cookie was renamed the Oreo Creme Sandwich. Ultimately, in 1974, the immortal Oreo Chocolate Sandwich Cookie was born, a name that should last forever or until it is changed again, whichever comes first.

Of course, the lack of definitive facts has not deterred Oreo scholars from speculating on why those four magic letters were thrown together. Michael Falkowitz, a representative of Nabisco

Brands Customer Relations, offers two of the more popular theories:

1. Mr. Adolphus Green, first chairman of the National Biscuit Company (founded in 1898 from the consolidation of the American Biscuit Co., the New York Biscuit Co., and the United States Baking Co.) was fond of the classics. The name "Oreo" is Greek for "mountain." It was said in early testing that the cookie resembled a mountain.

2. The name was derived from *or*, the French word for "gold." The original Oreo label had scrollwork in gold on a pale green background, and the product name was also printed in gold.

After the first printing of this book, we received several letters from Greek readers indicating that the Greek word for "mountain" is not *oreo* but *oros*. Furthermore, a Greek word that, phonetically, sounds like *oreo*, means "nice," "attractive," and even "delicious." Could this, and not Nabisco's "mountain theory," be the real answer to the origins of our number one cookie?

Submitted by Ronald C. Semone, of Washington, D.C.

In the illustration:

Funny Numbers © 1987

Have a Nice Read!

Funny Numbers: A Shocking Exposé of the Publishing World by A. Digit

Printed in U.S.A.
10 9 8 7 6 5 4 3 2 1

What Are Those Funny Numbers on the Bottom of Copyright Pages in Books?

Look at the bottom of the copyright page of this book. Unless someone at the typesetter's has played an elaborate practical joke on us, you should see a row of numbers with a few letters —something like this:

87 88 89 90 ??? 10 9 8 7 6 5 4 3 2 1

These funny numbers are simply a code designed to signify which printing of the book you have purchased. The number farthest to the right is the printing your have bought (in the example above, you would have bought the first printing). Harper & Row and some other publishers also mark the year of the printing, indicated by the number at the far left (in the example above, 1987). This practice is reassuring to paranoid writers, who assume that the shelf life of their works in bookstores will approximate that of *Tiger Beat* magazine on the newsstand. Those three question marks on our example stand for the three letters that Harper & Row uses to designate which of their printers handled the particular book.

When a book goes into a second printing, instead of redoing the whole copyright page, the printer merely deletes the "1" in the lower right corner and deletes the line that indicates that this was a first printing, if there is one. Some publishers put the lower numbers on the left and the higher ones on the right and omit the year of the printing altogether, but the principle is the same—the lowest number you see always conveys the print-run number.

The public often misunderstands the importance of printings. Ads blare, "Now in Its Fifth Printing!!!" as if a large number of printings guarantees a megaseller. Actually, multiple printings indicate that a book has surpassed expectations, but not necessarily that it has sold more than a book that never went into a second printing.

Submitted by Jonathan Sabin, of Bradenton, Florida.

Why Is 40 Percent Alcohol Called 80 Proof?

Before the nineteenth century, the technology wasn't available to measure the alcohol content of liquids accurately. The first hydrometer was invented by John Clarke in 1725 but wasn't approved by the British Parliament for official use until the end of the century. In the meantime, purveyors of spirits needed a way to determine alcohol content, and tax collectors demanded a way to ascertain exactly what their rightful share of liquor sales was.

So the British devised an ingenious, if imprecise, method. Someone figured out that gunpowder would ignite in an alcoholic liquid only if enough water was eliminated from the mix. When the proportion of alcohol to water was high enough that black gunpower would explode—this was the *proof* of the alcohol.

The British proof, established by the Cromwell Parliament, contained approximately eleven parts by volume of alcohol to ten parts water. The British proof is the equivalent of 114.2 U.S. proof. More potent potables were called "over proof" (or o.p.), and those under 114.2 U.S. proof were deemed "under proof" (or u.p.).

The British and Canadians are still saddled with this archaic method of measuring alcohol content. The United States's system makes slightly more sense. The U.S. proof is simply double the alcohol percentage volume at 60° F. For once, the French are the logical nation. They recognize the wisdom in bypassing "proof" and simply stating the percentage of alcohol on spirits labels. The French method has spread to wine bottles everywhere, but hard liquor, true to its gunpowder roots, won't give up the "proof."

Submitted by Robert J. Abrams, of Boston, Massachusetts.

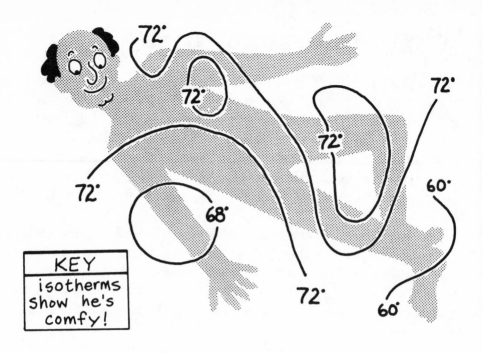

KEY
isotherms
show he's
comfy!

Why Are Humans Most Comfortable at 72° F? Why Not at 98.6° F?

We feel most comfortable when we maintain our body temperature, so why don't we feel most comfortable when it is 98.6° F in the ambient air? We would—if we were nudists.

But most of us cling to the habit of wearing clothes. Clothing helps us retain body heat, some of which must be dissipated in order for us to feel comfortable in warm environments. Uncovered parts of our body usually radiate enough heat to meet the ambient air temperature halfway. If we are fully clothed at 72° F, the uncovered hands, ears, and face will radiate only a small portion of our heat, but enough to make us feel comfortable. Nude at 72° F, we would feel cold, for our bodies would give off too much heat.

Humidity and wind also affect our comfort level. The more humid the air, the greater ability it has to absorb heat. Wind can also wreak havoc with our comfort level. It hastens the flow of the heat we radiate and then constantly moves the air away and allows slightly cooler air to replace it.

Submitted by Joel Kuni, of Kirkland, Washington.

Why Do They Call Large Trucks "Semis"? Semi-*Whats?*

The power unit of commercial trucks, the part that actually pulls the load, is called the "tractor." The tractor pulls some form of trailer, either a "full trailer" or a "semitrailer." According to Neill Darmstadter, senior safety engineer for the American Trucking Associations, "A semitrailer is legally defined as a vehicle designed so that a portion of its weight rests on a towing vehicle. This distinguishes it from a full trailer on which the entire load, except for a drawbar, rests on its own wheels."

Semi is short for "tractor-semitrailer," but most truckers use the term *semi* to refer to both the trailer alone and the tractor-semitrailer combination. Since the tractor assumes part of the burden of carrying the weight of the semitrailer, the "semi" must have a mechanism for propping up the trailer when the power vehicle is disengaged. The semitrailer is supported by the rear wheels in back and by a small pair of wheels, called the landing gear, which can be raised and lowered by the driver. The landing gear is located at the front of the semitrailer, usually just behind the rear wheels of the tractor.

Submitted by Doug Watkins, Jr., of Hayward, California.

Why Does San Francisco Sourdough Bread Taste Different from Other Sourdough French Breads?

This Imponderable has been a source of controversy for a long, long time. San Francisco sourdough French bread has exactly the same ingredients as any other: flour, salt, water, and natural yeast. Yet, somehow, it *is* different: the crust is dark and hard, but crumbly, and the taste more sour than the competition's.

The usual explanation for the unique San Francisco taste is the Pacific Ocean air, the winds, and especially the fog. Many of the old-time bakers still use brick ovens, and a mystique has built up around them.

The answer, however, can actually be traced to the "starter." Whenever a baker makes a batch of sourdough, some of the fermented dough is set aside as a starter, which will be used to leaven the next batch. In this manner, the action of the yeasts is maintained continuously. Some of the older bakeries have strains of starters dating back more than one hundred years.

A tourist at Fishermen's Wharf is literally eating a descendant of the bread consumed by forty-niners.

The use of starters did not originate in the United States. It is believed that the Egyptians, four thousand years before the birth of Christ, were exposing dough to airborne yeast spores to ferment. Until the advent of commerical yeasts and baking powders, most breads were leavened by using leftover dough from previous batches.

The majority of San Francisco bakeries use a proportion of about 15 percent starter. Little yeast is needed, because the starter contains natural yeast. Sourdough bread made with chemical yeast tends to lack the sourness and tang of the bread made with starter.

Scientists have also tried to pierce the mystique of San Francisco sourdough. In 1970, Dr. Leo Kline and microbiologist colleagues at Oregon State University isolated two organisms in sourdough: *Saccharomyces exiguus,* an acid-tolerant yeast; and a rod-shaped bacterium, resembling lactic-acid bacteria, which they suggested be named *Lactobacillus san francisco.* According to trade newspaper *Milling and Baking News,*

> The newly-discovered lactic acid bacteria causes souring. Lactic acids and acetic acids are produced by fermentation of carbohydrates in the flour and provide the sour flavor while the acetic acid primarily keeps spoilage and disease-producing bacteria from growing in the dough.
>
> Yeast cells do the leavening; carbon dioxide gas is produced by yeast during fermentation of carbohydrates in flour. Ethyl alcohol, also produced by the yeast cells, evaporates during cooking. The carbon dioxide provides the light, fluffy texture important in bread, biscuits and pancakes.

The specific bacterium *Lactobacillus san francisco* seems to be a new species, which probably explains why San Francisco sourdough is unique.

Submitted by Donald C. Knudsen, of Oakland, California.

Does the U.S. Postal Service Add Flavoring to the Glue on Postage Stamps to Make the Taste More Palatable?

The Postal Service doesn't intend the adhesive to have any particular flavor. The glue on U.S. postage stamps comes in only two "flavors," and not for reasons of taste.

The first type, used primarily on commemorative stamps, is simply a blend of corn dextrin (a gummy substance extracted from starch) and water. This solution is gentle on commemoratives, which are designed to last longer (in philatelic collections) than "regular" stamps.

The second type of adhesive, used on regular issues, such as the twenty-two–cent flag stamps, is a blend of polyvinyl acetate emulsion and dextrin. Added to this scrumptious taste sensation is a bit of propylene glycol, used to reduce paper curl.

Is the taste of the stamp glue reminiscent of another flavor? Dianne V. Patterson, of the Postal Service's Consumer Advocate's Office, points out that the polyvinyl acetate used for stamp adhesive is the basic ingredient in bubble gum.

Submitted by Joel Kuni, of Kirkland, Washington.

Why Do Wagon Wheels in Westerns Appear to Be Spinning Backward?

Motion-picture film is really a series of still pictures run at the rate of twenty-four frames per second. When a wagon being photographed moves slowly, the shutter speed of the camera is capturing tiny movements of its wheel at a rate of twenty-four times per second—and the result is a disorienting strobe effect. As long as the movement of the wheel does not synchronize with the shutter speed of the camera, the movement of the wheel on film will be deceptive. This effect is identical to disco strobe lights, where dancers will appear to be jerking frenetically or listlessly pacing through sludge, depending on the speed of the strobe.

E. J. Blasko, of the Motion Picture and Audiovisual Products Division of Eastman Kodak, explains how the strobe effect works in movies: "As the wheels travel at a slower rate they will appear to go backward, but as the wheel goes faster it will then become synchronized with the film rate of the camera and appear to stay in one spot, and then again at a certain speed the wheel will appear to have its spokes traveling forward, but not at the same rate of speed as the vehicle." This strobe effect is often seen without need of film. Watch a roulette wheel or fan slow down, and you will see the rotation appear to reverse.

Submitted by Richard Dowdy, of La Costa, California. Thanks also to: Thomas Cunningham, of Pittsburgh, Pennsylvania, and Curtis Kelly, of Chicago, Illinois.

Why Does Unscented Hair Spray Smell?

Let's differentiate between the major formulations of hair spray. A "regular, scented" formula contains fragrance added to give the spray a distinctive smell. "Fragrance free" refers to hair sprays without any fragrance added at all. Very few hair sprays are fragrance free; these products are designed to be hypo-allergenic for consumers sensitive to any fragrance.

"Unscented" hair spray not only *does* have a scent, but it also has added fragrance, a fragrance designed to mask the chemical base of the product. The difference between "unscented" and "scented" hair spray, then, is that "scented" hair spray contains more fragrance, more long-lasting fragrance, and a fragrance designed to be prominent.

Hair spray is 95 percent alcohol. John Corbett, of the Clairol Corporation, told *Imponderables* that neat alcohol doesn't smell like a dry martini, but rather like the rubbing alcohol used for cleaning cassette recorder heads. The prospect of spraying rubbing alcohol on your hair is an affront to your nose. The purpose of the unscented spray is to avoid challenging the more expensive, and desirable, fragrance of perfumes or colognes that the customer might apply.

Corbett added that he doubted that consumers cared much about how hair sprays smelled, as long as they weren't offensive. In the toiletry category, consumers seem to care passionately only about the smell of shampoos.

Sales for "scented" and "unscented" hair sprays are about even, with "fragrance free" products representing a tiny share of the market.

Submitted by Aleta Moorhouse, of Mesa, Arizona.

Why Does Heat Lightning Always Seem Far Away? And Why Don't You Ever Hear Thunder During Heat Lightning?

Heat lightning is actually distant lightning produced by an electrical storm too far away to be seen by the observer. What you see is actually the diffused reflection of the distant lightning on clouds.

You don't hear thunder because the actual lightning is too far away from you for the sound to be audible. There *is* thunder where the lightning is actually occurring.

Why Can't Hair Grow on a Vaccination Mark?

A vaccination mark is nothing more than scar tissue. A vaccination causes an inflammation intense enough to destroy the hair follicles in its vicinity. Any deep injury to the skin will destroy hair follicles and cause hair loss, a condition known to dermatologists as "scarring alopecia." One can easily transplant hair onto a vaccination mark, if desired, but one can never bring a dead hair follicle back to life.

Submitted by David Wilsterman, of Belmont, California.

What Kind of Hen Lays Extra-Large Eggs? What Determines the Size Categories of Chicken Eggs?

Although there are six official sizes of eggs, the smallest size a grocery store consumer is likely to encounter is the medium egg. Sizes are determined strictly by weight, as the chart below indicates:

Size	Minimum Weight Per Dozen Eggs
Jumbo	30 oz.
Extra-Large	27 oz.
Large	24 oz.
Medium	21 oz.
Small	18 oz.
Peewee	15 oz.

Small- and peewee-sized eggs are generally sold to bakers and food processors at a lower price per pound than larger eggs, so the prudent egg producer wants to encourage hens to lay big eggs. The Single-Comb White Leghorn, the most popular laying hen in the United States, eats approximately a quarter-pound of feed per day. It takes about four pounds of feed to produce a dozen eggs, so larger eggs are not without cost to the farmer.

The biggest variable in egg size is the age of the chicken. Generally speaking, the older the chicken, the larger the egg. Hens that start laying eggs prematurely tend to lay more but smaller eggs. Different breeds also tend to vary in size of eggs produced. Leghorns, for example, tend to lay larger than average eggs.

The weight of the bird is another factor in egg size. A pullet (a hen less than one year old) significantly underweight at sexual maturity will tend to produce small eggs. For this reason, farmers must pay attention not only to the quantity but the quality of feed given to hens. Feed without sufficient protein and fatty acids, while cheaper to supply, will yield smaller eggs. Hard evidence suggests that hatching environment also affects egg size. Heat, stress, and overcrowding all lower the size of eggs.

Consumers are often confused about the relative value of different sizes of eggs. Some feel that larger sizes have disproportionately more shell than smaller eggs (not true: shells constitute approximately 10 percent of the weight of all eggs). Which size will constitute the best buy is likely to vary from week to week and can be determined by a formula devised by the American Egg Board. Let's say large eggs cost 96 cents a dozen and a dozen extra-large eggs cost $1.05. Which is the better buy? First, find the price difference by subtracting the price of the smaller size from that of the larger. In this case, the price difference is $1.05 minus 96 cents, or 9 cents. Then divide the price of the smaller eggs by 8 to find the "magic number." In this case, 96 cents divided by 8 is exactly 12 (round off the number if it isn't even).

If the magic number is lower than the price difference, the

smaller eggs are a better buy. If the magic number is higher than the price difference, the larger eggs are a better buy. Because in the example 9 (the price difference) is less than 12 (the magic number), the extra-large eggs would be cheaper per weight than the large eggs.

You divide the price difference by 8 to find the magic number because egg sizes vary in increments of exactly 3 ounces. Large eggs (the one size that is always available in stores) are 24 ounces per dozen, so 24 divided by 3 equals 8, which when divided into the price of a dozen eggs provides the benchmark price for 3 ounces of eggs.

All of this makes perfect sense, even though we sense eyes glazing over as you read it.

Submitted by Helen M. Tvorik, of Mayfield Heights, Ohio.

Why Do Some Chickens Lay Brown Eggs and Others Lay White Eggs?

The color of eggs comes exclusively from the pigment in the outer layer of the shell and may range from an almost pure white to a deep brown, with many shades in between. The only determinant of egg color is the breed of the chicken.

Because white eggs are preferred in almost every region of the country, the Single-Comb White Leghorn has become by far the favorite egg-layer in the United States. The Leghorn is prized for many reasons: it reaches maturity earlier than most pullets; it utilizes its feed efficiently; it is relatively small (an important consideration when most chickens are kept in cages even smaller than New York City studio apartments); it is hardy, adapting well to different climates; and most important, it produces a large number of eggs. If more consumers went along with New England's preference for brown eggs, more breeds such as the Rhode Island Red, New Hampshire, and Plymouth Rock would be provided to produce them.

A simple test to determine the color of a hen's eggs is to look at her earlobes. If the earlobes are white, the hen will lay white eggs. If the earlobes are red, she will produce brown eggs.

Although many people are literally afraid to try brown eggs, they are no more or less nutritious or healthy than white ones. In fact, brown eggs have some cachet among health-food aficionados, which guarantees their higher cost, if not greater benefits.

Egg yolks also range dramatically in color, but yolk variations are caused by dietary differences rather than genetic ones. Yolk color is influenced primarily by the pigments in the chicken feed. If the hen gets plenty of yellow-orange plant pigments known as xanthophylls, the pigments will be deposited in the yolk. Hens receiving mash with yellow corn and alfalfa meal will lay eggs with medium yellow yolks. Those fed on wheat or barley produce lighter yolks. A totally colorless diet, such as white corn, will yield a colorless yolk. For cosmetic reasons alone, farmers avoid giving chickens a colorless diet, because consumers prefer a yellowish hue to their yolks.

Submitted by Jo Ellen Flynn, of Canyon Country, California.

How Did the Expression "Two Bits" Come to Mean 25 Cents? How Did "Two-Bit" Come to Mean "Cheap"?

"Bit," which has long been English slang for any coin of a low denomination, derived from the Old English word, *bite*, which meant a small bit or morsel. Before the American Revolution, English money was in short supply, so coins from all over Europe, Mexico, and South America were equally redeemable. Sailors and new immigrants assured a steady stream of non-English coins into the new country. Because there were so many different denominations, coins were valued by their weight and silver and gold content.

Spanish and Mexican coins were especially popular in early America. "Bit" became a synonym for the Spanish and Mexican coin, the *real*. The real was equivalent to one-eighth of a peso, or twelve and one-half cents. Particularly in the southwestern United States, where the Mexican influence was most strongly felt, Americans rarely called a quarter anything else but "two bits." Recognizing that U.S. coinage had no equivalent to one bit, Southwesterners usually referred to ten cents as a "short-bit" and fifteen cents as a "long-bit," and occasionally still do so today.

In Spain, a bit was an actual coin. Pesos were manufactured so that they could literally be cut apart. A peso, which equaled eight bits, could be cut in half to become two four-bit pieces. Cut in fourths, a peso became four two-bit pieces.

How did the term "two-bit" become synonymous with cheapness and tackiness (especially because, obviously, one bit is cheaper than two)? The first known use of this meaning, according to word whiz Stuart Flexner, was in 1856, referring to a saloon that was so cheap that a good, stiff drink could be had for . . . two bits.

Submitted by John A. Bush, of St. Louis, Missouri. Thanks also to: Tom and Marcia Bova, of Rochester, New York.

Why Did Volkswagen Discontinue Making the "Bug"?

At the time, most of us thought that the phasing out of VW Beetles was an insidious plot, designed to eliminate a model that lasted too long and thus reaped insufficient profits for the greedy automaker. Why try to sell us a cheap, dependable Bug, when they could peddle a more expensive, less charismatic Rabbit? But there was a simpler explanation: the VW Beetle had stopped selling.

Although the German Bug had been around since the 1930s, the first one didn't hit North American shores until 1949, when two brothers brought them home and soon decided to open a Volkswagen distributorship on the East Coast.

Five years later, only 8,000 Beetles were sold in a year, but the Bug soon started to take off. In 1955, sales reached 32,000 units. The peak years for the Bug were the mid-1960s: in 1968, Volkswagen sold 423,000 automobiles, the vast majority of them Bugs. But watch what happened to Beetle sales after 1968:

1969:	403,000
1970:	405,000
1971:	354,000
1972:	358,000
1973:	371,000
1974:	243,000
1975:	92,000

After a slow, but steady decline from its peak year, the popularity of the Beetle fell precipitously. Volkswagen was forced to bail out of the Bug business in the United States.

Speculations about the metaphysical reasons for the decline of the Beetle abound. Everything from growing materialism to the Vietnam War has been blamed for its demise. Larry Brown, a representative of Volkswagen, offers a more prosaic excuse: Japanese imports. In the late 1960s, the Japanese began to provide a stylish subcompact with better specifications than the Beetle, and for less money.

During its heyday, the VW Bug was designed to attract the thinking man or woman. The Beetle appealed to college professors and students, not only because it was cheap, but because it was emblematic of their rationality and refusal to buy into the car-as-fantasy-machine myth that Detroit had been perpetuating for decades. The irony, of course, is that the VW became a status symbol itself—the ultimate antiestablishment automobile. VW ads delighted in tweaking the pretensions of more expensive cars. The Beetle buyer felt confident that he was buying the steak, and not the sizzle.

Offered a rational alternative, these same buyers flocked to the Japanese imports and later to Volkswagen's own Rabbit, which offered better mileage, better handling, better leg and shoulder room, and a safer ride. The Beetle was superior only in its charm, in its charisma.

The charisma remains. Brown told *Imponderables* that he still receives calls from longtime owners of Beetles, asking him to come for a thirtieth birthday party or a 300,000-mile party. Magazines and clubs devoted to the Beetle keep the spirit alive. The Beetle is still manufactured in Mexico, and *exported* to Germany.

We asked Brown if the Beetle might be resurrected. After all, the death of convertibles was prematurely announced just a few years ago. Brown wasn't optimistic. He estimates that there are twenty thousand hardcore addicts who would buy a new Beetle immediately, but after that, it would be a hard sell. Volkswagen would have to sell a Beetle with the old specifications for approximately eight to ten thousand dollars today, overpriced for an entry-level car.

Instead, for 1988 Volkswagen has chosen to offer the Fox, a new entry-level model with a list price of under six thousand dollars. Intended to compete with the new Korean cars, as well as Japanese subcompacts, the Fox won't be the cheapest car on the block, the way the old Beetle used to be.

The race of so many full-line automobile companies to compete in the entry-level field indicates that there is still profit to be made in low-priced cars. Volkswagen probably would have clung to the Beetle indefinitely as long as it sold, but the Bug's demise, ironically, forced Volkswagen to expand its thinking and planning. A one-product company (the Karmann Ghia, VW's sports car, was never a big seller in the U.S.) is always in jeopardy.

The success of the Beetle was dependent on the serendipitous confluence of several factors: a bulging demographic group of baby boomers coming into driving age; a clever marketing and advertising campaign; and a growing wave of antiestablishment thinking. But most of all, there was that charisma. When charisma wanes, it's hard to regain that magic. Ask the makers of Flavor Straws. Or Screaming Yellow Zonkers.

Submitted by J. Spring, of Citrus Heights, California.

Why Are the Flush Handles on Toilets on the Left Side?

Have we finally found a product that was designed with the left-hander in mind? Of course not.

Most early flush toilets were operated by a chain above the tank that had to be pulled down by hand. Almost all of the chains were located on the left side of the toilet, for the user had more leverage when pulling with the right hand while seated.

When the smaller handles near the top of the tank were popularized in the 1940s and 1950s, many were fitted onto existing toilets then equipped with pull-chains. Therefore, it was cheaper and more convenient to place the new handles where they fitted standard plumbing and fixtures.

The handles offered the user a new dilemma: should one flush while seated or flush while standing? Although this subject is not often discussed in polite quarters, we are more that delighted to tread on delicate matters in order to stamp out Imponderability wherever we find it. Alexander Kira, in his wonderful book, *The Bathroom*, notes that in the "Cornell Survey of Personal Hygiene Attitudes and Practices in 1000 Middle-Class Households," 34 percent of respondents flushed the toilet while still seated and 66 percent flushed while standing up. Thus, it would seem that the majority of Americans flush either left-handed or else in an awkward right-handed crossover style. Would there be reason to switch handles over to the right side?

In *The Bathroom*, Kira argues that the current configuration discriminates not so much against right-handers as against flushing-while-seated types:

> Most flushing mechanisms are poorly located. . . . convenient only if the user flushes the closet after rising and turning around. A sizable number of persons prefer, however, for one reason or another (odor, peace of mind, and so on), to flush the closet while seated and after each bowel movement and must engage in contortions to do so. Since the water closet is presently also used for

standing male urination, this might be regarded as a justification for its location.

Kira sees the flushometer as no solution to our left-right problem. Generally used only in public bathrooms, flushometers are those levers that you never know whether you are supposed to operate with your foot or your hand. Evidently, people use both, making the flushometer unsanitary. The device's position, about eighteen inches off the floor, is awkward for either extremity.

Europeans have fared little better in tackling this design problem. Most European toilets have a pull-up knob located on top of the tank. The placement of the knob not only makes it most difficult to flush from a seated position, but it prevents using the top of the tank as a magazine rack or radio stand.

Alexander Kira's solution to all of these problems is Solomonlike in its ecumenicalism. He recommends a spring-loaded flush button set into the floor that would allow users to flush from either a seated or standing position, "before, during, or after elimination." These buttons can be operated electronically rather than mechanically, freeing them from the fate of the current flush handle, the placement of which is dictated by the demands of mechanics rather than the convenience of the user.

Submitted by Lisa R. Bell, of Atlanta, Georgia. Thanks also to: Linda Kaminski, of Park Ridge, Illinois.

Why Does the Price of Gas End in Nine-Tenths of a Cent?

No one we contacted in the oil or service-station businesses could find any reason to believe that gas isn't priced at $1.19.9 for the same reason that automobiles are priced at $9,999 or record albums at $8.98. As Ralph Bombardiere, the executive director of the New York State Association of Service Stations, Inc., put it, "There is and will always be a big difference between the price of 29.9 cents and 30.0 cents, and the same principle will follow through when the number reaches $1.29.9 and $1.30.0."

It is doubtful that sophisticated marketing surveys were ever undertaken by service stations or oil companies to establish the effectiveness of ending prices in nine-tenths of a cent, but the use of fractional prices goes back at least seventy years. C. F. Helvie, customer relations manager for the Mobil Oil Corporation, sent us a fascinating letter, the result of combing through Mobil's collection of photographs of old service stations and other reference materials.

Helvie found a photograph of a 1914 Texaco gas station that displayed a sign advertising gasoline for 14½ cents per gallon. The Mobil material suggests, but does not conclusively prove, that the practice of ending unit pricing of gas with nine-tenths started no earlier than the late 1920s and early 1930s.

The Great Depression decimated the demand for gasoline. More than 2.6 million cars and trucks were taken off the road, and the consumption of gasoline was down a billion gallons per year in both 1932 and 1933. Gas stations fought to survive. Helvie writes:

> Production at the time was running far above demand and the market quickly went into a serious oversupply situation. It was at that time that premiums such as candy, cigarettes, ash trays, dolls, and countless other giveaway items made their appearance at service stations. In such a competitive climate, it seems reasonable to assume that the gasoline marketers of the day would have been

attracted to the concept of fractional pricing. In addition, mechanical gasoline pumps, with computers that could be set to fractional prices, began to make their appearance at service stations at about the same time.

When prices zoomed at the gas pumps during the oil crisis of the 1970s and federal price and supply controls were imposed, individual stations lost the autonomy to set prices. The government issued mandated formulas for pricing, which resulted in unusual fractional amounts. Further compounding the problem was that, during this period, the price of gasoline went above one dollar per gallon, and most computers were incapable of handling prices of more than two digits. Until their computers could be modified, many service stations simply set their pumps to calculate half-gallon prices, which led to more strange fractions. Some stations chose to sell at a price per liter and maintained the usual nine-tenths fraction.

Consumers are accustomed to most retail establishments charging a cent or two less than a round number. Helvie indicated that his experience as a customer-relations expert was that "most motorists accept and understand gasoline prices ending in nine-tenths of a cent per gallon, but they react negatively to prices ending in other fractions."

Submitted by John D. Wright, of Hazelwood, Missouri. Thanks also to: Charles F. Myers, of Los Altos, California.

When I Open the Hot-Water Tap, Why Does the Sound of the Running Water Change As It Gets Hot?

The whistling sound you hear occurs with cold water as well, but is more common with hot water. Whistling occurs when there is a restriction of water flow in the pipes. According to Tom Higham, executive director of the International Association of Plumbing and Mechanical Officials, the source of the noise depends on the construction of the plumbing: "If the piping is copper, the cause is usually attributed to undersized piping. If the pipe is galvanized steel, noise is usually caused by a buildup of lime which reduces the area for the flow of the water." Water flow is restricted more often with hot water, as Richard W. Church, president of the Plumbing Manufacturers Institute, explains it, because "of additional air in the hot water formed when the molecules expand during the heating process."

The crackling noise you hear in the water heater is caused by lime accumulations in its tank. As the water heater expands and contracts, depending on the temperature, the lime breaks off and falls to the bottom of the tank. The water pipes simply transmit and amplify the glorious sound.

Submitted by Glenn Worthman, of Palo Alto, California.

The Measurement of "One Foot" Was Meant to Approximate the Length of a Man's Foot. How Did They Decide How Long a Meter Should Be?

The U.S. Constitution gives the Congress the power to fix uniform standards for weights and measures. Previously, little uniformity existed among different colonies or even among different countries in Europe or Asia. For example, King Henry I personally provided the nose and thumb that set the standard for the length of a yard, while other nations didn't even use the yard as a measure. Asian nations must have wondered if our "feet" really measured the length of a human foot.

Much of the clamor for a uniform system of measurement came from France. In 1790, during the French Revolution, the National Assembly of France asked the French Academy of Sciences to provide an invariable standard for all weights and measures. One committee responded quickly, urging that the Academy accept a decimal system as the simplest and most elegant solution. A subsequent committee recommended that the basic measure of length of such a system should represent a portion of the earth's circumference: a unit equal to one ten-millionth of the length of a quadrant of the earth's meridian (in other words, one ten-millionth of an arc representing the distance between the Equator and the North Pole).

This unit was later given the name *mètre*, from the Greek word *metron*, meaning "a measure." The meter was the foundation for all of the other measures, as Valerie Antoine, executive director of the U.S. Metric Association, Inc., explains:

> The unit of mass was to be derived by cubing some part of this length unit and filling it with water [thus, the "gram" became the mass of one cubic centimeter of water at its temperature of maximum density]. The same technique would also provide the capacity measure. In this way, the standards of length, mass, and capacity were all to be derived from a single measurement, infinitely reproducible because of natural origins, precisely interrelated, and decimally based for convenience.

The "metric system" did not catch on beyond France, at first, but its rigidity and standardization made it appealing to scientists and engineers throughout the world. Few people realize that as early as 1866, by Act of Congress, it was made "lawful throughout the United States of America to employ the weights and measures of the metric system in all contracts, dealing or court procedures." By the turn of the twentieth century, the supremacy of the metric system was assured among developed nations.

The advances in precision instruments made the original definition of the meter too fuzzy. The "Treaty of the Meter," an

1875 agreement, established a mechanism to refine and amend the metric system, and seventeen nations, including the United States, joined the "Metric Convention." Since 1893, the meter has been defined as the length of the path traveled by light in a vacuum during a time interval of 1/299,792,458 of a second (in other words, the speed of light in a vacuum is 299,792,458 meters per second). As the speed of light is unlikely to change in the near future, scientists are confident that the meter will have a long life as a standard measurement.

Valerie Antoine mildly reprimanded us for using the spelling "meter," which is an Americanized version of what most of the world—including other English-speaking countries—spells "metre."

Why Does the Moon Appear Bigger at the Horizon Than Up in the Sky?

This Imponderable has been floating around the cosmos for eons and has long been discussed by astronomers, who call it the moon illusion. Not only the moon but the sun appears much larger at the horizon than up in the sky. And constellations, as they ascend in the sky, appear smaller and smaller. Obviously, none of these bodies actually changes size or shape, so why do they *seem* to grow and shrink?

Although there is not total unanimity on the subject, astronomers, for the most part, are satisfied that three explanations answer this Imponderable. In descending order of importance, they are:

1. As Alan MacRobert of *Sky & Telescope* magazine states it, "The sky itself appears more distant near the horizon than high overhead." In his recent article in *Astronomy* magazine, "Learning the Sky by Degrees," Jim Loudon explains, "Apparently, we perceive the sky not as half a sphere but as half an oblate [flattened at the poles] spheroid—in other words, the sky overhead seems closer to the observer than the horizon. A celestial object that is perceived as 'projected' onto this distorted sky bowl seems bigger at the horizon." Why? Because the object appears to occupy just as much space at the seemingly faraway horizon as it does in the supposedly closer sky.

2. When reference points are available in the foreground, distant objects appear bigger. If you see the moon rising through the trees, the moon will appear immense, because your brain is unconsciously comparing the size of the object in the foreground (the tree limbs) with the moon in the background. When you see the moon up in the sky, it is set against tiny stars in the background.

Artists often play with distorting perception by moving peripheral objects closer to the foreground. Peter Boyce, of the American Astronomical Society, adds that reference points tend to distort perception most when they are close to us and when the size of the reference points is well known to the observer. We *know* how large a tree limb is, but our mind plays tricks on us when we try to determine the size of heavenly objects. Loudon states that eleven full moons would fit between the pointer stars of the Big Dipper, a fact we could never determine with our naked eyes alone.

3. The moon illusion may be partially explained by the refraction of our atmosphere magnifying the image. But even the

astronomers who mentioned the refraction theory indicated that it could explain only some of the distortion.

A few skeptics, no doubt the same folks who insist that the world is flat and that no astronaut has ever really landed on the moon, believe that the moon really *is* larger at the horizon than when up in the sky. If you want to squelch these skeptics, here are a few counterarguments that the astronomers suggested.

1. Take photos of the moon or sun at the horizon and up in the sky. The bodies will appear to be the same size.

2. "Cover" the moon with a fingertip. Unless your nails grow at an alarming rate, you should be able to cover the moon just as easily whether it is high or low.

3. Best of all, if you want proof of how easy it is to skew your perception of size, bend over and look at the moon upside down through your legs. When we are faced with a new vantage point, all reference points and size comparisons are upset, and we realize how much we rely upon experience, rather than our sensory organs, to judge distances and size.

We do, however, suggest that this physically challenging and potentially embarrassing scientific procedure be done in wide-open spaces and with the supervision of a parent or guardian. *Imponderables* cannot be held responsible for the physical or emotional well-being of those in search of astronomical truths.

Submitted by Patrick Chambers, of Grandview, Missouri.

If We See Mockingbirds During the Day and Hear Them at Night, When Do They Sleep?

At night, but off and on, and with an occasional nap during the day. Birds aren't as compulsive as humans are about their sleep hours, but then they don't have nine-to-five jobs. Birds also require much less sleep than humans, but then they don't have taxes to worry about either.

Actually, it has proved to be quite a challenge to determine the sleep patterns of birds. Laboratory experiments can't replicate the conditions they face in the elements, and any movement or sound the scientist makes during close observation will disrupt the sleep he is trying to measure.

No one has actually proved that sleep is physiologically necessary for birds. Its main benefit for them might be that standing still helps conserve energy: if a bird can't hear a potential predator hovering or see a worm ripe for the picking, it can't do anything about it. While sleep leaves them more vulnerable to predators, it is all that keeps birds from an exhausting 24-hour-a-day hunt for food.

Simply standing motionless with their eyes closed or open provides rest for most birds. Birds that live in the Arctic or Antarctic regions and have to contend with periods of twenty-four–hour sunlight, often take short catnaps throughout the day and night, but require no long sessions of sleep.

For diurnal birds, like mockingbirds, the daytime is full of activity, but they don't sleep peacefully throughout the dark hours, as anyone who has ever attempted to sleep near a male mockingbird knows all too well.

Submitted by Kathi Sawyer Young, of Encino, California.

Why Were Phillips Screws and Screwdrivers Developed?

The straight-bladed screwdriver was popular long before the advent of the Phillips. Was the Phillips merely a marketing ploy to make old hardware obsolete?

Fred A. Curry, a retiree of Stanley Works and now an educational consultant, has a large collection of Stanley tools and old catalogs. While trying to find an answer to our query, Mr. Curry found a 1938 article in Stanley's *Tool Talks*, which, to use a hardware metaphor, bangs the nail on the head:

> The most recent major improvement in screw design is the Phillips recessed head, self-centering screw and bolt. This type of screw is already extensively used in many of the major industries, and is even replacing the common wood screw for home repairs. Stanley has the No. 1 license to manufacture the screwdrivers, hand and

power driven bits required by the Phillips screw, and now offers a complete line of these Stanley quality drivers and bits.

The main selling point of the Phillips was clearly the self-centering feature. Straight-bladed screwdrivers tended to slip out of the screws' slots, ruining wood or other material, occasionally even injuring the worker. The recessed Phillips screws allowed a closer and tighter fit than the conventional slots. It may be harder, initially, to insert the Phillips screwdriver, but once it is in place, the Phillips is much less likely to slip.

Why Do Trucks Now Say Their Contents Are "Flammable" When They Used to Say "Inflammable"?

The prefix "in" usually means "not." If you are *in*sensitive, you are not sensitive. If you are *in*coherent, you are not coherent. If you are *in*flammable, you are not flammable.

Oops! You *are* flammable if you are inflammable.

The English language is less than a logical construct. "Flammable" and "inflammable" have identical meanings: "easily set on fire." So why did the trucking industry bother to change its warning notices?

Fire-insurance underwriters are usually given credit for starting the changeovers. They felt that foreigners, unaware of this exception to the usual meaning of "in-," might misconstrue "inflammable" signs, so they lobbied to change labels on containers and tanks to "flammable." Scientists, always sensitive to the need for international understanding, have also adopted "flammable."

Ironically, although the purpose of the change from "inflammable" to "flammable" was to facilitate the understanding of nonnative speakers, almost all of the international agencies responsible for regulating the labeling of (in)flammable materials, such as the United Nations, have chosen "inflammable"as their standard. A. N. Glick, president of the Conference on the Safe Transportation of Hazardous Articles (COSTHA), told *Imponderables* that the International Maritime Dangerous Goods Code of the International Maritime Organization uses the term "inflammable" but permits the use of "flammable" if there is a footnote reference.

The *Harper Dictionary of Contemporary Usage* had its panel of language experts (a group so concerned with preserving the English language that they still don't quite trust Edwin Newman) vote on whether they used "flammable." Most didn't, but they couldn't work up much enthusiasm for trying to fight its use, as it is less ambiguous to nonnatives.

I am surprised that nobody bothered to ask what an intelligent foreigner might think about a country in which companies bothered to put signs on their trucks announcing that the truck was carrying cargo that was *not* easily set on fire.

Submitted by Warrine Ahlgreen, of Tallmadge, Ohio. Thanks also to: Allen Johnson, Ph.D., of Kennewick, Washington.

Why Can't They Make Newspapers That Don't Smudge?

Reading a newspaper might be good for the mind, but it ain't great for the hands. After a bout with the Sunday paper, your hands are likely to look as if they have been engaged in a mud-wrestling contest rather than an intellectual endeavor.

What is that junk all over your hands? It is ink. And as much as these smudges annoy you, they bother the people within the newspaper industry even more. As Ralph E. Eary, who is responsible for the production and engineering of Scripps Howard's newspapers, told *Imponderables,* "Ink rub-off has been my mortal enemy for forty years. I have experimented with various inks, dyes, and water-based inks over the past twenty-two years and each comes up a failure."

Black news inks have changed little over the past forty

years. Inks consist of pigments, which produce colors, and "vehicles," liquids that carry the pigments. Conventional newspaper inks have an oil base. Oil never dries completely, which is why these inks smear on your hands and clothes. Black inks usually contain between 10 percent and 18 percent carbon black pigment content, with the balance consisting of mineral oil similar to automobile lubricating oil. Inks designed for letterpress machines have less pigment than ink used for offset presses.

Much hope was held out for the durability of water-based inks, but they have not proved to be a solution. In an article about ink for the journal of the American Newspaper Publishers Association, *Presstime*, technical writer Paul Kruglinski states the newspapers' continuing dilemma: "Ink rub-off is a relative problem: Its cause and elimination are not dependent on any one variable. The incidence and amount of rub-off hinge on the ingredients in inks, the kinds of inks used in each printing process and the type of newsprint used. It takes more than just changing chemicals to eliminate rub-off, researchers have learned."

Two factors have exacerbated the rub-off problem in recent years. The first is the changeover, by many newspapers, from letterpress to offset presses. In the letterpress process, the relief plate literally imprints the ink into the paper. The offset process works by what is called a "kiss" or "touch" impression, in which ink is deposited on the surface of the page, where it is more likely to smear.

The second and perhaps more significant trend over the past few decades has been toward publishers using heavier ink (adding extra pigment and oil to a particular area of page space) to make the paper more easily readable. The *New York Times*, for example, is extremely dark; the *Wall Street Journal* is printed with much lighter ink. Unfortunately, the *Times* and other newspapers pay a price for their high contrast—higher rub-off and higher "show-through" (the tendency of the print on the back side of a page to be visible on the front).

Newspaper publishers and ink manufacturers fight over who

is responsible for ink rub-off. The publishers blame the ink manufacturers for providing low-quality ink. The ink manufacturers insist that if the newspapers were willing to pay for better-quality ink, they would be glad to provide it.

The issue, clearly, is money. Now that most cities are monopolized by one paper, or by two papers owned by the same company, readers are literally a captive audience. It isn't clear to the newspapers that reduced rub-off would lead to increased sales. According to the American Newspaper Publishers Association, ink constitutes less than one percent of operating costs for most newspapers that don't publish in color.

Rub-resistant inks *are* more expensive. They work by neutralizing the carbon black in conventional inks by means of additives, such as resins and waxes. Resins trap the carbon black particles, making them stick to the surface of the newsprint. Wax works to cut down smearing by lubricating the surface of the page, reducing the friction between the ink and the fingers. The more resin and wax added to ink, the more rub-resistant it is— and the more expensive it is.

Conventional black ink designed for the letterpress process costs newspapers about thirty cents a pound; offset ink costs about fifteen cents more per pound. Most rub-resistant inks add at least ten cents more per pound to the bill. If these additives totally eliminated rub-offs, most newspapers would probably buy them, but as of now, they only improve the situation. The industry is still looking for rub-off–free ink.

Is there any solution to the rub-off problem? Ralph Eary, of Scripps Howard, and many other printers think the answer will probably come with flexography presses, which use a water-based ink. Eary believes that when the current generation of presses needs to be replaced, most publishers will choose flexo presses. Adds *Presstime*'s Paul Kruglinski,

> Letterpress and offset inks are said to "dry" through the dispersion of the vehicle into the newsprint. They actually don't dry; the fibers absorb the oil. But because the vehicle in flexo inks is water,

there is evaporation. Not only that, the latex additives bind the pigments in flexo inks to the surface of newsprint. With flexography, newspapers may be able to use a thinner newsprint stock for their products without quality degradation.

And we newspaper fanatics won't have to wear gloves to carry our treasures home.

Submitted by Jeff Charles, of St. Paul, Minnesota. Thanks also to: Cassandra Sherrill, of Granite Hills, North Carolina.

How and Why Do Horses Sleep Standing Up?

Horses have a unique system of interlocking ligaments and bones in their legs, which serves as a sling to suspend their body weight without strain while their muscles are completely relaxed. Thus, horses don't have to exert any energy consciously to remain standing—their legs are locked in the proper position during sleep.

Most horses do most of their sleeping while standing, but patterns differ. Veterinarians we spoke to said it was not unusual for horses to stand continuously for as long as a month, or more. Because horses are heavy but have relatively fragile bones, lying in one position for a long time can cause muscle cramps.

While one can only speculate about why the horse's body evolved in this fashion, most experts believe that wild horses slept while standing for defensive purposes. Wayne O. Kester, D.V.M., executive director of the American Association of Equine Practitioners, told us that in the wild, the horse's chief means of protection and escape from predators was its speed. "They were much less vulnerable while standing and much less apt to be caught by surprise than when lying down."

Submitted by Carole Rathouz, of Mehlville, Minnesota.

Why Is Seawater Blue and Tap Water Clear? Why Does the Color of the Ocean Range from Blue to Red?

White light consists of all the primary and secondary colors in the spectrum. Each color is distinguished by the degree to which it scatters and absorbs light. When sunlight hits seawater, part of it is absorbed while the rest is scattered in all directions after colliding with water molecules.

When sunlight hits clear water, red and infrared light absorb rapidly, and blue the least easily. According to Curtiss O. Davis of the California Institute of Technology's Jet Propulsion Laboratory, "only blue-green light can be transmitted into, scattered, and then transmitted back out of the water without being absorbed." By the time the light has reached ten fathoms deep, most of the red has been absorbed.

Why doesn't tap water appear blue? Curtiss continues: "To see this blue effect, the water must be on the order of ten feet deep or deeper. In a glass there is not enough water to absorb much light, not even the red; consequently, the water appears clear."

Thus if clear water is of a depth of more than ten feet, it is likely to appear blue in the sunlight. So how can we explain green and red oceans?

Both are the result not of the optical qualities of sunlight but of the presence of assorted gook in the water itself. A green sea is a combination of the natural blue color with yellow substances in the ocean—humic acids, suspended debris, and living organisms. Red water (usually in coastal areas) is created by an abundance of algae or plankton near the surface of the water. In open waters, comparatively free from debris and the environmental effect of humans, the ocean usually appears to be blue.

Submitted by Jim Albert, of Cary, North Carolina.

Why Don't Kitchen Sinks Have an Overflow Mechanism?

That little hole on the inside near the top of your bathroom sink or that little doohickey near your bathtub faucet is known in the plumbing trade as the "overflow." Its sole purpose is to prevent unnecessary spills when forgetful users leave water flowing unattended. Most bathtubs and bathroom sinks have such safety features, but we have never encountered a kitchen sink that did. Is there a logical reason?

Yep. Three, at least.

1. Most kitchen sinks, especially in homes, are actually double sinks. The divider between the double sinks is markedly lower than the level that would cause an overflow. Thus, excess

water in one of the sinks is automatically routed to the other side.

2. The kitchen sink is less likely than bathroom basins to go unattended for long periods of time. Because it takes so long to fill a bathtub, many a potential bather has answered the telephone, reached out and touched someone, and found much to his consternation that overflow mechanisms in bathtubs are far from infallible.

3. Perhaps the most important reason: kitchen sinks are usually made out of hard cast-iron surfaces, which tend to accumulate germs and fats more easily than china bathtubs, for example. Most kitchen overflows become quickly clogged, not only defeating the purpose of overflows, but creating unsanitary conditions.

Robert Seaman, the retired marketing manager of American Standard, told *Imponderables* that there is a current movement in the plumbing industry away from putting overflows into bathroom sinks. Germs can breed and spread inside overflows, and most get clogged eventually anyway. Many localities, however, have code requirements that mandate overflows in all lavatory sinks, where they are likely to remain until these codes are relaxed.

Submitted by Merrill Perlman, of New York, New York.

Why Do You Have to *Dry*-Clean *Rain*coats?

Actually, the majority of raincoats are washable. If the label indicates that a raincoat must be dry-cleaned, one or more components or fabrics of the coat are not washable. The most common offenders: linings (especially acetate linings), buttons, most wools, pile, satins, rubber, and canvas.

Most laymen assume that the care label instructions for rainwear refer to the effect of cleaning on water repellency. Actually, the water-resistant chemicals with which raincoats are treated are partially removed by both washing and dry-cleaning. Strangely, washing is easier on water repellency than dry-cleaning, as long as the detergent is completely removed through extra rinse cycles. According to Londontown Corp., makers of London Fog raincoats, the "worst enemies of water-repellent fabrics are (in this order) soil, detergents, and solvents." Dirt damages water repellency far more than cleaning, and stains tend to stick to raincoats if not eliminated right away.

Some of the solvents that dry cleaners use are destructive to water repellency. Before the original energy crisis, most dry-cleaning solvents were oil-based and were relatively benign to raincoats. When the price of oil-based solvents soared, the dry-cleaning industry turned to the synthetic perchloroethylene, which can contaminate water-repellent fabrics. Michael Hubsmith, of London Fog, said that if dry cleaners would rerinse garments in a clear solvent after dry-cleaning, the problem would go away. Likewise, if dry cleaners used clean dry-cleaning solution every time they treated a new batch of clothes, raincoats would retain their water repellency. But dry cleaners are as likely to blow the money for new solvent for every load as a greasy spoon is to use new oil for every batch of french fries.

Fred Shippee, of the American Apparel Manufacturers Association, adds that for many garments, clothing manufacturers have a choice of recommending either or both cleaning methods. Shippee speculates that some manufacturers might tend to favor dry-cleaning over washing for reasons of appearance. A washed raincoat needs touching up. A dry-cleaned, pressed raincoat looks great. When people like the way their garments look, they are likely to buy the same brand again.

What Is the Purpose of the White Half-Moons on the Bases of Our Fingernails and Toenails? And Why Don't They Grow Out with the Nails?

Those white moons are called lunulae. The lunula is the only visible portion of the nail matrix, which produces the nail itself. The matrix (and the lunulae) never moves, but new nails continually push forward, away from the matrix.

Why does a lunula appear white? Dermatologist Harry Arnold explains:

> The nail beds distal to the lunulae look pink because capillaries with blood in them immediately underlie the nail plate. The lunulae look white because the thin, modified epidermis of the nail bed is three or four times thicker there, being the busy factory where nail plate is manufactured. The lunula is avascular [without blood vessels], so it looks white.

Submitted by Joanna Parker, of Miami, Florida. Thanks also to: Jo Hadley, of Claremont, California.

Can Raisins Be Made Out of Seeded Grapes?

At one time, no doubt, raisins had seeds. Humans have eaten raisins for at least three millennia, presumably ever since someone was hungry enough to do a little experimentation with a cluster of sun-dried grapes. We do know that raisins were a valuable commodity long before the birth of Christ, especially in the Middle East, where foods that could withstand the hot sun and store indefinitely without spoilage were prized. We know that raisins were cherished in southern Europe, as well: in ancient Rome, two jars of raisins could fetch you a slave boy in trade.

Today, raisins have no seeds. When we pop a raisin into our mouth, we are saved that moment of nervous anticipation we encounter with table grapes, wondering whether we are about to bite into a hard pip. More than 90 percent of all raisins are made from Thompson seedless grapes, exactly the same table grape that is omnipresent in produce sections of the supermarket.

When they have reached the proper ripeness, in early autumn, Thompson grapes are taken from their vines and placed on paper trays to sun-dry. It takes about two to three weeks in the sun before the raisin reaches the correct degree of moisture (15 percent, as opposed to the 78 percent water content of table grapes), and the desired color and flavor. Four to five pounds of grapes sacrifice their lives to yield one pound of raisins.

About 6 percent of the Thompson seedless crop is taken to raisin plants for immediate processing. There the grapes are cured with sulfur dioxide to preserve their color and dried in ovens. The result is golden seedless raisins (also known as "goldens"), which are popular in baking recipes, especially fruit cakes. The grapes used for golden seedless are thus identical to those that make dark brown raisins.

The tiny currants used in hot cross buns and the tart sultanas are limited in availability and used primarily by bakers. Both are seedless.

But yes, a seeded grape can be, and is, used for making raisins. Approximately one percent of the total raisin crop is derived from the seeded Muscat grape. The Muscat is also the largest and sweetest grape used to make raisins, and is therefore prized for baking. The Muscat is sun-dried on paper trays like regular Thompson seedless grapes, but it must undergo an additional step during processing. The dried Muscat raisins are puffed with steam and passed between rollers that force the seeds out. The wrinkles do a nifty job of hiding the resultant scar tissue, which is why our readers might have assumed that all raisins are made out of seedless grapes.

Actually, one other surgical maneuver is performed on all raisins during processing. They must, of course, be cleaned, but their wrinkles assure that there will be hard-to-reach crevices where dirt could hide. So raisins are first washed in tanks of hot water, which opens up the wrinkles and ensures that they have been scrubbed behind their metaphorical ears.

Submitted by Henry J. Stark, of Montgomery, New York.

When a Fly Alights on the Ceiling, Does It Perform a Loop or a Roll in Order to Get Upside Down?

The problem, as David Bodanis states it in *The Secret House*, is that "Flies, like most airplanes, lose their lift when they try to go through the air bottom-side up, and become not flies, but sinks."

We would not venture an uninformed opinion on such a weighty subject. When confronted with a fly question, we of course immediately think of contacting the Canada Biting Fly Centre (or as Maurice Chevalier preferred to call it, Centre Canadien sur les Insectes Piqueurs). Its director, Dr. M. M. Galloway, was bold enough to offer a definitive answer: "A fly lands by raising the forelegs above its head, making contact with the ceiling and then bringing its second and hind legs forward and up to the ceiling. The fly thus flips with a landing."

Bodanis points out the extraordinary efficiency of this technique: "As soon as these two front legs contact the ceiling the fly will aerobatically tuck up the rest of its body and let momentum rotate it to the ceiling. The manoeuver leaves the fly's body suspended upside down, without it ever having had to do a full roll, a remarkable piece of topological extrication."

Submitted by W. A. Nissen, of Visalia, California.

How Can "Perpetual Care" Be Assured In Cemeteries After They Run Out of Space for New Plots?

The cemetery industry has long promoted perpetual care, the notion that your burial area will be tended, well, perpetually. But how can a cemetery continue to pay the expenses for perpetual care after its source of income, new burials, is eliminated?

Stephen L. Morgan, executive vice-president of the American Cemetery Association, explained how perpetual care is supposed to work:

> By law, most private cemeteries operate as endowed care cemeteries and are statutorily required to invest a portion of the proceeds from the sale of a lot [and usually, mausoleum sales], frequently a minimum of ten percent in many states [the range is 5–30 percent], into an irrevocable trust fund. The principal of the trust cannot be spent but the trust income is used for cemetery maintenance and repairs. In this manner, income for care and maintenance will be available long after all lots have been sold. The obligation is continuing and literally perpetual, hence the term "perpetual care."

John R. Rodenburg, vice-president of the Federated Funeral Directors of America, acknowledges that the principle often breaks down in practice, "as can be seen by looking at many inner-city and country cemeteries that have fallen into disrepair." In the past, small cemeteries were frequently abandoned after they stopped generating cash flow, which is why perpetual-care laws were established in the first place.

In many towns, the responsibility for maintaining cemeteries has fallen on churches, local civic groups, and associations of property owners. Church-owned cemeteries often hand over the tending of the cemetery to a nearby for-profit funeral director.

The standards of service provided by perpetual care vary from state to state, but are almost always minimal compared to the services rendered by active cemeteries or funeral parks. In most cases, perpetual-care statutes mandate that grass must be cut and rows plowed. There is no provision, necessarily, that the grass must be leveled or the grounds landscaped with plants or flowers. Nor do most states have a regulation insisting that snow be plowed away during the winter or even that the cemetery be passable for visitors. "Perpetual care" doesn't include the maintenance of markers or memorials, either.

One small-cemetery owner we talked to said that although the interest on his perpetual-care trust was significant (more than $10,000 annually), this money still represented less than what was needed to hire one full-time employee. How can anyone be expected to maintain a cemetery properly when the income generated by the perpetual-care trust doesn't pay for one maintenance worker?

What Is the Purpose of the Pinholes Around the Sides of Screw Caps on Soft-Drink Bottles?

The sole purpose of these holes is to vent the pressure from the bottle when it is opened. As the cap is unscrewed, it is important to release this "head space" pressure as fast as possible; without these tiny holes, there would be a danger of the cap flying off. Anyone who has ever been hit by an errant champagne cork will applaud this safety feature.

Submitted by Henry J. Stark, of Montgomery, New York.

Why Are Military Medals Worn on the Left?

Military historians generally trace the custom of wearing military decorations on the left breast to the Crusaders, who wore the badge of honor over the heart. Whether this spot was chosen for its symbolic purpose or to use the badge as a shield for the heart is unclear. We do know that the Crusaders carried their shields in their left hands, freeing the right hand for manipulating a weapon. (This poses an ancient Imponderable: did left-handed Crusaders carry their shield in their right hand, exposing their heart to the enemy?)

Military decorations are a relatively recent phenomenon and were originally worn at the neck or from a sash. According to S. G. Yasnitsky, of the Orders and Medals Society of America, the practice changed in the first decades of the nineteenth century. During the Napoleonic campaigns, many awards were given to and by the different governments that participated in these wars. More and more orders were created for the lower classes, as well as medals given to all classes of the military and civil participants, with the proviso that they were to be worn "from the buttonhole."

Many fighting alliances between countries were forged during the Napoleonic period, and decorations were exchanged frequently. Medal inflation was rampant. A good soldier could expect to be decorated not only by his own country but by an ally or two as well. Buttonholes were bursting. Only tailors were happy. What could be done about this crisis?

As Yasnitsky told us:

> Common sense prevailed. No one wanted to hide his gorgeous accumulation of gold and enameled awards, so several methods were tried out. Some had their jewelers make smaller copies of these medals, so that they would all fit into one prescribed space on their uniforms. Others—and this became the more popular method—would display their own country's decoration from the buttonhole, but mount the other awards so that they extended in a line from that buttonhole, from left to right.

Why Do Bicycle Tires Go Flat When the Bike Isn't Used for Long Periods of Time?

When spring beckons, we go down to the basement, looking for our trusty, rusty bicycle, which we haven't used since autumn. More often than not, we find two flat tires. Why?

1. Air escapes from the valve stem. Although a valve stem cover will help reduce the outflow, nothing can prevent leakage completely. As K. L. Campbell, of Firestone Tire & Rubber Company, explained, "No materials are completely impervious to migration of gases (such as air) through them when there is a pressure differential between the inside and the outside. The bigger the pressure differential, the faster the migration." The typical automobile tire will lose from one-half pound to one pound of air pressure per month, even when in regular use.

2. Inner tubes of bicycles are more porous than auto tires. No inner tube can be made totally airtight. Butyl rubber, the best type of material for reducing leaks in inner tubes, is the most impermeable rubberlike substance available (car tires are made with a butyl inner liner). Less expensive, nonbutyl rubber inner tubes tend to leak even more.

3. The actual volume of air in a bicycle tire is quite small. There might be about a pint of air at sixty pounds per square inch (psi) in a typical bicycle tire, compared to five gallons of air at thirty-five psi, in an auto tire. A small loss of air volume in a bicycle tire thus affects the bike tire much more than it would affect the auto tire.

4. Bike tires typically require about twice the air pressure of car tires, making it much harder for them to maintain high air pressure.

5. Tire pressure lowers as the temperature goes down. This demonstrates Amonton's law, which postulates that for a body of ideal gas at constant temperature, the volume is inversely proportional to the pressure.

6. Bikes contain more structural hazards to tires than cars do. To quote Huffy Corporation's manager of marketing research, Robert J. Fink, "A bike wheel provides thirty-six opportunities to cause 'pinholes' via the spokes and nipples. Car wheels do not (usually) have spokes."

7. Leaks in auto tires are much less noticeable than bicycle leaks. With a naked eye or even a good kick or squeeze, we could

never detect the usual one pound per month loss of air pressure. Why not? The sheer bulk of the car tire itself, primarily, for auto tires consist of many ply layers (actually, layers of rubberized fabric surrounded by a belt topped off with tread rubber). A bicycle tire is usually one layer of tread with an inner tube. The heavier bead of the auto tire, along with its solid rims, lack of spokes, and much lower air pressure all conspire to make the contrast between a level of thirty psi and a level of thirty-five psi visually and tactilely indistinguishable.

The bike industry has tried to reduce the leakage problems by introducing plastic tires, which, though less porous, yield a stiff, shock-laden ride. Porous rubber is likely to be with us for a long, long time.

Submitted by Pat Mooney, of Inglewood, California.

How Do They Print the "M&M" on M&M's Chocolate Candies?

While doing the radio promotional blitz for the first volume of *Imponderables,* we were inundated by questions about M&M's. Don't Americans have something less fattening to worry about?

We contacted the consumer affairs division of Mars Incorporated, and although they were as helpful and friendly as could be, mere flattery, bribery, and appeals to humanitarian instincts were not sufficient to pry away a definitive answer.

Despite wild theories to the contrary, the "M&M" *is* printed on each candy by machine, but the process is proprietary. The "M&M" insignia separates the Mars product from present and future knock-offs, so the company is understandably sensitive about guarding its technological secrets. Mars did reveal that the process is similar to offset printing, from which one could infer that the stamper does not strike the sugar coating of the candy directly. Many pill manufacturers print their logos with a similar offset technique.

We might as well take this opportunity to unburden our readers of some of the other weighty M&M Imponderables.

Why Are There No Seams on M&M's?

M&M's are coated by a process called "panning." After the individual pieces of chocolate are assembled, they are placed in a revolving pan that looks like a clothes dryer. As they rotate, the chocolates are sprayed with colored sugar. Cool air is blown into the pan to harden the coating. After evaporation, an even layer of dry shell is formed. The process is repeated several times to achieve the thickness that Mars desires. No seam shows because the coating is uniform and no cutting or binding of any kind was necessary to form the shell.

What Does M&M Stand For?

Two names—Mars and Murrie, the head honchos at M&M Candies in the early 1940s.

Why Are There More Brown M&M's Than Any Other Color, and How Do They Determine the Ratio of Colors?

M&M/Mars conducts market research to answer precisely these types of questions. Consumers have shown a consistent preference for brown M&M's, so they predominate.

Why Did They Take Away Red M&M's? Why Have They Put Them Back Recently?

Red M&M's were victims of the Red Dye No. 2 scare, and were dropped in 1976. Although Mars didn't actually use Red Dye No. 2 to color the red M&M's, the company was understandably concerned that the public might be frightened. Once it decided that consumers not only would accept the red M&M's again, but would welcome them back, Mars, Inc. complied.

Although many people know that red M&M's were dropped and then brought back, few realize that the mix of colors in plain M&M's is different from the peanut version:

Color	Percent in Plain M&M's	Percent in Peanut M&M's
Brown	30	30
Yellow	20	20
Red	20	20
Orange	10	10
Green	10	20
Tan	10	0

M&M's seem to be an endless source of Imponderables. As soon as you answer one, another pops out. Why would consumers like more peanut greens than plain greens in the mix? Why would tan, the worthy companion of plain oranges and greens, be shunned completely by peanut buyers?

Submitted by Gail Kessler, of Newton, Massachusetts. Thanks also to: Marley Sims, of Van Nuys, California.

How Do Manufacturers Decide Whether Freezers Go on the Top or the Bottom of Refrigerators?

Until the early 1950s, almost all freezer compartments were top-mounted. This was a logical arrangement, for the compressor of the refrigerator, the warmest single device in the appliance, was located on the bottom, furthest away from the coldest device—the freezer. Clearly, this was the most fuel-efficient configuration, for the refrigerator unit acted to cushion the impact of the heat transference. Placing the freezer next to the compressor is a little like placing an air conditioner next to the fireplace and running them both at the same time—much energy is wasted.

Mysteriously, in the 1950s, bottom-mounted freezers became the rage. The most common rationalization for the popularity of bottom-mounts was that the freezer was used less often than the refrigerator, so it made sense to place the least used compartment in the least convenient place. A more likely explanation was that by introducing bottom-mounts, refrigerator manufacturers were able to appeal to the inherent trendiness of American consumers. Bottom-mounts made a blah appliance sexy by adding a new design element. If we bought cars with V-8 engines and huge fins that got ten miles per gallon, why not buy a refrigerator that burned electricity but showed a little panache. At their peak, bottom-mounts commanded almost 50 percent of the American refrigerator market and were clearly the premium design for those of breeding and distinction—that is, until the introduction of the side-by-side refrigerator.

Side-by-sides quickly became the choice of all upstanding, upscale Americans and have never lost that position. Today, approximately 75 percent of all refrigerators manufactured are top-mounts; 23 percent are side-by-sides; and only 2 percent are bottom-mounts. One does pay dearly for the privilege of buying a side-by-side—they are usually priced hundreds of dollars higher than their rival designs.

As might be expected, side-by-sides tend to be bought by an

older and more affluent consumer. The top-mount sells dispro-portionately more to the younger and less affluent buyer. The bottom-mount market falls between them, but sales skew toward an older clientele.

If the main argument for the top-mount is its fuel efficiency, couldn't the compressor be placed on top of bottom-mount re-frigerators? Some manufacturers do move the compressor for bottom-mounts, but there are inherent disadvantages to this scheme that counteract any energy savings. If placed near the top, a compressor would waste prime space for food storage. Also, as Blaine Keib, a spokesperson for Amana Refrigerators, told *Imponderables*, economy of scale is achieved by allowing the guts of the machinery to be identical from one model to another.

Ultimately, whether to top-mount or bottom-mount is a less than profound question to refrigerator manufacturers. Currently, we are energy conscious, so top-mounts reign supreme. A bot-tom-mount fad could revive; if so, appliance makers will be pleased to oblige.

Submitted by Steve Thompson, of La Crescenta, California.

Why Do Hot Dogs Come Ten to a Package and Hot-Dog Buns Come Eight to a Package?

In order to answer this most frequently asked Imponderable, we must acknowledge that, to some extent, this is a chicken and egg question. Officials from the hot-dog and bun industries tended to be a tad defensive about the whole issue, so let's clear the air. We aren't trying to assign blame here, only to make this world a better place to live. But to achieve this harmony, it is necessary to delve into the messy history of hot dog and hot-dog bun packaging, and to let the chips fall where they may. As the cliché goes, *somebody* has to do it.

The hot dog, of course, is simply a form of sausage, and sausages have been with us at least as far back as the ninth century B.C. (they were mentioned in Homer's *Odyssey*). We won't even go into who created the first hot dog, or where it originated, because we don't want to jeopardize *Imponderables* sales in Frankfurt-am-Main, Germany, or Wien (aka Vienna), Austria. Suffice it to say that, by the late seventeenth century, "dachshund sausages," what we now call "hot dogs," were sold commercially in Europe.

No one knows for sure who was the first person to serve a dachshund sausage in a roll, but one popular story is that a German immigrant sold dachshund sausages, along with milk rolls and sauerkraut, from a pushcart in New York City's Bowery during the 1860s. However they were consumed, dachshund sausages took New York by storm. In 1871, Charles Feltman set up the first Coney Island hot-dog stand, and Nathan's later became an institution.

It was also a New Yorker who coined the term "hot dog," in 1901. On a cold April day during baseball season, concessionaire Harry Stevens was losing his shirt trying to peddle ice cream and cold soda, so he sent his salesmen out to buy dachshund sausages and rolls. Vendors sold them to frozen customers by yelling, "They're red hot! Get your dachshund sausages while they're red hot!" Sports cartoonist Tad Dorgan, sitting in the press box bereft of ideas, drew a cartoon with barking dachshund sausages nestled warmly in their buns. Dorgan didn't know how to spell "dachshund," so he substituted "hot dog." The cartoon was a sensation, and the expression "hot dog" stuck.

The hot-dog bun, in its current configuration, was introduced at the St. Louis "Louisiana Purchase Exposition" in 1904 by Bavarian Anton Feuchtwanger. At first, he loaned out white gloves to customers to handle his hot sausages, but when the gloves weren't returned he asked his baker brother for help and was soon presented with the slotted hot-dog bun we know today.

In the early twentieth century, hot dogs were purchased not in grocery stores, but only in butcher shops. They were stored in bulk boxes, and one simply told the butcher how many "dogs" one wanted to buy. From all evidence, hot dogs then were the same size as "conventional" hot dogs are today—approximately five inches long and about 1.6 ounces in weight. Certainly, by the time the hot-dog makers automated, this size was standard.

Not until the 1940s were hot dogs sold in grocery stores in the cellophane containers we see today. Almost all of the early hot-dog companies sold hot dogs in packages of ten, making each package a convenient one pound.

Perhaps the main reason the number of buns and hot dogs per package never matched was that when hot-dog buns were first introduced, hot dogs were being sold in butcher shops in varying quantities. Sandwich rolls traditionally had been sold in packages of eight. Kaiser rolls and hamburger buns, like hot-dog buns, had always been baked in clusters of four in pans designed to hold eight rolls. This practice, more than anything else, seems to explain why hot-dog buns usually come eight to a pack.

Today, pans are manufactured to allow ten or twelve hot-dog buns to be baked simultaneously, but Pepperidge Farm, for one, told us that these pans are relatively difficult to obtain. Ekco told *Imponderables* that their eight-bun pans heavily outsell other varieties.

It is clear that the number of buns or dogs in a package is more the result of tradition than energetic planning, but certain trends are rendering this Imponderable semiobsolete. Very quietly the bun industry, and more particularly the hot-dog industry, are introducing new sizes.

Many regional hot-dog companies have long sold packages of eight wieners, often calling them "dinner franks" because their larger size makes them more appropriate to serve as an entree for dinner than as a luncheon sandwich or snack. Several companies make quarter-pounders, sold four to a package. Kosher hot dogs have traditionally been larger, and thus come with fewer dogs per package. Armour, and many other companies, are introducing even bigger frank packages (Armour sells sixteen-ounce and twenty-four–ounce packages). In the South, hot dogs are often sold in bulk two-pound bags as well as in conventional cellophane packages.

Similar innovation is entering the bakery business. Continental Baking, the largest producer of hot-dog buns (and the parent company of Wonder bread), and American Bakery now sell ten-bun packages in many areas.

None of the many companies we talked to indicated that it knew (or cared) what its compatriots in the other field were doing. American Bakeries, like Wonder, is experimenting with different packages in different regions, but not in response to what hot-dog packagers are doing. Everyone seems to want to march to his own drummer.

Imponderables humbly suggests a summit meeting at a neutral site to discuss these differences that have created chaos. Until then, we will be stuck with orphan frankfurters, left without the shelter of a bun.

Submitted by Charlie Doherty, of Northfield, Illinois. Thanks also to: Lisa Barba, of Corona, California; Tom and Marcia Bova, of Rochester, New York; Kathy A. Brookins, of Sandusky, Ohio; Sharon Michele Burke, of Menlo Park, California; Paul Funn Dunn, of Decatur, Illinois; Kent Hall, of Louisville, Kentucky; David Hartman, of New York, New York; Mary Jo Hildyard, of West Bend, Wisconsin; Mary Katinos, of Redondo Beach, California; Joanna Parker, of Miami, Florida; Mary Romanidis, of Hamilton, Ontario, Canada; Terry Rotter, of Willowick, Ohio; Glenn Worthman, of Palo Alto, California.

Frustrables

or

The Ten "Most Wanted" Imponderables

There comes a time in any writer's life when he must share with his readers his innermost torments, his doubts, his fears. We have no shame in baring our soul and admitting what has kept us from realizing our hopes and dreams: the scourge of Frustrables (i.e., Frustrating Imponderables). These are Imponderables for which we could not find a definitive answer; or those for which we could find an answer that we were almost sure was true, but could not confirm. A reward of a free copy of the next volume of *Imponderables* will be given to the first reader who can lead to the proof that solves any of these Frustrables.

FRUSTRABLE 1: *Why Do You So Often See One Shoe Lying on the Side of the Road?*

Since we initially researched this Imponderable for our first book, we have spoken to countless officials at the Department of Transportation and Federal Highway Safety Traffic Administration. We have observed that Rich Hall devoted an entire chapter to the subject in his *Vanishing America* book without really answering the question.

We have even found out that there was another soul brave enough to tackle the subject, Elaine Viets, columnist for the St. Louis *Post Dispatch*. She devoted two columns to this Frustrable. In her first column, she advanced several plausible theories:

- They are tossed out of cars during fights among kids.
- They fall out of garbage trucks.
- Both shoes in a pair are abandoned, but one rolls away.

But being a good reporter, Viets wasn't satisfied with her own conclusions. She turned to her readers, who responded with their own guesses at the causes of what some called SSS (Single Shoe Syndrome):

- Discarded newlywed shoes (you *do* see single cans on the highway, come to think of it).
- A variation on the "fighting kids theory"—they are specifically thrown out of school buses, during fights or as practical jokes.

This is the best we've been able to come up with. Anybody else have a better explanation?

FRUSTRABLE 2: *Why Are Buttons on Men's Shirts and Jackets Arranged Differently From Those on Women's Shirts?*

The party line on this Imponderable is that it stems back to the days when ladies of means were dressed by their maids. Because most people are right-handed, it is easiest for right-handers to button their clothes from left to right, the way men's buttons are now arranged. The button arrangement for women was presumably changed to make it easier for the female (ostensibly right-handed) maid to button her mistress's clothes.

A few other theories are advanced less often. One is that women usually support babies with their left arm when breast-feeding, so it was more convenient for women to breast-feed in public from the left breast. In order to shelter the baby from the cold, the theory goes, the mothers covered the baby with the right side of the dress or coat; it behooved the clothesmakers, then, to make garments for women that buttoned up from right to left.

The last theory stems from the days when men carried swords. A man needed to be ready to lunge at a moment's notice, so he kept his right hand in his coat to make sure it was warm. He could only do this if his coat opened from left to right. But why couldn't women's coats conform to the men's styles?

Frankly, these stories seem a tad lame to us. Obviously, all such explanations are obsolete. Now that so many clothes are unisex, many garment manufacturers would prefer one button styling, yet inertia guarantees the status quo will linger on.

Can anyone offer any evidence about the true origins of the button Imponderable?

FRUSTRABLE 3: *Why Do the English Drive on the Left and Just About Everybody Else on the Right?*

The explanations we have encountered trace the disparity back to everything from English versus Italian railroads to Conestoga wagons. But no proof, anywhere.

FRUSTRABLE 4: *Why Is Yawning Contagious?*

The most asked Imponderable, and we have no good answer, only a few lame theories. Who studies yawning?

FRUSTRABLE 5: *Why Do We Give Apples to Teachers?*

We haven't gotten to first base with this Imponderable.

FRUSTRABLE 6: *Why Does Looking Up at the Sun Cause Us to Sneeze?*

Is this nature's way of stopping us from staring at the sun? Does looking up expose the nostrils to floating allergens?

FRUSTRABLE 7: *Why Does the First Puff of a Cigarette Smell Better Than Subsequent Ones?*

Even the cigarette companies' research departments can't answer this one.

FRUSTRABLE 8: *Why Do Women in the United States Shave Their Armpits?*

This phenomenon makes Gillette and Schick happy, but they can't explain it.

FRUSTRABLE 9: *Why Don't You Ever See Really Tall Old People?*

Yes, we know that most people lose a few inches over their life-span, and that our population has gotten much taller since today's septuagenarians were young. But we should see a few elderly people of above-average height. Do very tall people have higher mortality rates than average-sized folks? The big insurance companies, who don't keep separate figures on death rates by height, don't seem to know. Does anyone?

FRUSTRABLE 10: *Why Do Only Older Men Seem to Have Hairy Ears?*

Endocrinologists we spoke to couldn't explain this phenomenon. Help!

Acknowledgments

This second volume of *Imponderables* was made possible by the enthusiasm and participation of the readers who bought its predecessor. In less than one year, more than five hundred people wrote with their own Imponderables, their praise, their criticisms, and their corrections. All were greatly appreciated.

Their kindness, generosity, weirdness, curiosity, enthusiasm, and sense of humor energized me. What did I do to deserve a reader like Joanna Parker, who peppered me with charming letters, and then offered to track down the answer to a knotty Imponderable herself? It is thrilling for a writer, who labors alone, to find out that he is, indeed, reaching the audience he was hoping for. I promise to read every letter that is sent to me, and to answer all that have a self-addressed stamped envelope (and, I must admit, many that do not). To all the readers of the first *Imponderables*, thank you for making this book possible.

Rick Kot was doing me favors even before I worked with him. He did me his greatest favor by becoming my editor. Rick actively pursues good food, cares about popular music, and occasionally even laughs at my jokes. Who could ask for anything more? My agent, Jim Trupin, laughs less often at my jokes, but is otherwise an invaluable friend and partner. Kas Schwan continues to produce brilliant cartoons on demand. The Atlantic Ocean is likely to dry up before Kas runs out of creative ideas. To all of my new friends at Harper & Row, who have welcomed me with enthusiasm and good humor, thank you for the support.

When I get lost in the wonderful world of Imponderability, it puts a strain on my innocent friends and family. They want to talk about the meaning of life. I want to talk about why meatloaf tastes the same in every institutional cafeteria. They want to talk about why suffering exists. I want to talk about why you forget that a hat is on your head but it still feels as if it's on after you've taken it off. The following people helped me maintain my sanity over the last year while I've wrestled with these unfathomable problems: Lori Ames; Judith Ashe; Michael Barson; Ruth Basu; Jeff Bayone; Jean Behrend; Eric Berg; Brenda Berkman; Cathy Berkman; Kent Beyer; Josephine Bishop; Sharon Bishop; Jon Blees; Bowling Green State University's Popular Culture Department; Annette Brown; Herman Brown; Alvin Cooperman; Marilyn Cooperman; Paul Dahlman; Shelly de Satnick; Linda Diamond; Diana Faust; Steve Feinberg; Fred Feldman; Gilda Feldman; Michael Feldman; Phil Feldman; Ray Feldman; Kris Fister; Linda Frank; Seth Freeman; Elizabeth Frenchman; Michele Gallery; Chris Geist; Jean Geist; Bonnie Gellas; Bea Gordon; Dan Gordon; Ken Gordon; Christal Henner; Sheila Hennes; Sophie Hennes; Uday Ivatury; Carol Jewett; Terry Johnson; Sarah Jones; Mitch Kahn; Dimi Karras; Mary Katinos; Peter Keepnews; Mark Kohut; Marvin Kurtz; Claire Labine; Randy Ladenheim; all of my friends at the Manhattan Bridge Club; Jeff McQuain; Carol Miller; Julie Mears; Phil Mears; Steve Nellisen; Debbie Nye; Tom O'Brien; Pat O'Conner; Jeanne Perkins; Merrill Perlman; Larry Prussin; Lela Rolontz; Brian Rose; Paul Rosenbaum; Tim Rostad; Leslie Rugg; Tom Rugg; Kas Schwan; Patricia Sheinwold; Susan Sherman; Carri Sorenson; Karen Stoddard; Kat Stranger; Anne Swanson; Ed Swanson; Carol Vellucci; Dan Vellucci; Julie Waxman; Roy Welland; Dennis Whelan; Devin Whelan; Heide Whelan; Lara Whelan; Jon White; Ann Whitney; Carol Williams; Maggie Wittenberg; Charlotte Zdrok; Vladimir Zdrok; and Debbie Zuckerberg.

The word about *Imponderables* got spread by radio and television talk show hosts (and their producers) and by newspaper and magazine writers. To them, my thanks, not only for help promoting the book, but for providing me with a forum for communicating directly with potential readers. Special thanks for service and graciousness beyond the call of duty to: Sally Carpenter; Rick Dees; John Gambling; Alan Handelman; Carol Hemingway; Marilu Henner; Emily Laisey; Dave Larsen; Jann Mitchell; Beth Morrison; and Tom Snyder.

Most of my time while working on this book is devoted to research, digging for answers. In a few cases, books provided vital information, but most Imponderables could be solved only with the assistance of experts. Undoubtedly, executives at Armour and Hygrade and Wonder bread and Pepperidge Farm have better things to do than to talk to me about why there are ten hot dogs in a package and eight hot-dog buns in a package, but God bless them, they did. The following people generously provided help that led directly to the solutions to the Imponderables in this book: Dennis Albert, Westwood Products; Richard B. Allen, Atlantic Offshore Fishermen's Association; Frances Altman, National Hot Dog and Sausage Council; American Council of Otolaryngology; Dr. Harold E. Amstutz, American Association of Bovine Practitioners; Gerald Andersen, Neckwear Association of America; Beth Anderson, American Institute of Baking; Valerie Antoine, U.S. Metric Association; Jan Armstrong, International Tennis Hall of Fame; Darrell Arnold, *Western Horseman*.

Glen Bacheller, Dunkin' Donuts; Bob Baker, United Lightning Protection Association; Michele Ball, National Audubon Society; Jim

Baker, WABC-TV; Richard C. Banks, American Ornithologist's Union; Dr. Pat. A. Barelli, American Rhinologic Society; Roz Barrow, Harper & Row; Rajat Basu, Citibank; H. R. Baumgardner, American Retreaders Association; Professor Don Beaty, College of San Mateo; Ira Becker, Gleason's Gym; Linda E. Belisle, General Mills; Peter Berle, National Audubon Society; E. J. Blasko, Eastman Kodak; Bob Bledsoe, Texas Instruments; Ralph Bombadiere, New York Association of Service Stations; Peter Boyce, American Astronomical Society; Dan Brigham, Visa; John J. Brill, Northeastern Retail Lumbermen's Association; Larry Brown, Volkswagen; James E. Bures, Fanny Farmer Candies; Walter F. Burghardt, Jr., American Veterinary Society of Animal Behavior; Lieutenant Colonel James A. Burkholder, U.S. Air Force Academy; Thomas F. Burns, American Spice Trade Association; Kenneth H. Burrell, American Dental Association.

George F. Cahill, National Flag Foundation; Inge Calderon, American Supply Association; Dr. Bruce Calnek, Cornell University; Doug Campbell, Northern Nut Growers Association; K. L. Campbell, Firestone Tire and Rubber Company; Joan Walsh Cassedy, Transportation Research Forum; Molly Chillinsky, Coin Laundry Association; Richard W. Church, Plumbing Manufacturers Institute; Gary M. Clayton, Professional Lawn Care Association of America; Conference on the Safe Transportation of Hazardous Articles; Charlotte H. Connelly, Whitman's Chocolates; Tom Consella, John Morrell; Dr. John Cook, Georgia Dermatology and Skin Cancer Clinic; Rhoda Cook, Montana Outfitters and Guides Association; B. F. Cooling, American Military Institute; John Corbett, Clairol Corporation; B. W. Crosby, Pepperidge Farm; Fred A. Curry, Stanley-Proto Industrial Tools.

Neill Darmstadter, American Trucking Associations; Curtiss O. Davis, Jet Propulsion Laboratory; Jack D. DeMent, Dole Fresh Fruit Company; Mrs. David Doane, Dalmation Club of America, Inc.; Joseph M. Doherty, D.D.S., American Association of Public Health Dentistry; R. H. Dowhan, GTE Products Corporation; Dr. G. H. Drumheller, International Rhinologic Society.

Ralph E. Eary, Scripps Howard; James E. Eisener, Suburban Newspapers of America; Dick Elgin, Department of Agriculture; Dr. Elliot, American Dermatological Association; Kay Englehardt, American Egg Board.

Joseph D. Fabin, Department of Transportation; Dr. John Falk; Michael Falkowitz, Nabisco Brands; Fred F. Feldman, M.D.; Debbie Feldstein, National Academy of Television Arts and Sciences; Robert J. Fink, Huffy Corporation; Lynn Flame, London Fog; Howard R. Fletcher, Muscatine Memorial Park; Bob Ford, AT&T Bell Laboratories; Edward S. Ford, D.V.M., Grayson Foundation; Lynda Frank; Dudley Frazier, New American Library; William H. Freeborn, Assistant Secretary of State, Delaware; Don French, Radio Shack; David F. Friedman, Adult Film Association of America; Marvin M. Frydenlund, Lightning Protection Institute; Frye Boots.

Scoop Gallello, International Veteran Boxers Association; Dr. M. M. Galloway, Canada Biting Fly Centre; Dr. James Gant, Jr., International Lunar Society; J. Byron Gathright, American Society of Colon and Rectal Surgeons; Mary S. Gilbert, L'eggs Products; Glutamate Association; S. Gordon, Pavey Envelope and Tag Corporation; Amey Grubbs, Dude Ranchers Association.

Gerard Hageney, American Sugar Division, Amstar; E. E. Halmes, Jr., Construction Writers Association; Darryl Hansen, Entomological Society of America; Carl E. Hass, Winchell's; Waldo Haythorne; Jim Heffernen, National Football League; C. F. Helvie, Mobil Oil Corporation; Bob Henderson, Kansas State Department of Wildlife; Tom Higham, International Association of Plumbing and Mechanical Officials; Shari Hiller, Sherwin-Williams Company; Hal Hochvert, Bantam Books; Frank Holman; Sarah K. Hood, International Banana Association; Ellen Hornbeck; Dr. Andrew Horne, Federal Aviation Authority Office of Aviation Medicine; Harry Horrocks, National Lumber and Building Materials Association; Susan R. Hubler, House Ear Institute; Michael Hubsmith, London Fog; Donald Hull, International Amateur Boxing Association; Rob Hummel, Technicolor; George Hundt, Ekco.

Patrick C. Jackman, Bureau of Labor Statistics; Beverly Jakaitis, American Dental Association; John Jay, Intercoiffure America-Canada; James H. Jensen, General Electric Lighting Group; Bob Joseph, Red Lobster.

Stanley Kalkus, Naval Historical Center; Shirlee Kalstone; Jeff Kanipe, *Astronomy Magazine;* Dr. Morley Kare, Monnell Institute; Blaine Keib, Hanna Refrigeration; Bill Keogh, American Bakeries; Michael R. Kershow, Bicycle Manufacturers of America; Wayne Kester, D.V.M., American Association of Equine Practitioners; Felix Kestenberg, Misty Harbor; Robert C. Knipe, Textile Care Allied Trades Association; John A. Kolberg, Spreckels Sugar Division, Amstar Corporation; Al Konecny, U.S. Military Academy, West Point; Rick Kot, Harper & Row; Thomas J. Kraner, American Paper Institute.

Randy Ladenheim, William Morrow and Company; Eugene C. LaFond, International Association for the Physical Sciences of the Ocean; Robert E. Lee, International Boxing Federation; Thomas A. Lehmann, American Institute of Baking; B. Leppek, Huffy Corporation; Bernard Lepper, Career Apparel Institute; Belinda Lerner, National

Hockey League; Naomi J. Linder, General Foods; Barbara Linton, National Audubon Society; Leo A. Lorenzen, American Planning Service; Joseph J. Lorfano, American Newspaper Publishers Association; Patricia Lortz, National Association of Bedding Manufacturers; Susan A. Lovin, Institute of Transportation Engineers; Robert Lute III.

Alan MacRobert, Sky Publishing Corporation; Ruth Mankin, Delaware Chamber of Commerce; Bob Manning, Londontown Corporation; James A. Marchiony, National Collegiate Athletic Association; Edward P. Marion, Professional Football Referees Association; Nikki P. Martin, Reynolds Metals Company; Doug Matyka, Georgia-Pacific Corporation; Marsha McLain, Pet Incorporated; Thomas H. McLaughlin, Western Pet Supply Association, Inc.; Robert L. Meckley, Westinghouse Electric Corporation; Jay L. Meikle, California and Hawaiian Sugar Company; B. G. Merritt, Eveready Battery Company; Elizabeth Crosby Metz; Carla Mikell, Colgate Palmolive Corporation; Rick Miller, Kansas State University; Dr. William E. Monroe, American College of Veterinary Internal Medicine; Montgomery Elevator Company; James H. Moran, Campbell Soup Company; Professor Richard Moran, Mount Holyoke College; Stephen L. Morgan, American Cemetery Association; Jane C. Mott, General Motors Technical Center; Ruth Mottram, Mars, Inc.; Thomas R. Myers, See's Candies.

National Bath Bed and Linen Association; National Weather Association; New York Public Library; H. M. Niebling, North American Wholesale Lumber Association; James W. Nixon, Whitman's Chocolates.

Richard O'Connell, Whitman's Chocolates; Larry O'Connor, American Truck Dealers; John O'Regan, CBS-TV; Carl Oppedahl.

Eleanor Pardue, Hanes Hoisery, Inc.; Dr. Lawrence Charles Parish; Dennis Patterson, Murray Bicycle Manufacturing; Dianne V. Patterson, U.S. Postal Service; Pechter Fields Bakery; Polly A. Penhale, American Society of Limnology and Oceanography; Merrill Perlman, *New York Times;* Robert J. Peterson, American National Metric Council; Diane Pindle, Hygrade Company; Jack Pollack, Keith County *News;* P. M. Preuss, Ford Motor Corporation; Dr. R. Lee Pyle, College of Veterinary Internal Medicine.

Judy Radcoff, Sherwin-Williams Company; George Rapp, Jr., University of Minnesota, Duluth; Mike Redman, National Soft Drink Association; Gloria E. Reich, American Tinnitus Association; Jim Renson, Print and Ink Manufacturers; Jeffrey Reynolds, National Dog Groomers Association; Nelson Rimensnyder, U.S. House of Representatives Committee on the District of Columbia; Eugene W. Robbins, Texas Good Roads/Transportation Association; Beverly C. Roberts, Lawn Institute;

John R. Rodenburg, Federated Funeral Directors of America; Paul Rosenbaum; Lou Rothstein, Misty Harbor; Chuck Russell, Sharp Electronics.

Donna Samelson, Sun-Diamond Growers of California; Norman J. Sanchez; Sherry Sancibrian, Texas Tech University; Starr Saphir, New York Audubon Society; Armand Schneider, Federal Express; Stanley M. Schuer, Gasoline and Automotive Service Dealers Association; Henry Schwarzchild, Capital Punishment Project, American Civil Liberties Union; Janet Seagle, U.S. Golf Association; Robert Seaman; Fred Shippee, American Apparel Manufacturers Association; Joe Skrivan, Huffy Corporation; Gary D. Smith, Heinz USA; Richard N. Smith, National Bureau of Standards; Whitney Smith, Ph.D., Flag Research Center; Pedro Sole, Ph.D., Chiquita Brands, Inc.; Dick Spencer, *Western Horseman;* Cheri Spies, Continental Baking; Terry L. Stibal; Ed Stuart, Chrysler Motors; John J. Suarez, R.P.E., National Pest Control Association; Harold Sundstrom, Dog Writers Association of America; Virgil Swanson.

Lisa M. Tate, Distilled Spirits Council of the United States; Thomas A. Tervo, Stearns & Foster Bedding Company; Sue Thompson, AT&T Bell Laboratories; Tony Lama Company; Barbara Torres, Armour Foods; Anthony P. Travisono, American Correctional Association; Jim Trupin, JET Literary Agency.

Simone van der Woude, Consulate General of the Netherlands; Vermont-American Corporation; Elaine Viets, St. Louis *Post-Dispatch.*

Jim Warters, Professional Golfers Association; Eric S. Waterman, National Erectors Association; Julien Weil, Royal Crown Cola; Belinda Baxter Welsh, Procter & Gamble; Al B. Wesolowsky, *Journal of Field Archaeology;* S. C. White, National Hardwood Lumber Association; David K. Witheford, National Research Council, Transportation Research Board; Maggie Wittenberg; Merry Wooten, Astronomical League.

About a thousand people were contacted to gather information for this book. Not everyone was cooperative, but an astonishing percentage were. To those who, for whatever reason, preferred to remain anonymous, yet still provided information, I give my thanks.

WHEN DO FISH SLEEP?
and Other
Imponderables™ of
Everyday Life

For Phil and Gilda Feldman

Contents

Preface

Imponderables are mysteries that can't be answered by numbers, measurements, or a trip to the reference section of your library. If you worry about why the carbons on airplane tickets are red, or why tennis balls are fuzzy, or why yawning is contagious, you have been struck by the dread malady of Imponderability.

When we wrote the first volume of *Imponderables*, we weren't sure that there were others like us, who were committed to cogitating about the everyday mysteries of life. We needn't have worried. Most of the Imponderables in this book were submitted by readers of the first two volumes of Imponderables.

In *Why Do Clocks Run Clockwise?*, we introduced a new section, Frustables (short for "frustrating Imponderables") and asked for your help in solving them. Your response was terrific, but we don't want you to get complacent. We've got ten new Imponderables that we haven't been able to solve.

And because so many readers offered corrections and caustically constructive comments, we've added a letter section—we couldn't shut you up anymore even if we wanted to.

Would you like to win a free copy of the next volume of *Imponderables*? If you are the first to submit an Imponderable that we use in the next book, you will not only have the relief of finally having the answer to your mystery, but also a free, autographed copy of the book (along with, of course, an acknowledgment).

Why Do Roosters Crow in the Morning?

Because there are humans around to be awakened, of course. Does anyone really believe that roosters crow when they are by themselves? Nah! Actually, they speak perfectly good English.

Ornithologists don't buy our common-sense answer. They insist that crowing "maps territory" (a euphemism for "Get the hell out of my way and don't mess with my women—this is my coop"). In the spirit of fair play, we'll give the last word to one of those nasty ornithologist types (but don't believe a word she says), Janet Hinshaw, of the Wilson Ornithological Society:

> Most of the crowing takes place in the morning, as does most singing, because that is when the birds are most active, and most of the territorial advertising takes place then. Many of the other vocalizations heard throughout the day are for other types of communication, including flocking calls, which serve to keep members of a flock together and in touch if they are out of sight from one another.

Submitted by Rowena Nocom of North Hollywood, California.

Why Do Many Hotels and Motels Fold Over the Last Piece of Toilet Paper in the Bathroom?

This Imponderable was sent in by reader Jane W. Brown in a letter dated May 12, 1986. Jane was clearly a discerning seer of emergent popular culture trends:

> Staying in less than deluxe lodgings has led me to wonder why, and how, the custom of folding under the two outside corners on a roll of bathroom paper was begun. This operation creates a V on the last exposed edge of the tissue. I first noticed this bizarre sight in a LaQuinta Motor Inn. Then I stayed in some Holiday Inns while on a business trip. There, too, the bathroom paper had been tediously tucked in on the outside edges, the large V standing out, begging for attention. Recently, I upgraded my accommodations and spent several nights in a Marriott and an Intercontinental. Right: the bathroom paper was also arranged in this contorted fashion. Why?

Jane, enterprisingly, included an audiovisual aid along with her letter, as if to prove she wasn't crazy: a specimen of the mysterious V toilet paper. Since Jane wrote her letter, the folded toilet paper trick has run rampant in the lodging industry.

We contacted most of the largest chains of innkeepers in the country and received the same answer from all. Perhaps James P. McCauley, executive director of the International Association of Holiday Inns, stated it best:

> Hotels want to give their guests the confidence that the bathroom has been cleaned since the last guest has used the room. To accomplish this, the maid will fold over the last piece of toilet paper to assure that no one has used the toilet paper since the room was cleaned. It is subtle but effective.

Maybe too subtle for us. Call us sentimental old fools, but we still like the old "Sanitized for Your Protection" strips across the toilet seat.

Submitted by Jane W. Brown of Giddings, Texas.

　　　　　　　　　　　　　　DAVID FELDMAN

Why Do Gas Gauges in Automobiles Take an Eternity to Go from Registering Full to Half-full, and Then Drop to Empty in the Speed of Light?

On a long trek down our illustrious interstate highway system, we will do anything to alleviate boredom. The roadway equivalent of reading cereal boxes at breakfast is obsessing about odometers and fuel gauges.

Nothing is more dispiriting after a fill-up at the service station than traveling sixty miles and watching the gas gauge stand still. Although part of us longs to believe that our car is registering phenomenal mileage records, the other part of us wants the gauge to move to prove to ourselves that we are actually making decent time and have not, through some kind of *Twilight Zone* alternate reality, actually been riding on a treadmill for the last hour. Our gas gauge becomes the arbiter of our progress. Even when the needle starts to move, and the gauge registers three-quarters' full, we sometimes feel as if we have been traveling for days.

How nice it would be to have a gauge move steadily down toward empty. Just as we are about to give in to despair, though, after the gauge hits half-full, the needle starts darting toward empty as if it had just discovered the principle of gravity. Whereas it seemed that we had to pass time zones before the needle would move to the left at all, suddenly we are afraid that we are going to run out of gas. Where is that next rest station?

There must be a better way. Why don't fuel gauges actually register what proportion of the tank is filled with gasoline? The automakers and gauge manufacturers are well aware that a "half-full" reading on a gas gauge is really closer to "one-third" full, and they have reasons for preserving this inaccuracy.

The gauge relies upon a sensor in the tank to relay the fuel level. The sensor consists of a float and linkage connected to a variable resistor. The resistance value fluctuates as the float moves up and down.

If a gas tank is filled to capacity, *the liquid is filled higher than the float has the physical ability to rise.* When the float is at the top of its stroke, the gauge will always register as full, *even though the tank can hold more gasoline.* The gauge will register full until this "extra" gasoline is consumed and the float starts its descent in the tank. At the other end of the float's stroke, *the gauge will register as empty when the float can no longer move further downward, even though liquid is present below the float.*

We asked Anthony H. Siegel, of Ametek's U.S. Gauge Division, why sensors aren't developed that can measure the actual status of gasoline more accurately. We learned, much as we expected, that more precise measurements easily could be produced, but the automakers are using the current technology *for our own good:*

> Vehicle makers are very concerned that their customers do not run out of fuel before the gauge reads empty. That could lead to stranded, unhappy motorists, so they compensate in the design of the float/gauge system. Their choice of tolerances and calibration procedures guarantees that slight variations during the manufacturing of these components will always produce a combination of parts which falls on the safe side. The gauge is thus designed to read empty when there is still fuel left.

Tens of millions of motorists have suspected there is fuel left even when the gauge says empty, but few have been brave enough to test the hypothesis. Perhaps there are gallons and gallons of fuel left when the gauge registers empty, and this is all a plot by Stuckey's and Howard Johnson's to make us take unnecessary pit stops on interstates.

Submitted by Jack Belck of Lansing, Michigan.

DAVID FELDMAN

How Is the Caloric Value of Food Measured?

Imponderables is on record as doubting the validity of caloric measurements. It defies belief that the caloric value of vegetables such as potato chips and onion rings, full of nutrients, could possibly be higher than greasy tuna fish or eggplant. Still, with an open mind, we sought to track down the answer to this Imponderable.

Calories are measured by an apparatus called a *calorimeter*. The piece of food to be measured is placed inside a chamber, sealed, and then ignited and burned. The energy released from the food heats water surrounding the chamber. By weighing the amount of water heated, noting the increase in the water's temperature and multiplying the two, the energy capacity of the food can be measured. A calorie is nothing more than the measurement of the ability of a particular nutrient to raise the temperature of one gram of water one degree Centigrade. For example, if ten thousand grams of water (the equivalent of ten liters or ten thousand cubic centimeters) surrounding the chamber is 20 degrees Centigrade before combustion and then is measured at

WHEN DO FISH SLEEP? 269

25 degrees after combustion, the difference in temperature (five degrees) is multiplied by the volume of water (ten thousand grams) to arrive at the caloric value (fifty thousand calories of energy).

If fifty thousand calories sounds like too high a number to describe heating ten liters of water five degrees, your instincts are sound. One calorie is too small a unit of measurement to be of practical use, so the popular press uses "calorie" to describe what the scientists call "Calories," really kilocalories, one thousand times as much energy as the lowercase "calorie."

The calorimeter is a crude but reasonable model for how our body stores and burns energy sources. The calorimeter slightly overstates the number of calories our body can use from each foodstuff. In the calorimeter, foods burn completely, with only some ashes (containing minerals) left in the chamber. In our body, small portions of food are indigestible, and are excreted before they break down to provide energy. The rules of thumb are that two percent of fat, five percent of carbohydrates, and eight percent of proteins will not be converted to energy by the body.

Food scientists have long known the caloric count for each food group. One gram of carbohydrates or proteins equals four calories. One gram of fat contains more than twice the number of calories (nine).

Scientists can easily ascertain the proportion of fat to carbohydrates or proteins, so it might seem that calories could be measured simply by weighing the food. When a food consists exclusively of proteins and carbohydrates, for example, one could simply multiply the weight of the food by four to discover the calorie count.

But complications arise. Certain ingredients in natural or processed foods contain no caloric value whatsoever, such as water, fiber, and minerals. Foods that contain a mixture, say, of water (zero calories), fiber (zero calories), proteins (four calories per gram), fats (nine calories per gram), and carbohydrates (four calories per gram), along with some trace minerals (zero calories), are simply harder to calculate with a scale than a calorimeter.

Submitted by Jill Palmer of Leverett, Massachusetts.

DAVID FELDMAN

VN F U CN
RD THS CHRT
U STL MHT ND
SPCTCLS!

Who Put E on Top of the Eye Chart? And Why?

Professor Hermann Snellen, a Dutch professor of ophthalmology, put the E on top of the eye chart in 1862. Although his very first chart was headed by an A, Snellen quickly composed another chart with E on top.

Snellen succeeded Dr. Frans Cornelis Donders as the director of the Netherlands Hospital for Eye Patients. Donders was then the world's foremost authority on geometric optics. Snellen was trying to standardize a test to diagnose visual acuity, to measure how small an image an eye can accept while still detecting the detail of that image. Dr. Donders' complicated formulas were based on three parallel lines; of all the letters of the alphabet, the capital E most closely resembled the lines that Dr. Donders had studied so intensively. Because Donders had earlier determined how the eye perceives the E, Snellen based much of his mathematical work on the fifth letter.

The three horizontal limbs of the E are separated by an

equal amount of white space. In Snellen's original chart, there was a one-to-one ratio between the height and width of the letters, and the gaps and bars were all the same length (in some modern eye charts, the middle bar is shorter).

Louanne Gould, of Cambridge Instruments, says that the E, unlike more open letters like L or U, forces the observer to distinguish between white and black, an important consitituent of good vision. Without this ability, E's begin to look like B's, F's, P's or many other letters.

Of course, Snellen couldn't make an eye chart full of only E's, or else all his patients would have 20-10 vision. But Snellen realized that it was important to use the same letters many times on the eye charts, to insure that the failure of an observer to identify a letter was based on a visual problem rather than the relative difficulty of a set of letters. Ian Bailey, professor of optometry and director of the Low Vision Clinic at the University of California at Berkeley, says that it isn't so important whether an eye chart uses the easiest or most difficult letters. Most eye charts incorporate only ten different letters, ones that have the smallest range of difficulty.

Today, many eye charts do not start with an E—and there is no technical reason why they have to—but most still do. Dr. Stephen C. Miller, of the American Optometric Association, suggests that the desire of optical companies to have a standardized approach to the production of eye charts probably accounts for the preponderance of E charts. And we're happy about it. It's a nice feeling to know that even if our vision is failing us miserably, we'll always get the top row right.

Submitted by Merry Phillips of Menlo Park, California.

DAVID FELDMAN

Do the Police Really Make Chalk Outlines of Murder Victims at the Scene of the Crime? Why Do They Use Chalk?

As soon as law enforcement officials descend upon a murder scene, a police photographer takes pictures of the corpse, making certain that the deceased's position is established by the photographs. The medical examiner usually wants the body as soon as possible after the murder; the sooner an autopsy is conducted, the more valuable the information the police are likely to obtain.

Right before the body is removed, the police do indeed make an outline of the position of the victim. More often than not the body is outlined in chalk, including a notation of whether the body was found in a prone or supine posture.

A police investigation of a murder can take a long time, too long to maintain the murder site as it appeared after the murder. Forensic specialists cannot rely on photographs alone. Often, the exact position of the victim can be of vital importance in an investigation. By making an outline, the police can return to the murder scene and take measurements which might quash or corroborate a new theory on the case. Outline drawings may also be used in the courtroom to explain wound locations, bullet trajectories, and blood trails.

Herbert H. Buzbee, of the International Association of Coroners and Medical Examiners, told *Imponderables* that chalk is not always used to make outlines. Stick-em paper or string are often used on carpets, for example, where chalk might be obscured by the fabric. Carl Harbaugh, of the International Chiefs of Police, says that many departments once experimented with spray paint to make outlines, but found that paint traces were occasionally found on the victim, confusing the forensic analysis.

The ideal outline ingredient would be one that would show up, stay put, and do no permanent damage to any surface. Unfortunately, no such ingredient exists. Chalk gets high marks for leaving no permanent markings, but is not easily visible on many surfaces. Tape and string (which has to be fastened with tape) have a tendency to mysteriously twist out of shape, especially if they get wet.

None of these flaws in the markers would matter if murder victims were considerate enough to die in sites convenient to the police. Harbaugh says that on a street or highway any kind of outline will do. But what good is a chalk outline on a bed covered with linens and blankets?

Submitted by Pat O'Conner of Forest Hills, New York.

What Do Restaurants that Specialize in Potato Skins Do with the Rest of the Potato? What Do Restaurants that Specialize in Frogs' Legs Do with the Rest of the Frog?

In most restaurants, potato skins are a waste product, served as the casing of a baked potato or not at all. So we assumed that restaurants that specialized in potato skins used the rest of the potato to make mashed potatoes, boiled potatoes, or soups.

Our assumption was correct, but our correspondent mentions that potato skins are often served in bars that do not serve potatoes in any other form. Is it cost-effective for these establishments to serve the skins and dump the potato filling?

Most restaurants that serve potato skins buy the skins *only*, usually in frozen form. Linda Smith, of the National Restaurant Association, sent us a list of the biggest suppliers of potato skins. Most of these companies, not at all coincidentally, also supply restaurants with pre-cut cottage fries, hash browns, and O'Brien potatoes, among others. Ore-Ida isn't about to sell the skin and throw away the potato.

Anyone who has ever dissected a frog in biology class does not want to contemplate the idea of chefs picking apart an entire frog to get at its legs. Suffice it to say that restaurants buy only the legs of frogs. What suppliers of frogs' legs do with the rest of the frog is too gruesome for even us to contemplate.

Submitted by Myrna S. Gordon of Scotch Plains, New Jersey.
Thanks also to Sharon Michele Burke of Menlo Park, California.

If Water Is Heavier than Air, Why Do Clouds Stay Up in the Sky?

What makes you think that clouds aren't dropping? They are. Constantly.

Luckily, cloud drops do not fall at the same velocity as a water balloon. In fact, cloud drops are downright sluggards: They drop at a measly 0.3 centimeters per second. And cloud drops are so tiny, about 0.01 centimeters in diameter, that their descent is not even noticeable to the human eye.

Submitted by Ronald C. Semone of Washington, D.C.

Why Are There More Holes in the Mouthpiece of a Telephone than in the Earpiece?

We just checked the telephone closest to us and were shocked. There are thirty-six holes on our mouthpiece, and a measly seven on the earpiece. What gives?

Tucked underneath the mouthpiece is a tiny transmitter that duplicates our voices, and underneath the earpiece is a receiver. Those old enough to remember telephones that constantly howled will appreciate the problems inherent in having a receiver and transmitter close together enough to produce audible transmission without creating feedback.

Before the handset, deskstand telephones were not portable, and the speaker had to talk into a stationary transmitter. Handsets added convenience to the user but potential pitfalls in transmission. While developing the telephone handset, engineers were aware that it was imperative for the lips of a speaker to be as close as possible to the transmitter. If a caller increases

DAVID FELDMAN

the distance between his lips and the transmitter from half an inch to one inch, the output volume will be reduced by three decibels. According to AT&T, in 1919 more than four thousand measurements of head dimensions were made to determine the proper dimensions of the handset. The goal, of course, was to design a headset that would best cup the ear and bring the transmitter close to the lips.

One of the realities that the Bell engineers faced was that there was no way to force customers to talk directly into the mouthpiece. Watch most people talking on the phone and you will see their ears virtually covered by the receiver. But most people do not hold their mouths as close to the transmitter. This is the real reason why there are usually more holes in the mouthpiece than in the earpiece. The more holes there are, the more sensitive to sound the transmitter is, and the more likely that a mumbled aside will be heard three thousand miles away.

Submitted by Tammy Madill of Millington, Tennessee.

How Do Fish Return to a Lake or Pond that Has Dried Up?

Our correspondent, Michael J. Catalana, rightfully wonders how even a small pond replenishes itself with fish after it has totally dried up. Is there a Johnny Fishseed who roams around the world restocking ponds and lakes with fish?

We contacted several experts on fish to solve this mystery, and they wouldn't answer until we cross-examined you a little bit, Michael. "How carefully did you look at that supposedly dried-up pond?" they wanted to know. Many species, such as the appropriately named mudminnows, can survive in mud. R. Bruce Gebhardt, of the North American Native Fishes Association, suggested that perhaps your eyesight was misdirected: "If there are small pools, fish may be able to hide in mud or weeds while you're standing there looking into the pool." When you leave, they re-emerge. Some tropical fish lay eggs that develop while the pond is dry; when rain comes and the pond is refilled with water, the eggs hatch quickly.

For the sake of argument, Michael, we'll assume that you communed with nature, getting down on your hands and knees to squeeze the mud searching for fish or eggs. You found no evidence of marine life. How can fish appear from out of thin air? We return to R. Bruce Gebhardt for the explanation:

> There are ways in which fish can return to a pond after total elimination. The most common is that most ponds or lakes have outlets and inlets; fish just swim back into the formerly hostile area. They are able to traverse and circumvent small rivulets, waterfalls, and pollution sources with surprising efficiency. If they find a pond with no fish in it, they may stay just because there's a lot of food with no competition for it.

Submitted by Michael J. Catalana of Ben Lomond, California.

Why Do We Call Our Numbering System "Arabic" When Arabs Don't Use Arabic Numbers Themselves?

The first numbering system was probably developed by the Egyptians, but ancient Sumeria, Babylonia, and India used numerals in business transactions. All of the earliest number systems used some variation of 1 to denote one, probably because the numeral resembled a single finger. Historians suggest that our Arabic 2 and 3 are corruptions of two and three slash marks written hurriedly.

Most students in Europe, Australia, and the Americas learn to calculate with Arabic numbers, even though *these numerals were never used by Arabs*. Arabic numbers were actually developed in India, long before the invention of the printing press (probably in the tenth century), but were subsequently translated into Arabic. European merchants who brought back treatises to their continent mistakenly assumed that Arabs had invented the system, and proceeded to translate the texts from Arabic.

True Arabic numerals look little like ours. From one to ten, this is how they look:

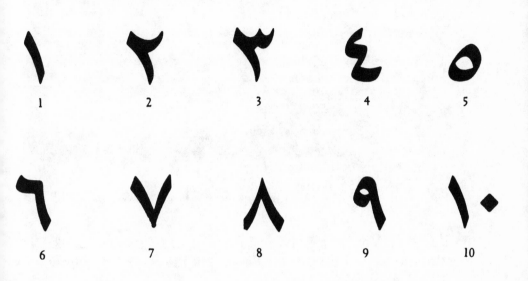

١	٢	٣	٤	٥
1	2	3	4	5

٦	٧	٨	٩	١٠
6	7	8	9	10

Submitted by Dr. Bruce Carter of Fort Ord, California.

WHEN DO FISH SLEEP? 279

When You Are Driving Your Car at Night and Look Up at the Sky, Why Does It Seem that the Moon Is Following You Around?

If you, like every other literate human being, have read *Why Do Clocks Run Clockwise? and Other Imponderables*, then you know why the moon looks larger on the horizon than up in the sky, even though the moon remains the same size. Clearly, our eyes can play tricks on us.

Without reference points to guide us, the moon doesn't seem to be far away. When you are driving on a highway, the objects closest to your car go whirring by. Barriers dividing the lanes become a blur. You can discern individual houses or trees by the side of the road, but, depending upon your speed, it might be painful to watch them go by. Distant trees and houses move by much more slowly, even though you are driving at the same speed. And distant mountains seem mammoth and motionless.

DAVID FELDMAN

Eventually, as you travel far enough down the highway, you will pass the mountains, and they will appear smaller.

If you think the mountain range off the highway is large or far away, consider the moon, which is 240,000 miles away and bigger than any mountain range (more than 2,100 miles in diameter). We already know that our eyes are playing tricks with our perception of how big and far away the moon is. You would have to be traveling awfully far to make the moon appear to move at all. *Astronomy* editor Jeff Kanipe concludes that without a highway or expanse of landscape to give us reference points "this illusion of nearness coupled with its actual size and distance makes the moon appear to follow us wherever we go."

This phenomenon, much discussed in physics and astronomy textbooks, is called the parallax and is used to determine how the apparent change in the position of an object or heavenly body may be influenced by the changing position of the observer. Astronomers can determine the distance between a body in space and the observer by measuring the magnitude of the parallax effect.

And then again, Elizabeth, maybe the moon really is following you.

Submitted by Elizabeth Bogart of Glenview, Illinois.

When Does a Calf Become a Cow?

The calf's equivalent of a bar mitzvah occurs after it stops nursing, usually at about seven to eight months of age. After they are weaned and/or when they reach twelve months, they are referred to as yearling bulls or yearling calves.

According to Richard L. Spader, executive vice president of the American Angus Association, "calves don't achieve full-fledged bullhood or cowhood until they're in production. We normally refer to a first calf heifer at, say, twenty-four months of age or older, as just that, and after her second calf as a three-year-old, she becomes a cow."

Bulls don't usually reach maturity until they are three. After they wean from their mothers, they are referred to as "yearling bulls," or "two-year-old bulls." Are we now all totally confused?

Submitted by Herbert Kraut of Forest Hills, New York.

When One Has a Cold, Why Does Only One Nostril at a Time Tend to Get Clogged (Even Though *Which* Nostril Gets Clogged Can Change at Any Time)? Come to Think of It, Why Do We Need Two Nostrils in the First Place?

The shifting of clogged nostrils is a protective effort of your nasal reflex system. Although the nose was probably most important to prehistoric man as a smelling organ, modern humans' sense of smell has steadily decreased over time. The nose is now much more important in respiration, breathing in O_2 to the nose, trachea, bronchi, lungs, heart, and blood, and ultimately the exchange of oxygen and carbon dioxide. As rhinologist Dr. Pat Barelli explains:

> A fantastic system of reflexes which originate in the inner nose sends impulses to the heart and indirectly to every cell in the body. These reflexes, coupled with the resistance of the nose, increase the efficiency of the lungs and improve the effectiveness of the heart action.

The most common reason for congested nostril switching is the sleep process. When we sleep, our body functions at a

DAVID FELDMAN

greatly reduced rate. The heart beats slower and the lungs require less air. Rhinologist Dr. Zanzibar notes that patients

> commonly complain that at night when they lie on one side, the dependent side of the nose becomes obstructed and they find it necessary to roll over in bed to make that side open. Then the other side becomes obstructed, and they roll over again.

When the head is turned to one side during sleep, the "upper nose" has the entire load of breathing and can become fatigued. According to Dr. Pat Barelli,

> one nostril doing solo duty can fatigue in as little as one to three hours, and internal pressures cause the sleeper to change his head position to the opposite side. The body naturally follows this movement. In this way, the whole body, nose, chest, abdomen, neck, and extremities rest one side at a time.

Bet you didn't know your schnozz was so smart. Our motto is "One nostril stuffed is better than two."

Submitted by Richard Aaron of Toronto, Ontario.

Why Do New Fathers Pass Out Cigars?

"What this country needs is a good five-cent cigar" might have been first uttered in the early twentieth century, but in the late seventeenth and early eighteenth centuries, cigars cost much more than five cents. According to Norman Sharp, of the Cigar Association of America, "cigars were so rare and treasured that they were sometimes used as currency."

Two hundred years ago, a baby boy was considered a valuable commodity. He would work the fields all day and produce money for the father, whereas a baby girl was perceived as a financial drain. At first, precious cigars were handed out as a symbol of celebration only when a boy was born.

By the twentieth century, some feminist dads found it in their hearts to pass the stogies around even when, drat, a girl was born. Now the ritual remains a primitive but relatively less costly act of male bonding—a tribute to male fertility while the poor mother recovers alone in her hospital room.

Submitted by Scott P. Frederick of Wilmington, North Carolina. Thanks also to Mike Bartnik of Omaha, Nebraska; and Dan and Patty Poser of San Luis Obispo, California.

DAVID FELDMAN

Now anybody can have dimples!
SMEE'S safety-sealed
press-on
DIMPLES
be "cute as a button..."
... in minutes!
before
after!
.99¢ or TAX

What Are Dimples? And Why Do Only Some People Have Them?

Dimples are a generic name for indentations of the skin. Dimples are produced when muscle fibers are attached to the deep surface of the skin, such as in the cheek or chin, or where the skin is attached to bones by fibrous bands, such as the elbow, shoulder, and back.

Dimples are most likely to appear where the skin is most tightly attached to the underlying bone. Anatomist Dr. William Jollie, of the Medical College of Virginia, indicates that "dimples probably are due to some developmental fault in the connective tissue that binds skin to bone."

So all this time we've envied those with dimples but didn't realize that they were exhibiting an anatomical flaw! And the tendency toward dimples seems to be hereditary. You have your father to blame, Michael Douglas.

Submitted by Donna Lamb of Stafford, Texas.

Why Do Bath Towels Smell Bad After a Few Days When They Are Presumably Touching Only Clean Skin?

Most towels are made of 100% cotton. While it's true that after a shower you have eliminated most of the germs and dirt from your skin, the process of rubbing a towel against the body rubs off dead skin that sticks to the moist towel. Towels become an ideal nesting place for the mildew endemic to humid bathrooms.

Most people flip a fan on or open the windows when showering but then turn off the fan or close the windows when they dry themselves. Jean Lang, director of Marketing at Fieldcrest, says it is much more important to promote circulation *after* the shower. Without dispersing the moisture, the bathroom becomes like a terrarium. The same type of mildew that afflicts plastic shower curtains attacks towels, especially if the towels have never dried completely from their last use.

We remember our windowless high school locker room with little nostalgia. The lack of ventilation and circulation led to mildew and smelly towels. We would have gladly endured the smell of garbage for the odious aroma of schoolmates' moist towels.

Submitted by Merry Phillips of Menlo Park, California. Thanks also to Paul Funn Dunn of Decatur, Illinois.

How Do Stamp Pads Keep Moist When They Are Constantly Exposed to the Drying Influence of Air?

The ink used in stamp pads has a glycol and water base, which forms a mixture that actually absorbs moisture from the air. On a humid day, this hygroscopic effect allows the stamp or stamp pad to replenish any moisture lost on dry days.

Submitted by Russ Tremayne of Auburn, Washington.

DAVID FELDMAN

Why Are Tupperware® Brand Products Sold Only at Parties? Couldn't They Make More Money by Selling the Stuff in Stores Too?

Until Earl Tupper came along, most housewares were made of glass, ceramics, wood, or metal—traditional, dependable materials. In 1945, Tupper established Tupper Plastics and tried to market his containers in retail stores.

Tupper's products bombed. Consumers feared that plastic material would prove flimsy, and they didn't understand or believe that Tupper's innovative airtight seal would keep foods fresh. Two salespeople with experience demonstrating Stanley Home Products on the party plan saw Tupper's products and convinced him that sales would mushroom if his plasticware were demonstrated. Early tests were highly successful. In 1951, Tupperware Home Parties was incorporated, and all Tupper products were removed from store shelves.

Now that the public has learned that Tupperware plastic is durable and effective, why doesn't Tupperware compete with less established brand names in K-Mart's and Macy's? Tupperware is convinced that the party approach has unique advantages. Lawrie Pitcher Platt, Tupperware's director of Public Relations and Community Affairs, explains:

> Tupperware brand products continue to be sold on the party plan because each dealer is like a teacher. He or she demonstrates the many subtle features designed into the pieces shown and discusses product care and the full lifetime warranty. Tupperware brand products are a lifetime purchase, unlike many products manufactured today, and it is management's belief that learning about use and care enhances the value to the customer.

Translation: The Tupperware dealer justifies the higher cost of its product.

As of 1989, Tupperware has 89,000 independent dealers in the United States alone and 325,000 in forty-two countries worldwide. With such a solid sales force base, Tupperware would jeopardize the revenue of its dealers by selling Tupperware brand products on a retail basis again. Why risk a retail rollout when Tupperware already has a dedicated sales force devoted solely to its product? Avon and Fuller Brush have experienced problems with direct sales of late, but Tupperware's success may be partly attributable to its party concept, in which the "sponsor" gets rewarded with free merchandise for throwing the party. And unlike many direct sellers, Tupperware doesn't necessarily invade customers' homes. About 25% of all Tupperware parties in the United States are now held outside the home.

Submitted by Charles Kluepfel of Bloomfield, New Jersey.

Why Do Monkeys in the Zoo Pick Through Their Hair All the Time? Why Do They Pick Through One Another's Hair?

In the wild, primates pick at their own hair frequently but for short periods of time. Usually, they are trying to rid themselves of parasitic insects, insect webs, or remnants of food.

Monkeys in captivity are much less likely to be riddled with parasites, but may be afflicted with another skin problem. Monkeys exude salt from the pores of their skin. The salt lands on loose bits of skin, and monkeys will often pick through their hair trying to shed the salty flakes.

A monkey, unlike a human, has no difficulty in scratching its back (or any other part of its body, for that matter). Most animal behaviorists assume that apes—be they gibbons or chimpanzees—search through one another's hair for purely social reasons. One psychologist, H. H. Reynolds, noted that chimpanzees are not altruistic or naturally cooperative: "Grooming behavior appears to be one of the most cooperative ventures in which chimpanzees engage."

Perhaps mutual grooming in monkeys is akin to the human handshake, whose original purpose was to signal that a potential weapon, the outstretched hand, would not turn into a clenched fist.

Why Is Cheddar Cheese Orange?

Unless they've been breeding some pretty strange cows in Wisconsin, we would expect cows to produce white milk. All the folks in the dairy industry assured us that they haven't bred a mutant race of cows just to produce orangeish cheddar cheese.

Cheddar cheese is artificially colored with natural ingredients, most commonly annatto, a seed obtained from the tropical annatto tree, found in Central America. Kraft, the largest seller of cheese in the United States, uses a combination of annatto and oleoresin paprika, an oil extraction of the spice paprika, to color its cheddar cheese. Depending upon the natural color of the milk and the amount of annatto added, cheese can be turned into a bright orange color or a more natural-looking yellow shade.

The only reason why cheesemakers color their product is because consumers seem to prefer it. Regional tastes differ, though. Some areas of the eastern United States prefer white cheese, while most of the rest of the country favors yellow. Kraft even makes white "American Singles," although the artificially colored yellow slices far outsell them.

Submitted by Christoper S. von Guggenberg of Alexandria, Virginia.

What Is the Circle Adjacent to the Batter's Box on Baseball Fields?

This area is known as the fungo circle. Coaches stand in the fungo circle during pregame practice and hit balls to infielders and, more frequently, outfielders.

Why confine the coach to stand in one small area? So he won't wear out the grass on the field!

Submitted by Terrell K. Holmes of New York, New York. Thanks also to Ronald C. Semone of Washington, D.C.

What Exactly Is One Hour Martinizing?

Countless millions have passed dry-cleaning stores with the words ONE HOUR MARTINIZING emblazoned on the sign and wondered: What the heck is "Martinizing"? Can it really be done in one hour? Is it painful, and if so, can an anesthetic be administered?

Don't worry. Be happy. Martinizing is a service mark of Martin Franchises, Inc., the largest chain of franchised dry-cleaning establishments in the United States. Martinizing was first registered with the U.S. Patent Trademark Office in 1950 by the Martin Equipment Corporation, a manufacturer of dry-cleaning machines.

The equipment business and trademarks were later sold to the American Laundry Machinery Company of Cincinnati, Ohio, also a manufacturer of cleaning equipment. Although Martinizing was once part of the sales division of the American Laundry Machinery Company, it has spun off into a separate entity, still located in Cincinnati.

Today if an aspiring dry cleaner wants the know-how and name recognition that a franchise can provide, he or she will likely choose Martin, since it is the best-known name in the dry-cleaning field, and start-up costs are relatively low.

What's special about One Hour Martinizing? As far as we can tell, nothing. They use the same chemicals, solvents, and cleaning methods as other dry cleaners, and can "Martinize" in one hour, just as most dry cleaners can handle a job in one hour.

The folks are relying on the notion that if you patronize another establishment, you can say your clothes have been dry cleaned but you can't brag that they've been Martinized.

Submitted by Dominic Orlando of Arlington, Texas. Thanks also to Peter B. Child of Seattle, Washington.

What Flavor Is Bubble Gum Supposed to Be? Why Is Bubble Gum Usually Pink?

Although in *Imponderables* we managed to ascertain the main flavors in Juicy Fruit gum, we have failed miserably at obtaining the constituents in bubble gum. Perhaps we are losing our powers of persuasion. The best we have been able to wangle from our sources is that "regular" pink bubble gum is a mixture of several natural and artificial fruit flavors.

We thought that the pink color of bubble gum would provide clues to the identity of the flavors, but we were disappointed again. Bubble gum was invented in 1928 by a lone entrepreneur, Walter Diemer, who was an accountant from Philadelphia. From the very beginning, Diemer artificially colored his gum pink. Why? "Because it was the only coloring I had handy at the time!" So much for the sanctity of pink bubble gum.

Now, of course, with Bubble Yum coming in flavors like Bananaberry Split and Checkermint, pink bubble gum looks old

DAVID FELDMAN

hat. But not quite yet. Good old pink bubble gum is still the best seller by far.

Submitted by John Geesy of Phoenix, Arizona.

Why Don't Traffic Signal Light Bulbs Ever Seem to Burn Out? Can We Buy Them?

To answer the second part of the Imponderable first: sure, you can buy the same bulbs that light our traffic signals. But you probably wouldn't want to buy them.

Yes, the bulbs found in traffic lights do last much longer than standard household bulbs. The traffic light bulbs are rated at eight thousand hours, compared to the standard one thousand hours. Incandescent lights can be manufactured to last any length of time. However, the longer life a bulb has, the less efficiently it burns. According to General Electric's J. Robert Moody:

> The incandescent light is like a candle. If you burn it dimly, the candle will last a long time. If you burn the candle on both ends, you get a lot of light but short life. The traffic signal light must use 100 watts to get 1,000 lumens [units of light]. To obtain the same 1,000 lumens a household lamp needs only 60 watts. At an electric rate of $0.10/Kwh, the electric cost for 100 watts is $10.00 per 1,000 hours. For the 60 watts the electric cost is $6.00 per 1,000 hours. Thus, the consumer saves $4.00 per 1,000 burning hours [or 40%] by using a household light bulb rather than a traffic signal light bulb.

Traffic signal bulbs are also specially constructed and are filled with krypton gas rather than the less expensive argon gas used in standard bulbs. Municipalities obviously feel the added expense of the special bulbs is more than offset by the cost of labor for replacing burned-out bulbs and the fewer dangerous situations created by malfunctioning traffic signals.

WHEN DO FISH SLEEP? 293

We're as lazy as the next guys, but even we figure it is worth changing bulbs to save nearly 50% on our lighting needs. Now if we could get a flashing red light, that might be worth it . . .

Submitted by Michael B. Labdon of Paramount, California.

Why Does Mickey Mouse Have Four Fingers?

Or more properly, why does Mickey Mouse have three fingers and one thumb on each hand? In fact, why is virtually every cartoon animal beset with two missing digits?

Conversations with many cartoonists, animators, and Disney employees confirm what we were at first skeptical about. Mickey Mouse has four fingers because it is convenient for the artists and animators who have drawn him. In the early cartoons, each frame was hand-drawn by an animator—painstaking and tedious work. No part of the human anatomy is harder to draw than a hand, and it is particularly difficult to draw distinct fingers without making the whole hand look disproportionately large.

The artists who drew Mickey were more than happy to go along with any conceit that saved them some work. So in Disney and most other cartoons, the animals sport a thumb and three fingers, while humans, such as Snow White and Cinderella, are spared the amputation.

And before anyone asks—no, we don't know for sure *which* of Mickey's fingers got lopped off for the sake of convenience. Since the three nonthumbs on each hand are symmetrical, we'd like to think it was the pinkie that was sacrificed.

Submitted by Elizabeth Frenchman of Brooklyn, New York.
Thanks also to R. Gonzales of Whittier, California.

DAVID FELDMAN

Why Don't Migrating Birds Get Jet Lag? Or Do They?

No, birds don't seem to suffer from jet lag. But then again they don't suffer from airport delays, crowded seating, inedible airline food, or lost luggage either.

Human jet lag seems to be bound inextricably to passing rapidly through time zones. Birds usually migrate from north to south, often not encountering any time change. Veterinarian Robert B. Altman speculates that if you put a bird on an airplane going east to west, it might feel jet lag.

But birds, unlike humans, don't try to fly from New York to Australia in one day. Some migrations can take weeks. Birds don't stretch their physical limits unless they have to (such as when flying over a large body of water). If they are tired, birds stop flying and go to sleep, while their human counterparts on the airplane choose between being kept awake by a screaming baby or the one movie they have assiduously avoided seeing in its theater or cable presentations.

Humans are particularly susceptible to jet lag when they travel at night. As a rule, migration doesn't upset birds' natural sleeping patterns. They sleep when it is dark and awaken when it is light. On airplanes, humans fall asleep only immediately preceding the meal service or the captain's latest announcement of the natural wonders on the ground.

Of course, migration isn't without some perils of its own. The National Audubon Society sent *Imponderables* an article detailing the migration habits of shore birds along the Delaware Bay. Many of these shore birds travel from their breeding ground in the Arctic to the southern tip of South America. The round trip can be in excess of fifteen thousand miles.

When the birds land in warmer climes, they engage in a feeding frenzy not unlike a season-long Thanksgiving dinner. The birds found in the Delaware Bay, who had often flown more than five thousand miles with little rest, often doubled their body weight in two weeks. An official of the New Jersey Division of Fish, Game and Wildlife is quoted as saying that the birds "get so fat they can hardly even fly." *New York Times* reporter Erik Eckholm describes these fatted birds as bouncing along "like an overloaded airplane when trying to take off."

Submitted by Chris Whelan of Lisle, Illinois.

Why Do Some Hard-Boiled Egg Yolks Turn Gray or Green When Soft-Boiled Eggs Don't Discolor?

The discoloring is caused by iron and sulphur compounds that accumulate when eggs are overcooked. Although gray egg yolks lack eye appeal, the iron and sulfur don't affect the taste or nutritional value of the eggs.

Probably the most common way of overcooking eggs is to leave the eggs in hot water after cooking. The American Egg Board recommends that after eggs are cooked either cold water should be run over them or they should be put in ice water until completely cooled. Cooling eggs in this manner will not only avoid overcooking but will also make the shells much easier to peel.

DAVID FELDMAN

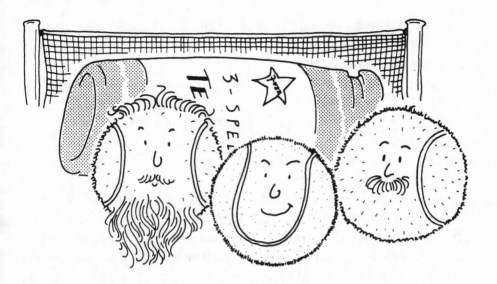

Why Are Tennis Balls Fuzzy?

The core of a tennis ball is made out of a compound consisting of rubber, synthetic materials, and about ten chemicals. The compound is extruded into a barrel-shaped pellet that is then formed into two half shells.

The edges of the two half shells are coated with a latex adhesive and then put together and cured in a double-chambered press under strictly controlled temperature and air-pressure conditions. The inner chamber is pressurized to thirteen psi (pounds per square inch), so that the air is trapped inside and the two halves are fused together at the same pressure.

Once the two halves have been pressed together to form one sphere, the surface of the core is roughened so that the fuzz will stick better. The core is then dipped into a cement compound and oven-dried to prepare for the cover application.

The fuzzy material is felt, a combination of wool, nylon, and Dacron woven together into rolls. The felt is cut into a figure-eight shape (one circular piece of felt wouldn't fit as snugly on a ball), and the edges of the felt are coated with a seam adhesive. The cores and edges of the two felt strips are mated, the felt is bonded to the core, and the seam adhesive is cured, securing all the materials and for the first time yielding a sphere that looks like a tennis ball.

After the balls are cured, they are steamed in a large tumbler and fluffed in order to raise the nap on the felt, giving the balls their fuzzy appearance. Different manufacturers fluff their balls to varying degrees. The balls are then sealed in airtight cans pressurized at twelve to fifteen psi, with the goal of keeping the balls at ten to twelve psi.

The single most expensive ingredient in a tennis ball is the felt. Many other sports do quite well with unfuzzy rubber balls. In the earliest days of tennis, balls had a leather cover, and were stuffed with all sorts of things, including human hair. So why do tennis ball manufacturers bother with the fuzz?

Before the felt is added, a tennis ball has a hard, sleek surface, not unlike a baseball's. One of the main purposes of the fuzz is to slow the ball down. The United States Tennis Association maintains strict rules concerning the bound of tennis balls. One regulation stipulates, "The ball shall have a bound of more than 53 inches and less than 58 inches when dropped 100 inches upon a concrete base." The fluffier the felt, the more wind resistance it offers, decreasing not only the bound but the speed of the ball. If the felt were too tightly compacted, the ball would have a tendency to skip on the court.

A second important reason for fuzzy tennis balls is that the fluffy nap contributes to increased racket control. Every time a tennis ball hits a racket the strings momentarily grip the ball, and the ball compresses. With a harder, sleeker surface, the ball would have a tendency to skip off the racket and minimize the skill of the player.

A third contribution of fuzz is the least important to a good player but important to us refugees from hardball sports like racquetball and squash. When you get hit hard by a fuzzy tennis ball, you may want to cry, but you don't feel like you're going to die.

Submitted by Dorio Barbieri of Mountain View, California.

DAVID FELDMAN

What Causes Floaters, or Spots, in the Eyes?

The innermost part of the eye is a large cavity filled with a jelly-like fluid known as vitreous humor. Floaters are small flecks of protein, pigment, or embryonic remnants (trapped in the cavity during the formation of the eye) that suspend in the vitreous humor.

The small specks appear to be in front of the eye because the semitransparent floaters are visible only when they fall within the line of sight. Most people might have specks trapped in the vitreous humor from time to time but not notice them. Eyes have a way of adjusting to imperfections, as any eyeglass wearer with dirty lenses could tell you. Floaters are most likely to be noticed when one is looking at a plain background, such as a blackboard, a bare wall, or the sky.

What should one do about floaters? An occasional spot is usually harmless, although sometimes floaters can be precursors of retinal damage. Most often, a home remedy will keep floaters from bothering you. The American Academy of Ophthalmology suggests:

> if a floater appears directly in your line of vision, the best thing to do is to move your eye around, which will cause the inside fluid to swirl and allow the floater to move out of the way. We are most accustomed to moving our eyes back and forth, but looking up and down will cause different currents within the eye and may be more effective in getting the floaters out of the way.

Although you may be aware of their presence, it is often surprisingly difficult to isolate floaters in your line of vision. Because the floaters are actually within the eye, they move as your eyes move and seem to dart away whenever you try to focus on looking at them directly.

Submitted by Gail Lee of Los Angeles, California.

Does It Ever Really Get Too Cold to Snow?

Having withstood a few snowy midwestern winters in our time, we're not sure we would want to test this hypothesis personally. Luckily, meteorologists have.

No, it never gets too cold to snow, but at extremely low temperatures the amount of snow accumulation on the ground is likely to be much lower than at 25 degrees Fahrenheit. According to Raymond E. Falconer, of the Atmospheric Sciences Research Center, SUNY at Albany, there is so little water vapor available at subzero temperatures that snow takes the shape of tiny ice crystals, which have little volume and do not form deep piles. But at warmer temperatures more water vapor is available, "so the crystals grow larger and form snowflakes, which are an agglomerate of ice crystals." The warmer the temperature is, the larger the snowflakes become.

What determines the size of the initial snow crystals? It depends upon the distribution of temperature and moisture from the ground up to the cloud base. If snow forming at a high level drops into much drier air below, the result may be no accumulation whatsoever. In the condition known as "virga," streaks of ice particles fall from the base of a cloud but evaporate completely before hitting the ground.

Submitted by Ronald C. Semone of Washington, D.C.

Why Do Dogs Have Black Lips?

You would prefer mauve, perhaps? Obviously dogs' lips have to be some color, and black makes more sense than most.

According to veterinarian Dr. Peter Ihrke, pigmentation helps protect animals against solar radiation damage. Because dogs don't have as much hair around their mouths as on most parts of their bodies, pigmentation plays a particularly important role in shielding dogs against the ravages of the sun.

According to Dr. Kathleen J. Kovacs, of the American Veterinary Medical Association, the gene for black pigment is dominant over the genes for all other pigments, so the presence of black lips is attributable to hereditary factors. If two purebred dogs with black lips breed, one can predict with confidence that their puppies will have black lips too.

Not all dogs have black lips, though. Some breeds have nonpigmented lips and oral cavities. James D. Conroy, a veterinary pathologist affiliated with Mississippi State University, told *Imponderables* that some dogs have a piebald pattern of nonpigmented areas alternating with pigmented areas. The only breed with an unusual lip color is the Chow Chow, which has a blue color. Conroy says that "the blue appearance of the lips and oral cavity is related to the depth of the pigment cells within the oral tissue."

Submitted by Michael Barson of Brooklyn, New York.

If Church and State Are Supposed to be Separated in the United States, Why Do We Swear On Bibles in Courts? What Happens if a Witness Doesn't Accept the Validity of the Bible?

The ritual of taking an oath with the right hand raised while placing the left hand on a holy object goes back to ancient times. Michael De L. Landon, secretary of the American Society for Legal History, sent us a picture of the Bayeux Tapestry, which depicts King Harold of England, who reigned from 1035–1040, taking an oath with both hands on a sacred object.

In the Middle Ages, before printed Bibles were commonly

available, Christians placed the left hand on a relic of a saint or some other sacred object and raised the right hand while taking an oath. Professor De L. Landon comments:

> the right hand raised and open, palm outward, is an internationally recognized gesture implying peace, honesty, and good intentions. In taking an oath, there is also probably the indication that one is pointing to heaven and calling upon God (or the gods) to be one's witness that one is sincere and telling the truth.

The English adopted the practice of having witnesses swear an oath on the bible before testifying. American law was based originally on an English common law that stipulated that only witnesses who believed in a Supreme Being could testify at a trial. The framers of the common law assumed that only the fear of an eternal punishment would ensure the honesty of the witness. Lord Coke, the leading English jurist of the early seventeenth century, went further and argued that nonconformists as well as atheists were *petui inimici* ("eternal enemies") and should be barred from testifying. Coke's position was adopted by the English for almost two hundred years, and although it became impossible to enforce the doctrine, Parliament did not actually remove the statute until 1869.

Most courtrooms have stopped using Bibles to swear in witnesses, for the ritual was always a ceremonial demonstration of good faith rather than a legally mandated procedure. Most courts traditionally have used King James Bibles, but have allowed Jews or Catholics to substitute versions that were acceptable to their faith.

The United States adopted the rule disqualifying disbelievers in the Federal Judiciary Act of 1789, which provided that no one could testify "who did not believe that there is a God who rewards truth and avenges falsehood." In 1906 Congress passed an amendment to allow states to determine their own rules for their own courts, although most states had already passed statutes voiding the disbeliever clause. Even today, a few states have not struck down the disbeliever clause; theoretically, an atheist could be barred from testifying in a trial in those states.

In his book *Church, State and Freedom*, Leo Pfeffer notes broader constitutional provisions ensure that no civil rights may be denied because of religious beliefs. Still, the issue hasn't been addressed squarely by the Supreme Court, and Pfeffer documents a scary application of how the nonbeliever clause has been applied in the past:

> in 1900 the Court upheld a Federal statute that required that the testimony of Chinese, in certain cases, be corroborated by that of white men, because of the 'loose notions entertained by [Chinese] witnesses of the obligation of an oath.' It would seem clear that if a defendant in a criminal case or a party in a civil case could not take the stand in his own behalf because of his religious beliefs or disbeliefs, he would be deprived of his liberty or property without due process of law and would be denied the equal protection of the laws in violation of the Fourteenth Amendment. Moreover ... the 'free exercise' clause of the First Amendment protects religious disbelief as well as belief ...

As might be expected, both the ACLU and Madalyn Murray-O'Hair's Society of Separationists have been in the forefront of litigation attempting to eliminate swearing on Bibles (as well as eliminating other elements of religion in the courts). The path of least resistance, for most jurisdictions, has been to abandon the use of Bibles.

One need not be philosophically opposed to the use of Bibles in the courtroom to note that a Bible has never been a guarantee of truthful testimony; perjurers have been swearing on Bibles for a long, long time.

Why Do Females Tend to Throw "Like a Girl"?

Not only do girls (and later, women) tend not to be able to throw balls as far as boys, but their form is noticeably different. If you ask the average boy to throw a baseball as far as he can, he will lift his elbow and wind his arm far back. A girl will tend to keep her elbow static and push forward with her hand in a motion not unlike that of a shot putter.

Why the difference? Our correspondent mentions that he has heard theories that females have an extra bone that prevents them from throwing "like a boy." Or is it that they are missing one bone?

We talked to some physiologists (who assured us that boys and girls have all the same relevant bones) and to some specialists in exercise physiology who have studied the underperformance of girls in throwing.

In their textbook, *Training for Sport and Activity: The Physiological Basis of the Conditioning Process*, Jack H. Wilmore and David L. Costill cite quite a few studies that indicate that up until the ages of ten to twelve, boys and girls have remarkably similar scores in motor skills and athletic ability. In almost every test, boys barely beat the girls. But at the onset of puberty, the male becomes much stronger, possesses greater muscular and cardiovascular endurance, and outperforms girls in virtually all motor skills.

In only one athletic test do the boys far exceed the girls before and after puberty: the softball throw. From the ages of five to sixteen, the average boy can throw a softball about twice as far as a girl.

Wilmore and Costill cite a fascinating study that attempted to explain this phenomenon. Two hundred males and females from ages three to twenty threw softballs for science. The result: males beat females two to one when throwing with their dominant hand, but females threw almost as far as males with their nondominant hand. Up until the ages of ten to twelve, girls threw just as far with their nondominant hand as boys did.

The conclusion of Wilmore and Costill is inescapable:

> Major differences at all ages were the results for the dominant arm ... the softball throw for distance using the dominant arm appears to be biased by the previous experience and practice of the males. When the influence of experience and practice was removed by using the nondominant arm, this motor skill task was identical to each of the others.

All the evidence suggests that girls can be taught, or learn through experience, how to throw "like a boy." Exercise physiologist Ralph Wickstrom believes most children go through several developmental stages of throwing. Boys simply continue growing in sophistication, while girls are not encouraged to throw softballs or baseballs and stop in the learning curve. As an example, Wickstrom notes that most right-handed girls throw with their right foot forward. Simply shifting their left foot forward would increase their throwing distance.

When forced to throw with their nondominant hand, most boys throw "like a girl." The loss in distance is accountable not only to lesser muscular development in the nondominant side, but to a breakdown in form caused by a lack of practice.

Submitted by Tony Alessandrini of Brooklyn, New York.

Given that the ZIP Code Defines the City and State, Why Do We Have to Include Both on Envelopes? Or Do We?

Jack Belck, the true zealot who posed this Imponderable, gave as his return address his full name, a street number, and 48858, with a note: "The above address is guaranteed to work."

Evidently it did. He received a letter we wrote to him in that lovely town, 48858.

But the question is a good one, so we asked our friends at the USPS to respond.

And they were a tad cranky.

Yes, they will deliver letters addressed by the Belcks of the world, but they aren't too happy about it for a couple of reasons. First of all, many people inadvertently transpose digits of the ZIP code. The city and state names then serves as a cross check. Without the city and state names, the letter would be returned automatically to the sender. Even if it is delayed, the postal service will reroute a letter with an incorrect ZIP code.

Secondly, Mr. Belck isn't quite right about one of his premises. In rural areas, more than one municipality might share the same zip code. City names can thus be of assistance to the local post office in sorting and delivering the mail.

Submitted by Jack Belck of 48858.

Why Do Telephone Cords Spontaneously Twist Up? What Can One Do About this Dreaded Affliction?

Spontaneously twist up, you say? You mean you sit on your sofa watching TV and suddenly the telephone cord starts winding like a snake?

After considerable research into the matter, we must conclude that telephone cords do not twist up spontaneously. You've been turning around the headset, Alan. We're not accusing you of doing this intentionally, mind you. As far as we know, twisting a headset is not even a misdemeanor in any state or locality. But don't try to blame your indiscretions on the laws of nature. Cords don't cause twisted cords—people do.

Now that we've chastised you, we'll offer the obvious, simple yet elegant solution. Remove the plug that connects the headset to the body of the phone. Hold the cord by the plug side and let the headset fall down (without hitting the floor, please). The cord will "spontaneously" untwist.

For those having similar problems with twisted lines connecting their phones to the modular jacks in the wall, simply unplug the line from the phone. If the line is sufficiently coiled, it will untwist like an untethered garden hose.

Submitted by Alan B. Heppel of West Hollywood, California.

Why Do Golf Balls Have Dimples?

Because dimples are cute?

No. We should have known better than to think that golfers, who freely wear orange pants in public, would worry about cosmetic appearances.

Golf balls have dimples because in 1908 a man named Taylor patented this cover design. Dimples provide greater aerodynamic lift and consistency of flight than a smooth ball. Jacque Hetric, director of Public Relations at Spalding, notes that the dimple pattern, regardless of where the ball is hit, provides a consistent rotation of the ball after it is struck.

Janet Seagle, librarian and museum curator of the United States Golf Association, says that other types of patterned covers were also used at one time. One was called a "mesh," another the "bramble." Although all three were once commercially available, "the superiority of the dimpled cover in flight made it the dominant cover design."

Although golfers love to feign that they are interested in accuracy, they lust after power: Dimpled golf balls travel farther as well as straighter than smooth balls. So those cute little dimples will stay in place until somebody builds a better mousetrap.

Submitted by Kathy Cripe of South Bend, Indiana.

DAVID FELDMAN

Why Don't Crickets Get Chapped Legs from Rubbing Their Legs Together? If Crickets' Legs Are Naturally Lubricated, How Do They Make that Sound?

If we rubbed our legs together for five minutes as vigorously as crickets do all the time, our legs would turn beet red and we would hobble into the bathroom searching for the talcum powder. How do crickets survive?

Quite well, it turns out. For it turns out that we can't believe everything we learned in school. Crickets don't chirp by rubbing their legs together. Entomologist Clifford Dennis explains:

> Crickets do not produce chirps by rubbing their legs together. They have on each front wing a sharp edge, the scraper, and a file-like ridge, the file. They chirp by elevating the front wings and moving them so that the scraper of one wing rubs on the file of the other wing, giving a pulse, the chirp, generally on the closing stroke.

On a big male cricket, the scraper and the file can often be seen by the naked eye. You can take the wings of a cricket in your fingers and make the chirp sound yourself.

No thanks. We'll take your word for it on faith.

Submitted by Sandra Baxter of Ada, Oklahoma.

Why Is a Navy Captain a Much Higher Rank than an Army Captain? Has This Always Been So?

When one looks at the ranks of the officers of the four branches of the American military, one is struck by how the Army, Air Force, and Marine Corps use the identical ranks, while the Navy uses different names for the equivalents. But there is one striking disparity: the Navy elevates the rank of captain.

Army, Air Force, Marine Corps	Navy
Warrant Officer	Warrant Officer
Chief Warrant Officer	Chief Warrant Officer
Second Lieutenant	Ensign
First Lieutenant	Lieutenant Junior Grade
CAPTAIN	Lieutenant
Major	Lieutenant Commander
Lieutenant Colonel	Commander
Colonel	CAPTAIN
Brigadier General	Commodore
Major General	Rear Admiral
Lieutenant General	Vice Admiral
General	Admiral
General of the Army or General of the Air Force	Fleet Admiral

The word "captain" comes from the Latin word *caput*, meaning "head." In the tenth century, captains led groups of Italian foot soldiers. By the eleventh century, British captains commanded

DAVID FELDMAN

warships. So the European tradition has been to name the head of a military unit of any size, on land or sea, a captain.

Our elevation of the English captain stems from English naval practice. In the eleventh century, British captains were not the heads of ships *per se*. Although captains were in charge of leading soldiers in combat aboard ship, the actual responsibility for the navigation and maintenance of ships fell upon the ranks of master. By the fifteenth century, captains bristled at deferring to the masters they outranked, and captains began to assume the responsibility for the ships heretofore claimed by masters. By 1747 any commander of a ship was officially given the rank of captain.

Meanwhile, on land most European countries named the commander of a company—of any size—captain. By the sixteenth century, military strategists felt that one hundred to two hundred men were the maximum size for a land unit in battle to be effectively led by one person. That leader was known as a captain.

From the inception of the United States military we borrowed from the European tradition. A captain was a company commander and indeed is so today. In the Air Force, a captain commands a squadron, the airborne equivalent of a company. But the Navy captain, because he has domain over such a big and complicated piece of equipment, has a legitimate claim to a higher rank than his compatriots in the other branches. As Dr. Regis A. Courtemanche, of the Scipio Society of Naval and Military History, put it,

> Navy captain isn't only a rank. The senior officer of a ship is always called "Captain" even though his rank may only be lieutenant. So a naval captain may have more responsibility than a military captain who usually commands only a small detachment in battle.

In 1862, the Navy realized that it was no longer practical to make captain its highest rank. They needed a way not only to differentiate among commanders of variously sized and equipped vessels but to reward those who were supervising the captains of warships. For this reason, the Navy split the rank of captain into three different categories. The commodore (and later, the rear admiral) became the highest grade, the commander the lowest, and the captain, once ruler of the seas, stuck in the middle of the ranks.

Submitted by Barrie Creedon of Philadelphia, Pennsylvania.

Why Do Astronomers Look at the Sky Upside Down and Reversed? Wouldn't It Be Possible to Rearrange the Mirrors on Telescopes?

Merry Wooten, of the Astronomical League, informs us that most early telescopes didn't yield upside-down images. Galileo's original spyglass used a negative lens as an eyepiece, just as cheap field glasses made with plastic lenses do now. So why do unsophisticated binoculars yield the "proper" image and expensive astronomical telescopes render an "incorrect" one?

Astronomy editor Jeff Kanipe explains:

> The curved light-gathering lens of a telescope bends, or refracts, the light to focus so that light rays that pass through the top of the lens are bent toward the bottom and rays that pass through the bottom of the lens are bent toward the top. The image thus forms upside down and reversed at the focal point, where an eyepiece enlarges the inverted and reversed image.

Alan MacRobert, of *Sky & Telescope* magazine, adds that some telescopes turn the image upside down, and others also mirror-reverse it: "An upside-down 'correct' image can be viewed correctly just by inverting your head. But a mirror image does not become correct no matter how you may twist and turn to look at it."

O.K. Fine. We could understand why astronomers live with inverted and upside-down images if they had to, but they don't.

Terrestrial telescopes do rearrange their image. Merry Wooten says that terrestrial telescopes can correct their image by using porro prisms, roof prisms, or most frequently, an erector lens assembly, which is placed in front of the eyepiece to create an erect image.

Why don't astronomical telescopes use erector lenses? For the answer, we return to Jeff Kanipe:

> Most astronomical objects are very faint, which is why telescopes with larger apertures are constantly being proposed: Large lenses and mirrors gather more light than small ones. Astronomers need every scrap of light they can get, and it is for this reason that the image orientation of astronomical telescopes are not corrected. Each glass surface the light ray encounters reflects or absorbs about four percent of the total incoming light. Thus if the light ray encounters four glass components, about sixteen percent of the light is lost. This is a significant amount when you're talking about gathering the precious photons of objects that are thousands of times fainter than the human eye can detect. Introducing an erector into the optical system, though it would terrestrially orient the image, would waste light. We can afford to be wasteful when looking at bright objects on the earth but not at distant, faint galaxies in the universe.

And even if the lost light and added expense of erector prisms weren't a factor, every astronomer we contacted was quick to mention an important point: There IS no up or down in outer space.

Submitted by William Debuvitz of Bernardsville, New Jersey.

Why Are the Rolls or Bread Served on Airlines Almost Always Cold While Everything Else on the Tray Is Served at the Appropriate Temperature?

We won't even comment on the *taste* of airline food (this is a family book). But if McDonald's can separate the cold from the hot on a McDLT sandwich, why can't the airlines get their rolls within about 50 degrees of the right temperature?

The answer lies in how airline meals are prepared aloft. The salad, bread, and dessert are placed on trays that are usually refrigerated or packed in ice. Entrees are loaded onto separate baking sheets. When it is time to start the meal service, the flight attendant who prepares the meals simply sticks the trays of entrees into ovens (not, by the way, microwaves).

The rolls are cold because they have been sitting all along with the salad and cake. Most airlines offer customers a choice of entrees. The flight attendant who is serving the meal simply

DAVID FELDMAN

selects the entree from the sheets they were cooked in and places it alongside the rest of the meal. Except for the entree choice, every flier's tray will look identical. Note that although most airlines vary the vegetable according to the entree, the vegetable is always cooked on the same plate as the main course because the entree plate will be the only heated element on the tray.

If the bread and salad taste cold, why doesn't the dessert? Airlines, almost without exception, serve cake for dessert. Michael Marchant, vice president of Ogden Allied Aviation Services and the president of the Inflight Food Service Association, told *Imponderables* that the softness of cake fools us into thinking it is being served at room temperature. The gustatory illusion is maintained because in contrast to the roll's hard crust, which locks in the coldness, the soft frosting of a cake dissipates the cold.

The folks in first class, meanwhile, are munching warm rolls, which have been heated. Certainly it is worth an extra five hundred dollars or so to get heated rolls, isn't it?

Why Do Chickens and Turkeys, Unlike Other Fowl, Have White Meat and Dark Meat?

Other birds that we eat, such as quail, duck, or pigeon, have all dark meat. Chickens and turkeys are among a small group of birds with white flesh on the breasts and wings.

Birds have two types of muscle fibers: red and white. Red muscle fibers contain more myoglobin, a muscle protein with a red pigment. Muscles with a high amount of myoglobin are capable of much longer periods of work and stress than white fibers. Thus, you can guess which birds are likely to have light fibers by studying their feeding and migration patterns.

Most birds have to fly long distances to migrate or to find food, and they need the endurance that myoglobin provides. All birds that appear to have all white flesh actually have some red fibers, and with one exception, all birds that appear to be all dark have white fibers. But the hummingbird, which rarely stops flying, has pectoral muscles consisting entirely of red fibers because the pectoral muscles enable the wings to flap continuously.

The domestic chicken or turkey, on the other hand, lives the life of Riley. Even in their native habitat, according to Dr. Phil Hudspeth, vice president of Quality and Research at Holly Farms, chickens are ground feeders and fly only when nesting. Ordinarily, chickens move around by walking or running, which is why only their legs and thighs are dark. They fly so little that their wings and breasts don't need myoglobin. In fact, the lack of myoglobin in the wing and breast are an anatomical advantage. Janet Hinshaw, of the Wilson Ornithological Society, explains why chicken and turkey musculature is perfectly appropriate:

> They spend most of their time walking. When danger threatens they fly in a burst of speed for a short distance and then land. Thus they need flight muscles which deliver a lot of power quickly but for a short time.

Next time you fork up an extra fifty cents for that order of all-white meat chicken, remember that you are likely paying to eat a bird that racked up fewer trips in the air than you have in an airplane.

Submitted by Margaret Sloane of Chapel Hill, North Carolina. Thanks also to Sara Sickle of Perryopolis, Pennsylvania; and Annalisa Weaver of Davis, California.

Why Haven't Vending Machines Ever Accepted Pennies?

In the second half of the twentieth century, when a child is more likely to think that penny candy is the name of a cartoon character rather than the actual price of a confection, it is hard to believe that in the early days of vending machines the industry would have loved to be able to accept pennies. When a candy bar cost five cents, vendors undoubtedly lost many sales when frustrated kids could produce five pennies but not one nickel. Now, when a candy bar might cost half a dollar, payment in fifty pennies might clog a receptacle. But why didn't vending machines *ever* accept pennies? We spoke to Walter Reed, of the National Automatic Merchandising Association, who told us about the fascinating history of this Imponderable.

The vending machine industry has always been plagued by enterprising criminals who inserted slugs or relatively worthless foreign coins into machines in the time-honored tradition of trying to get something for nothing. In the 1930s, a slug rejector was invented that could differentiate U.S. coinage from Mexican centavos of the same size. The slug rejector worked by determining the metallic content of the coin. Although the slug rejector could easily differentiate between silver or nickel and a slug, it couldn't tell the difference between a worthless token and the copper in a penny. For this reason, vendors hesitated to accept pennies in the machines.

The slug rejectors of today are much more sophisticated, measuring the serration of the coin, its circumference, its thickness, and the presence of any holes. Whereas the 1930s slug rejector was electromagnetic, current rejectors perform tests electronically.

The vending machine industry was instrumental in pushing for the clad-metal coins that were introduced in 1965. Since that year our quarter, for example, which used to be made of silver, now has a center layer of copper surrounded by an outer layer of copper and nickel. The copper-nickel combination reacts to the electronic sensors in vending machine rejectors much like silver. The government also loves the clad coins because the constituent metals are so much cheaper to buy.

Except in gumball machines, the vending machine industry has never accepted pennies, although they once gave pennies away to consumers. In the late 1950s, a cigarette tax was imposed that drove the retail price of cigarettes a few cents above its long-held thirty-five-cent price. Stores simply charged thirty-seven cents, but vending machines couldn't, for they were not equipped to return pennies.

Vendors had to decide whether to keep charging thirty-five cents and absorb the loss of the two cents on every pack, or charge forty cents and risk loss of sales when grocery stores could undercut them by 10%. So they compromised. Vending machines charged forty cents a pack, but pennies were placed in the pack to restore equity to the consumer.

Submitted by Fred T. Beeman of Wailuku, Hawaii.

Now that Most Products Sold in Vending Machines Sell for Fifty Cents or More, Why Don't Most Vending Machines Accept Half Dollars or Dollar Bills?

The problem with the half dollar is that the public does not carry it in its pocket. Half dollars are too bulky and heavy. Allowing half dollars would necessitate increasing the size of coin slots in the machines.

The American public loves quarters. Unfortunately, studies have shown that people resist putting in more than two coins in vending machines. And two quarters aren't enough to buy even a soft drink anymore.

So isn't the dollar bill acceptor the panacea? The technology exists to accept dollar bills in vending machines, but the same hassles that plague the consumer using dollar-bill changers are also a nightmare for the vendor. Bills must be placed in the proper position to be accepted. Worn or slightly torn bills are rejected routinely even though they are perfectly legal tender. And worst of all, dollar bills can't be counted easily by machine. The labor involved in counting paper money is not insignificant.

The vending machine industry lusts after the resuscitation of the silver dollar. Frustrated by the unpopularity of the Susan

B. Anthony dollar, trade groups are now pushing for a new gold-colored dollar with a portrait of Christopher Columbus on the obverse. The Treasury supports the proposal, for although coins are more expensive to manufacture than bills, they last much longer in circulation. Walter Reed points out that no other industrialized nation has an equivalent of a one dollar bill in paper currency anymore. The Canadians were the last to fall, with the Looney dollar, the same size as the ill-fated Susan B. Anthony, replacing their dollar bill.

Why Is a Blue Ribbon Used to Designate First Prize?

Most sources we contacted give credit to the English for introducing the blue ribbon. In 1348, King Edward III of England established the Order of the Garter, now considered one of the highest orders in the world. Ribbons had traditionally been used as a badge of knighthood. Members of the Order of the Garter were distinguished by wearing their dark blue ribbon on their hip.

A second theory presented by S. G. Yasinitsky, of the Orders and Medals Society of America, was new to us:

> Another version of the blue ribbon as meaning the highest achievement may have originated among British soldiers who practiced abstinence by belonging to the various army abstinence groups, especially in India, in the latter part of the nineteenth century. Their basic badge for the first six years' total abstinence was a medal worn on a blue ribbon. Hence a 'blue ribbon unit' was one which was comprised of all men who were sporting a blue ribbon in their buttonhole to denote their sobriety. 'Blue ribbon panel' and 'blue ribbon selection' followed this, I'm sure.

Yasinitsky and others have speculated that our ribbon color schemes might have had an astronomical basis. Blue, the highest award, represented the sky and the heavens, the highest point possible. Red (second prize) represented the sun, which was high up in the sky. Yellow (third prize) represented the stars, once thought to be lower than the sun. Yasinitsky mentions that runners-up in fairs and festivals are often given green ribbons as consolation prizes. The green color probably represents the lowly grass on the ground.

DAVID FELDMAN

What Is the "Cottage" in Cottage Cheese?

Food historians speculate that cottage cheese was probably the first cheese. And it was undoubtedly made by accident. Some anonymous nomad was probably carrying milk on a camel in the desert and at the end of the day found lumps rather than liquid. And much to the nomad's surprise, the lumps tasted pretty good.

According to the United Dairy Industry Association, cottage cheese was made in the home all over Europe as far back as the Middle Ages. "It was called 'cottage' because farmers made the cheese in their own cottages to utilize the milk remaining after the cream had been skimmed from it for buttermaking."

Submitted by Mrs. K. E. Kirtley of Eureka, California.

Why Are There So Many Ads *for* the Yellow Pages *in the* Yellow Pages?

Yellow Pages publishers are smart enough to realize that if you've got a copy of their directory in your grubby hands, you already are convinced of the efficacy of their medium. So why must they pummel us with promotional ads? Phone companies make profits from their directories by selling advertising space —you would think they'd rather have a local plumber buy a small display ad than toot their own horns.

The simple purpose of the promotional ads is to fill space between paid ads. Kenneth Hudnall, executive director of the National Yellow Pages Agency Association, explains why there is a need for filler:

> Mechanically, the composition of the Yellow Pages is quite involved. For a variety of reasons there will be small bits of space left at the bottom of a column of listings or between display ad-

DAVID FELDMAN

vertisements. Rather than leave this space blank, the publishers will throw in "justifiers" to fill up the space. And what is more natural than to put promotional copy for Yellow Pages in this space?

If all advertisements in the Yellow Pages were the same size, it would be easy for designers to lay out the directory without need for filler. But the ads, whether listings or display, come in all different sizes. A catering company won't want its advertisement stranded alone when all the other caterers in town are listed on the two pages before. Justifiers, then, have been a way to make the life of the designer easier and soothe the complaints of advertisers about the placement of their display ads.

One man, Arnie Nelson, had the kind of brilliant idea that can make fortunes: Why should Yellow Pages publishers "waste" the filler space when they could sell advertising in it? Nelson founded a company called Yellow Spots, Inc., whose purpose is to sell small-space display advertising to companies who traditionally do not advertise at all in the Yellow Pages.

According to Nelson and Yellow Spots executive Gabe Samuels, initially there was some resistance from the regional phone companies to giving Yellow Spots an exclusive right to sell display ads. But Yellow Spots mustered some strong arguments to convince them, the most compelling one economic: it would provide a windfall. According to Yellow Spots, anywhere from 6 to 20% of the Yellow Pages consist of filler. Adding 5 or 10% more to gross revenues through new display ads would be most profitable.

Some of the publishers were also reluctant to introduce a new type of advertising into a medium that had thrived without it for more than a hundred years. Nelson and Samuels argued that the Yellow Pages were actually used more by consumers as an information source, a magazine, rather than as an advertising medium. The editorial matter of the *Yellow Pages Magazine* are the directory listings. Yellow Spots would deliver the advertising, billboard ads without addresses or phone numbers. The ads that Yellow Spots would solicit were designed to promote a product rather than tell consumers where to buy it, thus not alienating Yellow Pages' traditional retail clients.

Yellow Spots' second obstacle was to convince corporations, mostly big, national advertisers, to promote their companies in a medium that had heretofore not been considered. There had never been a category in the Yellow Pages that would allow Coca-Cola to promote the image of its beverage, although local bottlers or distributors might have had their addresses and phone numbers printed.

So how did Yellow Spots attract national advertisers and have the temerity to ask up to $8 million from one potential client? They touted the unique advertising climate that the Yellow Pages presents:

- The circulation of all the Yellow Pages directories in the United States is about 100 million, 10 million more than there are homes in America. The Yellow Pages, of course, is usually used by more than one person.
- 50% of all customer references to the Yellow Pages result in a sale.
- 18% of all adults use the Yellow Pages at least once on any given day (and they average one and one-half uses per day). This is the equivalent of a rating of 18 on TV, emblematic of a successful show.
- Advertisers operate in a nonhostile environment in the Yellow Pages. Whereas the clutter of TV commercials is a bone of contention among viewers, users of the Yellow Pages do not feel oppressed by the number of ads. In a recent survey, 65% of Americans surveyed felt the number of ads in the Yellow Pages were "just about right"; 18% said they wished there were *more* ads; and only 8% complained there were too many ads.
- Yellow Pages are kept in the home all year long and, in many cases, much longer. Magazines—even those passed around within a family—tend to be thrown out within weeks.

Yellow Spots has already signed up Budget car and truck rentals and Sears Discovery card as major accounts, with others soon to follow. Although we admire the ingenuity of Yellow Spots, we're glad that the homely graphics of the promotional

DAVID FELDMAN

fillers won't totally disappear. Even Nelson and Samuels concede that they'll never take over all of the possible remnant space. They will be quite content with about 50 to 60% of it, thank you.

Submitted by Calvin Wong of Chapel Hill, North Carolina.

Why Is Flour Bleached?

Wheat isn't white. Flour is made out of wheat. So why is flour white?

First of all, all of the major flour producers, such as Pillsbury and General Mills, do make unbleached flour, which many breadmakers prefer. But the vast majority of flour sold to consumers is in the form of all-purpose bleached white flour, which is a combination of hard wheat flour (high in protein and best for making breads) and soft wheat flour (lower in protein and the best consistency for cakes and pastries).

Freshly milled white flour has a yellowish tinge, much like unbleached pasta, which consumers reject in favor of a pristine white. Flour processors have two ways to eradicate the yellow from wheat flour. If flour is stored and allowed to age naturally for several months, the yellow disappears as it is exposed to oxygen. But the cost of storing the bulky flour is prohibitive, so commercial flour is bleached artificially with bleaches such as benzoyl peroxide. Artificial bleaching works better than natural aging, which doesn't yield uniformity of color or maturation.

Mature flour produces better baking results and has a longer shelf life. So along with being bleached, all-purpose flour is artificially aged. While benzoyl peroxide merely bleaches flour, other agents such as azodicarbonamide and potassium bromide artificially age the flour as they bleach. The whole process is performed in twenty-four hours, and the bleach eventually decomposes into a harmless residue called benzoic acid when the flour is used.

WHEN DO FISH SLEEP? 325

Is there a down side to the bleaching process? Certain nutrients are lost, which is why all-purpose flour by law is enriched with nutrients. Some nutritionists are not sanguine about the results. The late Adele Davis was particularly rabid about the subject. She felt the machinery that grinds flour overheats it and gives it a precooked taste "comparable to last night's chops reheated." But she was particularly skeptical about the value of enriched flour:

> So-called "enriched" flour is my idea of outright dishonesty; at least 25 nutrients are largely removed during refining, and one-third of the original amount of iron, vitamin B and niacin may be replaced. Such flour is "enriched" just as you would be enriched by someone stealing 25 dollars from you and returning 99 cents.

Flour enrichment was mandated by the federal government in the early 1940s to compensate for the loss of nutrients that are eliminated from white flour. The flour industry contends that Adele Davis and other critics' objections to enrichment overstate the case. Although they concede that the bran and germ of wheat kernels in whole-wheat flour contain more nutrients than white flour, those nutrients lost (e.g., calcium, phosphorus, and potassium) tend to be found in other foods, and few consumers look toward baked goods as a source for these nutrients.

Although health-food advocates tend to belittle the nutritional value of white flour, the flour companies stress that bleaching in itself has never been a health hazard. The alternative to bleached flour, they say, is vastly more expensive flour.

What Is Goofy?

Goofy can't be a dog, claims our correspondent, or else he would look like Pluto, wouldn't he? Goofy is indeed a dog. Chihuahuas don't look like Doberman pinschers, so why should Goofy look like Pluto? Although we must admit that we don't know too

DAVID FELDMAN

many dogs who speak English and walk on two feet.

Pluto appeared several years before Goofy, in a tiny role in a Mickey Mouse short called "Chain Gang." Pluto's original name was Rover, and he was Minnie's dog, not Mickey's. But Mickey soon gained ownership, and Rover was renamed Pluto the Pup. Animator John Canemaker observes that Pluto's lack of speech and doglike walk were used to emphasize that Pluto was Mickey's pet and not his equal.

Goofy, on the other hand, was nobody's pet. His dogginess is indisputable, since his original name was Dippy Dawg. But Dippy had to pay his dues before he reached the summit of Goofyness. Dippy first played small roles in Mickey Mouse shorts in the early 1930s, and it wasn't until he was featured in the syndicated Mickey Mouse newspaper cartoons that he gained prominence in animated shorts.

Although Goofy was as loyal and loving as Pluto, he was not subservient. As his popularity grew, Goofy became a part of "The Gang," with costars Mickey Mouse and Donald Duck in a series of twelve cartoons in the late 1930s and early 1940s. Few remember that Goofy was married (to Mrs. Goofy) and that he was a proud parent (of Goofy, Jr.).

This Imponderable has been thrust at us many times since the release of the movie *Stand By Me*, in which a character muses about this question. How people can accept that a duck can survive being squashed by a refrigerator and then not believe that Goofy can be a dog, we'll never understand.

Submitted by Ashley Hoffar of Cincinnati, Ohio.

How Did the Toque Become the Traditional Chef's Hat? Does It Serve Any Functional Purpose?

Most men, in their daily lives, wear neither rags nor haute couture. We don a pair of pants and a shirt—maybe a sports coat or suit and tie if the occasion warrants it. But in the kitchen headware has always been schizophrenic. Cooks wear either ugly but functional hair nets or *toques blanches* ("white caps"), smart-looking caps with tops long enough to camouflage the heads of the entire Conehead family. Isn't there a middle ground? Why can't a chef wear a baseball cap or a derby? Can there possibly be a logical function for the shape of toques?

As early as the Roman and Greek Empires, master chefs were rewarded for their achievements by receiving special headware. For the ancients, laurel-studded caps were the honor.

In France up until the seventeenth century, chefs were awarded different colored caps depending upon their rank. Apprentices wore ordinary skull caps. During the early eighteenth century, Talleyrand's chef required his entire staff to don the

DAVID FELDMAN

toque blanche for sanitary reasons. The toque blanche was designed not only to keep the chef's hair from entering food but to register any stains upon the white background.

But this original cap was flat. The high hat gradually gained popularity not as a fashion statement, not to hide Mohawk hairdos, but to provide some ventilation for the head, as chefs frequently work under extremely hot conditions.

Viennese chef Antonin Careme, not willing to leave well enough alone, decided that the toque blanche needed still more oomph. He put a piece of round cardboard inside his toque to give the cap a stiffer, more dashing appearance. The cardboard has been replaced today by starch.

The toque blanche is no more functional than a hair net, and almost as silly looking. But as Shriners or Mouseketeers can testify, any hat bestowed upon someone as an honor is likely to be worn proudly by the recipient, regardless of how funny it looks.

Submitted by William Lickfield of Hamburg, New York.

When and Where Do Police Dogs Urinate and Defecate?

Our fearless correspondent, Eric Berg, notes that he trains his eyes for police dogs whenever he is in a big city and has yet to see nature call one of our canine protectors. "Have the police bred some sort of Bionic Dog?" Eric wonders.

Natural urges dog police dogs just as often as any Fido or Rover, but the difference is in the training; police dogs are much more disciplined than other dogs, or for that matter, most dog owners. Before the animals go on duty, trainers allow police dogs to run and go to the bathroom (well, not *literally* a bathroom) in the area where they are kept.

Part of the training of police dogs involves teaching the dog to control itself while on patrol and when in front of the public.

The dog is taught to signal when it has to "go," but is trained to keep itself under control in all circumstances.

Gerald S. Arenberg, editor of the official journal of the National Association of Chiefs of Police, alludes to the fact that "the dogs are given walks and care that is generally not seen by the public," the only hint we received that occasionally a dog might relieve itself while on duty.

Let's end this discussion here, before we run out of euphemisms.

Submitted by Eric Berg of Chicago, Illinois.

How Can Hurricanes Destroy Big Buildings But Leave Trees Unscathed?

Think of a hurricane as heavyweight boxer Sonny Liston, a powerful force of nature. A building in the face of Liston's onslaught is like George Foreman, strong but anchored to the ground. Without any means of flexibility or escape, the building is a sitting target. A building's massive size offers a greater surface area to the wind, allowing greater total force for the same wind pressure than a tree could offer.

But a tree in a hurricane is like Muhammad Ali doing the rope-a-dope. The tree is going to be hit by the hurricane, but it yields and turns and shuffles its way until the force of the hurricane no longer threatens it. In this case, the metaphor is literal: by bending with the wind, the tree and its leaves can sometimes escape totally unscathed.

Richard A. Anthes, director of the National Center for Atmospheric Research, offers another reason why we see so many buildings, and especially so many roofs, blown away during a hurricane. "Buildings offer a surface which provides a large aerodynamic lift, much as an airplane wing. This lift is often what causes the roof to literally be lifted off the building."

DAVID FELDMAN

We don't want to leave the impression that trees can laugh off a hurricane. Many get uprooted and are stripped of their leaves. Often we get the wrong impression because photojournalists love to capture ironic shots of buildings torn asunder while Mother Nature, in the form of a solitary, untouched, majestic tree, stands triumphant alongside the carnage.

Submitted by Daniel Marcus of Watertown, Massachusetts.

Why Are Downhill Ski Poles Bent?

Unlike the slalom skier's poles, which must make cuts in the snow to negotiate the gates, the main purpose of the downhill ski poles is to get the skier moving, into a tuck position . . . and then not get in the way.

According to Tim Ross, director of Coaches' Education for the United States Ski Coaches Association, the bends allow the racer "to get in the most aerodynamic position possible. This is extremely important at the higher speeds of downhill." Savings of hundredths of a second are serious business for competitive downhill skiers, even when they are attaining speeds of 60–75 miles per hour.

If the bends in the pole are not symmetrical, they are designed with careful consideration. Dave Hamilton, of the Professional Ski Instructors of America, reports that top-level ski racers have poles individually designed to fit their dimensions. Recreational skiers are now starting to bend their poles out of shape. According to Ross, the custom-made downhill ski poles may have as many as three to four different bend angles.

Funny. We haven't seen downhill skiers with three to four different bend angles in their bodies.

Submitted by Roy Welland of New York, New York.

Why Do So Many Mail-Order Ads Say to "Allow Six to Eight Weeks for Delivery"? Does It Really Take that Long for Companies to Process Orders?

This is a mystery we have pondered over ourselves, especially since these same companies that warn us of six-to-eight-week delivery schedules usually send us our goods within a few weeks. We talked to several experts in the mail-order field who assured us that any reasonably efficient operation should be able to ship items to customers within two to three weeks.

Many manufacturers farm out much or all of the processing of mail orders to specialized companies, called fulfillment houses. Some fulfillment houses do everything from receiving the initial letters from customers and obtaining the proper goods from their own warehouses to producing address labels, maintaining inventory control, and shipping out the package back to the customer.

DAVID FELDMAN

Dick Levinson, of the fulfillment company H.Y. Aids Group, told *Imponderables* that a fulfillment house should be able to gurarantee a client a turnaround of no more than five days from when a check is received until the package is shipped to the customer. A two- or three-day turnaround is the norm.

Do the mail order companies blame the post office? Why not? Everybody else does. But despite a few carpings, all agreed that even third-class packages tend to get delivered anywhere in the continental United States within a week.

Being paranoid types, we thought about a few nefarious reasons why mail-order companies might want to delay orders. Perhaps they want to create a little extra cash flow by holding on to checks for an extra month or so? No, insisted all of our sources.

How about advertising goods they don't have in stock? As checks clear, companies could pay for their inventory out of customer money rather than their own. It's possible but unlikely, said our panel. Stanley J. Fenvessey, founder of Fenvessey Consulting and perhaps the foremost expert on fulfillment, said that only a fly-by-night operation would try to get away with such shenanigans. He offered a few more benign explanations.

Sometimes a mail-order company, particularly one that specializes in imports or seasonal items, might run out of stock temporarily. By listing a delayed delivery date, the company forestalls complaints, even though it expects to deliver merchandise in half the stated time.

And in the magazine field, fledgling efforts sometimes try a "dry test," in which prospective subscribers are solicited by mail even though no magazine yet exists. Only if there is a high enough response rate will the magazine ever be produced.

The most compelling reason is the Federal Trade Commission's Mail Order Rule. The rule was established in 1974 after consumers complained in droves about late or nonexistent shipments of merchandise by mail-order operations. The President's Office of Consumer Affairs reported that the number of complaints registered against mail-order firms was second only to complaints about automobiles and auto services.

The Mail Order Rule states that a buyer has the right to

assume that goods will be shipped within the time specified in a solicitation and, "if no time period is clearly and conspicuously stated, within thirty days after receipt of a properly completed order from the buyer." Furthermore, when a seller is unable to ship merchandise within the time provisions of the rule, the seller must not only notify the buyer of the delay but also offer the option to the buyer to cancel the order.

Refunding money is not exactly any company's favorite thing to do, but the provisions about sending the notice of delay and option to cancel is perhaps more onerous to mail-order firms. Not only must the seller spend money on mailing these notices, but must somehow track the progress of each order to make sure it hasn't exceeded the 30-day limit. The bookkeeping burden is enormous.

Finally, we have arrived at the answer: By putting a shipping deadline of much longer than they think they will ever need, mail-order firms avoid having to comply with the provisions of the thirty-day rule whenever they run out of stock temporarily.

But don't these disclaimers discourage sales? After all, most items ordered by mail are available in retail stores as well. Dick Levinson suggests that most items ordered from magazines and newspapers are impulse items rather than necessities, and that most buyers are flexible about delivery schedules. Lynn Hamlin, book buyer for New York's NSI Syndications Inc., commented that space customers (those who order from newspapers and magazines) are less demanding than those who order from catalogs with toll-free phone numbers and who have the ability to ask a company operator how long the delivery will take. NSI advertisements guarantee shipment within 60 days, but usually are filled in two or three weeks. Ms. Hamlin notes that she has not seen any detrimental effect of the sixty-day guarantee on her company's sales, although she admits that around December 1, some potential customers might fear whether merchandise would arrive by Christmas.

Stanley Fenvessey informs us that about 75 to 90% of all catalog merchandise is delivered within two weeks, and insists

DAVID FELDMAN

that no large catalog house would ever print "six to eight weeks for delivery." One of Fenvessey's smaller clients, who owned a catalog company, printed "please allow four to five weeks for delivery" on his catalog. Fenvessey asked his client whether it really took this long to fulfill orders. The client replied that most orders were delivered in two weeks.

"So why put four to five weeks in the catalog?" asked Fenvessey.

"Because this way we avoid hassles when we are a few days late."

Fenvessey was convinced that the client couldn't see the forest for the trees. Fenvessey conducted a test in which two sets of catalogs were printed and shipped; the only difference between the two was that one announced that delivery would be between two to three weeks; the other, four to five weeks. The two to three week catalog drew 25% more orders, a huge difference.

Maybe many space advertisers are losing sales by scaring potential customers into thinking they're going to have to wait longer than they really will to get merchandise.

Submitted by Susie T. Kowalski of Middlefield, Ohio.

Why Are Silos Round?

The poser of this Imponderable, Susan Diffenderffer, insisted she had the correct answer in hand: "In a square silo, grain could form an air pocket and cause spontaneous combustion. There are no corners in a round silo."

Well, we think the spontaneous combustion theory is a tad apocalyptical, but you have the rest of the story right. Actually, at one time silos were square or rectangular. Fred Hatch, a farmer from Illinois, built a square wooden silo in 1873. But the square corners didn't allow Hatch to pack the silo tightly enough. As a result, air got in the silo and spoiled much of the feed. To the rescue came Wisconsin agricultural scientist, Franklin H. King, who built a round silo ten years later. The rest is silage history.

Why is it so important to shut air out of a silo? The mold that spoils grain cannot survive without air. Without air, the grass and corn actually ferment while in the silo, inducing a chemical change in the silage that makes it palatable all through the winter season.

Before silos were invented, cows gave less milk during winter because they had no green grass to eat. Silos gave the cows the lavish opportunity to eat sorghums all year long.

Submitted by Susan C. Diffenderffer of Cockeysville, Maryland.

Why Does Dialing 9 Usually Get You an Outside Line in a Hotel? And Why Does 8 Open a Long-Distance Line?

For many years we've been looking at want ads in the newspaper and seeing positions open for PBX operators. We've always wondered what the heck they did. "PBX" sure sounds threateningly high-tech. Little did we know that we were already experts in the field.

PBX systems are simply telephone lines designed for communication within one building or business that are also capable of interfacing with the outside world. Most large hotels have a PBX system. When you lift your phone up in your room, you become a PBX station user whether you like it or not.

Most PBX systems reserve numbers one through seven for dial access to other internal PBX stations. In a hotel, this allows a guest in one room to call another room directly. Decades ago, one might have dialed for the operator to perform this function, but hotels found that patrons preferred the greater speed of direct access; and of course, direct dialing saved hotels the labor costs of operators.

There is no inherent reason why 4 or 2 *couldn't* be the access code for an outside line or long-distance access, but Victor J. Toth, representing the Multi-Tenant Telecommunications Association, explains how the current practice began:

> The level "9" code is usually used by convention in all commercial PBX and Centrex as the dialing code for reaching an outside line. This number was chosen because it was usually high enough in the number sequence so as not to interfere with a set of assigned station numbers (or, in the case of a hotel, a room number).

Likewise, the 8 is sufficiently high in the number sequence to not interfere with other station numbers and has become the conventional way to gain access to long-distance services.

Toth adds that it is easy to deny level 9 class of service to a particular phone or set of phones if desired. Most hotels, for example, make it impossible for someone using a lobby phone to dial outside the hotel, let alone long distance.

Why Can't (Or Won't) Western Union Transmit an Exclamation Mark in a Telegram?

Many of the origins of the customs we now take for granted are lost in obscurity. We are thankful to Paul N. Dane, executive director of the Society of Wireless Pioneers, who led us to two gentlemen, W.K. "Bill" Dunbar, and Colonel Ronald G. Martin, who could answer these two Imponderables authoritatively.

Mr. Dunbar informs us that the original Morse code alphabet (but not the international code used for cablegrams and radiograms) did indeed provide for the exclamation mark: - - - - expressed it. "The early teletype machines with a three-row keyboard may not have provided for the exclamation mark, and although later equipment did, it might not have been capable of conveying the exclamation point into a Telex circuit."

According to Colonel Martin:

> It is very easy to cause an error during the transmission of a message with a lot of punctuation therein. Therefore, Western Union, in order to prevent lawsuits, abolished it.

Even if there were technological problems in printing an exclamation mark, a more compelling reason existed to shun it and other punctuation: Punctuation marks were charged as if they were words.

Submitted by Fred T. Beeman of Wailuku, Hawaii.

Why Do Telegrams End Sentences with STOP Rather than with a Period?

Western Union, throughout most of its history, has charged extra for periods as well as exclamation marks. But the reasons for the exclusion of periods and the inclusion of STOP are fascinating and highly technical. Bill Dunbar, president of the Morse Telegraph Club, explains:

> In certain instances the word STOP, when used as a period, was free. I believe this was the case with transoceanic cablegrams. Hollywood sometimes showed STOP in domestic telegrams, which may have given the impression it was common usage. At one time when competition between Western Union and Postal Telegraph was keen, STOP was free, but this did not last long and usually it was a chargeable word, so naturally it wasn't used much.
>
> The main reason for periods not appearing was a procedural one—the period was used to indicate the beginning and end of the body of a message. The preamble (i.e., call letters of sending office, the number of words in a message, type of service, and type of payment), origin city, the time and date were sent first. This was followed by the word TO, after which the receiving operator would drop down a line or two and move to the left of the page to write the address.

At the end of the address, a period was sent, signifying that the next characters would begin the text of the message. At the end of the message, the sender would send another period and say SIG (signature), and the copying operator would drop down two lines to write the signature; he would also add the time the message was copied. If there *was* a period in the message, it was converted to STOP for transmission.

The words TO, SIG and the periods were not written on the telegram, since they were procedural signals. Decimals were transmitted by sending the word DOT as 18 DOT 5. This might seem clumsy, but it eliminated any ambiguity as to whether a decimal point or the end of a message was indicated.

PERIOD must have been considered instead of STOP to signify the period, but probably was rejected for one simple reason: STOP is two letters shorter. Colonel Martin adds that the word PERIOD is more likely to cause confusion when a telegram concerns time.

Both Martin and Dunbar emphasize how important brevity of language and speed of transmission has always been to Western Union. But customers have proven to be just as frugal in their own way. Traditionally, Western Union charged a basic rate that allowed for ten free words. Any extra words or punctuation marks cost extra. Sometimes the need to squeeze a lot of information into ten words tested the ingenuity of the sender, as Mr. Dunbar's story illustrates:

> The story is told of a man who sent the following message: BRUISES HURT ERASED AFFORD ERECTED ANALYSIS HURT TOO INFECTIONS DEAD
> Translated it reads: "Bruce is hurt he raced a Ford he wrecked it Aunt Alice is hurt too in fact she's dead"

Writers who are paid by the word try to be as verbose as possible. But a writer who has to *pay* by the word will try to squeeze nineteen words into ten.

Submitted by Eileen LaForce of Weedsport, New York.

DAVID FELDMAN

Why Are Most Snack-Food Items, Such as Chips, Cakes, and Popcorn, Prepriced (on the Package) by the Manufacturers?

How often have you scoured the aisles of your local supermarket looking for the elusive item on your grocery list? You despair of ever finding what you need when you encounter a young man arduously arranging packages on the shelf. "Where can I find the artificial coloring?" you inquire.

"I don't know. I don't work here," replies the man.

Why can't you ever find the people who supposedly *do* work at the damn store? This poignant episode, repeated in grocery stores throughout the land, explains—believe it or not—why most snack items are prepriced by the manufacturers.

Most items in a supermarket, such as canned goods, are sent to the store by a warehouse distributor who handles many different brands. Snack-food manufacturers work on "store-door distribution," providing full service to retailers. Potato chips or popcorn are brought to the stores in trucks displaying the logo of one company. The agent for the manufacturer rids the shelves of any unsold packages with elapsed expiration dates, restocks, and straightens up the shelves to make the company's selling environment look attractive.

Retailers have come to expect this kind of full-service treatment from the snack-food industry. Next to the expense of cashiers, pricing items is one of the costliest labor costs of grocery retailers: Stores welcome prepricing by the industry.

Why do snack-food manufacturers go along with providing extra service to stores? Although manufacturers like retaining the control of pricing, according to Chris Abernathy, of the Borden Snack Group, fear of retail overcharging is not the main purpose for the practice. By stamping the price themselves, Borden and other snack-food companies can run citywide or regional promotions by cutting the price on the package itself.

Al Rickard, of the Snack Food Association, stresses that by stamping prices on packages themselves, manufacturers can guarantee *equality* of prices to outlets that sell their products. Snack foods are sold not only in grocery stores but in convenience stores, bowling centers, service stations, and other venues that are not used to putting price stickers on food items. Those establishments are more likely to sell snacks when they don't feel they will be undercut in price by supermarkets.

Most important, with store-door distribution manufacturers can assure themselves that their products are not languishing on the shelves because retailers are refusing to pull old goods. What all of the food items with prepricing have in common is their perishability. Most salted snack foods have shelf lives of approximately two weeks. Other prepriced items, such as doughnuts and bread, may have even shorter expiration dates. If they have to preprice snack items to guarantee the proper rotation of their goods, it is a small price to pay.

Submitted by Herbert Kraut of Forest Hills, New York.

Why Are the Commercials Louder than the Programming on Television?

Having lived in apartments most of our adult lives, we developed a theory about this Imponderable. Let us use a hypothetical example to explain our argument.

Let's say a sensitive, considerate yet charismatic young man —we'll call him "Dave"—is taking a brief break from his tireless work to watch TV late at night. As an utterly sympathetic and empathic individual, "Dave" puts the volume at a low level so as not to wake the neighbors who are divided from him by tissue-thin walls. Disappointed that "Masterpiece Theatre" is not run at 2:00 A.M., "Dave" settles for a rerun of "Hogan's Heroes." While he is studying the content of the show to determine what the character of Colonel Klink says about our contemporary society, a used-car commercial featuring a screaming huckster comes on at a much louder volume.

What does "Dave" do? He goes up to the television and

lowers the volume. But then the show comes back on, and "Dave" can't hear it. Ordinarily, "Dave" would love to forgo watching such drivel, so that he could go back to his work as, say, a writer. But he is now determined to ascertain the sociological significance of "Hogan's Heroes." So for the sake of sociology, "Dave" gets back up and turns the volume back on loud enough so that he can hear but softly enough not to rouse the neighbors. When the next set of commercials comes on, the process is repeated.

Isn't it clear? Commercials are louder to force couch potatoes (or sociological researchers) to get some exercise! When one is slouched on the couch, the walk to and from the television set constitutes aerobic exercise.

Of course, not everyone subscribes to our theory.

Advertising research reveals, unfortunately, that while commercials with quick cuts and frolicking couples win Clio awards, irritating commercials sell merchandise. And it is far more important for a commercial to be noticed than to be liked or admired. Advertisers would like their commercials to be as loud as possible.

The Federal Communications Commission has tried to solve the problem of blaring commercials by setting maximum volume levels called "peak audio voltage." But the advertising community is way ahead of the FCC. Through a technique called "volume compression," the audio transmission is modified *so that all sounds, spoken or musical, are at or near the maximum allowable volume.* Even loud rock music has peaks and valleys of loudness, but with volume compression, the average volume of the commercial will register as loudly as the peaks of regular programming, without violating FCC regulations.

The networks are not the villain in this story. In fact, CBS developed a device to measure and counterattack volume compression, so the game among the advertisers, networks, and the FCC continues. Not every commercial uses volume compression, but enough do to foil local stations everywhere.

Of course, it could be argued that advertisers have only the

DAVID FELDMAN

best interests of the public at heart. After all, they are offering free aerobic exercise to folks like "Dave." And for confirmed couch potatoes, they are pointing out the advantages of remote-control televisions.

Submitted by Tammy Madill of Millington, Tennessee.
Thanks also to Joanne Walker of Ashland, Massachusetts.

Why Is U.S. Paper Money Green When Most Countries Color-Code Their Currency?

Until well into the nineteenth century, paper money was relatively rare in the United States. But banknotes became popular in the mid-1800s. These bills were printed in black but included colored tints to help foil counterfeiters.

However, cameras then in existence saw everything in black, rendering color variations in bills meaningless when reproduced photographically. According to the U.S. Treasury, the counterfeiters took advantage:

> the counterfeiter soon discovered that the colored inks then in use could easily be removed from a note without disturbing the black ink. He could eradicate the colored portion, photograph the remainder, and then make a desired number of copies to be overprinted with an imitation of the colored parts.

Tracy R. Edson, one of the founders of the American Bank Note Company, developed the solution. He developed an ink that could not be erased without hurting the black coloring. Edson was rewarded for his discovery by receiving a contract from the U.S. government to produce notes for them. Edson's counterfeit-proof ink had a green tint.

In the nineteenth century, notes were produced by private firms as well as the treasury. But all notes, regardless of where they were printed, were issued in green, presumably to provide uniformity.

WHEN DO FISH SLEEP?   345

Could Edson have chosen blue or red instead of a green tint? Certainly. Although our sources couldn't tell us why green was the original choice, the treasury does have information about why the green tint was retained in 1929, when small-sized notes were introduced:

> the use of green was continued because pigment of that color was readily available in large quantity, the color was relatively high in its resistance to chemical and physical changes, and green was psychologically identified with the strong and stable credit of the Government.

And besides, "redbacks" or "bluebacks" just don't have a ring to them.

Other countries vary the coloring of their bills as well as their size. And why not? Different sizes would enable the sighted but especially the legally blind to sort the denominations of bills easily. But despite occasional rumblings from legislators, the Treasury Department stands by its greenbacks.

Submitted by Paul Stossel of New York, New York. Thanks also to Charles Devine of Plum, Pennsylvania; and Kent Hall of Louisville, Kentucky.

Why Do We Have to Close Our Eyes When We Sneeze?

We thought we'd get off easy with this mystery. Sure, a true Imponderable can't be answered by a standard reference work, but would a poke in a few medical texts do our readers any harm?

We shouldn't have bothered. We understand now that a sneeze is usually a physiological response to an irritant of some sort. We learned that there is a $10 word for sneezing (the "sternutatory reflex") and that almost all animals sneeze. But what exactly happens when we sneeze? Here's a short excerpt from one textbook's explanation of a sneeze:

DAVID FELDMAN

> When an irritant contacts the nasal mucosa, the trigeminal nerve
> provides the affect limb for impulses to the pons, and medullai
> Preganglionic efferent fibers leave these latter two structures via
> the intermediate nerve, through geniculate ganglion to the greater
> petrosal nerve, through the vividian nerve and then synapse at the
> sphenopalatine ganglion . . .

Get this outta here! Until Cliff Notes comes out with a companion to rhinology textbooks, we'll go to humans for the answers.

Our rhinologist friend, Dr. Pat Barelli, managed to read those textbooks and still writes like a human being. He explains that the sneeze reflex is a protective phenomenon:

> The sneeze clears the nose and head and injects O_2 into the cells
> of the body, provoking much the same physiological effect as sniffing snuff or cocaine. When a person sneezes, all body functions
> cease. Tremendous stress is put on the body by the sneeze, especially the eyes.

As Dr. G. H. Drumheller, of the International Rhinological Society, put it, "we close our eyes when sneezing to keep the eyes from extruding." While nobody is willing to test the hypothesis, there is more than a grain of truth to the folk wisdom that closing your eyes when you sneeze keeps them from popping out, but probably not more than three or four grains.

*Submitted by Linda Rudd of Houston, Texas. Thanks also to
Michelle Zielinski of Arnold, Missouri; Helen Moore of New
York, New York; Jose Elizondo of Pontiac, Michigan; Amy
Harding of Dixon, Kentucky; and Gail Lee of Los Angeles,
California.*

Why Don't Grazing Animals that Roll in or Eat Poison Ivy Ever Seem to Get Blisters or Itching in Their Mouths?

A few of the many veterinarians we spoke to had seen allergic reactions to poison ivy among animals but all agreed it was exceedingly rare. Poison ivy is not really poison. Humans develop an allergic reaction because of a local hypersensitivity to the oil in the plant. Veterinarian Anthony L. Kiorpes, a professor at the University of Wisconsin-Madison School of Veterinary Medicine, informed us that the same plant that may cause a severe reaction in one human may not affect another person at all.

Elizabeth Williams, of the University of Wyoming College of Agriculture, notes that she has never seen an allergic reaction in deer, but allows:

> It's possible some deer might be allergic to it but we just don't see the reaction because they are covered with hair. Or it may be that only a very few deer are allergic, and they learn to stay away from poison ivy.

DAVID FELDMAN

Veterinarian Ben Klein feels that most domestic animals have a built-in immunity to contact allergy dermatitis, such as poison ivy. Furthermore, that same hair Dr. Williams mentioned hiding an allergic reaction also shields the skin against potential reactions, according to veterinary dermatologist Peter Ihrke.

Why don't ruminants break out when they eat poison ivy or poison oak? Dr. Don E. Bailey, secretary-treasurer of the American Association of Sheep and Goat Practitioners, explains that even if these animals had a tendency toward allergic reactions, which they don't, the mucus membrane in their mouths is very thick and heavy.

The one animal that most often seems to contract allergic reactions to poison ivy is the dog. Dogs love to roll around in the worst imaginable things. Dr. Ihrke notes that most dogs can withstand the exposure to poison ivy but many of their owners cannot. The owners pet the dogs and come down with severe reactions. Similarly, an innocent vet will examine a dog and break out in a rash, the victim of a communicable disease that doesn't afflict the carrier.

Submitted by Karole Rathouz of Mehlville, Missouri.

Why Don't Queen-Sized Sheets Fit My Queen-Sized Bed?

Queen-sized beds expanded from 60″ x 75″ to 60″ x 80″ in the early 1960s. You would think that more than twenty-five years would be a sufficient amount of time to manufacture sheets large enough to cover the expanded surface area. And it was.

The problem is that sheets are designed to cover mattresses, and the linen industry has no control over what the mattress manufacturers are doing. And what the bed companies are doing lately is driving sheetmakers nuts. As Richard Welsh, senior vice president of Cannon Mills Company, succinctly summarizes:

The sheet industry has experienced problems with fitted sheets for all sizes, not only queen size. The problem is primarily due to the fact that mattress manufacturers have been increasing the depth of their mattresses. As one tries to get an edge on the other, they outsize them by half an inch. There are no standard mattress depths.

When Mr. Welsh first wrote to *Imponderables*, in December 1986, he complained about how the sheet industry, accustomed to fitting six-and-one-half- to seven-inch-deep mattresses, watched in horror as depth inflation hit. In the early 1980s, Cannon increased the length of their sheets to accommodate mattresses from eight to eight-and-one-half inches deep. But soon, the nine-inch barrier was broken. Cannon responded to this problem in 1987 by manufacturing sheets "guaranteed to fit." These sheets could cover a mattress nine-and-one-half inches thick.

But the mattressmakers never stopped. They invented a whole new genre of bed, the "pillow top" mattress, with pockets of polyester fill on top. Pillow tops have increased the crown space (the highest point of padding) on some mattresses to as high as one foot to twelve-and-one-half inches.

The standard queen-size flat sheet is now 90" x 102", which is more than sufficient to cover the 60" x 80" queen-size beds if they don't continue the creep upward. But creep they probably will. On the low end of the market, six-inch-thick mattresses still are available. If you have sheets that are longer than you need, have compassion for the sucker with the pillow top. The same sheet that is too long for you probably isn't long enough to tuck under his mattress.

P.S. It was inevitable. Fieldcrest and Wamsutta, among others, are now manufacturing sheets specifically for pillow top mattresses.

DAVID FELDMAN

Why Is There Cotton Stuffed in Prescription and Over-the-Counter Medicine Bottles? What Happens If I Take Out the Cotton? Why Aren't Alka-Seltzer Containers Stuffed with Cotton?

The main purpose of the cotton stuffed in medicine vials is to prevent rattling and subsequent breakage of pills during shipment. But why cotton? Because of its absorbency, cotton helps keep medications dry. David G. Miller, associate director of the National Association of Retail Druggists, points out that moisture will destroy most drugs.

Still, all the druggists we spoke to recommended taking out the cotton once the container is opened for use. Melvin T. Wilczynski, of the Lane Drug Company, explains that the absorptive characteristics of cotton, which help keep pills dry during shipment, also are capable of absorbing moisture from the environment. If the cotton gets wet and re-enters the bottle, the effectiveness of the medication is jeopardized.

WHEN DO FISH SLEEP?   351

Excess heat and light are also capable of breaking down medications. For this reason, it makes no sense to keep pills in the kitchen, where they are exposed to the heat of ovens, or outside the medicine cabinet in the bathroom, where they could be exposed to harsh light or space heaters.

At one time, Miles Laboratories did put cotton into Alka-Seltzer containers, but found that consumers couldn't be trusted. If you accidentally get an Alka-Seltzer tablet wet, you get premature fizz—a temporary thrill perhaps, but one that will do you no good when a bout of indigestion sets in.

Miles provides a styrofoam cushion to protect tablets during shipping, but they recommend throwing away the cushion once the bottle is opened. Although styrofoam is not as absorbent as cotton, it is perfectly capable of generating bubbles when wet.

Submitted by Andrew Neiman of Dallas, Texas.

Why Do Bagels Have Holes?

In *Why Do Clocks Run Clockwise? and Other Imponderables,* we explained why doughnuts have holes. We were pretty smug about our accomplishment too. Then a letter arrives from Jay Howard Horne asking us why bagels have holes. Will there ever be a stop to this mania for knowledge about hole origins?

Nobody knows for sure who created the first bagel. Chances are, it was an accident precipitated by a piece of yeast-laden dough falling into hot water. But we do know who first called a bagel a "bagel." In 1683, the first Viennese coffeehouse was opened by a Polish adventurer, who introduced a new bread called the *beugel*. When Austrians emigrated to the United States in the next two centuries, the beugel was re-christened the bagel.

So what was a Polish man doing opening a coffeehouse in Vienna and creating a hole-y bread?

DAVID FELDMAN

The king of Poland, Jan Sobiesky, had become a hero in Austria in the late seventeenth century by driving off armed invaders from Turkey. In their escape, the Turks left behind sacks of enough coffee to keep every citizen of Vienna up nights for a month, inspiring the opening of many a coffeehouse in Vienna.

The coffeehouse owner took a popular yeast bread called kipfel and reshaped it into the bagel shape we know and love today. The bread was meant to resemble the stirrups of brave King Sobiesky, who fought on horseback to save Vienna from the Turks. "Bagel" is derived from the German word for stirrup, "bugel."

Submitted by Jay Howard Horne of Pittsburgh, Pennsylvania.

Do the Digits in a Social Security Number Have Any Particular Meaning?

Now that the Social Security number has become a virtual citizenship identification number, paranoid types have become convinced that each digit is another way for Uncle Sam to poke into our private lives. No, the government can't tell by looking at our Social Security number whether we are registered Democrats or Republicans, whether we are in the highest income-tax bracket or are on welfare, or even whether we have committed a crime.

Under the current system, the first three digits of a Social Security number indicate the state of residence of the holder at the time the number was issued. The remaining digits have no special meaning.

Before 1973, Social Security numbers were assigned by local Social Security offices. The first three digits were assigned based on the location of the Social Security office rather than the residence of the issuee. Opportunists used to scoop up several different Social Security numbers by applying for cards at several different offices, which led to the current practice of issuing all numbers from the central Social Security office in Baltimore. According to Dorcas R. Hardy, commissioner of Social Security, the first three digits of a person's Social Security number are now determined by the ZIP code of the mailing address shown on the application for a Social Security number.

Although the first three digits of the Social Security number do not correspond exactly to the first three digits of that state's zip codes, the lowest Social Security numbers, like their ZIP code counterparts, start in New England and then get progressively larger as they spread westward. Numbers 001–003 are assigned to New Hampshire, and the highest numbers assigned to the 50 states are New Mexico's 585. The Virgin Islands (580), Puerto Rico (580–584, 596–599), Guam (586), American Samoa (586), and the Philippine Islands (586) are also assigned specific three-digit codes.

Until 1963, railroad employees were issued a special series of numbers starting with the digits 700–728. Although this practice is now discontinued, these numbers remain the highest ever issued. No one has ever cracked the 729 plus barrier.

Submitted by Douglas Watkins, Jr. of Hayward, California. Thanks also to Jose Elizondo of Pontiac, Michigan; Kenneth Shaw of San Francisco, California; and Rebecca Lash of Ithaca, New York.

Why Do the Light Bulbs in My Lamps Loosen After I've Put Them in Place?

An unscientific poll conducted by the Imponderables Research Board indicates that creeping bulb loosening is a problem for many, although a majority of respondents never faced the problem. Is some sadist running around loosening the bulbs of selected victims?

Perhaps, but a natural explanation is more likely. The greatest culprit in loosening light bulbs is vibration. Friction keeps the socket threads of a light bulb tightly fitted into the base threads of a fixture. J. Robert Moody, of General Electric, informed Imponderables that "vibration weakens the friction force, allowing the light bulb to back out of the socket on its own. If the vibration is intense, like on an automobile or an airplane, then a bayonet base must be used in place of the screw-threaded base."

Perhaps that incessant bass drone emanating from the

WHEN DO FISH SLEEP?   355

heavy-metal freak upstairs caused your problem. The only solution might be the purchase of a bayonet base for your lamp or a bayonet to use on your neighbor.

Submitted by Darryl Williams of New York, New York.

HOW Are Olives Pitted? How Do They Stuff Olives?

Until recently, the vast majority of olives were stuffed by hand. Olives were held in cups, and a crude machine operated with a foot treadle would punch out the pit while another element cut a hole on top of the olive simultaneously. A worker would then inspect the olive. If it was acceptable, she would take a pimento, onion, anchovy or other filling and manually stick it in the hole.

Obviously, olive companies were desperately in need of a high-tech solution to the slowness of their production line. Not only was the pitting and stuffing operation labor-intensive, but the machines would rip olives to shreds and leave pit fragments as a "bonus" for unsuspecting consumers. Even more damaging, the U.S. Food and Drug Administration would routinely refuse to allow importation of mangled olives (almost all green olives are imported from Spain).

Automation revolutionized the olive industry in the early 1970s. Modern machines, typically containing twenty-four separate stations, are capable of stuffing twelve hundred to fifteen hundred olives a minute. The olives are pitted in one movement, and the pimento is inserted with ease.

The down side to this otherwise lovely story is that automation has encouraged olive distributors to dump natural pimentos in favor of pimentos "enhanced" with paste and binders. These additives enable the pimento to be fashioned into an endless ribbon of red stuff. The machine then cuts the ribbon to exact specifications prior to stuffing the cavity, so that larger olives receive wider strips of pimento–red stuff. Of course, the pimento–red stuff tastes more like red stuff than pimento, but this is the price we pay for progress.

Machines now exist to sort olives by size, to inject brine into a jar, to pack olives in jars, to stuff olives with pimentos, to slice olives, and to seal olive jars. Until the 1980s almost all olives were packed into jars by hand. Fancy Spanish olives are often placed in geometric patterns to induce impulse purchases by consumers. According to Edward Culleton, of the Green Olive Trade Association, American consumers have never developed brand loyalty, so shoppers have traditionally been receptive to eye-catching arrangements of olives. About 90% of green olives are now packed by machine rather than by hand, so "place packs" (hand-packed jars) are likely to be a specialty item in the future. In fact, Spain now exports hand-pitted stuffed olives in beautiful crystal jars as a luxury gift item—and the olives are stuffed with real pimentos.

Submitted by Helen Tvorik of Mayfield Heights, Ohio.

Why Is One Side of a Halibut Dark and the Other Side Light?

With the price of halibut these days, we might assume that we are paying extra for the two-tone job. But nature supplies halibut with two colors for a less mercenary reason.

The eyeless side of the halibut is light, requiring no camouflage. But the side with eyes is dark. Like other flat fish that swim on one side, the halibut is dark on the side exposed to the light. Robert L. Collette, associate director of the National Fisheries Institute, describes the coloring as "a natural defense system." The dark side is at top "so that predators looking down upon halibut are less likely to detect their presence."

This camouflage system is adapted for fish and mammals that swim upright. They have dark backs and white undersides to elude their predators.

What Is the Difference Between a "Mountain" and a "Hill"?

Although we think you are making a mountain out of a molehill, we'll answer this Imponderable anyway. Most American geographers refer to a hill as a natural elevation that is smaller than 1,000 feet. Anything above 1,000 feet is usually called a mountain. In Great Britain, the traditional boundary line between hill and mountain is 2,000 feet.

Still, some geographers are not satisfied with this definition. "Hill" conjures up rolling terrain; "mountains" connote abrupt, peaked structures. A mound that rises two feet above the surrounding earth may attain an elevation of 8,000 feet, if it happens to be located in the middle of the Rockies, whereas a 999-foot elevation, starting from a sea-level base, will appear massive. For this reason, most geographers feel that "mountain" may be used for elevations under 1,000 feet if they rise abruptly from the surrounding terrain.

WHEN DO FISH SLEEP?

The *Oxford English Dictionary* states that "hill" may also refer to non-natural formations, such as sand heaps, mounds, or, indeed, molehills.

Submitted by Thomas J. Schoeck of Slingerlands, New York. Thanks also to F. S. Sewell of San Jose, California.

Why Aren't There License Plates on the Back of Many Big Trucks on the Highway?

Fewer than two-thirds of the fifty states require license plates on both the front and back of a commercial truck. Why do truckers, unlike automobile owners, only have to display one plate in many states?

Presumably, tractors will be pulling trailers most of the time, so the only time we are likely to see a tractor with two plates is when it is "deadheading" (not towing a trailer). Then, the back license plate is likely to be obscured by the trailer anyway, and be of little use to police.

Because many tractors are crossing borders constantly, the licensing of commercial tractors and trailers can be complicated. According to Jan Balkin, of the American Trucking Associations,

All trailers must have license plates from the state in which it is licensed. That state may not necessarily be the same as the state in which the tractor is licensed; carriers may license the tractor and trailer in different states, depending upon certain financial decisions as to which state(s) the carrier chooses.

DAVID FELDMAN

Why Do Mayors Hand Out Keys to Their City?

We've all seen those silly ceremonies on TV where a grinning mayor hands a three-foot-long key to a minor celebrity as flashbulbs pop. But we have always wondered: Why does the recipient need a key to the city? He's already *in* the city.

Actually, this ceremony has legitimate historical antecedents. In the Middle Ages, most large cities were walled. Visitors could enter and exit only through gates that were locked at sundown and reopened at dawn.

Mike Brown, of the United States Conference of Mayors, told *Imponderables* that gatekeepers used keys to open and close the gates. These keys were closely guarded, for they were crucial in preventing military attacks. If a key was passed to an honored visitor, it indicated total trust in him.

Today, a mayor no longer threatens the security of her domain by handing out the key to the city, and the honor is more likely a public relations stunt than in gratitude for service or accomplishment. But the meaning is the same. By handing out the key to the city, the mayor says, "Come back any time and you don't even have to knock. We trust you."

What Is the Purpose of the Beard on a Turkey?

All of our poultry experts felt that the beard has no specific anatomical function, but this doesn't mean the beard has no purpose. The beard is a secondary sex characteristic of the male, a visual differentiation between the sexes. How could a hen possibly resist the sexual allure of the beard of a strutting Tom?

Submitted by Mrs. Anabell Cregger of Wytheville, Virginia.

WHEN DO FISH SLEEP?   361

WHY Are Banking Hours So Short?

Nine to three, five days a week. Not a bad job if you can get it, eh? Short banking hours have always fit the needs of bankers and industry, but have not been convenient for retail customers. The banks are open only when the average person is working or going to school.

Mind you, workers in the bank industry don't get to leave the door at the stroke of three. Tellers, for example, must count cash and report their balances to a central processing center. Before automation, reconciling their books might have taken a little longer, but not significantly so.

Executives in the banking industry, who do not have to mind the day-to-day transactions of retail customers, have plenty of phone and social contacts to make after banking hours. When we posed this Imponderable to Joan Silverman, of Citibank, she was incredulous that we had not heard of the rule of 3/6/3.

"What is the rule of 3/6/3?" we asked.

"It's simple," she replied. "If you want to be a successful

362   DAVID FELDMAN

banker, you pay 3% to depositors; you charge 6% on loans to customers; and you hit the golf course by 3 P.M." Based on the interest rates mentioned, this obviously is a very old rule.

Government regulations once restricted the hours during which banks could be open for business. Gentleman bankers conducted most of their business on the golf course while tellers were back at the ranch settling their ledgers.

With computerization, there is no reason why banks couldn't have much longer hours. The tradition of the 9 A.M. to 3 P.M. Monday through Friday bank is preserved because of the bottom line: The banks figure that if they stay open later or open on weekends, they will increase retail customers' simple—and to the bank, often unprofitable—transactions, such as depositing or withdrawing money from checking and savings accounts. Most other businesses are closed on weekends and evenings—*they* don't have demanding, long hours.

Bank hours generally are extended only when there is a competitive marketing reason to do so, usually when a new bank or new branch needs to build new accounts and can advertise extended hours. Ohio's Banc One, Dayton, for example, opens many branches on Saturdays and even Sundays. Many of their branches are located in malls; before Banc One opened on weekends, it was often the only business closed in the whole shopping center. Much to Banc One's surprise, according to *American Banker:*

> the volume of teller activity during Sunday's four-hour shift has been greater than the amount of teller activity during a normal seven-hour weekday.

Obviously, if it were cost-effective for most banks to be open longer, they would do it. Automated teller machines have effectively opened the doors of many banks twenty-four hours a day anyway. Unlike bank employees, ATMs don't complain when they aren't excused to leave for the golf course at 3 P.M.

Submitted by Dorio Barbieri of Mountain View, California.
Thanks also to Herbert Kraut of Forest Hills, New York.

Speaking of ATMs ... When They Were Introduced, ATMs Were Supposed to Save Labor Costs for the Banks and Ultimately Save Money for the Customers. Now My Bank Is Charging Money for Each ATM Transaction. What Gives?

The banking industry is being squeezed from two sides. On the one hand, customers now demand interest on checking accounts and money-market rates on savings accounts. Yet they also want services provided for free.

While it is true that an ATM transaction generally is cheaper for the banks than the same transaction conducted by a teller, banks have spent a fortune buying and installing these machines. As David Taylor, of the Bank Administration Institute put it, "As the customer gets more and more convenience and control of his banking options, he will have to pay for each option one at a time." The alternative would be a return to having no service fees but also to customers getting lower interest rates

DAVID FELDMAN

on CDs and checking and savings accounts, which banks know would be suicidal for them. As bank deregulation accelerates and banks are allowed to compete with brokerages and other financial institutions, expect to see increasing service charges.

Most banks do not charge for ATM transactions. If there are two big banks in a town, each knows that if it charges for ATM transactions, the other bank will advertise that its machines are free. So the choice between free and pay ATMs is left to what the banking business calls "competitive reasons," which is fiduciary lingo for "if we think we can get away with charging for it, we will."

Why Does Granulated Sugar Tend to Clump Together?

It ain't the heat, it's the humidity. Sugar is hygroscopic, meaning that it is capable of absorbing moisture from the air and changing its form as a result of the absorption. When sugar is subjected to 80% or higher relative humidity, the moisture dissolves a thin film of sugar on the surface of the sugar crystal. Each of these crystals turns into a sugar solution, linked to one another by a "liquid bridge."

According to Jerry Hageney, of the Amstar Corporation, when the relative humidity decreases, "the sugar solution gives up its moisture, causing the sugar to become a crystal again. The crystals joined by the liquid bridge become as one crystal. Thus, hundreds of thousands of crystals become linked together to form a rather solid lump."

Although we can't see the moist film on sugar exposed to high humidity, it won't pour quite as smoothly as sugar that has never been exposed to moisture. But when it dries up again, the liquid bridge is a strong one. Bruce Foster, of Sugar Industry Technologists, told us that the technology used to make sugar cubes utilizes this natural phenomenon.

To make sugar cubes, water is added to sugar in a cube-shaped mold. After the sugar forms into cubes, it is dried out, and voilà! you have a chemical-free way to keep sugar stuck together.

Submitted by Patty Payne of Seattle, Washington.

Why Do Two Horses in an Open Field Always Seem to Stand Head to Tail?

Horses, unlike people, don't bother to make the pretense of listening to what companions have to say. And also, unlike humans, horses have tails. Rather than stand around face-to-face boring each other, figures the horse, wouldn't it be more practical to stand head to tail? This way, with one swish of the tail, a horse can rid its body of flies and other insects while knocking the bugs off of the head of the other horse.

In cold weather, horses are more likely to stand head-to-head, so they can help keep each other warm with their breaths. In this one respect, horses are like people—they are full of an inexhaustible supply of hot air.

Submitted by Mrs. Phyllis A. Diamond of Cherry Valley, California.

Why Does Your Whole Body Ache When You Get a Cold or Flu?

When a virus enters your bloodstream, it releases several compounds that mount your body's defense against infection. Interferon, interleukin, and prostaglandins are among the body's most

DAVID FELDMAN

valuable compounds. They raise a fever, shift the metabolism, and increase blood flow to areas of the body that need it.

Frank Davidoff, of the American College of Physicians, suggests that although science hasn't yet precisely defined their function, there is much evidence to suggest that these compounds are responsible for the aching feeling that accompanies colds and flus. More of the compounds are usually found in the bloodstream during the aching phase than before any symptoms start. And when doctors inject a purified form of each compound into a patient, many of the symptoms of a virus, including fever, sweating, and aching, occur without actually causing the entire illness.

These compounds are effective without anyone knowing precisely *how* they work, but there are logical explanations for *why* they work. Davidoff sums it up well:

> the aching and other symptoms seem to be the "price" that's paid for mounting a defense against the infection. Whether the price is inseparable from the defense isn't clear. Thus, on the one hand, the symptoms might actually be a holdover from some mechanism that was important earlier in evolution but that is unnecessary now in more complex creatures. On the other hand, symptoms like aching may be part and parcel of the defense; I don't believe anyone knows for sure.

Submitted by James Wheaton of Plattsburgh Air Force Base, New York.

How Did Romans Do the Calculations Necessary for Construction and Other Purposes Using Roman Numerals?

Our idea of a good time does not include trying to do long division with Roman numerals. Can you imagine dividing CXVII by IX and carrying down numbers that look more like a cryptogram than an arithmetic problem?

The Romans were saved that torture. The Romans relied on the Chinese abacus, with pebbles as counters, to perform their calculations. In fact, Barry Fells, of the Epigraphic Society, informs us that these mathematical operations were performed in Roman times by persons called "calculatores." They were so named because they used *calcule* (Latin for pebbles) to add, subtract, multiply, and divide.

Submitted by Greg Cox of San Rafael, California.

Why Do Some Ice Cubes Come Out Cloudy and Others Come Out Clear?

A caller on the Merle Pollis radio show, in Cleveland, Ohio, first confronted us with this problem. We admitted we weren't sure about the answer, but subsequent callers all had strong convictions about the matter. The only problem was that they all had *different* convictions.

One caller insisted that the mineral content of the water determined the opacity of the cube, but this theory doesn't explain why all the cubes from the same water source don't come out either cloudy or clear.

Two callers insisted that the temperature of the water when put into the freezer was the critical factor. Unfortunately, they couldn't agree about whether it was the hot water or the cold water that yielded clear ice.

We finally decided to go to an expert who confirmed what we expected—all the callers were wrong. Dr. John Hallet, of the Atmospheric Ice Laboratory of the Desert Research Institute in Reno, Nevada, informed us that the key factor in cloud formation is the temperature of the *freezer*.

When ice forms slowly, it tends to freeze first at one edge. Air bubbles found in a solution in the water have time to rise and escape. The result is clear ice cubes.

DAVID FELDMAN

The clouds in ice cubes are the result of air bubbles formed as ice is freezing. When water freezes rapidly, freezing starts at more than one end, and water residuals are trapped in the middle of the cube, preventing bubble loss. The trapped bubbles make the cube appear cloudy.

Why Are Most Pencils Painted Yellow?

Pencils came in various colors before 1890, but it was in that year the Austrian L & C Hardtmuth Company developed a drawing pencil that was painted yellow. Available in a range of degrees of hardness, the company dubbed their product Koh-I-Noor.

In 1893, L & C Hardtmuth introduced their Koh-I-Noor at the Chicago World's Colombian Exposition, and Americans responded favorably. Ever since, yellow has been synonymous with quality pencils.

Monika Reed, product manager at Berol USA, told *Imponderables* that although Berol and other manufacturers make pencils painted in a wide range of colors, yellow retains its great appeal. According to Bill MacMillan, executive vice president of the Pencil Makers Association, sales of yellow-painted pencils represent 75% of total sales in the United States.

Submitted by Robert M. Helfrich of Pittsburgh, Pennsylvania.
Thanks also to Beth Newman of Walnut Creek, California.

DAVID FELDMAN

Why Do You Have to Use #2 Pencils on Standardized Tests? What Happens If You Use a #1 Pencil? What *Is* a #2 Pencil?

If only we could blame our SAT scores on using #1 or #3 pencils! But it's hard to find any other besides #2s anyway.

All-purpose pencils are manufactured in numbers one through four (with half sizes in between). The higher the number, the harder the pencil is. Although the numbers of pencils are not completely standardized, there is only slight variation among competitors.

The #2 pencil, by far the most popular all-purpose pencil, is considered medium soft (compared to the #1, which is soft; to #2.5, medium; to #3, medium hard; and to #4, hard). Pencils are made harder by increasing the clay content and made softer by increasing the graphite content of the lead.

Why do some administrators of standardized tests insist on #2 pencils? Because the degree of hardness is a happy compromise between more extreme alternatives. A hard pencil leaves marks that are often too light or too thin to register easily on mark-sensing machines. Too soft pencils, while leaving a dark mark, have a tendency to smudge and thus run into the spaces left for other answers.

Even some #2 pencils might not register easily on mark-sensing machines. For this reason, Berol has developed the Electronic® Scorer. According to Product Manager Monika Reed, "This pencil contains a special soft lead of high electric conductivity," which eases the burden of today's high-speed marking machines.

Unfortunately, even the Electronic Scorer doesn't come with a guarantee of high marks, only accurately scored answers.

Submitted by Liz Stone of Mamaroneck, New York. Thanks also to John J. Clark of Pittsburgh, Pennsylvania; Gail Lee of Los Angeles, California; William Lush of Stamford, Connecticut; and Jenny Bixler of Hanover, Pennsylvania.

Why Do Fish Eat Earthworms? Do They Crave Worms or Will Fish Eat Anything that Is Thrust upon Them?

We have to admit, earthworms wouldn't be our first dining choice. What do fish see in worms that we don't see (or taste)?

R. Bruce Gebhardt, of the North American Native Fishes Association, emphasizes that just about any bait can entice a fish if the presentation is proper. Human gourmets may prefer a colorful still life on white china, but fish prefer a moving target. And they are a little less finicky than humans:

> A pickerel, for example, will attack a lure before it's hit the water. It must instantly assess the size of the bait; if it's a pine cone, it will worry about spitting it out after it is caught.

Most fish are attracted to food by sight, and prefer live bait. Fish are often attacking and testing as much as dining:

> It is unnecessary to *completely* convince the fish that the bait is alive. Most fish encountering anything strange will mouth it or closely examine it as potential food; the less opportunity it's liable to have, the more vigorously it will attack.

While the fisherman might think that every pull on his line means the fish finds his worm irresistible, the fish may well be

DAVID FELDMAN

nibbling the worm to determine the identity of the bait—by the time it finds out it has caught a worm, it's too late: It is hooked.

Our Imponderable also assumes that fish may go out of their way to eat earthworms, but Gerry Carr, director of Species Research at the International Game Fish Association, assures us that given a choice, most fish will go after food native to their environment:

> Nature is constituted in a way that everything has its place and is in ecological balance. Fish eat the foods that nature provides for them. The fly fisherman is acutely aware of this. He or she knows that trout, for example, at a certain time of year, seem to crave and feast on the type of nymphs that are hatching and falling into the water at that moment. Any other kind of artificial fly will not work, only the one that best imitates the hatch.
>
> Of course, not all fish are that finicky. Catfish eat anything that stinks. Logical! Their purpose in nature is to clean up the bottom, eliminating dead, rotting carcasses that rob water of oxygen and might cause all the fish to die. Nature's vacuum cleaner! And they survive because they have carved out or been given an ecological niche in the system that is not overly in competition with other species.

But why will worms attract even finicky fish? Carr continues:

> Worms, actually, are probably more of a side-dish in the diets of some fishes, a sort of aperitif. Worms look tasty, so the fish eats them. I do not think fish go looking for worms, specifically, unless they have got their appetite whet up for them by an angler conveniently drowning them.

Even if worms aren't native to a fish's environment, they fulfill most of the prerequisites for a favorite fish fast food. The size and shape are good for eating, and the fact that worms are wiggling when alive or look like they are moving even when dead adds to their allure. Carr mentions that barracudas cannot resist any appropriately sized bait or lure that is long and slender or cigar-shaped and moving at the right speed. "But offering them a worm that just sits there would be tantamount to a human asking for jelly instead of 'All-Fruit.' "

WHEN DO FISH SLEEP?   **373**

One other point needs to be stated. The popularity of earth-worms as bait is undoubtedly enhanced by the cheapness, easy availability, and convenience of them. As Gebhardt put it, "It's probably anglers' convenience that has given earthworms their reputation for delectability rather than petitions signed by fish."

Submitted by Roy Tucker of Budd Lake, New Jersey.

Why Are Stock Prices Generally Quoted in Eighths?

In *Why Do Clocks Run Clockwise? and Other Imponderables* we discussed the derivation of our expression "two bits." In Spain, a *bit* was one of the "pieces of eight," an actual pie-shaped slice of a peso. Two bits were one-quarter of a peso.

Spanish coins circulated freely in the New World before and during colonial times for at least two reasons. There weren't enough native coins to go around, and Spanish gold and silver specie were negotiable just about anywhere in the world (like in the good old days when foreign nations sought American dollars) because they were backed by gold.

Was it a coincidence that two bits of a peso happened to equal two bits of a dollar? Not at all. Peter Eisenstadt, research associate at the New York Stock Exchange archives, told *Imponderables* that when U.S. currency was decimalized in 1785,

> the U.S. silver dollar was established with a value equivalent to the Spanish silver peso. Though the official divisions of the dollar were in decimals, many continued to divide the new U.S. dollar into eighths and this practice was followed in securities trading.

Stocks were usually traded in eighths from the inception of securities trading in the United States in the 1790s. Eisenstadt believes that Americans simply borrowed the practice of quoting in eighths from the Europeans. As he notes, most early stock-brokers were part-timers, devoting most of their attention to the

DAVID FELDMAN

merchant trade, which had long quoted prices in eighths.

By the 1820s, stocks traded on the NYSE were universally quoted in eighths, but this was an informal arrangement; it became a requirement in 1885. The American and Pacific Stock Exchanges followed suit.

Although the history of our quoting stock prices in eighths makes historical sense, we don't understand why the exchanges still maintain the practice. When a stock dips to near zero, prices now are quoted in sixteenths and even thirty-seconds of a dollar, forcing financial tycoons to rely on their memory of grade-school fractional tables when doing calculations. And what happens when someone wants to sell his one share of stock quoted at 48⅜? Who gets the extra half-cent?

Wouldn't it make more sense to quote all stocks in hundredths of a dollar? Why should two-dollar stocks have to rise or fall more than ten percent at a time when a 2% change in most stocks is considered significant? Roy Berces, of the Pacific Stock Exchange, acknowledges that our system is probably archaic, but sees no groundswell for changing tradition.

Submitted by E. B. Peschke of St. Charles, Missouri. Thanks also to John A. Bush of St. Louis, Missouri; Christopher Dondlinger of Longmont, Colorado; and Dave Klingensmith of Canal Fulton, Ohio.

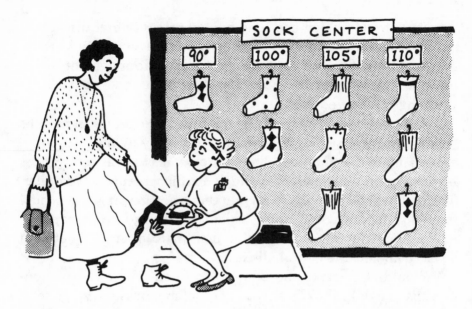

Why Are Socks Angled at Approximately 115 to 125 Degrees When the Human Foot Is Angled at About 90 Degrees?

Not all socks are angled, of course. Tube socks are "angled" at 180 degrees. Tube socks are so named because they are a straight tube of fabric closed on one end by sewing. The tube sock is constructed by "full circular knitting" (i.e., the knitting head on the machine knits in a full circle).

A tube sock doesn't contain a designated position for the heel, but more conventional socks do. Most socks are knitted with a feature called the "reciprocated heel." Sid Smith, president and chief executive officer of the National Association of Hosiery Manufacturers, told *Imponderables* how the reciprocated heel is made:

> Imagine a full circular knitting machine starting at the top of the sock and knitting in a complete circle all the way down the top of the sock, until it hits the point where the heel is to be knitted in. At this point, the machine automatically enters what is called the "reciprocated function." Instead of knitting in a complete circle,

DAVID FELDMAN

it knits halfway to each side and then back again, until the heel portion is knitted in.

After this is completed, the machine automatically reverts to full circular knitting to finish the sock. This reciprocation is what causes the finished sock to be angled.

The 115- to 125-degree angle of the sock, then, is the result of, rather than the purpose of, the knitting process. The fabrics used for socks will give or stretch to conform to the contours of the foot. Since a 180-degree tube sock can fit comfortably on the human foot, there is no reason why a conventional sock won't.

Submitted by Vernon K. Hurd of Colorado Springs, Colorado.

Why Do Cattle Guards Work?

No, there aren't demons underground shooting BB pellets between the bars of the cattle guards. Cows are afraid to walk where their feet can't get solid footing.

Our correspondent mentions that he has seen painted white strips used as cattle guards, presumably tricking cows into thinking that the unpainted area is a black hole. Cows are evidently as subject to phobias as cowboys and cowgirls.

Submitted by A. M. Rizzi of Torrey, Vermont.

Why Are There No A- or B-Sized Batteries?

Because they are obsolete. A- and B-sized batteries once existed as component cells within much larger zinc carbon battery packs. The A cells supplied the low-voltage supply for the filaments in the vacuum tubes used to supply power to early radios and crank telephones.

Of course, the descendants of the old A- and B-sized batteries are still with us. As electronic devices have gotten smaller, so have the batteries that power them. As might be expected, the A cell came first, then B, C, and D cells. The batteries were lettered in ascending order of size. James Donahue, Jr., of Duracell, Inc., says that as cells smaller than the original A cells were developed, they were designated as AA and then AAA cells. Donahue reports that there is even a new AAAA battery.

So the old A- and B-sized batteries are no longer in production. It's no use having a battery larger than the device it powers.

Submitted by Larry Prussin of Yosemite, California. And thanks also to Herman E. London of Poughkeepsie, New York; Nancy Ondris of Kings Park, New York; and Ronald Herman of Montreal, Quebec.

DAVID FELDMAN

What Are Those Little Plastic Circles (that Sometimes Have Rubber in the Middle) Found on the Walls of Hotels?

If you've noticed, those circles are located about three feet off the ground and usually near the entrance. They are called wall protectors, and their sole function in life is to keep doorknobs from slamming against the walls. And with some of the paper-thin walls we've encountered in motels, wall protectors may be responsible for keeping the structural integrity of the building intact.

Submitted by Carol Rostad of New York, New York.

Why Does Starch Make Our Shirts Stiff?

Starch is a type of "sizing," a filler used to add body, sheen, and luster to limp clothing. All shirts come off the rack with sizing, but sizing is water-soluble; every time the shirt is washed, sizing comes out of the shirt. The main purpose of adding starch, then, is to restore the original body of a garment.

The main ingredient in starch is wheat or, less frequently, corn. The grain is mixed with water, resins, and chemicals. As Bill Seitz, of the Neighborhood Cleaners Association, describes it, the starch is literally absorbed by the fabric. Cotton plus wheat is stiffer than cotton alone.

Norman Oehlke, of International Fabricare Institute, adds that starch also enhances soil resistance, facilitates soil removal for the next wash, and makes ironing easier.

Synthetic fabrics aren't as receptive to starch as all-cotton garments, so extra chemicals are added to the starch, such as polyvinyl acetate, sulfated fatty alcohols, silicones, and our personal favorite, carboxymethylcellulose.

Submitted by Kris Heim of De Pere, Wisconsin. Thanks also to Stanley R. Sieger of Pasadena, California.

How Does the Campbell Soup Company Determine Which Letters to Put in Their Alphabet Soup? Are There an Equal Number of Each Letter? Or Are the Letters Randomly Inserted in the Can?

We spoke to a delightful young woman at Campbell's named Ginny Marcin, who, astonishingly, did not have the answers to these questions at her fingertips. But she spoke to the vice president of Letter Distribution and obtained the following information.

DAVID FELDMAN

Campbell's makes two sizes of letters for their soups. Small letters go into some of the prepared soups (such as the Chunky line). Slightly larger letters bejewel their vegetable and vegetarian vegetable soups.

It is the stated intention of the Campbell Soup Company not to discriminate against any letter. All are equally represented. However, Campbell's cannot control the distribution of letters while inserting the letters and soup into the can, so irregularities can result. You might find a can with eight q's and only three u's, screwing up your plans to use the letters as Scrabble tiles.

Come to think of it, if the letters really are distributed randomly, why does Campbell's need a vice president of Letter Distribution?

Submitted by Tom Carroll of Binghamton, New York.

What Is the Purpose of Corn Silk?

These strands, which bedevil shuckers and flossless eaters alike, actually do have an important purpose. The longer threads of corn silk stand outside of the husk in tufts to collect pollen. The pollen then travels the silk to the ear of corn and fertilizes it.

Edith M. Munro, director of Information of the Corn Refiners Association, told *Imponderables* one of the critical factors exacerbating the loss in the corn harvest during the 1988 drought was that the "lack of moisture delayed the development of silks or dried the silks up, so that no silks were present when pollen was released." Without sufficient pollination, the growth of the corn is stunted, resulting in ears of corn with only a few kernels.

Submitted by Denise Dennis of Shippensburg, Pennsylvania.

DAVID FELDMAN

Why Are U.S. Government Department Heads Called "Secretaries" Instead of "Ministers," as in Most Other Countries?

The word "secretary" comes from the same Latin root as the word "secret." In medieval days, a secretary was a notary or a scribe, someone privy to secret and often important information. Over time, secretaries became not only men and women in charge of correspondence for an employer but trusted advisors to heads of state and royalty. So although today's office secretaries may now be a neglected and abused lot, Europeans have long called important officeholders "secretaries."

We wrote to several historians who were kind enough to unravel this Imponderable. They concurred that although Americans appropriated their governmental vocabulary from the English, no single term was used to describe cabinet-level officials in England at the time the United States Constitution was drafted.

The parliamentary-cabinet style government of England was not established until the early 1700s, and many of the titles from feudal governments still existed. Thomas L. Purvis, of the Institute of Early American History and Culture, elaborates on the mishmash of English titles:

> members of the cabinet carried titles both feudal and modern, such as Chancellor of the Exchequer and Prime Minister. Intermediate in age were the secretaries of various departments, such as the former Secretary of State for the Southern Department (whose purview extended over the American Colonies) and the ad hoc Secretary *at* War.

Americans, in their revolutionary ethos, were not about to give a nod to the hated English king and his ministers. The terms "president" and "vice president" were chosen to distinguish elected leaders from the dreaded monarchy.

None of the framers of the Articles of Confederation wrote why "secretary" was designated as the term for America's executive officers. The Department of the Treasury conducted an investigation into this Imponderable and found that the Library of Congress, the National Archives, and the Office of Protocol at the Department of State could provide no documentary evidence for the choice.

But all of our sources indicated that the attempt to distance the United States from any trappings of a monarchy contributed to the selection of "secretary." Samuel R. Gammon, executive director of the American Historical Association, told *Imponderables* that "the older English tradition of terming the monarch's chief executive assistants 'Principal Secretary of State' may also have been in their [the framers of the Constitution] minds."

"Secretary" was a solid, middle-of-the-road choice. As Purvis points out, the title seems honorific yet confers no indication of aristocracy and could be applied to any department in the government.

Submitted by Daniel Marcus of Watertown, Massachusetts.

Why Is Prepackaged Chocolate Milk Thicker in Consistency than the Chocolate Milk You Make at Home?

Gravity.

If you make a batch of chocolate milk at home and put it in the refrigerator to cool, you will notice something when you fetch it ten hours later. The chocolate sinks to the bottom.

All is not lost. Simply shaking up the container will redistribute the chocolate throughout the milk.

But this kind of separation is unacceptable in a commercial product, especially one that is sold in a transparent container. So commercial dairies use stabilizers and emulsifiers to assure that the chocolate and milk remain mixed. Although the job of the (usually natural) stabilizers and emulsifiers is to keep the chocolate from falling to the bottom of the carton, the by-product is a thicker consistency than home-style chocolate milk.

Submitted by Herbert Kraut of Forest Hills, New York.

Why Do Fingernails Grow Faster than Toenails?

This is not the kind of question whose solution wins Nobel Prizes for scientists or garners prestigious grants for research hospitals, yet the answer is not obvious. The average severed fingernail takes four to six months to grow back to its normal length. The average toenail takes nine to twelve months.

Dermatologist Dr. Fred Feldman says that although nobody knows for sure why toenails lag behind fingernails in growth, there are many possible explanations:

1. Trauma makes nails grow faster. Dermatologists have found that if a patient bites a nail down or loses it altogether, the traumatized nail will grow faster than on one left alone. Fingernails, in constant contact with many hard or sharp objects, are much more likely to be traumatized in everyday life than toenails. Even nonpainful contact can cause some trauma to nails. Because we use our fingers much more often than our toes, toenails do not tend to get the stimulation that fingernails do.
2. All nails grow faster in the summer than the winter, which suggests that the sun promotes nail growth. Even during the summer, most people cover their toenails with socks and shoes.
3. Circulation is much more sluggish in the feet than in the hands.

Our medical consultants did not suggest the obvious: The faster growth of fingernails is nature's way of providing us with a constant tool with which to open pistachio nuts.

Submitted by Dave Bohnhoff of Madison, Wisconsin.

Why Do We Dream More Profusely When We Nap than We Do Overnight?

According to the experts we consulted, we dream just as much at night as we do when we take a nap. However, we *recall* our afternoon-nap dreams much more easily than our dreams at night.

While we are dreaming, our long-term memory faculties are suppressed. During the night, our sleep is likely to go undisturbed. We tend to forget dreams we experience in the early stages of sleep. The sooner that we wake up after having our dreams, the more likely we are to remember them.

Any situation that wakes us up just after or during the course of a dream will make the sleeper perceive that he or she has been dreaming profusely. Dr. Robert W. McCarley, the executive secretary of the Sleep Research Society, told *Imponderables* that women in advanced stages of pregnancy often report that they are dreaming more frequently. Dr. McCarley believes that the perceived increase in dreaming activity of pregnant women is prompted not by psychological factors but because their sleep is constantly interrupted by physical discomforts.

Why Do Place Kickers and Field-Goal Kickers Get Yardage Credit from Where the Ball Is Kicked and Yet Punters Only Get Credit from the Line of Scrimmage?

Well, who said life was fair? It turns out that this blatant discrimination occurs not because anyone wants to persecute punters particularly but for the convenience and accuracy of the scorekeepers. Jim Heffernan, director of Public Relations for the National Football League, explains:

DAVID FELDMAN

Punts are measured from the line of scrimmage, which is a defined point, and it sometimes is difficult to determine exactly where the punter contacts the ball. Field goals are measured from the point of the kick because that is the defined spot of contact.

Submitted by Dale A. Dimas of Cupertino, California.

HOW Does a Gas Pump "Know" When to Shut Off When the Fuel Tank Is Full?

A sensing device, located about one inch from the end of the nozzle, does nothing while fuel is flowing into the gas tank, but is tripped as soon as fuel backs up into the nozzle. The sensing device tells the nozzle to shut off.

Because of the location of the sensing device and the relatively deep position of the nozzle, a gas tank is never totally filled unless the customer or attendant "tops off" the tank. Topping off tanks is now illegal in most states and is a dangerous practice anywhere.

Submitted by Stephen O. Addison, Jr. of Charlotte, North Carolina.

HOW Does the Treasury Know When to Print New Bills or Mint New Coins? How Does it Calculate How Much Money Is Lost or Destroyed by the Public?

There are more than two hundred billion dollars in coins and currency in circulation today in the United States. Determining the necessary timing for the minting and printing of new monies is therefore far from a simple task.

Most of the demand for new money comes from banks. When a bank receives more checks to cash than it can comfortably accommodate with its cash on hand, the bank orders new money from one of the twelve Federal Reserve Banks. Of course, the bank doesn't get the new money for free; it uses a special checkbook to order new cash. When a bank has excess cash, it can deposit money into an account at the Federal Reserve Bank to offset its withdrawals.

What happens when the Federal Reserve Bank itself runs out of coins or notes? It places an order with the U.S. Mint for new coins or the Bureau of Engraving and Printing for the new

DAVID FELDMAN

currency. So demand from individual banks, funneled through a larger "distributor"—a Federal Reserve Bank—is responsible for the decision to issue new currency.

The average life-span of a dollar bill is fifteen to eighteen months. Larger denominations tend to have a longer life because they are circulated less frequently. The perishability of paper notes is the second major factor in calculating the requirements for new currency. In 1983 alone, the twelve Federal Reserve Banks destroyed more than 4.4 billion notes, worth more than $36 billion. The constant retirement of defective bills explains why almost one out of every four notes the Federal Reserve Bank sends to local banks is a newly printed one.

Every time a Federal Reserve Bank receives currency from a local bank, it runs the notes through high-speed machines designed to detect unfit currency. The newest machines can inspect up to sixty thousand notes per hour, checking each bill for dirt by testing light reflectivity (the dirtier the note, the less light is reflected) and authenticity (each note is tested for magnetic qualities that are difficult for counterfeiters to duplicate).

Notes valued at $100 or less are destroyed by the local Federal Reserve Bank. Unfit bills used to be burned and processed into mulch (we kid you not), but they are now shredded and compressed into four-hundred-pound bales. Most of these bundles of booty are discarded at landfills. Federal Reserve notes in denominations of $500 or more are canceled with distinctive perforations and cut in half lengthwise. The local Federal Reserve Bank keeps the upper half of each note and sends the other half to the Department of Treasury in Washington, D.C. When the Treasury Department verifies the legitimacy of the notes, it destroys its halves and informs the district bank that it may destroy the upper halves.

Coins have a much longer life in circulation, but the Mint still produces more than 50 million coins a day (compared to "only" twenty million notes printed per day). A U.S. Mint official told us that shipping coins across country is not a trivial task logistically—five-hundred-thousand pennies, for example, are a tad bulky. Huge tractor-trailer trucks, up to 55 feet in length and

13½ feet high, are used to transport coins from the Mint to Federal Reserve Banks. Dimes, quarters, and half dollars are transported by armored carriers.

The demand process for coins works the same way as for paper notes. Although the Mint has learned that seasonal peaks run true from year to year (the demand for coins goes up during prime shopping seasons, such as Christmas), the Mint yields to the demands of its constituent Federal Reserve Banks.

Submitted by Hugo Kahn of New York, New York.

DAVID FELDMAN

What Is the Purpose of that Piece of Skin Hanging from the Back of Our Throat?

No, Kassie Schwan's illustration to the contrary, the purpose of that "hanging piece of skin" is not to present targets for cartoon characters caught inside other characters' throats. Actually, that isn't skin hanging down, it's mucous membrane and muscle. And it has a name: the uvula.

The uvula is a sort of anatomical tollgate between the throat and the pharynx, the first part of the digestive tract. The uvula has a small but important role in controlling the inflow and outflow of food through the digestive system. Dr. William P. Jollie, chairman, Department of Anatomy, the Medical College of Virginia, explains: "The muscle of both the soft palate and the uvula elevates the roof of the mouth during swallowing so that food and liquid can pass from the mouth cavity into the pharynx."

Dr. L.J.A. DiDio, of the Medical College of Ohio, adds that the uvula also helps prevent us from regurgitating our food during swallowing. Without the uvula, some of our food might enter the nasal cavity, with unpleasant consequences.

Submitted by Andy Garruto of Kinnelon, New Jersey.

WHEN DO FISH SLEEP?

Why Don't Birds Tip Over When They Sleep on a Telephone Wire?

A telephone wire, of course, is only a high-tech substitute for a tree branch. Most birds perch in trees and sleep without fear of falling even during extremely windy conditions.

The secret to birds' built-in security system is their specialized tendons that control their toes. The tendons are located in front of the knee joint and behind the ankle joint. As it sits on its perch, the bird's weight stretches the tendons so that the toes flex, move forward, and lock around the perch.

Other tendons, located under the toe bones, guarantee that a sleeping bird doesn't accidentally tip over. On the bottom of each tendon are hundreds of little projections. These fit perfectly into other ratchetlike sheaths. The body weight of the bird pressing against the telephone wire (or tree branch) guarantees that the projections will stay tightly locked within the sheaths.

Barbara Linton, of the National Audubon Society, adds that while this mechanism is most highly developed in perching

392   DAVID FELDMAN

birds and songbirds, many other birds do not perch to sleep. They snooze on the ground or while floating on water.

Submitted by Dr. Lou Hardy of Salem, Oregon. Thanks also to Jann Mitchell of Portland, Oregon.

Why Is It Sometimes Necessary to Stroke a Fluorescent Lamp to Get It to Light?

All fluorescent bulbs require a ground plane to start. If the fluorescent lamp is inside a metal fixture, any piece of metal, such as the reflector, can serve as a ground plane. Richard H. Dowhan, manager of Public Affairs for GTE Products Corporation, told *Imponderables* that the closer the ground plane is to the tube, the easier it is to start the fluorescent. "Placing your hand on the tube or stroking it creates a very effective ground plane." Magicians have been lighting "naked" fluorescent bulbs for quite a long time by serving as the ground plane.

But most of us aren't magicians, and most of us use fluorescent lamps inside of metal fixtures. Why do the lamps usually light with a flick of the switch at some times and then other times require a little massage? J. Robert Moody, of General Electric's Lighting Information Center, was kind enough to supply an answer that doesn't require a physics degree to understand.

Under normal conditions, fluorescent lamps should light without difficulty, with the electric current flowing inside the fluorescent tube. But if the lamp has a combination of a light coating of dust and a small amount of moisture from the air, the coating will allow "some of the electric current to flow on the outside of the tube, and the current on the outside of the bulb will prevent the lamp from lighting. Under this condition, stroking the tube will interrupt the flow of current on the outside of the tube and cause the light to come on."

Submitted by Harold J. Ballatin of Palos Verdes, California.

Why Is There an Expiration Date on Sour Cream? What's the Matter, Is It Going to Get More Sour?

We've gotten this Imponderable quite often on radio interviews, usually from smug callers sure that expiration dates are a capitalist plot to force us to throw away barely used sour cream. But mark our words: if you think sour cream is tart when you open it, just leave it in the refrigerator too long and taste the difference. As the expiration date on sour cream becomes a dim memory, bacteria acts upon the sour cream, making it unbearably tart. Given enough time, mold will form on the sour cream, even if it is properly refrigerated.

Sour cream has about a month-long life in the refrigerator. Wait much longer and we'll bet that you won't want to test just how sour cream can get. If you think we're wrong, there's one way to find out for sure.

Go ahead and taste it. Make our day.

394   DAVID FELDMAN

Who Translates the Mail When a Letter Is Sent to the United States from a Foreign Country that Uses a Different Alphabet?

If the United States Postal Service has problems sending a letter across town in a few days, we wondered how they contended with a letter sent to Nebraska from a remote village in Egypt. Does every post office hire a staff of linguists to pore over mail and route it in the right direction?

No, not every post office. But the USPS does employ linguists at their International Exchange Offices, located at the major ports (New York, San Francisco, Miami, and Boston) where foreign mail is received. All mail is separated and sorted at these border points and sent on its merry way.

We contacted some foreign consulates to find out how they solved the problem of indecipherable mail. A representative of the Greek consulate told *Imponderables* that if foreign mail is written in one of the international languages, multilingual personnel have no problem sorting it. If no postal worker can translate an address, the postal service will likely do what we did—call the embassy or consulate of the country of the sender and hope for the best.

Submitted by Charles F. Myers of Los Altos, California.

Why Do Roaches Always Die on Their Backs?

We couldn't believe that three readers actually had experienced the good fortune to see a dead roach and had torn themselves away from the subsequent celebration long enough to note the posture of the deceased insect. But we trudged on nevertheless, contacting entomologists who actually get paid to study stuff like this.

WHEN DO FISH SLEEP?   395

Professor Mary H. Ross, affiliated with Virginia Polytechnic Institute and State University, told *Imponderables* that when a roach dies, its legs stiffen and the cockroach falls on its side. Because most roaches have a flattened body form with narrow sides, the momentum of the fall rolls them onto their backs.

John J. Suarez, technical manager of the National Pest Control Association, adds that small cockroaches, such as the German and the brown-banded, are more likely to die on their backs. Larger cockroaches with lower centers of gravity, such as the American and the Oriental, occasionally die face down.

Needless to say, we can't guarantee the position of dead roaches contained in traps. Maybe the lifeless occupants of Roach Motels lie perfectly prone. Unfortunately, there is only one way to find out and only entomologists have the stomach for it. Please don't try to verify this at home!

> *Submitted by Gloria Stiefel of Orange Park, Florida. Thanks also to Irma Keat of Somers, New York; and Gregg Hoover of Morgan Hill, California.*

Why Does Warmth Alleviate Pain?

A caller on Tom Snyder's radio show posed this Imponderable. We had no idea of the answer, but it was surprising that so many physicians we spoke to didn't know the answer either.

We finally got the solution from Daniel N. Hooker, Ph.D., coordinator of Physical Therapy/Athletic Training at the University of North Carolina at Chapel Hill. His answer included plenty of expressions like "receptors," "external stimuli," and "pain sensors." So let's use an analogy to simplify Hooker's explanation.

If a pneumatic drill is making a ruckus outside your window, you have a few choices. One is to do nothing, which won't accomplish much until the drill stops. But another option is to go to your stereo and put on a Led Zeppelin record at full blast. The pneumatic drill is still just as loud—you may still even be able to hear it. But the music will certainly distract you (and for that matter, your next-door neighbors as well), so the drilling doesn't seem as loud.

Hooker emphasizes that most of us associate warmth with pleasant experiences from our youth. By placing heat on the part of our body that hurts we stimulate the sensory receptors, which tell our brain that there has been a temperature change. This doesn't eliminate the pain, but the distraction makes us less aware of the pain. As our body accommodates to the high temperature, we need fresh doses of warmth to dampen the pain. When we receive the renewed heat treatment, we *expect* to feel better, so we do.

Why Can't We Use Both Sides of a Videotape like We Do with an Audio Tape?

Don French, chief engineer of Radio Shack, is getting a little testy with us: "If you keep using me as a consultant on your books, we are going to have to start charging for my service!"

We have read all of the bestselling business management books. They all reiterate that most people aren't motivated by higher pay but by recognition of their effort and accomplishments. So to you, Don French, we want to acknowledge our heartfelt appreciation for the efforts you have expended in educating the American public on the wonders and intricacies of modern technology in our contemporary culture of today. Through your efforts, our citizens will be better equipped to handle the challenges and complexities of the future.

But not one penny, bub.

Luckily, Mr. French couldn't resist answering this Imponderable anyway.

It turns out that even though some audio cassette recorders require the tape to be flipped before recording on the other side, the recorder doesn't actually copy on both sides of the tape. It copies on the top side of the tape in one direction and the bottom in the other direction.

On videotapes, the audio is also recorded on a small portion of the top side of the tape. But the video, with a much higher frequency requirement and slower recording speed, needs much more room to copy, and is recorded diagonally on most of the remaining blank tape.

Submitted by Jae Hoon Chung of Demarest, New Jersey.

Why Are the Toilet Seats in Public Restrooms Usually Split Open in the Front?

This has become one of our most frequently asked Imponderables on radio shows. So for the sake of science and to allay the anxiety of unspoken millions, here's the, pardon the expression, poop on a mystery whose answer we thought was obvious.

Try as they might, even the most conscientious janitors and bathroom attendants know it is impossible to keep a multiuser public toilet stall in topnotch sanitary condition. Let's face it. Pigs could probably win a slander suit from humans for our comparing our bathroom manners to theirs. Too many people leave traces of urine on top of toilet seats. Men, because of a rather important physiological distinction from women, particularly tend not to be ideally hygienic urinators, but most sanitary codes make it mandatory that both male and female toilets contain "open-front" toilet seats in public restrooms. In fact, at one time, "open back" seats were mandated as well, but the public wouldn't stand (or sit) for them.

If they are more hygienic, why not use open-front toilet seats at home? The answer is psychological rather than practical. An open-front seat would imply to the world that one's bathroom habits were as crass as those employed by the riffraff who use public restrooms. Still, we would think that open-front toilet seats in home bathrooms might lessen the number of divorce-causing arguments about men keeping the toilet seats up.

Submitted by Janet and James Bennett of Golden, Colorado.
Thanks also to Tom Emig of St. Charles, Missouri; Kate McNeive
of Scottsdale, Arizona; and Tina Litsey of Kansas City, Missouri.

HOW Are the First Days of Winter and Summer Chosen?

This Imponderable was posed by a caller on John Dayle's radio show in Cleveland, Ohio. John and the supposed Master of Imponderability looked at each other with blank expressions. Neither one of us had the slightest idea what the answer was. What did it signify?

We received a wonderful answer from Jeff Kanipe, an associate editor at *Astronomy*. His answer is complicated but clear, clearer than we could rephrase. So Jeff generously has consented to let us quote him in full:

> The first day of winter and summer depend on when the sun reaches its greatest angular distance north and south of the celestial equator.

Imagine for a moment that the Earth is reduced to a tiny ball floating in the middle of a transparent sphere and that we're on the "outside" looking in. This sphere, upon which the stars seem fixed and around which the moon, planets, and sun seem to move, is called the celestial sphere. If we simply extend the earth's equator to the celestial sphere it forms a great circle in the sky: the celestial equator.

Now imagine that you're back on the Earth looking out toward the celestial sphere. You can almost visualize the celestial equator against the sky. It forms a great arc that rises above the eastern horizon, extends above the southern horizon, and bends back down to the western horizon.

But the sun doesn't move along the celestial equator. If it did, we'd have one eternal season. Rather, the seasons are caused because the Earth's pole is tilted slightly over 23 degrees from the "straight up" position in the plane of the solar system. Thus, for several months, *one hemisphere tilts toward the sun while the other tilts away.* The sun's apparent annual path in the sky forms yet another great circle in the sky called the ecliptic, which, not surprisingly, is inclined a little over 23 degrees to the celestial equator.

Motions in the solar system run like clockwork. Astronomers can easily predict (to the minute and second!) when the sun will reach its greatest angular distance north of the celestial equator. This day usually occurs about June 21. If you live in the Northern Hemisphere and note the sun's position at noon on this day, you'll see that it's very high in the sky because it's as far north as it will go. The days are longer and the nights are shorter in the Northern Hemisphere. The sun is thus higher in the sky with respect to our horizon, and remains above the horizon for a longer period than it does during the winter months. Conditions are reversed in the Southern Hemisphere: short days, long nights. It's winter there.

Just reverse the conditions on December 22. In the Northern Hemisphere, the sun has moved as far south as it will go. The days are short, while the lucky folks in the Southern Hemisphere are basking in the long, hot, sunny days.

The first days of spring and fall mark the vernal and autum-

DAVID FELDMAN

nal equinox, when the sun crosses the equator traveling north and south. As astronomer Alan M. MacRobert points out, the seasonal divisions are rather arbitrary:

> Because climate conditions change continuously, there is no real reason to have four seasons instead of some other number. Some cultures recognize three: winter, growing, and harvest. When I lived in northern Vermont, people spoke of six: winter, mud, spring, summer, fall, and freezeup.

Why Do Most Cars Have Separate Keys for the Ignition and Doors? Doesn't This Policy Increase the Chances of Locking Yourself Out of the Car?

The automakers aren't so concerned about *you* getting into your car. They are worried about thieves getting into your car.

Ford Motor Company, for example, now uses one key for the ignition and doors and a separate key for the glove compartment and trunk. Ford once used the same key for the door and the trunk, but changed. A Ford representative, Paul Preuss, explains:

> At one time, it was a relatively easy matter for a car thief to work open a car door and make an imprint so that it was possible to produce a key that also worked the ignition. Hence, a separate ignition key. Changing from a five-cut key to the present ten-cut key accomplishes the same thing. Five of the cuts activate the door lock and a different five operate the ignition. Taking an imprint of the door lock does not provide the proper cuts for the ignition lock.

General Motors also provides a separate key for doors and ignition and explains its decision as an attempt to foil aspiring thieves.

A two-key approach also allows the car owner to stash valuables in the trunk or glove compartment while leaving only the ignition key with a parking lot attendant or valet. And if you misplace the door key? Well, there's always the coat hanger.

Submitted by Doris Hosack of Garfield Heights, Ohio. Thanks also to Charles F. Myers of Los Altos, California; and Loretta McDonough of Frontenac, Missouri.

P.S. News Flash. Just as this book was going to press, we received a note from the Ford Parts and Service Division. Although the company felt that separate door and ignition keys made sense for security reasons, Ford is returning to its roots: "The consumer prefers one key for both door and ignition; therefore, we will phase in one key for both in the near future."

What's the Difference Between Popcorn and Other Corn? Can Regular Corn Be Popped?

There are five different types of corn: dent, flint, pod, sweet, and popcorn. Popcorn is the only variety that will pop consistently. Gregg Hoffman, of American Popcorn, told *Imponderables* that other corn might pop on occasion but with little regularity.

The key to popcorn's popping ability is, amazingly, water. Each popcorn kernel contains water, which most popcorn processors try to maintain at about a 13.5% level. The water is stored in a small circle of soft starch in each kernel. Surrounding the soft starch is a hard enamel-like starch. When the kernel is heated for popping, the water inside heats and begins to expand. The function of the hard starch is to resist the water as long as possible.

When the water expands with such pressure that the hard starch gives way, the water bursts out, causing the popcorn kernel to explode. The soft starch pops out, and the kernel turns inside out. The water, converted into steam, is released (fogging the eyeglasses of four-eyed popcorn makers), and the corn pops.

DAVID FELDMAN

The other four varieties of corn are able to store water effectively. But their outer starch isn't hard enough to withstand the water pressure of the expanding kernel, and so nothing pops.

Submitted by David Andrews of Dallas, Texas.

What Does It Mean When We Have 20–20 or 20–40 Vision?

The first number in your visual acuity grade is always twenty. That's because the 20 is a reference to the distance you are standing or sitting from the eye chart. The distance is not a coincidence. Rays of light are just about parallel twenty feet from the eye chart, so that the muscle controlling the shape of the lens in a normal eye is in a state of relative rest when viewing the chart. Ideally, your eyes should be operating under optimal conditions during the eye test.

The second number represents the distance at which a normal eye should be able to see the letters on that line. The third from the bottom line on most eye charts is the 20–20 line. If you can see the letters on that line, you have 20–20 ("normal") vision. A higher second number indicates your vision is subnormal. If you have 20–50 vision, you can discern letters that "normal" observers could see from more than twice as far away, fifty feet. If you achieve the highest score on the acuity test, a 20–10, you can spot letters that a normal person could detect only if he were 50% closer.

We also got the answer to another Imponderable we've always had about the vision test: Are you allowed to miss one letter on a line and still get "credit" for it? Yes, all you need to do is identify a majority of the letters on a line to get full credit for reading it. If only our schoolteachers were such easy graders.

How Does Yeast Make Bread Rise? Why Do We Need to Knead Most Breads?

Yeast is a small plant in the fungus family (that's ascomycetous fungi of the genus *Saccharomyces*, to you botanical nuts), and as inert as baker's yeast might seem to you in that little packet, it is a living organism. In fact, it works a little like the Blob, feeding and expanding at will.

Yeast manufacturers isolate one healthy, tiny cell, feed it nutrients, and watch it multiply into tons of yeast. One gram of fresh yeast contains about ten billion living yeast cells, thus giving yeast the reputation as the rabbit of the plant world.

To serve the needs of bakers, manufacturers ferment the yeast to produce a more concentrated product. But the yeast isn't satisfied to idly sit by in the fermentation containers—it wants to eat. So yeast is fed its favorite food, molasses, and continues to grow. A representative of Fleischmann's Yeast told *Imponderables* that under ideal conditions, one culture bottle of yeast holding about two hundred grams will grow to about one hundred fifty tons in five days, enough yeast to make about ten million loaves of bread.

After it has grown to bulbous size, the yeast is separated from the molasses and water and centrifuged, washed, and either formed into cakes or dried into the granulated yeast that most consumers buy. When the baker dissolves the yeast in water, it reactivates the fungus and reawakens the yeast's appetite as well.

Yeast loves to eat the sugar and flour in bread dough. As it combines with the sugar, fermentation takes place, converting the sugar into a combination of alcohol and carbon dioxide. The alcohol burns off in the oven, but small bubbles of carbon dioxide form in the bread and are trapped inside the dough. The carbon dioxide gas causes gluten, a natural protein fiber found in flour, to stretch and provide a structure for the rising dough without releasing the gas. When the dough doubles in size, the recommended amount, it is full of gas bubbles and therefore has a lighter consistency than breads baked without yeast.

By kneading the bread, the baker toughens the gluten protein structure in the dough, stretching the gluten sufficiently to withstand the pressure of the expanding carbon dioxide bubbles. You don't need to knead all dough, however; for instance, batter breads, which are made with less flour and have a more open, coarse grain, don't need it.

Submitted by Jim Albert of Cary, North Carolina.

Why Do Doctors Tap on Our Backs During Physical Exams?

We've always been suspicious about this tapping. From a patient's point of view, it has two strong attributes: It doesn't hurt and it doesn't cost anything extra. But nothing ever seems to happen as a result of the tapping. No doctor has ever congratulated us on how great our back sounded or for that matter looked worried after giving us a few whacks on the back. At our most cynical, we've even wondered whether this is a physical examination equivalent of a placebo: The doctor gets a break from the anxious gaze of the patient, and the patient is reassured that at least the back part of his body is O.K.

Doctors insist that there is a sound reason to tap our backs. Short of an X ray, the tap is one of the best ways to collect information about the lungs. The space occupied by the lungs is filled with air. The two lungs are contained in the two pleural spaces, full of air, and lung tissue itself contains air.

Dr. Frank Davidoff, associate executive vice president, Education, for the American College of Physicians, told *Imponderables* about the fascinating history of the practice of tapping:

> In 1754, a Viennese physician named Leopold Auenbrugger discovered that if you thumped the patient's chest, it would give off

a more hollow sound when you tapped over the air-filled lung space, and a more "flat" or "dull" sound if you tapped over a part of the chest that was filled with something more solid, like muscle, bone, etc. Auenbrugger's father was a tavern keeper in Graz, Austria, who used to judge the amount of wine left in the casks by tapping on them—the hollow note indicating air, the flat note indicating wine.

Auenbrugger found that by thumping a patient's chest—somewhat as his father rapped on a cask—abnormal lesions in the chest cavity, such as fluid or a solid tumor in the cavity where air-filled lung ought to be, produced a sound different from that given off in a healthy air-filled chest. Auenbrugger tested out his new method of physical diagnosis over a period of seven years of drumming on his patient's chests, and in 1761, he put before the medical profession the result of his experiments, in a book called *New Invention to Detect by Percussion Hidden Diseases in the Chest*.

Dr. Davidoff adds that the technique used today is virtually the same as the one Auenbrugger invented more than two hundred years ago.

Dr. William Berman, of the Society for Pediatric Research, says that the technique is a good, obviously cheap alternative to an X ray and has even other attributes. Tapping on the front of the chest can determine the size of a patient's heart, because the heart is much more solid than the lungs as it is muscular and full of blood.

Submitted by Richard Aaron of Toronto, Ontario.

Why Do Military Personnel Salute One Another?

Every Western military organization we know of has some form of hand salute. In every culture, it seems the inferior initiates the salute and is obligated to look directly into the face of the superior.

The origins of the hand salute are murky. In ancient Europe, where not only military officers but freemen were allowed to carry arms, the custom for men about to encounter one another was to lift their right hand to indicate they had no intention of using their sword. Many of our friendly gestures, such as tipping hats, waving, and handshaking, probably originated as ways of proving that one's hand was not reaching for a sword or a convenient rock.

By the time of the Roman Empire, salutes were a part of formal procedure among the military. Soldiers saluted by placing their right hands up to about shoulder height with the palm out. The hand never touched the head or headgear during the salute.

In medieval times, when knights wore steel armor that covered their bodies from head to toe, two men often encountered each other on horseback. To display friendship, two knights supposedly would raise their visors, exposing their faces and identities to view. Because they held their reins in the left hand, they saluted with their right (sword) hand, an upward motion not unlike the salute of today.

Whether or not our modern salute stems from the rituals of chivalry, we know for a fact that we Americans borrowed our salute from modern British military practices. In 1796, British Admiral Earl of St. Vincent commanded that all British officers must henceforth take off their hats when receiving an order from a superior "and not to touch them with an air of negligence." Although the British Navy made salutes compulsory, it didn't codify the precise nature of the salute. In many cases, inferiors simply "uncovered" (doffed their caps).

The American military salute has also undergone many changes over the years. At one time, Marines didn't necessarily salute with their right hand, but the hand farthest from the officer being saluted. Even today, there are differences among the branches. Although the Army and Air Force always salute with their right hand, Navy personnel are allowed to salute with the left hand if the right is encumbered. And while Air Force and Army men and women may salute while sitting down, Naval officers are forbidden to do so.

Even if the motivations of ancient saluters were to signal friendly intentions, the gesture over the years has been transformed into a ritual signifying respect, even demanding subjection, and a tool to enforce discipline. The United States Marine Corps, though, has maintained a long tradition of shunning any symbols of servility. In 1804, Marine Commandant William Ward Burrows knowingly discarded the European tradition of inferiors uncovering before superiors and issued this order:

DAVID FELDMAN

No Marine in the future is to take his hat off to any person. When the officer to be saluted approaches, he will halt, face the officer and bring his right hand with a quick motion as high as the hat, the palm in front.

As a Marine publication notes, Burrows' order did much for the esprit de corps:

We can be certain of one fact—the newly initiated salute was popular with enlisted personnel, for an English traveler of that period (Beachey) reported that "the Marines, although civil and well disciplined, boast that they take their hats off to no one."

Submitted by Wally DeVasier of Fairfield, Iowa. Thanks also to George Flower of Alexandria, Virginia.

Why Do Recipes Warn Us Not to Use Fresh Pineapple or Kiwifruit in Gelatin? Why Can We Use Canned Pineapple in Gelatin?

Both pineapple and kiwifruit contain enzymes that literally break down gelatin into a pool of glop. The enzyme in pineapple, papain, is also found in papaya and many other tropical fruits. According to the president of the California Kiwifruit Commission, Mark Houston, kiwifruit contains a related enzyme, actinidin, that similarly breaks down gelatin, preventing jelling.

Papain is a particularly important enzyme that has more functions than turning your Jell-O mold into a Jell-O pool. Papain is the active ingredient in meat tenderizers. Just as papain splits the protein in gelatin, it also attacks proteins in meat. Ever experience a stinging sensation in your mouth while eating a fresh pineapple? Papain is attacking your throat.

How can we contain this rapacious enzyme? Just as Kryptonite incapacitates Superman or garlic renders Dracula useless, so heat is the enemy of protein-splitting enzymes such as papain or actinidin. Canned pineapple can be used effectively in gelatin because the heat necessary to the process of canning fruit inactivates the enzymes. Canned pineapple might not taste as good as fresh, but it is much easier on the throat.

Submitted by Marsha Beilsmith of St. Charles, Missouri. Thanks also to David Freling of Hayward, California; and Susan Stock of Marlboro, Massachusetts.

Where Is Donald Duck's Brother?

"We see Donald Duck's nephews, Huey, Dewey, and Louie, but we never see their Dad, Donald's brother. Why not?" wails our concerned correspondent.

The main reason we never see Donald's brother is that he doesn't have one. He does have a sister with the infelicitous name of Dumbella. In a 1938 animated short, *Donald's Nephews*, Donald receives a postcard from his sister informing him that she is sending her "three angel children" for a visit.

Poor Donald, excitedly anticipating the arrival of Masters Huey, Dewey, and Louie, had no idea either that the little visit would turn into a permanent arrangement or, since his sister really thought they were little angels, that she had really earned her name. The three ducklings, indistinguishable in their personalities and equally adept in their propensity for mischief, continued to torture Donald and Scrooge McDuck in many cartoon shorts.

In a 1942 short, *The New Spirit*, Donald lists the three dependents in a tax form as adopted, indicating that Donald was a most generous brother, a certified masochist, and just as dumb as Dumbella.

Submitted by Karen S. Harris of Seattle, Washington.

DAVID FELDMAN

What Causes Bags Under the Eyes?

Let us count the ways, in descending order of frequency:

1. Heredity. That's right. It wasn't that night on the town that makes you look like a raccoon in the morning. It's all your parents and grandparents' fault. Some people are born with excess fatty tissue and liquid around the eyes.

2. Fluid retention. The eyelids are the thinnest and softest skin in the entire body, four times as thin as "average" skin. Fluid tends to pool in thin portions of the skin.

   What causes the fluid retention? Among the culprits are drugs, kidney or liver problems, salt intake, and very commonly, allergies. Cosmetics drum up more business for dermatologists and allergists than just about anything else. Allergic reactions to mascara and eyeliner are the usual culprits.

3. Aging. The skin of the face, particularly around the eyes, loosens with age. Age is more likely to cause bags than mere sleepiness or fatigue.

4. Too many smiles and frowns. These expressions not only can build crow's feet but bags. We can safely disregard this answer to explain Bob Newhart's bags, however.

Another less fascinating explanation for many sightings of bags under the eyes was noted by Dr. Tom Meek, of the American Academy of Dermatology, in the *New York Times:* "The circles are probably caused by shadows cast from overhead lighting. . . ."

Submitted by Stephen T. Kelly of New York, New York.

How Do Blind People Discriminate Between Different Denominations of Paper Money?

Sandra Abrams, supervisor of Independent Living Services for Associated Services of the Blind, points out that the government defines "legally blind" as possessing 10% or less of normal vision. Legally blind people with partial vision usually have few problems handling paper money:

> Individuals who are partially sighted may be able to see the numbers on bills, especially in certain lighting conditions. Some people with low vision must hold the money up to their noses in order to see the numbers; some people have been asked by members of the public if they are smelling their money. Other persons with low vision might use different types of magnification. Some people with partial sight have pointed out that the numbers on the top corners of bills are larger than those on the bottoms.

The U.S. government certainly doesn't make it easy for blind people to identify currency. Virtually every other nation varies the size and color of denominations. One reader asked

DAVID FELDMAN

whether a five-dollar bill *feels* different from a twenty-dollar bill. Although suggestions have been made to introduce slight differences in texture, a blind person can't now discriminate between bills by touching them.

Initially blind people must rely on bank tellers or friends to identify the denomination of each bill, and then they develop a system to keep track of which bill is which. Gwynn Luxton, of the American Foundation for the Blind, uses a popular system with her clients:

- One-dollar bills are kept flat in the wallet.
- Five-dollar bills are folded in half crosswise, so that they are appproximately three inches long.
- Ten-dollar bills are folded in thirds crosswise, so that they are approximately two inches long.
- Twenty-dollar bills are folded in half lengthwise, so that they are half the height of the other bills and sit down much farther in the wallet or purse than the other bills.

Machines have been created to solve this problem as well. The relatively inexpensive Talking Wallet reads out the denomination of bills it receives. The more expensive Talking Money Identifier can be hooked up to cash registers and be used for commercial use. Many newspaper vendors are blind, and the Money Identifier can save them from being shortchanged.

Blind people have so many pressing problems imposed on them by a seeing culture that identifying paper money is a minor irritant. As Sandra Abrams puts it, "Frankly, of all the things I do daily, identifying money is one of the easiest."

Submitted by Jon Gregerson of Marshall, Michigan.

When Not Flying, Why Do Some Birds Walk and Others Hop?

Birds are one of the few vertebrates that are built for both walking and flying. Physiologically, flying is much more taxing on the body than walking. Usually a bird without fear of attack by predators in its native habitat will eventually become flightless. New Zealand, an oceanic island with few predators, has flightless cormorants, grebes, wrens, and even a flightless owl parrot. As Joel Carl Welty states in *The Life of Birds*:

> Why maintain splendid wings if the legs can do an adequate job? This principle may well explain why birds who are good runners fly poorly or not at all. And some of the best fliers, such as hummingbirds, swifts, and swallows, are all but helpless on their feet.
>
> More birds are hoppers than walkers. Birds that walk or run characteristically possess long legs and live in wide open spaces. While the typical tree dweller has four toes on each foot, many walkers have only two or three. Most tree-dwelling birds are hoppers, because it is easier to navigate from branch to branch by hopping than by walking. Most birds that hop in trees will hop on the ground. Although each hop covers more ground than a step would, the hop is more physically taxing.

Dr. Robert Altman, of the A & A Veterinary Hospital, points out that some birds will hop or walk depending on the amount of ground they plan to cover. "For a few steps, it might be easier for a bird to hop from place to place as he would from perch to perch in trees. To cover longer distances, the bird would walk or run."

Submitted by Jill Clark of West Lafayette, Indiana.

DAVID FELDMAN

Why Does String Cheese "String" When Torn Apart?

If you read *Why Do Clocks Run Clockwise? and Other Imponderables,* and shame on you if you haven't, you know that newspapers tear easily in a vertical position because all the fibers are lined up in the same direction when pulp is put into the papermaking machine. String cheese works on exactly the same principle.

When producing string cheese, the cheese curd is formed into a large mass and then stretched mechanically. The stretching causes the protein fibers to line up in a parallel fashion. According to Tamara J. Hartweg, of Kraft, "This physical modification of the protein structure is what causes the stringing quality of the cheese. When peeled, the protein fibers, which are aligned in one direction, come off in strings."

Submitted by Lee Hand of Newbury Park, California.

Who Got the Idea of Making Horseshoes? Why are Horseshoes Necessary? What Would Happen If Horses Weren't Shod?

If horses weren't shod, they would probably have trouble getting served at fast-food establishments. Maybe they can get away with no shirts. But no shoes?

But seriously, folks, horses have the Romans to blame for the end of their barefoot existence. Horses were perfectly happy galloping around without shoes until the leaders of the Roman Empire decided that it would be a good idea to build paved roads. Without support, horses' hooves would split and crack on the hard pavement.

The paving of roadways hastened the time when horses, used to riding the range in the wild, were domesticated and forced to carry loads and pull heavy carts. These added burdens put strain on horses' feet, so the Romans used straw pads as the first horseshoes.

Karen L. Glaske, executive secretary of the United Professional Horsemen's Association, says that although evolution has bred out some of the toughness of horses' feet, many can still live a barefoot life:

> Shoes are not essential to a horse that is left to pasture or used only as an occasional trail mount. However, the stresses which horses' feet endure when jumping, racing, showing, or driving make it necessary for the conscientious owner to shoe the animal. It is a protective measure.

DAVID FELDMAN

Why Are Tattoos Usually Blue (With an Occasional Touch of Red)?

Most tattoos are not blue. The pigment, made from carbon, is actually jet black. Since the pigment is lodged *underneath* the skin, tattoos appear blue because of the juxtaposition of black against the yellowish to brown skin of most Caucasians. Although red is the second most popular color, many other shades are readily available; in fact, most tattoo artists buy many different colorings, premade, from Du Pont.

We spoke to Spider Webb, perhaps the most famous tattooist in the United States and leader of the Tattoo Club of America, about the prevalence of black pigment in tattoos. Webb felt that most clients, once they decide to take the plunge, want to show off their tattoos: Black is by far the strongest and most visible color. Webb added that in the case of one client, albino guitarist Johnny Winter, a black tattoo does appear to be black and not blue.

Submitted by Venia Stanley of Albuquerque, New Mexico

Why Is the Width of Standard Gauge Railroads Four Feet Eight-and-One-Half Inches?

When tramways were built in England to carry coal by cart or coach, the vehicles were built with wheels four feet eight-and-one-half inches apart. Legend has it that this was the same distance apart as Roman chariot wheels, but we doubt it for one important reason: There is a more logical explanation. Track gauges are determined by measuring from the *inside* of one rail to the *inside* of the other. However, the rails themselves occupied three-and-one-half inches of space. In other words, fifty-six-

and-one-half inches was almost certainly derived by starting with a measurement of five feet and deducting the width of the rails themselves.

When steam railroads were later constructed in England, the tramway gauge was retained for the most part, and in 1840 Parliament made it official, decreeing four feet eight-and-one-half inches as the standard gauge in Great Britain.

If only the United States were as logical. The first railroad in America, in Massachusetts, featured locomotives from England, built for standard gauge tracks, so the U.S. started with the same track dimensions. But no one in the fledgling American rail industry seemed to consider that it might be nice to have an interlocking system of compatible railways.

As companies from different states started their own lines, anarchy ruled. The Mohawk & Hudson stretched the standard gauge only one half inch, but the Delaware & Hudson featured a six-foot behemoth. In the early and mid-nineteenth century, gauges ranged between a little more than three feet to more than six feet.

Faced with incompatible rolling stock, long delays were common, yet to be preferred to the numerous accidents that ensued when engineers tried to roll locomotives on gauges a few inches too wide at the usual breakneck speeds.

When Union Pacific was about to be built, Abraham Lincoln tried to fix five feet—then the most popular width in the South and California—as the standard gauge for the whole country. But the established railroads in the North and the East objected on financial grounds and managed to lobby to retain fifty-six-and-one-half inches as the standard.

According to railroad expert Alvin Harlow in "The Tangle of Gauges,"

> In 1871 there were no fewer than twenty-three gages, ranging from 3 feet up to 6 feet on the railroads of the United States. Less than fifteen years later there were twenty-five; a considerable group of roads in Maine had been born only two feet wide, whilst

DAVID FELDMAN

a logging company in Oregon had built one that sprawled over 8 feet of ground.

The proliferation of gauges was caused not only by regional stubbornness but because no railroad company seemed willing to spring for the cost of converting its tracks. Finally, Illinois Central broke the logjam. In one wild, torchlit night, Illinois Central workers narrowed six hundred miles of track. Southern railroad companies, reluctant to adopt the Yankee standard, followed suit years later.

Even more difficult than relaying track was the task of refitting the rolling stock. Locomotives and cars were dragged into shops all along their routes. Harlow mentions that although the companies tried to return cars to their home lines for conversion, the logistics were a nightmare. Usually cars were converted wherever they were when the tracks were remodeled. Sufficient numbers of new workers had to be hired temporarily to have crews working twenty-four hours a day resetting locomotive truck wheels, removing the tires from truck wheels, and resetting them for the standard gauge.

A few gauges with oddball widths survived into the twentieth century, mostly in New England and the Pacific Northwest, but they were anomalies. The United States eventually rejected the "new and improved" and returned to the standard gauge of the English.

Why Is the Bathtub Drain Right Below the Faucet? Why Isn't the Bathtub Drain on the Opposite Side of the Bathtub from the Faucet?

"Wouldn't this configuration be easier for rinsing purposes?" asks our correspondent Pam Lebo. No doubt it would, but there are plenty of reasons why the plumbing industry is going to continue to make you and the makers of Woolite unhappy.

Now hard as it may be to believe, some people actually use the bathtub for bathing. These heathens would not appreciate having to sit on the drain (or for that matter, having the spigot clawing at their backs). John Laughton, of American Standard, raises another legitimate objection: A dripping faucet in Pam's configuration would cause a stain on the whole length of the bathtub.

Your dream configuration would have other practical drawbacks. Peter J. Fetterer, of Kohler Company, explains why:

> The bathtub drain is generally at the same location as the water supply because of the piping required for both. Drains and supplies run through buildings in plumbing chases, vertical spaces for pipes that move water from floor to floor. Drains are attached to vent pipes that run through the chases and vent to the outside of a structure. These chases use up living space and are kept to a minimum for economic reasons.

So must we resign ourselves to a lifetime of boring bathtubs? Not necessarily. Pam's configuration might attract some who take only showers, but it will probably never be popular. However, American Standard has created a bathtub that presents interesting possibilities for extracurricular activities besides rinsing. Their avant garde bathtub places both the faucet and the drain halfway along the bath with, offers John Laughton, "a back slope at both ends so that two could bathe together in comfort and save water." Save water. Sure, Mr. Laughton.

Submitted by Pam Lebo of Glen Burnie, Maryland.

DAVID FELDMAN

Do Fish Sleep? If So, When Do Fish Sleep?

Our trusty *Webster's New World Dictionary* defines sleep as "a natural, regularly recurring condition of rest for the body and mind, during which the *eyes are usually closed* and there is *little or no conscious thought or voluntary movement*." Those strategically placed little weasel words we have italicized make it hard for us to give you a yes or no answer to this mystery. So as much as we want to present you with a tidy solution to our title Imponderable, we feel you deserve the hard truth.

Webster probably didn't have fish in mind when he wrote this definition of "sleep." First of all, except for elasmobranchs (fish with cartilaginous skeletons, such as sharks and rays), fish don't have eyelids. So they can't very well close them to sleep. No fish has opaque eyelids that block out vision, but some have a transparent membrane that protects their eyes from irritants.

Pelagic fish (who live in the open sea, as opposed to coasts), such as tuna, bluefish, and marlins, *never* stop swimming. Jane Fonda would be proud. Even coastal fish, who catch a wink or two, do not fall asleep in the same way humans do. Gerry Carr, director of Species Research for the International Game Fish Association, wrote us about some of the ingenious ways that fish try to catch a few winks, even if forty winks are an elusive dream:

Some reef fishes simply become inactive and hover around like they're sleeping, but they are still acutely aware of danger approaching. Others, like some parrot fishes and wrasses, exude a mucus membrane at night that completely covers their body as though they've been placed in baggies. They wedge themselves into a crevice in the reef, bag themselves, and remain there, semi-comatose, through the night. Their eyes remain open, but a scuba diver can approach them and, if careful, even pick them up at night, as I have done. A sudden flurry of movement, though, will send them scurrying. They are not totally unaware of danger.

In many ways, fish sleep the same way we plod through our everyday lives when we are awake. Our eyes are open but we choose, unconsciously, not to register in our brains most of the sensory data we see. A fish sleeping is in a state similar to the poor fish depicted watching the slide show in Kassie Schwan's illustration. We stare at the screen with our eyes open, but our minds turn to mush. If a crazed assassin burst into the room, we could rouse ourselves to attention, but if someone asked us to describe what fabulous tourist attraction we were watching, we couldn't say whether it was Stonehenge or the Blarney Stone.

If you accept that a fish's blanking out is sleeping, then the answer to the second part of the mystery is that fish sleep at night, presumably because of the darkness. Anyone with an aquarium can see that fish can float effortlessly while sleeping. They exude grace—which is more than we can say for how most humans look when they are sleeping.

*Submitted by Karole Rathouz of Mehlville, Missouri. Thanks
also to Cindy and Sandor Keri of Woodstock, Georgia; and
Heather Bowser of Tulsa, Oklahoma.*

DAVID FELDMAN

Why Do We Seem to Feel Worse at Night When We Have a Cold?

For the same reason that your feet swell up and hurt after a long day standing up. To quote Dr. Ernst Zander, of Winthrop Consumer Products:

> Nasal obstruction, produced by a great variety of conditions, usually seems worse to a patient when he is lying down. This is because tissue fluids and blood tend to pool in the head more when he is recumbent than when he is standing.

Of course, one is generally more likely to feel tired and worn out at night. But the doctors who *Imponderables* consulted indicated that reclining for long periods of time will worsen symptoms—one reason why often we feel lousy despite the "luxury" of being able to lie in bed all day long when we are sick.

Why Do Many Dry Cleaning Stores Advertise Themselves as "French" Dry Cleaners? Is There Any Difference Between a French Dry Cleaner and a Regular Dry Cleaner?

To answer the last part of this Imponderable first, there is a BIG difference between a French dry cleaner and a regular dry cleaner: about one dollar per garment.

Sure, some justification exists for calling any dry cleaning establishment "French." Dry cleaning was supposedly discovered in the 1830s by one Jolie Belin, a Frenchman who reputedly tipped over a kerosene lamp on a soiled tablecloth and found that the oil eliminated the stains. The story of Jolie Belin might be apocryphal, but dry cleaning definitely started in France.

Most Yankees are so cowed by the image of anyone who can speak French and order fancy wines in restaurants that we not only entrust our best clothing to them but are willing to pay extra for the artistry of the French dry cleaner.

DAVID FELDMAN

We conveniently forget, though, that the owner of the French dry cleaning store is as likely to be Japanese as French. And the French dry cleaner is unlikely to tell you that there is absolutely no difference between the way he and the One Hour Martinizing store down the block cleans your clothes.

Submitted by Mrs. Shirley Keller of Great Neck, New York.

Why Do Kellogg's Rice Krispies "Snap! Crackle! and Pop!"?

Kellogg's Rice Krispies have snapped, crackled, and popped since 1928. Kellogg's production and cooking process explains the unique sound effects.

Milled rice, from which the bran and germ have been removed, is combined with malt flavoring, salt, sugar, vitamins, and minerals and then steamed in a rotating cooker. The rice, now cooked, is left to dry and temper (i.e., sit while the moisture equalizes). The rice is then flattened and flaked as it passes through two cylindrical steel rollers. The Krispies are left to dry and temper for several more hours.

The cereal then moves to a toasting oven. The flattened rice is now exposed to hot air that puffs each kernel to several times its original size and toasts it to a crisp consistency. This hot air produces tiny air bubbles in each puff, crucial in creating the texture of Rice Krispies and their unique sound in the bowl.

When milk is added to the prepared cereal, the liquid is unevenly absorbed by the puffs, causing a swelling of the starch structure. According to Kellogg's, "This swelling places a strain on the remaining crisp portion, breaking down some of the starch structure and producing the famous 'Snap! Crackle! and Pop!' "

Submitted by Kevin Madden of Annandale, New Jersey.

WHEN DO FISH SLEEP?   427

Why Do So Many Cough Medicines Contain Alcohol?

No, the alcohol isn't there to make you forget the taste of the cough medicine. *Nothing* could do that.

Some drugs don't mix well with water. Alcohol is the best substitute. Although the alcohol may help some people sleep, the alcohol in the recommended doses of most cough medicines isn't high enough to affect the average person (one teaspoon has less than 10% the alcohol of a shot of whiskey).

Why Do Letters Sent First Class Usually Arrive at Their Destination Sooner than Packages Sent by Priority Mail?

When we send a package through the United States Postal System, we have alternatives. We can send them third class (and for certain goods, fourth class) for considerably less than Priority Mail, the package equivalent of first-class mail. But our experience is that packages invariably take longer to arrive. So we asked the USPS why. Their answers:

1. Packages are canceled and processed by hand. Almost all letters are canceled and processed by machines. Letters are sorted by OCR (Optical Character Reader) machines capable of processing up to thirty thousand letters in one hour. These machines "read" the last line of the address and sort the envelopes by zip code. Even if the OCRs can't read a letter, another machine helps humans to do so. The letter is transferred to an LSM (Letter Sorting Machine), which pops up a letter one second at a time before a postal worker who routes the letter to the proper zip code.
2. Samuel Klein, public affairs officer of the United States Postal Service, says that if a package is larger than a shoe box or weighs more than two pounds, it must be delivered by a parcel-post truck, which also carries nonpriority packages.

DAVID FELDMAN

3. Postal workers inadvertently treat Priority Mail as fourth-class mail. Dianne V. Patterson, of the Office of Consumer Affairs of the USPS, warns that "If the Priority Mail or First-Class stamps or stickers are not prominently placed on the parcel, it stands a good chance of being treated as fourth-class mail."

It isn't hard to understand the tremendous logistical difficulties in delivering mail across a large country, or even why mail might be delivered more slowly than we would like. But it is hard to understand exactly how the post office discriminates between processing a first-class and a fourth-class delivery. In the days when airmail was a premium service and fourth-class mail was transported by rail, we understood the distinction. But are postal workers now encouraged to malinger when processing fourth-class mail? Are they taught to let it sit around delivery stations for a few days so as not to encourage customers to use the slower service?

Despite our grumbling, we've found the USPS to be dependable in delivering all the free books we sent out to Imponderables posers. But we'll share a nasty secret. The books we send out at Special Fourth Class (book rate) seem to arrive no later than the books we send by the costlier Priority Mail.

Why Isn't There a Holiday to Commemorate the End of the Civil War?

Reader Daniel Marcus, who sent in this Imponderable, stated the mystery well:

> We observe a national holiday to commemorate the end of World War I on November 11 [Veteran's Day], and newspapers always note the anniversaries of V-E and V-J Days regarding the end of World War II. The Revolutionary War is honored, of course, on July 4. Why isn't there a national holiday to celebrate the end of the Civil War, the second most important and only all-American war in our history?

Good question, Daniel, but one that assumes a false premise. Memorial Day (also known as Decoration Day), celebrated on the last Monday of May, now honors the dead servicemen and servicewomen of all wars. But originally it honored the Civil War dead.

In his book *Celebrations*, historian Robert J. Myers credits Henry C. Welles, a druggist in Waterloo, New York, for originating the idea of decorating the graves of dead Civil War veterans in 1866. Originally the holiday was celebrated on May 5, when townspeople would lay flowers on the servicemen's graves.

John A. Logan, commander in chief of the Grand Army of the Republic (a veterans' support group), declared in 1868 that Decoration Day should be observed throughout the country. New York State was the first to make the day a legal holiday in 1873. Although Memorial Day never officially became a national holiday, it is celebrated in almost every state on the last Monday in May.

As with most holidays, the average person does not necessarily celebrate the occasion with the solemnity the founders of the holiday envisioned. In his study of the Civil War era, *The Expansion of Everyday Life, 1860–1878,* historian Daniel E. Sutherland notes that the new Memorial Day conveniently filled the void left by the declining popularity of George Washington's birthday: "Brass bands, picnic lunches, baseball games, and general merrymaking soon attached themselves to the new holiday, as it became as much a celebration of spring as a commemoration of the nation's honored dead." Today, the holiday is more often viewed as a kickoff to summertime than a serious tribute to the war dead.

Southerners, as might be expected, didn't particularly cotton to the concept of the northerner's Memorial Day. They countered with Confederate memorial days to honor their casualties, and many southern states still observe these holidays today. Florida and Georgia's Confederate Memorial Day is April 26; and Alabama and Mississippi celebrate on the last Monday of April. Not coincidentally, the president of the Confederacy, Jefferson Davis, was born on June 3. Kentucky and Louisiana celebrate the day as a state holiday.

Submitted by Daniel Marcus of Watertown, Massachusetts.

Is It True that Permanents Don't Work Effectively on Pregnant Women?

No, it isn't true, despite the fact that our correspondent has been told that it *is* true by her hairdressers. And you are not alone; we have been asked this Imponderable many times.

Everett G. McDonough, Ph.D., senior vice president of Zotos International, Inc., is one of the pioneers of permanent waving (he has worked at Zotos since 1927), and he is emphatic. He has seen or read the results of fifty thousand to one-hundred thousand perms given in the Zotos laboratory over the past sixty years. He has never seen the slightest evidence that pregnancy has any effect on permanent waving. And for good reason:

> a hair fibre after it emerges from the skin has no biological activity. Whether it remains attached to the scalp or is cut off, its chemical composition will remain the same. In either case the chemical composition can be altered only by some external means.

Louise Cotter, consultant to the National Cosmetology Association, reiterated McDonough's position and explained how a permanent wave actually works.

> A hair is held together by a protein helix consisting of salt, hydrogen, and disulphide bonds. The words "permanent wave" refer to the chemical change that takes place when those bonds are broken by a reducing agent having a pH of 9.2. The hair, when sufficiently softened, is re-bonded (neutralized) with a solution having a pH of 7.0–7.9. This causes the hair to take the shape of the circular rod on which it is wound, creating full circle curls or a wave pattern, depending upon the size and shape of the rod.

Although Cotter says that poor blood circulation, emotional disturbances, malfunctioning endocrine glands, and certain drugs may adversely affect the health of hair, none of these factors should alter the effectiveness of a perm on a pregnant woman. Pregnancy isn't an illness, and none of these four factors is more likely in pregnant women. Even if a pregnant woman takes hormones that could conceivably affect the results of a perm, a cosmetologist can easily compensate for the problem.

John Jay, president of Intercoiffure, answers this Imponderable simply:

> I have never had a permanent-wave failure due to pregnancy. Should failure occur for whatever reason, pregnancy may be the most convenient excuse available to some hairdressers.

Submitted by Jeri Bitney of Shell Lake, Wisconsin.

Why Do Some Escalator Rails Run at a Different Speed from the Steps Alongside Them?

The drive wheel that powers the steps in an escalator is attached to a wheel that runs the handrails. Because the steps and the rails run in a continuous loop, the descending halves of the stairs and handrails act as a counterweight to their respective ascending halves. The handrails, then, are totally friction-driven rather than motor-driven.

If the escalator is properly maintained, the handrail should move at the same speed as the steps. The handrails are meant to provide a stabilizing force for the passenger and are thus designed to move synchronously for safety reasons. Handrails that move slower than the accompanying steps are actually dangerous, for they give a passenger the impression that his feet are being swept in front of him. Richard Heistchel, of Schinder Elevator Company, informed *Imponderables* that handrails were once set to move slightly faster than the steps, because it was believed that passengers forced to lean forward were less likely to fall down.

> *Submitted by John Garry, WTAE Radio, Pittsburgh, Pennsylvania. Thanks also to Jon Blees of Sacramento, California; Robert A. Ciero, Sr. of Bloomsburg, Pennsylvania; and David Fuller of East Hartford, Connecticut.*

Why Are There Lights Underneath the Bottom Steps of Escalators and Why Are They Green?

Those emerald lights are there to outline the periphery of the step on which you are about to hop or hop off. The majority of accidents on escalators occur when a passenger missteps upon entering or exiting the escalator. The lights, which are located just below the first step of ascending stairs (and the last step of descending stairs), are there to show the way for the unproficient escalator passenger.

Escalator lights are green for the same reason that traffic lights use green: Green is among the most visually arresting colors.

Submitted by John T. Hunt of Pittsburgh, Pennsylvania.

DAVID FELDMAN

Why Are Rented Bowling Shoes So Ugly?

We know that taste in art is a subjective matter. We are aware that whole books have been written about what colors best reflect our personalities and which colors go best with particular skin tones.

But on some things a civilized society must agree. And rented bowling shoes *are* ugly. Does anybody actually believe that maroon-blue-and-tan shoes best complement the light wood grain of bowling lanes or the black rubber of bowling balls?

Bruce Pluckhahn, curator of the National Bowling Hall of Fame and Museum, told us that at one time "the black shoe—like the black ball—was all that any self-respecting bowler would be caught dead using." Now, most rented bowling shoes are tricolored. The poor kegler is more likely to be dressed like Cindy Lauper (on a bad day) than Don Carter.

We spoke to several shoe manufacturers who all agreed that their three-tone shoes were not meant to be aesthetic delights. The weird color combinations are designed to discourage theft. First, the colors are so garish, so ugly, that nobody *wants* to steal

WHEN DO FISH SLEEP?   **435**

them. And second, if the rare pervert does try to abscond with the shoes, the colors are so blaring and recognizable that there is a good chance to foil the thief.

Of course, rented bowling shoes get abused daily. A bowling proprietor is lucky if a pair lasts a year. Gordon W. Murrey, president of bowling supply company Murrey International, told *Imponderables* that the average rental shoe costs a bowling center proprietor about $10 to $25 a pair. The best shoes may get rented five hundred times before falling apart, at a very profitable $1 per rental.

Even if rentals were a dignified shade of brown, instead of black, tan, and red, they would get scuffed and bruised just the same. Bowlers don't expect fine Corinthian leather. But can't the rented bowling shoes look a littler classier, guys? Isn't a huge 9 on the back of the heel enough to discourage most folks from stealing a shoe?

Submitted by Shane Coswith of Reno, Nevada.

What's the Difference Between Virgin Olive Oil and *Extra* Virgin Olive Oil?

We promised ourselves that we wouldn't make any jokes about virgins being hard to find and extra-virgins being impossible to find, so we won't. We will keep a totally straight face while answering this important culinary Imponderable.

We may have trouble negotiating arms reductions, but on one issue the nations of the world agree; thus, the International Olive and Olive Oil Agreement of 1986. This agreement defines the terms "virgin olive oil" and "extra virgin olive oil."

Any olive oil that wants to call itself virgin must be obtained from the fruit of the olive tree solely by mechanical or other physical means rather than by a heating process. The oil cannot be refined or diluted, but may be washed, decanted, and filtered.

DAVID FELDMAN

The lowest grade of virgin olive oil is semi-fine virgin olive oil, which is sold in stores as "virgin." This oil must be judged to have a good flavor and no more than three grams of free oleic acid per hundred grams of oil.

The next highest grade, fine virgin olive oil, cannot exceed one and a half grams of oleic acid per hundred grams and must have excellent taste.

Extra virgin olive oil must have "absolutely perfect flavour" and maximum acidity of one gram per hundred grams. According to José Luis Perez Sanchez, commercial counselor of the Embassy of Spain, extra virgin olives are often used with different kinds of natural flavors and are quite expensive, which any trip to the local gourmet emporium will affirm.

As with many other food items, the prize commodity (extra virgin olive oil) is the one that achieves quality by omission. By being free of extraneous flavors or high acidity, the "special" olive oil is the one that manages what wouldn't seem like too difficult a task: to taste like olives.

Submitted by Phyllis M. Dunlap of St. George, Utah.

Why Are There Cracks on Sidewalks at Regular Intervals? What Causes the Irregular Cracking on Sidewalks?

Believe it or not, those regularly spaced cracks are there to prevent the formation of irregular cracks.

We tend to see concrete as lifeless and inert, but it is not. Concrete is highly sensitive to changes in temperature. When a sidewalk is exposed to a cool temperature, it wants to contract.

Gerald F. Voigt, director of Engineering–Education and Research at the American Concrete Pavement Association, explains that concrete is very strong in compression but only one tenth as strong in tension.

> It would be much easier to break a piece of concrete by pulling on two opposite ends, rather than push it together. Cracking in concrete is almost always caused by some form of tensile development.
>
> In many cases the concrete slabs are restricted by the friction of the base on which they were constructed. This frictional resis-

DAVID FELDMAN

tance will put the slabs in tension as they contract; if the resistance is greater than the tensile strength of the concrete, a crack will form. Something has to give.

Without any form of restraint, the concrete will not crack.

Concrete tends to shrink as it dries, and tends to gain strength over time. Thus, sidewalks are most vulnerable to cracking the first night after the concrete is placed. Two strategies are employed to combat cracking.

Arthur J. Mullkoff, staff engineer at the American Concrete Institute, told *Imponderables* that properly positioned reinforcing steel is often used to reduce cracks. But the most effective method of minimizing cracks is to predetermine where the cracks will be located by installing joints in between segments of concrete.

Those spaces that threaten the well-being of your mother's back are a form of "tooled joints," strategically positioned cracks. These joints are placed in all types of concrete slabs. Gerald Voigt elaborates:

> The concrete is sawed or tooled to approximately one-quarter of the thickness of the slab, which creates a "weakened plane." The concrete will crack through the "weakened plane" joint, because that joint is not as strong. As you can see on almost any sidewalk, tooled joints are placed about every four to eight feet. These joints are placed to control where cracks develop and avoid random cracking which is usually considered unattractive. . . . Typically sidewalks are four inches thick; joint depth must be at least one-quarter of the sidewalk thickness.

Perhaps the most surprising element in the story of concrete cracks is that although so much effort is put into preventing them, cracks are not particularly troublesome. The National Ready-Mixed Concrete Association says that cracks rarely affect the structural integrity of concrete. Even when the cracks are wide enough to allow water to seep in, "they do not lead to progressive deterioration. They are simply unsightly."

Incidentally, our correspondent asked how the superstition "Step on a crack, break your mother's back" originated. We've

WHEN DO FISH SLEEP?   439

never found a convincing answer to this Imponderable, but Gerald Voigt offered a fascinating theory:

> Since a concrete sidewalk consists of many short segments (slabs) of white concrete, it can be imagined that it is like a human spine. The spine also consists of many short segments (vertebrae) of white bones. The weak links in each system are the joints. Stepping on a sidewalk crack, or joint, is analogous to stepping on the weakest area of the spine. I imagine if I were walking down a spine, I would avoid stepping on a vertebrae link, wouldn't you?

Submitted by Mrs. Harold Feinstein of Skokie, Illinois.
Thanks also to Henry J. Stark of Montgomery, New York.

Why Do We Have to Shake Deodorant and Other Aerosol Cans Before Using?

If you could see inside a can of deodorant, you would see that the ingredients are not arranged uniformly in the can. The propellant is not soluble and so won't mix with the active ingredients in the deodorant.

In many cases, you would see three or four levels of ingredients in a can. The top layer would contain the hydrocarbon gas used as a propellant. Other active ingredients, such as aluminum salt, emollient, and fragrance, also might seek their own level. By shaking up the can, you would guarantee spraying the proper proportion of ingredients.

Any effort expended in shaking the can is well worth the appreciation from friends and loved ones. But a stiff spray of hydrocarbon gas simply isn't sufficient to take care of a nasty body odor problem.

Submitted by Mark Fusco of Northford, Connecticut.

DAVID FELDMAN

Why Do Airlines Use Red Carbons on Their Tickets?

The dominant manufacturer of airline tickets is Rand McNally, the same company that makes maps and atlases. We spoke to Chris George, of Rand McNally's Ticket Division, who told us that there are two explanations for the tradition of red carbons.

In the early years of commercial aviation, black carbons were used. This we know for a fact. But Mr. George says the problem with black carbons was that in high humidity specks of black would fall off the ticket. Women, in particular, were upset that their hands or gloves were befouled with black crud. So the airlines did market research that revealed women did not object as much to traces of red on their hands because they were used to rouge and lipstick stains. This, Mr. George adds wryly, is the romantic explanation.

The unromantic explanation (a.k.a. the truth) is as follows: Once your ticket form is torn by the ticket agent, it is sent to the accounting department of the airline. The major carriers have long used optical scanners to read the serial numbers found on each ticket. An OCR (Optical Character Recognition) scanner can't read the ticket when black flecks of carbon land on the serial number because it can only register information printed in black ink. Much as a photocopier will not read blue ink, an OCR scanner won't read red ink. Who would have thought that accountants would be responsible for the daring flash of red on airline tickets?

In a time of high-tech stationery, why don't the airlines use carbonless paper? Part of the answer again relates to the OCR equipment. Carbonless paper contains blue specks that OCRs won't read. Furthermore, with chemically sensitized noncarbon paper, legibility is good for only about five copies. Old-fashioned carbon paper can render nine legible copies, sometimes necessary for the daunting itineraries of business travelers.

Now that most airlines are issuing automated ticket boarding passes—the ones that look like computer cards—the decline of the carbonized form is inevitable. Because not all ticket counters possess the equipment to issue these boarding passes, Mr. George predicts that the beloved red carbonized forms will continue to play a part in aviation for the foreseeable future.

Submitted by Niel Lynch of Escondido, California.

I Have a Dollar Bill with an Asterisk After the Serial Number: Is It Counterfeit?

The *Imponderables* staff will gladly accept your dollar bill if you don't want it. No, it's not counterfeit. You are holding a "star note," a replacement for a defective bill that has been destroyed.

In 1910, the Bureau of Engraving and Printing started printing ★ B and later ★ D as prefixes before the serial numbers of replacement notes. No star notes were issued for national bank notes, which were replaced by new notes that matched the missing serial numbers.

Now that notes are issued in series of one hundred million at a time, it is obvious why the Bureau would rather not have to renumber replacement notes, especially since, as Bob Cochran, secretary of the Society of Paper Money Collectors, told us, errors are quite common in the printing process:

> The most common errors are in inking, cutting, and in the overprinting operation. With inking there can be too much, not enough, or unacceptable smears. Notes are printed in sheets of 32; the back is printed in all green ink and then the face is printed in all black ink. If one side or the other is not registered properly, the designs will not match up on both sides after the sheets are cut up; if the registration is very poor, the notes will be replaced. A third separate printing operation adds the serial number and Treasury Seal; the major error possibilities are in inking and placement, since the basic note design already exists at this point.

You have probably noticed that serial numbers on U.S. currency are preceded by a letter. That letter designates which of the twelve Federal Reserve districts issued the note (this is why the letters span A through L). For example, all serial numbers preceded by D (the fourth letter of the alphabet) are issued by the Fourth District of the Federal Reserve (Cleveland). Here is a list of the twelve Federal Reserve Bank districts and the letter designations for each:

District	Letter	City
1	A	Boston
2	B	New York
3	C	Philadelphia
4	D	Cleveland
5	E	Richmond
6	F	Atlanta
7	G	Chicago
8	H	St. Louis
9	I	Minneapolis
10	J	Kansas City
11	K	Dallas
12	L	San Francisco

The star note enables the treasury to issue a new set of serial numbers rather than attempting to reassign all the missing serial numbers of defective notes. On U.S. notes, a star substitutes for the prefix letter. A replacement U.S. note might look like this: ★ 00000007 B. On Federal Reserve notes, a star substitutes for the letter at the end of the serial number, so that the location of the Federal Reserve district is kept intact: D 00000007 ★.

William Bischoff, associate curator of the American Numismatic Society, adds that there is one other use for the star note. The Bureau of Printing and Engraving uses printers with eight-digit numbering cylinders to produce one hundred million notes at a time. But for the one-hundred-millionth note, a ninth digit is needed. Rather than bothering to add another digit on the cylinder that would literally be used on one out of a hundred million notes, the one-hundred-millionth note is a hand-inserted star note.

To What Do the Numbers Assigned to Automotive Oil Refer?

Thirty years ago, 10–30 was considered a premium automotive oil. Today, one can buy 10–50 or even 10–60 oil, but few people know what these numbers mean.

The numbers measure the viscosity of the oil. The higher the number, the higher the viscosity (meaning the oil is less likely to flow). Although the viscosity of a liquid is not always directly correlated to thickness, high-viscosity oils are thicker than their low-viscosity counterparts.

The numbers on engine and transmission oils are assigned by the Society of Automotive Engineers. Their numbers range from 5W to 60. The W stands for winter. When a W follows a number, it indicates the viscosity of the oil at a low temperature. When there is no W following a number, the viscosity is measured at a high temperature.

All oil companies promote multigrade oils, which are designed to perform well in hot or cold temperatures. Thus 10W–40 doesn't indicate a range of viscosity, but rather the low viscosity of oil during winter (when one desires greater flow capabilities) and high viscosity in the summer.

Submitted by Tom and Marcia Bova of Rochester, New York.

When I Put One Slice of Bread in My Toaster, the Heating Element in the Adjacent Slot Heats Up as Well. So Why Does My Toaster Specify Which Slot to Place the Bread in If I Am Toasting Only One Slice?

Considering that the pop-up toaster has proven to be perhaps the most durable and dependable kitchen appliance, we were surprised to learn that toasting technology varies considerably from model to model. The earliest toasters browned one side of bread at a time; one had to decide when to flip the bread over by hand, a problem not unlike the momentous decision of when to flip over a frying pancake or hamburger.

Now that even the simplest pop-up toaster has a toast selector dial to allow the user to choose the preferred degree of doneness, most of the guesswork in toasting has been eliminated. We are not even allowed to select which of two or four slots to put in our one meager slice of bread. Why not?

Actually, nothing dire will result if you don't use the slot marked ONE SLICE. The worst that will happen is that the toaster will pop up an underdone or overdone piece. But why is the same well that manages to produce wonderful toast when it has company next door suddenly rendered incompetent when forced to work alone?

The answer depends upon the type of technology the toaster uses to determine doneness. The simplest toasters, now passé, worked from a simple time principle. The darker the brownness dial was set for, the longer the timer set for the toaster to heat the bread. Toasters that worked on a timer alone did not need a ONE SLICE notation because they always cooked the bread for the same amount of time, as long as the brownness dial wasn't changed. Using a timer alone guaranteed that a second set of toast would come out overdone, because the toaster was already warmed up yet toasted the second set for the same period of time as the first batch that was heated from a "cold start."

To solve the problem, appliancemakers inserted a thermostatic switch in toasters, which measured the heat of the toaster rather than the time elapsed in cooking. The thermostat alone caused a reverse problem. A second batch of bread would come out underdone because the first cycle had already caused the heating element to charge. The toaster didn't "know" that the second batch of bread hadn't been exposed to the toaster long enough; it knew only that the toaster had achieved the desired temperature.

The solution to the problem was to use a combination timer-thermostat. Today, the timer is not set off until the thermostat tells the timer that the toaster has reached the preset temperature (determined by the setting of the brownness dial). With this technology, it might take a minute for the thermostat to tell the timer to start ticking with the first set of toast but only a few seconds for the second or third.

We spoke to an engineer at Proctor-Silex who told us that most of their toasters have the thermostat close to—or in some cases, inside—the well that is marked ONE SLICE so the thermostat can do a more accurate job of "reading" the correct temperature for that slice. Some toasters that have ONE SLICE markings are "energy saver" toasters, specifically designed so that the heating element in the second slot will not be charged if it does not contain bread.

Sunbeam has long produced the 20030 toaster, an elegant two-slicer that selects the proper brownness of the bread by a radiant control that "reads" the surface of the bread to determine the degree of doneness. As far as we know, the Sunbeam 20030 is the only toaster that doesn't work on a time principle. The 20030 actually measures the surface temperature of the bread by determining its moisture level and can accurately measure the time needed to toast any type of bread. Wayne R. Smith, of

Sunbeam Public Relations, told *Imponderables,* "There's no point in having radiant controls in both slots when having a control in one slot works just as well."

Submitted by Lisa M. Giordano of Tenafly, New Jersey. Thanks also to Muriel S. Marschke of Katonah, New York; and Jim Francis of Seattle, Washington.

Why Are Almost All Cameras Black?

Black isn't the most obvious color we would pick for cameras. Not only is black an austere and a threateningly high-tech color to amateurs, it would seem to have a practical disadvantage. As Jim Zuckerman, of Associated Photographers International, explained, black tends to absorb heat more than lighter colors, and heat is the enemy of film.

Of course, there was and is no reason why the exteriors of cameras need to be black. For a while, chromium finishes were popular on 35 millimeter cameras, but professional photographers put black tape over the finish to kill any possible reflections. Sure, some companies now market inexpensive cameras with decorator colors on the exterior. Truth be told, the persistence of black exteriors on cameras has more to do with marketing than anything else. As Tom Dufficy, of the National Association of Photographic Manufacturers, told us: "To the public, black equals professional."

Submitted by Herbert Kraut of Forest Hills, New York.

Why Is There a Permanent Press Setting on Irons?

We buy a permanent press shirt so that we won't have to iron it. Then after we wash the shirt for the first time, it comes out of the dryer with wrinkles. Disgusted, we pull out our iron only to find that it has a permanent-press setting. Are iron manufacturers bribing clothiers to renege on their promises? Is this a Communist plot?

The appliance industry is evidently willing to acknowledge what the clothing industry is reluctant to admit: A garment is usually permanently pressed only until you've worn it—once. Wayne R. Smith, consultant in Public Relations to the Sunbeam Appliance Company, suggested that "permanent press" was chosen to describe the benefits of some synthetic materials be-

DAVID FELDMAN

cause "it has a far more attractive sound to consumers than 'wrinkle-resistant.' "

We know what Mr. Smith means. We've always felt that the difference between a water-resistant watch and a waterproof watch was that the waterproof one would die the moment *after* it hit H_2O.

What Causes Double-Yolk Eggs? Why Do Egg Yolks Sometimes Have Red Spots on Them?

Female chicks are born with a fully formed ovary containing several thousand tiny ova, which form in a cluster like grapes. A follicle-stimulating hormone in the bloodstream develops these ova, which will eventually become egg yolks. When the ova are ripe, the follicle ruptures and an ovum is released. Usually when a chicken ovulates, one yolk at a time is released and travels down the oviduct, where it will acquire a surrounding white membrane and shell.

But occasionally two yolks are released at the same time. Double-yolk eggs are no more planned than human twins. But some chickens are more likely to lay double-yolk eggs. Very young and very old chickens are most likely to lay double yolks; young ones because they don't have their laying cycles synchronized, and old ones because, generally speaking, the older the chicken, the larger the egg she will lay. And for some reason, extra-large and jumbo eggs are most subject to double yolks.

If a chicken is startled during egg formation, small blood vessels in the wall may rupture, producing in the yolk blood spots—tiny flecks of blood. Most eggs with blood spots are removed when eggs are graded, although they are perfectly safe to eat.

DAVID FELDMAN

Submitted by Lewis Conn of San Jose, California. Thanks also to Melody L. Love of Denver, North Carolina.

Why Are Barns Red?

We first encountered this Imponderable when a listener of Jim Eason's marvelous KGO-San Francisco radio show posed it. "Ummmmm," we stuttered.

Soon we were bombarded with theories. One caller insisted that red absorbed heat well, certainly an advantage when barns had no heating system. Talk-show host and guest agreed it made some sense, but didn't quite buy it. Wouldn't other colors absorb more heat? Why didn't they paint barns black instead?

Then letters from the Bay area started coming in. Donna Nadimi theorized that cows had trouble discriminating between different colors and just as a bull notices the matador's cape, so a red barn attracts the notice of cows. She added: "I come from West Virginia and once asked a farmer this question. He told me that cows aren't very smart, and because the color red stands out to them, it helps them find their way home." The problem with this theory is that bulls are color-blind. It is the movement of the cape, not the color, that provokes them.

Another writer suggested that red would be more visible to owners, as well as animals, in a snowstorm. Plausible, but a stretch.

Another Jim Eason fan, Kemper "K.C." Stone, had some "suspicions" about an answer. Actually, he was right on the mark:

> The fact is that red pigment is cheap and readily available from natural sources. Iron oxide—rust—is what makes brick clay the color that it is. That's the shade of red that we westerners are accustomed to—the rusty red we use to stain our redwood decks. It's obviously fairly stable too, since rust can't rust and ain't likely to fade.

The combination of cheapness and easy availability made red an almost inevitable choice. Shari Hiller, a color specialist at the Sherwin-Williams Company, says that many modern barns are painted a brighter red than in earlier times for aesthetic reasons. But aesthetics was not the first thing on the mind of farmers painting barns, as Ms. Hiller explains:

> You may have noticed that older barns are the true "barn red." It is a very earthy brownish-red color. Unlike some of the more vibrant reds of today that are chosen for their decorative value, true barn red was selected for cost and protection. When a barn was built, it was built to last. The time and expense of it was monumental to a farmer. This huge wooden structure needed to be protected as economically as possible. The least expensive paint pigments were those that came from the earth.

Farmers mixed their own paint from ingredients that were readily available, combining iron oxide with skim milk—did they call the shade "2% red"?—linseed oil and lime. Jerry Rafats, reference librarian at the National Agricultural Library, adds that white and colored hiding pigments are usually the most costly ingredients in paints.

K.C. speculated that white, the most popular color for buildings in the eighteenth and nineteenth centuries (see *Why Do Clocks Run Clockwise? and Other Imponderables* for more than you want to know about why most homes are and always have been painted white), was unacceptable to farmers because it required constant cleaning and touching up to retain its charm. And we'd like to think that just maybe the farmers got a kick out of having a red barn. As K.C. said, "Red is eye-catching and looks good, whether it's on a barn, a fire truck, or a Corvette."

Submitted by Kemper "K.C." Stone of Sacramento, California. Thanks also to Donna Nadimi of El Sobrante, California; Jim Eason of San Francisco, California; Raymond Gohring of Pepper Pike, Ohio; Stephanie Snow of Webster, New York; and Bettina Nyman of Winnipeg, Manitoba.

Why Are Manhole Covers Round?

On one momentous day we were sitting at home, pondering the imponderable, when the phone rang.

"Hello," we said wittily.

"Hi. Are you the guy who answers stupid questions for a living?" asked the penetrating voice of a woman who later introduced herself as Helen Schwager, a friend of a friend.

"That's our business, all right."

"Then I have a stupid question for you. Why are manhole covers round?"

Much to Helen's surprise, the issue of round manhole covers had never been important to us.

"Dunno."

"Guess!" she challenged.

So we guessed. Our first theory was that a round shape roughly approximated the human form. And a circle big enough to allow a worker would take up less space than a rectangle.

"Nope," said Helen, friend of our soon-to-be ex-friend. "Try again."

Brainstorming, a second brilliant speculation passed our lips. "It's round so they can roll the manhole cover. Try rolling a heavy rectangular or trapezoidal manhole cover on the street."

"Be serious," Helen insisted.

"O.K., we give up. Tell us, O brilliant Helen. *Why are manhole covers round?*"

"It's obvious, isn't it?" gloated Helen, virtually flooding with condescension. "If a manhole were a square or a rectangle, the cover could fall into the hole when turned diagonally on its edge."

Helen, who was starting to get on our nerves just a tad, went on to regale us with the story of how she was presented with this Imponderable at a business meeting and came up with the answer on the spot. With tail between our legs, we got off the phone, mumbling something about maybe this Imponderable

WHEN DO FISH SLEEP? 453

getting in the next book. First we get humiliated by this woman; then we have to give her a free book. Isn't there any justice?

Of course, after disconnecting with Helen we did what any self-respecting American would do: We tortured our friends with this Imponderable, making them feel like pieces of dogmeat if they didn't get the correct answer. And very few did.

Of course, we can't rely on an answer provided by the supplier of an Imponderable, even one so intelligent as Helen, so we contacted many manufacturers of manhole covers, as well as city sewer departments.

Guess what? The manufacturers of manhole covers can't agree on why manhole covers are round. Some, such as the Vulcan Foundry of Denham Springs, Louisiana, immediately confirmed Helen's answer but couldn't resist throwing a plug in as well ("Then, again, maybe manhole covers are round to facilitate the use of the Vulcan Classic Cover Collection").

But the majority of the companies we spoke to said not only do manhole covers not have to be round but many aren't. Manhole covers sit inside a frame or a ring that is laid into the concrete. Many of these frames cover the hole completely and are not hollow, so there is no way that a cover any shape could fall into the hole.

Most important, as Eric Butterfield, of Emhart Corporation, told *Imponderables*, manhole covers have a lip. Usually the manhole cover is at least one inch longer in diameter for each foot of the diameter of the hole.

Round manholes are more convenient in other ways. Lathe workers find circular products easier to manufacture. Seals tend to be tighter on round covers. And Lois Hertzman, of OPW, a division of Dover Corporation, adds that round manholes are easier to install because there are no edges to square off.

Everyone we spoke to mentioned that many manholes are not round. Many older manhole covers are rectangular. The American Petroleum Institute wants oil covers to be the shape of equilateral triangles (impractical on roadways, where this shape could lead to covers flipping over like tiddlywinks).

Engineers at the New York City Sewer Design Department

DAVID FELDMAN

could find no technical reason for round manhole covers. They assumed, like most of the fall-through theory dissenters, that the round shape is the result of custom and standardization rather than necessity.

So, Helen, we have wreaked our revenge. Perhaps your answer is correct. But then, maybe it is wrong. Maybe the real reason manholes are round is so that they can facilitate the use of the Vulcan Classic Cover Collection.

Submitted by Helen Schwager of New York, New York.
Thanks also to Tracie Ramsey of Portsmouth, Virginia; and
Charles Kluepfel of Bloomfield, New Jersey.

In *Why Do Clocks Run Clockwise?*, we broke down and admitted we were haunted and rendered sleepless by our inability to answer some Imponderables that were sent to us. Often we found fascinating explanations, tantalizing theories, or partial proof. But burdened by the strict ethical codes that the custody of the body Imponderability places upon us, we can't rest until we positively nail the answers to these suckers.

So we asked our readers for help with the ten most Frustrating Imponderables (or Frustables, for short). The fruits of your labors are contained in the following pages. But before you get totally smug about your accomplishments, may we lay ten more on you?

These are ten Imponderables for which we don't yet have a conclusive answer. Can you help? A reward of a free, autographed copy of the next volume of *Imponderables*, as well as an acknowledgment in the book, will be given to the first reader who can lead to the proof that solves any of these Frustables.

FRUSTABLE 1: *Why is Legal Paper 8½" × 14"?*

We have located the first company to manufacture a legal-sized pad. We've also contacted the largest manufacturers of paper and stationery and many legal sources. But no one seems to know the reasons for lengthening regular paper and dubbing it "legal size." And yes, we know that many courts have abandoned legal-sized paper and now use 8½" × 11".

WHEN DO FISH SLEEP?   **459**

FRUSTABLE 2: *Why Do Americans, Unlike Europeans, Switch Forks to the Right Hand After Cutting Meat?*

Did someone give the Pilgrims radical etiquette lessons on the *Mayflower?* Is there any sense to the American method?

FRUSTABLE 3: *How, When, and Why Did the Banana Peel Become the Universal Slipping Agent in Vaudeville and Movies?*

Vegetable oil would work better, no?

FRUSTABLE 4: *Why did the Grade E Disappear from Grading Scales in Most Schools?*

An F makes sense as the lowest mark (F = failure); but why did the E get lost?

FRUSTABLE 5: *How Did They Lock Saloon Doors in the Old West?*

Were saloons in the old West open 24 hours? If they weren't, a couple of swinging doors three feet off the ground wouldn't provide a heckuva lot of security. Were there barriers that covered the entrance, or are swinging saloon doors a figment of movemakers' imaginations?

FRUSTABLE 6: *Why Do So Many People Save* National Geographics *and Then Never Look at Them Again?*

A visit to just about any garage sale will confirm that most people save *National Geographics*. An unscientific poll confirms that nobody ever looks at the issues they've saved. What gives?

FRUSTABLE 7: *Why Do People, Especially Kids, Tend to Stick Their Tongues Out When Concentrating?*

Theories abound, but no one we contacted had any confidence about their conjectures.

FRUSTABLE 8: *Why Do Kids Tend to Like Meat Well Done (and Then Prefer It Rarer and Rarer as They Get Older)?*

Are kids repelled by the sight of blood in rare meat? Do they dislike the texture? The purer taste of meat? What accounts for the change as they get older?

FRUSTABLE 9: *Why Does Whistling at an American Sporting Event Mean "Yay!" When Whistling Means "Boo!" in Most Other Countries?*

WHEN DO FISH SLEEP?

FRUSTABLE 10: *Why Are So Many Restaurants, Especially Diners and Coffee Shops, Obsessed with Mating Ketchup Bottles at the End of the Day?*

We have been in sleazy diners where we couldn't hail a waitress if our lives depended on it and were lucky if our table was cleaned off. Where was the waitress? She was grabbing all the ketchup bottles and stacking them so that the remains of one bottle flowed into a second bottle.

Who cares whether the ketchup bottle on the table is one third filled or completely full? Doesn't the ketchup flow more easily out of a less than full bottle? Do restaurateurs mate ketchup bottles to please patrons, or do they have other, perhaps nefarious, reasons?

DAVID FELDMAN

Frustables Update

Captured!!! The Ten Frustables from Why Do Clocks Run Clockwise?

FRUSTABLE 1: *Why Do You So Often See One Shoe Lying on the Side of the Road?*

They say that every parent has a favorite. In this case, we'll admit it. This isn't only our favorite Frustable, it's probably our favorite Imponderable ever, partly because it has been a difficult "child." We spoke to endless officials at the Department of Transportation and the Federal Highway Safety Traffic Administration. All of them were aware of the phenomenon; none had a compelling explanation.

In *Why Do Clocks Run Clockwise?* we talked about some of

the theories proffered by readers of Elaine Viets, columnist for the *St. Louis Post-Dispatch:*

- They are tossed out of cars during fights among kids.
- They fall out of garbage trucks.
- Both shoes are abandoned at the same time, but one rolls away.
- They are disentangled, discarded newlywed shoes.
- They are thrown out of school buses and cars as practical jokes.

We asked if our readers could come up with anything better.

We needn't have worried. You guys came through in spades. Your answers fell into three general categories: theoretical, empirical, and confessional. So profound were your insights into this important subject that we have given thirteen of them official *Imponderables* Awards of Merit.

Award-Winning Theoretical Explanations

Best Supply-Side Argument by a Noneconomist. Provided by Stefan Habsburg of Farmington Hills, Michigan: "Because if there were a pair, someone would pick them up!"

Best Conspiracy Theory. Provided by Morry Markovitz of Croton Falls, New York:

If a lost pair of shoes were found intact, the shoe industry might lose a sale as these old shoes were pressed into service by a new owner. Has the shoe industry secretly hired "road agents" to scour the country-side, picking up one of each pair they find?

Best Explanation Involving Eastern European Influence Upon the One-Shoe Problem. Provided by Rick La Komp of Livermore, California: "Barefoot field-goal kickers decided they didn't need more than one shoe and threw the other away."

Best Explanation by an Obnoxious Anthropomorphic Cartoon Animal. Provided by David Selzler of Loveland, Colorado. David sent us a "Garfield" cartoon in which the cat muses, "Why do you find only one shoe in the trash? One shoe on a sidewalk? One shoe in the street?" He wonders about why people don't throw things away in pairs. So Garfield sees one shoe in a trash can and knocks on the door of the adjacent house. Guess who answers? A pirate with a peg leg.

Most Logical Theory. Provided by Russ Tremayne of Auburn, Washington, and Maria N. Benninghoven of Kensington, Maryland. Both of these readers assume that most shoes found on the side of the road are thrown out of moving cars. They also assume that most people toss both shoes out one at a time. Russ assumes it would be most natural to throw out the shoes with one dominant hand:

> Most people's hands aren't large enough to comfortably grasp a pair of shoes, even if the laces are tied. Therefore, one shoe gets thrown at a time as the vehicle continues to travel. Perhaps one shoe, thrown weakly, lands on the edge of the highway, while the other, thrown with more force, lands off the road to lie invisibly among tall grass or brush.

Empirical Theories

Best Exploitation for Personal Profit of the One-Shoe Phenomenon. Provided by R.E. Holtslander of Lake Wales, Florida.

> About 20 years ago when I lived in Missouri and was coming home from California on a windy day, I noticed a large cardboard box on the highway in New Mexico. Papers were flying from it. Shortly after that, I saw an almost new broom, so I pulled off the road and picked it up.
>
> Soon other things appeared by the road. I saw a shoe for the right foot. As I had a sore toe at the time and thought the shoe was big enough to give my foot comfort, I picked it up, too.
>
> I saw a man in a pickup truck at the side of the road. He too had stopped to retrieve something. From then on it was like a treasure hunt. I picked up several things and then he would pass us and then we would pass him. Soon we passed into Texas, and there I found the mate to the shoe I had picked up in New Mexico!
>
> I kept the shoes for several years and showed my guests a pair of shoes, one of which I got in New Mexico and the other in Texas . . .

Best Explanation for the Unsalutary Effect of Poor Nutrition and Sleeping Habits Upon the Retention of Shoes. Provided by Dave Sodovy of Hamilton, New York: Dave recounts the story that a few summers ago he had a job with two other kids who were the sons of the boss. Father and sons lived an hour's drive away from work, necessitating leaving their house at 7:15 because the boss wanted to get coffee and doughnuts to fortify him for the road. The sons retaliated for having to get up at this barbaric hour by sleeping through the trip.

> From this evolved a routine in which the time between waking up and later falling asleep in the car was spent in "semi-sleep."
>
> One morning, the two boys and their dad arrived as usual, but the younger son was wearing only one shoe! A few questions revealed the reason. In his state of semi-sleep, with one shoe on, one shoe in one hand, and a bag lunch in the other hand, he set the shoe on the roof of the car to open the car door.
>
> Since his main concern was to go to sleep in dad's car, he didn't retrieve his shoe—he just closed the door and got comfortable. Dad and his other son had been in the car waiting; the three took off as soon as my one-shoed friend closed the door. The shoe was still on the roof of the car, and apparently survived the 25- and 35-mph speed limits of the neighborhood in which they lived. Once on the highway, the shoe was doomed. Indeed, once the three arrived at work, they called Mom, who sought out the missing shoe, locating it on the side of the highway.
>
> I doubt that this is the definitive answer that you're looking for, but it does explain how at least one shoe got on the road by itself.

The Margaret Mead Field Research Award. Goes to Laurie McDonald of Houston, Texas. Laurie once lived in Providence, Rhode Island, and found scores of single shoes alongside the highway between Warwick and Pawtucket while driving to and from work. Laurie collected seventy shoes in a period of six months.

Among her discoveries were mostly tennis shoes, most left-footed; "very early on Sunday mornings, I would inevitably find a few brand-new patent leather platform shoes sitting upright on the side of the road, waiting to be plucked."

DAVID FELDMAN

In 1979, Laurie was inspired to write a series of short stories, consisting of hypothetical explanations of how single shoes landed off the highway. In one, the protagonist was a hippie, sticking out his hand to hail a car. Instead, the outstretched hand became a shooting target for unneeded boots of army servicemen.

Although Laurie offers no theoretical breakthroughs, we nevertheless owe her a great deal for proving conclusively that single shoes are deposited on the highway at an alarming rate, at least in Rhode Island.

Confessions

The "10-4, Good Buddy" Award. Goes to Robin Barlett of Erie, Pennsylvania. Robin writes:

> My husband is a truck driver and I went with him on a run. He got tired and pulled off to the side of the road to sleep, and I went back into the bunk and took my shoes off.
> We got up late at night and my husband had to go to the bathroom. Nobody was on the highway so he just hopped out to go and he must have kicked my shoe out, for it was not there when I tried to find it.

The Foot Out the Window Routine Award. Goes to Brian Razen Cain of Chipley, Florida, the last honest man in the world. Many readers theorized that single shoes are remnants of passengers who nap with one (or both) shoes dangling out car windows. But Brian was the only one to admit it. Brian fell asleep on the Florida Turnpike and woke up to find himself semishoeless. His response? The normal one: "I simply threw the other one out the window too."

The Dog Ate My Homework Award. Goes to Jay Lewis of Montgomery, Alabama.

> The shoes were dropped there by animals. Various beasties are attracted by the taste and smell of salt-impregnated leather. Since animals have trouble getting more than one shoe in their mouths,

WHEN DO FISH SLEEP?

they only carry one of the pair away. Where they finally discard it is where you see it—invariably without its mate.

C. Lynn Graham of Pelham, Alabama, adds that dogs tend to think that they will carry a shoe in their mouths forever. But as soon as they are distracted by a car coming down the road, the shoe pales compared to the chance to chase a passing car.

Surprisingly only one soul, Jennifer Ballmann of Jemez Springs, New Mexico, was willing to admit that she was the personal victim of doggy single-shoe syndrome. Two questions arise: Can a Saint Bernard carry two shoes at a time? Can a Pekingese carry one shoe at a time?

I Did it for the Sake of Science Award. Goes to an anonymous caller on a Detroit, Michigan, radio show hosted by David Newman. This caller, a paramedic, confessed that he was personally responsible for dropping several single shoes in the past week.

When administering CPR paramedics are trained to take off the victim's shoes, in order to promote better circulation. Many times in transporting a heart attack victim from a residence the shoes are taken off hastily and get lost before the patient enters the ambulance.

Will insurance companies pay for the missing shoes of patients not responsible for their loss?

The Motorcycles are Dangerous Even WITH a Helmet Award. Goes to Tom Vencuss of Newburgh, New York. Several readers speculated that single shoes were discarded wedding shoes. "Well," claims Tom, "not quite . . ."

> I was scheduled to be the best man at my cousin's wedding in Schenectady, New York, a two-hour ride from my home in Poughkeepsie. Prior to the wedding, I needed to make a quick run up to get fitted for my tuxedo. It was a beautiful afternoon so I decided to ride my motorcycle. I dressed in my normal riding gear but took a pair of dress shoes to wear at the fitting. I decided not to take a bag along since I would not be spending the night. So I strapped the shoes to the back of the bike.

DAVID FELDMAN

Several hours later, as I pulled into the parking lot for the tuxedo rental, I reached back to find only one shoe. The other, no doubt, was sitting lonely on a stretch of the New York State Thruway. Though it was an expensive afternoon, it did solve one of life's little mysteries.

Do we have the definitive, smoking-gun solution to this Frustable? We're afraid not. But after all, philosophers have been arguing over less important topics for thousands of years. Together we have raised the level of discourse on this topic to stratospheric heights. Maybe our grandchildren will find the ultimate answer.

Submitted by Julie Mercer of Baltimore, Maryland. Thanks also to Bess M. Bloom of Issaquah, Washington; and Sue S. Child of Red Bluff, Louisiana.

A free book goes to Laurie McDonald of Houston, Texas, to inspire her to conduct further hard research on this important topic. Thanks also to Elaine Viets of the St. Louis Post-Dispatch, *for her generosity.*

FRUSTABLE 2: *Why Are Buttons on Men's Shirts and Jackets Arranged Differently From Those on Women's Shirts?*

Of all the Frustables, none yielded less new ground than this one. Although more readers tried to answer this Frustable than any other but number three, few added much beyond the speculations we offered in *Why Do Clocks Run Clockwise?*

This much we know for sure: Buttons were popularized in the thirteenth century, probably in France. Before that, robes tended to be loose and unfitted and were fastened by strings, hooks, or pins.

Many readers said that men in the thirteenth century wore swords on the left hip under their coats. When they cross-drew their sword, they risked catching their sword if their garments were arranged right over left. By changing the configuration so that left closed over right, they could unfasten jacket buttons with their left hand and draw their sword with their right hand more quickly and safely.

An equal number of readers insisted that the different button configurations come from the custom of rich women having handmaidens who dressed them. Because clothes, as everything else, were designed for right-handers, the women's arrangement made it easier for maids to button their mistresses' blouses and dresses. Male aristocrats presumably dressed themselves.

The third popular answer is that women's button arrangement is most convenient for breast-feeding, so that the mother can unbutton her blouse with her right hand and rest the baby on her left arm.

None of the three popular explanations is convincing to us. All of the clothing historians we spoke to did not accept these pat answers either. Only the second theory explains why men's and women's buttons need to be different, and there is one inherent problem with this theory—many rich men were indeed dressed by servants. We don't put much stock in the breast-feeding theory either. One book we found mentioned that the women's arrangement made it easier for women who were breast-feeding while holding their babies in their right arms.

Much of the written material we have read on this subject mentions all three of these nonrelated theories, an indication to us that these explanations are based more on supposition after the fact than solid evidence. Robert Kaufman, reference librarian in the Costume Division at the Metropolitan Museum of Art in New York, told *Imponderables* that this Frustable has been among his most often asked questions. He and others have done considerable research on the subject and found no credible evidence to sustain any particular argument.

DAVID FELDMAN

A few readers offered some imaginative answers to this Frustable. A surprising number mentioned an intriguing variation of the handmaiden theory: By switching the button arrangement for the two sexes, it's easier for the two sexes to unbutton each other's clothing during a sexual encounter. Hmmmmmm.

Along the same garden path comes our favorite contribution to this discussion, from Erik Johnson of Houston, Texas: "The button arrangement is so that when a couple is driving in a car, with the man driving, they can peek inside each other's shirts."

Submitted by Julia Zumba, of Ocala, Florida. Thanks also to Kathi Sawyer-Young of Encino, California; Mathew Gradet of Ocean City, Maryland; Jodi Harrison of Helena, Montana; Sheryl K. Prien of Sacramento, California; Harry Geller of Rockaway Beach, New York; Terry L. Stibal of Belleville, Illinois; Mary Jo Hildyard of West Bend, Wisconsin; Tom and Marcia Bova of Rochester, New York; Robert Hittel of Fort Lauderdale, Florida; and many others.

FRUSTABLE 3: *Why Do the English Drive on the Left and Just About Everybody Else on the Right?*

Quite a few readers, justifiably, took us to task for the phrasing of this Frustable. By saying "just about everybody else" drives on the right, we didn't mean to slight the rest of the United Kingdom, Ireland, India, Indonesia, Australia, South Africa, Kenya, Thailand, Japan, and many other nations, all of which still drive on the left side of the road. But because most of these other countries adopted their traditions while a part of the British Empire, we wanted to give the "credit" where it was due.

So how did this left-right division start? All historical evidence indicates that in ancient times, when roads were usually narrow and unpaved, a traveler would move to the left when encountering another person on foot or horse coming toward them. This allowed both parties to draw their sword with their right hand, if necessary. If the approaching person were friendly, one could give the other a high five instead. Military policy, as far back as the ancient Greeks, dictated staying to the left if traveling without a shield, so that a combatant could use his left hand to hold the reins and need not brandish the sword or lance crosswise, risking the neck of the horse.

Richard H. Hopper, a retired geologist for Caltex, has written a wonderful article, "Why Driving Rules Differ," the contents of which he was kind enough to share with *Imponderables* readers. Hopper believes that the custom of mounting horses on the left-hand side also contributed to traffic bearing left. In many countries, pedestals were placed alongside the curbs of the road to help riders mount and dismount from their horses. These approximately three-feet-high pedestals were found only on the left side of the road. Long before the pedestals were erected, horsemen mounted and dismounted on the left, probably because their scabbards, slung on the left, interfered with mounting the horse; the unencumbered right leg could be more easily lifted over the horse.

Until 1300 A.D., no nation had mandated traffic flow. But Pope Boniface VIII, who declared "all roads lead to Rome," insisted that all pilgrims to Rome must stick on the left side of the road. According to Hopper, "This edict had something of the force of law in much of western Europe for over 500 years."

The movers and shakers of the French Revolution weren't excited about having a pope dictate their traffic regulations. Robespierre and other Jacobins encouraged France to switch to right-hand driving. Napoleon institutionalized the switch, not only in France but in all countries conquered by France.

Why did the United States, with an English heritage, adopt the French style? The answer, according to Hopper and many others, is that the design of late-eighteenth-century freight wagons encouraged right-hand driving. Most American freight wagons were drawn by six or eight horses hitched in pairs; the most famous of these were the Conestoga wagons that hauled wheat from the Conestoga Valley of Pennsylvania to nearby cities. These wagons had no driver's seat. The driver sat on the left-rear horse, holding a whip in his right hand. When passing another vehicle on a narrow ride, the driver naturally went to the right, to make sure that he could see that the left axle hub and wheel of his wagon were not going to touch those of the approaching vehicle.

In 1792, Pennsylvania passed the first law in the United States requiring driving on the right-hand side, although this ordinance referred only to the turnpike between Lancaster and Philadelphia. Within twenty years, many more states passed similar measures. Logically, early American carmakers put steering wheels on the left, so that drivers on two-lane roads could evade wavering oncoming traffic. Although Canada originally began driving on the left-hand side, the manufacture of automobiles by their neighbors to the south inevitably led to their switch to the right. Although Ontario adopted right-hand driving in 1812, many other provinces didn't relent until the 1920s.

Great Britain, of course, stayed with the ancient tradition of left-side driving and not just out of spite. Their freight wagons were smaller than Conestoga wagons and contained a driver's seat. Hopper explains why the driver sat on the right-hand side of the wagon:

> The driver sat on the right side of the seat so that he could wield his long whip in his right hand without interference from the load behind him. In passing oncoming wagons, the drivers tended to keep to the left of the road, again to be able to pass approaching vehicles as closely as necessary without hitting.
>
> In passenger carriages, the driver also sat on the right, and the footman, if there was one, sat to the driver's left so that he could quickly jump down and help the passengers disembark at the curb.

Needless to say, a coachman wouldn't have felt quite as secure sitting to the right of the driver. Every time a right-handed driver got ready to crack the whip, the coachman would have had to duck and cover.

The British built their cars with the steering wheel on the right because their wagons and carriages at the time still stuck to the left side of the road. Their foot controls, however, have always been the same as American cars.

Well more than a hundred readers sent responses to this Frustable, most of them containing fragments of this explanation. Hopper's article is the best summary of the conventional wisdom on this subject that we have encountered. But there are dissenters. Patricia A. Guy, a reference librarian at the Bay Area Library and Information System in Oakland, California, was kind enough to send us several articles on this subject, including a fascinating one called "The Rule of the Road" from a 1908 periodical called *Popular Science Monthly*. Its author, George M. Gould, M.D., argues that Americans had adopted right-hand side travel before the development of Conestoga wagons, as had the French, whose wagons were driven by postilion riders (mounted on the left-rear horse). Dr. Gould couldn't come up with a convincing theory for the switch and argued that this Imponderable was likely to be a Frustable for all time.

We include this dissent to indicate that we tend to lunge at any answer that neatly solves a difficult question. We can give you a logical reason why Americans and the French switched the traditional custom of driving on the left; but we wouldn't risk our already precarious reputations on it.

Submitted by Claudia Wiehl of North Charleroi, Pennsylvania. Thanks also to John Haynes of Independence, Kentucky; Kathi Sawyer-Young of Encino, California; Larry S. Londre of Studio City, California; David Andrews of Dallas, Texas; Hugo Kahn of New York, New York; Barbara Dilworth of Bloomsburg, Pennsylvania; Pat Mooney of Inglewood, California; Stephen Murphy of Smithfield, North Carolina; Frederick A. Fink of Coronado, California; and many others.

A free book goes to Richard H. Hopper of Fairfield, Connecticut.

DAVID FELDMAN

FRUSTABLE 4: *Why Is Yawning Contagious?*

After the publication of *Imponderables,* this question quickly became our most frequently asked Imponderable. And after years of research, it became one of our most nagging Frustables. We couldn't find anyone who studied yawning, so we asked our readers for help.

As usual, our readers were bursting with answers, unfortunately, conflicting answers. They fell into three classes.

The Physiological Theory. Proponents of this theory stated that science has proven that we yawn to get more oxygen into our system or to rid ourselves of excess carbon dioxide. Yawning is contagious because everybody in any given room is likely to be short of fresh air at the same time.

The Boredom Theory. If everyone hears a boring speech, why shouldn't everyone yawn at approximately the same time, wonders this group.

The Evolutionary Theory. Many readers analogized contagious yawning in humans to animals displaying their teeth as a sign of intimidation and territoriality. Larry Rose of Kalamazoo, Michigan, argued that yawning might have originally been a challenge to others, but has lost its fangs as an aggressive maneuver as we have gotten more "civilized."

Several readers pointed us in the direction of Dr. Robert Provine, of the University of Maryland at Baltimore County, who somehow had eluded us. You can imagine our excitement when we learned that Dr. Provine, a psychologist specializing in psychobiology, is not only the world's foremost authority on yawning, but has a special interest in why yawning is contagious! In one fell swoop, we had found someone who not only might be able to answer a Frustable but a fellow researcher whose work was almost as weird as ours.

Dr. Provine turned out to be an exceedingly interesting and generous source, and all the material below is a distillation of his work. As usual, experts are much less likely to profess certainty about answers to Imponderables than are laymen. In fact, Provine confesses that we still don't know much about yawning; what we do know is in large part due to his research.

Provine defines yawning as the gaping of the mouth accompanied by a long inspiration followed by a shorter expiration. This definition seems to support the thinking of some who believe the purpose of a yawn is to draw more oxygen into the system, but Provine disagrees. He conducted an experiment in which he taped the mouths of his subjects shut. Although they could yawn without opening their mouths, they felt unsatisfied, as if they weren't really yawning, even though their noses were clear and were capable of drawing in as much oxygen as if their mouths were open. From this experiment, Provine concludes that the function of yawning is not related to respiration.

In other experiments, Provine has proven that yawning has nothing to do with oxygen or carbon dioxide intake. When he pumped pure oxygen into subjects, for example, their frequency of yawning did not change.

476   DAVID FELDMAN

Provine's research also supports the relationship between boredom and yawning. Considerably more subjects yawned while watching a thirty-minute test pattern than while watching thirty minutes of rock videos (although he didn't poll the subjects to find out which viewing experience was more bearable— we wouldn't yawn while watching and listening to thirty minutes of fingernails dragged across a blackboard, either). Did the subjects yawn for psychological reasons (they were bored) or for physiological reasons (boredom made them sleepy)?

When Provine asked his students to fill out diaries recording their every yawn, certain patterns were clear. Yawning was most frequent the hour before sleep and especially the hour after waking. And there was an unmistakable link between yawning and stretching. People usually yawn when stretching, although most people don't stretch every time they yawn.

Yawning is found throughout the animal kingdom. Birds yawn. Primates yawn. And, when they're not sleeping, fish yawn. Even human fetuses have been observed yawning as early as eleven weeks after conception. The child psychologist Piaget noted that children seemed susceptible to yawning contagion by the age of two. It was clear to Provine that yawning was an example of "stereotyped action pattern," in which an activity once started runs out in a predictable pattern. But what's the purpose of this activity?

Although Provine is far from committing himself to an answer of why we yawn, he speculates that yawning and stretching may have been part of the same reflex at one point (one could think of yawning as a stretch of the face). Bolstering this theory is the fact that the same drugs that induce yawning also induce stretching.

The ubiquity of yawning epidemics was obvious to all the people who sent in this Imponderable. Provine told *Imponderables*, "Virtually anything having to do with a yawn can trigger a yawn," and he has compiled data to back up the contention:

- 55% of subjects viewing a five-minute series of thirty yawns yawned within five minutes of the first videotaped yawn, compared to the 21% yawn rate of those who watched a five-minute tape of a man smiling thirty times.

- Blind people yawn more frequently when listening to an audio-tape of yawns.
- People who read about yawning start yawning. People who even think about yawning start yawning. Heck, the writer of this sentence is yawning as this sentence is being written.

If we are so sensitive to these cues, Provine concludes that there must be some reason for our built-in neurological yawn detectors. He concludes that yawning is not only a stereotyped action pattern in itself, but also a "releasing stimulus" that triggers *another* consistently patterned activity (i.e., another yawn) in other individuals. Yawns have the power to synchronize some of the physiological functions of a group, to alter the blood pressure and heart rate (which can rise 30% during a yawn).

Earlier in our evolution, the yawn might have been the para-linguistic signal for members of a clan to prepare for sleep. Provine cites a passage in I. Eibl-Eibesfeldt's *Ethology*, in which a European visitor to the Bakairi of Central Brazil quickly noted how yawns were accepted behavior:

> If they seemed to have had enough of all the talk, they began to yawn unabashedly and without placing their hands before their mouths. That the pleasant reflex was contagious could not be denied. One after the other got up and left until I remained . . .

Yet, Provine is not willing to rule out our evolutionary theory either. Perhaps at one time, the baring of teeth sometimes apparent in yawning could have been an aggressive act. Or more likely, combined with stretching, it could have prepared a group for the rigors of work or battle. When bored or sleepy, a good yawn might have revivified ancient cavemen or warriors.

So even if Dr. Provine can't yet give us a definitive answer to why yawning is contagious, it's nice to know that someone out there is in the trenches working full-time to stamp out Frustability. If Dr. Provine finds out any more about why yawning is contagious, we promise to let you know in the next volume of Imponderables.

DAVID FELDMAN

Submitted by Mrs. Elaine Murray of Los Gatos, California. Thanks also to Esther Perry of Clarks Summit, Pennsylvania; Julie Zumba of Ocala, Florida; Jo Ellen Flynn of Canyon Country, California; Hugo Kahn of New York, New York; Steve Fjeldsted of Huntington Beach, California; Frank B. De Sande of Anaheim, California; Mark Hallen of Irvington, New York; Raymond and Patricia Gardner of Morton Grove, Illinois; Jim White of Cincinnati, Ohio; Renee Nank of Beachwood, Ohio; and many others.

A free book goes to Christine Dukes of Scottsdale, Arizona, for being the first to direct us to Dr. Provine.

FRUSTABLE 5: *Why Do We Give Apples to Teachers?*

This Frustable has remained remarkably resistant to reasoned replies. Although few readers could supply hard evidence to back their claims, a lot of people sure seemed to think they knew the answer to this one.

Two theories predominated. The most popular answer was the Biblical explanation. In Genesis, the forbidden fruit comes from the tree of knowledge. Although the forbidden fruit is never specified, the apple has over time been given that distinction. As Lou Ann M. Gotch of Canton, Ohio, puts it:

> the apple has come to signify knowledge. Perhaps by giving an apple to the teacher our children are admitting that they're little devils. Or perhaps they are intimating that the teachers could use a little more knowledge.

The second camp traces the custom to early rural America, when teachers were given free room and board but little pay. Students and their families traditionally brought something to

DAVID FELDMAN

contribute to the school and/or the teacher, be it wood for a fire or fruit for consumption.

But why an apple? As Georgette Mattel of Lindenhurst, New York, points out, apples were cheap and plentiful. Donald E. Saewert adds that the apple is the only fruit that can be stored for long periods of time without canning. In the winter, it might have been the only fresh fruit that was available in many areas. And Ann Calhoun of Los Osos, California, closes this argument with an impressive volley: "Sure would beat dragging a twelve-foot stalk of corn to school."

Both of these arguments are plausible but certainly not proven. Two readers sent us evidence of other possible solutions to this Frustable.

Ann Calhoun mentions that perhaps the apple-teacher connection was made up by an illustrator in one of the nineteenth-century illustrated magazines ("Every illustration I've seen . . . includes a very pretty young teacher, a blushing hayseed boy of nine, and a classroom of giggling sniggerers.")

Calhoun speculates that the boy gives the teacher an apple not as a symbol of knowledge but as a symbol of beauty. For according to ancient Greek legend, the highly prized golden apples that grew in the Garden of the Hesperus were awarded for beauty at the Judgment of Paris. Calhoun continues:

> In every Rockwellian illustration of this theme . . . the teacher is young and beautiful. Since older generations were heavily schooled in the classics (as ours is not) the teacher and kids would get the reference immediately. And yes, there are satiric variations with the teacher depicted as old, fat, gray, ugly, and scowling. The reason for her sour expression is that *she* also knows the original reference, knows the satiric content of the gesture and is about to send that little hypocritical, mendacious, miscreant presenter out behind the barn for a thrashing he so richly deserves. . . . I truly can't imagine a spindly young cleric presenting his medieval monkish tutor with an apple for beauty. Such impertinence would only earn him a thrashing outside the castle walls. So when and where did all this apple presenting and polishing start?

Good question. We've heard from only one person who dares to speculate on this. We received a fascinating letter from Henry C. Hafliger, member of the Board of Trustees of the San Jacinto Unified School District. He traces the custom back to Switzerland and cites the book *Bauerspiegel*, written by Jeremiah Gotthelf in the early nineteenth century. Gotthelf was a disciple of Johann Pestalozzi, the Swiss educator and reformer who had a tremendous influence on American education in the nineteenth century.

In effect, *Bauerspiegel* chronicles a Swiss equivalent to our rural explanation for the custom. Hafliger summarizes:

> when education was first offered to all classes of children in Switzerland, salaries of teachers were subsistence at best. Parents would supplement teachers' salaries with food, and one of the easiest foods to bring to school was the apple. Farmers would keep apples in their cellars all year long because in those days apples were not considered a dessert but a staple. Gotthelf writes that children soon learned that the child who brought the apple received the least amount of swats with the pointer or switch that the teacher always carried. The children from the poor families, some of whom did not have enough food themselves, were at a distinct disadvantage.

Hafliger's theory, then, was that the fruit was originally given on the premise that "an apple a day keeps the switch away."

Submitted by Malinda Fillingion of Savannah, Georgia. Free books go to Ann Calhoun of Los Osos, California; and Henry C. Hafliger of San Jacinto, California.

DAVID FELDMAN

FRUSTABLE 6: *Why Does Looking up at the Sun Cause Many People to Sneeze?*

Of all the Frustables, we came closest to getting a definitive solution to number six. Most of the people who responded were sun-sneezers themselves, and some said that just looking up at a bright light or even at the reflection from a car bumper was enough to set off the achoo mechanism.

The more than one hundred letters we received on this topic almost all carried some variation of the same theme. After a little digging, we found out that the most popular explanation was far from the only possible one.

We do know this much: Somewhere between 25 to 33% of the population is afflicted with "photic sneeze reflex." It is almost certainly a hereditary condition. Reader Margy D. Miller of DeKalb, Illinois, reports that she and all four of her children all sneeze when they first step out of doors into the bright sun.

The most accepted explanation for the photic sneeze reflex is that light signals that should irritate the optic nerves somehow trigger receptors that play a part in the sneezing process. The neural tracts for the olfactory and optic sensory organs lie adjacent to each other and have close (but not identical) insertion points in the brain.

When some people with this particular genetic predisposition encounter a bright light for the first time, the pupils do not contract as rapidly as they should, and the eyes are irritated. Somehow—neurologists we spoke to could not specify *how*—the olfactory and neural tracts cross-circuit.

The result: The nerves fool the brain into thinking that there is a foreign irritant in the nasal mucosa. The brain does what comes naturally; it tries to rid the sinuses of the phantom dust or pollen. The brain sends out a sneeze reflex.

Case closed?

Not quite. Reader John W. Lawrence, M.D., who specializes in internal medicine and rheumatology, gave us a variation of the above. He concurs that the original cause of the sneeze is

WHEN DO FISH SLEEP?   483

eye irritation, but believes that the tears caused by the irritation actually trigger the sneeze:

> Many people develop eye sensitivity to light. This sensitivity results in a lacrimal outburst (making of excess tears) in response to the irritation. The excess tears then run off down the lacrimal duct, which is present for this purpose. The lacrimal duct empties into the back of the nasopharynx. A drippage of liquid into the back of the nose triggers the sneeze.
>
> Only when tearing exceeds the lacrimal duct's capacity to carry runoff do tears overflow and "run down the cheeks."

William J. Dromgoole, a reader from Somerdale, New Jersey, sent us a newspaper clip indicating that scientists at Scripps Clinic and Research Foundation in La Jolla, California, have found evidence that certain allergy treatments for runny noses can cause photic sneeze reflex. Simply switching medications has rid some people of this mildly vexing problem.

Several readers have written to ask why they always seem to sneeze a particular number of times (sometimes twice, but usually three times). ENT specialists we talked to pooh-poohed it. Anyone have a theory to explain this phenomenon?

Submitted by Rick Stamm of Redmond, Washington. Thanks also to William Debuvitz of Bernardsville, New Jersey; and Lisa Madsden of Minneapolis, Minnesota.

A free book goes to James Miron, R.N., of Republic, Michigan.

DAVID FELDMAN

FRUSTABLE 7: *Why Does the First Puff of a Cigarette Smell Better than Subsequent Ones?*

As we indicated in *Why Do Clocks Run Clockwise?*, the research departments of the major cigarette companies couldn't (or wouldn't) answer this Imponderable. Similarly, the Tobacco Institute and the Council For Tobacco Research—U.S.A., Inc., claimed that although much research has been conducted on the sensory awareness of cigarette smoke, this phenomenon was neither universal nor verifiable.

Luckily, *Imponderables* readers aren't as reticent as the professionals in the field. We don't have a definitive answer to this Frustable, but readers supplied us with three plausible explanations.

The Physiological Theory. Richard H. Hawkins, D.D.S., president of Medical Innovators of North America, argues that the first puff of a cigarette smells best because the olfactory nerve endings within the nasal cavity are able to interpret the smell sensation only after a rest period. "With repeated puffs, the olfaction perception goes to zero." This argument might explain why a smoker derives increasingly less satisfaction from subsequent puffs, but doesn't explain why nonsmokers, who might find cigarette smoke irritating and obnoxious, find the aroma of the first puff pleasant.

Reader Albert Wellman of Santa Rosa, California, speculates that the difference between first puffs and subsequent ones is the physical process of burning the tobacco leaves. "I suspect that once the major portion of the chemical responsible for the 'good smell' of cigarette smoke has been vaporized by the first puff of smoke, there is not enough left in the tobacco to provide a comparable olfactory experience from the remainder of the cigarette."

Wellman also hypothesizes that perhaps the olfactory nerves are temporarily blocked by some other active biochemical agent in the smoke. This theory is bolstered somewhat by research that indicates that although olfactory organs are easily fatigued, the fatigue is limited to one particular flavor. Usually, the nose will respond to a new or different smell, and there are 685 different chemical compounds found in leaf tobacco smoke.

Most of the (little) hard research we have been able to find on the sensory response to cigarette smoke doesn't corroborate these physiological explanations. Dr. William S. Cain, of the departments of Epidemiology and Public Health and Psychology at Yale University, argues that smokers don't really "taste" cigarettes in the conventional sense. The four tastes—sweet, sour, salty, and bitter—don't play much of a role in cigarette enjoyment; of the four, only the bitter is perceived by the smoker.

But Cain argues that the sense of smell is not very important either, and in the last words of the following, hints at the problem posed in this Frustable:

> it matters little for smoking enjoyment whether the smoke is exhaled through the nose or through the mouth. Smell may play a role at the moment the smoker lights up, but adaptation rapidly blunts olfactory impact.

DAVID FELDMAN

The Tobacco as Filter Theory. Reader Jack Perkins of San Francisco, California, writes:

> As a long-time heavy smoker, I can tell you that the first puff not only smells better, it's milder. The reason for this is that the tobacco acts as a filter catching tars, nicotine, and chemicals. The further down you smoke, the greater the build-up of these substances, resulting in harsher smoke.

Rev. David C. Scott, of Bethany Presbyterian Church in Rochester, New York, agrees, adding, "The first puff has the advantage of being filtered both by the longest filter and cleanest filter. . . . Each subsequent puff both shortens the filter and dirties even more what remains. Andrew F. Garruto of Kinnelon, New Jersey, compares smoking the stub of a cigarette to making a pot of coffee through used grains.

All of these arguments explain why the purity of taste and smell deteriorate as a cigarette has been smoked. But none explains to the nonsmoker why the first puff smells fine but then deteriorates immediately.

The Burning Wood, Sulfur, and Butane Theory. Even if we can't confirm any of these theories for sure, we like this modest explanation the best. Perhaps the reason why the first puff smells better is that the aroma of the lighting agent, not the tobacco, is what we are responding to. We received this letter from Allison Rosenthal, of Rancho Palos Verdes, California:

> People have always loved the smell of burning wood. By burning tree branches, pine needles, and pine cones, many not only warm their houses but improve the smell therein. If you have ever gone for a walk in Mammoth [California] in the winter, you would surely be familiar with this wonderful scent. A burning match smells much the same, maybe even a little better. Not only do you have a form of wood on a match but also sulfur, which is very pleasing when mixed with wood smoke. If you use a large 'Diamond' wood match and pull on the cigarette hard enough when lighting it, you can actually taste the sulfur and wood mixture. Even though it doesn't taste so good, it *does* smell nice.

Although Allison Rosenthal hasn't noticed that the first puff of a lighter-lit cigarette smells better, several other readers, including Judith R. Brannon of Santa Clara, California, feel that the smell of butane is the hero. As connoisseurs of gas station fumes, we would agree.

The match/lighter argument is the only theory that explains how an odor perceived as pleasant by smoker and nonsmoker alike can suddenly turn unpleasant, at least for the nonsmoker. If the hard research in sensory reactions to cigarette smoke can be believed, what a smoker perceives as a response to the taste of the flavor of a cigarette is actually a camouflage, masking a chemical response to the relief from nicotine deprivation.

A free book goes to Allison Rosenthal of Rancho Palos Verdes, California.

FRUSTABLE 8: *Why Do Women in the United States Shave Their Armpits?*

The recorded history of armpit shaving is a spotty one indeed. The earliest reference we have found was that the ancient Babylonians, more than one thousand years before the birth of Christ, developed depilatories to remove unwanted body hair.

Julius Caesar reported that the early Britons "had long flowing hair and shaved every part of their bodies except the head and upper lip," but this quotation may refer only to men. We do know that barbers removed superfluous hair from the eyebrows, nostrils, arms, and legs from male customers around this time.

The first direct reference to the specific topic at hand is contained in Ovid's *Art of Love,* written just before the birth of

Christ: "Should I warn you to keep the rank goat out of your armpits? Warn you to keep your legs free of coarse bristling hair?"

In Chaucer's day (the fourteenth century), the mere sight of any hair was considered erotic. Women were required to wear head coverings; caps were worn indoors and out by women of all ages.

These ancient antecedents predict our current duality about body hair on women. On the one hand, underarm hair is considered unsightly and unhygienic, and yet on the other, sexy and natural.

None of the many razor companies or cosmetic historians we contacted could pinpoint when women first started shaving their armpits. The earliest reports concerned prostitutes during the gold rush days in California. Terri Tongco, among other readers, posited the theory that prostitutes shaved their underarms to prove they had no body lice, which were rampant in the old West.

Many older readers were able to pinpoint when their mothers and grandmothers started shaving their armpits. Not-so-old historian C.F. "Charley" Eckhardt of Seguin, Texas, is the only person we have found who has actually studied this Frustable:

> My paternal grandmother, born in 1873, and my maternal grandmother, born in 1882, did not shave their armpits. My wife's maternal grandmother (1898), my mother (1914), and my mother-in-law (1921) all did or do.
>
> Eadweard Muybridge's photographic studies of the nude human figure in motion and Hillaire Belloc's photographs of New Orleans prostitutes, all taken before or immediately after the turn of the century, show hairy armpits, as do nude photos of prostitutes known to have been taken in El Paso, Texas, prior to 1915. In addition, still photographs taken from pornographic motion pictures known to have been made prior to 1915 show the women with unshaven armpits, as do surviving pornographic photographs of the "French postcard" variety which are documented as having been made in the United States prior to 1915.
>
> Theatrical motion pictures released about and after 1915, including *Cleopatra* (starring Theda Bara), the biblical sequences

WHEN DO FISH SLEEP?

from D.W. Griffith's *Intolerance,* and several others, show shaven armpits. Something, then, happened about 1915 that would cause not merely stars but impressionable teenagers (as my wife's grandmother was) but not necessarily older family women (like my grandmothers) to start shaving their armpits.

So what caused these women to start shaving their armpits around 1915? Many readers, including Charley Eckhardt, give the "credit" to Mack Sennett:

> The first moviemaker to show the feminine armpit extensively in non-pornographic films was Mack Sennett, in his Bathing Beauty shorts . . . Sennett's Bathing Beauties had shaven armpits, and they are the first direct evidence we have of the armpit-shaving phenomenon. Whether or not Mack actually said 'That looks like hell—have 'em shave' is a moot point, though the statement is completely in character with what we know about Sennett.

We do know that flappers of the Roaring Twenties adopted the sleeveless clothing that seemed so daring in the Sennett shorts.

We heard from several women who were more concerned about why the custom persists rather than how and when it started. Typical was this letter from Kathy Johnson of Madison, Wisconsin:

> I am one of the apparently few U.S. women who has never shaved her armpits or legs. It never made logical sense to me, so why do it? I've heard the argument that shaving those regions is more sanitary. Then why, I volley back, don't men shave their armpits? Why, in fact, doesn't everyone shave their heads if lack of hair is so sanitary? Stunned silence . . .

Several psychologists and feminists have speculated that men like the shaven look because it makes women look prepubescent —young, innocent, and unthreatening. Diana Grunig Catalan of Rangely, Colorado, who subscribes to the prepubescent theory, speculates that "American women, unlike their European counterparts, were not supposed to do anything with all those men they attracted with their revealing clothing. A childlike, helpless look can be a protection as well as an attractant."

In defense of men, it has been our experience that many women have visceral reactions to the presence or lack of body hair in men. Why does the same woman who likes hair on the front of the torso (the chest) not like it on the back? Why is hair on the arms compulsory but excess hair on the hands considered repugnant? Are women, as well as men, afraid to face the animal part of our nature? Hairy questions, indeed.

Submitted by Venia Stanley of Albuquerque, New Mexico.

A free book goes to C.F. "Charley" Eckhardt of Seguin, Texas.

FRUSTABLE 9: *Why Don't You Ever See Really Tall Old People?*

This Imponderable-turned-Frustable was submitted by Tom Rugg, who stands six foot six inches and understandably has a vested interest in the answer.

Many readers sent us lists of reasons why people get shorter as they get older. Some of the reasons include gravity; the degeneration, rigidification, and compression of the vertebral column as we get older; osteoporosis; curvature of the spine. All of these phenomena explain why we might lose two or three inches over a lifespan, but don't explain why we haven't seen the six-foot-nine person who has "shrunk" to six foot six.

Several people wrote to say that improved nutrition has made our population taller than it used to be. Presumably, our generation will grow old and "really tall" with a lifetime of Twinkies and Diet Coke in our systems. Yes, we have grown taller but on average little more than a half inch in the last twenty-five years and fewer than two inches since the beginning of the century.

Dr. Alice M. Mascette of Tacoma, Washington, and Cindy West of Towson, Maryland, mentioned that a portion of our really tall population is afflicted with Marfan's syndrome, a genetic affliction of the connective tissue of the body. Sufferers of Marfan's syndrome have abnormally large hands and feet and a subpar heart. Many die of a ruptured aorta after an aneurism.

So far, these Marfan's syndrome sufferers—only a small fraction of all very tall people—are the only identifiable group of tall people who have been proven to have a short lifespan. But it is not at all clear that the tallness per se is what causes their deaths.

The way to unlock this Frustable is by asking: Do very tall people have shorter lifespans than other people? Surprisingly, there is no scientific data to support the proposition. We heard from more than fifteen doctors, health agencies, and insurance companies, and none of them study mortality based on height alone. Metropolitan Life conducts countless studies on the relationship between height-weight ratios and longevity, but doesn't feel that there is any reason to believe that tall people have a higher morbidity rate than the population as a whole.

In fact, the only quasi-scientific study we've seen (sent to us by reader David Jordan) that claims that very tall people live shorter lives was conducted by an aerospace engineer, Thomas T. Samaras. He tracked the lifespans of three thousand professional baseball players and found that the tallest players (six foot six or taller) lived, on average, to only the age of fifty-two. On the other hand, the shortest group (under five foot four) lived more than sixty-six years on average.

All of the medical and insurance experts we spoke to doubted the validity of Samaras' results, as well as his reasoning. Samaras speculated that the heart of a tall person must work overtime to pump blood a longer distance than a short person. Johns Hopkins University heart specialist Dr. Solbert Perlmutt disagreed with this argument and added, "Besides, you don't see mice living long. But you see elephants doing quite well."

DAVID FELDMAN

And evidently some old people only slightly shorter than elephants are doing pretty well, too, though the scarcity of the really tall old person is evidenced by the fact that of the hundreds of thousands of people who read *Why Do Clocks Run Clockwise?* only one person stepped up to the plate and offered himself as a specimen. Robert Purdin of Tinton Falls, New Jersey, is sixty-five (is that old?) and six foot five (is that really tall these days?).

Dr. Emil S. Dickstein of Youngstown, Ohio, says that he sees many tall old people, as does Gwen Sells, a member of Tall Clubs International. Reader George Flower, who once encountered a six foot seven man in his seventies, reminds us that Jimmy Stewart, if not "really" tall, is pretty tall.

But our favorite sighting was sent in by Andy Stone of Denver, Colorado, who told us about Randy "Sully" Sullivan, who weighs trucks at the Port of Entry in Cortez, Colorado:

> Sully is six foot ten inches. I've never asked his age but his hair is white, his posture stooped (that's right, stooped), and I estimate he's about seventy.

So, Tom Rugg, there's hope for you yet.

Submitted by Tom Rugg of Sherman Oaks, California.
Thanks also to Joanna Parker of Miami, Florida.

A free book goes to David Jordan of Greenville, Mississippi.

FRUSTABLE 10: *Why Do Only Older Men Seem to Have Hairy Ears?*

How appropriate that we saved the most frustrating Frustable for last. In *Why Do Clocks Run Clockwise?*, we mentioned that we consulted endocrinologists who professed ignorance on the subject. "If this condition is only found in males, why don't you speak to geneticists," they chimed in unison.

So we talked to geneticists. Guess what they said.

"Why don't you talk to endocrinologists? They'd know about this stuff."

So we put this in as our last Frustable and waited for the mail to roll in. It did.

Most of the mail had much the same answer as this one, from Bryan, Texas:

> I am Stacey Lero, a seventh grader at Anson Jones School. . . . We are studying genetics in science. On the Y chromosome there is a gene for hairy ears. It matures throughout your lifetime and as men reach the late forties or early fifties (sometimes earlier or later), it has matured enough to be expressed and the hair begins to grow. I hope I've answered your question.

What??? Heads of genetic departments at prestigious universities can't answer this Imponderable and Stacey Lero is studying it in a seventh grade science class? What's going on here?

Then several other readers, including Richard Landesman, associate professor of zoology at the University of Vermont, and R. Alan Mounier of Vineland, New Jersey, sent me clips from genetics textbooks that confirmed Stacey Lero's letter. One text said that hypertrichosis (excessive hair) of the ear is passed directly from father to son.

Feeling humbled by the knowledge of our readers, we consulted some more geneticists. They replied that the Y-chromosome theory had been largely discounted—no hard research supports this belief. "Why don't you talk to an endocrinologist," said one soothingly.

Are we the only ones who feel a little queasy about medical textbooks printing untrue facts? Or are scientists and doctors not believing what is in medical textbooks?

Peter H. Lewis, a reporter at the *New York Times*—the paper of record, for darn's sake—called us excitedly to say that they had run an article in 1985 about hairy ears being signs of susceptibility to heart attacks. In 1984, two doctors in Mineola, Long Island, reported to the *New England Journal of Medicine* that there was a "significant statistical link" between men (but not women) who had hair in their ear canal and people they had treated for coronary artery disease. The doctors did not overplay the significance of this finding. In fact, the hubbub their findings released prompted Dr. Richard F. Wagner and Dr. Karen Dineen to issue a poetic disclaimer:

> If on the ear there is a crease
> Do not assume that life will cease.
> If hair is noted in the ear,
> Do not assume that death is near.
> So, if when walking down the street
> An ear with hair and crease you meet,
> Don't give the gent a dreadful fright—
> Don't hint infarction is in sight.

Needless to say, the medical authorities we consulted would neither affirm nor deny the viability of the androgen theory.

We give up. Some Frustables are too frustrating even for us, and we're masochists.

We figure that Stacey Lero will be going to high school soon. She's obviously very bright and will probably become a science major in high school. She will then enter college, where she will become a double endocrinology/genetics major. She'll choose between MIT and Cal Tech for her graduate work. In the year 2011, Stacey will win the Nobel Prize for answering this Frustable. The world will be a better place. And it will all be due to that seventh-grade science teacher in Bryan, Texas. Well, and maybe a little to the inspiration provided by that free copy of *When Do Fish Sleep?*

A free book goes to Stacey Lero of Bryan, Texas.

Tuesday

Dear Dave ~
l believe l
have the
answer to
your question

US MAIL

24815

LETTERS

We have received more than two thousand letters since the publication of *Why Do Clocks Run Clockwise?*. Most of them posed Imponderables or tried to answer Frustables. But some corrected or added information to our answers or contained priceless comments about the topics in our first two volumes of *Imponderables*. Here are some of our favorites.

On the Relative Merits of Round vs. Flat Toothpicks

We commented that even the manufacturers of flat toothpicks couldn't provide any reason why they were superior to round toothpicks, except for their lower price. Who would have thought that this topic could rouse emotions? Some letters were thoughtful, others passionate.

Flat toothpicks have uses round ones don't have, such as smearing small amounts of various kinds of goo onto surfaces (epoxy cement is one) and in being able to enter crevices closed to round toothpicks. Flat picks, with their greater surface, are in my experience superior to round ones for testing doneness of cakes, custards and so on. . . .

MAX HERZOG
Augusta, Georgia

When I read your slam at flat toothpicks in *Imponderables*, I thought, "Gee, I hope I can find this guy's address so I can straighten him out." And lo and behold, there it was. You even invited comment. You must be a brave man. If you can't stand the thought of reading a defense of flat toothpicks, skip this part.

I *hate* round toothpicks, The damn things are too fat and too close to their little pointy ends, which means that they won't go between my teeth at the gum line far enough to push out the bits of whatever gets stuck in there. Flat toothpicks will. So what if I have to throw a few away when they break before I can accomplish much; they're cheap, as you pointed out.

Furthermore, being pointed on both ends, round toothpicks are worthless for polishing the front surfaces of my teeth, unless I chew them down a bit first. I think the makers of flat toothpicks should square off those big ends, but at least those ends aren't pointy as on those round jobbers, and I can do some good with them.

Whenever a restaurant has only round toothpicks, I take out my pocket knife and whittle 'em down so they'll go through the gaps. I haven't worked up the nerve yet to do this in front of the maître d', but one of these days I will, scattering toothpick slivers on the carpet, to make sure the message is absorbed.

ALAN M. COURTRIGHT
Seattle, Washington

On Why Countdown Leaders on Films Don't Count Down to One

Your information is correct until you reported that the number one is the start of the picture. Although there isn't a one on Academy Leader, the picture actually starts on what would be zero. The forty-seven frames of black film that follow the single frame bearing a "2" are for the projectionist to open the dowser and allow light through the projector. A quick "beep" is usually heard along with the number two, indicating that the sound is in sync with the picture.

In theaters that alternate between two projectors, there is a mark that appears in the upper right-hand corner of the picture, which tells the projectionist to start the other projector up to speed, and then a second mark, which is when the projectionist actually should change over to the new reel. This countdown leader allows a precise amount of time for the projector to get up to speed, so that when the changeover occurs the viewer will not have missed any of the movie.

BRIAN M. DEMKOWICZ
Chief Projectionist, IMAX Theater
Baltimore, Maryland

DAVID FELDMAN

On Why American Elections Are Held on Tuesday

Election day is not the second Tuesday in November but is the first Tuesday after the first Monday in November.

STEVEN J. RIZZO
Islip, New York

On Why Balls Are on Top of Flagpoles

I was always taught that the answer was longevity of the pole. In the days when flagpoles were wooden, the end grain of the wood was exposed if not capped by a ball or other type of finial. End grain absorbs dampness more readily than any other part of the wood. . . .

GAVIN DUNCAN
Tabb, Virginia

Several veterans, including retired Army Sergeant Robert E. Krotzer of Hephzibah, Georgia, wrote to say that they were taught that the purpose of the ball was to keep the flag from being caught on the pole when the wind blew the flag upward. The flag experts we spoke to admit that this is the reasoning the Army provides, but insist that even a sphere doesn't stop a flag from getting stuck on top of a pole.

On Why the Sound of Running Water Changes When Hot Water Is Turned On

I do not deny the validity of the causes you discussed, however the *pitch* of that sound at a given rate of flow depends on the density of the water. Hot water is substantially less dense than cold water. . . . The fundamental fact of physics is that different density fluids have different natural frequencies of vibration while flowing through a given orifice.

Just turn on any hot-water faucet that has been off long enough for the water content to get cold some distance down the pipe. Then stand back and listen. You will clearly hear a change in pitch as the hot water arrives. The change is sudden and cannot be explained by any adaptive change of the pipes. It is the direct result of the change in the natural frequency of the water itself. The noisier the flow the more noticeable the change.

STEFAN HABSBURG
Farmington Hills, Michigan

On Why We Aren't Most Comfortable in 98.6° F Temperature

In *Why Do Clocks Run Clockwise?*, you wrote we would feel most comfortable when it is 98.6° F in the ambient air—if we were nudists.

Not *exactly* so. Human beings use up caloric energy, derived from food, to make motions with our muscular bodies. This process yields a certain amount of excess energy in the form of heat. Our bodies radiate this excess heat into the ambient air. When severely overheated, our bodies hasten the action by evaporating sweat. But we must have a means to *keep* our body temperature at 98.6° F or we die of heat prostration.

If we were all nudists and the ambient air *everywhere* was 98.6° F, we'd feel discomfort the moment we began to move. Lacking a temperature differential in the ambient air, our bodies could no longer radiate heat easily. First we'd sweat, and then we'd all die.

The only hope to remain alive would be to remain as motionless as possible for as long as possible, but sooner or later the excess heat from involuntary motions (like the heart and lung muscles) would build up.

So a 98.6° F temperature wouldn't be "comfortable" very long. . . . We need a slightly lower temperature in the air sooner or later.

DON SAYENGA
Bethlehem, Pennsylvania

DAVID FELDMAN

On Bird Droppings

You can't get away with anything with Imponderables *readers. We simplified a little by calling the white stuff surrounding the black dot in bird droppings "urine." One reader noticed.*

Mammals and amphibians get rid of nitrogenous waste in the form of urea dissolved in water. This is the material we commonly call urine. Birds and reptiles cannot accomplish this. They get rid of their nitrogenous wastes in a white semisolid form called uric acid. This is the white material in the birds' droppings.

There are two reasons why birds and reptiles use uric acid for waste disposal. One is because it is a water conservation technique. The other reason is perhaps more important. Bird and reptile embryos develop inside a hard shell. If they were to produce water-soluble urea while developing, it would end up poisoning the embryo before it could fully develop and hatch.

This leads us to the answer of another interesting question, "What is that 'gooky' stuff inside the shell after a baby bird hatches?" It is the remains of what is called the "allantois," the garbage can where nonsoluble uric acid is deposited while the embryo is developing.

SANDY JONES
Manassas, Virginia

On the Purpose of the Half Moons on Fingernails

Although our explanation—lunula are trapped air and serve no biological purpose—was correct, one reader did find a way to use them:

When preparing a patient prior to surgery requiring a full anesthetic, I was told to remove all nail polish prior to admission. When I asked why, I was told that recovery room personnel can monitor blood pressure by observing changes in the color of half moons.

MICHEALE WILLIAMS
Portland, Oregon

WHEN DO FISH SLEEP?

On the Mysterious Fruit Flavors Contained in Juicy Fruit Gum

> When I was in college, I made the synthetic flavors of oil of pineapple (ethyl butyrate) and oil of banana (amyl acetate). I found when mixed in precisely a certain ratio, I got the distinct aroma of Juicy Fruit. . . .
>
> Incidentally, if one wishes to synthesize ethyl butyrate, be prepared. Butyric acid is one stinking, sickening smelling acid. But once mixed with ethyl alcohol and concentrated sulfuric acid, the ethyl butyrate emerges with a sweet pineapple aroma.
>
> HAROLD E. BLAKE
> Tampa, Florida

On the Purpose of Pubic and Underarm Hair

Most of the experts we contacted speculated that this body hair served as a sexual attractant. But in a letter to Human Evolution, *one reader dissented. We reprint part of the letter with his permission:*

> Pubic and axillary hair have been assumed to be biologically non-functional and therefore relegated to a role of mere sex attractants or to signal sexual maturity. Yet if one examines the action of axillary and pubic hair it can be seen that these patches serve as a kind of lubricant for arm and leg movements repectively and must have been retained in that capacity or evolved separately when other body hair was lost. One can easily observe the friction-reducing function of axillary hair by shaving under one arm and noting the added friction of the shaved arm. The fact that pubic hair extends up the abdomen beyond the point where it facilitates leg movement may mean that body hair was lost while our fore-bears were still walking in a crouch or on knuckles; for it comes into function, particularly the lateral portions, in that position. It would serve well for a semicrouched or sometimes-crouched proto-hominid that had lost most of its body hair. As our ancestral mothers began losing their body hair, fatty breasts and pubic and axillary hair could have all evolved simultaneously. The hair patches were selected for the purely biological function of reducing friction whereas general loss of body hair gave rise to the

DAVID FELDMAN

necessity of fatty breasts for providing the crucial psychological role of softness, comfort, and security for the infant.

NOEL W. SMITH
State University of New York
Plattsburgh, New York

On Why Ranchers Hang Old Boots Upside-down on Fence Posts

The longest chapter in Why Do Clocks Run Clockwise? *was a futile attempt to answer this Imponderable. We confirmed that Nebraska was the epicenter of boot-hanging activity. We even found the son of the man reputed to have started the practice. But even he didn't know why his father hung the boots. Some readers had their own ideas.*

Marla Bouton, of Kearney, Nebraska, sent us an article by Roger L. Welsch, professor of English and anthropology at the University of Nebraska–Lincoln, published in the October 30, 1983, Sunday World-Herald Magazine *of the Midlands. Along with repeating all of the theories we advanced, Welsch recounted many other stories he was told by boot-hangers, including the number of boots indicated the number of sons in the family; the toes point toward the nearest graveyard; the toes point toward the main house in case someone was lost in a snowstorm; and the boots are a token of good luck.*

Welsch concludes that although there may not be one single answer, hanging boots is probably some form of territorial marker. He notes that boot hanging is most prevalent in arid flatlands.

In a geography like this, long arrays of boots are striking, even stunning, and that is precisely their purpose. They are markers. They announce that someone lives here in this moonscape, that there are inhabitants, no matter how "deserted"—a perfect word, "deserted!"—things appear to be. . . .

Several readers insisted there was a more practical explanation for the custom.

The ranchers may be trying to stop the absorption of water. . . . In Alabama, a lot of farmers turn empty cans onto the tops of fence posts for this reason, or they will nail the tops that were taken from cans, onto the tops of the posts. This keeps the posts from absorbing large amounts of water when it rains. Wooden posts absorb quite a bit of water through the tops. Putting boots on the posts might prevent the wood from rotting prematurely.

C.A. "Junior" Weaver
Millbrook, Alabama

In West Virginia, some of the older farmers, including my grandparents, used to put on tin cans, old pieces of tires, roof shingles, or something else that would cover the top and hang down the sides of the fence posts.

This practice was done mostly to fence posts that still had bark on them. The farmers felt there was no reason to put objects on posts that had the bark stripped off.

Still asking why? Believe it or not, the reason was to keep the fence posts from rotting.

The idea was to keep the rain and snow from laying on the top of the post and soaking or running behind the bark. They believed the rain or snow would run down behind the bark, become trapped and rot the wood faster than if there was no bark at all on the posts. . . .

My husband and I have fence posts in our backyard (they are over 10 years old) and the bark has been stripped off. They show no signs of rot so far. They are so hard you can't hardly drive a nail into them.

Every once in awhile when I am traveling on some of the older, less busier country roads in the state, I see a fence with something on the top of the fence posts, and I remember asking my grandfather why he was doing it. I am glad that I was curious enough to ask because I may have helped you solve an Imponderable that seemed to be driving you nuts.

Elaine K. Southern
Clarksburg, West Virginia

DAVID FELDMAN

If most of our letters on this subject came from the South and the Midwest, we received at least one sighting considerably farther to the north.

I was very surprised to see this in your book as I thought this practice was only done in my old territory.

I was a district rep for a car manufacturer and my territory included the central east of Alberta, Canada. This included Drumheller and Trochu, two small towns on either side of the Deer River.

Drumheller is famous for being the site of one of the first large dinosaur finds in North America. It now has a large scientific museum that attracts thousands of visitors every year. Trochu is not famous for anything, although it does have a very good ice-cream stand open during the summer.

Anyway, the back road from Drumheller to Trochu is one of the most pleasant drives you can find on the prairie. . . .

After crossing the river and driving toward Trochu and the ice-cream stand, there is a rancher who has put hundreds of boots on his fencing along the road. I asked about them and was told that they were to stop the aging of the fence posts. If the tops of the posts are covered and not left exposed, they will last that much longer. And since I once had a job replacing an old fence, I can assure you that anything that can be done to make them last longer would be tried.

Kevan Taylor
Niagara Falls, Ontario, Canada

WHEN DO FISH SLEEP?

Acknowledgments

The single most gratifying part of my job is receiving the thousands of letters that readers of *Imponderables* have sent me. Your ideas have supplied most of the mysteries answered in this book. Your support and encouragement have supplied the inspiration.

I have kept my promise to answer all letters that have included self-addressed stamped envelopes. I'll continue the practice, but please be patient. When deadline pressure mounts, so does my response time. I cherish your letters and pounce on each one like a child encountering a wrapped birthday present.

In Harper & Row, I have a found a publishing house that provides me with all the benefits of a family—without the in-laws. Excepting that he is taller and wears clothes better than me, Rick Kot is all I could ask for in a person or an editor. His assistant Scott Terranella is exhibiting annoying tendencies toward becoming as perfect as Rick, but Scott has been so kind to me it's hard to get mad at him.

From the top down the folks at Harper & Row have been gratuitously nice to me. The publisher, Bill Shinker, has been constantly supportive and enthusiastic. The beloved Brenda Marsh and the sales reps (sounds like a Motown act!) have, wonder of wonders, gotten my books into the stores. Roz Barrow, with skill and graciousness, made sure there were enough books to ship to the stores. Steve Magnuson has been full of great marketing ideas. Debra Elfenbein, with a sharp mind and several sharp red pencils, helped tighten and focus this manuscript. The publicity department, headed by Karen Mender, helped thrust me upon an innocent North America. Special thanks to my publicist and rock 'n' roll heartthrob, Craig Herman, and to Allison Koop, Susie Epstein, and Anne Berman. And to the trinity in Special Markets, Connie Levinson, Barbara Rittenhouse, and Mark Landau: You have a friend for life, whether you like it or not.

In *Why Do Clocks Run Clockwise?*, I complained that my agent, Jim Trupin, didn't laugh enough at my jokes. I'm happy and proud to announce that he has corrected this egregious flaw and can now lay claim to be the last Renaissance man. Jim and his wife, Elizabeth, are two of my favorite people. Speaking of favorite people, Kassie Schwan, illustrator and semiprofessional gardener, continues to produce terrific illustrations. And the late (not dead, just late) Mark Kohut has taught me more than anyone about how the book business works. Lovely Joann Carney is the only person who has ever gotten me to sit in front of a camera for more than five minutes without wiggling uncontrollably, let alone to enjoy the process of being photographed.

Over the last few years, I've had a chance to meet an underpaid, unsung but fabulous group of people—booksellers. From the president and CEO of Waldenbooks, Harry Hoffman, to the managers of mall stores, Julie Lasher and Brian Scott Rossman; from B. Dalton's manager of Merchandise Planning and Communication, Mattie Goldberg, to all the folks at the Benjamins Bookstore in the Pittsburgh Airport, the booksellers I've met have been intelligent, committed, and inordinately good company. Thanks for providing me with an on-the-job education.

My friends and family have helped me survive a difficult year. Thanks to all who have lent support: Tony Alessandrini; Michael Barson; Rajat Basu; Ruth Basu; Jeff Bayone; Jean Behrend; Brenda Berkman; Cathy Berkman; Sharon Bishop; Carri Blees; Christopher Blees; Jon Blees; Bowling Green State University's Popular Culture Department; Jerry Braithwaite; Annette Brown; Arvin Brown; Herman Brown; Joann Carney; Janice Carr; Alvin Cooperman; Marilyn Cooperman; Judith Dahlman; Paul Dahlman; Shelly de Satnick; Linda Diamond; Joyce Ebert; Steve Feinberg; Fred Feldman; Gilda Feldman; Michael Feldman; Phil Feldman; Phyllis Fineman; Kris Fister; Linda Frank; Seth Freeman; Elizabeth Frenchman; Michele Gallery; Chris Geist; Jean Geist; Bonnie Gellas; Bea Gordon; Dan Gordon; Ken Gordon; Judy Goulding; Chris Graves; Christal Henner; Marilu Henner; Melodie Henner; David Hennes; Paula Hennes; Sheila Hennes; Sophie Hennes; Steve Hofman; Uday Ivatury; Terry Johnson; Sarah Jones; Mitch Kahn; Dimi Karras; Mary Katinos; Robin Kay; Stewart Kellerman; Harvey Kleinman; Mark Kohut; Claire Labine; Randy Ladenheim-Gil; Debbie Leitner; Jared Lilienstein; David Lynch; all my friends at the Manhattan Bridge Club; Phil Martin; Jeff McQuain; Julie Mears; Phil Mears; Carol Miller; Barbara Morrow; Phil Neel; Steve Nellisen; Millie North; Milt North; Charlie Nurse; Debbie Nye; Tom O'Brien; Pat O'Conner; Joanna Parker; Jeannie Perkins; Merrill Perlman; Joan Pirkle; Larry Prussin; Joe Rawley; Rose Reiter; Brian Rose; Paul Rosenbaum; Carol Rostad; Tim Rostad; Susie Russenberger; Leslie Rugg; Tom Rugg; Gary Saunders;

Joan Sanders; Mike Sanders; Norm Sanders; Cindy Shaha; Patricia
Sheinwold; Kurtwood Smith; Susan Sherman Smith; Chris Soule;
Karen Stoddard; Kat Stranger; Anne Swanson; Ed Swanson; Mike
Szala; Josephine Teuscher; Carol Vellucci; Dan Vellucci; Hattie
Washington; Julie Waxman; Roy Welland; Dennis Whelan; Devin
Whelan; Heide Whelan; Lara Whelan; Jon White; Ann Whitney; Carol
Williams; Maggie Wittenburg; Karen Wooldridge; Maureen Wylie;
Charlotte Zdrok; Vladimir Zdrok; and Debbie Zuckerberg.

Well more than one thousand educators, institutions, experts,
foundations, corporations, and trade associations were contacted for
this book. Because we can't go to reference books to get our answers to
Imponderables, we are dependent upon the generosity of the folks
listed below. Although many other people supplied help, those listed
below gave us information that led directly to the solution of
Imponderables in this book: Sandra Abrams, Associated Services for
the Blind; Richard B. Allen, Atlantic Offshore Fishermen's
Association; Dr. Robert D. Altman, A & A Veterinary Hospital;
American Academy of Dermatology; American Hotel and Motel
Association; Carl Andrews, Hershey Foods; Richard A. Anthes,
National Center for Atmospheric Research; Gerald S. Arenberg,
National Association of Chiefs of Police; Dr. Edward C. Atwater,
American Association for the History of Medicine.

Dr. Don E. Bailey, American Association of Sheep and Goat
Practitioners; Dr. Ian Bailey, School of Optometry, University of
California, Berkeley; Jan Balkin, American Trucking Associations; Dr.
Pat A. Barelli, American Rhinologic Society; Nancy Beiman, National
Cartoonists Society; Roy Berces, Pacific Stock Exchange; Dr. William
Berman, Society for Pediatric Research; Dr. William Bischoff,
American Numismatic Society; Ed J. Blasko, Eastman Kodak
Company; Dr. Peter Boyce, American Astronomical Society; Richard
Brooks, Stouffer Hotels; Edwin L. Brown, American Culinary
Federation; Bureau of the Mint, Department of the Treasury; Dr.
Walter F. Burghardt, American Veterinary Society of Animal Behavior;
Herbert H. Buzbee, International Association of Coroners and Medical
Examiners.

John Canemaker; Gerry Carr, International Game Fish
Association; Carel Carr, Yellow Pages Publishers Association; Helen
Castle, Kellogg's; Louis Chang; Bob Cochran, Society of Paper Money
Collectors; Linden Cole, Society of Actuaries; Linda W. Coleman,
Department of the Treasury, Bureau of Engraving and Printing; Robert

L. Collette, National Fisheries Institute; Dr. James D. Conroy, College of Veterinary Medicine; Charles T. Conway, Gillette Company; Philip S. Cooke, Inflight Food Service Association; Captain K.L. Coskey, Navy Historical Foundation; Louise Cotter, National Cosmetology Association; Danny J. Crawford, Marine Corps Historical Foundation; Edward Culleton, Green Olive Trade Association.

Hubert R. Dagley II, American College of Sports Medicine; Paul N. Dane, Society of Wireless Pioneers; Neill Darmstadter, American Trucking Association; Dr. Frank Davidoff, American College of Physicians; Professor Michael De L. Landon, American Society for Legal History; Brian M. Demkowicz, Maryland Academy of Sciences; Dr. Liberato John A. DiDio, International Federation of Associations of Anatomists; James J. Donahue, Duracell Inc.; Richard H. Dowhan, GTE Products; Don R. Duer, Still Bank Collectors Club of America; Thomas Dufficy, National Association of Photographic Manufacturers; W.K. Bill Dunbar, Morse Telegraph Club.

Susan Ebaugh, Serta Inc.; Dr. William G. Eckert, INFORM; Carole L. Edwards, Mobil Oil Corporation; Peter Eisenstadt, New York Stock Exchange Archives; Kay Engelhardt, American Egg Board.

Raymond E. Falconer, Atmospheric Sciences Research Center, SUNY at Albany; Dr. Fred Feldman; Dr. Barry Fells, Epigraphic Society; Stanley Fenvessey, Fenvessey Consulting; Peter C. Fetterer, Kohler Company; Deidre Flynn, Popcorn Institute; Bruce A. Foster, Sugar Industry Technologists; Don French, Radio Shack; Lester Frey, Villamarin Guillen.

Samuel R. Gammon, American Historical Association; Dr. James Q. Gant, International Lunar Society; Bruce R. Gebhardt, North American Native Fishes Association; Chris George, Rand McNally; Gerontology Research Center, National Institute of Aging; Karen L. Glaske, United Professional Horsemen's Association; Jacqueline Greenwood, Black & Decker; Patricia A. Guy, Bay Area Information System Reference Center.

Susan Hahn, United States Tennis Association; Dr. John Hallett, Desert Research Institute; Korynne Halverson, Evans Food Group; David A. Hamilton, Professional Ski Instructors of America; Lynn Hamlin, National Syndications Inc.; Darryl Hansen, Entomological Society of America; Carl Harbaugh, International Association of Chiefs of Police; Dorcas R. Hardy, Commissioner of Social Security; John Harrington, Council for Periodical Distributors; Tamara J. Hartweg, Kraft; Connie Heatley, Direct Marketing Association; Jim Heffernan,

National Football League; Richard Heistchel, Schinder Elevator Company; Jacque Hetrick, Spalding Sports Worldwide; Shari Hiller, Sherwin-Williams Company; Janet Hinshaw, Wilson Ornithological Society; Robert C. Hockett, Council for Tobacco Research; Dick Hofacker, AT&T Bell Laboratories; Greg Hoffman, Jolly Time; Beverly Holmes, Frito-Lay Inc.; Dr. Daniel Hooker, University of North Carolina at Chapel Hill, Student Health Service; Richard H. Hopper; Donald Hoscheit, Osco Drug; Mark R. Houston, California Kiwifruit Commission; Professor Barbara J. Howe, National Council on Public History; Kenneth Hudnall, National Yellow Pages Agency Association; Hyde Athletic Industries, Inc.

Dr. Peter Ihrke, American Academy of Veterinary Dermatology; International Bank Note Society; Helen Irwin, National Tennis Hall of Fame.

John Jay, Intercoiffure America; Dr. William P. Jollie, American Association of Anatomists; Larry Josefowicz, Wilson Sporting Goods Company.

Jeff Kanipe, *Astronomy*; Robert Kaufman, Metropolitan Museum of Art; Edward E. Kavanaugh; Dr. Thomas P. Kearns, American Ophthalmological Society; Michele Kelley, American Hotel and Motel Association; Dr. Anthony L. Kiorpes, University of Wisconsin, Madison, School of Veterinary Medicine; Dan Kistler, Christian Research Institute; Dr. Ben Klein; Samuel Klein, United States Postal System; Ken Klippen, United Egg Producers; Dr. Kathleen Kovacs, American Veterinary Medicine Association; Stanley Kranzer, Metropolitan Life.

Jean Lang, Fieldcrest; Keith Lattislaw, National Center for Health Statistics; John Laughton, American Standard; Mary Jane Laws, American Dairy Association; Cathy Lawton, Shulton Inc.; Dr. Beverly Leffers, Milton Helpern Institute of Forensic Medicine; Professor Alfonz Lengyel, Eastern College; Dick Levinson, H.Y. Aids Group; Peter H. Lewis, *New York Times*; Pierre Lilavois, New York City Sewer Department; Barbara Linton, National Audubon Society; Kenneth M. Liss, Liss Public Relations; John Loftus, Society of Collision Repair Specialists; Joan G. Lufrano, Foote, Cone & Belding; Lynne Luxton, American Foundation for the Blind.

William L. MacMillan III, Pencil Makers Association; Alan MacRobert, *Sky & Telescope*; Dr. M. Mackauer, Center for Pest Management; Joseph D. Madden, Drug, Chemical and Allied Trades Association; Reverend Robert L. Maddox, Americans United for

Separation of Church and State; Mail Order Association of America; William C. Mailhot, Gold Medal Flour; Michael Marchant, Ogden Allied Aviation Services; Ginny Marcin, Campbell Soup Company; Colonel Ronald G. Martin; Howard W. Mattson, Institute of Food Technologists; Dr. Robert McCarley, Sleep Research Society; James P. McCauley, International Association of Holiday Inns; Dr. Everett G. McDonough, Zotos International; William F. "Crow Chief" Meyer, Blackfeet Indian Writing Company; Mary D. Midkiff, American Horse Council; Jerry Miles, American Baseball Coaches Association; David G. Miller, National Association of Retail Druggists; Dr. Stephen Miller, American Optometric Association; Robert J. Moody, General Electric; Rita Moroney, Office of the Postmaster General; Pete Morris, C.H. Morse Stamp Company; Bill Mortimer, Life Insurance Marketing and Research Association; George Motture, Wise Foods; Meg Wehby Muething; Arthur J. Mullkoff, American Concrete Institute; Edith Munro, Corn Refiners Association; Gordon W. Murrey, Murrey International; D.C. Myntti, American Bankers Association.

Dr. David Nash, American College of Physicians; National Institute on Aging, National Institute of Health; Arnie Nelson, Yellow Spots; David Nystrom, U.S. Geological Survey.

Norman Oehlke, International Fabricare Institute; Carl Oppedahl.

Dr. Lawrence Charles Parish, History of Dermatology Society; Dianne V. Patterson, United States Postal System; William R. Paxton, Federal Railroad Administration; Peggy Pegram, Bubble Yum; Joy Perillo, AT&T Archives; Pillsbury Company; Leslye Piqueris, American Foundation for the Blind; Lawrie Pitcher Platt, Tupperware Home Parties; Bruce Pluckhahn, National Bowling Hall of Fame and Museum; Proctor-Silex; Dr. Robert Provine, University of Maryland; Roy S. Pung, Photo Marketing Association, International; Thomas L. Purvis, Institute of Early American History and Culture.

Jerry Rafats, National Agriculture Library; Dr. Salvatore Raiti, National Hormone and Pituitary Program; Monika Reed, Berol USA; Walter Reed, National Automatic Merchandising Association; Al Rickard, Snack Food Association; Bob Riemer, Gasoline and Automotive Service Dealers; R.J. Reynolds; Robert S. Robe, Scipio Society of Naval and Military History; Dr. Robert R. Rofen, Aquatic Research Institute; Tim Ross, U.S. Ski Coaches Association; Professor Mary H. Ross, Virginia Polytechnic Institute; Rosemary Rushka, American Academy of Ophthalmology.

Micael Saba, Attiyeh Foundation; Gabe Samuels, Yellow Spots;

José Luis Perez Sanchez, Commercial Office ot the Embassy of Spain; Ronald A. Schachar, Association for the Advancement of Ophthalmology; Schick Division, Warner-Lambert; Janet Seagle, U.S. Golf Association; William Seitz, Neighborhood Cleaners Association; Gwen Sells, Tall Clubs International; Dale Servetnick, Department of the Treasury; Norman F. Sharp, Cigar Association of America; Anthony H. Siegel, Ametek; Dr. M.S. Silberman; Joan Silverman, Citicorp; Dave Smith, Disney Company; Linda Smith, National Restaurant Association; Sid Smith, National Association of Hosiery Manufacturers; Wayne Smith, Sunbeam Appliance Company; Bruce V. Snow, Dairylea Cooperative; Dona Sorensen, Fleischmann's Yeast; Marshall Sorkin, Carter-Wallace; Richard Spader, American Angus Association; Dr. Bob Spanyer, American College of Physicians; John J. Suarez, National Pest Control Association; Amy Sudol, Chase Manhattan; Richard J. Sullivan, Olive Oil Group.

David Taylor, Bank Administration Institute; Thomas A. Tervo, Stearns and Foster Bedding; William D. Toohey, Tobacco Institute; Victor Toth, Multi-Tenant Telecommunications Association; Bob Toy, Telephone Pioneers of America; Jim Trdinich, National League.

Ralph E. Venk, Photographic Society of America; Dennis Vetock, U.S. Army Military History Institute; Elaine Viets, St. Louis *Post-Dispatch*; Gerald F. Voigt, American Concrete Pavement Association; Vulcan Foundry.

Al Wagner, AFC Computer Services; Debbie Walsh, American Federation of Teachers; Belinda Baxter Walsh, Procter & Gamble; Spider Webb, Tattoo Club of America; Monique Wegener, Lenders Bagel Baker; Richard H. Welsh, Jr., Cannon Mills; S.S. White Industrial Products, Pennwalt Corporation; Melvin T. Wilczynski, Lane Drug Company; Dr. Elizabeth Williams, Wyoming State Veterinary Laboratory; Dr. Jack Wilmore, University of Texas; Frank C. Wilson, American Orthopedic Association; Donald W. Wilson, U.S. Ski Educational Foundation; Jerry Wiseman, Atlantic Gelatin; Dr. Robert M. Wold, College of Optometrists in Vision Development; Merry Wooten, Astronomical League; World Impex Bowling.

S.G. Yasinitsky, Orders and Medals Society of America.

Dr. E. Zander, Winthrop Consumer Products; Linda Zirbes, Hyatt Hotels Corporation; Jim Zuckerman, Associated Photographers International.

And to my sources who, for whatever reason, preferred to remain anonymous, thanks for your contribution.

ACKNOWLEDGMENTS

WHY DO DOGS HAVE WET NOSES?
and Other Imponderables™ of Everyday Life

For Jim Trupin

Contents

CONTENTS   521

CONTENTS

CONTENTS

CONTENTS

CONTENTS

Preface

We live in an age of lasers and quarks. We are supposedly over-loaded with information. But there is much we don't know. Like why does a green bar of soap yield white suds? Or why have most airlines stopped serving honey roasted peanuts?

As long as there are humans, there will be Imponderables, little mysteries of everyday life that drive you nuts—until you get the answers. Our mission is to stamp out Imponderability; this isn't an easy task, but luckily our readers have made it a collaborative enterprise.

Virtually all of the mysteries in this book were sent in by readers of the first three volumes of *Imponderables*. In the Frust-ables section, readers offer their help in answering ten frustrat-ing Imponderables that we haven't been able to solve.

And for those of you who want to let us have it, the letters section is the place.

How do we entice potential coconspirators? If you are the first person to submit an Imponderable that we use in the next book, or are the first to solve a Frustable, you'll receive a free, autographed copy of the book, along with an acknowledgment.

What Are Gnats Doing When They Swarm?

Gnats are not the only living things that swarm. Birds do it. And bees do it. So it shouldn't be too surprising to learn that those gnats aren't freaking out or doing an insect variation of slam dancing when they swarm. Those are male gnats looking for female companionship.

Like the boys in *Saturday Night Fever*, flashing their gold chains and hairy chests, male gnats figure that no hot-blooded female anthropod could possibly resist their charms when they strut their stuff together. Amazingly, it works. At least, we can say with authority that there is no shortage of gnats.

One question persists, though. If the purpose of the swarming display is to find a female, why do all the males compete with each other in a swarm when the female of the species is probably telling her best friend, "When they're swarming, all boy-gnats look alike."

Maybe swarming isn't the most efficient means for male

gnats to find a mate, but then pack cruising in bars isn't the most efficient method either. Maybe male gnats, like their human counterparts, need friends along to steel their courage.

Submitted by Charles, a caller on the Larry Mantle show, KPPC-FM, Pasadena, California.

Why Do Manufacturers Place Underwear Labels Inside the Center of the Back Where They Rub Uncomfortably on a Person's Spine?

When we posed this imponderable to our illustrious illustrator, Kassie Schwan, she quickly answered, "So that you know which way to put your underwear on." Yes, Kas, but this begs the question. Which sadist decided that the label had to be put in a place designed to rub against our delicate backsides?

As usual with such matters, economics rears its ugly head. Underwear is a low profit margin item; manufacturers are eager to cut costs in any way possible. It is cheaper to print the size on a label attached to the garment than it would be to print the size on each polymer bag. This way, the label doubles as the size indicator at the retail store.

At least one person was willing to state that he was unashamed of the industry practice. George Weldon, of underwear giant Munsingwear, said that his company's labels are made of 100% cotton, and are so soft that consumers can't tell whether the label is on the outside or inside.

You know something? He's right. In the interest of science, we tested his thesis and found that we could not tell whether the label was on the outside, inside, or, in one case, torn off completely.

A caller on a talk show once pleaded: "Why can't manufacturers put the labels on the outside of the back?" Weldon says that Munsingwear considered it, but consumers fear exposing their size inadvertently to the scrutiny and amusement of the public.

Submitted by Kay Nelson of Huntington Beach, California.

When a Letter Is Sent from the United States to Greece, Does Greece Receive any Money from the U.S. for Delivering It?

Much to our surprise, yes.

Ernest J. Collins, of the USPS's Office of Classification and Rates Administration, explains what is called the "terminal dues system":

> Foreign countries receive reimbursement for mail they process and deliver which is in excess of the mail which they send to the United States. For example, if during a given period Greece sent to the United States 10,000 kilograms of mail and the United States sent 12,000 kilograms to Greece, there would be an imbalance of 2,000 kilograms. The United States would reimburse Greece for the extra 2,000 kilograms. The reimbursement rate is currently $3.28 per kilogram.

The system does not differentiate between the two types of international mail, "LC" (letters and cards) and "AO" (publications). The terminal dues system reduces to a formula of about a nickel for delivering one half-ounce letter and about 30 times that much for delivering a one-pound magazine. A USPS press release complains that

> this type of terminal dues structure does not represent the real costs of delivering these different kinds of mails, since half-ounce letters cannot be handled and delivered for a nickel and it does not cost $1.57 to deliver a single magazine.

This imbalance of payments has caused political problems in the international postal community. Industrial nations, such as the

United States, lobby for greater compensation for letters, while small countries want to preserve the status quo.

The reason for the disagreement, of course, is purely financial. The U.S. has a large net outflow of publications and a huge net inflow of letters and postcards. The U.S. must subsidize the delivery of its international letters while simultaneously paying much more to foreign countries to deliver American publications than it really costs them to process and deliver.

The United States Postal Service isn't the only government arm that loses money because of this terminal dues system. The IRS wants its share too. Many American publishers have found it cheaper to relocate their printing facilities in foreign countries than pay punitive international postage fees. Other publishers freight items to the foreign country and then pay that country's local postage rates.

Because the international organization that arbitrates these matters has a one-country/one-vote policy (like the General Assembly of the United Nations), the little countries were able to block efforts to increase compensation for delivering letters.

But a Solomon-like solution has been agreed upon and will go into effect on January 1, 1991. The current flat rate will be continued until a "threshold amount" of 150 metric tons of annual mail is sent out of a country (third world countries do not send out this much). After 150 metric tons, the compensation will better reflect the actual cost of processing and delivering that type of mail.

Submitted by Bob Hatch of Seattle, Washington. Thanks also to Sharon Roberts of Ames, Quebec.

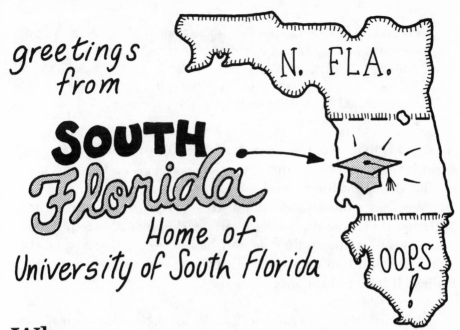

greetings
from

SOUTH
Florida
Home of
University of South Florida

N. FLA.

OOPS
!

Why Isn't the University of South Florida in Southern Florida?

Yes, folks. The University of South Florida is located in Tampa, smack dab in the middle (north-southwise, at least) of Florida. Maybe our simple peasant heritage is betraying us, but we too wondered why an institution of higher learning couldn't get its geographical location right.

We received a witty letter from Robert L. Allen, director of USF office of public affairs, in which he demonstrates that there was a modicum of logic in the name choice:

> When the University of South Florida was founded in 1956, there were already three other state-supported universities in Florida. They were Florida A&M University (Tallahassee) and Florida State University (Tallahassee), both in northwestern Florida, and the University of Florida (Gainesville) in north central Florida.
>
> At the time, the University of South Florida was the southernmost university in the Florida State University system. The pow-

ers that be did not foresee the establishment of universities in the southern part of the state. Since 1956, the University of Central Florida has been established in Orlando [not too far north of Tampa], Florida Atlantic University in Boca Raton and Florida International University in Miami [both far south of the University of South Florida].

Allen adds that "we generally describe our location as southwest Florida," which at least indicates that Tampa is on the west coast of Florida and still retains the USF initials.

We find it amazing that the trustees of the Florida school system didn't have the wisdom and marketing savvy to put more campuses in southern Florida long ago. After all, these campuses could have offered package deals of tuition plus Easter vacation frolics all for one low price.

Submitted by Jerry Kiewe of Lauderdale Lakes (far south of Tampa, by the way), Florida.

Why Are Racquetballs Blue?

Larry Josefowicz, of Wilson Sporting Goods Co., told *Imponderables* that the dark blue color is the most easily discernible. Light colors fade into the wooden floors and white or cream walls of a racquetball court. Considering how fast a racquetball moves during a game, the choice of colors becomes a safety, as well as a playability, issue.

Wilson and its competitors tested other colors, but none combined visibility with customer preference like the present color. Brad Patterson, executive director of the Racquetball Manufacturers Association, adds that at one time, black and dark green racquetballs were tested, but they marked the walls. Patterson doesn't see any other color stealing blue's thunder in the near future:

WHY DO DOGS HAVE WET NOSES?

The other reason it will be difficult to ever phase in any other color ball is simply player preference. It is akin to yellow tennis balls now [yellow tennis balls were also introduced to improve visibility, especially for indoor and nighttime tennis]. The players simply prefer blue, since that is the color they grew up with . . .

Submitted by Gary Fradkin of Carmel, New York.

Is There Any Rhyme or Reason to the Numbers Assigned to Federal Tax Forms? For Example, How Did the Most Prominent Form Get the Number 1040?

We heard from no less of a source than the chief of the Publishing Services Branch of the Internal Revenue Service, Hugh W. Kent, Jr. He prefaced his explanation by writing:

> We wish we could reciprocate with a Gothic tale of mystique, cloaked in a night fog like the one that hovered in the woods outside Dr. Frankenstein's castle.

Now we know the IRS has been accused of sadistic tendencies in the past, so as conscientious and heretofore unaudited taxpayers, we just want you, the reader, to realize that Mr. Kent is merely joking. He doesn't really wish to scare the hardworking taxpayers of America with ominous tales of nefarious IRS plots. On the contrary, he is demonstrating the fact that IRS officials have wonderful senses of humor. We're sure that Mr. Kent and the other fine people at the IRS understand that we were conducting legitimate business during that weeklong trip to Disney World last year. Researching Imponderables, you know.

Kirk Markland, also with the Publishing Services Branch, told us that the IRS decided on a four-digit numbering system for their forms. The rest, as Mr. Kent continues, is history:

> For stock, revision, and other control purposes, we number our forms in numerical sequence. Thus, when the first tax law

became effective in 1913, we merely numbered the new individual income tax form with the next number in sequence, which happened to be 1040. To preclude having large gaps in the sequential order of form numbers, our forms' numbering system allows us to reuse numbers as old forms become obsolete.

Neil Patton, chief of the Taxpayer Information and Education Branch of the IRS, sent us a copy of the first Form 1040, which was considerably simpler than today's "short form." One page asked taxpayers to itemize the types of income they accrued in 1913; another page asked about deductions in only seven categories. And the front page did not task the mathematical skills of the taxpayer: It asked him or her to subtract deductions from gross income, account for withheld taxes, and calculate the tax on a scale that will evoke nostalgia for all. The highest tax rate, for those earning more than $500,000 in net income, was all of six percent.

Submitted by Boyd Briskin of Riverside, California. Thanks also to Michael Gempe of Elmhurst, Illinois.

Why Does Wood "Pop" When Put on a Fire?

John A. Pitcher, director of the Hardwood Research Council, was kind enough to tackle this burning Imponderable:

> Wood pops when put on a fire because there are little pockets of sap, pitch [resin], or other volatiles that are contained in the wood. As the wood surface is heated and burns, heat is transferred to the sap or pitch deeper in the wood.
>
> The sap or pitch first liquefies, then vaporizes as the temperature increases. Gasses expand rapidly when heated and put tremendous pressure on the walls of the pitch pocket. When the pressure gets high enough, the pocket walls burst and the characteristic sound is heard.

Submitted by Patric Conroy of Walnut Creek, California.

WHY DO DOGS HAVE WET NOSES?

Why Does a Fire Create a Crackling Sound? Is There Any Reason Why a Fire Cracks Most When First Lit?

Of course, "pops" are not unrelated to "crackles." John Pitcher explains that the larger the sap or pitch pockets in the wood, the bigger the pop; but if there are smaller but more numerous pockets, the wood will crackle instead.

The reason most fires crackle most when first lit is that the smaller pieces of wood, used as kindling, heat up quickly. The inside sap pockets are penetrated and crackle immediately. Big pieces of wood burn much more slowly, with fewer, intermittent, but louder pops.

For those of you who are, pardon the expression, "would-be" connoisseurs of lumber acoustics, Pitcher provided *Imponderables* readers with a consumer's guide:

> There are distinct differences in the popping characteristics of woods. High on the list of poppers is tamarack or larch. Most conifers are ready poppers. On the other hand, hardwoods, such as ash, elm, and oak, tend to burn quietly, with only an occasionally tastefully subdued pop. You might call them poopers rather than poppers.

Submitted by Andrew F. Garruto of Kinnelon, New Jersey.

Why Did the Chinese First Use Chopsticks?

The conventional wisdom on this subject is that the Chinese consider it the chef's duty to carve meat or slice vegetables into bitesize morsels. Chopsticks were then invented to serve as efficient tools to pick up morsels of food and rice. But there is much evidence to suggest that their use was originally motivated not by aesthetics but by practical considerations.

Chopsticks were introduced sometime during the Chou Dynasty, probably a century or so before the birth of Christ. Until the Chou Dynasty, stir frying did not exist. But China faced a serious fuel (i.e., wood) shortage. Forests were cut down to clear land for agriculture to feed a burgeoning population.

Stir frying developed as the most efficient method to use the least amount of wood as fuel for the shortest period of time. Because the food was cut before stir frying, the meat and vegetables cooked much faster than by other methods.

During the Chou Dynasty, few people owned tables (a luxury, especially with the wood shortage), so a utensil was needed that would allow diners to eat with one hand only—the other hand was needed to hold the bowl of rice. Because most Chinese dishes have sauces, chopsticks enabled users to scoop up food without getting goop all over their fingers. And now chopsticks allow non-Orientals the opportunity to propel goop all over the tablecloths of Chinese restaurants.

And why did the Chinese decide to use chopsticks in the middle of this supposed wood shortage? Only some of the chopsticks were made of wood. More were made of ivory and bone.

Why Have Most Airlines Stopped Serving Honey Roasted Peanuts and Resumed Giving Away Salted and Dry Roasted Peanuts?

Sara Dornacker, media relations manager of United Airlines, told *Imponderables* that "cocktail snacks are rotated periodically to give frequent fliers some variety." United Airlines served honey roasted peanuts for five consecutive years but withdrew them for about one year while they gave "lightly salted peanuts" a chance. But in February, 1990, United brought back honey roasted peanuts and is hedging their decision now by alternating them with pretzels. Only time will tell whether passengers conditioned to legumes with their drinks will respond to starch.

But another source offers an alternative explanation for why honey roasted peanuts seem to have been withdrawn from most airlines' food service at around the same time. Phillip S. Cooke, executive administrator of Inflight Food Service Association, reports that passengers

> repeatedly commented in survey after survey that they did not like the smell created in the cabin when all of the passengers opened those little bags simultaneously. Apparently, honey roasted peanuts create a rather sickly sweet smell, although I must confess that I have never noticed it and it has certainly never bothered me personally.

AND OTHER IMPONDERABLES 545

It's never bothered us either. We were having a hard enough time trying to open up those blasted little bags with our fingernails and/or teeth.

Submitted by Deborah J. Huth of San Jose, California.

Why Don't Magazines Put Page Numbers on Every Page?

Magazine publishers *would* like to put a number on every page of their magazine. But many publishers freely agree to withhold pagination for full-page advertisements, particularly for "bleed" ads, in which the material covers the entire page. In a standard ad, an outside border usually allows for pagination without interfering with photographs or artwork. But many advertising agencies demand that their image-enhancing bleed ads not be marred by anything as mundane as a page number; publishers contractually accede to this requirement.

High-circulation magazines often publish many different editions. When you encounter letters after a page number (e.g., 35A, 35B, 35C), you are reading a section designed for a particular demographic or geographic group. Readers often find these editions annoying, because they impede the flow of the magazine (try finding page 36 when the regional edition occupies pages 35A through 35Q).

By customizing their editions, magazines can not only attract advertisers who might be uninterested or cannot afford inserting messages in a national edition, but can charge considerably more per thousand readers reached. If *Fortune* printed an edition targeted at accountants, for example, a software company with a new accounting package might be convinced to advertise in this edition but would not find it cost-effective to try the national edition. Even nonbleed full-page ads designed for regional or demographic editions are rarely numbered, since one ad might appear on several different page numbers in different editions.

J. J. Hanson, chairman and CEO of Hanson Publishing Group, Inc., adds that another reason for omitting pagination is that some ads are actually preprinted by the advertiser and inserted in the magazine: "Often those preprinted inserts are prepared before the publisher knows which page number would be appropriate." Scratch and sniff perfume strips and liquor ads with laser effects are two common examples.

At a time when one designer-jeans advertiser might book ten consecutive, nonpaginated pages, and regional, demographic, and advertising supplements can dot a single issue of a magazine, finding a page number can be a mine field for readers. But a gold mine for the publishers.

Submitted by Samuel F. Pugh of Indianapolis, Indiana. Thanks also to Karin Norris of Salinas, California; and Gloria A. Quigley of Chicago, Illinois.

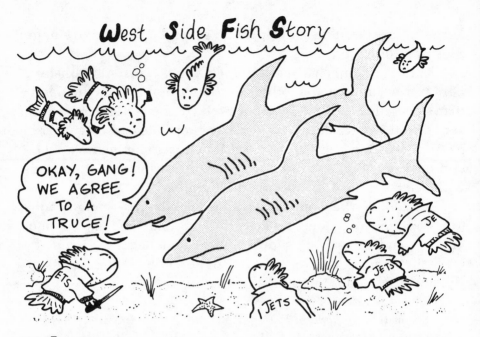

Why Don't the Small Fish in a Large Aquarium Have the Gills Scared out of Them Every Time a Big Fish, Such as a Shark, Swims By?

Every time we go to a public aquarium, we ask this question of anyone who looks even quasiofficial. We understand that a huge shark might not be a natural predator of a small fish. But then an elephant isn't *our* natural predator. And if an elephant started chasing us down the street, you'd better believe we would duck and cover.

Every one of those quasiofficials at the aquariums reported that the little fish didn't seem the least bit frightened by the sharks. We contacted some fish experts to discuss this phenomenon and in unison they echoed the same sentiments: Little fish don't tend to be any more frightened by sharks than mosquitoes are of humans.

Why not? Life in an aquarium, like the economy, is largely a matter of supply and demand. Little fish are not going to be

WHY DO DOGS HAVE WET NOSES?

eaten unless there is demand (i.e., hungry sharks). But aquarium heads, like some overactive presidents, tinker with the supply-demand equation. As an economist might put it, an aquarium is not a free market. The aquarium cuts demand by feeding the sharks, producing an artificial oversupply. R. Bruce Gebhardt, secretary and past president of the North American Native Fishes Association, explains:

> It doesn't behoove the manager of a public aquarium to replace smaller livestock all the time. It's too expensive and time-consuming . . . so the tank manager will feed the sharks. The sharks will come to rely on easy feeding rather than actually working for their food. If they're full, they're less likely to want to feed on other fish and make threatening moves towards them.

As the sharks (or other large predators) become progressively lazier, the small fish become emboldened, seeing themselves no longer as appetizers but rather as smaller but equal roommates in the tank. So the small fish comprise an ample but elusive supply for the sharks.

All of the authorities we contacted agreed that fish seem to have a developed sense or instinct that lets them know when they are in danger. Dr. Robert R. Rofen, of the Aquatic Research Institute, refers to the intelligence of fish ("they are smart enough to analyze whether they are in danger or not"). Gerry Carr, Director of Species Research for the International Game Fish Association, testifies to the adaptability of small fish:

> Little fish naturally do not want to be eaten and will vanish in a blink the moment the big fish begin to give off hunger signals. I don't know exactly how the little fish pick up on this, but they do. Maybe the shark's movements and vibrations change and this is picked up by the lateral line of the smaller fish. Maybe the shark's stomach growls (just kidding, but who knows). Fish have very active perception and can recognize and react to vibrations, temperature changes, and chemical changes in the water, all of which may play a part in alerting the potential sushi [Hey! We'll do the jokes here] meals of their impending danger.

AND OTHER IMPONDERABLES 549

One can observe large bass swimming casually in a lake with swarms of small fish that are their natural food, and the small fish will show no fear. But when the dinner bell rings, everything changes.

Carr adds that despite the shark's fearsome image, other fish, such as large groupers, would pose a much greater threat to small fish. Groupers are veritable vacuum cleaners in aquariums and are relatively oblivious to other fishes if they are well fed. Even sharks will backslide if in a frenzy or in the mood for a snack if the small fish make themselves easy prey.

Gerry Carr suggests that fishes, both large and small, "are not truly 'natural enemies' as we understand the term. The big fish just get hungry and eat the little fish. No grudge is involved and no offense is taken." Although it's futile to hold a grudge or take offense when you happen to be being digested in the offender's stomach at the moment.

But don't feel too sorry for the small fish. As Gebhardt points out, small fish

> can easily outmaneuver the shark in a relatively confined space. If they have reef structure to escape to quickly, they may be confident enough in their own invulnerability to swim unalarmed. If the fish are small enough, they wouldn't be worth the shark's effort. There's no point in a shark spending more energy chasing prey than he gets from eating it.

What Is the Purpose of the Orange Balls You Sometimes See on Power Lines?

Next to pairs of tied-up tennis shoes (why *do* kids throw them up there?), orange balls are the strangest artifacts found on power lines. But at least the orange balls, occasionally orange discs or bottles, do serve a purpose.

Power lines are thin and difficult for pilots to see. Many utility companies place balls on lines that are in the flight path of a nearby airport. After a snowstorm, the orange ball might be the only visible sign of the wires or utility poles.

WHY DO DOGS HAVE WET NOSES?

We spoke to Bill Sherrard, manager of publications at Long Island Lighting in New York, who told us that his company has placed balls on their wires for another safety reason. When birds are in migration patterns, the balls let our feathered friends know where the lines are. As even nonornithologists know, birds love to perch on power lines.

Submitted by J. Melville Capps of Somerville, Massachusetts. Thanks also to Rory Sellers of Santa Fe, New Mexico; and Janice Catania of Marlboro, New York.

What Is the Purpose of the Coloring on the Toes of Some Men's Socks?

A few sock manufacturers color-code their socks so that workers at their plants can discriminate between different styles. And some predyed yarns are knitted into the sock to indicate to the seamer exactly where he or she should place the seam when the toe is closed after the sock is knitted.

But the colored toes serve primarily a marketing function. Sid Smith, president and chief executive officer of the National Association of Hosiery Manufacturers, told *Imponderables:*

> . . . it is impractical, and nearly impossible, to provide a permanent label or printed information on each sock regarding its style, brand name, and other information. All of the required data is placed on the packaging, which is available to the consumer at the time and place of the retail purchase of the product. This is a reasonable and acceptable practice for the federal, state, and local regulatory agencies, and the hosiery industry, as all pertinent information is transferred to the consumer at the point of purchase.

The "packaging," usually a paper band stretched around once-folded socks, is presumably discarded by the consumer the first time he wears the socks. But if a man wears the socks for a while and likes them, how is he supposed to remember which brand they are? Often, the knitted-in coloring in the toe is the only means to identify the brand and/or the style of the socks. The phrase "they all look alike" could have been coined to describe the exasperation of the average man trying to find exactly what brand and style of black socks he bought 18 months ago.

Why do they place the coloring in the toe area rather than the heel or the ankle? Although hoity-toity designers now license their names for socks, consumers haven't yet shown a propensity for flaunting their hosiery preferences. The toe is chosen because when worn, the brand identification is well hidden from view. Smith adds that several companies do place pre-dyed colored yarns in other places on their socks, including the heel and the top band.

Submitted by Karen McNeil of Staten Island, New York. Thanks also to Kevin Olmstead of Warren, Michigan.

☆ Great New Shape!
☆ Fabulous Topography!
☆ Green, Green, Green!
☆ Off that beaten path!

Where Is Old Zealand?

The first thing we did after reading this Imponderable was to laugh for an extended period of time. Then we had a brilliant idea. We looked up "Zealand" in the dictionary. We found the following: "largest island of Denmark, between Jutland and Sweden."

We remembered that the first European to land on New Zealand was Abel Tasman, a Dutchman. Now we know that all of the famous explorers blundered upon their discoveries, but this was too much. Did Tasman actually name his island after the wrong country? Was he a traitor?

Not quite. Tasman worked for the powerful Dutch East India Company, which wanted to find new trading partners willing to part with gold or silver in exchange for Dutch cloth and iron (now you know why the Dutch East India Company was successful).

Dutch explorers had already found Australia, which they called "New Holland." But they didn't realize that it was an island; the company thought that New Holland might extend south to where Antarctica is located. Abel Tasman didn't find the long continent he expected, but he and his crew were the first to discover several islands. The first was what Tasman named Van Diemen's Land (after his Governor-General)—its name was later changed to Tasmania, for obvious reasons.

Sailing east from Van Diemen's, Tasman bumped into a big land mass that, much to his consternation, was occupied by Maori tribesmen who didn't cotton to European intruders. The Maoris paddled up to the strange boats in their canoes, shouting and sounding combat trumpets. The Dutch thought they were being met by a welcoming committee and blew their trumpets back! Eventually, the Dutch did get the message when tribesmen killed several of Tasman's men and made it impossible for the crew to explore the land.

Tasman's diaries record that he named his discovery "Staten Landt." Tasman theorized that this island was actually only a small part of a great continent stretching all the way from the South Pacific to the foot of South America. So he named his discovery after Staten, the land off the southern tip of Argentina.

The very next year, another Dutchman discovered that Staten was an island and not part of South America, so Staten Landt no longer was a suitable name for Tasman's discovery. The Dutch renamed the island "Zeeland" ("sea land"), not after the Danish island but after a province of the same name back in Holland.

Probably because of the Maori's unfriendly greeting, the Dutch didn't follow up Tasman's discovery until Captain James Cook's expedition in 1769. But Tasman, one of the few explorers not to impose his name upon any of his discoveries, was later honored by having not only the island of Tasmania but a bay and a sea named after him.

Submitted by Bill Sinesky of Orrville, Ohio.

Why Do Sonic Booms Often Come Two at a Time?

Sonic booms are caused by the displacement of air around an aircraft flying faster than the speed of sound. Even slow-moving aircraft can produce pressure waves ahead of and behind the aircraft that travel at the speed of sound. But once supersonic speeds are attained, pressure disturbances called "shock waves" form behind the aircraft and reach the ground in the form of a thunderlike sound.

Many parts of the airplane are capable of creating shock waves, even the wings. But as the distance between the airplane and a person on the ground increases, only two shock waves are felt—the bow shock wave and the tail shock wave. Bill Spaniel, public information coordinator of Lockheed Aeronautical Systems Company, sent a clipping from *Above and Beyond: The Encyclopedia of Aviation and Space Sciences, Vol. II,* that explains the phenomenon:

> As the distance between the airplane and the observer is increased, the distance between the bow and tail shock waves is also increased. A person on the ground may even hear two booms, with a time interval between the bow shock wave and the tail shock wave of one-tenth to four-tenths of a second.

These shock waves pattern themselves in a cone shape, and can be felt on the ground for miles on either side of the flight path.

If you haven't noticed an increase in sonic booms since the introduction of the Concorde, the explanation is that supersonic aircraft travel at heights often twice that of subsonic widebodies. Although just as many shock waves are created at 65,000 feet altitude as at 30,000 feet, the intensity of the sonic boom is diminished by the extra mileage down to the ground.

Submitted by Dr. J. S. Hubar of Pittsburgh, Pennsylvania.

Why Are Rental Cars So Cheap in Florida?

Yes, we've heard the first rule of success in business: "Location. Location. Location." Still, on Sundays we read the travel section of the *New York Times* and wonder why it costs more to rent a car for two days in New York City than it does to rent a car for a week in Florida. Why the huge discrepancy?

We contacted some of the biggest names in car rentals—Hertz, Avis, Alamo, and Thrifty—and they spoke as one. The answer is the first rule of pricing: "Competition. Competition. Competition." According to Dick Burnon, communications manager for Hertz:

> The Sunshine State is the biggest, most competitive car-rental market in the world. Consumers benefit from this extreme competition among car-rental companies, and the result is very low rates for leisure rentals.

Notice that Burnon refers to low rates for "leisure rentals." The heavy price competition is for vacationers, so the low rates are usually reserved for weekly rentals. Business travelers, usually on expense accounts, seldom need a car for a week, and pay for the privilege with much higher per-day rates. This explains why most rental-car companies demand that you keep the car for a minimum number of days for a weekly rental—that's right, it often costs more to rent the same car from the same agency for three days than for a week. Airlines demand that Supersaver fare recipients stay over Saturday nights at their destination, a similar attempt to weed out business customers.

Phyllis Schweers, manager of Consumer Services at Thrifty Rent-A-Car Systems, complains that there is an overabundance of rental cars in southern Florida. As long as the competition is so fierce in this attractive market, and the oversupply continues, prices will be artificially low.

Other markets that feature inexpensive car rentals include Arizona, California, and Nevada. All of these places are tourist magnets that feature warm weather yearlong, ensuring that the rental market will be a 12-month a year enterprise, enabling car-rental companies to amortize the cost of buying new fleets. In cold climates, such as New England, leisure rentals plummet in winter. Regardless of price, not too many people are motivated to go on pleasure drives through Vermont in March.

The thought occurs to us that if the rental companies can afford to rent cars in Florida for less than one-half the price they are charging in New York or Boston, perhaps they are making an exorbitant profit in New York and Boston.

Why Does the Oboe Give Pitch to the Orchestra During Tuning?

"Tradition" echoed our sources when asked this question. But this explanation isn't sufficient. After all, before the oboe was invented, harpsichords and violins gave pitch. Are there any practical advantages to the oboe?

It turns out there are. Margaret Downie Banks, curator of The Shrine to Music Museum and Center for Study of the History of Musical Instruments in Vermillion, South Dakota, says that the oboists' double reeds "are made specifically to play at the pitch to which the orchestra will be tuning," a perfect A. The reeds are difficult to make because of their extreme rigidity. But they also are much less flexible in pitch than most instruments and less likely to waver in pitch.

The tone color of the oboe is exceptionally pure. Norman Savig, music librarian of the University of Northern Colorado, puts it this way: "the oboe has a high-pitched, clear, penetrating

WHY DO DOGS HAVE WET NOSES?

sound." Even the farthest-flung member of a large orchestra has no problem hearing the oboe.

High technology has invaded orchestra tuning. Acoustical experts have long contended that oboes do not supply perfect pitch. More than twenty years ago, in his book *The Acoustical Foundations of Music*, John Backus argued the point: "More reliable tuning standards than the oboe are available to orchestras willing to sacrifice tradition for accuracy in intonation."

Most big orchestras now use electronic tuners. But the oboist, in a nod to tradition, still sets the tuning bar.

Alvin Johnson, of the American Musicological Society, argues that their lack of flexibility makes oboes just as accurate as electronic tuning forks, and he adds a parting shot: "The trick isn't to get in tune. It's to play in tune."

Submitted by Dr. Amy Bug of Swarthmore, Pennsylvania.
Thanks also to Manfred S. Zitsman of Wyomissing,
Pennsylvania.

Why Do Newspaper Columns Give Differing Dates for the Sun Signs of the Zodiac?

Although even many of the diehard practitioners don't profess to know *why* astrology "works," this doesn't keep them from being rigorous about *how* they work. Astrologers are faced with the same dilemma as calendar makers. The year and the zodiac are divided into 12 months/signs and 365 divided by 12 simply will not yield an even number.

But the signs of the zodiac are based on the movement of the sun, a heavenly body that is much more logical in its movements than the human calendar. Astrologer Debbi Kempton-Smith told us that the moment of the vernal equinox varies from year to year, so that the birth sign of a baby born at the exact same moment will one time be an Aquarius and another year be a Pisces.

When a newspaper column identifies the date parameters for a given sign, it means that babies born on this day in this year fall within that sun sign. To indicate a typical yearly fluctuation, Debra Burrell, of the New York School of Astrology, shared the precise moment the sun enters the sign of Pisces in three consecutive years:

> 1989: the Sun enters Pisces on February 18, 4:21 P.M., EST.
> 1990: the Sun enters Pisces on February 18, 10:15 P.M., EST.
> 1991: the Sun enters Pisces on February 19, 3:59 A.M., EST.

Like network television programming, astrologers choose to run on Eastern Standard Time.

Submitted by Panayota Karras of Huron, South Dakota.

How Do They Put the Holes in Macaroni and Other Pasta? Why Is Elbow Macaroni Curved?

After semolina is mixed with water and kneaded to make the wheat more smooth and elastic, the dough passes through dies —metal discs with holes. The size and shape of those holes determine what the finished pasta will look like. The National Pasta Association explains:

> Round or oval holes produce solid rods, such as linguine and spaghetti. When a steel pin is placed in the center of each hole in the die, the dough comes out in the hollow rods known as macaroni. For elbow macaroni, a pin with a notch on one side is used. The notch allows the dough to pass through more quickly on one side, causing it to curve slightly. A revolving knife attached to the die cuts the dough at frequent intervals into short lengths.

Submitted by Valerie Grollman of North Brunswick, New Jersey.

Why Are There So Many Pins in Men's Dress Shirts and How Are They Put In?

The next time you bellyache about removing all those pins from your newly purchased dress shirt, have some compassion for the poor souls who insert them. That's right, all of those pins are stuck in by hand. If you can figure out a way to mechanize the process, you'd have some willing buyers.

So if the shirt manufacturers are willing to pay the labor expense to insert all those pins, they are not there for frivolous reasons. The main functions of the pins are to protect the shirts from damage and to enhance the appearance of the shirts at the retail level.

Many shirts, even from domestic companies, are manufactured in Asia and sent to North America in container ships, stacked collar-to-collar. The collar pins are particularly crucial to retailers, since shirts are displayed in transparent packaging and the collar is the most visually striking feature of a shirt. Customers also have a tendency to grab shirts on the rack by the collar and the pins help prop them up. Most of the pins on the body of the shirt are there to prevent the shirt from unraveling as the garment gets manhandled at the store.

We spoke to Mark Weber, corporate vice-president for marketing of Phillips-Van Heusen, who told us that a great deal of thought is put into the look and feel of what seems to be rather simple shirt packaging. For example, research indicates that the sound of the tissue paper crinkling in a shirt package is appealing to the consumer, so some companies put in the tissue, which isn't essential to preserve the shirt.

Weber adds that there is a side benefit to placing so many pins in shirts: They act as a deterrent to customers opening up the package in the store.

Submitted by Laurie Ann von Schmidt of Winsted, Connecticut. Thanks also to John F. Gwinn of Cuyahoga Falls, Ohio, and Karen and Mark Landau of Valley Cottage, New York.

Is There Any Logic to the Numbers Assigned to Boeing Jets? What Happened to the Boeing 717?

The first Boeing airplane was, appropriately enough, assigned the number 1 in the late 1910s. From then on, Boeing has grouped its product lines in series.

The first series, numbers 1-102, featured mostly biplanes. The first pressurized airplane, the Boeing 307 Stratoliner, was part of the 300 series that also included the Boeing 314 Clipper seaplane. Many military planes were included in the 200 and 400 series (the B-17 bomber was also known as the 299; B-47 and B-52 jet bombers were part of the 400 series). Boeing reserved the entire 500 series for industrial products, such as gas turbine engines. GAPA and Bomarc missiles were grouped in the 600 series.

When the prototype for the 707 jet was being designed, it

was given a working number of 367-80. The intent was to disguise the jet as if it were just an update of the Boeing Stratocruiser. When the plane was ready to be unveiled, the 700 series was created in its honor.

Why was the first plane named the "707" instead of the "700"? According to Boeing, the name was picked

> simply because it was catchy. Since then, Boeing has built on that base of publicity and continued the naming sequence.
>
> The numbers are assigned in the order the airplane was designed, not by the number of engines or even dates of introduction. Hence the 727, which came before the 737, has three engines while the 737 has only two. The 767 was introduced into passenger service in late 1982, while the 757 came on the air transport scene in early 1983.

So what happened to the Boeing 717? Perhaps because the company didn't realize that their 7 _ 7 series would become a staple of the international aviation scene, Boeing assigned the 717 number to another jet—the KC-135, an aerial refueler produced for the United States Air Force. The Air Force still uses the 717, more than 25 years after it was introduced.

To forestall future questions—yes, 800- and 900-model series already exist, and have been assigned to such esoterica as lunar orbiters and hydrofoil boats.

Submitted by Fred Murphy of Menlo Park, California. Thanks also to David Goldsmith of Berkeley, California.

Why Do Fly Swatters Have Holes?

Elementary physics. The holes in fly swatter blades reduce wind resistance, thus increasing the velocity of the snap. The faster you snap the blade, the better your chances are of killing the varmint.

All of our varied fly-swatter experts agreed that lowering

wind resistance was the major function of blade holes, but we had a fascinating conversation with a man who dares to think even deeper thoughts. Jim Cowen is president of the world's largest manufacturer of fly swatters, Roxide International, Inc.

Roxide experiments constantly with different materials to increase blade speed. Cowen is particularly proud of his all-plastic swatter, which uses Lexan® resin, a General Electric polymer found in automobile bumpers. Lexan permits the shaft of the all-plastic swatters to "flex much like a pole vaulter's fiberglass pole would flex," increasing the chances of a quick and clean kill.

But not all of Roxide's customers prefer space-age technology. Cowen says that farmers, in particular, prefer all-metal swatters. Why?

> ... they feel the finer mesh in the all-metal fly swatter prevents the possibility of an 'air pillow' forming underneath the swatter blade which would literally push the fly out of the way before the swatter struck.

Regardless of material preference, all fly swatter users are united in their desire for a clean kill (after all, the holes in a fly swatter were not designed to act as a strainer), and Cowen assures us that there is a secret to ensuring "swatting success."

> An individual should hold the swatter blade several feet over a fly for ten seconds or so. In this time the fly will become accustomed to having something over his head, relax his springing/escape position and start to groom his tongue and his legs [usually to eliminate food particles]. When this occurs, the fly is otherwise "engaged" and a quick flick of the wrist will kill the unsuspecting insect.

And for those of you who are too squeamish to do the dirty deed yourselves, Cowen offers a more passive solution: fly paper. Roxide invented fly paper in 1861.

Submitted by Philip Writz of Abbotsford, Wisconsin.

Why Do We Have to Send So Many of Our Magazine Subscription Orders to Boulder, Colorado?

We always thought that New York was supposed to be the publishing capital of the United States, but we'll have to reconsider. If you want a subscription to either *New York* or *The New Yorker,* the magazines that chronicle the life of our publishing capital, you have to send your check off to Boulder, Colorado.

What's going on in Boulder that we should know about? A company named Neodata Services.

Neodata's president, Kurt Burghardt, told us how Neodata landed in Boulder, Colorado. Neodata, which began in 1949, was originally a division of *Esquire.* The Smart family, who owned *Esquire,* used to vacation in Estes Park, and would drive through Boulder on their way. The Smarts figured Boulder would provide good, cheap labor. In 1963, Neodata was incorporated as a separate company, and is now owned by Dun & Bradstreet Corporation.

About half of all subscriptions are processed by the magazines themselves. Some of the biggest publishers, such as Time-Life, can achieve the economy of scale necessary to save money by processing subscriptions themselves. The other half are handled by fulfillment houses such as Neodata. Neodata is the largest subscription fulfillment house in the United States, handling over 70 million subscribers to 260 magazines, including *U.S. News and World Report, Vogue, Consumer Reports, McCalls,* and *Ski.*

Magazine fulfillment is a big business. There are 290 million subscriptions to consumer magazines; Neodata has a 22 percent share of the market but has lost the fulfillment business of *Esquire.* Neodata's next biggest competitor, Communication Data Services, located in Des Moines, Iowa, has a 17 percent share and is owned by the Hearst Corporation, which, ironically, now publishes *Esquire.*

The big fulfillment houses maintain super computers to handle the millions of orders they must process. Neodata, for example, maintains production facilities in Ireland. When you send out a subscription card to Boulder, it might be shipped with hundreds of thousands of cards to Ireland, where workers will input the data and then transmit the information back electronically to Neodata's computers in Boulder. If you order a magazine through a discount mail-order house, such as Publishers Clearinghouse or American Family, it will send your order to a fulfillment house as well.

Because most magazines who hire fulfillment houses wish to preserve the illusion that they are servicing their own subscriptions, fulfillment houses toil in obscurity and keep a low profile. You will never see Neodata's name on a subscription form or an address label, but at least you will now know why you are sending a subscription to *The New Yorker* to Boulder, Colorado.

Submitted by Steve N. Kohn of Copperas Cove, Texas. Thanks also to Dr. Seth Koch of Silver Spring, Maryland; and Jim Eason of San Francisco, California.

What's the Difference between Electric Perk and Electric Drip Coffee?

Sarah Moore, of San Francisco's Hills Brothers Coffee, assures us that the exact same coffee beans are used for both blends. The only difference is that the percolator coffee is ground coarsely, and the drip coffee is given a finer grind.

In a percolator, the brewing water and beverage is recirculated through the grounds, potentially turning the liquid into sludge. Bridget A. MacConnell, of General Foods USA, explains: "Perk coffeemakers do not use filters, so if the grind was as fine as it is for drip coffeemakers (which do use filters), you would end up with coffee grounds in your cup."

Submitted by Terry Peak of Pierce City, Missouri.

Why Do Male Dogs Lift Their Legs to Urinate?

Contrary to popular belief, the reason dogs lift their legs isn't to avoid "missing" and squirting their legs by mistake. Whenever you ask an expert any question about animal behavior, be prepared to receive the answer "to map territory." So it is with the matter of dog urination.

Most dogs are compulsive in their urination habits and have favorite "watering holes." By lifting a leg, the urine flows up and out much farther, extending the boundaries of the male's "territory." From a dog's point of view, evidently, the bigger their territory, the better.

We talked to veterinarian Ben Klein about this Imponderable and he mentioned that the lifting of the leg seems to be linked to the testicular hormone. Puppies who have been castrated before the age of four months tend not to lift their legs to urinate, with no obvious ill effect.

We then asked Dr. Klein if this mapping works. Do dogs respect the territory of other dogs? Dr. Klein responded: "Not any more than people do." In other words, male dogs, like their macho human counterparts, are indulging in flashy but ultimately futile behavior.

Submitted by Wilma Lee Sayre of Cottageville, West Virginia. Thanks also to Adam Hicks of Potomac, Maryland; Villard Brida of Weirton, West Virginia; Bob Campbell of Pullman, Washington; and Lawrence Ince of Briarwood, New York.

Why Are Television Sets Measured Diagonally?

Rarely has any Imponderable elicited such hemming and hawing. But then we found the brave man who would utter what others were merely hinting at. So we yield the floor to Scott J. Stevens, senior patent counsel for Thomson Consumer Electronics, a division of General Electric: "... the diagonal measurement is larger than either the horizontal or vertical measurement, hence making the picture appear as large as possible to potential customers."

Submitted by John D. Claypoole, Jr. of Norwalk, Connecticut. Thanks also to Mike Ricksgers of Saxonburg, Pennsylvania.

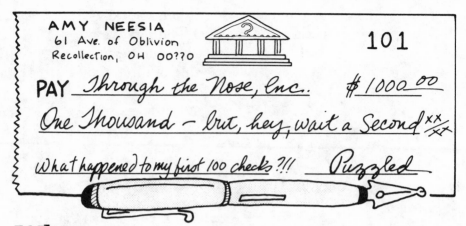

AMY NEESIA
61 Ave. of Oblivion
Recollection, OH 00??0

101

PAY _Through the Nose, Inc._ $ _1000 00_

One Thousand — but, hey, wait a Second xx/xx

What happened to my first 100 checks ?!!   _Puzzled_

When You Order Checks from a Bank, Why Is the First Check Numbered "101" Rather Than "1"?

We always assumed that the first check is numbered "101" because no one wants to cash a check numbered "1." It would be the financial equivalent of showing up in high school with lily-white sneakers or unbroken-in jeans.

And there is something to this theory. Fred Burgerhoff, of Deluxe Check Printers, told *Imponderables* that many businesses request checks starting with 1001 or 10,001, since no concern wants a customer or associate to think it just opened its doors.

Many individuals don't realize that they can also request their checks to start with any number they want. Some merchants are reluctant to cash checks with low numbers. Deluxe's Stuart Alexander remembers the days when many merchants put up signs stating they would not cash checks below number 500.

David Taylor, of the Bank Administration Institute, says that merchants and banks have good reason to be wary of new accounts. More than half of all check frauds occur within the first 90 days of an account being established. Taylor adds that most banks institute special procedures for scrutinizing checking accounts during this 90-day period, monitoring for suspicious deposits or withdrawals that might indicate a kiting operation.

Even if bank customers preferred their checks to start with "1," the check printers and banks would rather give them "101" instead. Stuart Alexander says that the numbering machines used by printers have a minimum setting of three digits, so that checks would have to read "001" rather than "1."

When you open a checking account, it takes several weeks before personalized checks can be issued, so you are given a starter kit including several unnumbered checks. But for bookkeeping purposes, banks don't want the numbers on personalized checks to conflict with numbers assigned by customers to the starter-kit checks.

Submitted by Jon R. Kennedy of Charlotte, North Carolina.

Why Won't or Why Can't One-hour Photo Developers Process Black-and-White Film in One Hour?

They could. But there isn't enough demand to make it a profitable enterprise.

But help may be at hand. Ilford's XP-1 black and white film can be processed by many one-hour color labs. According to Thomas J. Dufficy, of the National Association of Photographic Manufacturers, although they may not advertise it, many developers can print XP-1 on black and white paper in one hour, using the same equipment they do for color film.

Submitted by Nils Montag of Chicago, Illinois. Thanks also to Jena Mori of Los Angeles, California.

Do Submarines Have Anchors?

They sure do. Submarines need anchors for the same reason that other ships do. Any time a submarine needs to maintain its position on the surface but doesn't happen to be near a pier or another vessel, the anchor is used. Anchors aren't needed while submarines are submerged, but subs have to resurface sometime, so anchors come in handy.

One of our favorite correspondents, George Flower, who happens to be in the navy, wrote to us: "A submarine on the surface is a very unstable platform, as any sub sailor will be willing to tell you." We were under the misapprehension that an anchor would help stabilize a submarine, but Captain G. L. Graveson, Jr., public affairs director of the Naval Submarine League, disabused us of the notion. Captain Graveson told *Imponderables* that in a rough sea with the anchor down, the ship will tend to position itself perpendicular to the wind; to this extent, an anchor might help cut turbulence on the surface.

But Graveson claims that submarines aren't noticeably more unstable on the surface than other ships. He noted that the worst instability on a submarine is usually experienced in the process of diving or resurfacing; as the centers of gravity and bouyancy change, so do the complexions of some of the queasier sailors.

Submitted by Jim Kowald of Green Bay, Wisconsin.

Why Are There No Photographs in the *Wall Street Journal?*

On rare occasions there *are* photographs in the *Wall Street Journal,* but it is safe to say that if Clark Kent had worked for *WSJ* instead of the *Daily Planet,* Jimmy Olsen wouldn't have been Superman's confidant.

The *Wall Street Journal* was designed as a financial broadsheet and has never had an official policy against photographs. When it profiles a pillar of finance, the *Journal* usually illustrates the article with a dot drawing of the subject. But if an editor decides that a photograph is necessary to enhance the story, a photograph is included. Decades of tradition make it unlikely that an editor casually will order a photograph—the *Wall Street Journal* has never hired a staff photographer.

The first issue of the *Wall Street Journal* rolled off the presses on July 8, 1889; its first photograph appeared in 1927, when the obituary of the *Wall Street Journal*'s own drama critic and editor, James S. Metcalfe, was accompanied by a photograph of a painting of Metcalfe. Two years later, a photograph of an architectural sketch was printed. Not until later in 1929, when a photograph of William Hamilton accompanied his obituary, did the *Journal* print a portrait photograph.

In celebration of the fiftieth anniversary of its parent company, Dow Jones, precedent was broken and several photographs were inserted into one issue of the *Journal.* But after this burst of exuberance, photographs have appeared only intermittently, perhaps most often in obituaries. Occasionally a major world figure rates a photograph, such as Mao Tse-tung in 1976, but just as likely the honor will go to lesser subjects. The last photograph printed in the *Journal* was of Mary Alice Williams, Maria Shriver, and Chuck Scarborough, upon the premiere of their late, unlamented newsmagazine, "Yesterday, Today & Tomorrow."

Submitted by Steve Thompson of La Crescenta, California.

What Is the Purpose of the Yellow "VIOLATION" Flag Found on Parking Meters? When, if Ever, Does It Pop Up?

Any time we put a coin in a parking meter and turn the handle, the yellow "VIOLATION" flag appears, only to recede when our time is credited. On a bad day, the red "TIME EXPIRED" flag pops up if we haven't made it back to the car on time. And on a really bad day, a parking enforcement officer will notice the red flag and we will get a ticket.

But what is the need for a yellow "VIOLATION" flag when the red one signals an overtime charge? The yellow flag is there to signal the meter enforcement person that the meter is malfunctioning. If a coin gets jammed in a slot, or a driver tries to insert a foreign object into the slot, the yellow flag will not retract. While he or she is issuing tickets, the enforcement officer will notify a repair technician, who will either repair the meter on the spot or replace the mechanism with one that functions correctly.

Why does the yellow flag say "VIOLATION"? According to Dennis W. Staggs, manager of customer service at parking meter manufacturer, POM Incorporated, "City statutes make it a violation to park at a meter with the violation flag up, and in most cases, you will receive a ticket if you do park there."

Often, one can see drivers propping notes under their windshield wipers or surrounding parking meters with pieces of paper whining about how they would simply *love* to be able to put all sorts of money into the meter if only the contraption would cooperate. Little do they know that if the yellow flag is up on the meter, they have violated the law not only by inserting money into the meter but by parking in that spot in the first place.

Folks have been trying to "beat" parking meters since 1953, when they first appeared in the United States. William L. Kemp, manager of international sales administration at Duncan Industries, the largest manufacturers of parking control systems in the world, has been in the industry for 38 years, and explains how nefarious types have tried to circumvent the trusty yellow flag:

> In the early years of parking meters, motorists learned that if they put their coin into the meter and only partially turned the handle, ∴ . . the red flag would go down and the yellow flag would come up. They would park for a longer period of time than their coin purchase allowed, assuming the enforcement officer would think the motorist just forgot to turn the handle all of the way. The officer would turn the handle to prove to himself that there was in fact a coin in the coin handler. The coin then would drop and time would wind on the meter and the motorist gained all the extra time from when he parked the car until the time the officer pulled the handle!
>
> As the practice of partially turning the handle grew as motorists became aware of the method to cheat the city, it became necessary to post labels on the meters saying "POLICE WILL NOT TURN HANDLE," and from that time on, tickets were issued to the offenders and the practice died a natural death.

What interests us is that although one of the main purposes of the "VIOLATION" flag is to deter folks from parking in a given spot, few people understand the purpose of the yellow flag. We asked twenty-five people what the purpose of the yellow flag was. Not one knew the correct answer.

Submitted by Charles Myers of Ronkonkoma, New York.

AND OTHER IMPONDERABLES   575

Why Don't Woodpeckers Get Headaches?

Not a bad question, especially considering that we humans have no problem contracting migraines from metaphorically beating our heads against the walls. Luckily for woodpeckers, their entire bodies are designed to peck with impunity.

Although anatomical features differ among different species of woodpeckers, all of them have unusually thick skulls. But the species that peck most frequently have a special advantage: Their skull curves inward at the upper base of the bill so that the skull is not attached to the bill. Although their beaks can withstand the frequent hammering, the separation between the bill and the skull acts as a natural shock absorber.

Actually, the bills of woodpeckers are not nearly as fragile as they appear. Yes, the tip of the bill is narrow, but it is broad-based and remarkably sturdy; the pointed tip acts as a chisel.

If anything, the biggest danger to woodpeckers is flying debris, but Mother Nature has taken care of this problem, too.

Woodpeckers' nostrils are narrow slits so that flying wood chips won't land in their noses.

Submitted by Reverend Harry T. Rowe of Milton, West Virginia.

Why Do Electronics and Automobile Repair Shops Have Such Big Backlogs? Why Don't They Hire More Repair Technicians to Reduce Their Backlogs?

This syllogism seems indisputable:

1. If you need to repair your car (say, for body work) or a busted VCR, you are going to have to wait a long time for the privilege.
2. Repair work is a highly profitable business.
3. Therefore, it is in the self-interest of repair shops to do more repairs.

Sure, it costs money for repair shops to hire more technicians or add work benches (about $20,000 for a modern audio workbench and many times that for an automobile mechanic's bay), but isn't it cost-effective to add capacity when backlogs are so consistently high? Furthermore, a good facility that could also perform repairs quickly would gain more business simply because of the quick turnaround.

Surely, the repair industries must have thought these issues through. So why does it still take two weeks to get a repair done? According to Richard L. Glass, president of the Professional Electronics Technicians Association, the problem is that the public won't pay for added costs entailed in fast service. Obviously, any service business that guarantees immediate (or even same-day) repairs will by necessity have technicians idle at non-peak periods or technicians unqualified to perform particularly difficult repairs. Glass elaborates:

> We pay for ambulance drivers and firemen to sit and wait for accidents and fires. We don't pay for technicians to sit and wait

for higher than average incidences of service, or peaks in service demand. We find the public is outraged at $50 per hour labor fees by electronics technicians working on consumer products, yet IBM and Xerox technicians must charge $125+ on their calls, when in fact the consumer technician has a much more difficult job.

Sometimes repair facilities try to expand and meet resistance. John Loftus, of the Society of Collision Repair Specialists, told us that many communities won't give zoning clearances for collision repair facilities, so that even successful shops with good locations can't expand to handle increased business.

Mike Zazanas, of the Professional Audio Retailers Association, told *Imponderables,* with more than a little frustration, that in the repair industry the shops that have big backlogs tend to have the best technicians. Zazanas told us that if several qualified technicians walked into his store as he was speaking to us, he'd offer them jobs (and presumably put us on hold). But "it's impossible to find one." In the "old days," entry-level technicians were "screwdriver mechanics" or "tube jerkers" who simply replaced and tested tubes. With the advent of transistors, electronics, and chips, even lower-level technicians must have a higher level of education and expertise.

The crux of the problem, according to John Loftus, is more sociological than economic. Now that a formal education is necessary to become an electronics technician, most prospective technicians decide in school to become electronic engineers instead. Even though, in most cases, they would make as much money fixing equipment as designing it, engineering conjures up visions of white collars while technical work means blue collars and grimy hands. To many, a white collar means creativity and prestige; a blue collar signifies monotony and lack of education. Until this prejudice against technical work is combated, Loftus thinks the problem of attracting talented technicians will persist.

Because the space requirements of an electronics repair shop are more modest, everyone in the industry we contacted said that the major factor causing backlogs is a lack of qualified technicians. If they could find the technicians, retailers would gladly hire them.

The car repair picture is spottier. We contacted each of the Big Three automakers in the U.S., and none professed concern about a problem with the waiting time for repairs. Why should they add new bays to their service facilities when the new equipment is so expensive and, evidently, few are complaining to them about waiting a week to get a tune-up.

Why Does Sound Linger for a Few Seconds After You Unplug a Radio?

Dick Glass, president of the Professional Electronics Technicians Association, took a few minutes away from his repair backlog to give us the answer to this Imponderable:

> Sound lingers because filter capacitors charge up to the power supply voltage level, say 24 volts. The filter capacitors are extremely large so that any ripples in the power line voltage, or surges, will be smoothed out.
>
> Turning off the radio still leaves the capacitors charged up. Until the transistors or bleed-off circuits lower that voltage, the radio continues to operate as if it were connected to a battery. If you had a filter capacitor large enough, you could operate the radio for hours without it being plugged in and turned on.

Submitted by Dr. Charles Waggoner of Macomb, Illinois.

Why Are Three Consecutive Strikes in Bowling Called a "Turkey"?

"Turkey" has long been a favorite research project for word experts. Many books on etymology will go on at length about how a North American bird was named after a country in which it has never existed. They will speculate about how "talking turkey" originated.

But two of the stranger uses of "turkey" are not clearly documented. Although disparaging uses of "turkey" have existed since the nineteenth century, no one seems to know why the word came to describe a show business flop.

We've also been unable to find any written reference to the origin of the bowling term. But Mark Gerberich, director of operations of the Professional Bowlers Association, passed on the thoughts of PBA historian Chuck Pezzano, who knows as much as anyone about the subject:

> There used to be sweepstake tournaments during the holidays, Christmas and Thanksgiving. If a person bowled three strikes

against the heavier pins (usually four pounds), the crowd would scream "turkey" and the bowler would receive a live turkey for his or her performance.

Submitted by Elizabeth Skomp of Crawfordsville, Indiana. Thanks also to Carlos F. Lima of Middletown, Wisconsin.

Why Is Teddy Roosevelt Always Depicted Charging up San Juan Hill When There Were No Horses in Cuba During the Spanish-American War?

The poser of this Imponderable, Herb Clark, adds that there was no room for horses in the ships that took Roosevelt and his men to Cuba. So why this flight of fantasy by artists?

As much as we hate to quibble with a reader, we must make one amendment to your premise, Herb. True, there wasn't room on the ships to transport horses for the regiment. But there was room for the horses of a few key officers. Roosevelt's horse, Texas, was shipped to Cuba and Teddy did indeed ride the horse in the battle of San Juan Hill.

Submitted by Herb Clark of Hopkins, Minnesota.

Why Don't Planets Twinkle at Night?

What causes a heavenly body to twinkle? Alan MacRobert, of astronomy magazine *Sky & Telescope*, explains:

> Twinkling is caused by light rays being diverted slightly—jiggled around—by turbulence where warm and cool air mixes in the upper atmosphere. One moment a ray of light from the star will hit your eye; the next moment, it misses.

Our eyes fool our brains into thinking that the star is jumping around in the sky.

Stars are so far away from us that even when viewed through a sophisticated telescope, they look like single points of light. Even though planets may at first appear the same size as stars to the naked eye, they are actually little disks in the sky. Jeff Kanipe, associate editor of *Astronomy*, told *Imponderables* that "the disks of planets like Venus, Mars, Jupiter, and Saturn can be easily seen by looking at them with a pair of binoculars or a small telescope."

How does this difference in size between stars and planets affect their "twinkling quotient"? We've already established that stars appear to the eye as single points. Kanipe explains how that one point turns into a twinkle:

> When starlight passes through about 200 miles of Earth's atmosphere, the light-bending properties of the different layers of air act like lenses that bend and jiggle the rays to such an extent that the star's position appears to jump about very slightly, causing it to twinkle.

MacRobert contrasts the effect of refraction upon our view of a planet:

> The disk of a planet can be regarded as many points packed close together [yes, like a thousand points of light]. When one point twinkles bright for a moment another may be faint. The differences average out and their combined light appears steady.

Kanipe phrases it a little differently:

> A planet's light comes from every part of its disk, not just a single point. Thus, when the light passes through the atmosphere, the shift in position is smaller than the size of the planet's disk in the sky and the twinkling isn't as pronounced.

Still don't get it? Let's use a more down-to-earth analogy, supplied by Kanipe:

> From the vantage point of a diving board, a dime on the floor of the swimming pool appears to shift violently about because the water acts like a wavy lens that continuously distorts the rays of light coming from the coin. But a submerged patio table, say, looks fairly steady because the water can't distort the light rays coming from its greater surface area to the point that the table appears to shift out of position.

Submitted by Henry J. Stark of Montgomery, New York. Thanks also to Frank H. Anderson of Prince George, Virginia, and J. Leonard Hiebert of Nelson, British Columbia.

Why Do We Wake Up with Bad Breath in the Morning?

Most bad breath (or "fetid breath," as dentists like to call it) is caused by sulfur-bearing compounds in the mouth. How do they get there? And why is the problem worse in the morning?

Microorganisms in the mouth aren't fussy about what they eat. They attack:

Food left in the mouth.

Plaque.

Saliva found in the spaces between teeth, the gum, and on the tongue.

Dead tissue that is being shed by the mouth, gums, and tongue.

The microorganisms convert this food into amino acids and peptides, which in turn break down into compounds with a pungent sulfur odor.

Brushing the teeth helps rid the mouth of all of these food sources of the microorganisms. But the best defense is a regular salivary flow, the type you get by talking, chewing, or swallowing—the stuff that most of us do only when awake.

Eliminating cavities is not the only reason to floss. The longer food particles stay in the mouth, the more fetid the breath will be, so those six to ten hours of sleep are the perfect breeding time for bacteria and a threat to sensitive noses everywhere.

Submitted by Rowena Nocom of North Hollywood, California; Thanks also to Jason Glass of El Monte, California, and Richard Slonchka of McKees Rock, Pennsylvania.

How Do Carbonated Soft Drink Manufacturers Manage to Fill Bottles without Spilling Liquid?

Not all bottling methods work in exactly the same way, but the following scenario is typical.

Empty bottles are lifted on a platform that rises up to meet a filler. The fill height is preset by adjusting vent tubes on the filler. Margie Spurlock, manager of consumer affairs for Royal Crown Cola, explains it:

> These vent tubes have small holes in the side which are closed except for the one at the desired fill height. Beverage replaces air in the bottle as the air escapes through the vent tube hole. When the beverage covers the hole in the vent tube, the pressure is equalized and no more beverage is dispensed into the container.

Steve Del Priore, a plant manager at Pepsi-Cola's Brooklyn, New York, bottling facility, reports that no head forms on the liquid whatsoever. CO_2 is introduced as the liquid goes in the bottle so that the pressure is equalized. When the filler platform rises, a sealing rubber is put on that eliminates spillage.

Del Priore adds that the bottle caps, which are called "closures" in the soda trade, don't have threads until after they are applied; the sides of the closures are straight. But the aluminum is then stretched down with 500 pounds of pressure and small wheels shape the caps to insure that the bottle stays closed.

Submitted by Thomas I. Himmelheber of Abingdon, Maryland.

What Is the Purpose of Cigar Bands? Do They Serve Any Function Besides Advertising the Name of the Manufacturer?

The cigar band was introduced in 1854 by Gustave Bock, a European who emigrated to Cuba and helped develop the Cuban cigar industry. According to Norman F. Sharp, president of the Cigar Associates of America, Inc.:

> Bock began putting them on his cigars in 1854 in order to prevent them from being counterfeited. It seems that dealers in the days before bands would sometimes open his boxes and substitute inferior cigars for the Bock cigars.

A probably apocryphal story claims that the cigar band was developed to answer the complaints of the upper-class ladies of Cuba, who then freely smoked cigars but were bothered by the nicotine stains on their fingers. Another plausible theory suggests that the band helped keep the cigar wrapper intact in case the gum on the ends wasn't sufficient.

Today, of course, the cigar band's sole purpose is to advertise the manufacturer of the cigar, and many people collect bands as a hobby. Devotees of the stogie have long argued over whether the band should be removed when one smokes the cigar. In his book *The Cigar*, Z. Davidoff votes for removing the band but strikes a balanced tone:

> Sensitive as I am to this poetry of the band, I do recommend removing it after lighting the cigar, that is, after having smoked about a fifth of the cigar . . . the cigar is even more attractive in its nudity . . .
>
> If you prefer to smoke a cigar without its band to the halfway point or even three-quarters, go right ahead. It is not an offensive practice, and don't be upset by those who reproach you.

In these days of antismoking sentiment, being reproached for leaving on the cigar band is the least of a cigar smoker's worries.

Submitted by Douglas Watkins, Jr. of Hayward, California.

Why Is Easter Observed on Such Wildly Different Dates?

We don't know the exact day when Jesus was born or what day of the week the first Thanksgiving was observed (*see* "Why is the American Thanksgiving on Thursday?"), but at least we know when to expect to see them on our calendar every year. Easter's date varies so much because the timing of Easter is based on the lunar calendar.

Early Christians celebrated Easter on the same date as the Jewish Passover, but Christians, wanting to distance themselves from Jewish practices, changed the time of observance at the Council of Nicaea in A.D. 325. Like legislators everywhere, the Council was prone to pass some pretty complicated laws: Easter was henceforth to be celebrated on the first Sunday after the first full moon on or after the spring equinox (March 21).

Long before the resurrection of Jesus was celebrated, virtually every Western society celebrated the rebirth of nature in the spring. Ironically, one of the holiest Christian holidays is named after a pagan goddess. The name "Easter" derives from the Anglo-Saxon goddess Eostre, who governed the vernal equinox.

Submitted by Marilyn B. Atkinson of Grass Valley, California. Thanks also to Mojo Chan of Scarborough, Ontario, and Susan E. Watson of Jamestown, Rhode Island.

Why Do the Agitators in Washing Machines Go Back and Forth Rather than Spin 360 Degrees?

In order to loosen dirt from soiled laundry, the clothes must move in the machine. If the agitator spun continuously, centrifugal force would actually make the clothes stick in one spot. So the back and forth movement of most top-loading washing machine agitators actually moves the clothes more.

Submitted by Gabrielle Popoff of Rancho Santa Fe, California.

Why Do Most Hotels and Motels Place Exactly Three Sets of Towels in the Bathroom Regardless of the Number of Beds or Persons in the Room?

We've observed that most hotel/motel towel racks are designed to house two sets of towels. In most cases, the third set of towels is slung over the other two.

Why do innkeepers bother with the extra towels when the vast majority of rooms are occupied by one or two persons? James P. McCauley, executive director of the International Association of Holiday Inns, Inc., was kind enough to survey some hotel owners for us. This is what he heard:

> The answer seems to be seasonal or dependent on the availability of an indoor/outdoor pool or whirlpool. Most hotels/motels that have outdoor pools offer extra towels during the summer. Those hotels that offer an indoor swimming pool or whirlpool could have an extra set of towels in the room during the entire year. The more amenities offered, the more likely a third set of towels, or at least an extra-large towel.

We also heard from Richard M. Brooks, vice-president of rooms management at Stouffer Hotels and Resorts. In its resort properties, Stouffer actually requires four sets of towels in each room because most rooms are occupied by two people who will each likely need one towel for a bath and the other for a post-swim shower.

But most commercial hotels cater to single travelers. Brooks says that fewer than 25 percent of Stouffer's nonresort hotels are occupied by more than one person at a time. So hotels want to put in the fewest possible number of towels in each room. The expense can add up:

> By providing only three towels, hotels keep their investment in towels to a minimum. Remember, most good hotels keep three to four times the number of terry and linen items necessary in stock to be sure guests have a sufficient supply. In a typical Stouffer property, this usually means an investment of well over $250,000.

Submitted by Charles Myers of Ronkonkoma, New York.

Inside illustration signs (part of image):
LEAVE THAT PEACH FUZZ TO THE PEACH
SHAVE IT OFF; HOW-TO WE'LL TEACH
JUST WON'T MAKE THE LADIES SING
RAZOR STUB'S A FUNNY THING

Why Are Peaches Fuzzy?

We heard from about fifteen experts on peaches, all of whom agreed that the fuzz is there for a reason. Exactly what that reason is was considerably harder to nail down.

Perhaps the best consensus answer was provided by Charles D. Kesner, horticulturist at Michigan State University's College of Agriculture and Natural Sciences:

> Peaches are in the Rose family, genus Prunus, specie persica. Peach fuzz is genetic and likely selectively developed to give the fruit more resistance to insects and diseases. Although peach fruits do sustain some disease and insect damage, they are much more resistant than the nectarine which was developed by plant breeders with recessive genes for the fuzzless character. Therefore, a nectarine is simply a peach without fuzz.

Want some other theories?

The California Cling Peach Advisory Board adds that the fuzz also protects peaches from sunburn.

Clay Weeks, a peach specialist in the pomology department at the University of California, Davis, mentions that fuzz helps reduce potential water loss in the fruit.

Davis plant pathologist Dr. Joe Ogawa mentions that fuzz not only helps collect rain water for the fruit but also serves as a barrier against fungus as well as insects.

Perhaps the best evidence that nature provided fuzz for functional reasons is the contrast between peaches and its fuzz-less brother, the nectarine. Nectarines are far less sturdy than peaches. They are more susceptible to brown rot and tend to be bruised in transit more easily than fuzzy peaches.

Why Can't You Buy Canned Nectarines?

Fresh nectarines are a popular commodity. And we just learned that nectarines are essentially fuzzless peaches (with the difference of one recessive gene). So is there a technical reason why it is hard to can nectarines? Or is it a matter of lack of demand?

A little bit of both, it turns out. Only one person we contacted, Les Rose, vice president of operations for the Apricot Producers of California, claimed that nectarines can as well as freestone peaches. Rose contends that a lack of demand (as well as the higher prices fetched by fresh product) is responsible for the lack of canned nectarines.

But our other sources felt that technical considerations were more important. Nectarines tend to be very soft. Bill Johnson, manager of Information Services for the California Canning Peach Association, says that the mechanical processing required for canned fruits tends to ruin the texture of nectarines. The fruit bruises easily, leading to a poor appearance.

Ronald A. Schuler, president of the California Canning Peach Association, says that a processor in Fresno, California,

tried to can nectarines several years ago but couldn't avoid severe losses in yield because of the soft fruit.

The supply of nectarines also tends to be less bountiful than
peaches. According to Charles D. Kesner, horticulturist at Michigan State University's Northwest Michigan Horticultural Experiment Station, nectarines are highly susceptible to brown rot.
The expense of eliminating brown rot in humid climates is not
worth the cost, so domestic production of nectarines is confined
to the western United States.

Ronald A. Schuler says that "the canning of regular yellow
fleshed freestones is also moving toward extinction in the retail
can sizes." As consumers increasingly opt for fresh produce, the
bucks for the growers are in fresh rather than canned product.

Submitted by Douglas Watkins, Jr. of Hayward, California.

Why Do Dogs Love to Put Their Heads Out the Windows of Moving Cars? But Then Hate to Have Their Ears Blown Into?

Most of the people who have asked this Imponderable connect
these two questions, wondering why a dog loves speeding down
a freeway at 65 MPH (with its head totally exposed to the wind)
when it balks at a little playful ear blowing. But dog authorities
insisted the two Imponderables we were talking about mixed
apples and oranges.

Of course, nobody has been able to interview canines on the
subject, but the consensus is that dogs like to put their heads out
of car windows because they are visually curious. Many dogs are
not tall enough to have an unobstructed view of the outside
world from the front seat, and most dogs are too short to have
any forward or rearward view from the back seat. Poking their

WHY DO DOGS HAVE WET NOSES?

head out of the window is a good way to check out their surroundings and enjoy a nice, cool breeze at the same time.

But blowing in a dog's ear, even gently, can hurt it, not because of the softness of the skin or the sensitivity of the nerves, but because of the sound of the blowing. Veterinarian Ben Klein told *Imponderables* that one of the ways a dog is tested for deafness is by the vet blowing into the ear through a funnel; if the dog doesn't get upset, it's an indication of deafness. So while we may associate blowing into the ear of a dog as playfulness or to a human mate as a sexual overture, to the dog it is the canine equivalent of scratching a blackboard with fingernails. The frequency of the sound drives them nuts.

Dr. William E. Monroe, of the American College of Veterinary Internal Medicine, adds that the external ears of dogs are full of sensory nerves that help to prevent trauma injuries and preserve hearing:

> By preventing debris (sand, wood chips, etc.) from entering the ear canal, damage to the ear and hearing is prevented. Thus, avoiding air in the ear could have survival advantage.

The ear can't trap all the debris a dog must contend with. In fact, Dr. Klein mentioned that sticking their heads out of car windows is one of the major causes of ear infections in dogs.

Next thing we know, we'll have to install seat belts for dogs.

Submitted by Frederick A. Fink of Coronado, California. Thanks also to Allison Crofoot of Spring Valley, New York; Rich Williams of San Jose, California; Candace Savalas of New York, New York; Douglas Watkins, Jr. of Hayward, California; Melanie Jongsma of Lansing, Illinois; Jacob Schneider of Norwalk, Ohio; David Hays and Paul Schact of Newark, Ohio; and Roseanne Vitale of Port St. Lucie, Florida.

Why Do Many Brands of Aspirin Not Have a Safety Cap on Their 100-Count Bottles?

The Poison Packaging Act of 1970 mandated that if the contents of any packaged substance could pose a significant hazard to children, and if it is technically feasible, the package must contain a safety cap. Most of us have gotten used to trying to align those two confounded arrows and trying to exert enough leverage to flip the cap off. But if you don't have long fingernails, it's hard to get leverage; and if you have long fingernails, you don't have long fingernails for long.

A casual survey at our local drugstore reveals that the poser of this Imponderable was right. Many brands of aspirin have safety caps on all their sizes except the 100-count. What gives?

If we have problems opening the safety caps, you can imagine the problems that the elderly or sufferers of arthritis might have. So one of the provisions of the Poison Packaging Act authorized manufacturers to market one (but no more than one) size of packaging that did not comply with the safety-cap standard, as long as the package is conspicuously labeled with the words: "This package for Households Without Young Children."

Why have most aspirin marketers chosen the 100-count container for their noncomplying package? It's the most popular size. And although no one will say it on the record, we got the distinct impression that there are some nonelderly, nondisabled consumers who don't love the safety cap. By putting the easier-to-open cap on their most popular size, the companies ensure that their product will be competitive with other brands.

Thanks to Jean, a caller on the Ray Briem show, KABC-AM, Los Angeles, California.

Where Do Butterflies Go When It Rains?

Butterflies don't just prefer sunny days. They need sunlight in order to regulate their body temperature. Whether it is raining or not, when the sun is obscured or the sun sets, butterflies fly for cover immediately.

Just as human beings might duck for cover underneath the canopy of a tree, butterflies seek the protection of natural coverings. According to Rudi Mattoni, editor of the *Journal of Research on the Lepidoptera,* the favorite resting sites include the undersides of leaves or stems of bushes and on blades of grass.

Butterfly bodies are exceedingly delicate, so nature has provided them with other kinds of protection against the rain. When resting, the teardrop configuration of the butterfly prevents rain from pooling on the wings or body, and the surfaces of the butterfly's skin do not absorb water.

Richard Zack, curator/director of the James Entomological Collection at Washington State University, adds that many butterflies could not survive flying during a rainstorm. Not only does wind wreak havoc with their ability to fly, but the big rain-drops themselves would pose a major risk.

Submitted by Jennifer Martz of Pottstown, Pennsylvania.

Why Do You Sometimes Find Coffee Bags Hung on the Coat Hooks of Airplane Lavatory Doors?

Flight attendants do not take grounds out of cans to brew coffee for inflight service. They simply pop in bags, which look like huge tea bags, into the coffeemaker. Although more expensive, the coffee bags totally eliminate the potential problem of run-away coffee grounds if the flight attendant were to drop a can or the plane were to experience sudden turbulence. But why must the airline, or the flight attendants, hang these bags on the coat hooks of lavatory doors, as we have seen more and more of late?

We received two different answers to this Imponderable. The first comes from an expert on airplane food service, Phillip S. Cooke, Executive Administrator of Inflight Food Service Association:

> Consider the poor, harried flight attendant who often has to serve a fairly complicated meal service in a very short time and in a very confined space (the galley was not uppermost in the minds of aircraft designers!). Sometimes the only place to hang anything, and the only hook available during these rush periods is, you guessed it, that little hook just around the corner, or across from the galley—in the lavatory. The attendants certainly mean to retrieve the coffee bags at the conclusion of service, but they also sometimes forget.

A good theory, but this is one Imponderable for which we could indulge in hands-on research. Every time we encountered coffee bags on coat hooks, we asked the flight attendants why. And we got the same answer over and over again.

WHY DO DOGS HAVE WET NOSES?

As Phillip Cooke mentioned, in most nonwidebody planes, the coach galley is located at the rear of the plane, and lavatories are always nearby. Lavatories have a nasty habit of not smelling too great. Ingenious flight attendants hit upon a home remedy: coffee bags. Unused coffee grounds deodorize the lavatories for the comfort of the flight attendants and the passengers.

Airlines have to tread a thin line in treating the problem of smelly lavatories. Room deodorizers can be noxious in a big room, let alone in a tiny space without windows or good ventilation. Some airlines have chosen to use mild deodorizers, so flight attendants have been hanging coffee bags in self-defense.

Submitted by Charles Myers of Ronkonkoma, New York.

Why Is There No Interstate Number 1, 2, or 3 in the United States? Why Do You So Seldom See Highway 3s? Is There any Logical System to the Numbering of the Highway System?

Contrary to popular belief, interstate highways in the U.S. do not necessarily connect two different states. The criteria for roadways in the interstate system have more to do with technical requirements, such as the access to the highway (interstates must have totally public access), shoulders on both sides of the road, minimum width of lanes, etc.

Reader Mike Osenga is correct. The lowest-numbered interstate highway is 4, which connects Tampa and Daytona Beach in Florida, a distance of less than 150 miles. Interstate highway 5 runs up the entire west coast, from San Diego, California, to the Washington/Canadian border. What happened to numbers 1, 2, and 3?

The powers that be, namely the American Association of State Highway and Transportation Officials (AASHTO), determined that the principal north-south interstate routes should bear numbers divisible by five. Interstate highway 4, then, is the lowest even companion number to 5. Of course, even-numbered interstates run in an east-west direction, and odd-numbered ones in a north-south orientation.

But there are more rules to the numbering system than that. The lower odd numbers, such as Interstate 5, are located in the West and the lower even numbers in the South. Note that Interstate 10 runs through the southern United States, while numbers 90 and 94 cross the northern areas.

U.S. highways may duplicate the numbers already used for interstates, and odd and even numbers still indicate north-south and east-west routes, respectively. But strangely enough, the lower odd numbers are in the East (such as U.S. 1, which hugs the east coast) and the higher odd numbers, such as the Pacific Coast Highway, U.S. 101, are in the West.

Why is there a dearth of highway 3s? Although there may be no Interstate 3, there is a U.S. highway 3, which starts in New Hampshire, just south of Chartierville, Quebec, and meanders south to Boston, Massachusetts; but at 279 miles, it is one of the shortest U.S. highways. In fact, all the numbers between 1 and 27 have been taken for U.S. highways; 88 out of the first hundred numbers have been assigned. The highest U.S. highway number? 730.

The numbering of state highways isn't even this organized. Many states have even-numbered north-south routes and odd-numbered east-west highways. And if you pore over an atlas, you will notice that many states have no highway 3 or an inconspicuous highway 3. Why has 3 been singled out for obscurity and ignominy? All the sources we contacted indicated it was just a coincidence. Given the hodgepodge of numbering systems, we believe it.

Submitted by Mike Osenga of Brookfield, Wisconsin. Thanks also to William L. Chesser of Littleton, Colorado, and Tom Pietras of Battle Creek, Michigan.

AND OTHER IMPONDERABLES

Why Are There Expiration Dates on Fire Extinguishers?

No, the chemicals found in most portable fire extinguishers won't "spoil" like milk if left in past the expiration date. But according to Bill Fabricino, of BRK Electronics, "since most fire extinguishers use a pressurized gas for a propellant, the gas eventually will leak out through seals and render the extinguisher useless."

Submitted by Herbert Kraut of Forest Hills, New York.

Why Do Eyes Sometimes Come out Red in Photographs? Why Is This Particularly True of Cats' and Dogs' Eyes?

Have you ever seen "red-eye" in a professional's photographs? Of course not, because they know that paying customers want a portrait of the topography of their faces, not an intrusive journey into the blood vessels of their eyes.

Yes, the red you see is blood, and you get more red than you ever wanted to see because your flash bulb or flash cube is too close to the camera lens. Ralph E. Venk, president of the Photographic Society of America, says that the light from the flash "enters the lens of the eye directly and is then reflected off the back surface of the eyeball, the retina, and bounces back to the camera. The problem of red-eye is compounded because flashes are used in dark environments and the human eye automatically opens wider in the dark.

A few simple tips should banish red-eye from your lives:

1. Try holding the flash farther away from the lens axis. An extra three inches should do. Thomas J. Dufficy, of the National Association of Photographic Manufacturers, says that when camera makers noticed the problem with red-eye when flash

cubes were first introduced, they offered flash cube extenders, three-inch high posts that increased the angle between the camera lens axis and the flash cube.

2. When taking photographs in the dark, don't have subjects look straight into the camera. Notice that in group shots, the red-eye victim is always the one looking straight into the lens. Your subjects will also enjoy the photographic process more too, since an oblique angle lessens the chances of them being temporarily blinded by flashes.

3. A modest suggestion. Try not to take photographs when it is pitch black. Even without red-eye, they never seem to come out well anyway. Leave the cave photographs to the pros.

And why do cats and dogs seem to be especially prone to contracting red-eye in photographs? Both cats and dogs have larger and more open pupils than humans, which allow the flash to penetrate into their innocent retinas.

Submitted by Abby Mason of Canton, Ohio. Thanks also to Gene Newman of Broomall, Pennsylvania; Elanor Lynn of Worcester, Vermont; and Megan A. Martin of Chino, California.

Why Do Dogs Have Wet Noses?

To tell you the truth, we committed to this Imponderable as the title of the book before we had a definitive answer to it. When the deadline for the title faced us, we called some friends, Tom and Leslie Rugg, who have a large reference library about dogs, and asked them if there was any information in their books about dogs and wet noses. "Sure," they replied. They found several books that talked about sweat glands in dogs' noses that secrete fluid. The moisture of the nose evaporates as air is exhaled from the nostril, thus cooling off the dog.

Sounded good to us. Our title Imponderable was answerable.

An ethical dilemma nagged at us, though. We always claim that Imponderables are questions you can't easily find an answer to in books. And we like to find experts to answer our mysteries. Were we really going to allow our title Imponderable to be answered by other books? So we decided to confirm the answers supplied by the Ruggs' books.

Now we know where the phrase "Let sleeping dogs lie" comes from. The next month involved calls to numerous veterinarians, dog anatomists, zoologists, canine histologists, and even canine respiratory specialists. Without exception, they were gracious, knowledgeable, and interesting. But we have one serious complaint about dog experts, and scientists in general. They refuse to B.S.

How we long for the experts in the humanities and the social sciences, who have theories about everything and never let a lack of evidence get in the way of their pronouncements. But the most eminent dog researchers in the country, from prestigious veterinary schools like Cornell University and Iowa State University, insisted that we are closer to cloning human beings than we are to having a definitive answer to this Imponderable.

Here's what we do know. Most healthy dogs have wet noses most of the time. If a dog has a dry nose, it might just mean it has slept in a heated room, or buried its nose between its paws for an extended period. But it might also mean that the dog is dehydrated, often an early warning sign of illness. What causes the wetness in the first place? We heard three main theories:

1. The lateral nasal glands in a dog's nose secrete a fluid. Some of these glands are near the opening of the nostril and may be responsible for most of the moisture, but no one has proven how these secretions get to the tip of a dog's nose (there are no glands on the exterior of the nose).

2. Dr. Howard Evans of Cornell University believes that the wetness is probably a combination of secretions of the lateral nasal glands and the (nasal) vestibular glands.

3. Dr. Don Adams, a specialist in the respiratory system of canines at Iowa State University, adds that dogs often lick their noses with their tongues. Much of what we

perceive to be secretions on a dog's nose might actually be saliva.

So what function might a wet nose serve? Several theories here, too:

1. Most likely, the secretions of the nasal glands help the dog dissipate heat. Dogs do not sweat the way humans do. They dissipate most of their heat by panting with their tongues hanging out, evaporating from the moist surface of the tongue. While they pant, most of the air enters through their nose, which is more efficient than the mouth in evaporating water vapor. In his book *How Animals Work*, zoologist Knut Schmidt-Nielsen reports that

> in the dogs we tested, on the average about a quarter of the air inhaled through the nose was exhaled again through the nose, the remaining three-quarters being exhaled through the mouth. The amounts could vary a great deal, however, and at any given moment from zero to 100% of the inhaled air volume could be exhaled through the nose.

Schmidt-Nielsen's study indicated that exhaling through the mouth doubled dogs' heat loss, but when they were only slightly overheated, some dogs didn't pant at all. Schmidt-Nielsen indicated that the sole function of the nasal glands might be to provide moisture for heat exchange.

2. Lateral nasal glands contain odorant-binding particles that help dogs smell. Dr. Dieter Dellman of Cornell University told us that all animals can smell better when odors are picked up from a moist surface. Whether or not moisture on the *exterior* of a dog's nose actually aids in olfactory functions is not well established.

3. Dr. Adams thinks it is possible that the lateral nasal glands might be connected with salivary functions. He told us about a personal experience. Adams was measuring lat-

WHY DO DOGS HAVE WET NOSES?

eral nasal gland secretions one day (we thought we had a weird job!) and felt sorry for the poor dog stuck wearing an Elizabethan collar. Secretions were coming in a steady trickle, until Adams decided to reward the dog with a few pieces of sausage. All of a sudden, the lateral nasal glands sprung a leak. Adams doesn't claim to understand what the connection is yet, but such accidental discoveries explain why scientists aren't apt to spout off about definitive answers until they can prove the veracity of the theory.

4. The wetness is a cosmic joke meant only to spoil the life of anyone who writes about it. This, of course, is our theory.

So, dear readers. If you should see us on television or speaking on the radio, promoting this book, and the host asks this Imponderable, please be advised that though our answer might be short and glib and we appear to be carefree, don't let our glad expression give you the wrong impression. We are really shedding the tears of a clown.

Every time we provide the simple, ten-second sound bite that the host craves but that doesn't really answer this Imponderable with the complexity it deserves, we are being paid back for premature title selection.

Submitted by Kelly Marrapodi of Tucson, Arizona. Thanks also to Erin Johnson of Marietta, Georgia, and Mike Surinak of Tucson, Arizona.

Why Don't You Ever See a Used UPS Truck?

Our correspondent, Robert A. Waldo, notes that driving about, one often sees second-owner trucks that betray the identity of their original owners. Perhaps a "U-HAUL," "FRITO-LAY," or "RYDER" will peek through a new paint job.

UPS maintains three kinds of vehicles in its fleet of over 100,000: vans; tractor-trailers; and its familiar brown delivery trucks, which UPS itself calls "package cars." The trucks are manufactured to UPS' specifications by General Motors, Ford, and Navistar. Although the chassis may differ, the bodies of the trucks are identical. The "package cars" are scrupulously maintained and washed at least once every other day. The lifespan of a package car is astonishingly high—between twenty and twenty-five years.

The secret to the disappearing UPS truck is simple. According to Serena Marks, a public relations representative of the United Parcel System, "Because of our high safety standards, once a package car has been taken permanently out of service it is destroyed." Maybe if the automobiles and trucks we bought for ourselves lasted twenty-five years, we could afford to destroy them rather than trading them in.

Submitted by Robert A. Waldo of Bothell, Washington.

THE CLEAVER MEMORIAL WARD

QUIET

GUARDED   STABLE   GRAVE

What Are the Guidelines for Stating That a Hospital Patient Is in "Good" or "Critical" Condition? Are the Standards Uniform among Hospitals?

Much to our surprise, there aren't uniform standards. We contacted many hospitals' public relations departments and found that they were much more preoccupied with protecting the privacy rights of patients than they were with pinpointing their condition. All of the hospitals directed me to the American Hospital Association, which issues a brochure written by Mary Laing Babich called "General Guide for the Release of Patient Information by the Hospital," which is adapted from a chapter of *Hospitals and the News Media: A Guide to Good Media Relations.*

Babich's guide includes two conditions used to describe patients whose vital signs are stable and within normal limits, "good" and "fair." The patient in good condition is comfortable and the indicators are excellent. The "fair" patient may be uncomfortable, but the indicators are favorable. Many hospitals use "stable" or "satisfactory" as a synonym for "fair."

A patient in "serious" condition "may be unstable and not within normal limits." This patient is acutely ill but not necessarily in imminent danger. The prognosis for the "serious" patient is unclear.

The "critical" patient always has unstable and abnormal vital signs and may be unconscious. The indicators are unfavorable.

"Unconscious" and "dead" are the other two conditions listed. The former is used when a patient is brought into the hospital in this condition before the prognosis or vital signs of the patient are established. Everyone knows what "dead" means, but releasing this information can be a difficult problem. According to Babich's guidelines, the death of a patient is a matter of public record but the hospital has the obligation to notify the next of kin first: "Information regarding the cause of death must come from the patient's physician, and its release must be approved by a member of the immediate family (when available)."

Despite the proliferation of the American Hospital Association's guidelines, we've noticed that hospital spokespersons often improvise their own terms at press conferences. "Very critical" and "grave" have been offered, probably as gingerly attempts to answer the unstated question that reporters really want to know: "When is this famous patient going to die?"

Submitted by Glenn Worthman of Palo Alto, California.

Why Is a Watch Called a "Watch"? After All, Do You Have to Watch a Watch Any More than You Have to Watch a Clock?

Huh?

Let's see who's on first here. First we go to our trusty dictionaries, which inform us that the word "watch" has the same Old English etymology as the words "wake" and "awaken." Were the first watches alarm clocks? Probably not. Some word historians have speculated that the word derives from an Old English word meaning "to keep vigil" and that the naming of the timepiece had to do with the fact that they were carried by night watchmen.

But the most fascinating, if unverifiable, etymology was provided by Stuart Berg Flexner in his book *Listening to America*. When watches were introduced, clocks had no hour or minute hands. Rather, clocks struck on the hour—a totally auditory signal (indeed, "clock" derives from the Latin word *cloca*, meaning "bell"). But watches sported minute and hour hands. One had to literally watch the watch to find out what time it was.

Submitted by Corporal Dorwin C. Shelton of Tarawa Terrace, North Carolina.

What's the Distinction between a Clock and a Watch?

The difference isn't merely size. Some old pocket watches were bigger than our travel clocks of today. Clocks were invented in Italy in the fourteenth century and watches followed more than a century later.

From the beginning, clocks were weight driven. But the breakthrough that made watches possible was the invention of a different technology to drive the device—the mainspring made of coiled steel.

Now that both clocks and watches use new technologies, the distinction between the two often hinges on size, portability, and where the timepiece is displayed.

Submitted by Cuesta Schmidt of West New York, New Jersey.

How Did the Football Get Its Strange Shape?

If it weren't for the forces of civility, we might call the game "*head*ball" instead of football. For the earliest antecedent of football used human skulls as the ball.

The Danes occupied England in the early eleventh century. Shortly after the Danes were vanquished in 1042, an Englishman unearthed the skull of a buried Danish soldier and kicked it around his field. Others dug up Danish "headballs" and enjoyed the pastime of kicking them around but found the solidity of the object rather hard on the foot. So they looked for alternative sporting equipment. And they quickly found the obvious choice.

Inflated cow bladders, of course.

The game caught on and assumed the proportions of a mass psychosis. A bladder was dropped between two neighboring towns. If one team managed to kick the bladder into the center of the other's town, it won. Although contestants never touched the ball with their hands (indeed, they called the game futballe), they had no such compunctions about using their fists to hit each other.

King Henry II (1154–1189) banned the sport, not only to eliminate rampant vandalism and violence but because it posed a security threat. His soldiers were playing futballe instead of practicing their archery. For the next four hundred years, futballe was outlawed but continued to be played anyway.

The ban against futballe was lifted by James I (1603–1625), who bowed to the wishes of sportsmen. The game was legitimized by placing it in standardized playing fields and awarding points for passing the other team's goal. Cow bladders yielded to round balls. This game became known as Association Football. The shortening of the Association to Assoc. provided the slang expression "soccer," which is the sport's modern name.

The next historical development crucial to the history of American football occurred when a frustrated William Ellis, a college student in England, decided to pick up the soccer ball during a game and run with it. He scored the first illegal touchdown in 1823. Although at the time his behavior was not rewarded, his college is best known for his unsportsmanlike behavior. The name of his college: Rugby. (And now you know why this is the only sport whose name is often capitalized, at least when referring to English Rugby.)

Many early settlers in America played soccer, but the game caught on in the mid-nineteenth century among Ivy League colleges. Bob Carroll, of the Professional Football Researchers Association, sent us an entertaining account of how the shape of the American football evolved:

> The football got its shape before it was a football. The first intercollegiate game between Rutgers and Princeton in 1869 was no more football than roller derby is a steeplechase. They played soccer—and used a round soccer ball. When the college boys got to writing some rules in 1873, they specified that a "No. 6 ball" should be used.

WHY DO DOGS HAVE WET NOSES?

However, there were two No. 6 balls—a round one for soccer and one a bit more oblong for rugby. The reason these two different balls had evolved in England was that soccer, which depended upon kicking and "puddling" the ball along the ground, could only be played with a round (or "puddle-able") ball. In Rugby, though, a player could run with the ball before he kicked it. Well, it don't take a whole lot of smarts to figure out you can hold onto a fat, prolate spheroid easier than a fat sphere. Think of the fumbles if we played football with a basketball!

In 1874, the boys from McGill University in Canada taught the soccer players from Harvard how to play Rugby. Then Harvard taught Princeton, Yale and Columbia. In the early 1880s, Walter Camp pushed through rules that changed American rugby to American football. By 1883, touchdowns counted more than kicked goals, which meant the ball was soon tapered even more to make it even easier to run with.

The forward pass was legalized in 1906 and by 1913 became a fairly common occurrence [the emergence of the forward pass can be traced to a 1913 Notre Dame game against Army when Gus Dorais and the legendary Knute Rockne combined to pass for a dramatic victory]. That led, over a period of time, to more thinning of the ball so it could be passed and make those pretty spirals we all know and love. The more passing—the skinnier the football. If they keep changing rules to help the passers, by 2025, football will be played with a javelin.

Submitted by William Marschall of Edenton, North Carolina. Thanks also to Mike Pintek, KDKA, Pittsburgh, Pennsylvania; Jena Mori of Los Angeles, California; Fred White of Mission Viejo, California; and Patrick M. Premo of Allegany, New York.

HERE'S MY RING! I KNEW WE'D GET IT OUT WITH THE SNAKE!

Why Is the Piping under Kitchen Sinks So Circuitous? Why Is It "S"-Shaped? Why Not Just Have One Straight Vertical Pipe?

Believe us, Colleen, this is not a plot by the plumbing industry to sell you more piping. You want those curves.

The piping under sinks (and under lavatories, for that matter) is called a "P" trap. The curvy pipe dips down below the horizontal pipe so that a water seal is formed in the bend, assuring that water, and not air, will fill the area below the horizontal pipe.

Why would you want to create a deliberate water blockage? Because the water blocks sewer and other foul smells from drifting up the pipe and into the room.

And on occasion, the "P" trap blocks certain items from going downstream. Gary Felsinger, a marketing manager at Kohler Co., explains: "In some cases, the "P" trap also saves valuable rings from falling into the sewer when accidentally dropped down the drain."

Submitted by Colleen Uehara of San Jose, California.

What Is the Meaning of the Codes on Colored Stickers Affixed to Some Envelopes by the Post Office?

After the mail has been sorted at the post office, the mail is bundled according to its destination. The postal worker grabs a handful of mail and fastens it with a rubber band lengthwise and another rubber band widthwise. On the top of each bundle, he or she affixes a sticker that designates the following code:

"F" on a blue sticker stands for "firm." The whole bundle is addressed to one company.

"D" on a red sticker stands for "direct." All of the mail in that bundle is headed for one particular five-digit ZIP code.

"C" on a yellow sticker stands for "city." The mail is going to one city, and the first three digits are the same on each piece (e.g., all ZIP codes in Kansas City start with 641).

"3" on a green sticker stands for "3-digit area." Not all cities are large enough to claim exclusive rights to all three of the first ZIP code digits. "3" bundles are going to a Sectional Center Facility that might route the mail to several different towns or cities that share the same first three digits.

"A" on a pink sticker stands for "Area Distribution Center." Some cities have more than one three-digit ZIP code. The "A" is an attempt to send the bundle to the distribution center closest to where the mail is actually being delivered, even if it doesn't qualify for a "C" sticker.

We asked Karen E. McAliley, of the Consumer Affairs Department of the United States Postal Service, how postal workers decide which envelopes to place the stickers on. McAliley replied that it is the luck of the draw. Whichever envelope happens to be on top of the bundle receives the honor. The bundles are then hand-tossed into appropriate sacks and go their way.

Submitted by Dan Proper of Chapin, South Carolina.

Why Don't Food Manufacturers Put Their Street Address on Their Labels?

Because they don't have to. Why encourage crackpot letters? Why waste space on the label with a street address when you can increase the size of the words "New and Improved" on the label by one-eighth of an inch?

But manufacturers are required by the federal government to list their name, the city, state, and ZIP code of their company. They must put their street address on the label only if their place of business is not listed in a telephone or city directory. So if you want to write that nasty letter, and the street address isn't printed on the label, directory assistance can always locate the company for you.

Submitted by Carl Allen of Los Angeles, California.

AND OTHER IMPONDERABLES

At Weddings, Why Do We Congratulate the Groom and Wish the Bride Happiness? Is It Considered to Be Unlucky or Simply Poor Manners to Congratulate the Bride?

In our experience, the tradition makes sense. The groom deserves congratulations and the bride needs all the luck she can muster.

Several etiquette books we consulted continue to recommend the practice, even though it is rooted in the basest form of sexism. Jaclyn C. Barrett, of *Southern Bride,* told us that "Congratulations!" to the bride somehow is interpreted as "I can't believe you actually landed a man!" Still, all of our sources indicated that it wasn't considered unlucky to extend congratulations to the bride—just poor form.

Congratulating the groom, according to *Bride*'s associate editor Melanie Martini, stems from the ancient notion of marriage as the capture of a woman by a man. Saying "Congratulations!" to the groom is translated as "Nice trout!"

Submitted by Barrie Creedon of Philadelphia, Pennsylvania.

Why Are All Gondolas Black?

This Imponderable was thrown at us on Jim Eason's KGO talk show in San Francisco. We were totally stumped but many subsequent callers offered their theories, most having to do with the advantage of black in absorbing the sun. We were skeptical, since not too many boats we have ever seen were painted black.

We considered flying out to Venice to check out this Imponderable (a legitimate research expense, no?), but unfortunately we stumbled upon the answer before we obtained our passport.

The origins of these boats are obscure; no one can find the derivation of the word "gondola." Gondolas have probably existed since the eleventh century and probably were painted many different colors. But in 1562, a sumptuary law was passed in Venice mandating that all gondolas be painted black. Many sumptuary laws were primarily attempts to avoid extravagant or unnecessary expenditures. But during this period, the Catholic church encouraged the passage of laws that banned ostentation for its own sake, particularly in matters of dress and decoration.

Still, the Italian flash has always shone through in the gondola. For in contrast to its somber color, the gondola sports a gleaming ferro that decorates the upcurving prow of the boat. Nobody knows whether the seven metal prongs on the prow ever had a symbolic meaning or if they were purely ornamental, but the steel ferro has always undermined the intention of the sumptuary law.

Why Do Many Soft Drink Labels Say "5 Mg. or Less Sodium per 6 oz. Serving" When the Labels Also Claim the Drink Is "Sodium-free"?

As if to prove he wasn't crazy, Douglas Watkins sent us a Schweppes label with both of the claims stated above. With its usual gift of the mother tongue, the American government (specifically, the Food and Drug Administration) has declared that "sodium-free" doesn't really mean the drink contains no sodium but rather five milligrams or fewer per serving. Serving sizes can vary, but most soft drink companies use 6 ounces as the standard.

Even more obviously subjective terms have exacting sodium requirements. "Very low sodium" drinks contain 35 milligrams or less sodium per serving; "low sodium" drinks have 140 milligrams or fewer.

"Reduced sodium" claims must be backed up with proof

that the drink has reduced the original amount of sodium by at least 75 percent. "No salt added," "unsalted," and "without added salt" are all official terms that signify that no salt is added during processing when salt normally is used.

As much as it pains us to be fair to a bureaucracy, we must admit that it would probably be counterproductive for the FDA to insist that "sodium free" means absolutely no sodium. Many foods have trace amounts of sodium that pose no danger to people on even the most restrictive diets. Do we really need labels that proclaim "minuscule sodium"?

Submitted by Douglas Watkins, Jr. of Hayward, California.

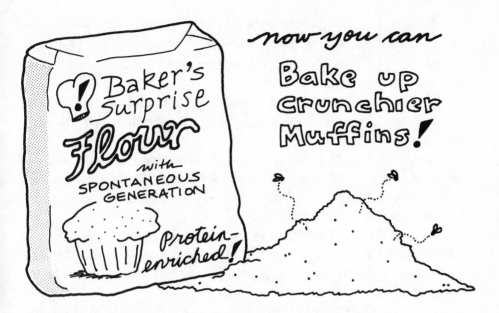

Why Do Bugs Seem to Suddenly Appear in Flour, Cornmeal, and Fruit? Where Do They Come From?

If you want to disabuse yourself of the notion that your house or apartment is a haven, a calm and clean refuge from the chaos of the outside world, consult David Bodanis' *The Secret House,* a study of the natural world inside our houses. With the help of scary, graphic photographs, Bodanis shows us that for every cockroach we might see scampering across our kitchen floor at night, there are thousands of bed mites, microscopic insects that subsist largely on a balanced diet of shedded human skin and hair.

Any time you slam a newspaper down on the dining room table or spray deodorant in the bathroom, you are traumatizing thousands of little critters. So it shouldn't be too surprising that the insects in our houses become interested in other types of food. Raw, unbleached flour may not be too appetizing to us, but compared to hair droppings, it becomes a reasonable alternative.

Many insects infest food before it is packaged, often in the form of eggs. According to Dr. George W. Rambo, of the National Pest Control Association, these insects are called "stored product insects." Everyone in the food industry expects a few insects and/or rodent hairs to infest many kinds of food; the Food and Drug Administration acknowledges the inevitability by mandating maximum limits.

Even if insects are not in the flour or fruit when you purchase it, they are attracted to the food once you bring it home. Flour might seem bland to you, but to grain mites or meal worms, it smells like ambrosia.

Many of the insects that infest flour, for example, are barely visible to the eye. It's a snap for a bug less than one-eighth of an inch long to intrude into packaging, especially after it has been opened.

So it's a losing fight. Our advice is to worry about the ones you can see and try not to think about the others.

Submitted by Karole Rathouz of Mehlville, Missouri. Thanks also to Jill Palmer of Leverett, Massachusetts; Scott Parker of Beaumont, Texas; Nicole Locke of Belmont, Massachusetts; Jane Doty of Tigard, Oregon; and Beverly Ditolla of Arvada, California.

Why Are the Large Staples Used to Fasten Cardboard Cartons Made of Expensive Copper?

They aren't. Carton staples are made out of steel wire. But they are finished with a very thin coating of a copper-sulfate solution, which gives the staples the appearance of copper. According to John Nasiatka, an engineer at the Duo-Fast Corporation, this is known as a "liquor" finish. Scrape a staple with a knife, and you will see how thin the coating is.

WHY DO DOGS HAVE WET NOSES?

The copper-sulfate coating is not applied for aesthetic reasons; it provides real, if limited, rust protection.

One company we contacted, Redmore Products, reports that it makes staples from wire with a heavy copper coating. These staples are designed for electric utilities. The extra copper provides a longer life and helps prevent electrolysis (and we're not talking about hair removal).

Submitted by Clifford Abrams of Evanston, Illinois.

Why Does *TV Guide* Start Its Listings on Saturday?

When *TV Guide* first began in 1953, Saturday was one of the nights that attracted the greatest number of television viewers. Such blockbuster shows as "The Jackie Gleason Show," "The Original Amateur Hour," "Your Show of Shows," and "Your Hit Parade" all appeared on Saturday.

Sunday was then an even bigger night, but sales of *TV Guide* weren't high on Sundays. Many cities had strict blue laws that forbade stores, including supermarkets, from conducting business on Sundays. *TV Guide* feared that consumers who couldn't buy the magazine on Sunday might forgo the purchase altogether. By listing programs starting with Saturday, *TV Guide* could attract working couples doing their grocery shopping on Friday night or Saturday.

Patrick Murphy, programming editor of *TV Guide*, told *Imponderables* that the original decision was made entirely by the editorial department, but now there are production reasons for keeping the listings starting on Saturday. Saturday is the networks' biggest sports day. Last-minute schedule changes are often made in line-ups for football and basketball games. By starting with Saturday, *TV Guide* can wait until the "last minute" to commit to printing which teams will be playing. And now that Saturday is one of the nights that draws the fewest viewers, shoppers who don't buy the magazine on Saturday might still buy it on Sunday (the night with the most sets in use), now that blue laws are a thing of the past.

Submitted by David Wedryk of South Holland, Illinois. Thanks also to David A. Kroffe of Los Alamitos, California.

Is There any Difference between a "NO OUTLET" and a "DEAD-END" Sign?

Not much. According to the *Manual on Uniform Traffic Control Devices,* there is no technical distinction between the two signs. But Harry Skinner, chief, Traffic Engineering Division of the Office of Traffic Operations at the Federal Highway Administration, says that there is a subtle difference in practice:

> the DEAD END sign will commonly be used for roads or streets that terminate within sight of the driver whereas a NO OUTLET is more often used to sign a road or street which is the only entrance and exit to a neighborhood.

Submitted by Donna M. Auguste of Menlo Park, California.

Why Do Ironworkers Wear Their Hard Hats Backwards?

Unless an inordinate number of ironworkers were absentminded baseball catchers on the side, we had no explanation for this Imponderable until we heard from James B. Ford, of Local 396 in St. Louis, and editor of *Journeyman Ironworker*.

Ford, an ironworker with 25 years' experience, swatted away the Imponderable with ease:

> ... the majority of the time, we are wearing welding goggles on the job. By wearing our hard hat backwards, it enables us to pull the goggles up onto our foreheads without removing the hard hat each time. Of course, we wear hard hats for safety reasons; so at the same time we are observing the safety rules, we have the convenience of easy goggle removal.

Submitted by Frank Overstreet of Fred, Texas.

Speech bubble (left): DARLING, THIS RED IS A BIT TOO COOL—

Speech bubble (right): BUT, SWEETNESS! RED IS SERVED AT IGLOO TEMPERATURE!

Why Is Red Wine Supposed to Be Served at Room Temperature and White Wine Chilled?

A recent article in the *New York Times* reported that despite expectations of a boom, wine sales had flattened in the United States during the 1980s. Although affluent Americans started buying much more wine in the 1970s, the industry's attempts to seduce average Americans with anything other than wine coolers obviously failed in the 1980s.

What happened? Although the average person might reply that he doesn't want to spend $6.00 for a bottle of wine in a liquor store, or $20.00 for the identical bottle at a restaurant, the same guy will spend $1.50 for a bottle of Evian water that tastes remarkably like tap water.

We think there is another possibility. The average person is afraid of wine and the whole rigamarole surrounding it. Who wants to take a special date out to a nice restaurant and proceed to mispronounce the name of the wine and then get a chilly look from the waiter when he orders *that* wine ("Was that red wine with fish?" the poor shlub wonders. "Or white wine with fish? And what do I do if I get a steak and she orders fish—order pink wine? Come to think of it, there is a pink wine—isn't there?"). And then, worst of all, our poor shlub has to pretend he knows what he is doing when the waiter or wine steward pours the wine in his glass for inspection. He knows that the waiter knows that he doesn't have the slightest idea how to even pretend that he is actually judging the quality of the wine rather than merely attempting to avoid looking like a bumbling idiot.

All this and then you have to pay through the nose for the privilege of being humiliated. Personally speaking, we'd still rather order wine out in a restaurant than at home. We have a remarkably poor record of extracting the cork intact. When more wine comes with screw-tops, we'll consider becoming enologists.

One of the great truths handed down to us from Mount Olympus is that it is a cardinal sin to chill red wine. We've read this rule scores of times but without an explanation. We are happy to announce that we found some wine experts who could explain the practice and clear away some of the mystique. We yield the floor to Sam Folsom, of San Francisco's Wine Institute:

> Red wine contains a number of natural acids, most notably tannin [tannic acid], and other components that aren't found in white wine. This is because red wines are fermented with the grape skins, while white wines are not. Many of these natural acids are found in the skin of the grape.
>
> When red wine is chilled, these natural acids are exacerbated, while the grape flavors are masked. This results in a wine that tastes harsh without any other flavor components. At room temperature, the natural acids are much more in balance with the grape flavors, making the wine much more appealing. White wines are refreshing chilled and don't suffer the same flavor imbalances when chilled because they do not contain tannin and other acids.

We spoke to Barbara Mader Ivey, national director of Women on Wine, a woman who proves that it is possible to be an expert on wine and have a sense of humor at the same time. She confirms that most red wines taste best at room temperature but suggests common sense. If your room happens to be a nonairconditioned one in Palm Springs during the summer, a sweetish nouveau beaujolais will not be at its best at "room temperature." And although chilling enhances most white wines, she suggests that good wine will have a fine flavor at any room temperature; if anything, most people err on the side of overchilling white wine.

Submitted by Roy Welland of New York, New York. Thanks also to Charles Myers of Ronkonkoma, New York.

Why, After a Call on a Pay Phone, Does One Hear a Click That Sounds Like the Money is Coming Back Down to the Refund Slot?

We dare say that if we plumbed deep into our souls, we would admit that we have, on more than one occasion, heard the unmistakable sound of coins dropping after completing a call and checked the refund slot to make sure our quarter hadn't come back. Of course, we fully intended to reinsert the quarter. We just wanted to make sure that our quarter didn't fall into the wrong hands and thereby shortchange the phone company. Right?

The sound you hear after hanging up the phone is indeed the sound of your coin(s) falling down. Shelly Gilbreath, of Southwestern Bell Telephone, explains:

> When the call is complete, and the customer at the coin phone hangs up, or the call times out, an audible "click" is heard. This "click" is the sound that the coin phone equipment recognizes as a signal to allow the money to drop from the reservoir into a small metal compartment inside the coin phone. There are employees within the phone companies that come around and unlock the front of the coin phone [we answered the mystery of why you

never see these employees in *Imponderables*], and collect the coins that are in the compartment.

Submitted by Todd Nickerson of Londonderry, New Hampshire.

Why Do So Few Houses in the South Have Basements?

Weather. Architect Bill Stanley told *Imponderables* that many southern communities have high water tables that can flood basements. In wet areas, some houses are built on stilts to forestall the potential problem.

But basements are more practical in colder climates and don't cost that much extra to build. Dennis McClendon, managing editor of the American Planning Association's *Planning* magazine, and a transplanted southerner, explains why:

> Southern homebuilders don't have to go very far below ground to place the house's foundation below the frost line. To avoid heaving and cracking, a house's foundation must go below the frost line (the depth to which the ground can be expected to freeze).
>
> Building codes in the North typically require foundations several feet below ground level. Since the builder has already had to excavate that deep for foundations, it makes sense to treat the foundations as walls and finish the space inside as a basement. It also makes connection to water and sewer lines (which must be below the frost line) easier. Tradition also plays a part: Home buyers who are used to the space a basement provides expect one in a new home.

Submitted by Jon R. Kennedy of Charlotte, North Carolina.

Why Is Sugar an Ingredient in Most Commercially Packaged Salt?

It is? So we wondered when we received Stephanie Drossin's Imponderable. We went to our cupboard and found our container of Morton's salt.

Waddya know? Dextrose is listed as an ingredient. We immediately dispatched a letter to Morton International and received an enlightening response from advertising/sales promotion supervisor Kathleen M. Reidy:

> Dextrose is added to Morton Iodized Table Salt in order to ensure optimum salt flavor characteristics and to stabilize the iodide. Iodide is added as it is vital to the proper function of the thyroid gland and in the prevention of goiter.
>
> Actually, the amount of dextrose in salt is so small that it is dietetically insignificant. Morton Iodized Table Salt contains 0.04 percent dextrose or 40 milligrams per 100 grams of salt.
>
> For many years dextrose was also added to Morton Plain Table Salt. However, dextrose was removed from Morton Plain Table Salt in 1980 to allay the fears of those concerned with their sugar intake.

We don't know about iodide stabilization, but we will confirm that adding sugar to just about anything ensures optimum flavor. Whenever we're cooking and faced with a dish that just doesn't work, sugar seems like a mystical cureall.

But now that we've made both sodium and sugar out to be nutritional bad guys, and now that we've let the cat out of the bag about sugar in salt, we're anticipating the launching of a new product, Diet Salt. That's right. Salt with artificial sweetener.

Sure, salt isn't fattening. But by saving those milligrams of sugar over ten years, you will have saved enough calories to indulge yourself in a whole Hershey's Kiss.

Submitted by Stephanie Drossin of Philadelphia, Pennsylvania.

AND OTHER IMPONDERABLES 631

Is It True That Women Who Live Together Tend to Synchronize Their Menstrual Cycles? If So, Why Does This Happen?

Yes, it's true. In a 1971 article in *Nature*, M. K. McClintock provided hard research to confirm what women had long claimed: Women who live together tend to have synchronous cycles. Subsequent researchers have corroborated McClintock's findings. Nobody can explain the phenomenon yet, but many possible explanations have been eliminated.

The American College of Obstetricians and Gynecologists led us to a 1989 article in the *American Journal of Human Biology* that confronts this Imponderable head-on. Written by three medical doctors (B. B. Little, D. S. Guzick, and R. M. Malina) and one anthropologist (M. D. Rocha Ferreira), "Environmental Influences Cause Menstrual Synchrony, Not Pheromones" reports the findings of a fascinating research experiment.

They studied 127 female college students who lived in a group of 12 houses that surrounded a common courtyard. The study was conducted in the fall and none of the women had lived together during the summer.

The conclusions were startling. During the first month of coresidence, the day of menstrual onset deviated from the mean by an average of 13.7 days. During the next month, the average deviation declined to 2.6 days! Although a high degree of synchrony was achieved in one month of coresidence, the second month added only 0.3 day increase in synchrony.

By collecting all kinds of demographic and personal information, the researchers were able to rule out any other obvious correlations. They found no statistical correlation, for example, between synchrony and age, exercise patterns, or years since menarche. Other studies have shown that mothers, daughters, and sisters do not tend to have a higher than expected number of synchronous menstrual periods unless they live together.

Previous investigators suggested that pheromonal influences might have caused synchrony. But one of this study's findings tends to dispute this theory: Living in the same house tended to slightly increase synchrony, but explained only a small part of the variance. If the pheromonal secretions were the key to menstrual cycles,

> roommates and coresidents should have been significantly synchronized and women who did not live together should not have been synchronized. In contrast, the results of this study indicate that a large component of the variation in menstrual cycling is environmental (i.e., shared variance), perhaps as much as 91%. Thus, coresidence may be a surrogate for common environmental effects on synchrony, and not necessarily an opportunity for exposure to pheromones.

The researchers of this study don't speculate on precisely what these environmental factors are. It wasn't diet, because each house planned its own menus, so college "mystery meat" isn't the answer. Perhaps the shared hours and routine (all the women

AND OTHER IMPONDERABLES   633

had a midnight curfew and a ban on male visitors after hours) contributed. So although we don't yet know the etiology of synchronous cycles, at least, as Kassie Schwan's illustration suggests, we know that they can be conveniently efficient.

Submitted by Rocco Manzo of St. Louis, Missouri.

Why Are Blueprints Blue?

Not because architects wanted to dabble in primary colors. No one would disagree that white lines on blue paper aren't easy to read.

But the paper is cheap. The salts used in blueprint processing are what turns them blue when developed. Dennis McClendon, of the American Planning Association, told *Imponderables* that the silver salts used in photography yield a nice black tone that reads well against white paper. But silver salts are expensive and difficult to develop.

About one hundred years ago, original architectural drawings were done with pen and ink, a costly, labor-intensive process. So the technology of blueprinting was developed to reproduce originals relatively cheaply; blueprinting technology didn't change much for almost a century.

Blueprinting was a wet process in which the original pen and ink drawing was made on translucent tracing paper. The paper was put in contact with paper coated with a ferro (iron)-prussiate (salt) mixture. This coating turned the finished blueprint blue.

The blueprint was then exposed to ultraviolet light, developed in potash, rinsed in water, and dried. Originally, the prints were left out in the sun to dry, but later they were artificially exposed in blueprint machines using carbon arcs or mercury vapor lamps. The original pen and ink lines reproduced as white and the blank areas reproduced as solid blue.

The blueprinting process proved to be cheap, relatively fast, and reliable. Only one problem loomed: Nobody liked reading blueprints.

To the rescue came the diazo process. Diazo materials are coated not with iron and prussiate salts but with diazonium salts and a coupler (which eventually colors the print) that are developed in ammonia fumes. The biggest advantage of the diazo process is that after the drawing is exposed to ultraviolet light, the clear portions of the original are rendered white (or light) and the opaque markings appear dark (usually blue). One can read "whiteprints" without eyestrain.

By the late 1950s, the diazo process, which had been invented in the late 1920s, had largely displaced blueprinting as a favored means of reproducing architectural drawings. Many architects and most laymen still nostalgically refer to whiteprints as "blueprints."

Soon there may be nostalgia for whiteprints. For diazo reproduction is losing its market share to LDXCs (large document xerographic copiers). The machines themselves are very expensive, but most architectural firms love their convenience. If nothing else, LDXCs don't leave the reproduction room smelling like ammonia. Now that they have been turned into an anachronism, blueprints have a right to be blue.

Submitted by Herbert Kraut of Forest Hills, New York. Thanks also to Laurence Ince of Briarwood, New York.

How Can Babies Withstand Higher Body Temperatures Than Their Supposedly Hardier Parents?

When adults spring a high fever, they are likely to be very sick. But babies often spike to high temperatures without serious repercussions. Babies' temperatures respond more quickly, more easily, and with much greater swings than adults'.

Why? Our body has a thermostat, located in the hypothalamus of the brain. When we are infected by bacteria or a virus, toxins interfere with the workings of the thermostat, fooling it into thinking that 103 degrees Fahrenheit, not 98.6 degrees, is "normal." With a baby, a 103-degree fever doesn't necessarily mean a more severe illness than a 101-degree fever.

Babies simply do not possess the well-developed hypothalamus that adults do. Temperature stability and regulation, like other developmental faculties, steadily increase as the baby ages.

Fever is a symptom, not the cause of sickness. In fact, fever is both a bodily defense against infection and a reliable alarm.

The first reaction of most parents to their babies' fevers is to bundle them up like Eskimos, especially when taking them outside. Mother and father don't always know best. Fever isn't really the enemy and shouldn't be treated as such. The body is trying to fight infection by raising the temperature. Swaddling the baby actually interferes with the heat loss that will eventually ease the fever.

Submitted by Ron Pateman of Chicago, Illinois.

What Accounts for the Varying Amounts of Static Electricity from Day to Day? Why is There More Static Electricity in the Winter Than During the Summer?

With the help of Richard Anthes, president of the University Corporation for Atmospheric Research, we can lay out the answer to this Imponderable with a logical precision that Mr. Wizard would admire.

1. Static electricity relies upon the buildup of an electrical charge difference between two objects and the sudden release of this difference in an electrical spark.
2. In order to build up a charge difference sufficient to create static electricity, there should not be much electrical conductivity in the air.
3. The conductivity of moist air is greater than the conductivity of dry air.
4. Relative humidity inside houses or other buildings is usually much lower in the winter than the summer.
5. Therefore, static electricity is more likely to occur in the winter than in the summer.

Static electricity can occur in the summer if the humidity happens to be low that day or if air conditioning dehumidifies the air inside.

Submitted by Reverend Ken Vogler of Jeffersonville, Indiana.

Why Do We Kiss Under the Mistletoe?

The innocuous mistletoe plant, now used to cop a cheap kiss or two, was once considered to be a sacred plant by the ancient Druids. They believed that mistletoe could cure sicknesses and shield its owner from evil forces such as witches or ghosts. Druids gathered the plant at winter solstice, just days before we now celebrate Christmas. With great solemnity and ritual, they cut the mistletoe with a golden sickle reserved solely for this purpose.

So sacred was the mistletoe to the Druids that they never allowed the plant to touch the ground, which probably explains why we still hang mistletoe over our doorways. The Druids believed that by placing the mistletoe over their doorways, they could not only protect the health and safety of all who passed through but also promote romance and fertility. If a boy kissed a girl under the mistletoe and gave one of the plants's white berries to the kissee, the ritual meant they would get married within the year.

Ironically, although mistletoe is now associated with Christmas, the Christians in Celtic regions, ashamed of their pagan antecedents, did everything possible to dissociate themselves from the belief in the power of mistletoe. But the practice took hold. And although a buss under the mistletoe no longer promises marriage, at least we've retained the fun part of the ritual.

Submitted by Brian Hart of Bala Cynwyd, Pennsylvania. Thanks
also to Jeffrey R. Reder of Mahopac, New York; Gail Lee of Los

Angeles, California; Karin Norris of Salinas, California; Nadine
L. Sheppard of Fairfield, California; and Jena Mori of Los
Angeles, California.

What Do the Numbers on Pasta Boxes Mean?

The biggest marketers of packaged pastas, such as Ronzoni,
Prince, and Mueller's, make such a bewildering array of pastas
that numbers were assigned to help consumers discriminate
among the varieties. Unfortunately, each company has their own
system, and the numbers are arbitrarily assigned.

Frank Taufiq, vice-president of quality assurance for the
Prince Company, told *Imponderables* that his company makes
more than 80 different shapes and sizes of pasta. All are given
numbers, in the hope that it will be easier for the consumer to
remember numbers 56 and 57 than that they signify mostaccioli
and mostaccioli with lines, respectively.

We have seen shoppers with glazed expressions trying to
find the pasta variety that they once enjoyed but cannot remember or even pronounce if they did remember. The numbering
system would undoubtedly help more people find the right pasta
if supermarkets arranged pasta on their shelves in numerical
order.

We once found a supermarket that placed all of Campbell's
soups in alphabetical order. We might not have bought more
soup as a result, but we sure spent less time in the soup aisle.

Submitted by Tom and Marcia Bova of Rochester, New York.
Thanks also to Howard Givner of Brooklyn, New York.

How Do Worms Survive During the Winter? Can They Crawl and Find Food?

They do just fine, thank you. Richard Zack, curator/director of the James Entomological Collection in Washington, explains:

> Worms continue to live and crawl around during the winter, usually below the freeze level. Their activity does slow and they would appear relatively inactive as compared to the summer. Remember, in most of our country the ground rarely freezes to much of a depth and snow is actually a good insulator from freezing temperatures and winds. If a worm were to be caught in frozen ground it would remain inactive, but alive, until the ground thawed.

Submitted by Robert Commaille of Bethel, Connecticut.

Why Do Worms Come out on the Sidewalk After It Rains?

What's with this sudden obsession over worms? Are the nineties going to be the Decade of the Larva?

What do you think the worms are coming out for? Their health? In fact, they are. Except for those that live as parasites, most worms live by burrowing little holes in the ground. When it rains, those little holes fill with water. If the worms didn't get out of the holes, they'd drown. Worms may be creepers, but they're not dolts.

Why do they congregate on the sidewalk after a rain? Two reasons. Sidewalks provide more solid support than dirt or grass during a rainstorm. But if you read our discussion of why ants congregate on the sidewalk (in *Why Do Clocks Run Clockwise?*), you've probably guessed the other explanation. The sidewalk provides a nice white background for us to see dark objects, worms, and insects. But if you investigated the grass adjacent to the sidewalk, you would find many worms trying to stay above water, wishing they had made it to the sidewalk.

Submitted by Mike Arnett of Chicago, Illinois. Thanks also to Karole Rathouz of Mehlville, Missouri; John P. Eichman of Yucaipa, California; Willard Wheeler of Upland, California; and Tom Trauschke of Whitehall, Pennsylvania.

Why Don't Place Settings Use Serrated Knives?

In *Imponderables,* we discussed how mean old Cardinal Richelieu decreed in the seventeenth century that all dinner knives must have rounded edges in order to eradicate the serious social problem of dinner guests picking their teeth with sharp-edged knives. Ever since, the western world has been stuck with knives up to the task of spreading butter but inappropriate for cutting meat.

Now that there isn't too much danger of folks using their knives as toothpicks, might we go back to the old days of pointed knives? Why must we have separate "steak knives" to perform the chore for which knives were originally intended? Even rounded, serrated knives would cut meat more easily than the typical dinner knife and would still be able to spread butter effectively.

The reason our wish is but a pipe dream comes from Robert M. Johnston, who represents the Sterling Silversmiths Guild of America:

> The serration in a knife aids in its cutting. The serration is also apt to damage fine china and therefore is seldom used on a place knife in silverware.

Submitted by Richard Aaron of Toronto, Ontario.

Is There Any Meaning to the Numbers in Men's Hat Sizes?

Yes. But please don't ask for the full story—it is very complicated.

The American hat size is based on a measurement of the circumference of the head. The average man's head is about 23 inches in circumference. Divide 23 by pi (3.1416) and you get a number resembling 7⅜, a common hat size. The English, French, and Italians all have their own systems, also based on the circumference of the head.

In practice, most American hat manufacturers determine their sizes by measuring the length of the sweat band inside the hat and dividing by pi.

Submitted by Herman E. London of Poughkeepsie, New York.

What Is the Purpose of the Small Hole in the Barrel of Cheap Stick Pens?

We were first asked this question by a caller on Tom Snyder's syndicated radio show. Tom Snyder, upon hearing the question, proceeded to laugh his patented Tom Snyder laugh (or is it his Dan Ackroyd laugh?) and we knew we had to find the answer.

Susan Thompson, of A. T. Cross, makers of noncheap pens, told us that the innocuous little hole is of vital importance to a stick pen. Without the hole, a vacuum would be created in the pen as the ink was used and the pen wouldn't write.

R. F. Rhode, physical laboratory supervisor for Sheaffer Pen, concurs that if no air were allowed to enter the assembly and the parts of the pen were airtight, the pen would not write. Rhode adds that the hole serves another important function: equalizing the atmospheric pressure inside and outside the pen. Without equalized pressure, sensitive ballpoint pens tend not to write and start leaking (for more on leaking, see below).

Submitted by Vince Tassinari of West Springfield, Virginia.

Union of **P**reoccupied **S**cientists **A**nnual **M**eeting

TODAY
seminar
on
memory
skills

Tonight
dance
featuring
the
ink spots

What Causes Ink "Hemorrhages" in Pens?

Remember all the way back to the last Imponderable, when we were rambling on about air pressure? Here's the payoff. Air pressure is usually the culprit in the leaks of aqueous fountain pens. Sheaffer Pen's R. F. Rhode explains:

> If the pen is only partially filled with ink, there is considerable air in the sac or cartridge that holds the main ink supply. If there is a pressure change caused by a temperature change or an altitude change, and the pen is held point down or horizontal, the air expands and the pressure caused by this forces the thin aqueous ink out of the feeding system onto paper, clothing, etc.

O.K. Maybe the folks featured on *Lifestyles of the Rich and Famous* use fountain pens and jet to Aspen and have to suffer through the agonies of altitude adjustment. But why do the cheap pens that most of us use leak all the time?

Once when we were teaching, we bought a ten-pack of guaranteed student-torture devices, red pens. All ten of these beauties hemorrhaged within a few weeks. Infuriated, we sent eight of the leaky corpses back to the manufacturer, demanding a refund. We got back a curious note, along with ten fresh replacements, acknowledging the defects but saying in effect, "What do you expect from cheap pens? If you want a pen that doesn't leak, buy a good pen."

A malfunctioning ballpoint is the most likely cause of a stick pen's hemorrhage. Why do ballpoints malfunction? Common reasons include: manufacturing defects; excessive pressure by the user; dropping the pen; and temperature shifts. Pilot Corporation's Mimi Clark adds that leaking can also occur if the ink is too viscous and/or the size of the point is not sufficient to accommodate the ink flow coming down the barrel.

Ballpoint refills also have leaky tendencies. R. F. Rhode explains why:

> Usually this occurs on the larger diameter ballpoint refills that contain a follower-type material on top of the ink column. If there is a "break" in this follower-type material, ink will leak out the back end of ballpoint refills. Another cause can be excessive accumulation of ink around the ball in the tip—this is known as "leaking" or "gooping."

"Gooping" may be slang, but when the ink that is supposed to be in your pen is all over your hands and papers, no word is more descriptive.

Submitted by Gerald P. Cuccio of Downsview, Ontario.

Why Don't Women's Blouses Come in Sleeve Lengths, Like Men's Shirts?

Because there is no standard sleeve length for women's blouses. Cory Greenspan, of the Federation of Apparel Manufacturers, explains that the "appropriate" length of a woman's sleeve varies depending upon the dictates of the fashion designer and the purpose of the outfit. Men's long-sleeve shirts are designed to be worn with a jacket so that the sleeve will hang just below the wrist line when the wearer is standing. But women wear long-sleeve blouses with other garments or no covering at all.

Women have a much wider choice of blouses than men do of dress shirts. If each blouse came with sleeve sizes, retailers would have to cut down on their selection in order to provide all the different sizes. While men are content with the usual boring solids and stripes, even the dressiest of women's blouses are available in a wide range of colors and textures.

For the same inventory reasons, most men's shirts are now sold with "average" sleeve lengths. While the neck size is specified (e.g., 16), the "average" sleeve length may be 32/33. We expected to hear that the actual sleeve length of a 32/33 shirt is 32½ inches. But Mark Weber, of Phillips-Van Heusen, told *Imponderables* that the actual length is always the higher of the two numbers (in this case, 33 inches). By using "average" sleeve lengths, retailers can cut the number of different sizes of the same style shirt in half and use the saved space to display a greater variety of styles.

> *Submitted by Melanie Jongsma of Lansing, Illinois. Thanks also to Robert A. McKnight of Jennings, Missouri.*

Why Are the American Quart and Gallon Smaller than the British Imperial Equivalents?

The American colonists adopted most of the weights and measures of Old England, including the British system of liquid measurements (pints, quarts, and gallons). In the eighteenth century, the English used two different gallons: the ale gallon

WHY DO DOGS HAVE WET NOSES?

(282 cubic inches) and the wine gallon (231 cubic inches). The American colonists adopted the English wine gallon from the beginning and so it has remained.

But the English had to do *something* to punish the Americans for the Revolution, so they decided in 1824 to abandon their two-tier gallon system and to switch to the British Imperial gallon, which is equivalent to the volume of ten pounds of water at a temperature of 62 degrees Fahrenheit (or to put it more precisely if less memorably, the equivalent of the nice round number of 277.42 cubic inches).

The U.S. government decided not to switch and the result is that today Americans, shocked by the high price of petrol in Great Britain, are slightly relieved by getting a little more gasoline in an Imperial gallon. Joan Koenig, of the Office of Weights and Measures at the U.S. National Bureau of Standards, adds that the British are in the process of adopting the metric system, another indication that the Empire ain't what it used to be.

Submitted by Richard Speiss of Winnipeg, Manitoba.

Why Is That Piece of Tissue Paper Included in Wedding Invitations?

When wedding invitations come back from the printer, along comes a box of tissue paper that seems to serve no discernible purpose. Any prospective bride will tell you that one of the less than thrilling chores in the prewedding grind is hand-inserting a sheet of tissue paper inside each invitation. Why bother with the stuff?

According to Melanie Martini, associate editor of *Bride's* magazine, at one time the tissues did serve a practical purpose: to keep ink from smudging. Modern printing techniques have rendered the tissues obsolete in theory but not in practice. For some reason, that piece of tissue veritably reeks of class and tradition, so few brides leave it out.

Occasionally, brides at small weddings will use calligraphy on the invitations. In this case, the tissues might help blot the ink, as did the tissue papers of yore. But no less an authority than Elizabeth Post, in *Emily Post's Complete Book of Wedding*

WHY DO DOGS HAVE WET NOSES?

Etiquette, says that the tissue paper may be discarded with impunity.

Submitted by Harrison Leon Church of Lebanon, Illinois.
Thanks also to Donna J. Budz of San Diego, California.

Why Does Neptune's Moon Triton Orbit "in Reverse?"

Our old astronomical all-star, Jeff Kanipe, associate editor of *Astronomy,* was willing to answer this Imponderable on the proviso that we made clear there is no such thing as "reverse" or "forward" in outer space, any more than there is an up and down. As usual, Jeff wrote such a clear and fascinating explanation that we'll let him speak for himself.

In our solar system, most moons orbit their master planets in the same direction that the planets spin. If you could look down on Earth's north pole from space, you'd see that we rotate counterclockwise, from west to east. This is why the sun, moon, and stars seem to "rise" in the east and "set" in the west from Earth.

The moon, too, orbits Earth west to east, although because we complete one rotation (one day) more quickly than the moon can complete a single orbit (about 27.3 days) it looks as if the moon is fixed in the sky. But if you note the moon's position over a few nights, you'll see that it moves eastward with respect to the stars. The planets also orbit the sun in a west-to-east direction as seen from the north pole of the solar system. Astronomers refer to this motion as "direct."

Triton, Neptune's largest moon, doesn't orbit its master planet with a direct motion. Triton orbits in the direction opposite Neptune's spin and orbit. Astronomers think that a gravitational tug-of-war in the early solar system reversed Triton's orbit.

Four and a half billion years ago, Triton was in its own orbit around the sun, and Neptune was in a slightly greater orbit just beyond Triton. Being the more massive of the pair, Neptune's gravity pulled on Triton whenever the smaller planet passed by. Over millions of years, the distance between Neptune and Triton closed until Neptune exerted more gravitational influence on Triton than the sun.

Finally, during one orbit in which the two bodies passed particularly close to one another, Neptune's gravity wrenched Triton out of its orbit. Triton swung out ahead of Neptune and then fell back toward the planet along an elliptical orbit. That orbit, however, was in a clockwise direction, opposite the rotational spin and orbital direction of Neptune.

Submitted by Cheryl Topper of Brooklyn, New York.

Why Do Mis-hits of Golf Shots, Especially Irons, Sting So Badly and for So Long?

As if the pathetic trajectory of your ball weren't punishment enough, a mis-hit in golf is likely to be accompanied by a sustained stinging sensation in the hands. If a shot hurts, you either haven't struck the center of the ball or, even more likely, you haven't hit the ball with the sweet spot of the club. Dr. John R. McCarroll, of the Methodist Sports Medicine Center, explains:

> Hitting the toe or the heel of the club causes more stress to be sent up the shaft and radiated into the hand. It is essentially like holding on to a vibrating hammer or like being hit with a hammer on the hands because the stress comes up and causes the hands to absorb the shock.

John Story, of the Professional Golfers' Association of America, explains that not all golf clubs are alike when it comes to inflicting pain on the duffer. A mis-hit on a driver (or any other wood) is much more forgiving than the iron, which has a harder head and therefore creates much more vibration. The vibration from the mis-hit of a driver gets lost in the long shaft.

Dr. McCarroll adds that advances in club manufacturing have lessened the problem of hand stings: "The newer shafts such as graphite and casted clubs cause less pain to your hands than the classic forged club with a metal shaft."

Submitted by Ron Musgrove of San Leandro, California.

What Exactly Is Happening Physiologically When Your Stomach Growls?

You've got gas in your stomach even when you (and others) aren't aware of it. You swallow gas as you eat and drink, and as you continuously swallow saliva. Some gas lands in your stomach through bacterial fermentation.

Imagine your stomach and intestines as a front-loading washing machine in a laundromat. Instead of clothes, water, and detergent whooshing around, there are solid foods, liquids from your diet, water, digestive fluids, and gas constantly churning and contracting, even when you are not aware of it. This churning kneads and mixes the food and enzymes, making it easier for the stomach and intestines to digest and absorb the food.

But just as the excess water and suds must be eliminated from the washer, so must the food left in the stomach. These contractions enable the residue to move to the lower gut, where it is formed into feces.

Dr. Frank Davidoff, of the American College of Physicians, describes the arduous travels of gas in the stomach:

> Now when bubbles of gas and liquid are mixed together in a hollow, muscular tube and the tube contracts in waves, massaging the contents along the way, pushing portions of the mixture through narrow, contracted gut segments, the result is gurgling, splashing, and squeaking of all kinds—borborygmi, growls, rumblings—whatever you want to call them.
>
> Your stomach seems to growl more when you're hungry because part of the physiological condition of hunger is an increased muscular activity of your gut, as though it were anticipating the incoming meal, getting ready to move it along.

Of course, the washing machine metaphor breaks down just about now. The washing machine doesn't particularly care whether it continues to get fed, and unlike our stomachs, we're not constantly stuffing clothes, water, and detergent down its throat while it is still trying to work off its current load.

Submitted by Karen Lueck of Tulsa, Oklahoma. Thanks also to Ronald C. Semone of Washington, D.C.; Margaret MacDonald of San Francisco, California; Karl Valindras of Petaluma, California; and David A. Bohnke of Monroeville, Indiana.

Are You Ever Going to Answer the 12 Most Frequently Asked Irritating Questions?

A wise person once said: "There is no such thing as a stupid question." We would like to add a corollary. "Maybe, but there sure are some questions that we don't want to hear."

We are goodhearted by nature. We wake up in the morning with a smile on our face and love in our hearts. But nothing will turn our rosy optimism into irritability more than facing any of these UnImponderables.

There are only a few criteria for selecting Imponderables for these books:

1. They must present genuine mysteries that most people would not know the answer to.
2. The mysteries should deal with everyday life rather than esoteric, scientific, or philosophical questions.
3. They are "why" questions rather than who/what/where/when trivia questions.

            WHY DO DOGS HAVE WET NOSES?

4. Seminormal people might be interested in the questions and answers.
5. They are mysteries that aren't easy to find the answer to, especially from books. Therefore, they are questions that shouldn't have been written about frequently.

Some of the most frequently asked Imponderables are ones that meet criteria one through four but fail miserably at number five. If someone else has answered them, they aren't really Imponderables anymore!

The bane of our existence is when a comedian like George Carlin, Steven Wright, or, worst of all, Gallagher, offers a witty rhetorical question. The result: One week later, our mailbox is stuffed with folks clamoring for an answer. And there is no way to answer these questions without denuding them of their humor or wit. When we try, we feel like academics trying to describe why the Marx Brothers are funny.

In the fervent, desperate hope that we can slow down to a trickle the flood of people asking these most frequently asked UnImponderables, we offer our quick answers to the following would-be Imponderables that aren't really Imponderables at all.

1. WHY *Do We Park on Driveways and Drive on Parkways?*

This is our least favorite UnImponderable, especially because we have already answered it ourselves in *Who Put the Butter in Butterfly?* We have graciously consented to allow us to quote our own answer:

> One of the main definitions of *way* is "a route or course that is or may be used to go from one place to another." New York's Robert Moses dubbed his "route or course that was used to go from one place to another" *parkway* because it was lined with trees and lawns in an attempt to simulate the beauty of a park. The *driveway*, just as much as a *highway* a *freeway*, or a *parkway*, is a path for automobiles. The driveway is a path, a *way* between the street and a house or garage.

AND OTHER IMPONDERABLES

2. IF *7-11 Stores Are Open 24 Hours, Why Do They Need Locks on the Doors?*

Originally, 7-11 stores were open from 7:00 A.M. until 11:00 P.M., thus providing the name for the chain. Of course, these stores needed locks every day because they were used, logically enough, to lock the doors. But occasionally, locks are needed even in stores open 24 hours.

What if a single employee in a small-town location has to go to the bathroom? What if an urban store wants to provide security? What if the store is shut down because of an emergency, such as an earthquake? Locks come in handy.

3. WHY *Is There No Channel 1 on Televisions?*

Actually, at one time, there was a channel 1. But the FCC gave back the band to its original users—mobile radios. TV bands are much wider than radio bands; and as anyone who has a radio with TV-audio reception knows, the TV band is just an extension of the FM frequencies.

4. WHY *Does the Water Drain out of a Bathtub in a Counterclockwise Direction North of the Equator and Clockwise South of the Equator?*

Any physics book, astronomy book, or dictionary will give you the answer to this. The earth's rotation deflects moving bodies to the appropriate direction. This was discovered by nineteenth-century French engineer Gaspard de Coriolis.

The question is whether or not the Coriolis effect is strong enough to influence the spiraling of drains. Many other factors, such as wind patterns, the configuration and irregularities of the tub (in our tub, the water usually drains clockwise), and the circulation of the water as it fills the tank, affect the rotation of the drainage more.

Scientists have proven that water "remembers" its circulatory patterns long after it appears to be still. One scientist went to the effort of not draining water until it rested for eight days.

Under these conditions, M.I.T. physicist Ascher H. Shapiro found that the vortex repeatedly drained in a counterclockwise direction. His results were confirmed by a team at the University of Sydney, who found that the circular tub consistently drained clockwise "down under."

Most scientists agree that the Coriolis effect does not apply to the movements of larger bodies of water, such as rivers and streams. But one place you cannot confirm the Coriolis effect is in toilets. The force of the flush is much, much greater than the whimper of the Coriolis effect.

5. WHY *Can't We Tickle Ourselves?*

Psychologists have wrestled with this one since Freud but haven't really gotten very far. Many psychologists believe that elements of surprise, aggressiveness, and sexuality must be present to induce a laugh. As much as we may love ourselves, it isn't so easy to surprise ourselves with a tickle.

6. WHY *Is a Hamburger Called a "Hamburger" When It Doesn't Contain Ham?*

Because the dish isn't named after the meat but after the city where it was popularized—Hamburg, Germany.

7. WHY *Do Foreign Pop and Rock Performers Sing with an American Accent?*

Most of the early British superstars, such as John Lennon, Paul McCartney, and Mick Jagger, were ardent devotees of American blues and rhythm-and-blues singers. They consciously imitated the phrasing of their musical influences. Listen, by comparison, to the vocals of Peter Noone of Herman's Hermits or Gerry Marsden on "Ferry Cross the Mersey," and you'll see that not every British pop singer tried to repress his or her native accent.

Punk and new wave bands of the 1970s and 1980s made a

AND OTHER IMPONDERABLES   657

conscious attempt to assert their English diction and phrasing. One would never mistake the Sex Pistols, the Clash, or the Pet Shop Boys for American bands.

Performers on the European continent have found it tough to get any exposure on British or American radio without recording in English. So Scandinavian bands like Roxette, Abba, and A-Ha have taken the path of least resistance and recorded in English—in some cases, not even understanding the meaning of the lyrics they were singing.

8. WHY *Do Men Have Nipples?*

Some have argued that nipples are a vestigial organ, one that some time in our evolution may disappear altogether in men. The appendix is another organ that might have served a more important function in our bodies than it does today, where it exists mainly to provide high standards of living for surgeons.

Males actually have the anatomical equipment in place to provide milk, but it lies dormant unless stimulated by estrogen, the female hormone. Might men have suckled babies in the distant past?

9. WHY *Do They Carve Moons on Outhouse Doors?*

In his book *More of the Straight Dope*, Cecil Adams questions the premise of this often-asked Imponderable, and we side with him. There is no evidence to suggest that the custom preceded depictions of outhouse moons in cartoons, particularly Al Capp's "Li'l Abner." On occasion, recently built outhouses are "mooned" in the mistaken impression that a cherished tradition is being upheld.

Adams concludes his discussion with the most telling point. The question isn't so much why a moon is there as why a carving is on the outhouse: "The reason there's a hole in the first place is a lot simpler: it provides ventilation."

10. WHAT *Sadist Invented the Necktie? And What Supposed Function Did It Serve?*

This particular sadist wisely decided to remain anonymous. As for function, we have found no proof whatsoever that neckties ever had any purpose in life other than to look pretty. The Neckware Association of America agrees.

The modern necktie is a variation of the cravats first worn by Croatian mercenaries who took France by storm with their masochistic fashion statement in the seventeenth century. The English modified the French style and, typically, made ties as uncomfortable as possible, leading inevitably to the American Revolution.

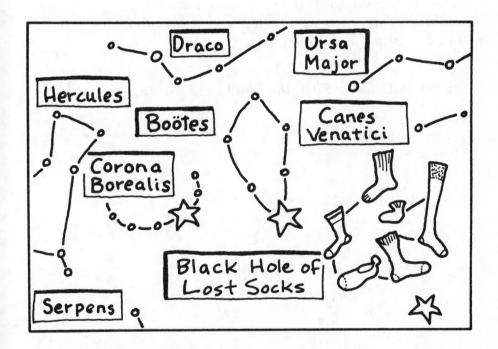

11. WHATEVER *Happened to the Missing Sock . . . ?*

If we could answer this question, we'd be in line for a Nobel prize and would be featured on "Sixty Minutes." No more being chained to the word processor.

AND OTHER IMPONDERABLES

But enough fantasy. We do have one theory that we will humbly propose. We lose pens all the time and find ourselves buying new ones constantly. But even though we wind up with single, unmatched socks in our drawers, we don't seem to replenish socks with the same rapidity as pens.

We had always assumed that we were losing socks caught on the sides of the washer or dryer. Callers on talk shows have proposed that socks meet, escape from the laundry room, and elope, never to be seen again. But the question nags . . . if they are disappearing one at a time, why don't we have to buy new socks all the time?

Maybe socks are mating in the washing machine but are actually giving birth to offspring during the spin cycle. Perhaps we are not losing socks but gaining one at a time.

Maybe we've been dealing with Imponderables and Un-Imponderables for a little too long.

12. WHICH *Came First, the Chicken or the Egg?*

The egg.
Then the chicken.
Then the sock.

Why Does the Phone Company Use that Obnoxious Three-Tone Signal before the Recording Tells You That They "Cannot Complete Your Call as Dialed"?

The phone company prefers to identify the three-tone signals as "Special Information Tones," but we like to call them "Ear-Splitting Shrieks from Hell." A busy signal sounds like the *Moonlight Sonata* compared to these ESSFHs.

AT&T's Dick Hofacker agrees with us on one point: these signals weren't meant for human consumption, but for machines with less sensitive auditory systems. Actually there are several different Special Information Tones, which serve different purposes:

    1. They convey to fax and computerized calling systems (also known as automatic dialers) that they've dialed a nonworking number. Only after this message has been

conveyed to machines do humans, with ears now only semi-intact, learn from a synthesized voice machine that they've just wasted their call.

2. The phone company is capable of monitoring how many times the "cannot complete your phone call as dialed" message is reached. Phone companies monitor how often Special Information Tones are activated in any particular trunk of phone cables. If the count is high, it might be the first indication that a phone line has been severed.

3. The special information tone is capable of telling the phone company how many calls a given disconnected number attracts. While a phone company might reassign a residential phone number in three months, the former phone number of a big retail store might continue to attract calls for a year or more. By calculating the number of calls made to an "old" number, the phone company can accurately assess when to reassign the number to a new company.

4. A Special Information Tone also precedes the recording "All circuits are busy. Please try your call again later."

Even though each three-part Special Information Tone has a slightly different frequency and precedes a different announcement, in two ways they are uniform: They may not bother machines, but all the Ear-Shattering Shrieks from Hell are not going to be easy on your ears. And all of them will convey bad news. Wouldn't it be more humane to have the verbal recording precede the Ear-Splitting Shriek from Hell?

Submitted by Peter J. Mastrantuono of Woodbridge, New Jersey.

Why Do Doctors Always Advise Us to "Drink Plenty of Liquids" When We Have a Cold?

Has anyone ever told you *why* it is important to drink plenty of liquids when we have a cold? The simple answer is: to prevent dehydration.

Dr. Frank Davidoff, of the American College of Physicians in Philadelphia, was willing to tell us not only why we should all be good boys and girls and drink those liquids but why we get dehydrated in the first place, and why it is important not to be.

When we feel sick, we tend not to feel like eating or drinking, which can leave us dehydrated. But fever also causes water loss.

No, if your body temperature is two degrees higher than normal, water in your body doesn't evaporate noticeably faster. But fevers speed up the metabolism. As a result, you blow off more carbon dioxide and you need more oxygen to run your body, so you breathe faster. Every time you breathe you give off moisture. You are literally blowing off water, as well as "hot air" when you breathe, just as a whale's spout blows off water. Davidoff points out that "spit valves" on brass wind instruments are necessary in order to release condensed water because the air blown through the horns is so moist.

A high fever can be dangerous in and of itself, so the body tries to fight it off. The body's main defense is to evaporate moisture off and through the skin. Sometimes the moisture is imperceptible; sometimes it's a spritz (which is why we are usually sweaty when we have a fever); and other times, when a fever is finally breaking, it can be a drenching.

Drinking "plenty of liquids," then, is a way of replenishing the water lost by evaporation, sweating, and breathing. Medically, avoiding dehydration is especially important, as Davidoff explains:

Dehydration isn't a desirable state at any time, but in the presence of an infection, like a cold, it can be particularly aggravating, even dangerous.

1. Dehydration can make you feel generally bad, adding to the debility from the infection.

2. Dehydration can bring on or aggravate constipation; since bed rest and decreased food intake also cause constipation, this can be a bad combination.

3. Finally, and most important, dehydration thickens the mucus secretions from sinuses and bronchial passages. Thick secretions can block drainage from sinuses and lungs. Blocked drainage leads to discomfort and worsening infection in sinuses and to collapse of lung tissue and, worst of all, progressive infection in the lungs, which can become pneumonia.

Submitted by Daniel T. Placko Jr. of Chicago, Illinois.

Why Do Colored Soaps and Shampoos Yield White Suds?

Judging from our mail, this Imponderable is Uppermost on the minds of our readers lately. God knows why, but it is.

Here's the scoop. Very little dye is put into soap or shampoo to color them. As College of San Mateo physics professor Donald Beaty puts it, "When it's in the bottle, the light that is used to view the liquid passes through a considerable thickness of colorful shampoo or liquid soap." But once you make suds, the water-soluble dye is highly diluted. The percentage of dyed color contained in the original product is greatly reduced. Beaty adds that nothing magical "happens" to the colorant in the dye:

> Light that reflects from the surface of each soap bubble will contain the same ranges of colors as the light used to illuminate the lather. We tend to perceive the reflected light as white light if the incident light is normal room light or daylight.

Sally Miller, a consumer services representative of soap and shampoo behemoth Procter & Gamble Company, told *Imponderables* that manufacturers could easily put enough colorant into bar soaps or shampoos to yield colored suds, but their research indicates that "most consumers find white lather preferable for applying to the skin or the hair." A high concentration of dye could also stain towels and turn a demure blonde Prell user into a green-haired Cyndi Lauper lookalike.

Submitted by Dave Calicchia of West Palm Beach, Florida. Thanks also to Mary Cannon, of Chandler, Arizona; Barry Rhodes, Gene Mace, and Jim Hill of Ucon, Idaho; Jodie Masnick of Howell, New Jersey; Danny Brown of Flora, Illinois; Steve Attig of Las Vegas, Nevada; Johanna Tiefenbach of Waldron, Saskatchewan; and Nancy Fukuda of Monterey, California.

Why Do Most People Wear Wristwatches on Their Left Hand?

At first, we thought: This is obvious. Most people are right-handed and use the right arm more often than the left. Therefore, they are more likely to damage the watch while wearing it on their dominant hand.

We spoke to several experts about the subject, including horologist Henry Fried, Bulova's Pat Campbell, and Lowell Drutman of Timex. They concurred with our theory but added a couple of their own. "Have you ever seen a right-handed person trying to buckle up a leather strap on his right wrist?" asked Drutman. "They aren't very successful." Try it. He's right.

But all three also offered another theory that helps explain why many left-handers wear their watches on their left hands, too. Ever since the days of the pocket watch, the stem (the round part you wind) has been placed adjacent to the "3" (on the right-hand side of the watch). This location makes it awkward to wind the clock with the left hand, whether you are left-handed, right-handed, or ambidextrous. Whether generations of windless watches will change wrist preferences is a matter for sociologists of the future to keep tabs on.

Fried reports that no watchmaker has ever tried to market a "left-hander's" watch, although an occasional iconoclastic designer has placed the stem on the "9" side.

Submitted by Margaret McCallion of Londonderry, New Hampshire. Thanks also to Jim LaBelle of South Bend, Indiana, and Sharon Roberts of Amos, Quebec.

AND OTHER IMPONDERABLES   667

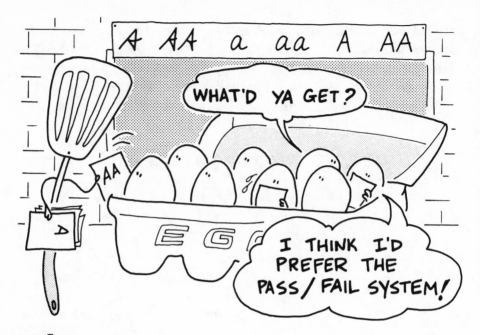

What Do the Grades of Eggs Signify? What's the Difference Between "A" and "AA" Eggs?

We get frustrated when we can't find answers to Imponderables, but sometimes we are driven nuts when we are provided too much information. The USDA sent us several healthy-sized handbooks on egg grading, and they were as hard to decipher as the instruction booklets that come with VCRs.

These handbooks are serious affairs. the first page of one of them provides definitions of words and terms used throughout the book, esoteric words like "person" (defined as "any individual, partnership, association, business trust, corporation, or any organized group of persons, whether incorporated or not") and "quality" ("the inherent properties of any product which determine its relative degree of excellence"). You get the idea. So when answering this Imponderable, it was no mean feat to separate the shell from the egg white here, and that is no yolk.

Most of the eggs sold over the counter in supermarkets are

"AA" grade, the highest distinction. The next grade is "A," followed by "B." "C," the victim of grade inflation, has been phased out. Eggs must pass criteria in four different categories before they can receive the "AA" grade:

1. Shell—Both "A" and "AA" grades must have clean, unbroken shells with a "practically normal appearance." "B" quality eggs may be slightly stained (1/32 of the surface if localized, or 1/16 if scattered). Grade "B" eggs may be abnormally shaped or have a ridge or thin spots.

2. The air cell—The air cell is the space between the shell membranes that is usually found in the large end of an egg. When an egg is held large end up, the depth of the air cell can't exceed 1/8″ in a grade "AA," 3/16″ in a grade "A," and 3/16″ in a grade "B."

3. Egg Whites—Grade "AA" eggs must have a clear and firm white. Grade "A" whites must be clear and "reasonably firm" with a "fairly well-defined yolk outline when the egg is twirled." Grade "B" eggs not only can appear weak and watery but can contain small blood and meat spots.

4. Yolks—"AA" yolks stand up tall and blend into the surrounding white. "A" yolks are round and upstanding and have a more discernible outline. Grade "B" yolks are enlarged and flatted and marred with germ development.

Egg grades have nothing to do with egg size. A pee wee with a relatively small air cell will receive an "AA" while a jumbo with a flat yolk will get a low passing "B."

How are they tested? While eggs used to be graded by hand candling, most inspections are now done by machine.

Submitted by Eric Borgos of Northampton, Massachusetts.
Thanks also to Rick DeWitt of Erie, Pennsylvania.

Since Blood is Red, Why Do Veins Look Blue?

We got into trouble with some readers when we gave a slightly facetious explanation of the expression "blue-blooded" in *Who Put the Butter in Butterfly?*, so we'll play it straight here. In fact, we'll let one of our favorite medical authorities, Dr. Frank Davidoff, associate executive vice-president of the American College of Physicians, take the floor:

> Veins look blue because they are fairly large blood vessels, full of blood that has been stripped of its oxygen load, and close enough to the surface of your skin to see the blue color of this blood.
>
> Inside the red blood cells that make up about 40% of your blood volume is the oxygen carrying pigment called hemoglobin. As the red cells pass through your lungs, the hemoglobin picks up oxygen and binds it, turning bright red in the process. The oxygen-hemoglobin combination is called "oxyhemoglobin." This oxyhemoglobin is pumped on out of your heart under pressure through the large muscular blood vessels called arteries.
>
> Out in the tissues, red cells with their oxyhemoglobin ultimately pass on through tiny blood vessels called capillaries, where they give up their oxygen to cells for use in metabolism. (The skin is rich in capillaries, which is why healthy, non-pigmented skin is pink; a sudden rush of extra oxyhemoglobin into dilated blood vessels in skin causes the phenomenon of blushing).
>
> As hemoglobin loses its oxygen, it turns a dark purplish blue —deoxyhemoglobin—which collects in larger and larger veins on its way back to the heart. While the biggest veins are deep in the tissues (they tend to run paired with the largest arteries), some fairly large veins lie just under the skin, where you can appreciate their blueness if there isn't too much brown skin pigment (melanin) to hide the color.

Submitted by Mrs. R. D. Harvey of Gulf Breeze, Florida. Thanks also to Jae Hoon Chung of Demarest, New Jersey, and Ron Pateman of Chicago, Illinois.

Why Does Just About Everything Look Darker When it Gets Wet?

Come to think of it, reader Russell has a point. Drop some water on your new cream-colored blouse and you get a dark spot. Have a clod standing near you spill his Perrier on your navy blue blazer and the light liquid somehow manages to make the coat's dark color even darker. Why is this so?

Elementary physics, it turns out. You lose the true color of the garment in three ways:

1. Even a thin coating of water will force light coming toward the garment to refract within the water film. The available light is thus disbursed.

2. The reflection on the surface of the water itself causes incoherent light scattering.

3. A combination of the two points above ensures that there will be less light available on the surface of the jacket to reflect back to your eyes. Thus the spot will appear darker than the rest of the jacket that doesn't have to compete with water in order to reflect light.

Submitted by Kathleen Russell of Grand Rapids, Michigan.
Thanks also to Kent Parks of Raleigh, North Carolina.

PILGRIM, Inc.
"Making the most of America's traditions"

Why Is the American Thanksgiving on Thursday? Was the Original Thanksgiving on Thursday?

Although latter-day cynics might conclude that Thanksgiving was set on Thursday in order to wangle a four-day weekend, little evidence supports that. In fact, we don't know what day of the week the Plymouth Colony's first Thanksgiving was celebrated.

But we do know that Plymouth's first Thanksgiving was held in mid-October, 1621, and lasted three days. Other colonies held their Thanksgiving celebrations on different days of the week. And all the colonies occasionally declared one-shot thanksgivings on varying days of the week following special blessings or tragedies in their communities.

In 1668, the Plymouth General Court declared that Novem-

WHY DO DOGS HAVE WET NOSES?

ber 25 be declared an annual day of thanksgiving. This proclamation lasted all of five years.

Most New England colonies held their own thanksgivings on either Wednesday or Thursday, probably to distance the holidays from the Sabbath. Colonists were, appropriately enough, puritanical about intruding upon the Sabbath in any way, so not only was Sunday ruled out, but so were the day of preparation (Saturday) and the day after (Monday). Friday was a fast day of the Catholic church, and the Puritans wanted no connection or identification with Catholic practices.

Thursday was known in Boston and a few other northeastern towns as "lecture day", when ministers gave religious lectures in the afternoon. Since some citizens were already taking time away from their work to attend these meetings, perhaps "lecture day" was the reason Thursday beat out Wednesday as the popular choice for Thanksgiving.

The first *national* Thanksgiving celebrated the American victory over the British at Saratoga in 1777. Samuel Adams prevailed upon the Continental Congress to declare a day of thanksgiving. But several colonies continued to celebrate their local versions as well.

George Washington issued the first presidential proclamation of Thanksgiving, designating Thursday, November 26, 1789, as the day of celebration. With the exception of John Adams' attempt at one Wednesday Thanksgiving on May 9, 1798, all national Thanksgiving days since 1789 have been celebrated on Thursday.

But no uniform date was selected for Thanksgiving until Abraham Lincoln declared that starting in 1863, the last Thursday in November would be the national day. His proclamation was motivated by not only the Union's victory in the Civil War but the pressure exerted by the passionate editorials of women's magazine editor Sarah Josepha Hale, who relentlessly promoted the issue for over 35 years. Lincoln never stated why he chose Thursday, but presumably he was following the tradition of the Puritans and, later, George Washington.

For some reason, presidents haven't been able to stop tinkering with the date of Thanksgiving. Andrew Johnson experimented with the first Thursday of December, 1865, as a new date. Johnson relented and returned to Lincoln's last Thursday in November the next year, but he was impeached anyway. Ulysses S. Grant preferred the third Thursday in November, 1869. Seventy years later, Franklin Delano Roosevelt pulled a U.S. Grant and proclaimed Thursday, November 23, rather than November 30, as Thanksgiving Day.

But traditions were too settled by then. Many states observed Thanksgiving on the last Thursday anyway. FDR realized he was waging a useless and meaningless fight and cooperated with Congress when it passed a joint resolution placing Thanksgiving on the fourth Thursday in November. Ever since, not even Richard Nixon has tried to move it.

Submitted by Rick DeWitt of Erie, Pennsylvania. Thanks also to Richard Miranda of Renton, Washington.

Why Are the Valve Stems on Fire Extinguishers Pentagonal?

We were confronted with this Imponderable on a radio show, and we asked if any listeners had ever seen a pentagonal wrench. The answer: square wrenches, sure; hexagonal wrenches, of course. But a five-sided wrench? Nope.

We should have figured it out. Fire hydrants with five-sided valve stems were designed precisely because pentagonal wrenches are not generally distributed. Since only fire hydrants require five-sided wrenches, the general population doesn't own them.

And more specifically, vandals don't own them. Even vandals have discovered you can't easily open a five-sided valve stem if you are using a square or hexagonal wrench.

Not that the lack of proper tools has kept vandals from trying. New York City firefighter Brenda Berkman told *Imponderables* that kids use conventional monkey wrenches of all kinds to try to open hydrants during the summer. Even when they don't succeed in opening the hydrants, they sometimes strip the nuts. David Cerull, president of the Fire Collectors Club, adds that some cities are installing special collars around the valve stem to keep vandals away.

Why Are Most Receipts from Cash Registers Printed in Purple?

According to Robin Pierce, business products division manager of Citizen CBM American Corp., the answer, appropriately enough for a cash register, concerns the preservation of cold cash. Purple ink, because of the chemical constituents that make up the oil base, has a longer life than any other color. The longer the ink lasts, the longer the purple ribbons last, and the more money the shopkeepers save.

And those of us who have the propensity for arriving at the checkout line of a supermarket at precisely the time when the checker decides to change ribbons also applaud the idea of long-lasting ink, be it purple or chartreuse.

Submitted by Joseph Blake, Jr. of Ottawa, Kansas.

How Do Kangaroos Clean Their Pouches?

If you think the illustration above is a bit gross, consider the actual answer. According to Rick Barongi, curator of mammals at the Sans Diego Zoo, kangaroos use their forefeet to open their pouches wide and then proceed to stick their heads in and lick their pouches clean!

After the mother gives birth, keeping the pouch clean requires some effort, for joeys stay in the pouch for many months (up to seven or eight months for the largest kangaroos). After that, joeys pop out for walks and a snack but return to the mother's pouch when hungry. The joeys will continue to enter the pouch until they can no longer squeeze into it or their mothers no longer make them welcome.

Exactly what is the mother cleaning out of her pouch? Miles Roberts, deputy head of research at the National Zoological Park, told us that along with the expected epidermis flakes that accumulate, a waxy substance forms in the pouch that the kangaroos try to lick off. When the pouch is occupied by her joey, the mother's cleaning activity increases; not only does mom have to lick off the usual debris but also the joey's droppings.

And to think we complain about changing diapers.

Submitted by Terri Rippey of Saint Joseph, Missouri.

Why Aren't All Beer Bottle Caps Twistoffs? Are There Any Advantages to Nontwistoff Caps?

Yes, there is one disadvantage to twistoff caps. You may have noticed that with rare exceptions, bottles without twistoff caps are imports. Twistoffs are made out of aluminum, a soft metal. L. Van Munching, Jr., of Van Munching & Co., U.S. distributors of Heineken beer, told *Imponderables* that soft caps can be loosened in transit with the danger of beer and/or air leaking out of the bottle.

But Phil Katz, of the Beer Institute, says that the domestic beer industry has found few problems with twistoff caps. Consumers have a strong preference for twistoffs, and since they cost no more than conventional closures, the domestic beer industry has been happy to comply.

Much of the impetus for the twistoff technology came from bottle manufacturers. After can manufacturers developed the pull tab for their containers, consumers no longer wanted to bother with the inconvenience of bottle or can openers. The bottle industry needed to offer a cap that could be opened with the hands or risk losing even more market share to aluminum cans.

Why Won't the Contents of a 13-Ounce Bag of Coffee Fit into a 16-Ounce Coffee Can?

This Imponderable is less theoretical than it may seem at first, since "gourmet" coffee packaged in 13-ounce bags has become a popular item. Consumers like the security of storing coffee in a sturdy, tightly closed coffee can. But they become frustrated when they can't fit the bag's 13-ounces of coffee into a container that will supposedly hold three ounces more. Have coffee sellers been ripping us off with undersize containers all these years? And how could the original pound of coffee fit into the 16-ounce can if it now will not hold 13 ounces of the bagged coffee?

The answer, says John Adinolfi, of the National Coffee Association of U.S.A., has nothing to do with fraud and a lot to do with "density":

> The 13-ounce bag may contain coffee with a much lower density than the coffee packed in the 16-ounce can. This may be especially true if the coffee was processed utilizing a newer "fast roast" technique which produces a much lower density. In addition, in the packaging process, ground coffee is vibrated vigorously to compact it so it can be packaged efficiently.

Bridget A. MacConnell, of General Foods, adds that a vacuum is drawn on coffee bags, which acts to further compress the coffee:

> When you open the vacuum bag and pour the coffee out, you reduce the density of the coffee as you pour it—the agitation loosens it. If you tap the can after you've poured the coffee in, that will reduce the level somewhat, but probably not enough to fit the entire 13 ounces.

Many coffee cans have been downsized from 16 ounces to 13 ounces. Perhaps coffee marketers have been decreasing the size of their cans to help stamp out this Imponderable, but somehow we have a gut feeling that might not have been their primary motivation.

Submitted by Carolyn Ehrlich of Little Neck, New York.

How Do Men Produce Falsetto Voices?

We received a nifty response from Dr. Michael J. D'Asaro, a speech pathologist in Santa Monica, California:

> Falsetto voice, which is the highest portion of the pitch range, is produced by an extreme contraction of the laryngeal muscles and elevation of the larynx, permitting only a very short segment of the vocal cords to vibrate, a portion furthest forward in the length of the vocal cords.
>
> The rest of the vocal cords are held stationary and the short segment that vibrates vibrates at an extremely high frequency, as do shorter strings in musical instruments.

Singers can be trained to drift from their usual pitches into the falsetto range without interrupting the vibration, but D'Asaro says that in the untrained voice, "there is often a break in vibration similar to the voice breaks associated with voice change in males at puberty."

Why Don't You Ever Hear Women Singing Falsetto?

We pride ourselves on the fact that we don't find interesting facts in books or magazines and then build Imponderables around them. We always start with genuine mysteries and then try to find the answers.

This Imponderable is the first one we've ever used that was sent in by a source. Dr. D'Asaro added this tidbit as a sidebar to his answer to the last Imponderable. But since we had never thought about this question before, and wish we had, and since we had no idea of the answer, we'll break precedent:

AND OTHER IMPONDERABLES   679

... there is no counterpart to falsetto in the female voice. The female vocal mechanism, being much smaller than the male, naturally vibrates at a higher frequency. It typically can vibrate no higher than the soprano range, although there are a few notable exceptions in singers with extreme ranges.

Submitted by Dr. Michael J. D'Asaro of Santa Monica, California.

What Unit of Measurement Is Indicated by the Numbers on Nonreal-Time Counters on VCRs and Audio Tape Recorders? Are the Settings Uniform on the Recorders of Different Companies?

Now that new taping equipment usually comes with electronic rather than mechanical counters, we don't understand why every recorder isn't equipped with a real-time counter. On VCRs, for example, if you know the length of the first of two shows you have taped, with a real-time counter you can stop the tape at the exact point where the second show begins. God forbid we should have to endure the major strain of reversing and fast-forwarding with our remote control to find a program!

Consultation with our electronics experts gave us the expected response. The counters on VCRs and audio tape recorders are not calibrated for any specific length of time. And the settings are not uniform from company to company. As TDK's Robert Fontana puts it: "Switching to another tape deck with index numbers logged from another will likely render havoc. Consistency and compatibility are not virtues of such counters."

In fact, the counters on recorders vary from machine to machine within the same company. And we have learned from painful experience that a count of 100 at the beginning of the tape doesn't signify the same amount of time as 100 at the end of the tape. Fontana summarizes: "Counters serve no purpose other than to index what's on the tape when that tape deck is used."

What Determines Whether a Letter with Insufficient Postage Will Be Sent to the Addressee or Back to the Sender?

Believers in Murphy's Law assume that the rule of thumb is: If *I* sent the letter with insufficient postage, I'll get it back; but if I'm the addressee, *I'll* get it back. But why go through life with such a paranoiac attitude? If there is anything we can trust in this world, even more than Murphy's Law, it is that our postal system will have a rule and regulation concerning every possible eventuality.

In general, the policy is simple. If there is postage affixed to a letter or parcel, but it is insufficient, the mail will be "promptly dispatched" to the addressee postage due. If the addressee agrees to pay the discrepancy, all is fine with the world. If the addressee refuses payment, the mail is returned to the sender who must, on first-class mail, pay the additional postage due and remail the piece. Senders of any other class must pay not only the deficiency but the forwarding postage, if any, and the return postage.

Many letters are sent bearing no postage whatsoever. In some cases, the stamps have fallen off. Others go naked because of neglect or forgetfulness. These pieces are marked "returned for postage" and returned to the sender.

The USPS has had difficulty in the past with jerks trying to send mail without having to pay for the privilege. A common method of freeloaders is deliberately to not affix a stamp and to reverse the address and the return address, hoping that the mail will be "returned" to the intended recipient. But sometimes even the most innocent person forgets to affix a stamp on an envelope without a return address. The postal system is cracking down on fraud, so the innocent person won't get his letter delivered. According to the *Domestic Mail Manual* of the USPS,

> If no return address is shown, or if the delivery and return address are identical, or if it is determined that the delivery address and the return address, while different, are actually for the same person or organization, the piece will be disposed of . . .

The *Domestic Mail Manual* covers all kinds of contingencies that even *Imponderables* readers might not think about. For example, what if an absentminded person accidentally slips her "prepaid" Federal Express package into a USPS collection box? The post office is actually kind enough to call its competitor and say, "Yo! We've got business for you. You have until the close of the next workday to pick it up." If Federal Express doesn't pick it up (not too likely), the USPS returns it to the sender postage due.

Ah, but what postage fee should they charge? Luckily for the sender, they charge first-class rather than Express Mail prices:

> Compute the postage-due amount from the point at which the unpaid matter entered the mailstream to the sender's location. If the entry point is unknown, compute the postage due from where the matter was first found in the mailstream to the sender's location. . . . Do not deliver such mail to the addressee, or provide address-correction or forwarding service.

And what happens when the post office damages a stamp or envelope? It depends upon whether the envelope has already been canceled. If it is apparent to postal workers from the cancellation that a stamp once was affixed to the envelope, the piece is treated as if the stamp were still there.

And what happens if you buy some stamps that aren't sticky enough to stay on an envelope? Or those stamps you bought during a heat wave have curled up because of humidity? The

USPS will gladly exchange stamps at full value, "but only for an equal number of stamps of the same denomination. . . . Each such transaction is further limited to stamps with a total value of $100 or less from each customer."

Submitted by Paula Chaffee of Utica, Michigan.

Why Does the Cold Water That Comes Out of the Bathroom Faucet Seem Colder than the Cold Water from the Kitchen Faucet?

The operative word in the question is "seem." All of our plumbing experts claimed that it just ain't so.

Gary Felsinger, marketing manager of the faucets and fittings division of Kohler Co., offered a few plausible theories: "Water temperature could be affected by the length of pipe run, the type of insulation, and perhaps heating ducts that are many times installed under the cabinet where the kitchen sink is installed." But these conditions would only affect a tiny fraction of homes and apartments.

Jim Datka, of American Standard, mentioned to us that bathroom water faucets tend to get used more often than kitchen faucets. Perhaps the posers of this Imponderable were working with an already cold water faucet in the bathroom? Or were seeking cold water after having run hot water—perhaps after doing the dishes?

Plumbers we spoke to tended to pooh-pooh the premise of this Imponderable. They all pointed out that water in the house comes from one source, and that the water is at the same temperature when it enters the house.

The experts' explanations make sense to the Dr. Spock in us, but not to our Scotty. Because, darn it, the cold water in our bathroom *does* seem colder than the cold water in our kitchen.

Readers, is the cold water colder in your bathroom than in your kitchen? Does anybody have any theories to explain either the reality or the perception of this only semi-resolved Imponderable?

Submitted by Joni E. Ray, Karen K. Kinonen, and Bill M. Quillard of Vancouver, Washington. Thanks also to Caroline Corenzo, of Worcester, Massachusetts.

Is There any Particular Reason Why Boats and Airplanes Have Red Lights on the Left Side and Green Lights on the Right?

The origins of this practice are obscure. Wayne Young, of the Marine Board of the National Research Council, suggests that side lights might be a descendant of the system originally used for hand buoys. As far back as 1889, the International Marine Conference agreed on a uniform coloring system, subsequently changed by a League of Nations subcommittee in 1936 to the current Uniform System of black buoys with green or white lights on the starboard side and red buoys with red or white lights on the port side.

In practice, the color scheme of side lights makes right-of-way decisions a snap for pilots or navigators, using color associations we have all known since childhood. B. Scott Coe, of *Sail* magazine, explains the "stop and go" theory:

> Picture a four-way stop. The boat to your right has the right of way. Looking at him, you see his left, or port side, which shows a red light. This means you stop, he goes. Presumably he sees your green (starboard) light and will go. If you look at the boat on the left of you at the crossing, you see his green light. This means you go and he stops. Presumably, that boat is seeing your red (port)

light and will stop. An old sailing ditty goes: 'If to starboard red appear, 'tis your duty to keep clear.'

Side lights also enable airplanes and ships to pass each other in the dark. Rexford B. Sherman, director of research and information services at the American Association of Port Authorities, wrote *Imponderables* that he believes:

> the explanation lies with navigational "rules of the road" that require ships or aircraft to pass each other on the right side. Thus the position of the lights vis-a-vis an approaching vessel or airplane would indicate whether your craft is properly positioned in relation to the other.
>
> Of course, air traffic controllers endeavor to prevent planes from passing each other too closely. Still, the side lights, which can be seen from a surprisingly long range, enable a plane to detect the presence and flight direction of nearby aircraft.

Submitted by Wally De Vasier of Fairfield, Virginia. Thanks also to Andrew Kass of Staten Island, New York.

How Do They Get the Mint Flavoring on Toothpicks?

Long ago, toothpick manufacturers decided that hand-rolling toothpicks in mint flavoring might be a tad labor-intensive. So they spray the flavor on the toothpicks.

Submitted by Elizabeth L. Wendling of Richfield, Ohio.

What Is the "Bias" Referred to in High Bias Audio Tape? Is High Bias Superior to Low Bias?

We heard from Robert Fontana, customer/technical service manager of tape giant TDK Electronics Corp.:

In layman's language, bias is a technical term that describes the ultrasonic signal that is mixed with the audio signal during recording. Its purpose is to facilitate a high fidelity recording onto magnetic tape. The absence of bias would yield a recording that sounds substantially inferior to the source.

High bias and low bias are . . . descriptions of the amount of bias required to make a good recording onto tape. Different tape formulations require different amounts of bias. Hence, normal bias, high bias, and metal bias denote different types of tape formulations whose bias requirements are different.

A high bias recording has a higher voltage signal applied than the normal bias type.

William J. Goffi, of Maxell, told *Imponderables* that high bias tapes capture more highs and lows than normal bias tape, and is generally more sensitive. This sensitivity makes it the proper choice for recording music, while low bias tape is usually sufficient for capturing voice.

Submitted by Jim Kowald of Green Bay, Wisconsin.

What Precisely Is Sea Level? And How Do They Determine Exactly What It Is?

Painstakingly. Obviously, the sea level in any particular location is constantly changing. If you measure the ocean during low tide and then high tide, you won't come up with the same figure. Wind and barometric shifts also affect the elevation of the seas.

But the oceans are joined and their height variation is slight. So geodesists (mathematicians who specialize in the study of measurement) and oceanographers settle for an approximation. Because the cliché that "water seeks its own level" is true, geodesists worry more about sea level variations over time than between places. Measurements are taken all over the globe;

there is no one place where sea level is determined. One sea level fits all.

The National Geodetic Survey defines "mean sea level" as the "average location of the interface between ocean and atmosphere, over a period of time sufficiently long so that all random and periodic variations of short duration average to zero." The U.S. National Ocean Service has set 19 as the appropriate number of years to sample sea levels to eliminate such variations; in some cases, measurements are taken on an hourly basis. Geodesists simply add up the 19 years of samples and divide by 19 to arrive at the mean sea level.

The mean sea level has been rising throughout most of the twentieth century—on average, over a millimeter a year. On a few occasions, sea level has risen as much as five or six millimeters in a year, not exactly causing flood conditions, but enough to indicate that the rise was caused by melting of glaciers. If theories of the greenhouse effect and global warming are true, the rise of the global sea level in the future will be more than the proverbial drop in the bucket.

Submitted by Janice Brown of Albany, Oregon. Thanks also to Wendy Neuman of Plaistow, New Hampshire; Noel Ludwig of Littleton, Colorado; Jay Howard Horne of Pittsburgh, Pennsylvania; Charles F. Longaker of Mentor, Ohio; and Mrs. Violet Wright of Hobbes, New Mexico.

Why Do Basketballs Have Fake Seams? Do They Have a Practical Purpose or Are They Merely Decorative?

A caller on a radio talk show asked this question indignantly, as if the ball industry were purposely perpetrating a fraud, at worst, and foisting unnecessary decoration on a ball, at best. Before you accuse basketball manufacturers of making a needless fashion statement, consider that most basketball players need all the help they can get manipulating a basketball. A basketball is too big for all but the Kareems and Ewings of the world to grasp with their fingers. Those "fake" seams are there to help you grip the ball (similarly, quarterbacks make sure their fingers make contact with the seams when passing).

Basketball manufacturers make two kinds of seams, narrow and wide. National Basketball Association professionals prefer the narrow-channel seams, while many amateurs, particularly young people with small hands, use wide-channel seams.

Why Are Lakes Windier at Midday than During Morning or Night?

Richard Williams, a meteorologist at the National Weather Service's National Severe Storms Forecast Center, has actually paid cash money to buy *Imponderables* books (we knew there was something we like about him), and sent in his own Imponderables in the past. And now he was kind enough to send us a detailed letter on the subject at hand.

Williams emphasizes that it is windier over land as well as lake during midday. However, the wind increase is accentuated over the relatively smooth, open surface of a lake.

> Often, the lowest layers of the atmosphere are at rest during the night and more active or turbulent by day. At night, particularly on clear nights, the earth's surface cools along with the adjacent lowest layers of the atmosphere. The lower layers cool faster than the higher layers, producing a "stable" temperature regime with cool air at ground level and relatively warmer air above the surface.
>
> Under these conditions a temperature inversion will form a few hundred feet above the earth's surface. An inversion is a vertical zone in which temperatures rise with increasing altitude ver-

WHY DO DOGS HAVE WET NOSES?

sus the normal cooling. The inversion serves as a barrier or boundary—separating the near-surface air from wind flow aloft. Often at night, calm or very light wind flow will occur at ground level even though the winds aloft continue with little change in speed from day to night.

After sunrise, if the day is sunny or at least partially so, the sun warms the ground. In the lowest layers of the atmosphere, warm, turbulent mixing occurs and the inversion boundary disappears. Once this happens, the general wind flow resumes at the surface. Winds that were probably present during the night just a few hundred feet above the surface can again be felt at ground level. *The midday increase in winds is most pronounced over water where there is less resistance to wind flow.*

Another effect occurs along a coastline and over large lakes. Above a large body of water, local land-to-water wind circulations develop due to the unequal heating of water and land surfaces. This differential heating during the afternoon produces a water-to-land breeze, known as the sea breeze or lake breeze. At night a weaker land-to-water low level breeze can occur: the land breeze.

Submitted by C. Loewenson of New York, New York.

Why Does Wool Obtain Its "Distinctive" Smell When It Gets Wet?

"Distinctive," heh. What delicacy of expression.

When alive, all sheep manufacture lanolin, a secretion from the sebaceous glands—the equivalent of human perspiration. Lanolin collects in the wool and prevents it from drying out. That's the good news. But the bad news is that lanolin helps impart the "distinctive" smell of sheep when they get wet.

Almost all of the lanolin should be removed in the processing of wool. After wool is sheared and graded, the next step is the washing and scouring of the fibers. The wool runs through a series of rakes that comb out foreign material and a series of tubs filled with a detergent solution. After the wool is cleaned, it passes through several water rinses that remove the lanolin. Then the wool passes through squeeze rolls and is hot-air dried.

If the scouring process is insufficient, too much lanolin may be retained in the wool. Or if the chemicals used in the scouring process are too strong, it may degrade the fibers. Both problems could cause smelly products.

Our guess is that your question refers to a bulky wool sweater rather than, say, a pair of worsted pants. Representatives of The Wool Bureau and the American Wool Council both mentioned "oil wool" as the likely inspiration for this Imponderable.

Oil wool is intentionally not totally scoured in processing because the natural grease makes knitting easier. The famous Aran Island sweaters of Ireland are notorious "stinkers." Note that wool overcoats usually don't have a problem when it rains because modern scouring and finishing technology remove virtually all of the wool's lanolin.

Submitted by Pierre Jelenc of New York, New York.

Why Does the Groom Carry the Bride over the Threshold?

With the price of housing being what it is today, we think it might be more appropriate to have the real estate broker carry both the bride and groom over the threshold of their new home.

This superstitious countercharm dates back to the Romans, who believed that spirits resided at a home's entrance. Stephanie de Lys, in her book *A Treasury of American Superstitions*, writes that the Romans believed good and evil spirits slugged it out at the threshold. They also believed that if one walked into the house with the left foot first, evil would triumph; if the right foot came first, the good spirits would predominate. So why don't the bride and groom simply take care to put their right foot forward when entering their new abode?

Those Romans were just a tad sexist, as de Lys explains: "The groom, knowing that a woman in a highly emotional state is very apt to be careless, took no chances, and picked her up in his arms and carried her into the house."

Submitted by Marge Fener of Hempstead, New York.

Why Is There Aluminum Foil on the Neck of Champagne Bottles?

According to Irving Smith Kogan of the Champagne Association, the aluminum foil is there to cover up the less than thrillingly attractive wiring that helps keep the cork under pressure (the French word for the wire is *muselet*, which means "muzzle").

Before the days of aluminum foil, lead was used to cover the wire muzzle. Kogan adds that triangular "weep holes" were added to rid the lead of condensation. Even now, some champagne makers add triangular- or diamond-shaped holes to the foil for decorative purposes and as a nod to tradition.

The muzzle was a late nineteenth-century addition to champagne making. Before then, corks were hammered into place and secured by hand-tied twine.

We had heard a rumor that the foil was there to obscure the occasional bottle of champagne that had a short fill. But Kogan assured us that in this high-tech age, the possibility of a short fill is highly unlikely. Champagne is given its dosage injection at the same table where the cork is inserted. There isn't enough time for the champagne to bubble away.

What Kind of Container Holds the Rain Measured by Meteorologists?

You can set a bucket outside in your backyard, let the precipitation accumulate, and measure the bucket with a ruler. But after a while the thought is likely to occur to you: How big is the container supposed to be? Sure, it will take more rain to fill an inch of a big bucket than a thin beaker, but then the larger circumference of the bucket will also trap more water. Hmmmm. This isn't as simple as it first seemed.

It turns out that meteorologists don't let this stuff worry them too much. They use many different devices to measure rainfall. Perhaps the most common is the eight-inch rain gauge, a simple metal cylinder with an eight-inch-diameter top. The water is funneled from the outside cylinder into a smaller inner gauge. The water in the inner gauge is measured by a calibrated wooden or metal stick (which can convert the contents of different-sized gauges into the "inches" we hear about in weather reports). By funneling the water into the narrow inner gauge, the vertical scale is expanded, allowing accurate reading of rainfall to the nearest hundredth of an inch.

Richard Williams, meteorologist for the National Weather Service, told *Imponderables* that most of his agency's offices use another method: weighing rain in a bucket and using a mathematical formula to convert weight into hundredths.

Williams adds that in a third type of gauge, rainfall is not collected at all:

> As it falls, each one-hundredth inch of precipitation fills a small metal "bucket." The bucket fills, tips over, and then empties.

Each fill/empty cycle triggers an electrical contact and the number of "tips" is charted to determine the rainfall. This is particularly useful in determining the rate of rainfall and in making a permanent chart of the event.

Other variables affect accurate measurement of rainfall. But the most important problem is wind. Ground-level gauges will collect more rain, and tend to be more accurate, than those above ground, especially if accompanied by an antisplash grid. If the rain gauge is set above the ground, high winds can create uneven distribution of rain and splashing of water onto, rather than into, the gauge.

The problems in measuring rainfall are minor compared to measuring snowfall. Wind is a particular problem since blowing snow, rather than falling snow, might accumulate in gauges, particularly ground-level gauges. The temperature when the snow was formed, wind patterns, and how long the snow has been caught in the gauge may determine whether snow accumulates in air-filled, feathery layers or is compacted down to a tight, dense pack. Since the density of fallen snow varies tremendously, scientists require some way to compare snowfalls accumulated under different conditions.

Meteorologists use several techniques to deal with these problems:

1. Snow boards. These boards are put out on the ground. The accumulation is measured on an hourly basis and then cleaned off. This labor-intensive method assures a reading before the snow can pack down. But any one board might not be representative of an area, so many must be used if an accurate assessment of precipitation is important.

2. Weighing. Essentially the same technique we discussed with rain gauges. A heating element is put into a gauge (often a standard rain gauge) so that the snow melts. The water is then weighed and converted into "inches."

3. Snow pillows. These immediately record the weight of the snow that accumulates above them without converting the snow into water.

Submitted by Ted Roter of Los Angeles, California. Thanks also to Valerie M. Shields of Danville, California.

What Does the "FD&C" Found on Food and Shampoo Labels Mean?

The "FD&C" on the label assures that the dyes used in the product have the stamp of approval of the U.S. government. Although since nobody seems to know what in the heck "FD&C" means, it's not clear how much assurance is really provided.

The letters stand for Food, Drug, [and] Cosmetic. In 1938, the Food, Drug, and Cosmetic Act gave the FDA the authority to regulate the dyes used in these three categories of products. At the present time, seven dyes may be used in all three; 26 dyes are approved for drugs and cosmetics only; and two "Ext." dyes ("D" and "C") are approved for drugs or cosmetics designed for external use only (e.g., a skin lotion) and not subject to accidental or incidental ingestion (e.g., lipstick).

Submitted by Patrick Chambers of Grandview, Missouri.

How Can Fingernails and Hair Grow After Someone Dies?

They can't. But that doesn't stop this ancient myth from persisting.

We'll give you the real story. But don't read this while eating, please. And remember, this Imponderable wasn't our idea. We just pursue truth anywhere we find it.

The tissues of a corpse dry out rather quickly. As the skin dries out, it shrinks, but hair and nails don't break down as quickly as the surrounding skin. If the same quantity of hair, for example, surrounds a partially shrunken/evaporated skull, the hair will apppear to have grown.

We once spoke to a funeral director who honestly believed that men's beards grew after they died. Why else, he asked, would we sometimes have to shave them more than once before the funeral? The answer, of course, is that the hair didn't grow, but the stubble that might have been obscured at the time of death now showed through after the surrounding skin had shrunk.

The "nail illusion" is heightened because the skin around the fingers and toes tends to dry out particularly quickly, just as it is the first to wrinkle and expand when wet (a phenomenon we discussed in *Why Do Clocks Run Clockwise?*).

Not all corpses dry out in this way. If a corpse is kept in a moist place, it can develop adipocere, a fatty, waxy substance. Corpses with adipocere do not tend to display the hair or nail illusion.

Submitted by Loretta McDonough of Frontenac, Missouri, who is probably sorry she ever asked.

What Is the Purpose of the White Dot on the Frog of a Violin Bow?

For those unfamiliar with the term, the frog of a bow (used for any string instrument) is the screw that secures the hair of the bow and keeps it away from the stick at the point where the player holds the bow. In England, the frog is called the "nut";

the frog serves much the same purpose as a nut in American hardware terminology. While the frog is now adjustable so that the tension of the bow hair can be modified, it was originally fixed.

Although the frog serves a vital function, the sole purpose of the white dot is to look pretty. In fact, one lover of music once carried this decorative function to extremes. Alvin Johnson, of the American Musicological Society, related the following story about one of our titans of industry.

Henry Ford was an eccentric man and rich enough to indulge his idiosyncrasies. Ford loved square dancing and used to invite a string quartet of quite exalted fiddlers from his local symphony orchestra to play for him in his mansion. Ford and his dance partners were listening to square dancing played on four Stradivari violins. Ford insisted on putting in a diamond to decorate the frog of each bow.

Submitted By Garland Lyn of Windsor, Connecticut.

Why Does Traffic on Highways Tend to Clump Together in Bunches?

Four factors conspire to create clumps:

1. Moderately heavy or heavy volume of traffic.
2. Uneven speeds of vehicles.
3. The unwillingness of slow vehicles to move to the right-hand lane(s).
4. Uneven flow of traffic onto the highway.

Most clumps are caused when fast drivers pull up to slower-moving vehicles and can't get around them to pass. On an empty highway, one car can't block faster cars from passing. But on an already crowded highway, a relatively slow-moving car is as likely to be found in the left lane as the right lane. Alongside other vehicles traveling at approximately the same speed, they form a shield as impermeable as the defensive line of the Chicago Bears.

Richard Cunard, engineer of traffic and operations at the Transportation Research Board, told *Imponderables* that uneven traffic flow onto freeways from onramps can also cause clumps to form. When a green light on a major access road allows scores of cars to enter a highway at the same time, the slow-moving vehicles traveling in the right-hand lane scamper to the left to avoid slowing down to accommodate the newcomers. Fast-moving cars in the left-hand lanes then try to find faster hunting ground to their left. The result: a chain reaction in which all vehicles try to avoid the worst possible eventuality, an American tragedy—traveling at a slower rate than they would wish.

In an attempt to counteract the effect of inflowing traffic upon congestion and clumping, some cities have installed traffic lights on their onramps that restrict traffic flow onto freeways. The more sophisticated systems contain sensing devices that monitor the traffic in the right-hand lane of the freeway. Only when there are openings in the right-hand lanes do the sensing devices "tell" the signal at the onramp to turn green.

Clumps form just as easily on an interstate with two lanes in each direction as on urban freeways. On a two-lane road with even moderately heavy traffic, a few slow drivers who refuse to pull over to the right are sufficient to create clumps that can cause traffic jams for miles behind. Of course, these interstate highways carry signs that say "Slow Traffic—Keep Right.

But what is "slow traffic"? Is a driver traveling at the speed limit a slowpoke? Must you pull over everytime a joy rider going 80 miles per hour bears down on you? If you prize your rear bumper, the answer is yes. And yielding to the speed demon on your tail also accomplishes the task of helping to eradicate the scourge of clumping.

Submitted by John Benson of Auburn, California.

Why Do Home Doors Open Inward While Doors in Public Buildings Open Outward?

Interviewers sometimes ask us what percentage of the folks who pose an Imponderable also supply the answer. Our reply: fewer than one percent.

Many times, readers have given us leads or provided incorrect information. Good Imponderables are harder to find than answers anyway, and it takes us just as long to verify a theory proposed by a reader as it does to do original research.

But we're proud to announce that this Imponderable is a one-percenter. Dorothea McGee posed this Imponderable and after consulting with several architects, we know that her answer below was right too.

> Public buildings are obliged to have "panic bars" that open the door outward in case of fire or emergency. If a crowd is pushing to get out, the mob does not have to be backed away from the door to get out. Such doors are very expensive and have concealed hinges.
>
> At home, if confronted with an emergency, you are not faced with a large crowd pushing at once. Even in case of fire, you could get the family to move back enough to open the door.
>
> But in order to get large pieces of furniture into the house, you want easily removed doors. Since all you have to do is knock out the pin to take the door down, the pin has to be inside, where burglars can't reach. Also, you can put up a storm door without having the two doors bang into each other.

Architects have assured me that there are ways to install storm doors with outward-opening doors and that skilled burglars can get furniture out of just about any house they want, but the convenience of the outward-opening door for residences is clear. Architect Bill Stanley notes that at one time residential doors were barred from within to prevent intruders from pulling them open.

Submitted by Dorothea McGee of Paterson, New Jersey.

When Glass Breaks, Why Don't the Pieces Fit Back Together Perfectly?

We received a wonderful response to this Imponderable from Harold Blake, who you might remember from *When Do Fish Sleep?* as the gentleman who spent some time in college simulating the aroma of Juicy Fruit gum. It's nice to know that Mr. Blake, now a retired engineer, is still trying to find the solutions to the important things in life.

They key point Blake makes about this Imponderable is to remember that while glass appears to be inflexible, it does bend and change shape. If you throw a ball through a plate glass window, the glass will try to accommodate the force thrust upon it; it will bend. But if bent beyond its limits, glass shatters or ruptures.

At the point that the glass breaks, the glass's shape is distorted but the break is a perfect fracture—the parts would fit back together again. But as soon as the glass shatters, the parts begin to minimize their distortion and return to the unstressed state.

When the pieces return to their unstressed state, the fracture is no longer "perfect." Like a human relationship, things are never quite the same after a breakup.

Blake points out that other seemingly inflexible materials show the same tendencies as glass. Ceramics, pottery, and metals, for example, also distort and then return to a slightly altered "original" configuration.

Submitted by Charles Venezia of Iselin, New Jersey.

Guess who brushed with ...

expiro • DENT
Tooth paste

We don't need a "use by" date—it's BAD now!

Why Is There No Expiration Date on Toothpaste? Does Toothpaste Ever "Go Bad"?

After we received this Imponderable from a caller on a radio talk show, we were reminded of a personal experience. We once found large tubes of Colgate toothpaste on sale at a discount store for 49 cents apiece. Not ones to pass up a gift horse, we bought a couple of tubes only to discover, when we brought them home, that the toothpaste was manufactured in Venezuela. All the writing on the packaging was in Spanish.

We worried about exactly how old the toothpaste was. So we dumped the toothpaste in the cabinet under our bathroom sink and didn't think about it for a couple of years until one day we had run out of toothpaste. Searching for a fresh tube, we encountered one of the old Spanish language tubes? Was it safe to use?

No sign of an expiration date could be found on the tube. We opened the cap. It smelled okay. We had a social commitment that night and mulled over the alternatives. What was more important, our health or fresh breath?

So, of course, we brushed our teeth with the aged tooth-paste. And we lived.

Many foods and all drugs are normally marked with an expiration date. But toothpaste isn't quite a drug and isn't quite a food. What is it? With luck, an effective decay preventive dentifrice, of course!

Both Colgate and Crest informed us that toothpaste has no expiration date. The flavor might change slightly over the years (although the Colgate didn't), but it remains effective as a cavity fighter.

Procter & Gamble was kind enough to send a list of the ingredients in Crest toothpaste; as you will see, there is nothing in the paste that seems perishable (or appetizing):

Ingredient	Function
Sodium Fluoride	The active ingredient; protects the teeth against cavities.
Hydrated Silica	The abrasive of Crest; polishes and cleans the teeth.
Sorbitol and/or Glycerin	Prevents paste from hardening and keeps Crest smooth and creamy.
Trisodium Phosphate & Sodium Phosphate	These buffers keep Crest at a neutral pH of 7.
Sodium lauryl sulfate	Foaming agent; penetrates and loosens deposits on tooth surface.
Titanium Dioxide	Makes toothpaste opaque.
Xanthan Gum & Carbomer-940 or Carbomer-956	These hold the toothpaste together.
Sodium Saccharin	Sweetener
FD&C Blue #1	Colorant
Regular Flavor	Imparts a wintergreen taste.
Mint Flavor	Imparts a spearmint taste.
Gel Flavor	Imparts a sweet spice taste.
Water	The medium into which the ingredients are dissolved.
Mica (Crest for kids only)	Sparkles

Why Do Apples and Pears Discolor So Quickly When Peeled?

Our theory about this Imponderable is simple. We have had it drummed into our heads by teachers, parents, and nutritionists that the peels of fruits are the "best" part for us, full of vitamins and fiber. The spotting of fruits is nature's way of forcing the point—who is going to peel an apple when one is stuck with leopard-skin flesh?

But pomologists (who study fruits, not hands) insist on a more technical explanation. The discoloration in fruits, including peaches, apricots, and bananas, as well as apples and pears, is caused by oxidation. The catalyst for the oxidation is an enzyme, polyphenol oxidase.

According to John B. Williams, of California Apple Products, Inc., polyphenol oxidase occurs naturally in all sugar-producing fruits in varying amounts: "The amount of this enzyme will determine how quickly the browning occurs. The peel of most fruits will not allow oxygen to penetrate in sufficient quantities to act as a catalyst for the enzyme." Banana peels are more porous than apple or pear skins, allowing oxygen to penetrate into the fruit while the skin is still in place. The sturdier apple peel is unlikely to discolor unless it is bruised or cut open.

Submitted by Launi Rountry of Brockton, Massachusetts. Thanks also to Debby Birli of Richmond Heights, Ohio.

Why Do You Usually See Revolving Doors Only in Big Cities?

The main purpose of revolving doors, according to Mike Fisher, vice-president of sales and marketing for door manufacturer

Besam Inc., is to help preserve conditioned air (heat in winter and air conditioning in the summer), thus saving money on energy bills. The constant opening and closing of conventional doors plays havoc with temperature regulation.

Most tall buildings, of course, are found in big cities and almost any skyscraper is going to have revolving doors. Why? The taller a building is, the more "stack pressure" is exerted, forcing hot air to rise more than it normally would during cold weather. Stack pressure creates the wind tunnel effect you often find on the ground floor of skyscrapers.

Revolving doors are not cheap. The lowliest model might cost $8,000 or $10,000, while the revolving doors at Trump Plaza cost more than $100,000 apiece. In order to justify the price of a revolving door, owners want to see tangible savings in their energy bills.

Fisher argues that revolving doors can quickly become cost-efficient. The Newark airport recently installed revolving doors in a terminal's entrance and found that the cost of the doors was paid back in only three years.

Ray Sowers, of Tubelite, adds that revolving doors also lend a patina of prestige to a building, and that not all purchases can be attributed to cold-blooded, bottom-line considerations. Sowers has noticed that if his company has installed a revolving door in a building, Tubelite often gets an order from a building across the street. The revolving door is a bit of a status symbol.

Several of our sources mentioned that it was difficult to convince many architects in the warmer climes to install revolving doors, for they do not seem as concerned about losing air conditioning in the summer as they are about losing heat in winter, even though the energy loss can be just as expensive and uncomfortable. But this explains why revolving doors are comparatively scarce in even large cities in the South and West.

The day of revolving doors in small cities and even small towns might be at hand. Fisher is particularly excited about two comparatively new applications of automatic revolving doors. In airports, they are prized for their security advantages in directing traffic flow in one direction. And there is a real chance that many supermarkets might install automatic revolving doors. D'Agostino, a chain in New York City, has recently installed them in several of their stores, in order to better regulate both the conditioned air in the stores and, most importantly from an economic standpoint, the fragile temperature control of their refrigerated cases. If the door manufacturers can convince Kroger and A&P that it is cost-efficient to install automatic revolving doors, the premise of this Imponderable will soon be obsolete.

Submitted by Rosemary Mangano of Flushing, New York and Ed Hammerschmidt of Casper, Wyoming.

Why Are You Instructed to Put Cold Water into an Automatic Drip Coffeemaker?

Since coffeemakers eventually heat water to 190–200 degrees Fahrenheit, hotter than the hot water out of a tap, we never understood why it made a difference what temperature water is put into the coffeemaker. All of the coffee experts we contacted concurred: The only reason you need to put cold water into a coffeemaker is because the brewed coffee will taste better.

Hot water has a tendency to taste flat and stale. Hot water pipes tend to be corroded, contributing off-tastes to the water. Cold water tends to be full of oxygen and desirable minerals, yielding a more flavorful cup of coffee.

The rule of thumb in the coffee industry is that you shouldn't put water into a coffeemaker that you wouldn't want to drink straight. According to the National Coffee Association of U.S.A., zeolite-type softened water is a particular failure when used to brew coffee.

Submitted by Reverend Dale Huelsman of Wellington, Ohio.

What Accounts for the Great Difference in Climate between the Atlantic Coast and Pacific Coast of the U.S.?

If you are like us, you glaze over during weathercasts on the local news. The intricacies of the weather map, complete with air flows and troughs, strike us as no easier to comprehend than quantum physics. Why waste five valuable minutes on a weather report when all we want to know is whether we need an umbrella or an overcoat? After all, the four minutes saved could be devoted to more important news, like a graphic depiction of another grisly murder or a juicy political scandal.

"It Never Rains in Southern California," warbled Albert Hammond in his 1972 gold record. Not quite accurate, Albert, but not a bad meteorological generalization from someone who spent most of his life in Gibraltar. The weather is more moderate on the left coast and certainly much warmer in winter. Why is this?

The one principle we have managed to glean from those weathercasts is that the prevailing winds in North America move from west to east. We inherit the weather from the west of us. The sea is much slower to change in climate and temperature than land masses. Although the Pacific Ocean has its share of storms, they are relatively infrequent and are usually associated with moderate weather. So the West Coast receives relatively infrequent storms and moderate weather.

Sol Hirsch, executive director of the National Weather Association, told *Imponderables* that the Rocky Mountains are most responsible for the colder and stormier weather of the east coast (and the Midwest, for that matter):

> The weather in the east is determined by storm systems developing from the Rockies eastward that are generally moving in easterly or northerly directions, due to the rotation of the earth. In addition, the area east of the Rockies is exposed to cold air coming from Canada whereas cold air west of the Rockies is infrequent.

The collision of multiple fronts east of the Rockies manufactures storms and makes the weather patterns volatile and difficult to predict.

Of course, the volatility of weather in the East makes the job of a weathercaster considerably dicier than his West Coast counterpart's. If a weathercaster in southern California predicts "85 degrees and partly cloudy" during the summer and "75 degrees and partly cloudy" during the other three seasons, he won't be too far wrong.

Why Do Some Oranges Have an Extra Wedge of Fruit?

You won't find that extra piece of fruit on most oranges. The technical name for the extra piece is the "secondary fruit," and along with its seedlessness and visible navel, it is one of the genetic characteristics of the navel orange.

Catherine A. Clay, an information specialist for the Florida Department of Citrus, told *Imponderables* how the wedge develops:

> All citrus fruit starts out as a blossom on the tree. Each blossom has two sets of ovaries. With many varieties of citrus, the fruit grows around only the primary ovaries and excludes the secondary ovaries. However, with the navel variety and some mandarin oranges such as tangerines, the fruit grows over both sets of ovaries. The cone-shaped section, or secondary fruit, within the navel is actually an undeveloped "twin" of the primary fruit. The secondary fruit will never become a fully developed fruit.

Secondary fruits can be found in some varieties of grapefruits, temple oranges, and tangelos.

Navel oranges grown in humid, subtropical climates, such as Florida, the Caribbean, and parts of South America, tend to have larger navels and secondary fruit than those produced in drier climates with cool winters (e.g., California, South Australia, and Israel). The larger opening of the Florida navel causes problems with cultivation of the crop, for it provides a convenient nesting area for insects, mites, and fungi. Although the pests may enter through the small fruitlet, they can penetrate and eventually contaminate the primary fruit.

Submitted by Jim Seals of Belton, Missouri.

How Do the Trick Birthday Candles (That Keep Relighting after Being Blown Out) Work?

Michael DeMent, Product Spokesperson for Hallmark, told us that the wicks of their Puff Proof® Candles are treated with magnesium crystals. The crystals retain enough heat to reilluminate the wick after candles are blown out.

Because the magnesium-treated wicks retain heat so well, Hallmark recommends extinguishing the candles permanently by dipping them in water.

DeMent shocked us (and in this job, we're not easily shocked) by telling us that practical jokers aren't the only customers for trick birthday candles. Some penurious types view them not as trick candles but as *reusable* candles. After the candles are blown out for the first time, they gather the candles and pinch the wicks with their hands or surround them with a paper towel or other material so that the heat is allowed to radiate around the other object. They then rebox the candles and use them another time.

Not only is the birthday boy or girl deprived of a little fun, but my guess is that the honoree isn't going to get a Porsche or a VCR as a gift from such a cheapskate.

Submitted by Angel Rivera and Dodde Stark of Atlantic Highlands, New Jersey.

Why Doesn't Honey Spoil?

How many foods can you think of that don't spoil AND don't have a long ingredient list full of words with four or more syllables on their labels? Bees may be nasty little insects, but they sure know how to produce a durable product.

By far the most important reason honey doesn't spoil is its high acid content. Ordinary yeasts and bacteria simply can't survive in the acidic environment.

According to Dr. Richard Nowogrodzki, of the Office of Apiculture at Cornell University, honey has a very high osmotic pressure, which means that foreign microorganisms that enter honey rapidly lose water. Yeasts literally dehydrate and die. Nowogrodzki adds that one group of fungi, the osmophilic yeasts, can survive in honey but cannot grow to cause spoilage unless the water content increases to levels above those usually found in stored honey.

In order to protect the honey even when the moisture level increases, bees also add an enzyme (glucose oxidase) to the nectar when they are transforming it into honey. Nowogrodzki explains:

> This enzyme is inactive in honey unless the honey becomes diluted; in diluted honey the enzyme catalyzes a reaction that turns some of the glucose into glutonic acid (thereby further increasing the acidity of the honey) and hydrogen peroxide, which is a common household disinfectant that kills bacteria and fungi (including osmophilic yeasts).

Spoilage of honey is actually the result of fermentation. When the sugar-tolerant yeasts act upon the sugars in honey, alcohol and carbon dioxide is created. Spoilage is most likely to occur after honey has granulated, because the liquid remaining in the nongranulated honey contains too much water. Since honey yeasts will not grow below about 52 degrees Fahrenheit, storing honey in temperatures of 50 degrees or lower is a safe way to prevent granulation.

Scientists have long known that by simply keeping the water level of honey below 17 percent and/or by heating the honey to 145 degrees for about a half-hour, fermentation can be prevented.

Submitted by Douglas Watkins, Jr. of Hayward, California.
Thanks also to Robert M. Chamberlin of Rochester, Minnesota,
and Cary L. Chapman of Homeland, California.

HOW Did the "Grandfather" Clock Get Its Name?

Dutch astronomer Christian Huygens created the weight and pendulum clock in the mid-seventeenth century. He died long before his invention was dubbed the "grandfather clock."

Two hundred years later, in the United States, Pennsylvania German settlers considered the weight and pendulum clock (often called a long-case clock) a status symbol akin to the BMW or satellite dish of today. The popularity of floor clocks soon spread throughout the country.

But the name shift began in 1876, when popular Connecticut songwriter Henry Clay Work produced his masterpiece, "My Grandfather's Clock," which contained the immortal lyrics:

> My grandfather's clock was too long for the shelf,
> So it stood ninety years on the floor.

Clock owners shrugged off the sarcastic tone of Clay's song and adopted "grandfather" proudly, marking a rare case when a 200-year-old technology was renamed.

Submitted by Alex Soto of Potsdam, New York.

What Happens to the Little Punchings That Are Created by the Perforations in Postage Stamps?

Our correspondent adds that he worked for the postal system for 32 years, retired in 1979, and could never get an answer to this question. We're happy to report that we have found the answer. Now you can enjoy your retirement in peace.

Peter G. Papadopoulos, philatelic programs analyst at the Stamp Administration and Advisory Branch of the United States Postal Service (try to fit that title on a postage stamp!), told us that these hole punchings are called "chad." Environmentalists won't be too happy about the fate of chad: "They are sucked up by a vacuum during the perforation process and destroyed with other scrap paper."

Submitted by J. J. Feuhrer of San Diego, California. Thanks also to Dwight Siemens of Clovis, California.

Why Do We Carve Jack-o'-Lanterns on Halloween?

The modern celebration of Halloween has ancient and paradoxical roots. All Hallow's Day (also known as All Saint's Day) was proclaimed by Pope Gregory III in the eighth century. The new holiday was created for a practical reason: The Church had more martyrs and saints to honor than there were days of the week.

But long before the Christian celebration took hold, Druids had observed October 31 as Sambain ("summer's end"), the end of the Celtic year, a celebration of the summer's harvest, and an appeasement to the sun god and the god of the dead. The Druids believed that the souls of everyone who died in the last year dwelled in the bodies of animals. Only on October 31 would their souls reappear to visit their relatives.

Unfortunately, these revisits weren't congenial family reunions. Rather, the dead were thought to come back as witches, ghosts, and hobgoblins, and to wreak havoc across the land. The tradition of lighting bonfires on Halloween stems from the Druids' belief that the fires would frighten away evil spirits.

As Christian belief overcame pagan superstition in Ireland and Scotland, celebrants took over the role of mischief makers from supernatural apparitions. In the early United States, Halloween was not a big deal. Early settlers were mostly Protestants who didn't observe All Saint's Day back in Europe. But with the Irish immigration of the 1840s, America received citizens steeped not only in Catholic educations but with remnants of some of the Druid practices of Sambain.

One of the oldest Sambain traditions was for celebrants to carry a jack-o'-lantern. In Scotland, turnips were used; in Ireland, large potatoes and rutabagas were popular. But in the United States, pumpkins were much more abundant. The jack-o'-lantern was carried all during the night, not left on a windowsill as a sitting duck for roving kids. The scary faces carved on the pumpkins were presumably there to replicate the goblins and evil spirits once believed to rule on Sambain.

Why is the lantern called Jack? Nobody really knows for sure, although Irish legend claims that the Devil once came to claim the soul of a no-good man named Jack. But Jack outsmarted the Devil several times and stayed alive. When Jack eventually died, neither heaven nor hell would claim Jack.

Consigned to an afterlife without a home, Jack begged the Devil for a live coal to provide light so he could navigate in limbo. The Devil, who, as always, was a soft touch when it came to Jack, gave him a piece. Jack put the coal into a turnip. And Jack is still walking around with his lantern until either heaven or hell will open its door to him.

Submitted by Debby Birli of Richmond Heights, Ohio. Thanks also to John Bova of Cheektowaga, New York.

What's the Difference Between a Fast and a Slow Busy Signal on the Telephone?

According to Shelly Gilbreath and Ray Bombardieri, of Southwestern Bell Telephone, a fast busy signal, most often heard when trying to place a long-distance call, indicates that there isn't enough equipment available to process your call:

> The fast busy signal signifies that all trunks either receiving originating call signals, or all the trunks to the terminating end, are engaged and are at a capacity load. If the originating caller were to hang up and try again within a few moments, the call would most likely go through.
>
> Whether or not the party on the receiving end is engaged on the phone has no bearing on if you hear a fast busy signal.

The fast busy signal, a nonverbal variation of the prerecorded message "all circuits are busy," signals 120 times per minute, compared to the less feverish pace of the "regular" busy signal, which sounds 60 times per minute. Of course, the slow busy signal simply indicates that the person on the other end of the phone has found someone more interesting to talk to at the moment than you.

Submitted by Mike Luxton of Long Beach, California.

Where Does the Wax Go in Dripless Candles?

Into the flame itself. There are 67 different grades of paraffin, ranging from extremely soft (with low-temperature melting points) to extremely hard (with high-temperature melting points). Conventional candles use candles with such low melting points that most will melt in the sun.

Dripless candles use hard paraffin and longer wicks, so that no wax is in direct contact with the flame and so the wax around the wick won't melt or drip.

Submitted by Chuck and Louisa Keighan of Portland, Oregon. Thanks also to Stephen J. Michalak of Myrtle Beach, South Carolina; Mike Hutson of Visalia, California; Richard Roberts of Memphis, Tennessee; and Beth Kennedy of Exeter, New Hampshire.

How Did the Heights of Light Switches Become Established? Why Are They Located a Foot Above the Door Knob?

William J. Stanley, a member emeritus of the American Institute of Architects, is much amused by this Imponderable. He agrees that it would make much more sense to place light switches on the wall adjacent to the door knob, so that they could be reached more easily in the dark. But there is a reason for our illogical height standards:

> If you ask a real estate salesman about this he will probably claim that the purpose is to keep the switch out of the reach of small children. But this is not the real reason.
>
> Nearly all houses have the electrical distribution lines in the "attic" or ceiling joist space, from which individual circuits are dropped down inside the wall cavity. But some building codes require that the space between wall studs must be fire-blocked at or near midheight. The light switch boxes are placed just above the fire blocking to save the cost of making a hole through the blocking for the wire.

Stanley adds that many modern versions of building codes now allow the blocking to be lowered (or in some cases, eliminated altogether), allowing:

. . . the switches to be placed opposite the door knobs where they belong. The small amount of extra wire that this would require does not seem like a sufficient reason to perpetuate this anachronism. Of course, you may still have trouble getting an electrician or builder to admit that they are just cutting corners, based on an old rule that people had become accustomed to!

We wondered whether the height standards for light switches were standard throughout the world. They aren't. New York architect Nick Fusco, who has spent time in Japan, reports that not only the light switches but the door frames of Japanese residences are placed lower than their Western counterparts. Tourists might not notice the difference because many hotels built to cater to foreigners are built to a "higher" standard.

Submitted by John Clark of Pittsburgh, Pennsylvania.

Why Does the Difference between 75 Degrees and 80 Degrees in Water Temperature Feel Quite Severe When a Five-Degree Difference in the Ambient Air Barely Registers?

The conductivity of water is much higher than air. If the water in a swimming pool is colder than body temperature, the water will conduct heat quickly away from our bodies. If it is warmer, such as in a hot tub, the water just as rapidly transfers heat to the body. Difference in temperature in the ambient air transfer heat in the same directions but at a much slower rate.

Richard A. Anthes, president of the University Corporation for Atmospheric Research, emphasized to *Imponderables:* "It is the rate of conduction of heat that we sense as heat or cold."

Submitted by Glenn Worthman of Palo Alto, California.

SORRY, BUT OUR MIRROR IS STUCK ON THE "NIGHT" POSITION !!!

What Happens When You Flip the Day/Night Switch on the Rear-View Mirror of an Automobile? Why Do You See Only Lights When the Mirror is in the "Night" Position?

The best explanation we found for this Imponderable was supplied by Thomas J. Carr, director of safety and international technical affairs for the Motor Vehicle Manufacturers Association of the United States, which represents Chrysler, Ford, General Motors, Honda of America, Navistar International, Paccar, and Volvo North America. Carr disillusioned us about the reflective qualities of glass, but then solving Imponderables often involves disabusing ourselves of the innocence of youth:

> With a day/night mirror in the day position, the image is "seen" on the reflective coating that covers the back of the glass. In effect, the visual image passes through the glass to the highly efficient reflective coating and then back out to the viewer. About 80 percent of the incident (incoming) light is reflected with the mirror in the "day" position.

When the mirror is in the "night" position, the reflective coating that was used in the "day" position is tilted away so that the front surface of the mirror glass becomes the reflector. Because glass is a much less efficient reflector, only about 4 percent of the incident light actually reaches the viewer's eyes. Because so much less of the light is transmitted in this position, most of the background that provides reference cues to place a following vehicle in the scene is lost. You only see the lights of the vehicle and perhaps its outline.

Submitted by Kevin A. Shaw of Cincinnati, Ohio. Thanks also to Susan Irias of River Ridge, Louisiana, and Michelle Madsen of McMinnville, Oregon.

What Vegetables Are Used in Vegetable Oils?

If a company is selling 100% corn, peanut, or safflower oil, it will trumpet the identity of the vegetable in marquee-sized letters on the label. So it is natural that most consumers, when faced with the words "vegetable oil" on a label, assume that the contents consist of either a "bad" oil, such as the cottonseed, coconut, or palm oil that cardiologists are constantly warning us about, or a blend of several different vegetables.

In fact, until recently, many vegetable oils were blends. But now all the major brands, such as Wesson and Crisco, as well as most generic or store-brand vegetable oils, use 100% soybean oil in their "vegetable oil."

Although soybean oil has most of the characteristics of the "good" oils, the North American consumer hasn't yet embraced soybeans but will pay a premium for corn oil or peanut oil. Until consumers are convinced that soybeans are more desirable than "vegetable oil," soybeans will continue to forego star billing on the label and appear only in the fine print.

Submitted by Muriel S. Marschke of Katonah, New York.

WHY DO DOGS HAVE WET NOSES?

Why Do Toilets in Public Restrooms Make an Explosive Noise When Flushed?

Perhaps this isn't the most uplifting Imponderable of all time, but we're not judgmental types. If you wonder about a question, even a bathroom Imponderable, it's our job to, well, eliminate it.

The biggest difference between home and public toilets is that most home units work on gravity. But toilets in public restrooms utilize line pressure (created by turning the flush valve) so that the water pressure is much greater than a gravity-driven toilet.

Increasing the line pressure does not use any more water per flush. So managers and owners of big buildings are willing to put up with the sonic booms in exchange for the assurance that "customers" won't have to flush more than once.

We spoke to Jim Datka, of giant American Standard, which makes toilets for homes and institutions. He added that a couple of other factors exacerbate the "explosion" made in public restrooms. The acoustics in most public bathrooms couldn't be better for magnifying and echoing sounds: ceramic tiles; metal stalls; and not a shred of fabric to absorb the noise. Also, the metal flush valve is left exposed in the public restroom, instead of being obscured in a china tank, which helps swallow the cacophony in your home.

One more Imponderable down the drain.

Submitted by Mike, a caller on the Ray Briem show, KABC-AM, Los Angeles, California.

Why Is the Bottom of One- and Two-Liter Cola Bottles Black? Is the Black Bottom Piece There for Functional or Aesthetic Reasons?

The "base cup" is very much a practical and integral part of a bottle. M. Claire Jackson, of Coca-Cola USA, explains:

> The polyethylene terephthalate bottles are manufactured in a two-step process. They are first injection molded into a "preform" that looks like a test tube threaded at one end. The preform is then reheated and "blow-molded" into its final shape and size.

Because the bottoms of most plastic bottles are rounded, they will not stand upright without the base cup.

Why are the base cups black? In most cases, the black cup signifies that the bottle contains a dark beverage, such as a cola or root beer. Most lemon-lime and ginger ale bottles have green bases. Many companies that market flavored seltzers color-code their base cups (e.g., red for raspberry flavored, yellow for lemon, orange for mandarin orange), making it much easier to select your favorite flavor from crowded aisles of the supermarket.

Because it is a neutral color, black has become the "default" color for base cups. Margie A. Spurlock, manager of consumer affairs for Royal Crown Cola Co., told *Imponderables* that black tends to be visually compatible with the colors of most trademarked logos. And economics might enter the picture: "Some bottlers buy bare plastic bottles and label them as they are filled. Basic black affords them the option of buying in larger quantities for a better price."

Submitted by Marguerite McLeod of Braintree, Massachusetts.

Where Does the Sound of a Telephone Ring Emanate From? Why Does the First Ring Sometimes Start in the Middle While Other First Rings Go On as Long as Subsequent Rings? Why Do Receiving Parties Sometimes Pick up the Phone before the Caller Hears a Ring? Why Do Some American Phones and Many Foreign Phones Ring Twice in Succession?

The answer to all four of these Imponderables lies in the circuitry of the switches (also known as "central offices") of local phone companies. The ringing signal comes from the switches, not your telephone.

Ever notice how regular and rhythmic a phone ring is? That's because the ringing signal is precise and symmetrical—a constant cycle of four seconds of silence alternating with two seconds of ringing. When you dial the first three digits of a local number on a touch-tone phone, the sophisticated routing system is already directing your call to the appropriate switch in the receiver's area. By the time you punch in the last four digits, the switch quickly triggers the ringing mechanism on the receiver's line, and that same switch closest to the receiver's end trips a signal to start a ring on your phone.

But the ring signals to the caller and the receiver are not always precisely synchronized. If the circuits are overloaded, the switch that sends a signal to the receiver may be incapable of sending the same message back to the caller at that instant. If so, another switch is tripped and the caller's ring cycle will be different from the receiver's.

Because the ringing cycle is silent twice as long as it generates noise, the caller and receiver are exactly twice as likely to hear a full ring as a shortened one. So when the receiving party picks up the phone immediately upon hearing the phone ring, there is a chance he picked up before the caller heard a ring (when the caller was at the end of the four-second silent phase of the cycle). The next time this happens, compliment the receiver on his or her quick reflexes, and don't assume you have just undergone a paranormal experience.

Double-ring phones used to be much more common. Dick Hofacker, of AT&T Bell Laboratories, told us that multirings used to signal party-line users which particular customer was being favored by a call. PBX systems sometimes used multiring signals to indicate whether a call was coming from an in-house or external party. Local phone companies can set their switching equipment to execute single or double ringing codes; the switches at the receiver's end determine what kind of ring both parties hear. Nobody we spoke to could explain why many European countries favor double rings. Until recently, our esteemed publisher, HarperCollins, favored them. All we know is that it is rather easy, as Shelly Gilbreath, of Southwestern Bell Telephone explained, to set the codes to be "spaced differently, with short or long and/or fast or slow pulses."

Submitted by Mark Carroll of Nashville, Tennessee. Thanks also to Henry J. Stark of Montgomery, New York; Jon R. Kennedy of Charlotte, North Carolina; and Dr. Fred Feldman of Pacific Palisades, California.

Why Don't Barefoot Field Goal Kickers and Punters Get Broken Feet?

Jeff Atkinson, a former National Football League kicker, told *Imponderables* that most kickers detest the drag of a shoe, for the faster a kicker can get his foot through the ball, the farther he can kick it. Although most football kickers favor sleek, tight-fitting soccer shoes, a minority favor kicking in the buff. The thought is enough to make you cringe.

But barefoot kickers don't break their feet. Why not? In the now omnipresent soccer-style field goal kick, the foot meets the ball not on the toes but well above them, where the laces of the shoe would be if they were wearing shoes, and a little to the left of center (for right-footed kickers). Sports physician John R. McCarroll adds that if the kick is properly executed, the ball is struck by a flat surface of the most stable parts of the foot.

Why are there fewer barefoot punters than place-kickers? Because punts are executed on the outside rather than the inside of the foot. If you kick a punt on the same spot as a place-kick, the ball won't spiral properly. The outside of the foot is a little more susceptible to pain and injury than the inside of the foot, so there are fewer barefoot punters.

Atkinson says that the one time barefoot kickers often regret their choice is when kicking off. The most pain a kicker is likely to sustain is not from the football but from the hard plastic that holds the ball, which players sometimes hit accidentally.

Submitted by Dr. Roger Alexander of San Diego, California.

Why Is the Hot Water Faucet on the Left and the Cold Water Faucet on the Right?

This earth-shattering question is undoubtedly one of our ten most often asked Imponderables. But it has another distinction. This is the first Imponderable we have ever resuscitated from the dead-Imponderables file.

All of our usual plumbing experts struck out when faced with this Imponderable. "Tradition," they would say. "The cold water faucet has to be on one side or the other, doesn't it?" commented the less patient. Despairing of ever getting an answer, we expunged this Imponderable from our rolls and assumed that the answer would be lost in antiquity forever.

Then one night, on the Ray Briem Show in Los Angeles, a caller asked this Imponderable for the eight-millionth time and we verbally shrugged our shoulders. But then a plumber from a rural area called and expressed disbelief that we didn't know the answer. Here is a summary of what he said:

> You young whippersnappers. Don't you remember when there wasn't such a thing as a hot water faucet? Cold-water-only faucets placed the knob or lever on the right. Why not? Most people are right-handed. When hot water plumbing was introduced, it made sense to keep the cold water on the right and place the hot water on the left.

Makes sense to us. The anonymous plumber added that he still encounters a few cold-water-only sinks on his job. The knob or lever is always on the right.

We called our trusty old plumbing experts to verify the plumber's tale and they admitted that his explanation made sense to them. But since they haven't manufactured cold-water-only faucets for many a moon, we can't prove that this answer is the full explanation.

> *Submitted by Josh Gibson of Silver Spring, Maryland. Thanks also to Kyle Tolle of Glendale, Arizona; Mike Ricksgers of Saxonburg, Pennsylvania; Tom Pietras of Battle Creek, Michigan; Ted M. O'Neal of Wilmington, North Carolina; Gina Guerrieri of Shawnee, Oklahoma; Jean Harrington of New York, New York; Oree C. Weller of Bellevue, Washington; and many others.*

Why Are Weigh Stations on Highways Always Closed? Why Bother Building So Many of Them?

Drivers of overweight trucks have two big advantages over the enforcement officers at weigh stations: mobility and technology.

If every weigh station were open all the time, law-abiding truckers would be slowed intolerably. If the stations were spaced further apart but were always manned, canny drivers would take a circuitous route to bypass the weigh station. Because the weigh station is by definition stationary, and truckers almost always have an optional route to bypass the stations, state highway officials must find tactics to counter the mobility of the overweight trucks.

The technology that gives an advantage to the truckers is the citizens' band radio. Perhaps the CB is no longer a national fad, but it is still the primary source of intelligence for truckers. With truckers informing those behind them of where open weigh stations are located, keeping one weigh station open for a long period of time makes as much sense as printing the location of the weigh stations at the state border.

So how do officials strike back? By reclaiming the element of surprise. David J. Hensing, deputy executive director of the American Association of State Highway and Transportation Officials, told *Imponderables* that weigh stations are typically operated in the range of "an average of four hours a week at random times, although the level of use can vary widely from state to state and from station to station." By constantly shifting enforcement personnel, truckers are less likely to have fresh information about the location of open weigh stations, and by randomizing the staffing patterns, states make it impossible for truckers to figure out when weigh stations are open. The officials have found it more cost-effective to build 20 weigh stations open only 5 percent of the time than to build one station open all the time, and this method catches many more overweight trucks.

Officials are fighting back in other ways too. Many states are increasing their use of temporary scales that are set up at random times and locations and are experimenting with weigh-in-motion technologies that can weigh a truck without the driver knowing it.

So the next time you pass the "WEIGH STATION" sign with the "CLOSED" strip below it, rest assured that your enforcement officials are not off fishing, but somewhere else down the road doing their job.

Submitted by William Lush of Stamford, Connecticut.

Frustables

The 10 Most Wanted OR Imponderables

"Frustables" is short for "frustrating Imponderables," mysteries that have defied our frequent efforts to answer them. It isn't easy for us to admit that we can't hit a home run every time. In fact, sometimes we can't even lay down a sacrifice bunt. Sure, we've found some fascinating theories or bits of evidence that might lead to an answer to the ten Frustables you are about to read. But we don't have the proof to publish any answers.

So we throw our fragile ego onto the collective expertise and brilliance of our readers. Can you help? As always, we offer a reward of a free, autographed copy of the next volume of *Imponderables,* as well as an acknowledgment for your help in alleviating our frustration, to the first person who can lead to the proof that solves any of these Frustables. If you seek inspiration, following this section you can see how readers contended with the Frustables posed in *When Do Fish Sleep?*

Good luck with these new Frustables. You'll need it.

FRUSTABLE 1: *Does Anyone Really Like Fruitcake?*

We get some variation of this question quite frequently: Why does fruitcake exist? Why do nonprofit organizations sell fruitcakes for fundraisers when no one likes fruitcake? Why do people give fruitcakes as presents? (And yes, we've heard the story that there is only one fruitcake in the world which gets passed from person to person).

There might not be one definitive answer to such a complex phenomenon. But can anyone explain the proliferation of a product that no one seems to want? Or are there readers out there brave enough to publicly profess their love of fruitcake? Maybe we could publish your address and have all the unopened fruitcakes of the world sent to you.

**FRUSTABLE 2: *Why Does the Stroking of Index Fingers
Against Each Other Mean "Tsk-Tsk"?***

Why the stroking motion? Why not, say, the ring fingers?

**FRUSTABLE 3: *We Often Hear the Cliché: "We Only Use 10
Percent of Our Brains." How Was It Determined that We
Use 10 Percent and Not 5 Percent or 15 Percent?***

Is there any scientific basis for this claim? If so, who made it and
when was it established.

**FRUSTABLE 4: *Where, Exactly, Did the Expression "Blue
Plate Special" Come from?***

We assume that there was a restaurant that actually did serve
specials on blue plates. But where the heck was it?

**FRUSTABLE 5: *Why Does the Traffic in Big Cities in the
United States Seem Quieter than in Big Cities in Other
Parts of the World?***

The transportation officials we spoke to denied that the premise
is true. But this question from a reader confirms our experiences,
too. Any ideas?

**FRUSTABLE 6: *Why Do Dogs Tilt Their Heads When You
Talk to Them?***

When we were researching out title Imponderable, we asked
many experts what they thought about this Frustable. Several
mentioned that dogs do not tilt their heads when listening to
each other "arf." Why do cocker spaniels cock their heads when
listening to our cockeyed ravings?

FRUSTABLE 7: *Why and Where Did the Notion Develop that "Fat People Are Jolly?"*

From Santa Claus to Mama Cass, this stereotype is rampant. Why?

FRUSTABLE 8: *Why Do Pigs Have Curly Tails?*

We've been trying to find an answer to this since *Why Do Clocks Run Clockwise?* Does the curl serve any function whatsoever?

FRUSTABLE 9: *Why Does the Heart Depicted in Illustrations Look Totally Different than a Real Heart?*

Where did the fanciful shape come from?

FRUSTABLE 10: *Where Do All the Missing Pens Go?*

Not to be confused with the missing sock issue, the problem of misplaced pens seems far more serious to us. Everyone we talked to thinks that they are a "net" loser of socks. So who picks up all the pens that we all lose? What happens to them? Will the person or persons who has all our pens admit it? Or give them back?

Frustables Update

As this book is being written, eight months have passed since the publication of *When Do Fish Sleep?* in hardbound, so readers of the paperback edition haven't had a chance yet to solve the ten Frustables posed in it. We've been flooded with responses to some of the Frustables but a few Frustables have attracted only a trickle.

So this section will often be a progress report rather than the last word on many of these Frustables. In the next volume of *Imponderables*, we promise to keep you informed of any breakthroughs in our neverending endeavor to stamp out Frustability. We also encourage any readers of this book who haven't read *When Do Fish Sleep?* to add your comments to these 10 Frustables.

Our thanks to all who contributed their solutions, especially those we haven't been able to include by name.

FRUSTABLE 1: *Why is Legal Paper 8½" × 14"?*

What is especially frustrating about this Frustable is that the question seems like it would yield an easy answer. Yet the legal historians and paper companies we've contacted haven't been able to answer it. Even answers like Amboy, Washington, Kenneth McGoffin's—"Because it makes perfectly balanced paper airplanes"—started to sound good to us.

We heard from Dana Walker, of Ampad, a division of Mead Company, who claims that Ampad was the first company to produce the legal pad, at the beginning of the twentieth century:

> A Durham judge, tiring of penciling horizontal lines on scratch pads, wanted printed lines and a left vertical line for his marginal notes. So a hurried trip to the founder of the American Pad &

Paper Co., at Holyoke, produced the #369 legal pad of today, #369 because [Ampad's] Mr. Bockmiller lost first $3, then $6, then won $9 the previous night at poker.

Peter Bishop, Ampad's manager of marketing, confirms that the #369 pad measured 8″ × 14″, but can't explain the rationale behind the extra three-inch length.

Many readers speculated that the extra length was there to provide room for legal signatures (more cynical types insisted the extra length was there to compensate for lawyers' uncalled-for verbosity). But the most convincing argument came from one of our favorite correspondents, Fred Beeman, who lives in beautiful Kahului, Hawaii:

> When legal briefs were originally prepared in the early days of the U.S. legal system (on standard 8½″ × 11″ paper), there was never enough room at the bottom of the page for the notary public to place his statement of certification, and to emboss his seal, thus giving authenticity to a particular document. This could not be done on a separate piece of paper; it had to be done on the actual document itself.
>
> The more enterprising notaries would simply make their certifications on a separate sheet of paper (near the topmost portion). With scissors, they would cut off the top portion and use adhesive tape to affix that certification to the original document. Others, not as enterprising, would simply return the entire document(s) to the client, saying, "Leave approx. 3″ at the bottom for my certifications!".
>
> Eventually, some bright individuals decided that the solution was simply to make court documents about 3″ longer, so the "certification space" would already be there, and instruct secretaries to prepare documents as if the paper were 8½″ × 11″ in length.
>
> This worked. Secretaries would prepare documents as before, and the 3″ space would be at the bottom when the document was removed from the typewriter for a judge's signature, notarization, or whatever.

We can't verify this theory, but it's certainly the most plausible we've heard.

Maybe our favorite piece of correspondence concerning this Frustable came from the Association of Records Managers and Administrators' Project ELF ("Eliminate Legal-Size Files"). The lobbying efforts of Project ELF helped convince the Judicial Conference of the U.S. to adopt letter-size paper (8½" × 11") as a standard in all Federal Courts, effective January 1, 1983. Most state court systems have followed suit. Project ELF claims that the costs of duplicating paper sizes and then housing correspondence in needlessly large file cabinets can increase the administrative operating cost of business and government up to 25 percent.

Submitted by Tristan MacAvery of Davis, California. Thanks also to William B. Katz of Highland Park, Illinois; Lisa Lipson of Sacramento, California; Joseph S. Blake, Jr. of Ottawa, Kansas; Joey Garman of Hanover, Pennsylvania; Jerry Kiewe of Lauderdale Lakes, Florida; Major Harry Malone of Lawton, Oklahoma; and Richard B. Stacy of Tucson, Arizona.

A free book goes to Fred T. Beeman of Kahului, Hawaii.

FRUSTABLE 2: *Why Do Americans, Unlike Europeans, Switch Forks to the Right Hand After Cutting Meat?*

We received several impassioned letters, defending the American style of switching hands. We still don't think it makes any sense, even if *we* switch hands, too.

Most of the serious theories boiled down to three camps. The first group saw the fork switching as an attempt to do what most table etiquette attempts—separating humans from their natural tendency to gorge as much food as quickly as possible. Perhaps Pat Steigman of Tyler, Texas, put it best:

> By having to switch hands, the diner is forced to put down his knife before eating the bite. Since he is not allowed to cut more than one bite at a time, he will again be forced to switch hands after the bite is eaten to cut his next bite. All of this hand switching is meant to slow down the eating process to a socially acceptable speed. Now, with just a glance, it is easy to discern those of proper breeding at the dinner table.

The most popular answer to this Frustable dates the custom back to the American Revolution and an interesting conspiracy theory. Judy Swierczak of Lahaina, Hawaii, offers her version:

... it developed as a secret signal during the American Revolution. It allowed other Revolutionaries to recognize their compatriots when dining in a group. If you all switched cutlery, then it was safe to talk about your activities. If some didn't switch, everyone kept their mouths shut. It was an innocuous gesture, but highly significant.

Although about ten readers offered this theory, none were able to cite sources for this information. Sounds apocryphal to us.

We buy a third theory, which is that until the mid-1700s, America was a forkless society. Hand switching, then, was once not a matter of manners but of necessity. Several readers told us about references to this subject in archaeologist James Deetz's *In Small Things Forgotten*, James Cross Giblin's *From Hand to Mouth*, and J. C. Furnas' *The Americans: A Social History of the United States 1587–1914*. We also found a short discussion of the subject in David E. Sutherland's *The Expansion of Everyday Life*.

Lou-Ann Rogers of Bethlehem, Pennsylvania, summarizes Giblin's explanation:

...forks did not come to America until the mid-1700s. Until that time, people used spoons and knives. Initially the knives were sharp and were used to stab meat—the spoon pressed the meat down while it was being cut and lifted to the mouth (yes, on the knife!).

Then the sharp knives were replaced by rounded knives [we explained how this happened in Europe in *Imponderables*] that couldn't be used to transfer cut meat to the mouth. Thus, the spoon was still used to hold onto the meat while cutting it but then the knife was laid aside, the spoon put into the right hand and used to take the meat to the mouth. When forks came to the New World, people kept switching the way they had when using spoons.

Dale Neiburg of Laurel, Maryland, adds that forks, (which, like all cutlery, were imported from Europe) were not plentiful in the United States until the mid-1800s, whereas Europeans quickly integrated forks as an eating utensil:

AND OTHER IMPONDERABLES   737

Europeans, who went straight from knife to fork, hold the fork—
and unconsciously think of it—as a modified knife. Americans,
who went through an intervening "spoon phase," think of the fork
and use it as a modified spoon.

Neiburg's theory also explains why Europeans generally hold
their fork tines down, while Americans point the tines upward.

Although we may never find direct, conclusive proof of the
"missing fork" theory, it sure beats anything else we've heard.

*Submitted by Shirley Keller of Great Neck, New York. Thanks
also to Peter DeMuth of Denver, Colorado; Robert W. Purdin of
Tinton Falls, New Jersey; Ronald Walker of Covina, California;
and Abner Fein of Wantagh, New York.*

A free book goes to Lou-Ann Rogers of Bethlehem, Pennsylvania.

FRUSTABLE 3: *How, When, and Why Did the Banana Peel Become the Universal Slipping Agent in Vaudeville and Movies?*

Progress Report: No progress at all. Help!

FRUSTABLE 4: *Why did the Grade E Disappear from Grading Scales in Most Schools?*

We heard from a lot of you about this one, and it became abun-
dantly clear that grading scales vary throughout the United
States and have been changing at least since the turn of the
century.

Only one theory was advanced that could explain why just
about all school systems have eradicated the E from report cards.
And we must admit that we were too innocent and ethical to
have ever thought of the suggestion of Patti A. Willis of Endicott,
New York, and many other readers:

Back in the old days, when report cards were hand-written and
not a computer printout, a simple stroke of the pen could turn a

failing grade, F, into an excellent grade, E. The temptation was just too great for some children to resist.

In Endicott, E equals excellence. But in many school districts, E meant one slim step above failure. Russell Tremayne, a retired high school teacher from Auburn, Washington, told how and why the E was banished from his system:

A, B, C, D, and F were performance grades, indicating how a student had worked. They could be used as grades of record, entered upon a school transcript. The E, however, was a predictive comment, a sort of early warning. While the E could be used on the report card at midterm, it could not be used as a semester grade; it had to be converted to an F on the final transcript.

Trying to evaluate at midterm, a teacher was in a quandary as to how to grade a borderline student. If he gave the pupil an E, "a warning of possible failure," the student's response was usually the negative, "If I'm failing, I'll quit working."

If the teacher, trying to encourage the student, gave him a D and then, seeing the student slack off severely, gave him an F at semester time, the student (and often his parents) would cry foul, claiming that the teacher could not give a final F without having issued an interim E warning.

So the troublesome E was banished, and administrators, teachers, parents, and pupils were retaught that a D meant passing but in danger of failing should work deteriorate. A student could go from a D at midterm to an F at the semester's end without statistical contradiction or anyone's emotional flip-out.

Jeff Gay of Middleboro, Massachusetts, and Kenneth N. Burgess of Oakdale, Louisiana, report that at one time in their school systems, E also indicated a failing performance but one that showed effort.

But the majority of the correspondents felt that the E was eliminated to avoid confusion between E as a low grade and E as "excellent." Pamela L. Gibson of Belleville, New Jersey, mentioned that her elementary school used an E(xcellent), V(ery) G(ood), S(atisfactory), P(oor), and U(nsatisafactory) system. Gibson believes that "the A through F system was abolished in my school to prevent children from being traumatized by receiving the dreaded F."

Charles Northrop sent us his 1965–1966 report card from Campbell, California, with an unusual system of E (outstanding work), S+ (very satisfactory progress), S (progress compares favorably with ability), S− (below expected progress), and N (needs improvement, capable of doing much better). But J. Orrville Smith beats Charles by almost fifty years with our first reported use of E as excellent. He attended elementary school in Portsmouth, Virginia, from 1918 to 1926, where the grading scale was E(xcellent), V(ery) G(ood), G(ood), F(air), P(oor), and, ignominiously, V(ery) P(oor).

We heard from Tom Schoeck, who has spent more than 35 years working in education. He attended a private elementary school with an interesting grading policy:

> Academic subjects were graded, in descending order, A–B–C–D–F, while the non-academic areas (gym, music, art, and most important—"comportment"—later called "conduct") were graded E–S–U, for Excellent, Satisfactory and Unsatisfactory.
>
> Heaven forfend we should ever bring home a report card with a U in conduct! My understanding is that the E–S–U system predated the A–F system and was earlier in use for all subjects. But with the need or opportunity for more objectively precise sorting of students' performance levels arising sometime between the turn of the century and World War I (or even earlier in some areas of the country), somewhat "finer" classifications were needed. All this has been solved now, of course, with the emergence of numerical equivalents for letter grades, the 4.0 system, bell curves, standard deviations, etc.

Perhaps our favorite letter on this Frustable comes from Mike Schramm of Syracuse, New York, who demonstrates that an ingenious, underachieving student can make the best out of a failing grade, providing his parents are sufficiently credulous:

> My father went to high school in Rochester, New York, in the late 1930s and early 1940s. His report cards showed a grading system with A, B, C, D, and E (with no F's).

When I asked him about E, he said that some kids were able to convince their parents that E meant "excellent." This made for embarrassing confrontations with parents who thought their children were doing just fine, only to be told otherwise. A parent who would believe this might be likely to have a child who would get a lot of E's.

A free book goes to Mike Schramm of Syracuse, New York, for making us laugh.

FRUSTABLE 5: *How Did They Lock Saloon Doors in the Old West?*

Most of the many people who wrote us about this Frustable gained their knowledge about saloon doors not from historical research but from westerns on TV and movies or from visits to theme parks. Just about everyone knew that the swinging doors were not all that separated the saloon from Front Street, but only David Di Mattia of Yonkers, New York, worried about whether all of his totally logical explanations were less important than the needs of the entertainment industry:

> The swinging door was not the only door that shared the same door frame. When saloons were closed, full-length double doors (with or without pane glass) were used to provide security after business hours or on days closure was mandated by blue laws.
> The swinging saloon door served a few purposes for such a business establishment. Its half-length allowed patrons to see incoming or existing customers while still providing a modest amount of privacy for those imbibing inside. They also allowed for continuous air flow to help alleviate smoke and heat build-up during peak business hours. Finally, *maybe the swinging doors provided a safe throughway for movie and TV stuntmen.*

The only problem with the solutions proposed by almost everyone who wrote is that they were wrong. Our old friend, historian and writer C. F. "Charley" Eckhardt, who specializes in the American West, wrote:

AND OTHER IMPONDERABLES   741

The swinging doors of a Western saloon are the exterior doors only in Hollywood. If you'll take a magnifying glass to "Front Street" pictures of almost any western town, you'll find that most saloons had ordinary front doors like every other business in town.

Yes, saloons *did* have swinging doors—but they didn't open onto the street. *In most saloons, you entered through an ordinary lockable door at the front.* This brought you into the "cigar apartment," where the owner-manager's private offices were usually located and where you could buy cigars and package liquors—bottles wrapped in brown paper and tied with a string. There was then a partition, sometimes very elaborate, often scrollworked and leaded-glassed, with a pair of swinging doors in it. When you went through the swinging doors, you went from the cigar apartment into the saloon proper.

Eckhardt sent us photocopies of the *Brunswick–Balke–Collender Illustrated Catalog of Bar Fixtures, 1891*, including a floor plan for a single-story, single-lot saloon, that clearly shows that the swinging doors separate the saloon from the cigar apartment, not the street; the swinging doors cannot be seen from the outside. So much for the ventilation and privacy theories.

If you want to see examples of saloon exteriors, Charles Gerald Melton of Providence, Rhode Island, sent us a letter indicating that there are several verbal and pictorial references to saloons in the Time-Life *Old West* series. Pictures in *The Loggers, The Rivermen*, and *The Townsmen* show saloons with nonswinging exterior doors, although Melton points out that many kept their doors open 24 hours a day.

Ann Calhoun of Los Osos, California, won't be dissuaded by something so flimsy as hard evidence, though. She provided a fanciful history of the swinging door in saloons. She claims that the swinging doors were substitutes for curtains that were originally placed on the bottom half of saloons' windows to block the view inside. And somehow, she has managed to make this a feminist, ageist, and temperance issue:

> If you've ever noticed, swinging doors are always placed a
> few inches below the eye level of the average adult male, which

would put them a few inches above the eye level of the average adult female and completely block the view of the average whippersnapper. Unless, of course, he faked a broken shoelace at the precise moment of passing the forbidden door, bent down and *then* caught a glimpse of the nekkid lady over the bar.

As civilization progressed (?), electricity powered overhead fans, glass windows became cheap and plentiful, God invented air conditioning and swinging doors soon disappeared (unless the establishment was going all Yuppie, trendy, and thematic-kitschy), only to be replaced by often incredibly ornate sand-blasted glass windows and doors. Yet the theory still remained: If you're tall enough to see above the swinging doors, you're old enough to go inside and buy yourself a drink. If not, go home and have a nice glass of milk and some of Mommy's cookies.

Even today, ever walk past a self-respecting saloon, one worthy of the name? The place resembles a bunker expecting incoming artillery rounds! The only time the front door is *ever* open is when they're closed for business, the help is mopping the floors and swilling out the toilets and they desperately need cross ventilation lest the workers become stricken by the Lysol fumes . . .

So you can't trust everything you see on television or movies! How did they lock saloons in the Old West? With keys.

Submitted by Maria Katinos of Los Angeles, California.

A free book goes to C. F. Eckhardt of Seguin, Texas.

FRUSTABLE 6: *Why Do So Many People Save* National Geographics *and Then Never Look at Them Again?*

"What is this Frustable?" moaned reader Ann Calhoun, who waxed freely over Frustable 5. "Do I look like a psychiatrist?"

Well, no. In fact, this Frustable, which drew more mail than all but number 10, attracted dozens of different explanations for why people save the magazine, but few readers would play armchair shrink and speculate about why we save reading material that we will never pick up again.

We even got a few letters from folks who claimed that they actually did go back and read old *NG*s. Sure. But most Frustablebusters spoke with the detachment of cultural anthropologists.

The most popular response was that in almost every way, *National Geographic*s resemble books to be saved indefinitely rather than disposable magazines. As evidence, they point to:

- the flat spine
- the volume numbers and subjects, printed on the spine for easy reference, implying the issues are meant to be saved
- the glued binding

- the heavy, glossy paper stock
- foldout maps
- their ability to stand up like books
- and of course, the exquisite coffee-table booklike color photography

We also heard from students and parents of students, perhaps most entertainingly from four Oregon State University students: Tara Boehler, Brenda Miller, Krista Hess, and Jennifer Crocker:

> We are always encountering maniacal instructors who assign outrageously long and detailed papers (due by the end of the week) that require not only research but also visual aids. So we trot to our closets or under our beds and drag out the ole *National Geographic* stack and start cutting.

In support of the OSU contingent, William Kelso adds that the subject matter of *National Geographic* makes them worth having around: "An article on a geographic area or species of animal will still be more or less valid ten years later."

Mike Babin, technical services librarian of the Port Arthur [Texas] Library, reports that people actually do read back issues of *NG*:

> ... they just don't read *their* copies. *National Geographic* is not self-indexed ... it's much easier and convenient to go to your local library, which does have the index, and find the article wanted. I've found that most people are very good about remembering that they've read an article in the magazine, but not so good about remembering when they read it.

So much for the invaluable subject headings and volume and number notations on the flat spine of the magazine that were the excuse for saving the issues in the first place.

So if most of the people who subscribe to and save *National Geographic*s don't reread them, why do they save them? Ann Calhoun, our reluctant psychiatrist, turns unrepentant capitalist and suggests that the thinking runs along the lines of "Better hold onto these—someday they're going to be worth a lot of money." Little do these hoarders know that hundreds of thousands of others are simultaneously trying to dump their collections upon a yawning public.

H. E. Todd of Portland, Oregon, and others suggest that perhaps saving *NGs* has something in common with keeping old *Playboy* and *Penthouse* collections, although Todd admits that the latter have "higher frontal nudity density."

Paul Ruggerio of Blacksburg, Virginia, was not the only but certainly the youngest reader (at age 12) to suggest that shelves full of *National Geographic* have a certain snob appeal. Paul tells us not to feel inferior when we see a shelf full of the magazine in a neighbor's house:

> Don't let it get to you because deep down, you know that your secret stash of yellow magazines is sending the same message. And besides, they've never read any of their *National Geographics* either.

Perhaps we are cockeyed idealists, but we would like to think that the untold stacks of *National Geographics* are testimony to the noblest yearnings of the human spirit (and to the most Western of all negative emotions—guilt). We go along with reader William Kelso:

> The subject material of *National Geographic* is informative, educational, and uplifting: the sort of thing *we know we should be reading*. But other things always seem more pressing—quarterly sales results, centerfolds in skin magazines, etc. So we tell ourselves that we'll keep the *Geographics* and read them when we get around to it. Guilt is what keeps them on the shelf.

The same process (along with a healthy dose of laziness) also explains why 90 percent of our books remain on our shelves at home. How many of the books in your collection have you re-read? What makes you think you will go back to the novel that you couldn't make it halfway through in high school—especially when you know you won't be tested on it?

Submitted by Wendy Rath of Sandy, Utah.

A free book goes to William Kelso of Mercer Island, Washington.

FRUSTABLE 7: *Why Do People, Especially Kids, Tend to Stick Their Tongues Out When Concentrating?*

Those of you who based your responses on pure speculation were clearly floundering. You probably didn't realize that actual scientific research has been conducted on this subject. Two strong theories emerge that have little in common with each other:

 1. Sticking out the tongue is an unconscious signal to onlookers to stay away. Deborah Ledwich of Arthur, Ontario, was the first to write us about this:

> Whenever we see a person concentrating on something with the tip of his tongue protruding, we tend to be reluctant to speak to him or disturb him. Therefore, the sticking out of the tongue is a psychological signal (from the person who is concentrating on his task) to other people that he is busy and doesn't want to be disturbed. It works very effectively most of the time, too.

Experiments conducted with teachers indicated that students were less likely to approach the desk of the teacher when the teacher had his or her tongue sticking out.

 Chances are, the students didn't consciously register the tongue position of their teacher, but the process may be unconscious for the "tonguer" and the "tonguee." We find one major problem with this theory, though—it doesn't explain why people still stick out their tongues when they are alone.

 2. Remember Lily Tomlin's Edith-Ann character, the little girl who stuck her tongue out when concentrating? We heard from several people who indicated that there was a physiological explanation for the wayward tongue. Evan A. Ballard and E. Wilson Griffin III, two physicians at the Jonesville Family Medical Center in Jonesville, North Carolina, were the first and most qualified to discuss this theory. Here's what they wrote:

> Why do Michael Jordan and other talented human beings (including my five-year-old son) wiggle and waggle a pro-

truding tongue while performing tasks requiring concentration and dexterity?

The answer lies in the location in the brain of control of hands and mouths. The cerebral cortex is the site in the brain where complicated tasks and thoughts are integrated. Each part of the body is represented in the cerebral cortex at a certain area. It so happens that the area of the cortex controlling the tongue is immediately adjacent to the area controlling the hands. [Does this reasoning sound familiar? It's virtually the same explanation for the Frustable we answered in *When Do Fish Sleep?*: Why does looking up at the sun cause many people to sneeze?]

The reason for this is more than simply coincidence. Theory has it that man evolved his incredible dexterity with his hands (especially his opposable thumb) as he was developing his speech capacity. Speech, of course, requires much dexterity of the tongue and mouth in general. Since the areas of the brain controlling the hand and the mouth are adjacent to each other as well as performing closely related functions, many of their neurological pathways are interconnected. Activity in the neurons controlling the hand often leads, inadvertently, to activity in neurons controlling the mouth.

The tongue and the hands, therefore, are extremely closely related functionally and spatially in the brain, even though they are at some distance from each other in the body. Does this explain why some of us find our hands producing wild gestures when we are earnestly trying to express ourselves verbally?

Adding fuel to Ballard and Griffin's theory is the observation that many musicians stick out their tongue when doing fine picking (e.g., Roy Clark, B. B. King).

Why do kids, in particular, tend to stick out their tongues? Probably because they haven't yet learned that it is socially unacceptable behavior.

Finally, we can't resist sharing a story sent to us by H. E. Todd:

My daughter, a physician, was sticking out her tongue while water skiing one day. Asked if she did this when performing a difficult medical procedure and if so, if it might interfere with patient confidence, she replied, "Why do you think we doctors wear masks?"

Submitted by Malinda Fillingion of Savannah, Georgia. Thanks also to Ruby Clasby of Federal Way, Washington.

A free book goes to Drs. Evan A. Ballard and E. Wilson Griffin III of Jonesville, North Carolina; and Deborah Ledwich of Arthur, Ontario.

FRUSTABLE 8: *Why Do Kids Tend to Like Meat Well Done (and Then Prefer It Rarer and Rarer as They Get Older)?*

Two main schools of thought predominated, with many supporters for each. But there was precious little evidence to support either of these theories:

1. Kids associate rare meat with blood and, unconsciously, the fact that they are eating a once-living animal. But how does this explain why kids lose this fear as they get older?
2. Kids have extremely sensitive taste buds and prefer the blander taste of a burnt burger to the gamy taste of a rare piece of meat. Maybe. But the taste experts we consulted couldn't find any evidence to support this theory.

Anybody have a better explanation, or hard evidence, to support either of these two theories?

FRUSTABLE 9: *Why Does Whistling at an American Sporting Event Mean "Yay!" When Whistling Means "Boo!" in Most Other Countries?*

Never has a Frustable bored so many. The few speculations we received are too lame to report to a family audience. Do we have any anthropologists out there who can help us with this one? We can't seem to get to first base (boo!) on this one.

AND OTHER IMPONDERABLES 749

FRUSTABLE 10: *Why Are So Many Restaurants, Especially Diners and Coffee Shops, Obsessed with Mating Ketchup Bottles at the End of the Day?*

In *When Do Fish Sleep?*, we whined about our problem hailing a waitress to take our order because she was too busy stacking ketchup bottles. We questioned whether customers really care about having full bottles of ketchup in front of them. After all, half-full bottles flow more easily. Why do restaurateurs demand that their staff waste their time with this time-consuming activity?

We were deluged with responses. We heard from restaurateurs, waiters, and waitresses, but especially from *ex*-waiters and *ex*-waitresses, a contingent large enough to form a politically powerful lobbying group if they ever got organized.

They let us know in no uncertain terms that mating ketchup bottles was far from their favorite activity. But they were pressured to, as it is variously called, "mate," "marry," "stack," or "consolidate" ketchup bottles at the end of their shifts. The letter from Barrie Creedon of Philadelphia, Pennsylvania, was typical:

In any restaurant, "side work," any work you are not paid for (e.g., cleaning, stocking, stacking) is a major source of hostility among the staff. The opening crew thinks the closing crew is a bunch of lazy slobs and vice versa.

However, it is my experience that the biggest, toughest, most terrifying waitresses are always on the opening shift [remember, the thoughts expressed in this letter do not necessarily reflect the sentiments of the author, who has the utmost respect and veneration for opening-shift waitresses]. And if their ketchup bottles aren't nice and clean when they take them from the refrigerator, they can become *extremely* unhappy. So you work like there's no tomorrow on the bottles the night before in case there is a tomorrow, because if one of these women gets mad, it's not a pretty sight.

Many correspondents insisted that customers do indeed prefer full bottles, perhaps because the customer perceives a clean, full bottle as new. Annie Lloyd of Mercer, California, argues the case:

No one wants to use anything, including ketchup, that hundreds of strangers have used before him. So keeping the ketchup bottles full give the customer the illusion of having a new bottle that no one else has used prior to his arrival.

Kate Levander of Minneapolis, Minnesota, explains why it's so hard to catch the attention of a waiter when a coffee shop is about to close:

Ketchup bottles, unlike humans, take a long time before the mating process is complete. It takes quite a while for the inverted top bottle to glop all the ketchup into the bottom bottle.

Waiters and waitresses just don't want to wait until the lower ketchup bottles are full so they can go home. They have been *waiting* all day—on people asking for more ketchup.

Levander adds that while it may be true that full bottles of ketchup are slower to pour for the customer, half-full bottles make the marrying process much faster for the waiters.

Many restaurants do not simply consolidate the contents of

used bottles and replace them with factory-sealed bottles. Heinz and many other brands sell large #10 cans and two-gallon bags of ketchup for restaurant use; however, these large containers are not designed for use in refilling used bottles. Beth Adams, of Heinz public communications, says that her company does not condone the practice for hygienic reasons.

But this doesn't stop most restaurants. Heidi Cheney of Caldwell, Idaho, wrote us that the restaurant in which she worked used a funnel to collect upended bottles and poured the collected ketchup into [we hope] rinsed, recycled bottles.

All but the tackiest eateries do try to rinse off bottles. But Beth Adams observed that she has seen bottle necks cleaned with dirty rags. Not too hygienic.

Let's face it. The bottom line on this Frustable is the bottom line. Restaurants can save money by consolidating. Henry Verden, a professional restaurant manager from Elmhurst, Illinois, explains:

> #10 cans are much cheaper than buying smaller 10- or 12-ounce bottles. Since large cans would be, to say the least, impractical on tables, the restaurant will make an initial investment in bottles and then refill them from the #10 cans. Refilling ketchup bottles then becomes simply a matter of restocking every evening, just as you refill sugar shakers, napkin dispensers, and salt and pepper shakers.
>
> Stock rotation is the reason for "mating" the bottles. Simply refilling partial bottles would leave older ketchup in the bottom of every bottle. By combining partial bottles you leave empties to infuse fresh ketchup into the system without mixing it with old ketchup, which would shorten the shelf life of the fresher product. The bottles containing the older ketchup will be used up in the normal course of business.

Verden ends on an ominous note: "It also provides a manager with a project to keep waitresses, waiters, and bus people busy during slow periods."

And our saloon-door expert, Charley Eckhardt, who once owned a café, adds his two bits. If you don't use the big cans to dispense the ketchup, consolidating helps keep track of inventory: "Once you've consolidated the ketchup into as few bottles as possible, the empties tell you how much ketchup you've used and how much you need to buy." According to Beth Adams, one of the reasons Heinz is upset about ketchup "marriage" is that some less than reputable restaurants use Heinz bottles on the tables but fill them with off-brands in the kitchen. In this case, Heinz loses out twice: the restaurant buys neither the high-profit-margin 14-ounce bottles nor the bulk ketchup.

All this commotion, remember, is about ketchup, not exactly the most important element of any dining establishment. Melanie Morton of Branford, Connecticut, wrote us a particularly witty letter about her travails with ketchup mating. She writes that while demanding patrons are trying to flag a waitress at the end of her shift,

> she's tired, her feet hurt, and she wants to count her tips. And those precariously balanced bottles have a tendency to tip over when left unattended.
>   . . . It's the wonderful details like this in the restaurant business that made me leave it.

A free book goes to Henry A. Verden of Elmhurst, Illinois, and Melanie Morton of Branford, Connecticut. And special thanks to the many other former and current waiters and waitresses who sent equally good letters.

LETTERS

We are used to receiving letters with criticisms or corrections, but not from folks saying that our title was wrong!

In the early 1800s, the Waterbury Clock Co. of Waterbury, Connecticut, offered for sale a clock much like the Seth Thomas school clock. The main difference is that the Waterbury clock ran counterclockwise. The dial was made with the numerals fixed backwards.

These clocks were hung on the rear wall of barber shops. With the customer sitting in the barber chair facing large mirrors, the clock appeared "normal."

The Waterbury Clock Co. was destroyed by fire in 1880.

JOHN PARISEAU
Jewett City, Connecticut

But the concept lives on:

To be absolutely correct, the title of your book should be *Why Do MOST Clocks Run Clockwise?* . . . A barbershop clock which runs counterclockwise is still sold by a company named Klockit, in Lake Geneva, Wisconsin . . .

PAUL J. KRAHE
Erie, Pennsylvania

In When Do Fish Sleep?, *we answered an Imponderable about why automobiles require separate keys for the ignition and doors. We heard from a reader who thought two keys might be two keys too few:*

My old 1958 Chevy Yeoman station wagon had no less than *four* keys: ignition; doors; glovebox; and tailgate. The keys were all square-headed, too—you couldn't tell them apart by touch in the dark, like you can with modern keys.

The keys came in handy once, though. Some smart aleck in a '61 Impala parked behind me, blocking me in a parking space. My tailgate key fit his doors and my glovebox key fit his ignition. I drove his car about half a block, parked it by a fireplug and locked it up.

CHARLEY ECKHARDT
Seguin, Texas

In When Do Fish Sleep?, *we wrote about an accountant named Walter Diemer who invented bubble gum. But we erred in calling him an entrepreneur. A relative of Mr. Diemer's wrote to clarify:*

Mr. Diemer, who is 85 and lives in Lancaster, was a cost accountant with the Fleer Corporation. The company was attempting to develop its own base for making gum, and the lab was right near his office. He discovered that some of the rubber base mixes bubbled when chewed and set about systematically varying ingredients until he came up with one that chewed well and bubbled consistently. He had no knowledge of either chemistry or food. His finding was serendipitous and the development of the finished product the result of a great deal of trial and error experimentation.

BRUCE C. WITTMAIER
Lancaster, Pennsylvania

In When Do Fish Sleep?, *we discussed why only older men seem to have hairy ears. We allowed a misstatement by a reader to pass without notice. Several readers wrote us with thoughts similar to the following letter:*

I must dispute the comment that color blindness and pattern baldness are traits of the Y chromosome. Actually, the opposite is true. The most common forms of color blindness (those affecting the green and red cones), the two most common forms of hemophilia, and pattern baldness are all traits of the X chromosome. Then why are these problems generally associated with men? Because women, who have two X chromosomes, have two chances of getting a good allele, while men have only one.

DAVID S. RALEY
Germantown, Maryland

758   WHY DO DOGS HAVE WET NOSES?

In Why Do Clocks Run Clockwise?, *we discussed why there "21 guns" in a 21-gun salute. Several readers were disturbed with the fact that we didn't make it clear that there are 21 SHOTS in the salute, not necessarily 21 separate guns. We couldn't resist sharing this story passed along by a reader about a supposed Commodore Joseph E. Fyfe, who commanded a cruiser squadron operating in the Mediterranean during the closing years of the nineteenth century:*

> Fyfe brought his ships into Gibraltar early one morning and delivered the salute required by current regulations. The gunner of the flagship goofed and a salute of twenty-*two* guns was sounded.
>
> When reproached by the Brits for this gaffe, the Commodore replied that he had ordered 21 guns for Queen Victoria and one gun for Mrs. Joseph E. Fyfe.
>
> JOHN H. KAUFMAN
> *Coronado, California*

Although several doctors and several medical textbooks we consulted confirmed that those half-moons (lunulae) on our fingernails are white because of trapped air, we are ready to bow to the many doctors who wrote to us to disagree:

> . . . The lunula is the outermost, and therefore only visible, portion of the nail matrix. The rest of the matrix lies hidden beneath the proximal nail fold (the fold of tissue that ends in the cuticle).
>
> The function of the lunula, and the rest of the matrix, is well known: The matrix is what produces the nail plate (the nail itself). This is why the lunula never moves. New nail is continually formed, and continually pushed forward, away from the matrix.
>
> DIRK M. ELSTON, M.D.
> *Newport News, Virginia*

But why are lunulae white?

> The lunulae of nails are not white because of trapped air. The lunulae are white because the matrices of the nails lie beneath them—a different tissue from the nail beds.
>
> The nail beds distal to the lunulae look pink because capillaries with blood in them immediately underlie the nail plate. The lunulae look white because the thin, modified epidermis of the

nail bed is three or four times thicker there, being the busy factory where nail plate is manufactured. The lunula is avascular [without blood vessels], so it looks white.

HARRY L. ARNOLD, JR., M.D.

Although we received our information about the naming of Oreo cookies from several sources at Nabisco, a few readers took us to task for our explanation. We made a one-letter mistake in our spelling that might be crucial:

... The Greek word for "mountain" is *not* "*oreo,*" but "*oro.*" It makes me doubt that the cookies we know today had ever been shaped like mountains, or else they would be called *Oro* cookies.

I have a Greek friend who has always insisted that the cookies must have been named by a Greek man, because the word *oreo* is, in fact, a word in modern Greek. *Oreo* means "nice," or "pleasant," even "appetizing."

Seeing this familiar word on a cookie box is what originally prompted my friend to buy Oreos when he first came to America ...

KATHERINE CALDWELL
Crosswicks, New Jersey

Reader Richard Sassaman of Bar Harbor, Maine, was kind enough to send us a review of a book we had already read: The Pencil: A History of Design and Circumstance, *written by Henry Petroski. Petroski attributes the omnipresence of yellow pencils to the mid-nineteenth century, when pencil makers faced a shortage of graphite. A German company, A. W. Faber, found a new and exclusive source of superb graphite in Siberia, near the Chinese border. Faber's competitors, without access to Faber's stash, colored their pencils yellow to hint at the oriental association that only Faber actually enjoyed.*

In When Do Fish Sleep?, *we discussed why telephone cords seem to twist up spontaneously. One reader has a simple theory that makes sense to us:*

Right-handed people answer the phone by picking it up with their right hand [not us, but we won't protest too vigorously].

Typically, about thirty seconds to a minute into the conversation, though, they transfer the phone to their left ear in order to free their right hand to do other things, such as taking notes. When they put the phone down, presto! Exactly one twist has been added to the phone cord. This adds up rather quickly.

GEOFFREY A. LANDIS
Brook Park, Ohio

In our discussion of why the sound of running water in pipes changes as it gets hot (in Why Do Clocks Run Clockwise?*), we quoted a plumbing official who said that one of the reasons the phenomenon exists is "because of additional air in the hot water formed when the molecules expand during the heating process." Our source had it wrong. One of the many letters to correct this point came from a chemist at Purdue University:*

Nothing could be further from the truth. Molecules do not expand like Ballpark Franks. The explanation of the additional air in the hot water has its origin in the solubility of air itself in water. The solubility of air in water varies with the temperature of the water and the pressure of the gas above the water.

Therefore, as the temperature of the water increases, the solubility of the air in the water becomes lower. This would cause the air to come out of solution as a gas, hence the additional air in the hot water.

MARCY HAMBY
West Lafayette, Indiana

We discussed why women wear such uncomfortable shoes, especially high heels, in Imponderables. *We stressed highfalutin Freudian interpretations, but many women saw it as more of a feminist issue. We received a dissertation on the subject, part of which is found below:*

In heels, a woman stands with her weight centered on the balls of her feet. This throws forward the postural axis that normally runs down through the (anatomical) heels. In order to still stand straight, she must unconsciously make several muscular changes, which in concert tend to pull in her stomach, thrust out her behind, and tighten and emphasize her calves.

"What's wrong with that?" you ask malely. Not much, except

AND OTHER IMPONDERABLES 761

for the slight, continual, unnatural exertion required just to stand straight. The woman is not perfectly relaxed standing still, which has a subliminally inhibiting effect. She has few options for shifting her weight unobtrusively if she must stand for a long time (try it!), so she stands *still*. It's tiring, so she wants to sit down . . .

Now, walking in high heels. . . . The shoe heels hold up her feet's heel, but because her weight is pushed forward, she cannot rest it on her feet's heels as she walks. The effect is to shorten her stride and to bring her feet closer together with her toes nearly touching the imaginary line one might draw along between her footprints; to keep her balance she must exaggerate the transfer of weight from side to side. If she is still keeping her shoulders back and head up, she must swing her hips side to side; if she ignores her upper body, she's more likely either to lurch and fall forward or to buckle at the ankles and fall sideways . . .

LINDA DUPLANTIS
Bloomington, Indiana

So what does the "high-heel walk" mean? Linda Duplantis thinks the heels were meant to inhibit the movement of the women who wear them. If nothing else, most women prefer sitting down to hobbling on heels. A similar conclusion was echoed by another reader:

It is the preference of the heterosexual male for the high-heeled woman and her shapely legs and distinctive walk, and not necessarily a woman's vanity, that has caused the uncomfortable shoe to continue to flourish. Note the company policy within some corporations that all of its women executives are required to wear high heels. That isn't women's vanity; that's male ego and the desire to continue his sexual fantasies.

. . . Having a spinal disorder that requires that I wear flat shoes, it is interesting to note the cultural biases of men, women, the clothing industry, and employers to flat shoes. My personal observation, at 50+ years of age, is that there will never be sexual equality as long as women continue to wear high-heeled shoes. They probably will continue wearing them as long as men consider them attractive on a woman.

LINDA KIRKHAM WALTON
San Jose, California

High heels weren't the only footwear you had on your mind. There are two Imponderables from Why Do Clocks Run Clockwise? *that just won't go away: Why do some ranchers hang old boots on fenceposts? And why do you so often find one shoe lying on the side of the road? Most of you who wrote about the boots repeated points made in our* When Do Fish Sleep? *Frustables Update, particularly the argument that the boots are there to prevent water rot. But we received several letters, mostly from Colorado and Wyoming, with another point:*

> I grew up on a ranch in the mountains of Colorado, and old boots were (and probably still are) hung on fenceposts. It was a tradition to hang the boots there when a new pair was purchased so that another ranchhand who might have been down on his luck, or for any reason had a worse pair of boots, could try them on. If they preferred your old boots, they could keep them or hang them back on the fence for someone else to try.
>
> Eventually someone would get sick of seeing the boots up there and take them down or tell one of the kids (usually me) to throw them away.

MITCHELL DAVIS
Springfield, Virginia

But not all our readers' stories about boots on fenceposts were quite so heartwarming:

> I once lived on a small farm with several friends. One day an unknown person placed a single old boot on our pasture fence. We took a liking to it and continued the practice, using the ubiquitous single shoes we would find along the road. Before too long, the entire length of pasture fence had a shoe on every post.
>
> It had been a few years since I moved, but upon returning for a visit I learned of some new developments. One night *all* the shoes mysteriously disappeared. A neighbor, noticing the absence, approached the house. Upon seeing my former roommates' dog—the recent recipient of a "punk" haircut—the neighbors decided it was all part of some kind of satanic ritual, and called the police.

BILL COOK
Oakville, California

Unfortunately, the police never seemed to catch the felons. The correspondence about the "one shoe" syndrome veers toward the bizarre. One reader spotted the article in the syndicated column "News of the Weird," about a business professor at a college in Dubuque, Iowa,

> ... who stole shoes from students at universities in two states over a five-year period by snatching them in libraries when students left their tables for short breaks. . . .

The professor claimed he donated the pilfered shoes to the homeless, but police found 80 pairs of shoes in his apartment.

> ... An apparently unrelated rash of shoe thefts (one shoe at a time) occurred in the Boston Public Library earlier last year.
>
> Mrs. Louise Russell
> *Chicago, Illinois*

And another reader can give a personal testimonial to the one-shoe theft epidemic that threatens the stability of the world as we know it:

> I used to work for Gold Circle, a discount store similar to K-Mart. I was a "price change associate." My job was to change price tags in all departments. Part of my job was daily restraightening of the various store sections and assistance in quarterly and annual inventories.
>
> During the two quarterly inventories and one annual inventory in which I participated, I found over 300 "pairs" (of various sizes and styles) missing the right or the left shoe. I questioned the department manager and store manager. They said, and had documented police reports to prove it, that many people in the past, rich and poor alike, had entered the store and taken only the right or left shoe. In some cases, they threw down their old worn out shoe and just walked out of the store.
>
> Since manufacturers will only sell pairs to a retail outlet and styles change so rapidly, the Gold Circle chain was stuck with an unusable stock item on the books. Each store was told to purge

unusable stocks (i.e., throw in the trash) to make room for good stock and take a tax write-off . . .

JOSEPH A. RAUBAR
Amherst, New York

One daring gentleman tried to synthesize the two Impondera-bles that REFUSE TO DIE:

I can solve both Imponderables. The shoes lying by the side of roads fell off fenceposts! Or someone found a shoe on the side of the road and put it on a fencepost!

GREGORY REIS
Torrance, California

Our favorite letter of the last year proved to be a humbling one. It's bad enough to occasionally write a passage that other people can't understand. But what about when a reader asks a question about what we've written that proves that WE don't understand our own writing?:

I have read your book *When Do Fish Sleep?* to my children. On page 210 in the section on right- or left-hand driving, there is a puzzling sentence: "These pedestals [that once helped riders mount horses on public roadways] were found only on the left side of the road."

One of my sons asked which was the left side of a north-south road? The east or the west? The two boys hootingly averred that any fool knew it was east.

As a former air navigator, I was asked to arbitrate. I urged the children to think it over analytically and bring me the results. I then applied ointment, bandages, and one tourniquet to the results.

Please publish an answer soon. I'm running out of splints.

SAM E. STUBBS
Brampton, Ontario

Well, Mr. Stubbs, after reading your letter, we weren't feeling so well ourselves. But we felt much better after speaking to Richard Hopper, our main source for the answer to this Frust-able. We did know one fact about the pedestals on roadways:

They were located adjacent to curbs but abutted houses (and buildings) and were used primarily by the occupants of those houses (and buildings).

According to Hopper, when a horse was led out to be mounted, the horse was already facing "left" so that it could be properly mounted from the left (nobody with any sense wants to mount a horse so that one's legs kick over the horse's head in the process). As we said in When Do Fish Sleep?, Hopper has found much evidence that both pedestrian and horse traffic had traditionally kept to the left anyway, so that the right hand could be used to wave a hand in friendly greeting or a knife in less friendly situations.

So the answer to Mr. Stubbs' children's question (Which was the left side of a north-south road?) is: It depends on which direction the horse is going. If the horse is heading north, then the left side is west; if the horse is heading south, the left side is east.

Mr. Stubbs, you may now remove your splints.

Acknowledgments

It's thank-you time again. And once again, my first and most important thanks go to you, the readers. Not just for buying the books but for sharing your Imponderables, your criticisms, your answers to the Frustables, and your words of encouragement. The only way I have of gauging what you like and don't like about the *Imponderables* books is by reading your letters. Your correspondence make my work worthwhile.

Harper & Row may have just transformed itself into HarperCollins but luckily almost all of the people who have supported me in the past are still around for me to thank. Rick Kot may now be a senior editor, but he will always be younger than me. I also hope he will always be my editor. Rick's terrific and helpful assistant, Scott Terranella, has now ascended into the dizzyingly exciting field of publicity. Now, Sheila Gillooly is charmingly and ably doing her best to make my life easier. Debra Elfenbein is a lively and talented production editor; but then again, if I said something negative about her, she'd probably red-pencil the offending item.

Everyone at HarperCollins has been terrific to me, and I would say this even if it didn't score brownie points. Bill Shinker understood the concept of *Imponderables* at the outset and has been enthusiastic and supportive ever since. Brenda Marsh, Zeb Burgess, Pat Jonas, and all the HC sales reps have done a tremendous job; most people who love books don't know how to sell them. These folks do, and with grace and good humor. Steve Magnuson, Robert Jones, and the marketing staff ingeniously strategize about how to foist my books upon an innocent public.

Speaking of foisting upon an innocent public, that is the full-time job of the publicity department. It takes a special person to peddle the tomes of authors with bloated egos to jaded radio and

TV producers. Everyone in the department has been wonderful. Karen Mender leads these special (demented?) types with humor and skill. Thanks to Craig Herman, who is the guy stuck with foisting me.

Connie Levinson, Barbara Rittenhouse, and Mark Landau, of Special Markets, have been, at various times, valuable salespeople, helpers, advisers, psychotherapists, and friends. Thanks for your help. I'm grateful to the entire staff of Special Markets, especially Mary Clifford, for her unsolicited help.

I don't have to be too effusive about my agent, Jim Trupin, since the dedication of this book will probably humor him for a while. Oh, what the heck! He's great. But he'd better continue to treat me well, or I'll complain to his wonderful wife and partner, Elizabeth.

With every book, Kassie Schwan's cartoons get wittier and our collaboration more effortless. I promise to try to provide an Imponderable in every book that will enable you to draw a fish.

Mark Kohut and Susie Russenberger are not only good friends but mentors who have helped me navigate the treacherous waters of publishing.

I've been so busy working this year that I've neglected some friends and family, but they've been there for me. Thanks to all who have lent support: Tony Alessandrini; Michael Barson; Sherry Barson; Rajat Basu; Ruth Basu; Jeff Bayone; Jean Behrend; Brenda Berkman; Cathy Berkman; Sharon Bishop; Carri Blees; Christopher Blees; Jon Blees; everyone at Bowling Green State University's Popular Culture Department; Jerry Braithwaite; Annette Brown; Arvin Brown; Herman Brown; Joann Carney; Janice Carr; Lapt Chan; Mike Chelst; Don Cline; Alvin Cooperman; Marilyn Cooperman; Judith Dahlman; Paul Dahlman; Shelly de Satnick; Charlie Doherty; Laurel Doherty; Joyce Ebert; Pam Elam; Andrew Elliott; Steve Feinberg; Fred Feldman; Gilda Feldman; Michael Feldman; Phil Feldman; Ron Felton; Phyllis Fineman; Kris Fister; Linda Frank; Seth Freeman; Elizabeth Frenchman; Michele Gallery; Chris Geist; Jean Geist; Bonnie Gellas; Richard Gertner; Amy Glass; Bea Gordon;

Dan Gordon; Ken Gordon; Judy Goulding; Chris Graves; Adam Henner; Christal Henner; Lorin Henner; Marilu Henner; Melodie Henner; David Hennes; Paula Hennes; Sheila Hennes; Sophie Hennes; Larry Herold; Carl Hess; Mitchell Hofing; Steve Hofman; Bill Hohauser; Uday Ivatury; Terry Johnson; Sara Jones; Allen Kahn; Mitch Kahn; Joel Kaplan; Dimi Karras; Maria Katinos; Stewart Kellerman; Harvey Kleinman; Mark Kohut; Claire Labine; Randy Ladenheim-Gil; Debbie Leitner; Vicky Levy; Jared Lilienstein; David Lynch; Patti Magee; Jack Mahoney; everyone at the Manhattan Bridge Club; Phil Martin; Chris McCann; Jeff McQuain; Julie Mears; Phil Mears; Carol Miller; Barbara Morrow; Phil Neel; Steve Nellisen; Millie North; Milt North; Charlie Nurse; Debbie Nye; Tom O'Brien; Pat O'Conner; Joanna Parker; Jeannie Perkins; Merrill Perlman; Joan Pirkle; Larry Prussin; Joe Rawley; Rose Reiter; Brian Rose; Lorraine Rose; Paul Rosenbaum; Carol Rostad; Tim Rostad; Susie Russenberger; Leslie Rugg; Tom Rugg; Gary Saunders; Joan Saunders; Mike Saunders; Norm Saunders; Laura Schisgal; Cindy Shaha; Patricia Sheinwold; Kathy Smith; Kurtwood Smith; Susan Sherman Smith; Chris Soule; Kitty Srednicki; Karen Stoddard; Bill Stranger; Kat Stranger; Anne Swanson; Ed Swanson; Mike Szala; Jim Teuscher; Josephine Teuscher; Laura Tolkow; Carol Vellucci; Dan Vellucci; Hattie Washington; Julie Waxman; Ron Weinstock; Roy Welland; Dennis Whelan; Devin Whelan; Heide Whelan; Lara Whelan; Jon White; Ann Whitney; Carol Williams; Maggie Wittenburg; Karen Wooldridge; Maureen Wylie; Charlotte Zdrok; Vladimir Zdrok; and Debbie Zuckerberg.

We contacted about 1,500 corporations, educational institutions, foundations, trade associations, and miscellaneous experts to find the answers to Imponderables that books couldn't answer. We are delighted to say that most sources are becoming more open about sharing information on the record. Although many other people supplied help, all those listed below gave us information that led directly to the solution of the Imponderables in this book. Heartfelt thanks to all: Beth Adams, H. J.

Heinz Company; Dr. Don Adams, Iowa State University; John H. Addington, Fire Equipment Manufacturers Association; John Adinolfi, National Coffee Association; Alamo Rent-A-Car; Stuart Alexander, Deluxe Check Printers; Robert C. Allen, University of South Florida; American Dental Association; Curt Anderson, Sunkist; Jeff Atkinson, Avis.

Rich Barongi, San Diego Zoo; Jaclyn Barrett, *Southern Bride;* J. W. Batchelder; Tara Baugher, West Virginia University; Prof. Donald Beaty, College of San Mateo; Gene Beaudet, *Metalworking News;* Brenda Berkman, New York City Fire Department; Peter Bishop, Ampad; Harold Blake; Jeanette Blum, Public Relations Society of America; Boeing Company; Ray Bombardieri, Southwestern Bell Telephone; Charles A. Bookman, Marine Board; Dr. Albert F. Borges; G. J. Bozant, Fire-End & Croker Corporation; Larry J. Bramlett, National Office Products Association; John D. Brock, Southern Diazo Equipment Company; Ed Bronikowski, National Zoological Park; Richard M. Brooks, Stouffer Hotels; Fred Burgerhoff; Kurt Burghardt, Neodata Services; Dick Burnon, Hertz Corporation; Dr. Kenneth H. Burrell, American Dental Association; Debra Burrell, New York School of Astrology.

Pat Campbell, Bulova Watch Company; Candle Works; Thomas J. Carr, Motor Vehicle Manufacturers Association; Gerry Carr, International Game Fish Association; Bob Carroll, Pro Football Researchers Association; David Cerull, Fire Collectors Club; Joyce Christie, Institute of Public Utilities; Mimi Clark, Pilot Corporation of America; Catherine A. Clay, Florida Department of Citrus; S. Scott Coe, *Sail;* Ernest Collins, United States Postal System; Prof. Richard Colwell, Council for Research in Music Education; Phyl R. Condon, National Football Foundation and Hall of Fame; Mark T. Conroy, National Fire Protective Association; Philip S. Cooke, Inflight Food Service Association; John Corbett, Clairol; Jim Cowen, Roxide International; Richard Cunard, Transportation Research Board.

Dr. Michael D'Asaro; Jim Datka, American Standard; D. Datello, Sharp Electronics; Dr. Frank Davidoff, American College of Physicians; William F. Deal, International Bottled Water Association; Steve Del Priore, Pepsi-Cola Bottling Company of New York; Dr. Dieter Dellman, Iowa State University; Michael DeMent, Hallmark Cards; Nora DiPalma, American Standard; Sara Dornacker, United Airlines; Art Douglas, Lowell Corporation; Leslie D. Downs, Cosmetic, Toiletry and Fragrance Association; Lowell Drutman, Timex Corporation; M. J. Duberstein, NFL Players Association; Thomas Dufficy, National Association of Photographic Manufacturers; Barbara Dwyer, USDA.

Carole L. Edwards, Mobil Oil Corporation; Linda Eggers, Maytag Company; Kay Engelhardt, American Egg Board; Dr. J. Worth Estes, American Association for the History of Medicine; Dr. Howard Evans, Cornell University.

Bill Fabricino, BRK Electronics; Dr. Fred Feldman; Gary Felsinger, Kohler Company; Peter C. Fetterer, Kohler Company; Mike Fisher, Besam Inc.; George Flower; Sam Folsom, Wine Institute; Robert Fontana, TDK Electronics Corporation; James B. Ford; Don French, Radio Shack; Henry Fried.

John A. Gable, Theodore Roosevelt Association; Dr. James Q. Gant, International Lunar Society; Stan S. Garber, Selmer Company; R. Bruce Gebhardt, North American Native Fishes Association; Mark Gerberich, Pro Bowlers Association of America; Glenn Gibson, American Honey Producers Association; Shelly Gilbreath, Southwestern Bell Telephone; Martin Gitten, Consolidated Edison; Anne Glasgow, National Society of Professional Surveyors; Dick Glass, Professional Electronics Technicians Association; William Goffi, *Advertising;* Capt. James E. Grabb, American Society of Naval Engineers; Capt. G. L. Graveson, Naval Submarine League; Barbara Green, Greater New York Hospital Association; Cory Greenspan, Federation of Apparel Manufacturers; Jacqueline Greenwood, Black & Decker; Steve Gregg, Coffee Development Group; Phyllis Grotell, Wool Bureau.

Dr. Robert Habel, Cornell University; Dr. John Hallett, Desert Research Institute, Atmospheric Ice Laboratory; Joseph Hanson, *Folio;* John Harrington, Council for Periodical Distributors; Sylvia Hauser, *Dog World;* David J. Hensing, American Association of State Highway and Transportation Officials; Sanford Hill, American Orthopedic Society for Sports Medicine; Sol Hirsch, National Weather Association; Dick Hofacker, AT&T Bell Laboratories; Jim Hutchison, American Paper Institute.

Embassy of Italy; Barbara Mader Ivey, Women on Wine.

M. Claire Jackson, Coca-Cola; Bill Johnson, California Canning Peach Association; Alvin H. Johnson, American Musicological Society; Robert M. Johnston, Sterling Silversmiths Guild of America; Chris Jones, Pepsi-Cola; Pat Jones, American Association of Port Authorities; Larry Josefowicz, Wilson Sporting Goods Company.

Thomas J. Kallay, Edison Electric Institute; Jeff Kanipe, *Astronomy;* Phil Katz, Beer Institute; Kerry Keller, Center for Christian Studies; William Kemp, Duncan Industries; Debbi Kempton-Smith; Rose Marie Kenny, Hammermill Papers; Hugh Kent, Jr., Internal Revenue Service; Dr. Charles Kesner, Northwest Michigan Horticulture Station; Dr. Ke Chung Kim, Frost Entomological Center, Pennsylvania State University; Dr. Ben Klein; Kevin Knopf, Office of Tax Policy, Department of Treasury; Joan Koenig, Office of Weights and Measures, National Bureau of Standards; Milo Kovar, Astro-Psychology Institute; Thomas P. Krugman, California Cling Peach Advisory Board.

Langenberg Hat Company; John T. Leadmon, Department of the Navy; Dick Levinson, H. Y. Aids Group; Joseph M. Lichtenberg, National Pasta Association; John Loftus, Society of Collision Repair Specialists.

Bridget A. MacConnell, Yuban Coffee; Alan MacRobert, *Sky & Telescope;* Keith Markland, Internal Revenue Service; Serena Marks, United Parcel System; Melanie Martini, *Bride's;* Rudolf H. T. Mattoni, Lepidoptera Research Foundation; James P. McCauley, International Association of Holiday Inns; Karen E. McAliley, United States Postal System; Dr. John R. McCarroll, Methodist Sports Medicine Center; Dennis McClendon, American Planning Association; Frank McDonough, Amerex Corporation; Jody L. Messersmith, Forster Manufacturing; Sally Miller, Procter & Gamble; Dr. Stephen Miller, American Optometric Association; Mr. Coffee; Dr. William E. Monroe, American College of Veterinary Internal Medicine; Sarah Moore, Hills Brothers Coffee, Inc.; Patrick Murphy, *TV Guide*.

John Nasiatka, Duo Fast Corporation; Neckwear Association of America; Embassy of New Zealand; Dr. Richard Nowogrodzki, Cornell University.

Dr. Joe Ogawa, University of California, Davis.

Brad Patterson, Racquetball Manufacturers Association; Neil Patton, Internal Revenue Service; Chuck Pezzano; Robin Pierce, Citizen/CBM America; John A. Pitcher, Hardwood Research Council; Ellen Powley, International Horn Society; Project ELF, Association of Records Managers and Administrators; Roy S. Pung, Photo Marketing Association, International.

Dr. George W. Rambo, National Pest Control Association; Jean C. Raney, American Wool Council; Dr. R. Reed, Redmore Products; Robert M. Reeves, Institute of Shortenings and Edible Oils; Miles Roberts, National Zoological Park; Robot Industries; Dr. Robert R. Rofen, Aquatic Research Institute; Carol Rostad; Prof. Neal Rowell, University of South Alabama; Leslie Rugg; Tom Rugg.

Angela Santoro, *Wall Street Journal;* William Schanen III, *Sailing;* Ronald A. Schuler, California Canning Peach Association; Phyllis Schweers, Thrifty Rent-A-Car System; Norman F. Sharp, Cigar Association of America; Sheaffer Pen; Linda D. Shepler, Sunkist; Rexford B. Sherman, American Association of Port Authorities; Bill Sherrard, Long Island Lighting Co.; Jan Shulman, American Hospital Association; Wayne Smith, Sunbeam Appliance Company; Sid Smith, National Association of Hosiery Manufacturers; Ray Sowers, Tubelite-Indal; Bill Spaniel, Lockheed Aeronautical Systems Company; Margie Spurlock, Royal Crown Cola Company; Dennis W. Staggs, POM Inc.; Bill Stanley; Amy Steiner, American Association of State Highway and Traffic Officials; Dr. Al Stinson, Michigan State University;

John J. Suarez, National Pest Control Association; Amy Sudol, Chase Manhattan; Peggy Sullivan, Music Educators National Conference.

Farook Taufiq, Prince Company; David Taylor, Bank Administration Institute; Dr. Kristin Thelander, University of Iowa; Susan Thompson, A. T. Cross; Susan Tildesley, Headware Institute of America; Randy Troxell, Allied Specialty Company; Catherine Turner, United States Postal System.

Pamela Van Hine, American College of Obstetrics and Gynecology; L. Van Munching, Jr., Heineken; H. T. Vande Kerkhoff, United States Submarine Veterans of World War II; Ralph E. Venk, Photographic Society of America; Roberta Vesley, American Kennel Club.

Dana Walker, Ampad; Mark Weber, Phillips Van Heusen Corporation; Clay Weeks, University of California, Davis; S. C. White, National Hardwood Lumber Association; William O. Whitt, Association of Edison Illuminating Companies; David Williams; Dr. Elizabeth Williams, Wyoming State Veterinary Laboratory; John Williams, California Apple Products Inc.; Richard Williams; Dr. Jack Wilmore, University of Texas; William D. Winter, Jr., Lepidopterists' Society; Eleanor Wulff, International Guild of Candle Artisans.

Wayne Young, Marine Board.

Dr. Richard S. Zack, Washington State University; Dr. E. Zander, Winthrop Consumer Products; and Mike Zazanas, Professional Audio Retailers Association.

And to sources who preferred to remain anonymous, thank you for your help.

Parting Notes

We get the following questions so often in our mail, we thought we'd include our answers to help you understand how *Imponderables* works:

WHY *Didn't You Print My Imponderable in the Last Book?*

Could be a lot of reasons. The biggest mistake most people make is sending in questions that have already been discussed in other books or magazines. If we already know the answer, it isn't an Imponderable anymore. Also, a good Imponderable should be a mystery of *everyday* life, not a theoretical problem, a trivia question, or a query that could be answered by a trip to the dictionary: We're more interested in "why" questions than "who," "what," or "where" questions. And just because you don't see your Imponderable answered in the last book doesn't mean it won't be in the next book.

CAN *I Send in More than One Imponderable at a Time?*

Absolutely. As many as you want. We've received letters with several hundred Imponderables!

DO *You Personally Read Every Letter You Receive?*

Every word.

DO *You Respond Personally to Every Letter?*

Yes, if a self-addressed stamped envelope is enclosed. But depending upon deadline pressures, it might take longer than we'd like. If you don't want or need a personal reply, save the money and send a postcard or a letter without a SASE.

I *Just Bought a Copy of* Why Do Clocks Run Clockwise? *Is It Too Late to Send a Response to the Frustables?*

Probably. We answer the Frustables of one book in the next edition. But if you have something to add to our answers, we always seek corrections and additions. As a rule of thumb, if it is three years or more since the copyright date of the book you are reading, it's too late to send in your answers.

WHAT'S *The Best Time to Send in Imponderables?*

Anytime. We collect Imponderables on a continuing basis. Even if you send in a question after we've stopped researching a current book, we'll save it for the next one.

AFTER *the Name of the Person Who Submitted an Imponderable, It Sometimes Says "Thanks also to" — What Does That Mean?*

It means that the people listed sent in the same or a similar Imponderable after the person who received the "submitted by" credit.

WHO *Is Reponsible for Imponderables That Aren't Credited To Anyone?*

Unattributed Imponderables are usually our ideas, but they also come from anonymous callers on radio talk shows.

WHY *Don't You Group the Imponderables Together by Subject?*

We didn't want to give *Imponderables* the feel of reference books, even if that's the section where they are usually placed in bookstores. We want you to read the book not knowing what to expect next. But if readers feel strongly about this. we'd like to know.

HOW *Can We Make Your Life Easier?*

O.K., we'll admit it. Nobody has ever asked us this question. But may we make one request? Please don't send us money in the mail. We are not equipped to sell books by mail order, and we don't want you to be disappointed if we can't process an order quickly. Most bookstores will special-order books upon request.

Index

Cameras, black color of, 447
Candies, shapes of chocolate, 24–25
Candles, 714–715
   relighting, 708
Canned nectarines, 591–592
Capital punishment, hours of
   executions and, 34–36
Captain, Navy and Army rank of,
   310–312
Cars, *see* Automobiles
Carton staples, 622–623
Cartoon characters
   Donald Duck, 412
   Goofy, 326–327
   Mickey Mouse, 294
Cash register tapes, 675
Cattle guards, effectiveness of, 377
Cemeteries
   financal strategies of owners
      of, 95–99
   perpetual care and, 221–222
Chalk, outlines of murder victims
   in, 273–274
Champagne bottles, 692–693
Channel 1 Television, 656
Check numbers, 570–571
Cheese
   cheddar, orange color of, 289–290
   string, 417
Chef's hat, purpose of, 328–329
Chickens, white and dark meat of,
   315–316
Children, taste in meat, 749
Chocolate
   Easter bunnies, 116
   milk, consistency of, 384–385
   shapes of, 24–25
Chopsticks, 544–545
Cigar bands, 586–587
Cigarettes, first puff of, 485–488
Cigarettes, odor of, 38
Cigars, new fathers and, 283–284
Civil War, commemoration of,
   430–431

Climate, 705706
   and basements, 630
Clocks, 609–610
   counterclockwise, 757
   "grandfather," 710
   hand movements, 150
   numerals, 151–152
Clouds
   location of, 275
   rain and, 152
Coastal climate, 705–706
Coca-Cola, containers for, 157–159
Coffee, 567
   in airplane lavatories, 596–597
   13-ounce bags, 678
Coin sound in pay phones, 629–630
Colds
   body aches and, 366–367
   clogged nostrils and, 282–283
   liquids during, 662–664
   symptoms at night of, 425
Cold water, 683–684
   coffee made from, 705
Color
   of blood, 670
   of blueprints, 634–635
   of cash register tapes, 675
   of gondolas, 618–619
   of pencils, 760
   of plastic bottle bottoms, 720
   of racquetballs, 540–541
   of side lights, 684–685
   of sock toes, 551–552
   wetness and, 671
Commercials, television, loudness
   of, 343–345
Communication Data Services, 566
Concentration, tongues stuck out,
   747–748
Condition of hospital patients,
   607–608
Construction sites, pine trees and,
   147–148
Consumer Price Index, 159–161

Copper staples, 622–623
Copyright pages, strange numbers
     on, 175–176
Coriolis effect, 656–657
Corn silk, purpose of, 382
Cottage cheese, 321
Cotton in medicine bottles, 351–352
Cough medicine, alcohol in, 428
Countdown leader, film and, 9
Courtrooms, Bibles in, 301–303
Cows
     calves and, 281–282
     milking positions and, 128–129
Cracks on sidewalks, 437–440
Credit card slips, 129–130
Crickets, chapped legs and, 309–310
Crowing of roosters, 265
Curad bandages, wrappers of, 58
Currency, color of, 345–346
Customized magazine editions,
     546–547
Cuts, paper, pain and, 103–104

Dalmatians, firehouses and, 162–163
Dangerous Curve signs, placement
     of, 119–120
Dates for zodiac signs, 559–560
DC, AC and, 21–22
"Dead end" signs, 625
Dehydration from colds, 662–663
Delaware, incorporations in, 153–157
Dentist offices, smell of, 41
Deodorant aerosols, shaking of, 440
Deodorizers, coffee bags as, 596–597
Diazo process, 635
Dimples,
     facial, 285
     on golf balls, 307308
Discoloration of fruit, 703
Doctors, back tapping of, 407–408
Dogs
     black lips of, 300–301
     body odor in, 40
     circling of, 2–3

Dogs (*continued*)
     in cars, 592–593
     laryngitis in, 53–54
     listening, 730
     urination of, 567–568
     wet noses, 602–603
Donald Duck, 412
Doors
     opening direction, 699
     revolving, 703–705
     to saloons, 741–743
Double-yolk eggs, 450–451
Doughnuts
     handling in stores, 164
     origins of holes in, 62–64
Downhill ski poles, shape of, 331
Drain, spiraling of water from,
     656–657
Drains, location of bathtub, 421–422
Dreams, nap versus nighttime, 386
Dress shirts, new, pins in, 561–562
Drip coffee, 567, 705
Dripless candles, 714–715
Driveways, 655
Driving, left- and right-hand side of
     the road, 238, 471–474
Dry cleaning
     French, 426–427
     garment labels and, 59–60
     One Hour Martinizing, 290–291
     raincoats and, 216–217
Dyes, regulation of, 695

E
     on eye charts, 271–272
     as school grade, 460, 738–741
Ears
     of dogs, 592–593
     hairy, 239, 493–495
     popping in airplanes, 130–132
     ringing, causes of, 115–116
Earthworms as fish food, 372–374
Easter, chocolate bunnies and, 116
Easter, date of, 587–588

Hat tricks, hockey, 165–166
Height restrictions, fences and, 2830
Height, voice pitch and, 70
High bias audio tape, 685–686
High-heeled shoes, 761–762
Highways
    numbering systems, 598–599
    shoes found on, 236–237
    traffic flow, 697–698
    weigh stations, 725–726
Hills, mountains versus, 359–360
Hockey
    hat trick in, 165–166
    Wayne Gretzky uniform in, 18
Holes
    in fly swatters, 563564
    in pasta, 560
    in pen barrels, 643
    stamp perforations, 711
Holidays
    Easter, 587–588
    Halloween, 712–713
    Thanksgiving, 672–673
"Holland," versus "Netherlands,"
    use of, 65–66
Honey, 709–710
Honey-roasted peanuts, on airplanes,
    545–546
Horses
    mounting of, 765–766
    posture in fields, 366
    shoes, 418
    sleeping posture of, 212
Hospitals, condition of patients,
    607–608
Hot dog buns, number of, 232–235
Hot water, noise in pipes of,
    199–200
Hotels
    plastic circles on walls of, 379
    toilet paper folding in
        bathrooms, 266
    towels in, 588–589
Humidity, and static electricity,
    637–638

Hurricane, trees and, 330–331
Hypothalamus, and body temperature,
    636

Ice cubes, cloudy versus clear,
    368–369
Icy roads, use of sand and salt on,
    12–13
Imperial measures, British, 646–647
Imponderables, criteria for, 654–655
"Inflammable," versus
    "flammable," use of, 207–208
Inheritance patterns, 758
Insects, in home, 621–622
Insufficient postage, 681–683
Internal Revenue Service, tax form
    numbers, 541–542
Interstate highway numbers, 598–599
Inventor of bubble gum, 758
Iodide in salt, 631
Irons, permanent press settings on,
    448–449
Ironworkers' hard hats, 626
Irritating questions, 654–660
Ivory soap, purity of, 46–47

"J" Street, Washington D.C. and, 71
"Jack," "John" and, 43
Jack-o'-lanterns, 712–713
Jell-O, fruit in, 411–412
Jet lag, birds and, 295–296
"Jetsam," versus "flotsam," use of,
    60–61
Juicy Fruit gum, flavors in, 504

Kangaroo pouches, 676–677
Ketchup
    bottles of, 44–45
    restaurants mating of, 462,
        750–753
Keys
    automobile, 403–404, 757–758
    to cities, 361

Peanuts served by airlines, 545–546
Pencils
    color of, 370, 760
    numbering of, 371
Pennies, vending machines and,
        316–318
Pennsylvania Department of
        Agriculture registration, 121–122
Pens
    hole in barrel, 643
    leaking, 644–645
    missing, 731
Pepper, white, source of, 135–136
Percolator coffee, 567
Periods in telegrams, 339–340
Permanent press settings on irons,
        448–449
Permanents, pregnancy and, 432–433
Perpetual care, cemeteries and,
        221–222
Phillips screwdriver, 206–207
Photographs
    red eyes in, 600–601
    in *Wall Street Journal*, 573–574
Physical exams, back tapping and,
        407–408
Pine nuts, shelling of, 94
Pine trees, construction sites and,
        147–148
Pineapple in gelatin, 411–412
Pinholes, bottle cap, 223
Pins in new dress shirts, 561–562
Planets, 582–583, 649–650
Plumbing
    sound of running water and,
        501–502
    under-sink pipes, 614–615
Poison ivy, grazing animals and,
        348–349
Police dogs, urination and
        defecation of, 329–330
Pop singers, accents of, 657–658
Popcorn, other corns versus, 404–405
Pork and beans, pork in, 19

Post Office, U. S.
    international rates, 537–538
    regulations, 681–683
    stickers on envelopes, 615–616
    translation of foreign mail and, 395
Postage stamp perforations, 711
Postage stamps, taste of, 182
Potato skins, 274–275
Potholes, causes of, 27
Power lines, orange balls on, 550–551
Pregnancy, permanents and, 432–433
Press conferences, microphones in,
        11–12
Priority mail, first class versus,
        428–429
Processing of black-and-white film,
        571
Pubic hair, purpose of, 146, 504–505
Public restroom toilets, 719
Punts, measurement of, 386–387

Quart measures, 646–647
Queen-size sheets, 349–350
Questions, irritating, 654–660

Racquetballs, color of, 540–541
Radio, unplugged, 579
Railroads, width of standard
        gauges of, 419–420
Rain
    butterflies in, 595–596
    measurements of, 693–694
Raincoats, dry-cleaning of,
        216–217
Raisins
    cereal boxes and, 123
    seeded grapes and, 218–219
Ranchers, hanging of boots on
        fence posts by, 505–507
Razor blades, hotel slots for, 113
Rear-view mirrors, 717–718
Recorder counters, 680–681
Red wine, serving temperature,
        628–629

Smell of wet wool, 690–691
Snack foods and prepricing, 341–342
Snakes, tongues of, 106
Sneezing
   and eye closure, 346–347
   looking up and, 238
Snow
   and cold weather, 300
   measurement of, 694
Soap
   colored, white suds from, 664
   Ivory, purity of, 46
Soccer, 612–613
Social security numbers, 353–354
Socks
   angle of, 376–377
   colored toes, 551–552
   lost, 659–660
Sodium in foods, 619–620
Soft drink bottles
   bottom color, 720
   filling of, 585
Soft drinks
   containers for, 157–159
   pinholes on bottle caps of, 223
   sodium in, 619–620
Sonic booms, 555
Sounds
   after radio is unplugged, 579
   of burning wood, 542–543
   of pay phones, 629–630
   of public toilets, 719
   sonic booms, 555
   telephone rings, 721–722
   telephone tones, 661–662
   water in pipes, 761
Sour cream, expiration date on, 394
Sourdough bread, San Francisco,
   180–181
Southern houses, basements in, 630
Soybean oil, 718
Spanish–American War, 581
Speed limit, 55 mph, 143
Speedometers, 144–145
Sporting events, whistling at, 749

Staining, paperback books and, 93–94
Stamp pads and moisture retention,
   286
Stamps, postage, taste of, 182
Staples, copper, 622–623
Starch on shirts, 380
Stars, twinkling, 582–583
State highway numbers, 599
Static electricity, 637–638
Stir frying, 544–545
Stock prices as quoted in eighths of
   a dollar, 374–375
Stocking runs
   direction of, 124–125
   effect of freezing upon, 125–126
Stomach, growling, 652–653
STOP in telegrams, 338–339
Stored product insects, 622
Stouffer Hotel towels, 589
String cheese, 417
Submarine anchors, 572–573
Subscriptions to magazines, 565–566
Suds, white, from colored soaps, 664
Sugar
   clumping together of, 365–366
   in salt, 631
   spoilage of, 85
Summer, first day of, 401–403
Supersonic aircraft, 555
Surgeon, color of uniforms of, 86
Swarming of gnats, 535–536
Swatting of flies, 563–564

Table manners, 736–738
Tall people, aging and, 491–493
Tasmania, 554
Taste, sense of, in children versus
   adults, 461
Tattoos, color of, 419
Tax form numbers, 541–542
Teachers, apples for, 238
Teflon, 3
Telegrams
   exclamation marks and, 338–339

Telegrams (*continued*)
    periods and, 339–340
Telephones
    busy signals, 714
    dialing 9 to get outside line,
        337–338
    holes in mouthpiece, 276–277
    public, coin sounds, 629–630
    sound of ring, 721–722
    Special Information Tones,
        661–662
    touch tone keypad for, 14–15
    twisted cords, 307, 760–761
Telescopes, inverted images of,
    312–313
Television Channel 1, 656
Television commercials, loudness
    of, 343–345
Television set measurements, 569
Temperature
    of babies, 635–636
    differences in, 716
    human comfort and, 178–179
    inversions, 688–689
    of water, 683–684
        for coffee, 705–706
    of wine, 627–628
Tennis balls and fuzz, 297–298
Tennis, scoring in, 3–5
Terminal dues system (postal
    rates), 537–538
Thanksgiving, 672–674
Three way light bulbs
    burnout of, 104
    functioning of, 105
Throat, uvula, purpose of, 391
Throwing, sex differences in, 304–306
Tickets, red carbons on airline,
    441–442
Tickle of self, 657
Timepieces, 609–610
Tinnitus, causes of, 115–116
Tires
    automobile tread, disposition of,
        72–74

Tires (*continued*)
    bicycle, 224–226
    white wall, 149
Tissue paper in wedding
    invitations, 648–649
Toasters, one-slice slot on, 445–447
Toenails, growth of, 385
Toes of socks, colored, 551–552
Toilet paper, folding over in hotel
    bathrooms, 266
Toilet seats in public restrooms,
    399–400
Toilets
    flush handles on, 195–196
    public, flushing of, 719
    seat covers for, 83
Tongues, sticking out of, 461,
    747–748
Toothpaste expiration date, 701–702
Toothpicks
    mint flavored, 685
    round versus flat, 499–500
Toques, purpose of, 328–329
Towels, smelly, 286
Traffic control
    55 mph speed limit and, 143
    traffic lights and, 126–127
Traffic flow, 697–698
Traffic noise, 730
Traffic signal light bulbs, 293–294
Traffic signs, placement of
    dangerous curve, 119–120
Traps under sinks, 614–615
Tread, disposition of worn, 72–74
Treasury, printing of new bills by,
    388–390
Triton, orbit of Neptune, 649–650
Trucks
    license plates on, 358
    origins of term "semi" and, 179
Tuning pitch for orchestras, 558–559
Tupperware and home parties,
    287–288
"Turkey" in bowling, 580–581

Turkeys
  beards on, 361
  white versus dark meat, 315–316
TV Guide, 623–624
20-20 vision, 405
21-gun salutes, 68–70, 759
Twinkling of stars, 582–583
Twist-off bottle caps, 577–578
Twitches during sleep, 67
"Two bits," origins of term, 191–192
Two by Fours, measurement of, 87–88

Underarm hair, human, 146
Underwear labels, 536–537
Uniforms, surgeons', 86
Unimponderables, 654–660
United States highway numbers,
  598–599
United States Postal Service
  international rates, 537–538
  regulations, 681–683
  stickers on envelopes, 615–616
University of South Florida, 539–540
Unscented hair spray, smell of, 184
UPS trucks, 605–606
Urination of dogs, 567–568
Uvula, purpose of, 391

Vaccination marks, hair growth
  and, 186
Valve stems on fire hydrants, 674–675
Vegetable oils, 718
Veins, blue, 670
Vending machines
  half dollars and, 318–319
  pennies and, 316–318
Venice, gondolas, 618–619
Videotape versus audio tape, 398–399
Violin bows, frogs of, 696–697
Virgin olive oil, 436–437
Vision, 20-20, 405
Voices
  causes of high and low, 70
  falsetto, 679–680

Volkswagen Beetles, elimination
  of, 192–194

Wagon wheels in film, movement
  of, 183
Wall Street Journal, 573–574
Warmth, its effect on pain and,
  396–397
Warning labels, mattress tag, 1–2
Washing machine agitators, 588
Washington D.C., "J" Street in, 71
Watches (timepieces), 609–610,
  666–667
Water
  bathtub drain, 656–657
  color of, 213
  for coffee, 705
  hot and cold faucets, 723–724
  sound in pipes, 761
  temperature of, 716
    cold, 683–684
Weather patterns, 705–706
Weddings
  etiquette, 618
  invitations, 648–649
Weigh stations, 725–726
Western Union
  exclamation marks and, 338–339
  periods and, 339–340
Wetness, and color, 671
Whips, cracking sound of, 74
Whistling at sporting events, 461, 749
White paint on homes, 100–102
White pepper, source of, 135–136
White-wall tires, thickness of, 149
White wine, serving temperature,
  628–629
Window envelopes, 111
Winds, 688–689
Wine, 627–629
Winter
  first day of, 401–403
  worms in, 640
Wisdom teeth, purpose of, 137